EMERGING FROM THE CAVE

The URBAN PATTERN

CITY PLANNING
AND DESIGN

by

ARTHUR B. GALLION
DEAN OF THE SCHOOL OF ARCHITECTURE
THE UNIVERSITY OF SOUTHERN CALIFORNIA

IN COLLABORATION WITH

SIMON EISNER

CHAPTER TITLE SKETCHES BY
ANTHONY FIALKOWSKI

D. VAN NOSTRAND COMPANY, INC.
LONDON   NEW YORK   TORONTO

NEW YORK
D. Van Nostrand Company, Inc., 250 Fourth Avenue, New York 3

TORONTO
D. Van Nostrand Company (Canada), Ltd., 228 Bloor Street, Toronto

LONDON
Macmillan & Company, Ltd., St. Martin's Street, London, W.C. 2

DEDICATED
TO THE
FUTURE
GENERATION

PREFACE

Those of us who live in cities find our daily existence conditioned largely by the physical environment of the urban community. This book is about that environment and how it is planned and built.

In the minds of most of us the planning of our cities is assumed to be some remote affair of our local government customarily identified with the administration of a zoning ordinance or with street-widening projects and traffic control. If any attention at all is given to civic design, it is usually associated with a rare project for a municipal plaza, a city hall, or a boulevard improvement.

These affairs seem to be generally accepted by the people as necessary civic activities, but public response is marked more by a spirit of indifferent tolerance than by active interest. Since the people are actually seeing their cities growing less and less desirable as places in which to live and work, this attitude is not surprising but it suggests the need for not less planning but more public understanding and effective planning.

In tracing the historical development of the physical form of cities it is apparent that the social order of the times has invariably fixed its impression upon the shape —the form and arrangement—of cities. The cities we build today are the great designs produced by our democratic society; the urban environment—the living and working environment of the whole urban population—is linked with the welfare of democratic institutions. Nearly every enterprise in which people engage, whether it is domestic or production and trade, is affected by and, in turn, shapes the design of cities. Real estate and finance, the social sciences and economics, the law, public administration and political science, architecture and building, engineering and the arts, all are woven into the physical pattern of the city.

This book attempts a critical examination of the processes by which cities are planned and built, appraises some of the results, describes some of the defects, and poses a few suggestions which may be sufficiently provocative to warrant more than passing attention. If this study should contribute to a clearer realization of democratic responsibility for the condition of our urban environment, it will have performed a share of its intended job. Perhaps, in time, a common purpose may thus emerge more clearly for the businessman, the worker, the politician, and the administrator of urban affairs, which will change public complacency into informed and active participation by the people in the improvement of their cities and generate activity in city planning directed toward the community welfare and prosperity.

The author and his collaborator, Simon Eisner, are indebted to the many who have contributed to the rich sources of information and ideas upon which this book has drawn. We record our sincere gratitude to those who have been quoted and to those from whom illustrations have been obtained.

Arthur B. Gallion

Los Angeles, California
March, 1950

CONTENTS

PART **VI**
NEW HORIZONS

PART I

THE CITY
OF THE PAST

The People, Yes,
Out of what is their change
from chaos to order
and chaos again?
—*Carl Sandburg*

THE DAWN
OF URBANIZATION

From Cave to Village. When Paleolithic man moved from his cave into the shelters he constructed of boughs and leaves, he was making the first step toward urbanization. Then Neolithic man cultivated plants, domesticated animals, and introduced agriculture. He created possessions in the form of crops, animals, and tools, and possessions bred rivalry, which in turn brought the need for protection. Families collected into friendly groups and formed villages in which the agrarian population enjoyed the advantages of mutual protection. The villages were located on sites offering the natural protection of elevated terrain, islands, peninsulas, or they were surrounded with barricades and moats. One of the earliest known villages was built upon piles in a Swiss lake.

Man was a gregarious being. He sought the companionship of his fellowmen and devised group entertainment and sports. The stronghold of the village became an appropriate sanctuary for the altar of his deity. It provided a place for worship, a meeting place for assembly, and a center for trade. The environment became popular, and urbanization had begun.

Political Formation. The village brought something new to the lives of primitive man. It introduced the necessity for mutual responsibility and co-operation. There were various interests common to all the inhabitants, and they were merged into a form of society, a social and political organization.

Man did not adjust himself with the utmost grace to the self-discipline that this responsibility imposed upon him. He retained his primitive instincts for self-preservation and superstition. Personal rivalry flared within the village, and the most powerful assumed the role of tribal leadership, maintaining communal order with the aid of the cudgel. Rivalry spread between villages, armed conflict ensued, and the barricades were transformed into fortified walls. Several villages came under the domination of the victorious tribe, and its leader rose to a position of ruler. In time, empires were created, and rulers took the titles of king and emperor.

Society has been forged in the crucible of natural forces. Being a natural entity himself, man has inflicted upon himself many of the evils and hardships he has suffered. He has faced the necessity to improve economic security, correct social mal-

adjustments, discard mass superstitions, or resist seizure of power by autocrats bent
upon personal glory and self-aggrandizement. The conflicts have occurred with varying
degrees of pressure upon humankind and under a variety of circumstances.

Evolution of Physical Form. Evolving from these conflicts the development of
cities has marked the culture of a people. Sensitive to the surge between oppression
and justice, the physical form of cities has been shaped by the economic, social and
political forces of society. The degree to which freedom or slavery has dominated the
lives of men, the manner in which war has been waged, the instruments of destruction
and defense, the tools for peaceful pursuits and the way they have been used, the consideration, neglect, or disdain men have shown their fellowmen, all account for the
kind of cities Man has built for himself, and their effect on urban development may
guide us in charting our future enterprise in city building.

Historians have attempted to isolate and codify the variations in the patterns of
cities. However, their development almost precludes such classification. Adjectives
like organic and inorganic, irregular and geometrical, magical and mystical, formal
and informal, medieval and classic, are often so obtuse they obscure rather than clarify
the distinctions, or they describe a form without the substance. The primary distinction
in the pattern of cities is marked by the transitions from a slave to a mercantile economy and from slingshot to gunpowder warfare.

Two basic forms are discernible: the walled town and the open city. Within these
basic forms a wide variety of patterns has been woven, each color and design shaped
by the character of society at the time.

Few cities in which great cultures thrived began with a plan. They developed by a
process of accretion—the growth was irregular in form, sensitive to changes in the
habits of people, and dynamic in character. They began as free cities which men settled by voluntary choice. Geometrical form was introduced according to the manner in
which the land was apportioned among the inhabitants. Colonial cities founded by
great states were given a formal pattern predetermined by a ruling authority. Privileged landowners platted their land for allocation to settlers, the plots being generally
regular in form, almost static in character.

Within these various patterns we may find similar social, economic, and political
habits and customs. Neither the presence nor the absence of geometrical form has
affixed itself upon a people or a period as a conclusive expression of society. It is
rather the manner in which the forms have been manipulated and the purpose for
which they have been devised that give significance to the physical patterns of cities.

With the ebb and flow of civilization the irregular and geometrical patterns have
been grafted one upon the other. Villages which grew into cities because of geographic, economic, or social advantages may show evidence of geometrical forms
superimposed upon an irregular pattern, or an informal system may have been
grafted upon a city having an original pattern of gridiron streets. Cities have been
subjected to the process of continuous remodeling through the ages, and the variety of
forms is the result of forces which dominated during the successive periods of their

history. We find the motives of city builders, from emperors to subdividers, reflected
in the designs they have stamped upon the city.

We have been accustomed to measuring a civilization by the monuments it produced.
Certain cultural characteristics are revealed by these structures, but it is not enough to
observe the monuments alone. The city is not the palace, the temple, or a collection of
art objects. If we are to discern the characteristics of a civilization, we cannot confine
our attention to the rulers; we must observe the affairs of the people. The city means
the whole people who inhabit it, the entire collection of the houses the people live in,
the shops in which they work, the streets they traverse, and the places in which they
trade. To separate the palace from the dwellings of the populace is like removing
a phrase from its context. When the palace is related to the lives of the people, it
may provide quite a different interpretation than when it is observed as an isolated
monument.

More than the great structures that impress us, it is the dwellings of the people that
mark the culture of cities. Civilization is not measured by inventions alone; it is measured rather by the extent to which the people share the benefits these inventions make
possible. Progress is not gauged by comparison of an aboriginal village with a modern
city; it is more accurately appraised by the degree to which the people have participated in the advantages of each. Standards and quality are relative, and it is the contrast between the environment of the privileged and that of the poor which provides the
yardstick of the freedom and happiness enjoyed by the people in any period.

History reveals a lag between moments of great social ideals and the structures that
reflect them. Institutions of social and political justice or oppression gather a momentum which carries beyond their zenith. The substance of these institutions, the freedom they have nurtured or denied, may have altered or vanished by the time the physical
structure of the urban environment they engendered is finally completed. Frequently,
the powerful human forces which produced a city have begun to change or disappear
before the physical form of the city has modified. An environment which emerged from
a society of high ideals may then become the dramatic scene of decline. The city form
may remain after the substance of the society has vanished or been replaced.

Stability, in the sense of a sameness of human conduct, a *status quo* of human institutions, has not long endured. Humanity must continuously have new cultural food upon
which to nourish, or it decays. Civilization has not remained static for any protracted
period. During periods in history when the social and political institutions were molded
to the welfare of the people they provided the very climate of freedom in which the
baser instincts of humanity could forge and wield the tools of oppression, inequality,
and injustice. Unless this tide was stemmed, civilization turned in the direction of
decline. We observe these trends in ancient cities, in medieval cities of the Middle Ages,
in the Baroque Period, and there is evidence of their presence in our cities today.

Cities of Ancient Lands. Early civilization spread along the fertile valleys of the
Nile, Tigris-Euphrates, and Indus Rivers where food, water, and transportation were
at hand. A series of great and small empires rose, waged wars, and fell. Supremacy

shifted from one kingdom to another, each adding its contribution to the evolution of
the civilized world, but one characteristic was shared in common by all these civiliza-
tions. Moved by mystic superstition, the people were slaves of the ruling class, and
they bowed before the reigning king as before a deity. All possessions of the kingdom,
the land, and its benefits were subject to the will of the ruling monarch and his
appointed emissaries.

In Egypt the lives of the people were dedicated to the Pharaoh. The towns they built
in the third millennium B.C. were erected upon his order. They housed the slaves and
artisans engaged in building the great pyramids—the royal tombs of kings and nobles.
Like huge barracks the cells and compartments of sun-dried bricks were crowded about
common courtyards. Narrow lanes served as open drainage sewers as well as passageways to the dwellings. Walls surrounded the towns. Because the kingdom was broad
and mighty, they were probably built primarily for protection from seasonal floods
rather than the armies of invading enemies.

Concurrent with the Pyramid Period of Egypt permanent towns of burned brick
were built along the Indus Valley. In Mohenjo-Daro and Harrapa the streets were
arranged in a regular pattern and, as in Egypt, the dwellings were compactly built
about interior courts. The heights of buildings were established in proportion to the
width of streets, one and two stories predominating. Sanitation was of a relatively
high order; a system of underground sewers extended about the towns, and there is
evidence that disposal lines were connected to the dwellings. But all trace of the civilization that produced these cities has apparently vanished, and it remains a matter of
conjecture whether the peoples who occupied them influenced the city building of the
Near East in subsequent centuries.

In the second millennium B.C. Egyptian kings built great temple cities on the banks of
the Nile. Monumental avenues, colossal temple plazas, and rock-cut tombs remain as
mute testimony to the luxurious life of kings and nobles in Memphis, Thebes, and
Tel-el-Armarna, but few snatches of recorded history describe the city of the people.
Time and the elements have washed away the clay huts and tenements in which the
people dwelled. The dramatic Avenue of the Sphinxes in Thebes and the broad temple
enclosure, one-third mile wide and one-half mile long, in Tel-el-Armarna tell a vivid
story of powerful autocrats, while historians piece together fragmentary remains of
the homes of people and conclude that slums spread about the towns.

A series of empires rose in Mesopotamia, and humble villages along the valley of
the Tigris and Euphrates Rivers became monumental cities of the kings. Each was
heavily fortified to resist the siege of many enemies. The stately palace-temple
dominated the city, and the people lived their urban existence in the shadows of slavery
and superstitious religion. Economic hardship added to the burden of the masses.
According to Bemis and Burchard a skilled artisan in ancient Sumeria could obtain
housing for 5 or 6 per cent of his income, but the poorest dwellings cost unskilled
workers as much as 30 and 40 per cent of their subsistence allowance.[1]

[1] The Evolving House, Volume I, *A History of the Home*, Bemis and Burchard, 1933–36.

ANCIENT EGYPT

AN
EGYPTIAN
HOUSE

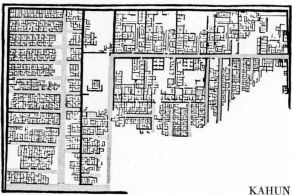

KAHUN

The city of Kahun, Egypt, dating from about 3000 B.C. and built for the slaves and artisans assigned for work on the Illahun pyramid, was hardly more than an assembly of cells arranged in rectangular blocks to which narrow alleys gave access. The apparent difference in the size of these cells indicates a distinction in class among the inhabitants, the more commodious dwellings occupying the upper-right quarter of the town.

Time and the ravages of weather have washed away the clay villages, and little is known of the average dwelling of the Egyptian. Deductions from sparse records indicate that the simplest dwelling was a single cell of sun-dried bricks and plaster covered with a roof of reeds. The city dwelling, such as the humble houses in Kahun, was probably a group of small rooms surrounding a diminutive courtyard in which the cooking and other domestic activities were performed. This court may have been used as a work area for the craftsmen.

The climate was favorable to outdoor living, and stairs led to the roof which was the most desirable space for living and sleeping. In the finer houses of the noblemen, these roof areas were apparently developed with gardens, lavishly furnished and covered with awnings.

A ventilating device, known as the "mulguf," was installed on the roof to provide some degree of cooling for the interior rooms. Probably olive oil lamps provided light, and such heat as was necessary was obtained from charcoal braziers. While sun-dried brick was the principal material with which the towns were built, the Egyptians, being fine masons, probably constructed the dwellings of nobles with stone and plaster.

A Monastery
B Bath

N

O FEET 500

MOHENJO-DARO

Excavations at Mohenjo-Daro in the Indus Valley have revealed the remains of a large city built about 3000 B.C. It is apparent that a relatively advanced civilization flourished in this city. Houses ranged in size from two rooms to mansions with numerous rooms. The map shows the archeologists' assumption that a major street ran in the north-south (First Street) and east-west (East Street) directions. Areas shown in black have been excavated and indicate the intricate plan of narrow roads. Buildings were of masonry, streets were paved, and considerable evidence of sewer drainage from dwellings has been uncovered. The principal buildings excavated are a public bath and a monastery.

KING SOLOMON'S TEMPLE AND CITADEL, JERUSALEM, c. 900 B.C.

The splendor of the temples and palaces of the kings in contrast to the congested dwellings of the populace. (*Restoration by Dr. John Wesley Kelchner*)

BABYLON

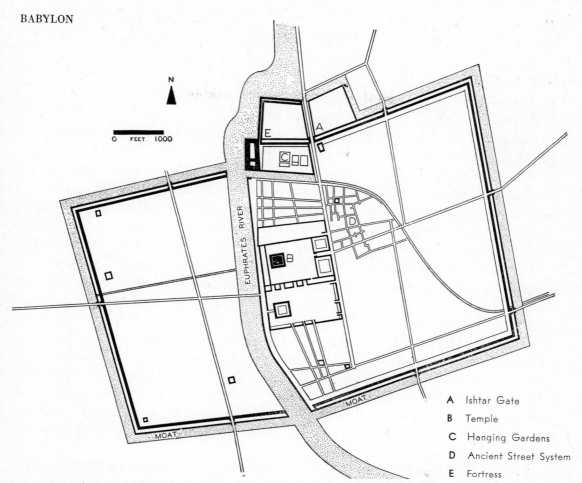

A Ishtar Gate

B Temple

C Hanging Gardens

D Ancient Street System

E Fortress

In the sixth century B.C. Babylon was a large city spanning the Euphrates River. Surrounded by great walls and a moat, it was a monumental city of kings—the processional avenue leading to the magnificent Ishtar Gate, the Temple, and the Hanging Gardens of Nebuchadnezzar's Palace. When Babylon was but a village, the streets were probably irregular; as it grew into a flourishing city, the avenues were laid with a more regular form as described by Herodotus. At that time the palatial monuments were built and the dwellings increased in height and crowding.

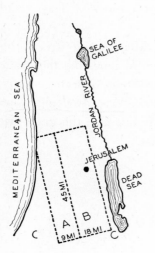

REGIONAL PLANNING IN ANCIENT TIMES

While in captivity in the sixth century B.C., the Israelites planned their return to Jerusalem and Ezekiel described in his book (Ezekiel 25:45) the plans desired by God for the allocation and use of the land upon their return. Within their land, from Dan to Beersheba, an area of 10,000 by 25,000 reeds (18 by 45 miles) was to be set aside for the priesthood and within it was to be the sanctuary of worship. An area 5,000 by 25,000 reeds (9 by 45 miles) was to be set aside for the people of the city. The land on both sides of these areas was reserved as princely lands.

There was no indication of the precise location of the boundaries and it is probable that Ezekiel understood God's wishes were directed more to the area of land needed for the production and distribution of abundant goods than the exact location surrounding the city of Jerusalem. Perhaps the amount of land allocated to production for the people of the city was less than that for the priests since Jerusalem was a crossroads for trade routes and the people derived considerable wealth from the resulting commercial enterprise in which they were engaged. The princely lands supported the kings who maintained residences on the Mediterranean and the Dead Sea as well as Jerusalem. The land described by Ezekiel lies within the area we identify today as Judea.

A Lands for City People   **B** Lands for Priests   **C** Lands for Princes

Seeking to improve the lot of the common people, the great King Hammurabi, in 2100 B.C., codified his laws of justice. In Old Babylon we observe the dawn of building regulations. The codes of Hammurabi meted harsh punishment to irresponsible builders. According to the king's decree, if the wall of a building should fall and kill the son of the occupant, the life of the builder's son would be sacrificed—the doctrine of "an eye for an eye, a tooth for a tooth."

Out of the slums of thriving imperial cities were carved triumphal avenues connecting magnificent city gates. King Sennacherib built his temples and palaces in seventh-century Nineveh. The processional avenues, great walls, monumental gates, and hanging gardens of Nebuchadnezzar's palace were the vivid spectacle of Babylon in the sixth and fifth centuries described by Herodotus. This Greek historian also told of the narrow streets lined with the three- and four-story dwellings of the populace. Behind the avenues, laid in regular pattern at right angles to each other, were the crowded houses of the people. Of more concern to the vanity of rulers was the monumental spectacle of the great edifices with which they adorned their cities.

Perhaps the physical environment of the home did not weigh heavily upon the people in ancient times. Undoubtedly a beneficent desert climate cleansed the insanitary surroundings in these southern lands. But, human nature being what it is, we can reasonably suspect that the violent contrasts in social caste, the servitude in which the multitude languished, and the restriction from participation in public affairs were as responsible for the continuous wars, revolts, and conquests, as the insatiable appetites of kings for power.

A more enlightened society appears to have been cultivated in the islands of the Aegean Sea. Kings reigned over city-states, but these rulers were apparently not accorded the distinction of deification as in eastern lands. In contrast to the austere detachment of royal palaces in Mesopotamia, the palace served as a center of community life in Aegean culture. On the island of Crete the town sites offered natural protection. Ancient cities, like Cnossus, were not surrounded by walls. The people enjoyed free access to the sea and entered into trade with other lands. On the mainland of Greece, however, cities needed the protection of ramparts; the cities of Tiryns and Mycenae were heavily fortified.

These early cities of the Aegean were irregular in form. Meandering streets followed the rugged topography of the sites. The streets were narrow lanes but they were paved with stone. Excavations have revealed highly developed systems of water supply, sanitation, and drainage for the palace and many of the houses. Most dwellings were one-story in height and, although densely built, the towns did not reach the great size and congestion which were apparent in cities of the Near East.

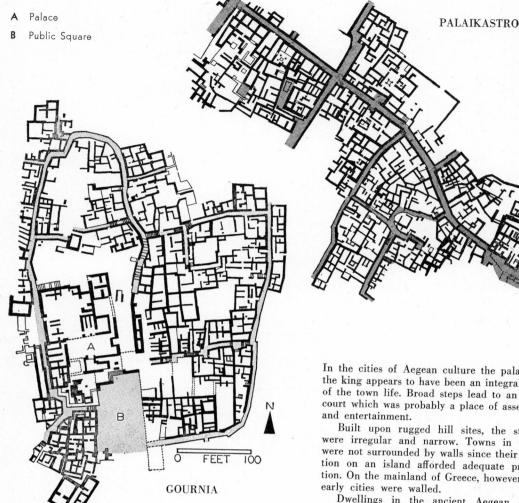

A Palace
B Public Square

PALAIKASTRO

N

0   FEET   100

GOURNIA

In the cities of Aegean culture the palace of the king appears to have been an integral part of the town life. Broad steps lead to an open court which was probably a place of assembly and entertainment.

Built upon rugged hill sites, the streets were irregular and narrow. Towns in Crete were not surrounded by walls since their location on an island afforded adequate protection. On the mainland of Greece, however, the early cities were walled.

Dwellings in the ancient Aegean cities comprised a few small rooms about a living room called the "megaron." This room opened into a small light court, or a portion of the ceiling itself was open. Rain water from the roof was collected in a cistern in this area. The poor houses were probably confined to the "megaron" and vestibule, with access to the roof for expansion of the living area. The larger houses contained a number of rooms and courtyards. There is evidence of bathing facilities within some of the better houses, and palaces of the Minoan period were equipped with drains. One-story buildings prevailed, the construction being mud brick on stone foundations.

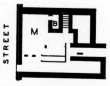

STREET

M

B

EARLY CRETAN HOUSE

B Bath
M Megaron

O

M

B

COURT

STREET

CRETAN HOUSE, c. 2000 B.C.

CHAPTER 2

THE CLASSIC CITY

Government by Law. On the mainland of Greece the virile shepherds from the north mingled with the Aegean peoples, merged with their city-states, and gradually absorbed them within their culture. A wealthy landowning noble class rose in power, and during the eighth century B.C. leaders from this group appropriated much of the influence previously exercised by the kings. The palace citadel disappeared, and temples dedicated to the gods of their religion replaced them upon the acropolis. The nobles assumed the power of kings, dominated the cities, and brought oppression to the peasant class. Seeking relief in other lands, the peasant group opened new avenues of colonization and trade. A merchant middle class emerged. Feuds between this new economic group and the city-dwelling nobles forced the selection of a common leader, and in the seventh century the Tyrants of Athens came into power.

Although they were themselves of the noble class, the Tyrants maintained their leadership by their support of the common people. Estates of the nobles were redistributed among the people, and a strong land-holding peasant class developed. Under the successive leadership of Solon, Pisistratus and Clisthenes, the principle of law evolved as a basis of social conduct. A new form was given to political organization of the community: a government of laws determined by the people.

During the fifth century B.C., with the inspired leadership of Pericles, democracy and a high order of morality took root in Athenian citizenship. Political education was extended by way of free speech and assembly. Magistrates were elected to execute the laws, and public service was vested with dignity. Sovereignty of the people was assured and protected by a body of laws to which all agreed and were subject. The deep sense of individual responsibility was expressed in the vow of Athenian citizenship:

I will not dishonor these sacred arms; I will not abandon my comrade in battle; I will fight for my gods and my hearth single-handed or with my companions. I will not leave my country smaller, but I will leave it greater and stronger than I received it. I will obey the commands which the magistrates in their wisdom shall give me. I will submit to the existing laws and to those that the people shall unanimously make; if anyone shall attempt to overthrow these laws or disobey them, I will not suffer it, but will fight for them, whether single-handed or with my fellows. I will respect the worship of my fathers.

The Democracy of Athens. Inspired by the political genius of Pericles the democracy of Athens in the fifth century acquired a soul. It required wise citizenship to retain this quality, and philosophers like Socrates strove to cultivate the wisdom and intelligence. Although Socrates sometimes disapproved of the laws and thought some of them bad, he insisted upon the obligation of the citizenry to abide by them until they were revised. Esteem for the law was expressed in the words of the great orator Demosthenes:

The whole life of men, whether they inhabit a great city or a small, is ordered by nature and the laws. Whilst nature is lawless and varies with individuals, the laws are a common possession, controlled, identical for all. . . . They desire the just, the beautiful, the useful. It is that which they seek; once discovered it is that which is created into a principle equal for all and unvarying; it is that which is called law.

Athenian democracy of the fifth century was described by Glotz[1]

as the exercise of sovereignty by free and equal citizens under the aegis of law. The law, which protects the citizens one against the other, defends also the rights of the individual against the power of the State and the interests of the State against the excesses of individualism. Before the last years of the fifth century there is no sign that liberty has degenerated into anarchy or license, nor is the principle of equality carried so far as to entail the denial of the existence of mental inequalities.

Democracy in the Age of Pericles produced that inherent dignity of the individual born of free speech, a sense of unity with one's fellowman, and a full opportunity for participation in affairs of the community. The Athenian citizen experienced the exhilaration of freedom and accepted the challenge of responsibility it thrust upon him with honor and with pride. The discovery of freedom gave impetus to the search for truth as honest men desire it. Philosophy was nurtured, and there were no depths which the wise and intelligent were afraid to plumb. Reason was encouraged, logic invited, and science investigated. There was no truth which might be discovered and remain undisclosed. Inspired by this atmosphere it was no wonder great philosophy was born; only in freedom can such greatness be cultivated, not freedom from care but freedom of the spirit. This was the environment of culture which produced Socrates, Plato, and Aristotle.

The affinity between freedom and spiritual values was symbolized in the temples built upon the acropolis. In them was reflected the exalted stature of democratic man. Some four centuries later another philosopher, this one from Bethlehem, was to recreate the spiritual values demonstrated by the Greeks at the height of their democracy.

The Humble City. During the early years when democracy was flowering, the Greek city was a maze of wandering unpaved lanes lacking in drainage and sanitation. Water was carried from local wells. Waste was disposed of in the streets. There were

[1] *The Greek City and Its Institutions*, Gustave Glotz, Kegan Paul, Trench, Trubner & Company, Ltd., 1929.

THE ACROPOLIS, ATHENS

The temple rather than the palace of rulers dominated the ancient Hellenic city and a meeting place for political assembly of the people—the *pnyx*—was added to the urban pattern. As the power of kings diminished and democracy expanded, the houses of the people and the community facilities established for their use assumed greater importance in the city plan.

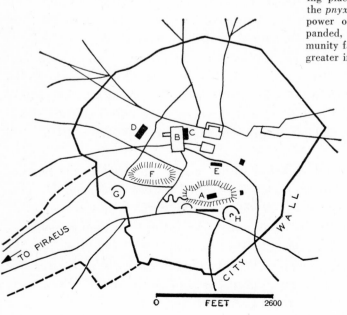

ANCIENT ATHENS

A Acropolis

B Agora

C Stoa

D Theseum

E Prytaneum

F Areopagus

G Pnyx

H Theater of Dionysus

no palaces and, with the exception of the temples, public buildings were few and simple. The common assembly place was the *pnyx*, an open-air podium where the citizens met to consider affairs of state. The agora, or market place and center of urban activity, was irregular in form. There was little distinction between the dwellings of the well-to-do citizen and his less privileged fellowmen. The few rooms that comprised the house were grouped about an interior court behind windowless façades facing the random streets. Most towns were surrounded by protective walls.

For the Greek citizen the temple was the symbol of his democratic way of life, the equality of men. Upon the temples he lavished all his creative energies, and in them we find a refinement of line and beauty of form that expressed the dignity and humility of the Athenian. In later and less happy days Demosthenes reflected upon this period of the fifth century. "These edifices," he said, "which their administrations have given us, their decorations of our temples and the offerings deposited in them, are so numerous that all efforts of posterity cannot exceed them. Then in private life, so exemplary was their moderation, their adherence to the ancient manners so scrupulously exact, that, if any of you discovered the house of Aristides or Miltiades, or any of the illustrious men of those times, he must know that it was not distinguished by the least extraordinary splendor."[2]

Hippodamus. It was natural that an atmosphere of philosophy should impel a search for order in the city. It was a topic that engaged the attention of teacher-philosophers and politicians alike. In the latter part of the fifth century an architect from Miletus, by the name of Hippodamus, advanced positive theories about the art and science of city planning. He has been credited with the origination of the "gridiron" street system, although this is not entirely accurate. A semblance of geometrical form had been present in early towns of Egypt, Mesopotamia, and the Indus Valley, and a formal rectangular pattern was used, in part, for rebuilding some Greek cities after their destruction by the Persians in the sixth century. The gridiron pattern was vigorously applied by Hippodamus to obtain a rational arrangement of buildings and circulation.

The city plan was conceived as a design to serve all the people. The individual dwelling was the common denominator. Blocks were shaped to provide appropriate orientation for the dwellings within them. The functional uses of buildings and public spaces were recognized in the arrangement of streets. They provided for the circulation of people and vehicles without interference with the orientation of dwellings or the assembly of people in the market place.

Superimposing the rigid geometrical form of the Hippodamian street system upon the rugged topography of the sites occupied by most Greek cities created numerous streets so steep they could be negotiated only with steps. Since the movement of people was almost entirely on foot, this did not present the problem we might assume today although there were probably some puffing Grecians who reached the top of a long climb to attend a political meeting in the assembly hall. The principal traffic streets,

2 *Ibid.,* p. 302.

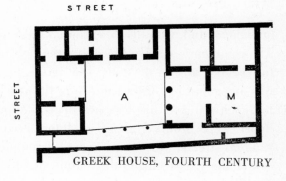

GREEK HOUSE, FOURTH CENTURY

K Kitchen   A Atrium
M Megaron   S Shop
L Living Room

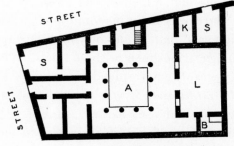

LATE GREEK HOUSE

A Old Agora
B New Agora

OLYNTHUS

The town of Olynthus conveys some idea of the transition in city development during the late fifth and early fourth centuries in Greece. Excavations indicate a dual town; the earlier portion with an irregular layout of streets, the complete plan not having been uncovered. An agora was situated here, and the remains of a *bouleuterion* (assembly) have been found. The dwellings were small and irregular in form. This part of the city may be the original plan occupied first by the Boeotians and later by the Chalcidians prior to the last quarter of the fifth century when the city grew in importance as a Greek "polis." The Hippodamian plan was probably developed after this time, the principal streets laid in a north-south direction about 300 feet apart and connected by east-west streets of narrow width some 129 feet apart. The city was razed by Philip of Macedon in 348 B.C. and did not rise again.

The climate in Greece was more rigorous than the countries we have previously observed. Protection from heat, cold, and dampness was a more important factor. The house of early times was centered about the hearth and contained a minimum number of rooms to heat. The hearth was situated in the central room called the "atrium." An opening in the roof permitted the smoke to escape and rain water from the sloping portion of this roof was collected here. There is no indication of sanitary provisions or water supply other than that collected in the atrium.

The Olynthus houses show the improvement which developed in both interior arrangement and relation to the street system. All dwellings were oriented uniformly, although the room arrangement varied somewhat. In general the rooms of the dwellings opened into a courtyard and faced to the south. The north wall gave protection from winds. The principal southern exposure was advantageous in winter because of the low angle of the sun which permitted it to penetrate the interiors; in summer the high altitude of the sun was a protection from the extreme heat. It will be noted that this orientation was applied uniformly to all dwellings regardless of the relation of the houses to the street. This rational treatment of planning was not again repeated until the housing program in Europe following World War I.

The later towns enjoyed paved streets and underground drains. The houses were generally two stories in height and some were equipped with baths connected to the drainage system. The cistern was prevalent in most houses and rain water was collected from the roof. The drainage system was apparently not intended for sewage disposal and sanitation was continued with cesspools and portable latrines.

There is a remarkable similarity in the dwellings thus far excavated in Olynthus, the standards being fairly uniform. Principal shopping was undoubtedly conducted in the agora, although there is evidence of small individual shops connected to some of the dwellings. These may have been the workrooms of craftsmen as well as market shops.

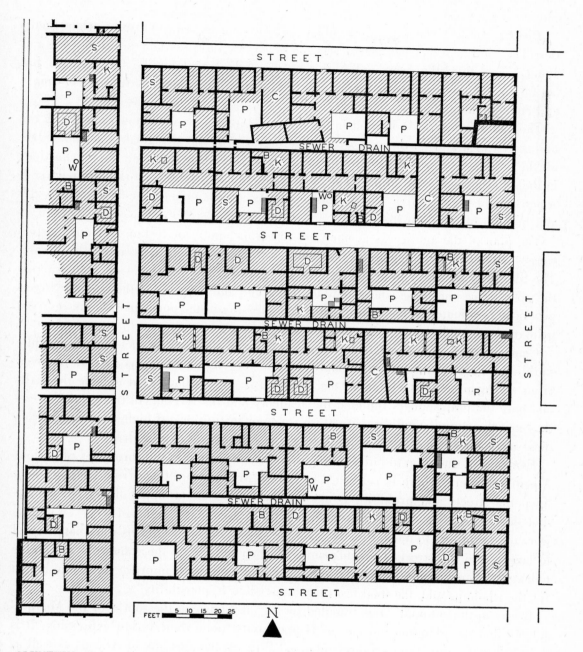

OLYNTHUS—Detail plan of shaded area in general plan on opposite page.

B Bath **C** Storage or Stable **D** Dining Room **K** Kitchen **P** Patio **W** Cistern **S** Shop

however, were placed to allow the circulation of the few horse-drawn vehicles which entered the town.

Public Space. The expanding affairs of government required appropriate facilities. The agora, or market place, was the center of business and political life, and about it were lined the shops and market booths. Accessible from the agora square, but not facing upon it, were the assembly hall (*ecclesiasteron*), council hall (*bouleuterion*), and council chamber (*prytaneum*).

The agora was usually located in the approximate center of the town plan, with the major east-west and north-south streets leading to it. It was designed to accommodate all the citizens who would have business in the market place or attend public functions in the adjacent public buildings. The open space enclosed by the agora occupied about 5 per cent of the city area, the dimensions being approximately one-fifth of the width and breadth of the town itself.

The plan of the agora was geometrical in form. Square or rectangular open spaces were surrounded by colonnaded porticoes sheltering the buildings about the square. The plan was arranged to avoid interference between the movement of people across the open space and those who assembled for trade and business in the market. Streets generally terminated at the agora rather than crossing it, the open space being reserved primarily for pedestrian traffic and circulation.

Common open space in Greek cities was largely confined to enclosure for public buildings. Because the city was small in area, the city dweller was not far removed from the open countryside about the town. Olive groves flourished outside the walls and here the philosophers founded the academy and the lyceum. In these quiet groves they met their pupils and set the pattern for later institutions of higher learning. From these academies came the first university, the Museum of Alexandria.

Evidence of attention to building regulations is recorded in the chronicles of various Athenian writers. There is reference to laws restricting buildings from encroachment upon the streets and prohibitions against the projection of upper floors beyond the first floor walls. These are forerunners of the present-day "rights-of-way." Windows were not permitted to open directly upon the street, and water drains were not allowed to empty into the street. Though primitive when judged by the standards acceptable today, the Greek towns demonstrated a conscious effort to improve the environment for the whole people, the final test of genuine civic responsibility.

It was in the colonial cities founded by the city-states on the shores of the Mediterranean that the planning theories of Hippodamus found their fullest expression. It is recorded that Hippodamus himself planned Piraeus, the port city of Athens, as well as Thurii and Rhodes. The old established cities were remodeled in parts, the agora assuming a more orderly form as new buildings were erected for public affairs, but the colonial cities had the benefit of planning prior to their settlement. Although they were founded by a mother city-state, they enjoyed a degree of political autonomy, becoming a part of the confederation of Greek cities which comprised the Athenian "Empire."

The Size of Cities. Athens, in the fifth and fourth centuries, had a citizen population of some 40,000 and a total population of between 100,000 and 150,000 including slaves and foreigners. Most Greek cities, however, were relatively small. Only about three towns exceeded 10,000 persons during the thriving Hellenic Period. It was a theory of Hippodamus that this was an appropriate size, and Plato later concluded it should range between 5,000 and 10,000. In the settlement of colonial towns it was customary to dispatch about 10,000 colonists from the mother city-state. The glorious metropolis with its teeming millions is undoubtedly an exaggerated description of the actual number of people who dwelt in urban communities in ancient times. The metropolis, as we know it, is of comparatively recent origin.

A number of factors bore upon the size of a city and the population it could support. The food and water supply was a primary consideration. The tools for cultivating the soil, the means for transporting the products, and the source and methods for distributing the water supply established limits on the urban population which could be accommodated in a single group. As long as people were dependent upon the primitive hand plough, the horse-cart, and gravity flow of water, it was not feasible to gather in great numbers and maintain adequate standards of urban hygiene. Hellenic towns relied primarily on local watercourses, wells, and springs, but supplemental supply was sometimes available through conduits from more remote sources in higher surrounding hills.

The Dwellings. In their houses the Greeks sought quiet privacy. Most of the social contacts and all business affairs were carried on outside the home. Small merchants frequently had shops adjacent to their houses, but business and politics were generally conducted in and adjacent to the agora. Sports and recreation were concentrated in the gymnasium; drama and festivals in the theater. Feasts and other celebrations seldom occurred in the private dwelling. There was usually a small altar in the home, but religious exercises and worship took place in the temples. Consequently, the house was unpretentious in its appointments and, as has been previously mentioned, there was little distinction between the dwellings in the town. A display of affluence was not consistent with the tenets of democracy in the fifth century.

Early houses were enclosed about a central hearth. A hole in the roof allowed the smoke to escape and it also permitted the collection of rain water in the cistern. In late Hellenic towns sanitation was improved by the pavement of streets and installation of underground drains from dwellings. The town maintained reservoirs, but there was no distribution system. With the improvement of drainage, however, there was an increasing number of homes with private baths. Disposal of sewage was apparently not provided for, and the portable latrine and private cesspool continued in use. Terracotta braziers supplemented the hearth as a source of heat in the larger houses.

Care in planning the dwelling was not less because of its simplicity. On the contrary, as the center of family life, the proper arrangement of rooms in relation to the site received attention from builders and philosophers alike.

The climate urged emphasis upon orientation of the dwelling. The maximum amount

PRIENE

A Agora

B Temple of Athene Polias

C Theater

D Stadium

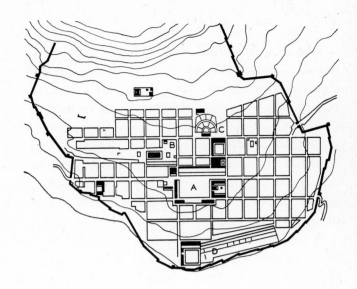

These cities demonstrate the Hippodamian plan as it developed toward the end of the Hellenic Period. The agora occupies the approximate geographical center of the town. About it are the temple shrines, public buildings, and shops. The dwelling blocks are planned to provide the appropriate orientation of houses in a manner similar to that shown at Olynthus. Recreation and entertainment facilities are provided in the gymnasium, stadium, and theater. The contours of the site indicate that some of the streets were very steep, steps being frequently required, but the main streets connecting the gates and the agora were generally placed so that beasts of burden and carts could traverse them readily.

MILETUS

A Agora

B Theater

C Stadium

D Port

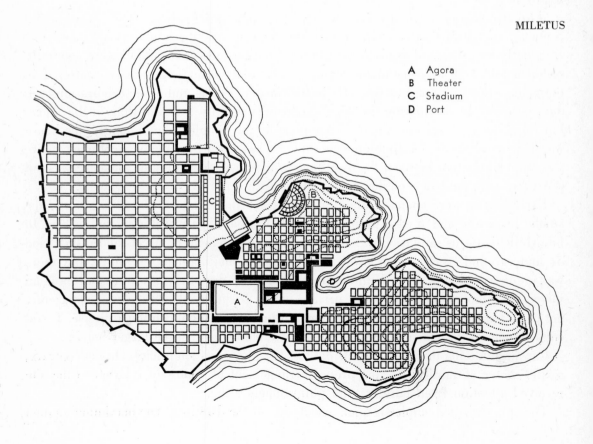

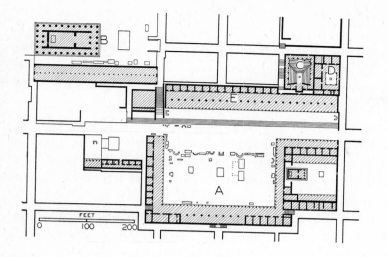

THE AGORA OF PRIENE

A Market Place

B Temple of Athene Polias

C Ecclesiasteron

D Prytaneum

E Stoa

The market place was designed for freedom of pedestrian movement, streets generally by-passing or terminating at the open space. Service to the shops was sometimes provided from the exterior streets surrounding the market place.

The agora was treated as a series of exterior rooms; although rectilinear in form, the spaces were not symmetrically arranged.

The shrines and public buildings were located about the agora. The *bouleuterion* was the meeting room for the city council, the *prytaneum*, the private chambers for the Council, and the open-roof *ecclesiasteron*, the public assembly hall, these public buildings being accessible from the agora but seldom directly form the market place. In the plan of Miletus the *bouleuterion* and *prytaneum* are shown, but it is believed that the *ecclesiasteron* also served as the *bouleuterion* in Priene.

THE AGORA OF MILETUS

A Market Place

B Bouleuterion

C Prytaneum

D Stoa

E Port

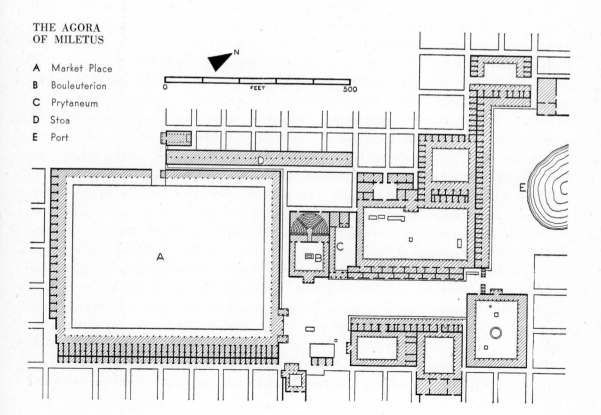

of sunshine that could be invited into the dwelling was desirable in the winter months, and if the rooms were shielded from the cold north winds, heat could be conserved. Conversely, the heat in summer was relieved when the direct rays of the sun were excluded. These criteria were satisfied in the plan of the Greek house.

The principal rooms were faced to the south, opening upon the private courtyard. A colonnade projected from the rooms to shelter them from the high summer sun. The north wall of the house was punctured with only a few small windows. This plan form was used in practically all dwellings in the town, whether the street entrance occurred on the north, south, east, or west.

Chroniclers of the period referred to the importance of proper orientation. Aristotle wrote, "For the well-being and health . . . the homesteads should be airy in summer and sunny in winter. A homestead possessing these qualities would be longer than it is deep; and the main front would face south." According to Xenophon in his *Memorabilia*, Socrates applied the following reasoning to the dwelling arrangement. "When one builds a house must he not see to it that it be as pleasant and convenient as possible? And pleasant is to be cool in summer, but warm in winter. In those houses, then, that look toward the south, the winter sun shines down into the *paestades* [court portico] while in summer, passing high above our heads and over our roofs, it throws them in shadow."

The effect of these criteria was a planning system that sprung from the elements of the individual unit—the home—applied uniformly throughout the town plan. This consistent treatment is unique in urban planning; we do not find it recurring for 2,400 years when a similar relation between the dwelling and the site was recognized in the vast housing program in Europe following the First World War.

Decline of the City. It cannot be assumed that political affairs always ran smoothly in the Age of Pericles. Teachings of the Sophists were disturbing to some of the well-established customs. A little man by the name of Socrates subjected many of the prevailing habits to severe questioning. He insisted upon inquiry and application of reason to the activities of men. He desired that the individual should cultivate an insight into truth, that he should become neither stronger than the state nor subservient to it. Socrates raised some questions about the existence of the gods.

There were some good democrats who believed he was wrong in raising these questions; they had suffered from uprisings of the oligarchic party and feared lest the faith in democracy be weakened. They brought charges against Socrates for impiety and subverting the youth of Athens. There were those who loved this wise man whose only ambition was the quest for truth. They appealed to him to flee his accusers as was the custom, but Socrates would not. He had suggested changes in the habits of men which would improve their lot, and if these were unlawful he would remain to face the people. Found guilty, he was sentenced to die, and in 399 B.C. he drank the hemlock.

The lesson of Socrates has been repeated in history. The institutions of men must change or decay, grow or wither. Socrates showed a way for men to continue command of their destiny by seeking truth. He strove to improve the institutions that they might better serve the people, and for this his fellowmen found him guilty of treason. More confidence in the strength of democracy would not have caused him to be so accused; more confidence might have saved democracy itself.

During the fourth century there was evidence of growing indifference toward the responsibility of government. Accustomed to liberty the people were taking it for granted, and they inclined to allow affairs to run themselves. Freedom guaranteed by democracy was coming to mean that "the people has the right to do what it pleases." Some people were, in the words of Demosthenes, "even building private houses whose magnificence surpasses that of certain public buildings."

Well-to-do citizens spent more of their time in their country villas, whereas the common people found the difficulty of earning a living more absorbing than participation in public affairs. The middle class was disappearing, and a wide gap was growing between those with money and those without it. Plato and Aristotle saw a degeneration of the democracy of Pericles. They perceived a growing abuse of individual liberty and became increasingly critical of democracy itself. Others were gripped with cynicism while maintaining the fight for democracy. Demosthenes said:

The objection may be raised that it was a mistake to allow the universal right of speech and a seat in the council. These should have been reserved for the cleverest, the flower of the community. But here again it will be found that they are acting with wise deliberation in granting even the baser sort the right of speech, for supposing only the better people might speak, or sit in council, blessings would fall to the lot of those like themselves, but to the commonalty the reverse of blessings. Whereas now, anyone who likes, any base fellow, may get up and discover something to the advantage of himself and his equals. It may be retorted, "And what sort of advantage either for himself or for the people can such a fellow be expected to hit upon?" The answer to which is, that in their judgement the ignorance and baseness of this fellow, together with his good will, are worth a great deal more to them than your superior person's virtue and wisdom, coupled with animosity. What it comes to, therefore, is that a state founded upon such institutions will not be the best state; but given democracy, these are the right means to secure its preservation. The people, it must be borne in mind, does not demand that the city should be well governed and itself a slave. It desires to be free and to be master. As to bad legislation it does not concern itself about that.

Glotz gives the following description of the alarming developments of this period in the fourth century:[3]

But in Greece as a whole there existed almost everywhere a glaring contrast between the equality promised by the constitution and the inequality created by social and economic conditions.

The power of money was spreading and corrupting morality. . . . Agriculture was commercialized to such an extent that by progressive eviction of small peasants and the concentration of estates in the same hands the system of large estates was recreated. Rhetoricians, advocates and artists, who had formerly reckoned it a dishonor to commercialize their talent, now felt no scruples in selling their goods as dearly as possible. Everything could be bought, everything had its price, and wealth was the measure of social values. By gain and by extravagance fortunes were made and unmade with equal rapidity. Those who had money rushed into pleasure-seeking and sought every occasion for gross displays of luxury. The newly rich were cocks of the walk. Men specu-

3 *Ibid.*, pp. 311, 312.

lated and rushed after money in order to build and furnish magnificent houses, to display fine weapons, to offer to the women of their family and to courtesans jewels, priceless robes and rare perfumes, to place before eminent guests and fashionable parasites fine wines and dishes prepared by a famous chef, or to commission some popular sculptor to carve their bust.

What happened to public affairs when "love of money left no one the smallest space in which to deal with other things, to such an extent that the mind of each citizen, passionately absorbed in this one purpose, could attend to no other business than the gain of each day" (Plato). Politics also was a business concern; the most honest worked for a class, the others sought for themselves alone the profits of power and barely concealed their venality. We are dealing with a time when "riches and rich men being held in honor virtue and honest men are at a discount," when "no one can become rich quickly if he remains honest" (Plato). Were these merely the capricious outbursts of a philosopher in love with the ideal or of a character in a comedy? Listen to the terrible words uttered before a tribunal: "Those who, citizens by right of birth, hold the opinion that their country extends wherever their interests are, these obviously are people who will desert the public good in order to run after their personal gain, since for them it is not the city which is their country, but their fortune."

The struggle between democracy and oligarchy was renewed, and Isocrates sums up the growing conflict between the widely separated classes:

Instead of securing general conditions of well-being by means of mutual understanding the anti-social spirit has reached such a pitch that the wealthy would rather throw their money into the sea than relieve the lot of the indigent, while the very poorest of the poor would get less from appropriating to their own use the property of the rich than from depriving them of it.

The Hellenistic City. The Peloponnesian Wars weakened Athens financially, and corrupt politicians began to gnaw at the moral fiber of the people. Athens became easy prey for a conqueror and succumbed to the Macedonian armies of Alexander the Great. But the essential qualities of wisdom, logic, and reason, the sensitive, esthetic character of democratic days, had sunk its roots deep into the soil of Athens. The Greeks were conquered by mighty armies, but their culture dominated the conqueror. Greek influence spread throughout the Mediterranean shores, and the Hellenistic period brought new city building—the planning and architecture patterned after the great works of the Greeks.

Old cities flourished and new cities were founded. Pergamon, Alexandria, Syracuse, and Candahar grew large and populous; the humble quality of the Hellenic city vanished. The city became the scene of luxury, ruddy with the display of empire. Magnificent public buildings—the odeion, the treasury, the library, the prison—were added to the agora. The assembly retained its traditional place among these monumental structures, but it remained, as Percy Gardner[4] expressed it, for the citizens "to exercise such functions (a mere show of autonomy) as the real rulers of the country . . . left to them." Baths, palaestrae, and stadia were built for entertainment and festival. Gardens and parks were introduced from the Orient. An entourage of royalty built fine villas in the urban environs, and distinctions in caste grew more apparent.

Small kings, wealthy families, and ambitious foreigners desirous of acclaim within this frame of monumental splendor bestowed generous gifts upon the city.

[4] *The Planning of Hellenistic Cities*, Percy Gardner.

Restoration by A. Zippelius. *Bettmann Archive*

The city of Priene was rebuilt during the 4th century B.C. and illustrates the transition from the Hellenic period to the Hellenistic Age. Having suffered the political disunion of the Greek states, it revived with the spread of Greek culture under Alexander the Great.

In this town we perceive the great influence of the Greeks upon their Macedonian conquerors while we also detect the effect of imperial domination. Alexander was a pupil of Plato, embraced the ideals of Hellenic culture with fervent enthusiasm, and determined to extend them throughout the world. The physical improvement in Greek cities reflected the deep roots of Hellenic culture and exhibited the refinement of the Athenian tradition. The Hippodamian plan introduced a more orderly arrangement of the city than was present in the early Hellenic development. The physical facilities for public assembly, the market place and the theater, the planning of sites for satisfactory orientation of dwellings, the buildings of temples, paved streets, sanitation and water supply were improved, and the forms of these facilities expressed the subtle esthetic arrangement and consummate skill possessed by the Greeks.

But changes from the Hellenic tradition were also in evidence, and the Hellenistic Age was the period during which these changes occurred. The slave system had always been the foundation of society in the world, and whereas it continued during Athenian supremacy, the feature of Greek democracy was the introduction of a government of laws decided by citizens in public assembly. The Hellenistic Age, however, departed from this process and returned to a state of imperialism. After Alexander's successful military expansion and in the face of his burning ambition to extend the culture of the Hellenes, he succumbed to the spell of personal power. As has since happened in the world, this power dominated his life, destroyed him and his empire, and his achievements.

Consistent with imperialism the cities of the Hellenistic Age were embellished with the display of a growing monarchy. More and more support for city development came from the noble class desirous for acclaim as benefactors. Distinction between the ruling class and the populace returned to the city and the physical facilities became more lavish, more grand and monumental in scale. The open-air meeting place—the *pnyx*—of the early Greek town was replaced by the *agora* and assembly hall; thence more and richer buildings were added through beneficent gifts from minor rulers and royal satellites. Priene was a city of only some 4,000 people, but it was equipped with relatively copious facilities. The gymnasium and stadium were introduced, temples were built and improved, and new public buildings were donated in return for popular favors.

When the ruling genius of Alexander disappeared social disintegration was inevitable. Imperial rule had drained the initiative and dissipated the strength of society. These forces were at work in towns like Priene where the refined quality of Hellenic culture shifted to the luxuriant excesses of the Hellenistic Age and set the stage for the decline of a great period in the history of mankind.

Empty honors were accorded for their beneficence. The great stoa at Priene was the gift of a king of Orophernes of Cappadocia. Here, one by the name of Zosimus staged a festive dinner for the whole citizen population of the city in return for receipt of the "dignity of Stephanephorus". According to Pausanias the *bouleuterion* at Megalopolis was named after Thersilius who dedicated it, and the donor of the *bouleuterion* at Elis was one by the name of Lalichmium.[5] Inscriptions bear a quantity of evidence of this surge for popularity through these magnanimous gestures of philanthropy. The genuine character of the Hellenistic city was, in the third and second centuries B.C., degenerating into a hollow form of a decaying social structure.

Roman Prowess. In their early migrations to the Italian peninsula, the Greeks had founded cities. Like other peoples on the shores of the Mediterranean, the Romans drew upon the Greek culture planted there. They grafted Hellenic forms upon the irregular patterns of their villages and used these forms for the new towns they founded in the near and far reaches of their broad empire.

The Romans were calculating organizers. They excelled in technical achievement and were skilled engineers and aggressive city builders. But they had not the philosophy of the Greeks. Preoccupied with conquest, administration was their prime business and they devised political organization which has continued to this day. Intense builders with a flair for gargantuan scale, their works were not graced with the refinement of line and form or the creative spirit of the Athenians. Greek forms were reduced to mechanical formulae which could be readily applied like parts arranged upon graph paper.

With inventive genius the Romans solved technical problems created by the congregation of great numbers of people in cities. They developed water supply and distribution, drainage systems, and methods of heating upon which the health of the masses depended. The great aqueducts for transport of water over tremendous distances and the underground sewers like Cloaca Maxima were feats of engineering skill and prowess. The great highways paved with stone represented the tireless efforts of intense builders.

Monuments and Diversion. The Forum Romanum of the Republic had a human scale. Its proportions and form undoubtedly caused the citizen to feel he was a part of the activity that took place there. Here the individual and his identity were merged with "Rome". The buildings were not so overwhelming in size that they humbled the individual. The common people had their share of hardships, but one can imagine the Gracchi pleading their case in the Senate for an equitable distribution of the land and its benefits. The citizen understood the religion of his temples, and he was proud of the triumphs of the Roman legions abroad. He could participate in the business affairs of the basilica and perhaps engage in the money-lending enterprise carried on there. He felt himself to be one of the actors in this drama as a Greek had been in his assembly and agora.

[5] *The Political Meeting Places of the Greeks*, William A. McDonald, Johns Hopkins Press, 1943.

POMPEII

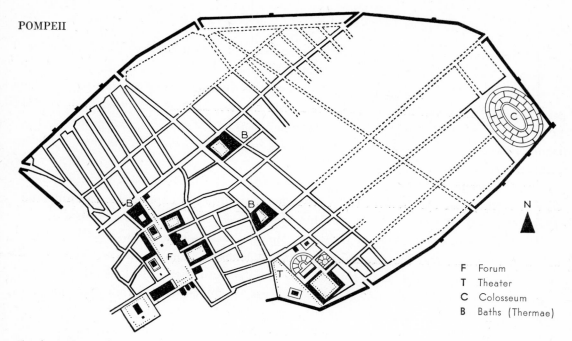

F Forum
T Theater
C Colosseum
B Baths (Thermae)

The forum lies in the center of an irregular street system suggesting the probability that the more regular pattern was established as the town grew in population and extended its area. The variety of building types about the forum was unified with a continuous colonnade. The rectangular shape, according to Vitruvius, was adapted to the use of the forum for gladiatorial demonstrations and other public events. The colonnade supported a balcony for observers.

THE APPIAN WAY OF ANCIENT ROME

TransWorld Airways

This citizen of early Rome saw gracious living like that in Pompeii and Herculaneum or the busy life and fashions of Ostia. He observed distinctions in class among the dwellings but took these for granted in a day when a slave economy was all he had thus far witnessed in history. If the citizen was not blessed with wealth, he could nevertheless indulge himself in the various common forms of entertainment the community offered—the gay combat in the colosseum, the drama in the theater, or a festival in the forum.

But the scene changed for the Roman citizen. World conquest was the ambition of Rome, and the citizen saw great riches flow into his capital. He saw intrigue absorb the military and political leaders and he saw the public lands and wealth won in campaigns appropriated by them. He saw monuments erected in dedication of great victories, and the triumphant entry of generals from abroad.

The Roman citizen saw emperors crowned and he saw them build new fora which dwarfed his Forum Romanum. He saw each new forum exceed in size the one that preceded it. The Forum of Augustus was greater than the Forum of Julius Caesar; the Forum of Vespasian matched that of Augustus; and the Forum of Trajan was the most magnificent of all. He saw the Palace of Augustus crown the Palatine and the Golden House of Nero span acres.

He saw his attention to social and economic inequities diverted by institutions for pleasure rather than culture. He saw the huge colosseum where carnal displays were staged for the excitement of a populace which might otherwise have grown restless. He saw the Circus Maximus where 150,000 persons could revel in the bloody combats of gladiators.

The scale of all these structures, the spaces they enclosed, and the architectural fitments with which they were adorned appalled the Roman citizen. It was not the plan of a city which he saw emerging, but a series of ever greater monuments to the glory and deification of his rulers. Even the colonial cities followed the form of the military camp.

Slums and Decay. Diversion was afforded the citizen, but he saw his city grow congested. He saw men, like Crassus, profess to be civic leaders but speculate in the land and build huge tenements. He saw the city crowded with slums to become fuel for disastrous fires. The height of buildings reached six, seven, and eight floors and Emperor Augustus found it necessary to decree a limit of 70 feet for all tenements. According to the Constantin Regionary Catalog there were 46,602 blocks of apartments and only 1,797 private houses in Rome in the fourth century after Christ.

This Roman citizen saw nobles, the returning heroes, and the rulers move to great estates and comfortable villas in the country. The Empire had grown so broad and so fat no enemy could reach them. Luxury and display were imported from the Orient, and the leaders grew soft. The city-dweller lived in slums while the affluent enjoyed leisure in the country. No strong and healthy men with convictions remained to defend the Empire, and Rome gradually merged with the camp of barbarians from the north. Civilization descended into the Dark Ages.

The lesson of Rome and the cities it built is well stated by Henry Smith Williams:[6]

During the entire ages of Trajan and the Antonines, a succession of virtuous and philosophic emperors followed each other; the world was in peace; the laws were wise and well administered; riches seemed to increase; each succeeding generation raised palaces more splendid, monuments and public edifices more sumptuous, than the preceding; the senatorial families found their revenues increase; the treasury levied greater imposts. But it is not the mass of wealth, it is on its distribution, that the prosperity of states depends; increasing opulence continued to meet the eye, but men became more miserable; the rural population, formerly active, robust, and energetic, were succeeded by a foreign race, while the inhabitants of towns sank in vice and idleness, or perished in want, amidst the riches they had themselves created.

[6] *The Historian's History of the World*, Henry Smith Williams, The Outlook Company, 1904.

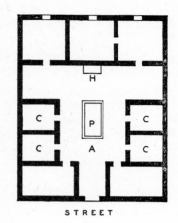

EARLY ROMAN HOUSES

A	Atrium	S	Shop
B	Peristyle	E	Entrance Vestibule
C	Bed Cubicles	L	Living Room
H	Hearth	D	Dining Room
P	Reservoir	K	Kitchen

Pompeii was a city largely devoted to residences. It was not a metropolis, as was Rome, and did not suffer the congestion of a large city. In it we find a wide range of dwelling facilities. The early "Roman" dwelling adopted the atrium (A) from Greece. Houses of the more affluent added the feature known as the "peristyle" (B) and this was sometimes extended into a garden. The House of Pansa shows these several elements. It occupies an entire block. Along the side street there were attached some small apartment-dwellings which convey some idea of the contrast between accommodations of the wealthy occupant in the main house and the poorer artisans or slaves. The street front of the houses was usually devoted to shops. From the entrance door a vestibule (E) opened into the *atrium* (A) in which the *impluvium* (P) for the collection of rain from the roof was located. Here guests were received and business affairs conducted. A passage connected the *atrium* and the peristyle, the heart of family life. Open to the sky, it was surrounded by a colonnade. Various rooms opened from the peristyle: the lounge (L), dining room (D), and sleeping rooms (C). Beyond the peristyle was the garden. Portions of the house had sleeping rooms on the second floor for slave quarters.

Heating was provided generally by charcoal braziers carried from room to room, but an ingenious device called the *hypocaust* was installed in some buildings. It was a series of ducts through which warm air was circulated from a central furnace. Cooking was done with charcoal on a stone stove. Lighting was obtained from oil candelabra.

While the public baths (*thermae*) occupied an important place in the social life of Romans, some of the houses were equipped with bathing facilities. Copper pipes have been found, although drain pipes have not been considered adaptable for sewage disposal. Construction was of stone, brick, and wood, and window glass was apparently in fairly common use.

LATE ROMAN HOUSE—House of Pansa

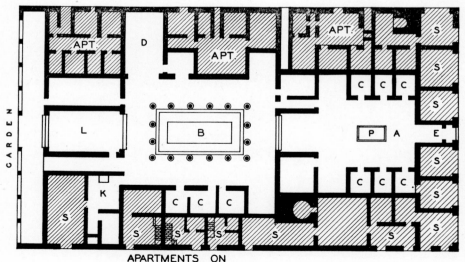

APARTMENTS ON
SECOND FLOOR

ROME

The original settlement of Rome lay on the banks of the Tiber near the later Forum Romanum. From this center, protected by the surrounding hills, the city fanned out in all directions. It became the scene for a series of ever-greater projects glorifying the military leaders and emperors. In addition to the temples, fora, and palaces, huge facilities for entertainment were built for diversion of the masses—the baths, colossia, theaters, stadia, and the circus.

There is no indication that the street system in Rome was other than an irregular pattern typical of great cities which grew by accretion. In contrast to a small city like Pompeii, Rome grew in population, suffered speculation in land and buildings, became congested, and was overrun with slums. Buildings increased in height until Augustus found it necessary to decree a height limit of 70 feet.

O FEET 1000

A	Forum Romanum	J	Baths of Trajan
B	Forum of Emperors	K	Baths of Diocletian
C	Palace of the Emperors	L	Theater of Pompey
D	Colosseum	M	Theater of Marcellus
E	Circus Maximus	N	Pantheon
F	Cloaca Maxima	O	Tomb of Hadrian
G	Claudian Aqueduct	P	Circus Flaminius
H	Baths of Caracalla		

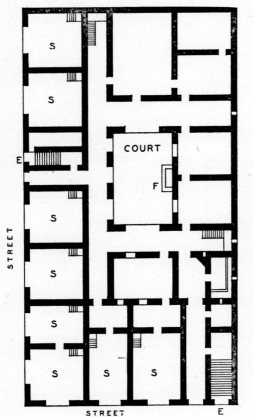

Ostia, the seaport for Rome, was likewise crowded and contained many apartments. The House of Diana is an example. It was five stories high, built of brick masonry, although many of the tenements in Rome were constructed of wood and were serious fire hazards. In the House of Diana there was a row of apartments facing the exterior and a row facing the interior court. A balcony surrounded the third floor. Water was supplied to the tenants at a fountain in the courtyard, and it is probable that a latrine was located on the first floor whence waste could be disposed. Shops were on the ground floor with interior stairs leading from each to an apartment above.

There is evidence of apartment buildings more commodious than this example, but there were undoubtedly many tenements offering less space. One poet spoke of the necessity for him to climb 200 steps to reach his dwelling.

S Shop   E Entrance   F Fountain

APARTMENT HOUSE, OSTIA

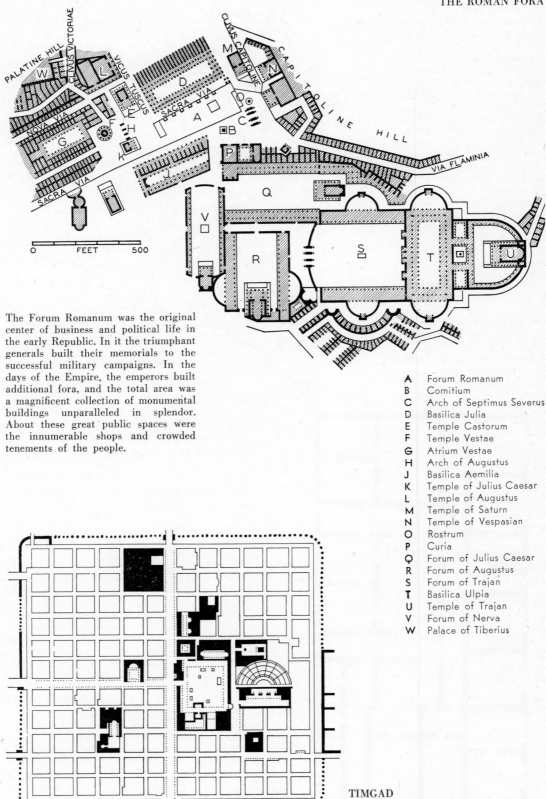

The Forum Romanum was the original center of business and political life in the early Republic. In it the triumphant generals built their memorials to the successful military campaigns. In the days of the Empire, the emperors built additional fora, and the total area was a magnificent collection of monumental buildings unparalleled in splendor. About these great public spaces were the innumerable shops and crowded tenements of the people.

A	Forum Romanum
B	Comitium
C	Arch of Septimus Severus
D	Basilica Julia
E	Temple Castorum
F	Temple Vestae
G	Atrium Vestae
H	Arch of Augustus
J	Basilica Aemilia
K	Temple of Julius Caesar
L	Temple of Augustus
M	Temple of Saturn
N	Temple of Vespasian
O	Rostrum
P	Curia
Q	Forum of Julius Caesar
R	Forum of Augustus
S	Forum of Trajan
T	Basilica Ulpia
U	Temple of Trajan
V	Forum of Nerva
W	Palace of Tiberius

TIMGAD

The Pattern of a Roman Camp

THE MEDIEVAL TOWN

Out of the Dark Ages. By the fifth century after Christ the Roman Empire had crumbled under the weight of luxury, pomp, and ceremony. Western civilization declined, trade disintegrated, and the urban population returned to rural life. Cities shrank in size and importance, and social and economic confusion followed.

Barbaric rulers established city-states and formed the nucleus of future nations. The economy was rooted in agriculture, and the rulers parceled their domains among vassal lords who pledged military support for the kingdom. The people were dependent upon the land for their subsistence and entered a state of serfdom under their lords. The feudal system was the new order.

Wars among the rival feudal lords were frequent. Strategic sites were sought for their castles, and within these fortified strongholds the serfs of the surrounding countryside found protection. Through centuries of the Dark Ages monasteries served as havens of refuge for the oppressed, and the church strengthened its position during these trying times. This influence combined with the power of the feudal lords renewed the advantages of communal existence within the protective walls. Invention of the battering ram and catapult increased the danger from enemies, forced the construction of heavier walls, and gave increased impetus for a return to urban life. The countryside was not safe, and fortifications were extended to include the dwellings that clustered about the castle and monastery.

Castle, Church, and Guild. Movement to the towns brought a marked revival of trade about the eleventh century. Advantages accrued to the feudal lords—in return for protection they collected higher rent for their land. Many new towns were founded, and sites of old Roman towns were restored. Urban life was encouraged by the lords; they granted charters which secured certain rights and privileges of citizenship to the urban dwellers. This new form of freedom was attractive to those who had lived their lives in serfdom.

Then the merchants and craftsmen formed guilds to strengthen their social and economic position. Weavers, butchers, tailors, masons, millers, metalworkers, car-

CARCASSONNE

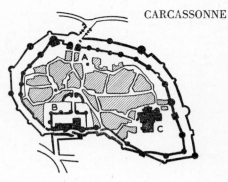

A   Market Square
B   Castle
C   Church of St. Nazaire

NOERDLINGEN

A   Cathedral Plaza
B   Moat

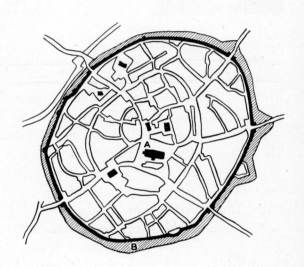

Medieval cities of the twelfth and thirteenth centuries usually had irregular street patterns and heavy walls. Carcassonne was restored by Viollet-le-duc in the nineteenth century. In it we see the castle (B) with its own moat and walls, the market place (A), and the Church of St. Nazaire (C). The plan of Noerdlingen shows the radial and lateral pattern of irregular roadways with the church plaza as the principal focal point of the town. The city of the Middle Ages grew within the confines of the walls. While the population was small, there was space in the town, but when it increased the buildings were packed more closely and the open spaces filled. Sanitation and water supply remained the same. The result was intolerable congestion, lack of hygiene, and pestilence.

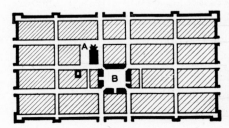

MONTPAZIER

A   Cathedral Square   B   Market Square

During the thirteenth and fourteenth centuries colonial cities were founded by young empires to protect their trade and provide military security. They were platted for allocation of sites to settlers and the regular plan is a distinct contrast to the informal development of the normal medieval town.

CARCASSONNE

penters, leatherworkers, glassmakers, all established regulations to control their production, maintain their prices, and protect their trade. A new social order was in the making—a wealthy mercantile class was rising to challenge the power of the feudal lords.

The early medieval town was dominated by the church or monastery and the castle of the lord. The church plaza became the market place and, with citizenship bestowed upon the people and merchant guilds established, the town hall and guild hall were built on or adjacent to the market plaza. The castle was surrounded by its own walls as a final protection in the event an enemy penetrated the main fortifications and entered the city.

Distinction between town and country was sharp, but this demarcation and the small size of the city provided ready access to the open countryside in times of peace. Aiding the protection of cities, the town sites were usually on irregular terrain, occupying hilltops or islands. The town was designed to fit the topographic feaures. The circulation and building spaces were molded to these irregular features and naturally assumed an informal character.

The roads radiated generally from the church plaza and market square to the gates, with secondary lateral roadways connecting them. The irregular pattern was probably consciously devised as a means to confuse an enemy in the event he gained entrance to the town. Although the battering ram and the catapult were instruments for assault upon the heavy fortifications and hot oil poured from the battlements was a means for mass defense, hand-to-hand combat was the principal form of military action. In the maze of wandering streets the advantage rested with the inhabitants against an enemy unfamiliar with the town arrangement.

The Picturesque Town. The abbés and artisans were sensitive to the form and materials of the buildings they erected. Under their guidance, care was exercised in the placement of, and relation between, the structures of the town. Buildings assumed a functional character in both form and location. They were not built to be "picturesque"; that quality emerged from the consideration given to town building by its builders. Accidents of vista and contrasts of form and color resulted from the contours of the land and the ingenious selection of the sites for each structure. The commanding position of the cathedral or church gave a singular unity to the town, a unity strengthened by the horizontal envelope of the encircling walls.

The entire town was treated with a structural logic that characterized the architectural treatment of the Romanesque and early Gothic buildings. Open spaces—the streets and plazas—developed as integral parts of the sites upon which the buildings were erected. With the exception of a few main roads between the gates and the market place, streets were used as pedestrian circulation about the town rather than traffic arteries as we know them today. Wheel traffic was generally absent on all but the main roadways.

Medieval Dwellings. Conservation of heat in the cold climates and the restrictive area of the town caused the houses to be built in connected rows along the narrow

MONT ST. MICHEL

It was the church rather than the palace that dominated the medieval town. Encircled by its protective walls, the town was small. In later days the battlements were elaborately engineered, as in Middleburg, and the populace was further separated from the open spaces about the town.

MIDDLEBURG

SEGOVIA

streets. Behind these rows of dwellings open space was reserved and in them the domestic animals were kept and gardens cultivated. The workshop and kitchen occupied the ground floor of the dwelling. Here the merchants and craftsmen operated their enterprises and manufactured their goods. There was little distinction between classes among the population of the early medieval town. The workers lived in the homes of their employers as apprentices in the trade or business. The living and sleeping space was on the second floor of the dwelling. The simple plan provided little privacy within the house. Some of the burghers enjoyed separate sleeping rooms, but the accommodations were universally simple and modest in their appointments. The chimney and fireplace replaced the open hearth of the ancient house. Windows were small and covered with crude glass or oiled parchment. Facilities for waste disposal within the dwelling were not usually provided, although some of the houses were equipped with privies. Construction was of masonry or wood frame filled with wattle. Thatch covered the roofs, and the fire hazard caused some towns either to prohibit this type of roofing or to encourage fire resistant materials by offering special privileges for the use of fireproof materials. Streets were usually paved and maintained by the owners of property facing upon them. This may account, in part, for their narrow width.

Medieval Institutions. Meditation and study characterized the monastery. It was extended to research by scholars intent upon the cultivation of professional skills. Monasteries and the guilds combined to form the university, and here were welcomed those who desired to study in withdrawal from the market place. Here also were conducted research and training in law, medicine, and the arts. Universities were assisted by the growing wealth of the merchant class. The universities at Bologna and Paris were founded in the twelfth century and those at Cambridge and Salamanca in the thirteenth century. The churches also established hospitals in which the sick could receive care and treatment not theretofore available to the people.

Life in medieval cities had color, a color visible to all the people. The church provided pageantry and gave drama to the life of every man. It was an institution in which all men could participate, giving inspiration and adding a measure of beauty to the existence of the people. It lifted people above baseness and encouraged better deeds. It offered music and meditation. The sense of participation produced a picturesqueness in life reflected in the picturesqueness of the towns. The people—merchants, artisans, and peasants—mingled in the market place, the guild hall, and the church; a human scale pervaded the informal environment of the city of the people.

There were innumerable hardships suffered and endured by the people of the Middle Ages, but in the early towns they did not lose the sense of intermingling. Each man had the feeling of being an active citizen in his community. This attribute of the urban environment—a social well-being—was, however, soon to be dissipated.

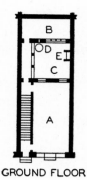

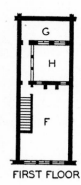

GROUND FLOOR   FIRST FLOOR

MEDIEVAL HOUSE
TWELFTH CENTURY

A Shop
B Kitchen
C Courtyard
D Well
E Privy
F Living Hall
G Sleeping Room
H Court

E Entrance to First Floor
H Living Hall— Store Room Below
C Chapel— "Solar" (Sleeping Dormitory) Above

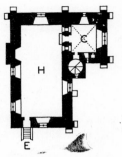

SMALL NORMAN MANOR
FIFTEENTH CENTURY

THE MEDIEVAL DWELLING

The medieval dwelling was conceived as an individual fortress. Before congestion overtook the town, the average dwelling was two stories in height. The work-room and storage were on the first floor or "basement." Sometimes the kitchen was also located here. Living, dining and sleeping took place on the second floor. Masonry was the usual construction, although wood frame filled with wattle and clay and roofed with thatch was not infrequent. It was the forerunner of the half-timber construction later used to a great extent.

As crowding increased, each building lot was used more intensively. Rooms were grouped about a tiny interior courtyard in which a cistern was located. Interior privies were sometimes provided, although there was no sewage disposal, refuse being discarded in the streets or in cesspools beneath the dwelling floors. Heating was provided by a fireplace, and lighting was obtained from wicks dipped in fish oil.

Continued intensity in the use of land raised the height of buildings to three and four stories. Half-timber construction permitted the projection of upper floors beyond each lower floor to further exaggerate the congestion.

For comparison, a small manor house is shown. It contained a "hall" and chapel on the second floor. All living, dining and cooking were performed on this floor. A dormitory, or "solar," was located in the tower above the chapel. A drain pipe was imbedded in the wall for disposal of waste. The windows had no glass and were protected with shutters. The lower floor was a vaulted store room. The manor houses were extended in size and formed the nucleus of villages in many cases.

SIENA

The informal vista of the medieval town. The streets were primarily for people on foot.

CHILHAM

A village square in Tudor England. Always desiring to preserve the quiet repose of their beautiful countryside, the villages of England did not mar the natural landscape setting.

C. H. Ferris

CHAPTER 4

THE NEO-CLASSIC CITY

Mercantilism and Concentration. The number of towns increased rapidly during the Middle Ages, but they remained relatively small in population. Many had only a few hundred people, and the larger cities seldom exceeded 50,000 inhabitants. The physical size was restricted by the girth of the fortifications, water supply, and sanitation, the distance across the town seldom exceeding a mile. Water was available at the town fountain. There was no sewage disposal, and all drainage was by way of the streets.

As long as the population remained small, these apparent deficiencies presented no serious problem. Communication between towns was slow, facilities for transport were cumbersome, and necessity for mutual assistance in times of conflict urgent. The towns were built within ready reach of each other. Most were within a day's journey apart and frequently a round trip to a neighboring town could be made on foot in a single day.

World travel and trade, however, brought a concentration of people to centers situated on main crossroads. During the fourteenth century Florence grew from 45,000 people to 90,000 people, Paris from 100,000 to 240,000, and Venice reached 200,000. Successful merchants consolidated their interests in several towns, and moneylending helped their enterprise. Commerce increased between towns and countries. The danger of military aggression gradually diminished, and safety for travel increased.

The mercantile economy expanded, and the power of the feudal lords declined. Ownership of the land gradually shifted to a new caste of noblemen, the wealthy merchants. The church accumulated a vast domain and there emerged two privileged classes, the nobles and the clergy. The guilds declined and medieval serfdom disappeared, but the facilities for processing materials and goods—the mills, ovens, presses—came into the possession of the noble class. The peasants were required to pay tolls of various sorts for the use of these facilities. The feudal economy had been rooted in the land, and the new economy was dominated by the possession and control of money.

Congestion and Slums. The growing population forced a congestion within the cities not present in earlier days. The traditional height of two stories for dwellings changed to three and four stories. The upper floors were projected beyond the first floor, and the roofs often spanned the street width. Open space within the interior blocks of dwellings was built up. Population density increased without change in the systems of water supply or sanitation.

Wheel traffic increased. The narrow streets became congested, dark, and filth-ridden from refuse thrown from dwelling windows, and provision for elimination of waste remained inadequate. The call of *gare de l'eau* was familiar in France and, contracted to the anglicized "gardy loo," it became equally familiar in Edinburgh. Excreta were disposed of in cesspools beneath dwelling floors; there or in the streets it was left to ripen for fertilizer. Odors from filth in the streets was overcome by keeping the windows or shutters closed. Ventilation was by way of the chimney only. Disease spread rapidly in times of epidemic; in the fourteenth century the Black Death, a pestilence of typhus, took the lives of nearly half the urban population.

During this period the cities reverted to a condition inferior to the days of Rome a thousand years before. The manor house of the nobleman grew spacious while the typical dwelling of the poor remained cramped and was moved higher into the attic. The first sewer was installed in London after the Black Death. Water closets were not introduced until the sixteenth century in Spain, France, and England, and it was early in the seventeenth century when water supply was connected to dwellings in London. Fire hazards were prevalent everywhere. As a precautionary measure an ordinance in London, in the thirteenth century, required that slate or tile roofs replace the usual reed and straw. It is interesting to note a similar order that appeared in the American Colonies at a somewhat later date. It read:

New Amsterdam, 15 December 1657:
   The Director General and Council of New Netherland to All, who shall see these presents or hear them read, Greeting! Know ye, that to prevent the misfortunes of conflagrations, the roofs of reeds, the wooden and plastered chimneys have long ago been condemned but nevertheless these orders are obstinately and carelessly neglected by many of the inhabitants. . . . The said Director General and Council have decided it to be necessary, not only to renew their former ordinances, but also to amplify the same and to increase the fines. . . .[1]

Overcrowding within the small dwellings of the poorer people further increased the hazards to health and the spread of epidemics. In 1539 an Act of Parliament mentioned that "great mischiefs daily grow and increase by reason of pestering of houses with divers families, harboring of inmates, and converting great houses into tenements, and erection of new houses."

Gunpowder. In the fifteenth century gunpowder was invented, and new techniques of warfare were introduced. The feudal lords had relied upon citizen-soldiers to man the crenellated parapets in time of siege, but the new weapons of attack and defense required larger numbers of trained professional soldiers. Military engi-

[1] *Housing Comes of Age*, Straus and Wegg, Oxford University Press, New York, 1938.

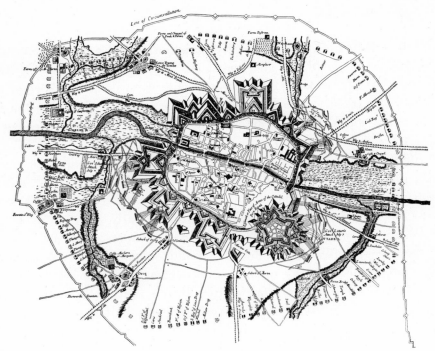

TOURNAY

The invention of gunpowder marked the beginning of the end of the walled town. Prior to development of cannon a dry or water moat surrounded the town walls and provided adequate protection from besieging enemies. Gunpowder increased the range of effective attack and forced the building of ramparts beyond the walls to extend the distance between the town and the attacking forces. Military engineering became an important phase of town building and complicated systems of water moats and ramparts were devised outside the main walls of the city. These broad spaces forced the enemy into more distant positions for their cannon.

The plan of Tournay illustrates the elaborate system of defense fortifications and shows the siege of that city by the Duke of Marlborough in 1709. The position of mortars and cannon, together with their range, is indicated in this plan.

In the late 18th and early 19th centuries long range artillery was greatly improved and the old systems of walls, moats, and ramparts were reduced in effectiveness for military defense, and the form of the city underwent drastic alterations. The walls and ramparts were levelled, the moats were filled-in and boulevards were built in the open space as in the famous Ringstrasse encircling the original town of Vienna. These spaces separated the old town from the surrounding suburbs but, as in Paris, they were gradually built-up in response to the ruthless speculation of the late 19th century and open space disappeared from the city.

VIENNA

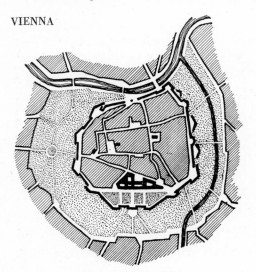

Vienna before 1857

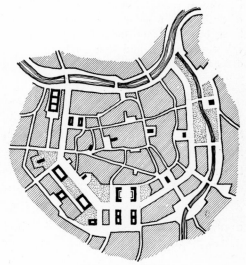

Vienna after 1857

neering became a science. Fortifications were extended, and heavy bastions, moats, and outposts were built. Extension of the area occupied by the fortifications created a "no-man's-land", and separation between town and country became more distinct. Open space outside the walls was further removed from the urban dweller. People came to the cities in large numbers to participate in the expanding commercial enterprise and fill the ranks of professional armies.

The Renaissance. In France the kings achieved a semblance of national unity in the fifteenth century. Elsewhere cities remained provincial dukedoms with wealthy merchant families wielding control over them. It became the ambition of rulers to display their affluence and power by improving their cities. They engaged in intellectual pursuits, drawing upon the classic heritage of Rome for this cultural activity. The noble families of Florence, Venice, Rome, and Lombardy desired to embellish their cities; the Medicis, Borgias, and Sforzas built themselves new palaces on which were draped the classic motifs. A formalism was grafted upon the medieval town although the buildings retained the characteristic fortress quality of the Middle Ages. The basic form of cities did not change, but the structure was decorated with façades of classic elements.

The Church participated in this movement. Residence of the Popes was re-established in Rome, and work on the Vatican Palace was begun. Pope Julius planned to replace the old basilica of St. Peter with a great church which would become the center of Christendom.

Feverish preoccupation with the arts gripped the merchant princes, churchmen, and the kings. Practice of the arts became a profession. The system of apprentice training in Italy prepared men to work in a variety of artistic fields. An apprentice to a painter would also work in the shop of a goldsmith; a sculptor would study architecture. Versatility was a characteristic of the artists and their services were given encouragement. Leonardo da Vinci practiced all the arts and became a planner, military engineer, and inventor as well. Kings, merchant nobles, and Popes were patrons of the arts and bid heavily for the services of the growing number of practitioners.

The strange anonymity of the master-builders of medieval towns no longer prevailed in the Renaissance. Robert de Luzarches, William of Sens (Canterbury Cathedral), Geoffrey de Noyes (Lincoln Cathedral), Jean-le-Loup, and Henrico di Gambodia (Milan Cathedral) are seldom recorded in the history of medieval town building, whereas a host of individuals received personal recognition in the Renaissance and later periods. The names of Brunelleschi, Alberti, Bramante, Peruzzi and Sangallo in Italy, and Bullant, de l'Orme, Lescot in France, are as well known as their works. Many others achieved world renown; their names were more prominent than the patrons who commissioned their works. Mansart, Bullet, Blondel, Lemercier, de Brosse, Le Notre, Percier, and Fontaine in France; Bernini, Longhena, Borromini, Palladio, Michelangelo, Raphael in Italy; Inigo Jones, Christopher Wren, the Brothers Adam in England; all these artists enjoyed the confidence and patronage of Popes, kings, and merchants.

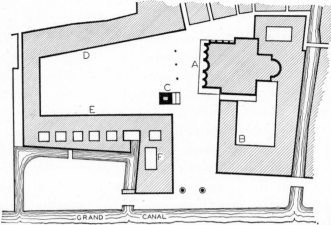

PIAZZA OF ST. MARK'S

A Cathedral
B Palace of the Doges
C Campanile
D Procuriatie Vecchia
E Procuriatie Nuove
F Libraria Vecchia

Formal plazas of the Renaissance were carved out of the medieval town and given monumental scale and form reminiscent of classic antiquity. Exterior space was enclosed with formal façades, and the shapes were modelled like sculptural pieces isolated from the rest of the city.

PIAZZA OF ST. PETER'S

A Piazza
B Cathedral
C Vatican

PIAZZA OF ST. PETER'S FROM THE CATHEDRAL

Monarchy and Monumentalism. The monumental character of the classic returned to the city. Every form had its centerline, and every space its axis. The structural quality of the Middle Ages was replaced by a classic sculptural form, modeled symmetrically. The "barbaric" art of medieval cities was forsaken. With haughty disdain Molière called it:

> The rank taste of Gothic monuments,
> These odius monsters of the ignorant centuries,
> Which the torrents of barbarism spewed forth.

The axis and the strong centerline symbolized the growing concentration of power. Kings of France became monarchs, wealthy merchants in Italy became autocratic dukes, large landowners in England became lord barons, and the Popes became benevolent partners of all. Louis XIV of France gave voice to the spirit of the times when he shouted his famous words, *"L'État, c'est moi."*

Out of the cramped medieval town were carved formal "squares." The modeling of spatial forms absorbed the attention and skills of designers and planners, and classic elements were ingeniously assembled to form the spaces. Michelangelo created the Campodiglio on the Capitoline Hill in Rome, Bernini designed the huge Piazza of St. Peter's, the Piazza di San Marco in Venice was completed, Rainaldi built the twin churches on the Piazza del Popolo, the Place Royale (now Place des Vosges) and Place des Victoires were built in Paris.

Long-range artillery removed the advantage of the old walls for military defense. Louis XIV ordered Vauban, his military engineer, to redesign the defense system. Vauban tore down the walls and built earthwork ramparts beyond the city. Within the leveled space of the old walls boulevards and promenades were laid. The famous Ringstrasse of Vienna occupied the open space left when the city walls of that city were demolished. Cities were opening up, and the city of the Middle Ages was being released from its clutter. Transition from the Renaissance Period to the Baroque Period was in process.

The Baroque City. An air of grandeur permeated the courts of kings. Louis XIV ordered Le Notre to design the gardens of Versailles. Here was space of unparalleled proportions, scale of incomprehensible size. Here was the conception of a man who, having achieved domination over the lives of men, confidently set about to become the master of nature. The egotism of rulers knew no limitations, nor could it brook a hint of equality; Louis XIV threw the wealthy financier, Foucquet, into prison for his temerity to build a château almost as fine as the king's.

In the eighteenth century the Baroque city expanded, and dominance of the ruler intensified. The avenues of Versailles focused upon the royal palace, whereas the whole city of Karlsruhe as well as Mannheim revolved about the palaces and great gardens of the royalty.

Plazas of the seventeenth century had been designed as isolated, enclosed spaces. They were now opened and less confined, as though moved by a desire to recapture the

VERSAILLES

A Palace
B Gardens
C Town

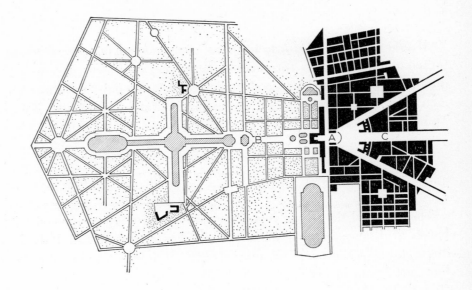

THE BAROQUE CITY

The centerline and the axis symbolized the mighty power of the monarch. Louis XIV ordered the removal of his palace from the congested city of Paris to the open hunting grounds of Versailles, and he ordered the avenues to radiate from his magnificent palace. The entire city of Karlsruhe was designed to revolve about and radiate from the Prince's palace. After the fire of 1666 Christopher Wren proposed a monumental plan for the rebuilding of London. He conceded the new power dominant in England by placing upon the major focal point the Stock Exchange. But the plan was not accepted; the necessary adjustment of property boundaries and prices could not be resolved.

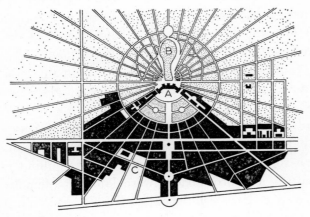

KARLSRUHE

A Palace
B Gardens
C Town

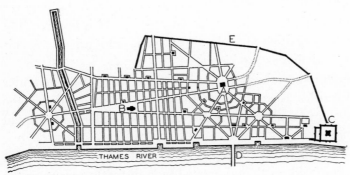

LONDON (Christopher Wren's Plan)

A Stock Exchange
B St. Paul's Cathedral
C Tower of London
D London Bridge
E Old Walls

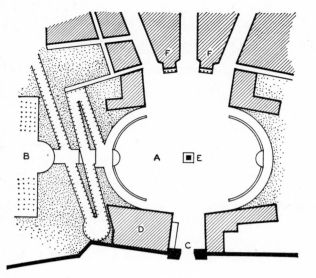

PIAZZA DEL POPOLO, Rome

A Piazza   D Church of Santa Maria del Popolo
B Pincio Hill and Gardens   E Obelisk
C Porto del Popolo   F Twin Churches by Rainaldi

During the Baroque period, the desire for unconfined space gripped the city rulers and their designers. The tremendous Place de la Concorde, designed by Gabriel, was created as part of the Paris extension plan to exalt King Louis XV. No longer was it a plaza framed with buildings like Place Vendome. It was rather a campus between other open spaces, the Tuileries Gardens, the Champs Élysées, and the River Seine. The Plazas in Nancy were linked with a broad avenue of trees which was itself a plaza. Piazza del Popolo exhibited the same characteristics in three dimensions. A series of garden terraces continued the open space up the Pincio Hill on one side, and open space extended the vista on the other.

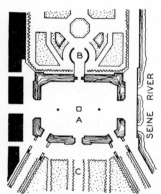

NANCY

A Place Stanislas
B Place Carriere
C Place Royale

A Place de la Concorde
B Tuileries Gardens
C Champs Élysées

PLACE DE LA CONCORDE, Paris

PLACE VENDOME
Paris

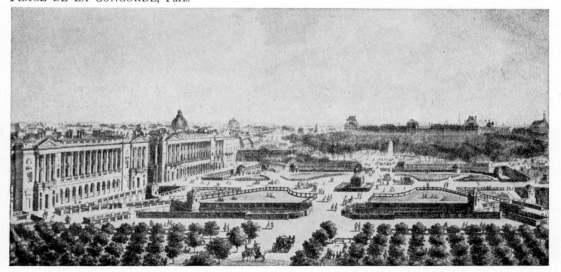

space of the countryside. Design shifted from walled-in architectural forms to an extension and expansion of open space. Jules-Hardouin Mansart, architect for the palace buildings at Versailles, designed the Place Vendôme with greater dimensions than previous squares in Paris. The three squares by Héré de Corny in Nancy were connected, the continuity of open space emphasized by colonnades and enhanced by a tree-lined avenue.

Probably the most dramatic example of the new surge to penetrate the city with open space was the Place de la Concorde designed by Jacques-Ange Gabriel during the reign of Louis XV. In this square, space is almost completely released. It flows from the gardens of the Tuileries and the Louvre on one side into the broad avenue of the Champs Élysées begun by Louis XIV to connect Paris with his palace at Versailles. The scale is further amplified by the Seine river lying along one side. Opposite the river is the only group of buildings facing this tremendous square.

Another departure in urban design was the Piazza del Popolo in Rome designed by Valadier. A three-dimensional transition of space was obtained with a series of terraces linking the lower level of the square and the gardens on the Pincio Hill above. Continuity replaced the enclosure of open space as the new direction in civic design.

In England the classic revival came later than elsewhere, the Tudor style having absorbed the Renaissance shock. Recoiling from the hazards of overhanging upper stories, a building ordinance in 1619 decreed that the walls of buildings would henceforth be built vertically from foundation to roof. Timed with the onrushing wave of classic formalism, this law aided the introduction of the "Italian Style" ushered in by Inigo Jones, its leading exponent.

The landowning class had tempered the rise of monarchy in England and the monumentalism of the "grand plan" did not quite take root there. Christopher Wren attempted it in his plan for rebuilding London after the fire of 1666. He went so far as to place the Stock Exchange at the symbolic focal point of his plan instead of the traditional palace or cathedral. Even this acknowledgment of the domination of mercantilism in England was not enough to offset disagreement over the necessary reapportionment of property values destroyed in the fire.

Formalism permeated the English Renaissance, but it was expressed in terms of quiet repose rather than striking grandeur. This quality is observed in the simple curved building forms facing broad open spaces of the Circus and Royal Crescent in Bath designed by John Wood, the younger. The same quality was built into the undulating surfaces and free curving forms of Lansdowne Crescent, also in Bath. John Nash carried on these curving plan forms overlooking spacious open parks in his designs for the Park Crescent and Regent's Park developments in London.

Formalism was unobtrusively introduced in the enclosed squares of London during the eighteenth century. They were intended not as impressive plazas, but as places for the quiet relaxation of the surrounding residents. These simple, though formal, open spaces were created largely by builders who would be classified today as "speculators"; they were in the business of subdividing land and building homes. Many are unknown, as in the case of Lansdowne Crescent in Bath, but two prominent builders in London were James Burton and Thomas Cubitt and they lent a dignity to their profession by the work they performed.

Behind the Façades. The fine rows of formal dwellings and squares in England, the monumental vistas, royal gardens and the palaces of France, the well-modeled piazzas in Italy, all had been built for the upper classes, the wealthy merchants, and the kings. The lot of the people of lesser means had not been substantially improved. It was not the purpose of the builders of the Baroque town to engage in reforms. They were concerned with such improvement of the urban environment that would maintain the prestige and glory of their exalted position in society. The broad avenues provided more than satisfaction of the ego and vanity in despots, more than delightful promenades for the elegant carriages of the aristocrats; they were strategic means with which to impress the populace with the power and discipline of marching armies.

Behind the fine façades of the plazas and wide avenues dwelt the congested urban population. The city lacked sanitation, sewers, water distribution, and drainage. Epidemics and pestilence were frequent, and the poverty was appalling. A breach was widening between the aristocracy and the masses. Fratricidal wars of religion and social restlessness of the seventeenth century were followed by the stamp of the despotic heel and the courtiers. Oppression brought revolutions in the eighteenth century. The Baroque city had unfolded its grand open spaces and they were overlapping upon the people. Another change was taking place: machines were replacing handcraft methods for making goods for trade.

Colonial Expansion—America. Aided by the mariner's compass, courageous explorers in the fifteenth and sixteenth centuries extended the net of colonial empires over the face of the globe. The eyes of people everywhere looked toward the new world in North America for relief from oppression and chaos. Colonies in the Americas were settled by pioneers impelled by a burning desire for freedom. Far removed from the mother-countries and with a whole great land as an ever-widening frontier to the west, the settlements did not grow as permanent fortified towns. Strong forts were established at some early settlements—Havana, San Juan, St. Augustine, New Amsterdam—but the barricades thrown up as protection from attack by Indians offered no impediment to the development of villages in the way that fortifications had restricted the growth of medieval cities in Europe.

The initial settlement was sometimes irregular in plan; the Wall Street district in Manhattan retains the pattern of the early settlement of New Amsterdam about 1660, and Boston streets meandered about the Common. But most of the towns were platted in advance for allocation of the land to settlers. The people who ventured across the sea to this new land sought opportunities from which they had been deprived in their homeland. Freedom meant the right to their land and possessions for their households. The principal occupation was agriculture; the towns were small and within walking distance from all parts to the countryside about them.

The quiet New England towns reflected the modest character of the puritan. The

BATH

Lansdowne
Crescent

A The Circus

B Royal Crescent

C Victoria Park

Open space was sought in England as on the continent. The handsome forms facing broad, informal park spaces are shown in Lansdowne Terrace, the Circus, and the Royal Crescent in Bath.

The formal squares in the residential districts of Bloomsbury, London, were not monumental in design or size, but they identify a conscious effort to improve the environment in cities.

These were developments for the upper classes, not the poor. The king ordered the Regent's Park Project in London as a place of dignified town houses for the well-to-do. The contrast in living environment is indicated in the plan of the Bloomsbury district, the contrast between the rows of two- and three-story residences about the "squares," and the crowded buildings in the network contiguous to the Bloomsbury development.

The Royal Crescent

British Information Service

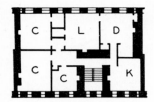

APARTMENT
EIGHTEENTH CENTURY

A Russel Square
B Bedford Square
C Bloomsbury Square
D British Museum

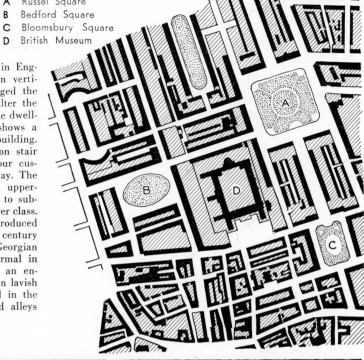

Revival of classicism and a law in England requiring exterior walls to run vertically from foundation to roof changed the appearance of houses but did not alter the crowded multi-family flats and humble dwellings of the poor. The illustration shows a plan of an eighteenth-century flat building. It is six stories high with a common stair to each dwelling unit, not unlike our customary "walk-up" apartments of today. The accommodations were designed for upper-middle class families, but lent itself to subdivision into smaller units for the poorer class.

The residential public gardens introduced by land developers of the eighteenth century were surrounded by the handsome Georgian façades of fine dwellings. While formal in design, these open spaces provided an environment of quiet dignity rather than lavish display. Behind these dwellings and in the older sections of narrow streets and alleys lived the less prosperous.

BLOOMSBURY, LONDON

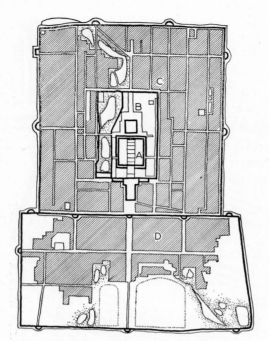

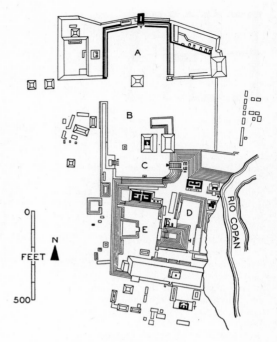

PEKING, China

    A Forbidden City
    B Imperial City
    C Tartar City
    D Chinese City

Within each of the cells surrounded by streets in the sketch is a maze of narrow minor roads, also laid out in rectilinear form.

COPAN, Honduras
  A Great Plaza
  B Middle Court
  C Court of Hieroglyphic Stairway
  D Eastern Court
  E Western Court

There is little record of ancient cities of the Orient. Mohenjo-Daro in 3,000 B.C. had a fairly regular layout of streets, and cities surrounding the great temples of Angkor Vat and Angkor Thom were probably laid in a formal pattern. The power of feudal rulers was maintained with military force in China as elsewhere in the world, and we see the stamp on the plan of Peking.

    Although Peking was founded at an earlier date, the present plan stems from the medieval period about the eleventh century. The original city of the Tartars was extended with the addition of the Chinese city. The Forbidden City of the Emperor lies in the center. The dwellings are cramped and crowded along an intricate system of regular narrow alleys, but the royal gardens and lakes occupy a large area of the city.

    In South and Central America there arose the highly developed civilizations of the Incas, the Aztecs, and the Mayas. Macchu-Picchu is an Incan city of stone perched, terrace on terrace, upon a dramatic mountain site. Only the great temple groups of the Mayas remain. Copan is such a group and it probably served as the combined civic, religious and recreational center for the surrounding population. The people must have lived in dwellings of wood, plaster, and thatch, there being no evidence of habitations. A two-caste society—nobles and slaves—the produce from agriculture was allocated in three parts, one part for the nobles, one part for the slave-workers, and one part as a reserve supply in the event of drought or disaster.

HOPI PUEBLO, Shupolovi

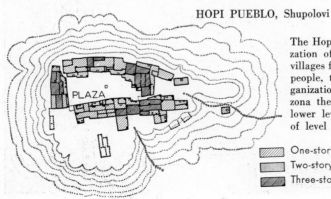

The Hopi Indian village of Shupolovi was the organization of a clan or group of clans who built their villages for protection from their enemies. An agrarian people, their society was communal in political organization. Perched atop the mesas of northern Arizona the people sought their scant water supply at lower levels where they carefully tilled small plots of level land.

    One-story Buildings
    Two-story Buildings
    Three-story Buildings

center was the meeting house and the Common, and each family had its own dwelling, albeit humble. The environment was one of beauty in simplicity—communities of neighbors. In the South the towns were settled by folks also eager to improve their lot, but they reflected the stamp of the Crown. Class distinctions, while dormant for a time, were retained, and formality characterized the life and pattern of the towns.

In Williamsburg, Virginia, the quiet though formal repose of an English town was transplanted to a new land. Through the beneficence of John D. Rockefeller, Jr., it was recently restored and offers an impression of the early colonial town. Williamsburg was settled in 1633, and in 1693 the College of William and Mary was granted a charter and located there. The town became the capital of the Virginia Colony in 1699.

The surveyor, Theodorick Bland, laid out the city with formal axes adapted from the aristocratic mode in Europe. The Duke of Gloucester Street was the main avenue, extending from the College to the Capitol building. A "green" was placed at right angles to this street and terminated at the palace. The town was subdivided into residence lots of one-half acre each. It was a formal plan, but it neither revolved about monumental features nor was it overpowered by them. A human scale pervaded the environment; the town appeared to exist for the people who lived there rather than the rulers who dominated it.

Early Philadelphia and Baltimore may have enjoyed this quality, but it is not apparent in their plans. The City of Brotherly Love was planned by the surveyor, Thomas Holme, for William Penn in 1682. It was a rigid gridiron street pattern extending between the Delaware and Schuylkill Rivers. Two main streets, Broad and Market, bisected the plan in each direction and intersected at the public square in the center of the town. A square block was allocated for a park in each quadrant.

The plan had little distinction. Penn expected it to be a town of single houses and shade trees. By the middle of the eighteenth century, however, it was common practice to build the houses from lot line to lot line and the open spaces were lost within the walls of brick that lined the gridiron streets. Continuous rows of buildings shut off access to the rear of the property, and alleys were cut through the center of the blocks. Then dwellings were built along the alleys, only to become the quaint and narrow business and residential streets for which the city is known today.

The aristocratic paternalism that characterized the early settlements in the southern colonies was reflected in the plan of Savannah, Georgia. Laid out in 1733 by James Oglethorpe, the plan was a rectilinear street system liberally interspersed with park squares along the avenues. The streets linked these parks and created continuity of open space when the town was built with single houses. It has since been forsaken by the intensive building coverage of the intermediate blocks.

Trade and shipping thrived in the North and settlers flocked to the Colonies. Landowners opened subdivisions and platted lots for sale and lease. Rights to pasture and timber on adjacent land were sometimes granted to purchasers of lots in the new towns. Such a development was Lansingburgh on the Hudson, surveyed by Joseph Blanchard for the large landowner, Abraham Lansing. This, like many others, was a speculative

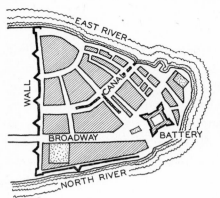

NEW AMSTERDAM

The Dutch settlement of New Amsterdam was built on the tip of what is now known as Manhattan, New York City. The pattern of its streets in 1660 still exists—Broadway (called Breedeweg by the Dutch), Broad Street, and Wall Street. The almost medieval irregular street plan and the canal are reminiscent of the Dutch towns in Europe.

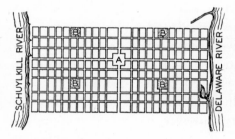

A Market Square
B The Capitol
C Governor's Palace
D College of William and Mary
E Bruton Parish Church
F Duke of Gloucester Street

WILLIAMSBURG

Settled in 1633, the town of Williamsburg was founded in 1699 as the capital of the Virginia Colony. It was laid out by the surveyor Theodorick Bland. The main street, Duke of Gloucester Street, was 99 feet wide and extended from the College of William and Mary to the Capitol. The land was subdivided in lots of about one-half acre in size. The town had a population of between 3,000 and 4,000 people. The quiet formality of the town was English. The spaces are not "grand"; they have a human scale.

PHILADELPHIA

William Penn commissioned the surveyor Thomas Holme to lay out the city in 1682. A rigid gridiron plan was adopted. Two major streets crossed in the center of the town and formed a public square. A square block park was placed in each of the four quadrants. The early dwellings were single-family houses. In the middle of the eighteenth century it became common practice to build dwellings on the side lot lines resulting in continuous rows of buildings which cut off access to the rear yards. Alleys were then cut through the center of the blocks. These alleys have since become streets.

A City Square
B Park

SAVANNAH

Laid out in 1733 by Oglethorpe, Savannah was a regular pattern of rectangular streets with park squares liberally spotted in alternate blocks. The plan is similar to Philadelphia with a more generous allocation of open spaces.

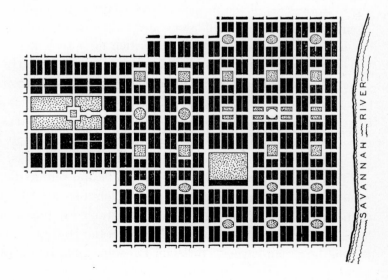

venture; the plan was a gridiron with a Common reserved in the center as in the New England villages. Profiting from the precedent in Philadelphia, alleys were platted in the original subdivision.

The gridiron plan adopted for these towns was not only the simplest form to survey, but it was not an unsatisfactory form for the small village. A sense of unity was maintained by the close relation of all dwellings to the town square and to the agricultural land on the outskirts. It was when this same pattern was extended endlessly that the monotony of the checkerboard lay heavily upon the town.

A small settlement begun in 1649 on the banks of the Severn River in Maryland received the name of Annapolis in 1694. It was the first city in America to adopt diagonal avenues and circles as the basic plan form but was followed by a more dramatic display, the classic plan for Washington, D.C., by Major Pierre Charles L'Enfant.

From Radials to Gridiron. After deliberation of an appropriate location for the capital of this new nation it was decided to avoid existing urban centers such as New York and Philadelphia. Ambitious for the future of their newly founded country, the founding fathers selected a site along the banks of the Potomac River, removed from the commercial environment of established cities. L'Enfant, a young French designer, was commissioned to prepare a plan for the new capital city. With his background in the baroque atmosphere of Paris and inspired by the spirit of the American cause, it was natural that he should conceive of this new city on a grand scale woven into a pattern of geometrical order. Such a plan appealed to the aristocratic tastes of men like Washington and Jefferson, and it was such a plan that was adopted by them in 1791.

Following the example of their capital city, a number of cities wrapped themselves in the radial plan, a system of diagonal streets overlaid upon a gridiron pattern. Joseph Ellicott, brother of Andrew Ellicott who surveyed Washington, D.C., planned the city of Buffalo in 1804. He adopted a form of diagonal streets crossing a gridiron pattern at the central square near the Lake Erie waterfront. After the fire of 1805, Judge Woodward and Governor Hull in 1807 prepared a plan for Detroit. It was a grand complex elaborated with concentric hexagonal streets and containing most, if not all, the myriad forms used in Washington, D.C. To implement the plan, owners of property destroyed in the fire were ceded larger sites conforming to the new layout. New plans in 1831 and 1853 drew away from the original idea and, with the exception of a few spots like Grand Circus Square, there is little apparent form in the city today.

Among the other cities with diagonal streets were Indianapolis and Madison. Both these cities were based upon the gridiron, but diagonals ranged from the center to the four corners of the plan. The center in Indianapolis was an open circle; in Madison the focal point was the Wisconsin State Capitol building.

In the midst of this wave of radial planning a significant development occurred in New York City. In 1800 the city surveyor and architect, Joseph Mangin, proposed a plan for extension of the city to the north. His plan provided for major north-south streets with squares and plazas somewhat reminiscent of Washington, D.C. It also

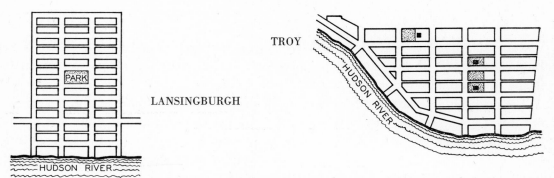

LANSINGBURGH

TROY

Speculative subdivisions were undertaken in the northern colonies in response
to the influx of settlers. One of these was Lansingburgh on the Hudson laid
out by Joseph Blanchard, a surveyor, for Abraham Lansing, a landowner. Purchasers of town lots were allotted
rights to adjoining pasture and timber land. The plan follows the gridiron of Philadelphia with a Common
which was typical of New England towns. Alleys were planned in the original development.

Troy was founded in 1786. It was also a speculative venture and employed the rectangular plan of streets
and alleys.

ANNAPOLIS

Founded in 1694, this little city was the first in this country to adopt
the diagonal street plan inspired by the monumental effects in
France.

WASHINGTON, D. C.

The plan by Pierre L'Enfant, approved by Washington and Jefferson, began a series of city
planning projects in which diagonal and radial streets were
superimposed upon the typical
gridiron layout. The city was
designed as a huge monumental
setting for the Federal government of a new nation.

L'ENFANT'S PLAN OF WASHINGTON, D. C.

BUFFALO

In 1804 Joseph Ellicott, a surveyor, laid out the city of Buffalo on the shores of Lake Erie. He copied the diagonal streets of Washington, D. C., with the plazas and circles of that city.

DETROIT

Judges' and Governor's Plan for Detroit, 1807.

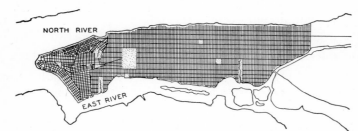

NEW YORK CITY

After turning down a proposal of the city surveyor and architect, Joseph Mangin, in 1800, a commission was appointed to arrive at a plan in 1811. Their plan was a rigid gridiron street pattern laid upon the irregular topography of the city. Open space was not generously allocated. A military parade ground of 69 acres, 55 acres for a public market, and 5 small parks were the only open areas provided in the plan. Despite the "uncommonly great" price of land, explained as the reason for the economy of open space, the layout of streets can hardly be construed as economical; they occupy some 30 per cent of the land area. This harsh and uncompromising plan is reflected in the city of today in which open space has all but completely vanished. It was not until the middle of the nineteenth century that the great Central Park was definitely established in the plan.

Fairchild Aerial Surveys, Inc.

suggested a treatment for the waterfront about Manhattan. But Mangin's plan was not adopted.

Instead, an official commission prepared a plan in 1811. This commission was composed of three members, two of whom were lawyers and landowners and the third a surveyor. They proposed a rigid gridiron street system to be laid over the entire island irrespective of the topography and extensive waterfront. Only one angular street was retained—Broadway. The position of the commission was quite clear: "Straight-sided and right-angled houses," they reported, "are the most cheap to build and the most convenient to live in."[2]

The matter of economy obviously guided the commission in its deliberations and dictated its conclusions. They found that "the price of land is so uncommonly great," and their proposal for retention of open space was indeed frugal. A reservation of 69 acres for a military parade ground, 55 acres for a public market, and five small parks was the limit of open area the commission deemed feasible.

Assuming that the major traffic would continue to move back and forth between the Hudson and East Rivers, the east-west streets, 60 feet in width, were spaced but 260 feet apart. This extravagance was offset, however, by economy of streets in the opposite direction; north-south streets, 100 feet wide, were spaced at distances ranging from 600 to 900 feet.

The commission's appraisal of traffic flow was hardly accurate as the reverse direction it has since taken readily attests. Nor did it reflect particular optimism for the future of this great city. But it is the economy of the commission that poses the most pertinent issue because it bears strong resemblance to that practiced in later and less happy days of urban planning.

It will be recalled that Peter Minuit purchased the entire island of Manhattan from the Indians in 1626. At that time he paid the astounding sum of $24. When the commission laid out its plan in 1811, most of the land was still devoted to agriculture. The commission, however, considered that the price of land was then "uncommonly great." Guided by the economy of a surveyor's rod and chain, the island was mapped in a huge checkerboard. The ultimate cost of fitting the topography, "broken by hills and diversified by watercourses," to this pattern of land subdivision was overlooked, to be sure, and the reservation of 30 per cent of the land for streets was possibly explained by the extensive frontage it provided for the sale of lots. But can the omission of ample open space be construed as economy?

The commission surely expected the city to continue the growth it was then enjoying: they obviously did for they so mapped it for subdivision and sale. Even though the land had been developed with single-family houses on individual lots, the open space in the 1811 plan would have been inadequate. Forty-five years later (1856), 840 acres were purchased for Central Park, and it cost the taxpayers of the city $5,500,000.

This is the variety of economy that distorts the planning of our cities today. It is this experience in the practice of economy from which we are obliged to learn and

2 *Early Town Planning in New York State*, Turpin Bannister, American Society of Architectural Historians.

profit. Is it economical to avoid the reservation of open space in the name of practical planning only to find the land value has become so dear we cannot afford the space when the need is urgent? The value of learning from yesterday is to prepare today for a better tomorrow.

There were those who protested the formlessness of the commissioners' plan. Many agreed with Henry R. Aldrich when he claimed its inspiration was "the great facility which it provides for the gambling in land values and ready purchase and sale of building blocks" which had "wrought incalculable mischief." It was an omen of the fate to befall the American city in subsequent years.

PART II

THE

INDUSTRIAL CITY

Sir, if you wish to have a just notion of the magnitude of this city, you must not be satisfied with seeing its great streets and squares, but must survey the innumerable little lanes and courts.

—*Samuel Johnson*

CHAPTER 5

THE INDUSTRIAL REVOLUTION

Handcraft to Machines. With the nineteenth century came the dawn of the Machine Age. Until that time all goods had been processed and assembled by hand. Shops were modest and generally located in the home of the proprietor. The number of employees was small, and there was maintained a close relationship between worker and employer.

There had always been those who worked with inventions. The Renaissance had been such a period; gunpowder, the printing press, and the processing of various materials were important developments of that time. Ways were devised to improve the simple hand machine, but in 1765 Watt invented the steam engine and, with it, mechanical power became independent of hand operation. Enterprising proprietors applied this power to the work in their shops, and production of goods increased. With production increased, trade expanded, the shop moved from the home into separate quarters— the factory—and the distinction between employee and employer widened.

In 1776 Adam Smith set forth his theories of capitalism. With the advent of machines driven with mechanical power a new era was born. Mercantilism moved into the capitalism of the industrial system. The number of employees in proportion to the owners increased rapidly, and trade unions among workers, in contrast to the medieval guilds of proprietors, were formed.

Invention of the machine touched off feverish activity; belt-line production absorbed the attention of industrial management, and repetition of operations replaced the variety of handcraft. Each machine had its job, and each man his machine. With each new device production per worker jumped; mass production made it possible for more people to have more things, or their counterparts, than had ever been available to them before. The size of factories grew and the number of workers employed by each factory owner also increased. The factory was like a magnet, drawing about it an ever-increasing belt of workers' dwellings, schools, and shops.

Transportation. The industrial system was dependent upon the transportation of raw materials to the factory and finished products to the consumers. Before the invention of the steam engine, goods were hauled in wagons and towed on river barges. Beginning in 1761 the inland waterways were linked by a system of canals in the United States, and in 1809 Fulton built his steamboat, the *Clermont*. In 1825 the first steam railroad was operated for public transportation in England, and a line was laid in the United States in 1829. Industrial production increased while domestic and foreign commerce expanded. Between 1850 and 1880, export trade from the United States increased from $17,000,000 to $100,000,000.

In the crowded city, the horse-drawn carriage trundled the people leisurely about the streets. The *voiture-omnibus* for passenger transportation was introduced to Paris in 1819 and was adopted, as the "horse-car", in New York City in 1831. In 1832 some rail lines were used by the horse-car, but the rail-less vehicle continued in use for a long time.

Traffic congestion paralleled the increase in population density, and in 1867 an elevated cable car was built in New York City. A steam train replaced the cable in 1871, but congestion was hardly diminished. Extending their rails beyond the city, the steam railroads offered some relief. Suburbs sprung up along them and invited those commuters who could afford the time and luxury of escape from the city centers.

The electric street railway replaced the horse-car about 1885, and thenceforth became the principal urban transport. By 1917 there were 80,000 cars and 45,000 miles of track in American cities. As a result, the population scattered somewhat about the periphery, but congestion persisted. In 1895 an electric elevated line was installed in Chicago and, shortly thereafter, in New York and Philadelphia.

Still failing to untie the knotty problem of traffic and transportation, the electric railway went underground. In 1897 a short line was built in Boston, and the first major subway was started in New York City in 1904. As we are sadly aware today, these developments aided and abetted congestion. The cities spread, population grew, and transportation only intensified concentration in the urban centers.

When Daimler invented the internal combustion engine in 1885, transportation was beginning another step into the tangle of urban traffic. There were four automobiles registered in the United States in 1895; in 1900 there were 8,000; in 1940, 32,000,000. The automobile split the city open at the seams, and to this day we are frantically trying to hold it together with patches on a worn-out fabric.

It is recorded that Leonardo da Vinci tinkered with a toy flying machine, but in the nineteenth century men themselves took to the air and by 1903 they were flying in heavier-than-air machines. In 1927 Lindbergh spanned the Atlantic Ocean, and in 1938 Howard Hughes flew around the world in 3 days, 19 hours, 8 minutes, and 10 seconds. Today commercial planes are traveling to every part of the earth, carrying 60 passengers at 300 miles per hour, and soaring into the stratosphere. How long can the city remain congested?

Communications. Civilization has moved at the rate man has communicated his ideas. In ancient times men sent their messages by "runner". The printing press and postal service were initiated in the fifteenth century, and the thoughts of men could be recorded for all to see and read. Their transmission, however, depended upon the carrier on foot or horseback.

The industrial revolution sprung wide the door of man's inventive genius. The will to communicate with each other hung by a strand of copper wire. By 1850 messages were being ticked off on a telegraph key. Then, on March 10, 1876, Professor Alexander Graham Bell sat in his laboratory and spoke into a gadget. His assistant, listening at the other end of a wire, heard the words, "Mr. Watson, come here, I want you." Men could talk to each other on the telephone, and the effect of space and time was drastically altered.

By the end of the first quarter of the twentieth century the miracle of radio not only further changed the effect of time and space, it exploded them in the face of civilization, and adjustment is still far from complete.

Public Health and Safety. In ancient times the tragedy of epidemics aroused rulers to improve the physical environment. Primitive though they were, there were efforts to provide drainage and distribute water in the cities of Crete and the Indus Valley. It was not until the cholera plague of the Middle Ages had violently reduced the urban population in Europe that sanitary sewer connections and water distribution were provided as a public service.

Measures for the public health and safety were extended during the nineteenth century. The first system of water supply by gravity flow was installed in Boston in 1652. By 1820 pumping systems were in general use, and methods for the disposal and treatment of sewage were improved. The heavy coverage of buildings on the land reduced the natural drainage of the city, but extensive street paving permitted effective cleaning and storm sewers augmented the sanitary equipment. Urban hygiene in the factory town did not lag for lack of facilities. It was simply outstripped and nullified by the congestion of people and the intensity of land use.

Public thoroughfares in towns of the Middle Ages were dark and foreboding lanes. An occasional oil lamp hanging from a corner building was the only light to guide the stranger through the night. Artificial gas lighting appeared in London in 1812 and by 1840 was in common use for lighting city streets. The first central generating plant for distribution of electricity was placed in operation in 1882. Thenceforth electricity replaced gas for street lighting.

Electricity illuminated the highway and residential street. It made the "great white way" that brightens the city of today, but it also brought the gaudy display of signs and advertising that flash at night and droop hideously by day. With degenerate taste they sell the wares of commerce and industry but reduce the city aspect to that of a cheap bazaar.

Services for the health, safety, and convenience of the urban population advanced farther in a period of less than 100 years than in all past history. This tremendous progress and the actual living and working conditions of the industrial city present a bewildering contrast. Glorification of the industrial system and the fruits of its new-born activity blinded people to the ruin and havoc spreading across the urban community.

The Factory Town. The steam locomotive extended its rails between the raw products, the factory, and the cities of consumers all over the land. The railroad with its sprawling yards penetrated the town with a network of tracks. Every amenity of urban life was sacrificed to the requirements of industrial production. The factory with its tentacles of railroads and shipping was the heart and nerve center of the city. Port cities on the ocean, lakes, and rivers prospered, drawing to them ships laden with coal and ore and sending from them shiploads of manufactured goods. Railroads and ships joined at the factories, and the waterfront became the industrial core of the city.

The impact of the industrial revolution was first felt in England. The new industrial economy brought exploitation of the poor and, with poverty, came the slums. New slums, mechanical slums, row upon row of crowded workers' houses in the shadow of the factory, all were added to the traditional slums of the seventeenth century in Europe. The degraded environment of the factory town hung like a cloud over urban life for the next century and a half. Engrossed in the technical processes of industrial production, the homes of the people were neglected. Writing in 1865, Dr. Clifford Allbutt described the slums he saw:

This is no description of a plague-stricken town in the fifteenth century; it is a faint effort to describe the squalor, the deadliness, and the decay of a mass of huts which lies in the town of Leeds, between York Street on the one side and Marsh Lane on the other; a place of "darkness and cruel habitations," which is within a stone's throw of our parish church, and where the fever is bred. These dwellings seem for the most part to belong to landlords who take no interest whatever in their well-being. One block perhaps has fallen years ago by inheritance to a gentleman in Lancashire, Devonshire, or anywhere; another to an old lady; a third, perhaps, to an obscure money-lender. Meanwhile, the rotten doors are falling from their hinges, the plaster drops from the walls, the window frames are stuffed with greasy paper or old rags, damp and dung together fester in the doorways, and a cloud of bitterness hangs over all. To one set of houses, appropriately named Golden Square, there is no admission save by alleys or tunnels, which are only fit to lead to dungeons; so that for perhaps half a century or more the winds of heaven have never blown within its courts.

In the new land across the sea there was a vast source of natural resources and an energetic people inspired by a new-won freedom. The industrial revolution swept across America unimpeded by traditions. Then one could hear the echo of events in Europe. As the economy shifted from agrarian to industrial, the people and the resources were soon to experience the throes of exploitation and the struggle for a decent living environment.

The air of American towns became polluted with smoke and grime from belching chimneys of the new age. Railroads ate into the core of cities, waterfronts were ruined, soot covered the village, and sewage lined the beaches. Buffalo, Chicago, Detroit, St. Louis, all devoted their splendid sites on lakes and river waterfronts to the industrial plants, the railroads, and the tankers of the new factory system. The land was platted and advertised as "desirable sites for industry."

Immigration from foreign lands invited the building of tenements. Into them the newcomers crowded, grateful for some place to live in this country of promise. Industrial growth in the large centers induced the people to remain in cities rather than migrate to the more healthful environment of rural communities, and the inevitable result was the creation of slums.

There was an exception to the concentration in congested cities. A large supply of labor was needed to obtain the raw products for manufacture, and "company towns" sprung up at mining and lumber camps in various parts of the country. They occupy an infamous place in the annals of American town development. Living in deplorable shacks and shanties, the workers' families were subject to the will of a single employer for their livelihood. Shelter, food, and clothing were supplied through and at terms prescribed by the mining company. The depths to which these communities sunk, and in which many still remain, is a shameful blot on the American scene.

Building tenements for rent was a profitable enterprise in the nineteenth century. Excessive building coverage on the land and crowding of dwellings within the buildings brought about population congestion with unbelievable acceleration. The population density in London was 265 persons per acre in 1870. It was 23 per cent higher than this in New York City, 326 persons per acre, which then had only one-third the total population of London.[1]

Standards of land use were lax. The first law to regulate tenement building came to New York in 1867, but only faint improvements were forced upon speculators. Planning persisted at a deplorably low level; the "railroad" plan was typical of the early tenements and it had no more evil rival in the world. The usual lot width was 25 feet, with a depth of 100 feet. Built to the side property lines of these narrow lots, the "railroad" plan covered as much as 90 per cent of the area. The small space remaining at the rear was used for privies, no sanitation being provided within the building. With four apartments on each floor, and five or six stories high, only one room in each dwelling enjoyed light and air; all other rooms had no exterior exposure.

The unbearable living conditions imposed on the poor did not go unnoticed. A competition was sponsored in 1879 by the "Plumber and Sanitary Engineer" for a "model" tenement. The results were touched with irony. The winning plan, by James E. Ware, Architect, was the prototype of the later accursed "dumbbell" plan which covered 85 per cent of the lot and resorted to a narrow interior light shaft along the property lines. Despite subsequent legislation "outlawing" these buildings, innumerable still remain to afflict the City of New York.

The Utopians. The industrial city was shrouded in gloom. Class distinctions of the eighteenth century were present, but the new economy forged links between them. The fate of the privileged classes was inextricably woven with the welfare of the masses. The upper classes recognized this, and philanthropy assumed new proportions. Efforts to relieve the burdens of the working classes pierced the haze all through the nineteenth century.

As early as 1797 the Society for Bettering the Conditions of the Poor was formed in England. While there were nostalgic recollections of the formal city, the struggle

[1] *American Cyclopedia,* 1875, Vol. XII, p. 382.

 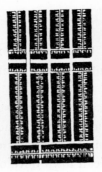 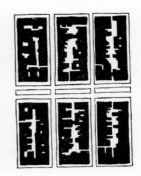

The Seventeenth Century City
The Picturesque Slum

The Nineteenth
Century City
The Mechanical
Slum

The Twentieth
Century City

Among the deplorable slums of the nineteenth-century factory town in England, the two-story row-house predominated. Stretching in long rows with small backyards and narrow streets, the living environment was dreary and monotonous. Crowding on the continent, however, was even more severe as indicated in the sketch of a tenement block in Vienna. Built to a height of four and five floors, it was typical to place a double row of dwellings within the block, the interior row facing on a narrow interior court on both sides. While it has been customary to assume that European slums were more crowded than housing in this new world, the tenement block in New York City does not confirm such a notion. The sketch shows a combination of the "railroad" and the "dumbbell" tenements, many of which still remain despite the fact that they were outlawed in 1901.

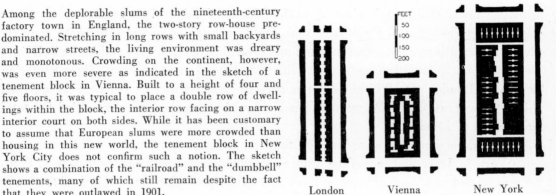

FEET
50
100
150
200

London   Vienna   New York

STOKE–ON–TRENT, England

British Information Service

TENEMENTS OF THE INDUSTRIAL CITY

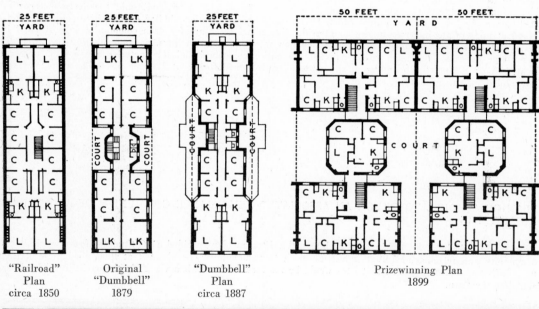

Picturesque slums gave way to mechanical slums in the nineteenth century. Rows of dwellings were built in the shadows of the factories. A typical workers house in England was two stories high; living, cooking and dining took place on the first floor, sleeping rooms were on the second. The wash room and privy were attached in the rear. In Holland crowded flats in 2 and 3 story buildings were typical.

Tenements took different forms in various countries, but they all had one characteristic in common—excessive land coverage. In New York the "railroad" plan became as bad as any and was in general use about the middle of the nineteenth century. It was outmoded by the "dumbbell" plan developed from the Competition of 1879. The typical lot in New York City was 25 feet wide and 100 feet deep. The "railroad" plan spanned the full width from lot line to lot line; the depth varied but generally covered 90 per cent of the lot area. There were four apartments on each floor and the buildings were six and seven stories high.

Privies were in the rear yard. Rooms were in tandem, and, since there was no light along the side property line, only one room in each apartment had outside exposure. The "dumbbell" plan, or "double-decker" offered little improvement except for the concession of a narrow light well along the side property lines. This feature allowed some semblance of light and air into the rooms, but it is difficult to believe much could filter down to the dwellings buried on the lower floors, and what air found its way into these wells must have been foul. Sanitation was improved to the extent of providing two common water closets on each floor. The "dumbbell" plan was outlawed by the Tenement House Act of 1901. This "New Law" was patterned after the competition requirements of the C.O.S. in 1899. Illustrated is the winning design by R. Thomas Short, Architect. The land coverage was reduced to 70 per cent of the lot area, and the tendency to use wider lots was generated; lots of 50 feet in width began to replace the 25-foot widths. Sanitary conveniences were provided in each dwelling. Light and air were provided in all rooms by interior courts instead of light wells, and the dwelling room arrangement was improved.

English Row-House   Dutch Flat

"Railroad" Plan circa 1850

Original "Dumbbell" 1879

"Dumbbell" Plan circa 1887

Prizewinning Plan 1899

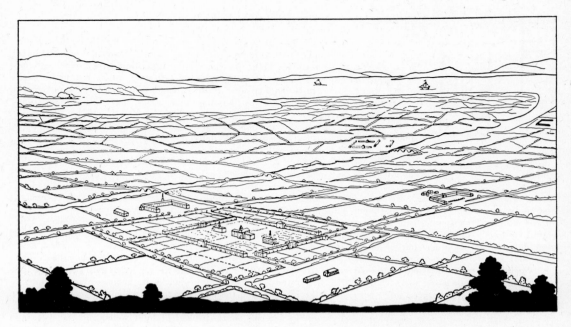

In 1816 Robert Owen, an English industrialist moved by the problem of the ill-housed industrial workers and increasing unemployment, proposed a plan for a community which he believed could become self-supporting and reduce the heavy cost of public relief. Owen further proposed that similar communities could be established at appropriate intervals in the countryside. Communal buildings for each community were situated in the center of a broad Common. About this Common were rows of dwellings, and surrounding the dwellings were large gardens. The main road encircled the entire compound and the factories and workshops were located along the outside boundary of the community. Designed for about 1200 people, each community was surrounded by an agricultural area of between 1000 and 1500 acres to supplement industrial employment.

PLAN OF A MODEL TOWN FOR AN ASSOCIATED TEMPERANCE COMMUNITY OF ABOUT 10,000 INHABITANTS

Proposed in 1849 by J. S. Buckingham, architect, this Utopian plan specified a multitude of features within the community and recommended that industries using "steam engines" be situated at least one-half mile from the town. It was also suggested that sites would be reserved for "suburban villas" in the agricultural land surrounding the town.

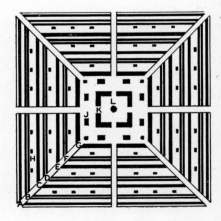

A 1000 houses 20 feet wide

B Arcade for workshops

C 560 houses 28 feet wide

D Retail shops

E 296 houses 38 feet wide

F Winter promenade arcade

G 120 houses 54 feet wide

H Schools, baths, dining halls

J Public buildings, churches

K 24 mansions 80 feet wide

L Central square

to improve the living environment of the working people moved steadily on. The depressing condition of housing for the poor impressed some industrial leaders who sensed the problems it presented to the future of the industrial economy. The first half of the century was marked by protests against the "sordidness, filth, and squalor, embroidered with patches of pompous and vulgar hideousness," and a number of Utopian communities were proposed. One such scheme was that of Robert Owen.

Owen was the proprietor of a cotton mill at New Lanark. He was familiar with the problems of industrial management, having successfully introduced reforms in the working conditions, hours, and wages for employees in his plant. However, Owen saw beyond these reforms and, in 1816, he set forth an unusual plan for a co-operative community combining industry and agriculture.

Dwellings were grouped about a large open space in which he located the communal buildings. Surrounding the dwellings were large gardens, and this entire area was encircled by a main roadway. On one side of the compound were the factories and workshops. Beyond, on all sides, was the agricultural belt ranging from 1,000 to 1,500 acres. The village was designed for about 1,200 people. Owen intended his plan for the unemployed, assuming that the community would become self-supporting and thereby reduce the heavy cost of public relief.

Another of the Utopians was J. S. Buckingham who, in 1849, wrote a treatise entitled *National Evils and Practical Remedies*. In this work he displayed his plan for a "model" town for an "Associated Temperance Community of About 10,000 Inhabitants." Buckingham adhered to the current distinction of class, placing the finer houses near the center of his plan, receding in class to the humble dwellings and workshops about the periphery.

The Utopian proposals were not executed, but they focused attention upon the growing evils of the urban environment. In 1844 the Rochdale Pioneers formed the first consumers' co-operative organization. In the same year the first Royal Commission on Health and Housing was appointed in England and the first Public Health Act was passed in 1848.

By the middle of the century severe epidemics were spreading over England and continental countries. The ruling classes could insulate themselves from many undesirable features of urban living, but they were not immune to disease. Spurred by alarm, the royalty engaged in a few paternal developments. Prince Albert in England, Louis Napoleon III in France, and the Berlin Building Society under Prince Wilhelm in Germany built some "model" dwellings.

These projects represented two extremes. In the congested areas six- and seven-story tenements were repeated with little improvement in plan and design than previous buildings; they could only decay into more slums with the passing of time. The other extremity was the suburb of single houses built on the outskirts of the cities. The intention of these dwellings was encouragement of home-ownership. Being too expensive for the vast number of low-paid workers, they reverted to the usual middle-class suburbs. The prospect of selling these dwellings at handsome profits further removed them from the income group most in need of improved housing. Consequently, there were no solutions in these spurts of activity.

The Model Towns. Recognizing the desirability of good housing for their workers and stimulated by the unexecuted proposals of the Utopians, some "model" communities were undertaken by industrial owners. One of the earliest of these "towns" was Bessbrook, built in 1846 for workers in the linen mills near Newry, Ireland. In 1852 Sir Titus Salt built Saltaire for some 3,000 workers in his textile mill near Bradford, England. Extensive community facilities were introduced in this development. In 1865 the Krupp family began the first of several "model" villages for workers in their munitions and iron factories in Essen, Germany.

George Cadbury, a chocolate manufacturer, moved his plant from Birmingham to a rural site and began the town of Bourneville in 1879. While this community was initiated as a "company" town it was converted to an autonomous village about 1900 and has some 2,000 dwellings today. The land has remained in the single ownership of the village. In France, another chocolate manufacturer, M. Menier, built a workers' colony at Noisel-sur-Seine near Paris in 1874. Similar communities were built in France by the Anzin Mining Company for mine workers at Valenciennes, and M. Schneider et Cie., for their Creusot Steel Mills near Fontainebleau. Others were developed at the Crespi Cotton Mills near Capriate, Italy, and Agneta Park near Delft, Holland, in 1883 for the Van Marken Yeast and Spirit Works.

In 1886, Lever Brothers, famous makers of soap, built Port Sunlight near Liverpool. The site for this project was 550 acres, and large blocks were employed with interior gardens and play areas, a forerunner of later planning. Another project that foreshadowed subsequent developments was Creswell, built by Percy Houfton in 1895 for his Bolsover Colliery. A hexagonal pattern was used, the houses facing inward on the gardens. Sir Joseph Roundtree, cocoa manufacturer, built Earswick near York in 1905. This, like Bourneville, was made a community trust. It was planned by Barry Parker and Raymond Unwin, architects prominent in the new direction of town planning.

Some industrialists in America sought to improve the housing for their workers, probably the best known being Pullman, Illinois, built in 1881. It was built as a permanent town in conjunction with the plant for manufacture of Pullman sleeping cars.

The "model" towns of the industrialists in the nineteenth century were so few in proportion to the real problem of housing in the factory centers that they contributed little to the solution of that problem. They were flavored with a paternalism similar to the "model" dwellings built by the royalty at an earlier date. They did demonstrate some planning arrangements from which later communities were to profit, but the rarity of the projects rather emphasized the disparity between the living standards which were possible in the industrial era and the low level to which housing for most of the urban population had degenerated.

There can be no claim to city planning during this era. The fervor for industrial expansion had blotted out the original plans for cities in America, and only remnants can now be seen. Ambitious proposals like the Judges and Governors plan for Detroit remained as diagrams of what might have been. Even the distinction between major and minor arteries established in the early Detroit plan, for example, was abandoned in favor of a standard street width of 66 feet.

The only plan that remained was Washington, D. C., and it was fraught with difficulties. The Capitol building and President's Palace had been placed upon the sites selected for them, but further developments were hardly appropriate to the dignity and grandeur of L'Enfant's plan. In Lincoln's time the streets were still muddy roads; Pennsylvania Avenue, intended as a broad and monumental promenade, was lined with nondescript commercial buildings and shops. The Capitol building faced east, overlooking the barren marshland which was destined to become the slums of the city.

The gridiron plan of New York City was the beginning of a sterile urban character. The movement "Westward ho!" gripped the pioneers and with them strode the land surveyors. By the time this great trek had moved across the United States the vast land had been mapped in a gargantuan gridiron of mile-square sections. The pattern of land division was thoroughly bound in a legal straight jacket of readily recorded deeds. Natural features, rivers, mountains, and valleys were ignored. Henceforth the grid became the basic pattern of farms, villages, towns, cities, and counties. Desirability of the land was measured by its prospects for quick and profitable turnover. Subdivision practices were conveniently designed to enhance these prospects, and the pattern of future development of cities was fairly sealed in this package of the gridiron plan.

The Horizon of Improvement. As the nineteenth century wore on governments in Europe assumed more and more responsibility for the improvement of the city. The British Housing Law of 1890 empowered the state and local authorities to condemn land and build dwellings for rent to the working class. In response to the growing strength of the trade union movement in Germany a law of 1889 granted privileges to co-operative housing developments, using funds derived from social insurance which had been inaugurated by Bismarck. At an earlier date, legislation was enacted in Holland to provide for the loan of public funds to "public utility societies" engaged in housing, and a similar program was begun in Stockholm, Sweden, in 1879. The "public utility society" is somewhat similar to the "limited dividend company" in the United States, but was subject to closer state supervision in Europe because of the greater degree of financial assistance it received from the government.

These various measures set the stage for the more enlightened era to follow in the next century. There also began a program of social work on behalf of decent housing which was to extend into the twentieth century. Miss Octavia Hill launched her crusade for the underprivileged in London in the latter part of the century— a practical program based upon the idea that good and continuous management could improve living even in existing tenements.

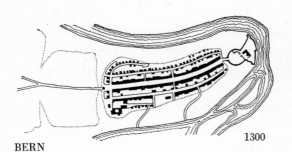

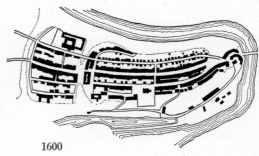

BERN   1300   1600

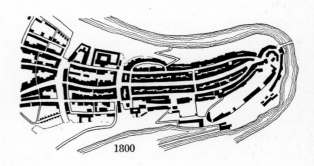

1800

The early medieval town had space within and about it. With the increase in trade and the rise of mercantilism the city form remained the same, but open space was built up. The methods of water supply, drainage, and waste disposal remained the same, but more and more people were crowded into the city. It has continued to grow in population as have other cities, but, while it extended its boundaries, the process of congestion has increased in intensity of land use. Current undesirable congestion has been bearable only with the vast improvement in water distribution, public utilities of gas, electricity, sewage disposal, and mechanical inventions.

Just as the medieval town became crowded with the increase in trade, the new towns gradually became congested with the development of commercialism. The plan of New Haven shows it as an open residential community until the industrial revolution. In the last hundred years, however, the street system has changed only slightly, but the land has been built-up until little open space remains.

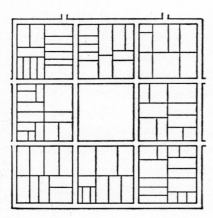

1641

NEW HAVEN

1812   Today

Stirred by the gallant efforts of such crusaders as Jacob Riis, there developed a growing protest against the congested tenements in America. The hideous "railroad" and "dumbbell" tenements on 25-foot lots had spread over New York City, but there were signs of mild and spotty reforms. As early as 1871 the Boston Co-operative Company began a modest program of rental houses for city workers, and other "model" dwellings were attempted.

In 1894 the publication of some plans for tenements by the Architect Ernest Flagg aroused wide interest. These plans provided broader light courts than the standard practice; they reduced the length of interior corridors and improved the exposure of the rooms. A competition for better housing was held by the Improved Housing Council in 1896. It was won by Mr. Flagg with a plan requiring a lot 50 feet in width but accommodating the same number of apartments per floor as the "dumbbell" plan on the same area of land. The rooms in each apartment were larger, and their exposure and arrangement were enhanced.

With this impetus to improve low-cost housing, the Tenement House Committee of the Charity Organization Society conducted a competition in 1899. The program specified certain basic planning standards to be followed by the competitors. Among the prescribed requirements were a maximum lot coverage of 70 per cent, large light courts, and a minimum volume of air per occupant within the dwelling. The winning design was submitted by the architect, R. Thomas Short.

This competition spurred renewed efforts for reform and culminated in the passage of the Tenement House Act of 1901, commonly known as the "New Law" in New York City. The act was modeled after the standards of the competition, and fairly established the 50-foot lot in subdivision practice.

Progress became more visible when the twentieth century opened. Several organizations were formed for the purpose of building better housing for the low-income worker. One of the most notable was the City and Suburban Homes Company of New York. Starting business in 1896 and assisted by Ernest Flagg, it has since built some 3,500 apartment units. The by-laws of the company are worthy of note; its purpose was: "To offer to capital a safe and permanent investment and at the same time to supply wage earners improved homes at current prices."

In 1879 the Washington Sanitary Improvement Company was established in Washington, D. C. It was followed in 1904 by the Washington Sanitary Housing Company and these organizations have built nearly 1,000 apartments for rental to families of low income in the capital city.

Movement to the Cities. The factory system brought more and more people to the urban centers. While rural areas in England were decreasing in population from 10,000,000 in 1821 to 9,500,000 in 1936, cities were gaining from 4,000,000 to 37,000,000. In Germany the rural population dropped from 23,000,000 in 1821 to 19,000,000 in 1936, and urban population increased from 2,000,00 to 48,000,000 in the same period. The industrial metropolis and congestion became synonymous. Between 1800 and 1900 urban population in Europe grew between 300 and 400 per cent. At the beginning of the nineteenth century, London had a population of 1,000,000; at the beginning of the twentieth century it was 7,000,000. During the same period Paris grew from 700,000 to 3,000,000, and Berlin from 172,000 to 4,000,000.

The population of the United States was largely agrarian at the beginning of the nineteenth century. Only about 5 per cent of the people lived in towns, and they were small communities. In 1790 there were but two cities with a population as large as 25,000. The inauguration of regular steamship service between Europe and America in 1840 helped to feed the factory system with immigrants seeking the freedom of this land. By the middle of the century 20 per cent of the people lived in cities. From that time forward the acceleration was rapid, and in 1940 there were 3,464 urban communities with 56.5 per cent of the total population of the country. Four hundred and twelve cities had more than 25,000 population. Of these, twenty three ranged between 250,000 and 500,000; nine were between 500,000 and 1,000,000, whereas five exceeded 1,000,000.

The Spiral of Land Values. The century saw the formation of land companies and the beginning of "real estate" as a business. Land prices boomed as city population jumped by leaps and bounds, and speculation was rife with expansion to the suburbs. Land values in Berlin doubled between 1865 and 1880. In one twenty-year period, land values in London increased one-third. With this increase in land values came increased congestion. Between 1836 and 1886, the density of population in Paris increased threefold. The density of people in London was 265 per acre in 1870, and, at the same time, there were residential areas in New York City with a density of 326 people per acre.[2]

During the latter part of the nineteenth century speculation in land flourished. Land valuations pyramided at a fantastic rate. Accommodation of the growing urban population in the expanding city became more and more difficult. Increasing the density in tenements only further inflated the value of land, which in turn bred higher values. The vicious cycle was in motion.

In New York land values were $742,000,000 in 1870. In 1872 they were $797,000,000. By 1927 they had risen to $7,780,000,000, and in 1932 they were $10,150,000,000. A study by Homer Hoyt showed a similar sequence, although less regular, in Chicago. The valuation of land for the 211-square-mile area occupied by that city ran the following course:[3]

1833 .... $	168,000	1861	60,000,000
1836	10,500,000	1897	1,000,000,000
1842	1,400,000	1926	5,000,000,000
1856	125,000,000	1932	2,000,000,000

[2] *Ibid.*
[3] *100 years of Land Values in Chicago,* Homer Hoyt, University of Chicago Press, Chicago, 1933, Table LXXX, Appendix III.

The chaotic effect of this violent sequence of higher density followed by higher land cost can hardly be understated. The movement of the tide has been stemmed only with occasional economic depressions, but these intervals have been followed by immediate recuperation of inflated land values. It is apparent that little hope for any modification of this cycle can be expected as long as the legal framework for the urban environment permits unlimited population densities.

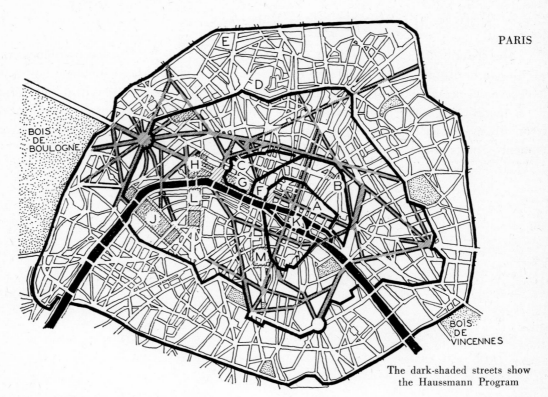

PARIS

The dark-shaded streets show
the Haussmann Program

Wall **A** Built by Philip Augustus, Twelfth century	**F** The Louvre	**L** The Invalides
Wall **B** Built by Charles V, Fourteenth century	**G** The Tuilleries	**M** The Luxembourg
Wall **C** Built by Louis XIII, Seventeenth century	**H** The Champs Élysées	
Wall **D** Built by Louis XV, Eighteenth century	**J** The Champs de Mars	
Wall **E** Built by Napoleon III, Nineteenth century	**K** The Île de la Cité	

Beginning as a fortified town on the small island in the Seine River, Paris was known as Lutetia by the Romans. At the time of the Norman invasion in the ninth century the town had expanded beyond the original *Île de la Cité* and was fortified on both sides of the Seine. The fortifications were extended by Philip Augustus in the twelfth century (Wall A). The left bank (south) was the principal location for churches and colleges, the commercial center lying on the right bank. The kings made their residence on this bank, and in the fourteenth century Charles V built Wall B to contain more adequately this growing part of the city. At the east end of the town was the tower known as the Bastille; at the west end, on the banks of the Seine, was the Louvre which became the royal palace.

The Louvre was extended in the sixteenth century under Henry II, and the Tuileries Gardens were created. The power of the monarch was growing, and the Renaissance was ushered in. Henry IV built the Place Royal, and in the seventeenth century Louis XIII had the walls expanded to contain the Tuileries Gardens (Wall C).

During the reign of Louis XIV, the Sun King, Paris grew rapidly, and court life extended its influence. Vauban reduced the fortified walls, and the ramparts were transformed into promenades, the first of the *Grands Boulevards*. The Tuileries Gardens and the Louvre were enlarged, and the initial stage of the Champs Élysées was built into the "suburbs" to the west. The Place des Victoires and Place Vendôme were built. Monumental quais were created along the Seine. King Louis XIV, however, moved his court and residence to Versailles where he built the great palace and gardens.

The city expanded further under Louis XV who built the Place Louis XV (Place de la Concorde), Rue Royale, and Church of the Madeleine. Streets were widened and new avenues built for fine residences. The Champs de Mars was also established, and in the latter part of the eighteenth century the new Wall D was built to contain the growing city.

Following the Revolution the industrial development of the city increased. The outskirts of the city were built up, and a new Wall E was built in 1840. Under Napoleon III, the huge program by Baron Haussmann was carried out. The principal portion of this is indicated in heavy shading. Many new avenues were cut through the city and boulevards created on the sites of old walls.

As Paris developed, the city underwent remodeling under each of the monarchs but it will be observed that the greatest projects in each successive period were those along the fringe of the city. The great open spaces that distinguish the city today were developed in advance of the city expansion, and the walls extended to include them as the city spread about them. Even as late as Haussmann, boulevards were carved out of the city, but the most expansive spaces were those like the Champs Élysées and the Place de l'Étoile, and boulevards radiating from them were laid across open fields. The rapid growth of Paris has spread the city in all its suburbs and absorbed the open spaces including those created when the walls of 1840 were leveled in the latter part of the nineteenth century.

CHAPTER 6

THE CITY OF
CONTRASTS

Last of the Baroque. Repeated outbreaks of the people caught in the tangled industrial city were a source of annoyance to the ruling class in Europe. In the midst of the orgy of urban expansion, a development of monumental proportions was undertaken in Paris. Sensitive to the restlessness of the working classes, Napoleon III proposed to open broad avenues through the slums in which discontent festered. In devising his plan he was not unmindful of the advantage these open spaces would provide his soldiers in controlling mob violence.

Georges-Eugène Haussmann, a bureaucrat in the city administration, was selected, in 1853, to take charge of the huge program. The result was an amazing demonstration of administration and organization. The entire boulevard system of Paris was planned and executed in a period of seventeen years and under the most strenuous circumstances. Haussmann was resisted, on the one hand, by a city council reluctant to appropriate the necessary funds and, on the other, by bourgeois property owners affected by his broad strokes of planning.

Haussmann was aware of the need to design for the traffic of a new industrial age. He laid out the new streets in long sweeps cutting through the maze of winding medieval lanes. With these avenues he connected old plazas and created new plazas. He laid out the radiating avenues across the open fields from the Place de l'Étoile, he laid out the Bois de Boulogne, he carved out the monumental Avenue de l'Opéra and many other grand boulevards.

The program engineered by Haussmann was stupendous. It transformed Paris and gave it much of the color of that great city. But can it properly be called planning? A series of masterful projects were executed. Haussmann intended to improve the circulation of traffic, and the broad avenues that were opened through the congested districts were an improvement. He had the conception of scale appropriate for the new city: he saw it as a complex wanting unification. But the tradition of monuments was deeply rooted in the process of city building. It was not long since the revolution

79

against tyranny, and an emperor was again the ruler. The tree-lined avenues and vistas meant to impress rather than serve the people.

The time was not ripe for solving the new urban problems. Mixed land uses were not changed, and the avenues became continuous shopping streets along the ground floor with dwellings on the upper floors. There was no separation between land uses as in the earlier London residential developments about Bloomsbury, which were by-passed by traffic arteries and shopping streets. The scheme of Haussmann was gargantuan in scale, but it was too late to become an effective monument to the ego of a monarch, and too early to solve the planning of the industrial city. It was the swan song of the Baroque city.

Mid-Victorian Mediocrity. There was a depressing consistency about the factory town of the nineteenth century. It bred mediocrity in every aspect of life; mediocrity was its characteristic. Vast areas of mean dwellings lay under a pall of smoke; an atmosphere of haze hung over the environment. Peaks of creative inspiration were few and far between. Monotonous order was a natural result of rigid organization of people and things. The mid-Victorian Period signifies bad taste and dull, routine life. Here and there a pseudo-gayety pierced the haze, but it was fluffy with gray frills touched more with half-concealed vulgarity than genuine pleasure. The urban environment reflected the bawdy "can-can" rather than the graceful waltz. A film of grime and soot covered it, and the wide range from wealth to poverty meant little more, in a cultural sense, than the difference between more or little bric-a-brac in the cluttered surroundings. The cultural energy of the city was sapped by the gigantism of industrial development. The factory was like a monster that spewed forth its products and then reached out to clutch them in its expanding claws.

Glorification of the machine was complete, and man had created a master. This was significant to him. He had proved his power. Here was a creature of man that could produce anything. It had no need for a brain; it was automatic. It had no limitations; it could even destroy man himself. And man was tremendously proud of his achievement.

Proof of the mediocrity of the age were the few who recognized it. William Morris and John Ruskin cried out against it; Charles Dickens wove it into his classic stories; muckraking reporters like Lincoln Steffens exposed it; Octavia Hill and Jane Addams fought it with vigorous social work. They saw the dulling of man's creative spirit, the shift from quality to quantity as a measure of success. They perceived it in all its shabby elegance and grime—the nineteenth century industrial city.

Apparently, man can move in an atmosphere of mediocrity for just so long, and then an awareness of a cultural vacuum dawns. Unfortunately he may only peer, rather than search, for the absent quality, and he often fabricates a substitute, an artificial air of pomposity that serves rather well and takes much less trouble than the search for culture. To achieve culture it might be necessary for him to forego temporarily some material advantages in which he so firmly believes. So he ingeniously contrives to have both.

This happened in the transition twilight of the nineteenth century.

The City Beautiful. World Fairs had proved a great way to place the products of industry before the people and it was proposed to hold one in Chicago in 1893. The Columbian Exposition, as it was called, was to demonstrate amply the great industrial empire and to give pedigree to this new empire. What more natural way to accomplish this than by clothing it in the robes of classic form? Had this not been the "cultural" drape for the great days of the past? Was this not an appropriate cloak for a new era when men could produce more than at any time in history? With this new power men could reproduce classic structures that would surpass the emperors. This was a natural conclusion in the nineteenth century and it was true. Mediocrity had taken its toll in taste as in exploitation. A reaction was inevitable, and it was violent.

It was a natural paradox that out of the smoke, soot, and grime of the cities, this Fair would be called "White City." Cities were cramped, monotonous, and ugly; the Fair would be big, broad, and beautiful. The Fair would be everything the urban environment was not, and it was a huge success. It did all the things it purported to do and something more. It launched a movement of "classic revival" in this country which was to portray all the contrasts conceived in the nineteenth century and born in the twentieth.

Daniel Burnham, the chief architect for the Columbian Exposition, uttered the magic words that marked the new era: "Make no little plans." The fair rolled up a tidal wave of "city planning" and it swept across the land. Every large city planned to become the "City Beautiful." Burnham was commissioned to prepare a plan for San Francisco after the earthquake and fire of 1906. The Commercial Club of Chicago engaged him for the plan of that city in 1909. He did one for Manila and Baguio in the Philippines, and he was an active member of a commission of architects who renewed the plan of Washington, D. C.

Other cities followed suit. Plans were of colossal scale with monumental proportions. Axes shot off in all directions terminating with proposed buildings that put the visions of past kings to shame. Great plazas and broad avenues, generously punctuated with monuments, were almost a civic obsession. The "City Beautiful" was the Grand Plan reincarnate; the *École des Beaux Arts* in Paris was the fountainhead for the designers of this period and the plans had to be big to be beautiful.

Civic centers became a popular theme. Nearly every city had its Civic Center Plan—open space landscaped in the traditional fashion, fountains distributed about plaza and garden, public buildings limited in number only by the size and ambition of the city, topped off with a frosted dome terminating a long and broad vista.

All this activity was performed in something of a vacuum. An air of haughty detachment pervaded the planning, an isolation from the affairs of people and community activities. A monument or public building blithely placed in the middle of an important traffic artery suggests the characteristic paradox. It was as though the planners had determined that the people must adjust themselves to the mighty formal arrangement. It failed to occur to them that the entire development of a city was essentially a derivative of human needs. The Civic Center conception itself was one of removal from the life of the community rather than a functional entity within it. Removed from channels of enterprise, civic affairs had an air of divorcement. The grandiose buildings were imposing, not inviting. They held the spellbound citizen at arm's length. They did not fit the city, its life, its habits, or its manners; theirs was an air of disdain rather than dignity.

Then these great structures became so laden with excess "architectural" expense, it was almost too much to bear. The citizen could really not afford the sums of money they cost. There were some grand gestures made and executed, but the lavish plans were largely destined for respectable storage in the archives of a more modest city hall. Most of the work that reached the stage of execution was necessarily and haphazardly remodeled later to fit the requirements of traffic and circulation ignored in the original planning.

The seeds of city planning had nevertheless been planted. Planning organizations sprung up in various parts of the country. A Town Planning Board was established in Hartford, Connecticut, in 1907. In 1909 the first National Conference on City Planning was held. This was followed in 1911 with the founding of the National Housing Association. By 1913 there were official planning boards in 18 cities in the country, and in the same year Massachusetts led off with the first state legislation that made city planning a mandatory responsibility of local governments: all cities with a population of 10,000 or more were required to establish a Planning Board.

The City of Commerce. Meanwhile the real city was shoving its sprouts through these pleasant but fortuitous efforts. The technical "know-how" of industrial production had been learned. The industrial system was no longer primarily a technical problem; it was now a commercial process. Financing and distribution were the new emphasis. Selling the rapidly produced merchandise and financing the expanding facilities to produce more were transforming the system into a financial empire. Factory management turned its attention from production of goods to commercial organization, banking, national and world-wide trade associations. The nature of commodities and their production methods gave way to ticker-tape and figures in a set of books. The businessman—the tycoon of commerce—became the main cog in the new era. Statistics, business cycles, bookkeeping, financing, and the stock market were the stock-in-trade of those who strove for success. Trade in commodities rather than the commodities themselves was what counted now. The city began to bristle with buildings sheltering acres of floor space for business. The skyscraper was the dramatic manifestation of the commercial city.

It was apparent that affairs must be operated on a practical basis. Cities must work, the ornamental must be discarded, and only the useful could be tolerated. Land cost money, buildings cost money, services cost money, and so did time. These required attention of practical men, not dreamers. It was well and good to have ideas about a "City Beautiful," but it was far more important that they pay dividends.

To answer these demands there emerged the "city engineer," the practical man who

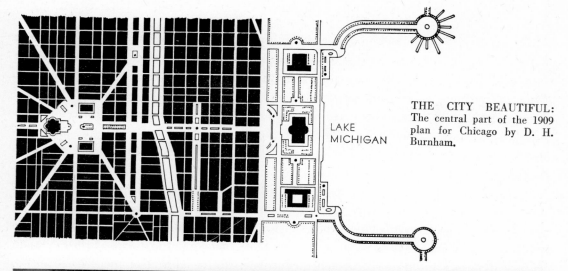

THE CITY BEAUTIFUL:
The central part of the 1909
plan for Chicago by D. H.
Burnham.

LAKE
MICHIGAN

American Airlines

THE INDUSTRIAL CITY: Gary, Indiana.

The City Beautiful and the Industrial City grew up together in
the nineteenth century. The problems of the growing metropolis
were not solved and the crowded City of Commerce emerged to
complicate further the urban pattern.

SILHOUETTE, ANCIENT TO MODERN

PYRAMID OF GIZEH   PARTHENON   COLOGNE   WOOLWORTH   RADIO   EMPIRE
                                         CATHEDRAL   BLDG   CITY   STATE
                                                                          BLDG

could make surveys and calculations, determine the size of sewer, water, and drainage systems, lay out rail lines, streets, walks, curbs. City planning became an engineering process engaging practical men free from dreams. These qualifications appealed to civic and business leaders and instilled confidence in their judgment and businesslike manner. It was this individual that businessmen desired for the responsibility of planning within budget limitations. They had received a huge dose of grand planning, proposals to embellish the city with architectural trappings costing more than the problems they were intended to solve.

There was merit in this position; the "City Beautiful" was not frowned upon, it was simply too expensive. Awed by the monumental dreams, impressed by the vision, it was not with disrespect that the proposals were sidetracked. These great designs had simply lost all connection with the commercial city that was growing up in the twentieth century. It was a thing apart, detached, unrelated to the affairs of men. It solved no problems, and there was a subconscious recoiling from the classic mold into which it would cast the physical environment.

The city was a business proposition, and it must pay dividends. Land took on a new value. There was a time when it was sold as "lots." The value was later measured in terms of street frontage, a price per front foot. It was now being measured by the *square* foot. Every square foot of land had a value and none could be wasted. Building coverage was intense; layer upon layer of floor space was piled upon the land.

Despite resistance to the monumental planning of the "City Beautiful," the classic treatment had made a deep impression. It gave an appearance of pedigree which was itself an asset to the business world. The value attached to every square foot of land for commercial use opposed the fine balance between the buildings and open space of classic planning. But the appearance could be captured, however, so remnants of the classic revival were hung upon the façades of buildings and each thus became a fit associate for its neighbor along the street. It was a sham, to be sure, but the street assumed a stylish front and the value of land behind the façades was protected.

As in architecture and the arts, city planning acquired a Queen Anne front and a Mary Ann back. The street became a canyon embellished with a galaxy of styles cutting through mountains of building bulk. The appearance of dignity was achieved without the loss of a square foot of land.

Washington, D.C., is not a typical American city, but it dramatically displays the contradictions of the twentieth century. The job of government in a great democracy attracted an expanding population to the capital city. With the people came commercial enterprise, and the forces of conflict were set; the commercial city and the classic city were diametrically opposed.

The pseudo-classic planning for activities of the Federal government was vigorously maintained. In 1901 the MacMillan Commission was appointed to restore the original character of the L'Enfant plan. Some results were obtained. The railroad which had been cut across the Mall was removed, and the present site for the Union Station was established. There was agreement on a uniform limit for the height of future buildings.

American Airlines

NEW YORK CITY

New York City illustrates the exaggerated chaos of the City of Commerce in the industrial age.

WASHINGTON, D. C.

A city of monumental compromise between the classic and the commercial city. At the lower left are the Supreme Court and the Library of Congress; above them, the Capitol and the Mall to the Washington Monument beyond. In the upper center is the monumental "triangle," and the Union Station is in the lower right corner.

To preserve these accomplishments the National Commission of Fine Arts was appointed in 1910 by President Theodore Roosevelt. It was followed in 1926 by creation of the National Capital Park and Planning Commission.

These commissions performed yeomen services to the preservation of the classic city, but that city had changed. A new age had arrived, immature but nonetheless a moving force. Commercialism with its entourage of shops, hotels, office and loft buildings, entertainment and residential development, traffic and transportation descended upon the city. Above all, the evaluation of land and the intensity of development that had overtaken other cities could not be denied in the capital city.

Commercial enterprise paid respects to the monumental street system which had been laid down. Into this framework the features of the new city were squeezed and fitted. Classic façades were likewise draped upon the street fronts, but behind these fronts formless building space was heaped upon the land, even as in other cities.

The contradiction between the classic and the commercial city was clearly apparent. To protect its character of monumental buildings and planning, the Federal reservation was necessarily isolated from the remainder of urban development. With this separation the prescription of uniform building height and style, building sites, forms, and open space could be rigidly controlled.

The paradox of the city was substantially complete. The execution of a plan for the capital of a great democratic government could be accomplished only by freezing its form into a preconceived and inflexible mold. The reason for the paradox had apparently escaped notice.

It was falsely assumed that a planning "style" could be transferred from another age and adapted to a new set of conditions. It was overlooked that periods of culture in the past have been identified by the special stamp of character they evolved from within the framework of each. Great cultures have not been so recognized because of their similarities with previous periods, but because of the distinctive qualities they have contributed to the progress of civilization.

The false premise upon which the plan of Washington, D. C., has evolved is magnified by the design of the structures themselves, the insistence upon classic forms without regard for the essential arrangement of interior space. Exterior space is equally oblivious to the functional elements of the city. The classic courtyards, their prototypes treated with fine paving or gracious gardens, have in Washington become oil spotted parking lots filled with automobiles. The Federal reservation of classic monumentalism is hollow and unnatural; the commercial city, warped into the pattern of its streets, is equally artificial.

The Need for Regulation. *Laissez-faire* took deep root in the affairs of men as the commercial city formed. The new attitude of practicality presented something of a contradiction in urban building. It became increasingly apparent that if freedom was to avoid license some order must be established. In practical terms this meant the adoption of rules and regulations which, in turn, implied certain curbs upon *laissez-faire*.

We have observed that regulations over city building were not new in the annals
of history. King Hammurabi codified his rules of justice in 2,000 B.C. The Greeks had
regulations pertaining to the building of dwellings. The Romans established height
limits for tenements. Towns of the Middle Ages adopted various regulations like the
restrictions against fire hazards and projecting upper stories.

The sad condition of housing that developed with the factory system in the nineteenth
century forced the enactment of many laws to curb abuses. Restrictions applying to
commercial and industrial buildings were rare, and with the advent of the skyscraper
the need for appropriate regulations became more and more apparent.

Regulations for light, air, and lot coverage, though lax, were accepted for residential
buildings, but commercial structures were permitted to occupy as much as 100 per cent
of the lot area for the entire height. Steel construction and elevators pushed buildings
higher. Light and air could penetrate on the street frontage only, and this diminished
as buildings rose, floor upon floor, into the air.

Regulations increased in number and scope during the early part of the twentieth
century. Codes establishing standards of construction, mechanical, and electrical instal-
lations were adopted to protect the public health and safety. Fireproof construction was
required where congestion was most acute. Protection was assured for public rights-of-
way.

Mixed land uses, the indiscriminate placement of stores and shops in residential
areas, induced premature depreciation of land values and residential neighborhoods.
The necessity to exercise some measure of public control over land use was pressing.

Zoning. There was some precedent for zoning. When town walls in Germany were
leveled in the nineteenth century, building regulations designated "belts" in which
apartments and single houses could be built about the periphery of the ramparts. Protection from encroachment of undesirable land uses had been attempted in America.
Exclusive residential sections in some middle-western cities were planned as courts
entered through monumental gates and "block ordinances" were framed to restrict
improvements to high-class residences. Height limits were placed on buildings in
Boston in 1903—125 feet in the central district and 80 feet elsewhere. In 1909 Los
Angeles adopted a regulation dividing the business area into seven "industrial" districts.
The remainder of the city was declared to be residential and in this area "laundries"
were excluded. After a piece of land, in which a brick industry was located, was annexed
to the city another ordinance was enacted to prohibit brickyards in residential districts.
Both these ordinances were upheld in the California courts.

These cases were hardly more than experimental gestures, but the chaotic growth
of cities made it imperative that positive steps be taken to bring some order into the
urban pattern. It is a fortunate characteristic of humankind that when leadership is
needed there is usually available someone willing and capable of assuming the responsibility. Such a man was Edward M. Bassett, an attorney in New York City. To
Mr. Bassett goes credit for a public service on behalf of the urban population. He
undertook a thorough investigation of the power of the people to regulate their own

destiny and worked diligently on the preparation of a legal instrument whereby the people could exercise effectively their powers to control the use of land in the urban community.

Mr. Bassett defined zoning as "the regulation by districts under the police power of the height, bulk, and use of buildings, the use of land, and the density of population." With this clear-cut purpose, the first comprehensive zoning ordinance in this country was enacted by New York City in 1916. There is no better testimony to the remarkable thoroughness of Mr. Bassett and his colleagues than the subsequent history of zoning in the courts. Tested in a number of cases in later years, the principle of zoning was upheld in every court.

One of these cases is particularly significant. It fairly confirmed the democratic nature of planning, and established it as an instrument with which the people could order the destiny of their cities. In his opinion on the "Euclid Case"[1] Justice Sutherland of the U. S. Supreme Court said:[1]

Until recently urban life was comparatively simple; but with the increase and concentration of population, problems have developed, and constantly are developing, which require additional restrictions in respect to the use and occupation of private lands in communities. Regulations, the wisdom, necessity and validity of which, as applied to existing conditions, are so apparent that they are now uniformly sustained, a century ago, or even a half century ago, probably would have been rejected as arbitrary and oppressive.

Little need be added to the words of Supreme Court Justice Sutherland.

Zoning had a profound effect upon American cities. For the first time there was created an instrument with which to control the use of land in urban areas. It is characteristic of this technique that it protects the general welfare of the people by protecting that of each individual citizen.

There was nothing in the nature of zoning that confined it to urban development alone. It was essentially a device for planning—the execution of a plan—and as such could be applied at any scale and for any land requiring public control over its use. It has been applied to counties in a manner similar to that of cities, and it has been adapted as a means for conservation of natural resources. In 1929 the State of Wisconsin empowered counties to establish districts in which agriculture was excluded from submarginal lands and forestry and recreational development encouraged within these privately owned lands.

Zoning is a vital part of the urban machinery, but it can fail through abuse, misuse, and resistance to essential changes in the urban pattern for the general welfare.

Extension of Public Services. The industrial revolution changed the city into a metropolis. The urban population became the multitude, and the supply of basic human wants to this multitude required highly organized services. Transportation via common carriers, roads, water supply, sewage disposal and drainage, communications, power and illumination, all vastly expanded in scope. Their impact upon the public health

[1] *Village of Euclid, Ohio* v. *Ambler Realty Company*, 272 U. S. 363, November 22, 1926.

and safety increased accordingly. Being thus colored with the public interest, some of these services were subject to public regulation; others were embraced in public ownership.

Public works to control or harness natural resources for the community at large were not new. We will recall the dikes, reservoirs, and irrigation projects along the Nile; the aqueducts, sewers, and roads built by the Romans as public projects. This responsibility disappeared for a time during the Feudal Period but returned toward the end of the Middle Ages. Limited though they were, water supply and sewage disposal were then considered public responsibilities.

In the early history of this country many of the highways were private toll roads. They were transferred to public ownership and control, and the sewerage system and drainage remained a public responsibility. There are other public services, however, which are owned and operated as private enterprises. Because of their impact upon the common welfare, the continuity of their service is essential and they enjoy a monopoly guaranteed by franchise. Known as *public utilities,* they are subject to regulation by public authority.

The railroads, street railways, and other forms of common carriers, the telephone, telegraph, and radio are with some exceptions regulated public utilities. The same is true of electric power, illumination, and gas distribution. The supply of water is generally owned by the public, although there are exceptions.

The "social" control of utility services is an important factor in the future of urban development. It is therefore pertinent to understand the position of our courts in dealing with this phase of democratic procedures.

In 1876 Chief Justice Waite of the U. S. Supreme Court set forth the theory of public interest in private property. The case[2] was that of a grain operator who violated a local statute controlling the rates for storage. The court held that the enterprise was "affected with the public interest" because of the dependence of the public upon it and the consequent right of the public to exercise authority over its operations. Justice Waite stated,

When, therefore, one devotes his property to a use in which the public has an interest, he, in effect, grants to the public an interest in that use, and must submit to be controlled by the public for the common good, to the extent of the interest he has thus created.

Chief Justice Taft confirmed this position in a later case[3] with this opinion:

In a sense, the public is concerned about all lawful business because it contributes to the prosperity and well-being of the people. The public may suffer from high prices or strikes in many trades, but the expression "clothed with the public interest" as applied to a business means more than that the public welfare is affected by continuity or by the price at which a commodity is sold or a service rendered. The circumstances which clothe a particular kind of business with a

[2] *Munn* v. *Illinois,* 94 U. S. 113.
[3] *Charles Wolff Packing Company* v. *Court of Industrial Relations of the State of Kansas,* 262 U. S. 522 (1923).

public interest, in the sense of *Munn* v. *Illinois* and other cases, must be such as to create a peculiarly close relation between the public and those engaged in it, and raise implications of an affirmative obligation on their part to be reasonable in dealing with the public.

It will be observed that enterprise engaging in public service assumes a dual obligation. The first is to supply all the needs of the public implied by the nature of the service, and the second is to provide the services at a cost reflecting reasonable but not excessive profit. This status of a public utility—a public service for which it enjoys a monopoly—imposes obligations beyond the scope of the usual private enterprise. Public utilities become an integral part of city planning, and successful development of the city is largely dependent upon the effectiveness of their operations.

CHAPTER 7

THE LIVING ENVIRONMENT

Patrick Geddes. Ever present among the complicated urban activities of the nineteenth century was the effort to improve the living environment. Urban speculation and its disintegrating effect upon the environment of man had aroused the public consciousness during the century. The critical essays of eminent men in the literary world—John Ruskin, Thomas Carlyle, Lord Shaftesbury, Charles Dickens, Engels, and Benjamin Disraeli—shed light on the issues with the force of their insight and talent.

Among those who spoke out against the evils at the turn of the century was Patrick Geddes. In 1892 Geddes founded the Outlook Tower in Edinburgh, and through this medium he presented the whole complex of urban life. He insisted upon a view of all phases of human existence as the base of operations, an integration of physical planning with social and economic improvements.

This principle does not sound unfamiliar today, but it was new when Geddes expressed it. As a contemporary of his said: "There was a time when it seemed only necessary to shake up into a bottle the German town-extension plan, the Parisian Boulevard and Vista, and the English Garden Village, to produce a mechanical mixture which might be applied indiscriminately and beneficently to every town in this country. Thus it would be 'town-planned' according to the most up-to-date notions. Pleasing dream! First shattered by Geddes, emerging from his Outlook Tower in the frozen north, to produce that nightmare of complexity, the Edinburgh Room at the great Town-Planning Exhibition of 1910."

Patrick Geddes gave voice to the necessity for what was later to become Regional Planning.

The Garden City. There was another who rose above the throng at the end of the century. He was Ebenezer Howard. Disturbed by the depressing ugliness, haphazard growth, and unhealthful conditions of cities, he had an idea which he set forth in a little book entitled *Tomorrow*, published in 1898. The idea was the Garden City.

In this book Howard described a town in which the land would remain in the single ownership of the community. The dwellings would be distributed about a large central court in which the public buildings would be located. The shopping center would be on the edge of the town and industries on the outskirts. The city would have a population of some 30,000 people in an area of 1,000 acres. Surrounding the entire city would be a permanent belt of agricultural land of 5,000 acres.

Rather than failing of execution as did the proposals of the early Utopians, Ebenezer Howard, before his death in 1928, saw his idea become reality. The Garden City Association was formed in 1899 and in 1903 the First Garden City, Limited, a limited dividend society, obtained 4,500 acres of land 34 miles from London and began the city of Letchworth. It was designed for a maximum population of 35,000 with an agricultural belt of 3,000 acres. In thirty years this town had grown to a population of 15,000, with more than 150 shops and sixty industries, and had paid 5 per cent dividends on the invested stock. At a later date a second garden city, Welwyn, was started. The site was 2,400 acres and it was designed for a population of 40,000. In fifteen years it had a population of 10,000, with fifty industries.

These cities followed the scheme of Ebenezer Howard, the agricultural belt remaining a permanent protection and not a reservation for continued expansion of the urban area usually considered the only usefulness of vacant land on the periphery of cities. These towns have had the added advantage of retaining, for the benefit of the population itself, the increment of increased value of land created by a growing and prospering community.

There is a difference between the usual joint-stock company and Garden City, Limited, which developed Letchworth. The principal object of the latter is to create a town for the benefit of the community. In so doing, the rights of the shareholders to dividends on their stock are limited (5 per cent in Garden City, Limited) and profits earned above the dividends are applied to the benefit of the whole community. The company is in a position of public trustee rather than a private landlord. It has proven a sound, but not a speculative, investment. Land for all development purposes is leased for a period of ninety-nine years. The town government is the Urban District Council of fifteen members, elected by the residents, and of these five members retire annually and are eligible for re-election.

Another feature distinguishes Letchworth. Development and growth of the Garden City are reversed from the practices of the usual speculative city. Aside from the merits of planning in either type of town, zoning in Letchworth determines the use of specific areas and only those uses are permitted; only factories and workshops are built in the industrial zones, and shops in the commercial zones. In the speculative town any use of a lesser economic character is permitted in its zoning provisions; dwellings are found in industrial and commercial zones, and these mixed uses are largely responsible for the sad state of the urban environment. The overdeveloped center and underdeveloped periphery of the speculative town are absent in Letchworth. Open spaces remain for development as the need arises and for the appropriate use provided in the plan.

Of the 1,500 acres of the town contained within the rural belt, 935 acres are reserved for residential use, 170 acres for industry, 60 acres for shopping, and the remainder for parks and roads. There are some 4,000 dwellings in the town of which the Urban District Council has built 1,300 cottages for workers.

The Common Denominator. The house a family lives in is the common denominator of the city; it is the fiber of the city. The link between it and city building is so close the two are almost synonymous. Industrial and commercial enterprise strengthen the structure of the city, but it is the community of homes that marks the health, even the civilization, of a people.

Haussmann ripped through the slums of Paris with his boulevards, civic centers were planned for American cities, the impressive garb of classic façades was hung on the streets of the commercial city, and zoning was devised as the legal instrument to lend stability to the urban framework. But housing, the manifestation of the inner structure of civilization and the culture of people, remained as always the "left-over" in the urban plan.

Had zoning come early rather than late the urban predicament might have been much different. It is not exactly practical to plan a city after it has been built. Planning implies a program before an act, but zoning was adopted after the city had taken shape and zoning could hardly accomplish more than freeze the mixture. There was no chance to prescribe the ingredients before they had been poured together and well stirred. It was inevitable that housing should become the excrescence of urban land use.

City planning was first an urge to improve the esthetic pattern of the urban environment. Then zoning made of it a statistical exercise and a marathon of prognostication. These movements were necessary and valuable, but they did not improve the environment of the people and that is the purpose of city planning. Housing has thus become the principal instrument to attain that objective. It brings into focus the social, economic, and esthetic aims and needs of the urban population. It consequently becomes a political responsibility.

After World War I the housing shortage became a major crisis in Europe. Building inactivity through the war years had left the people of all countries with not only a shortage of dwellings, but monetary systems that, through inflation and war debt, needed transformation. It was essential that governments take a hand.

Public policy with respect to housing had made considerable progress in European countries during the nineteenth century. The groundwork for public assistance had been laid. Financial aid was available to private enterprise through public utility societies and trade union co-operatives. Local public authorities were empowered to provide housing for the lowest income families. The exercise of condemnation by public authorities was an accepted instrument to enforce housing improvement, and cities in a number of countries had acquired large areas of vacant land outlying the built-up city.

The housing program restored to the minds of men that standards of living are more than a load of mechanical equipment surrounded by walls of a building and covered by a mortgage. The family and its dwelling had been engulfed by the tidal wave of the industrial revolution. It emerged from the war as the primary unit of design in city development.

The record of this program is of historic importance. The performance in each country assumed similar characteristics, but each deserves some attention for the remarkable progress it represents in the total pattern.

England. In England the Housing Act of 1919 superseded the Act of 1890 in response to the "Homes for Heroes" campaign. It provided for subsidies by the Ministry to local authorities for clearance of slums and building low-cost housing. During the twenties and early thirties the purposes of this Act were consolidated and extended. Compensation to owners in built-up areas declared ready for clearance was restricted to the market value of the land, and no payment was made for the substandard structures on the site. Standards of occupancy were established to prevent overcrowding of families within dwellings, and local authorities were vested with police power to order improvements in physically substandard dwellings or their demolition.

The housing program had given strong impetus to enactment of the Housing and Town Planning Act of 1909 which, with subsequent amendments, became the Town and Country Planning Act of 1932. This was a comprehensive piece of legislation. Local authorities were not only empowered to prepare and enforce plans for the urban area, but typical of the British pride in their rural countryside, the Act provided for the preservation of rural areas and important buildings. It further implemented the co-operative planning for two or more separate political subdivisions—cities and counties—where they required such treatment as a region.

The Housing Act of 1936 brought the relationship between housing, slums, and city planning into clearer focus. The local authority is required to prepare a plan for redevelopment of blighted areas, in which these areas are related to the general plan for the city. Such an area may then be declared suitable for redevelopment and the authority is empowered to acquire the land, in whole or in part, and arrange for its rebuilding by private enterprise or public authority. The terms on which this declaration may be made are that at least fifty working-class houses are contained in the area; at least one-third of the dwellings are overcrowded or physically unfit, congested, or unsatisfactory for renovation; that the area is suitably located for housing, in part, for industrial workers; and that redevelopment of the entire area is necessary to establish adequate standards of low-rent housing in the area.

The effectiveness of the British program is demonstrated by performance. According to the 20th Annual Report of the Ministry of Health, there were 3,998,366 dwellings built in England between the end of the war and 1939. Of this number, 2,455,341 were built by private enterprise, 430,481 were built by private enterprise with some degree of government assistance, and 1,112,544 were built by local authorities.

Slum clearance was an important phase of the program in England. However, apartment buildings three to five stories in height were considered necessary in order to restore ample open spaces in the residential plan, and this was contrary to the traditional dwelling of the English people. The cottage and garden was the type of dwelling

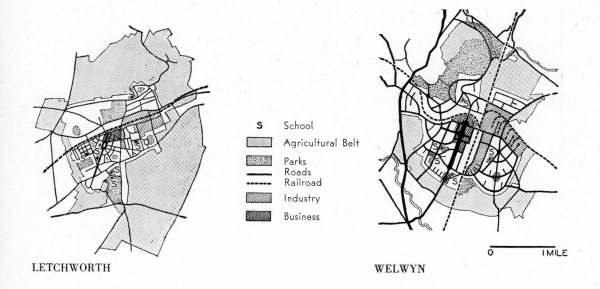

S   School

Agricultural Belt

Parks

Roads

Railroad

Industry

Business

LETCHWORTH

WELWYN

0   1 MILE

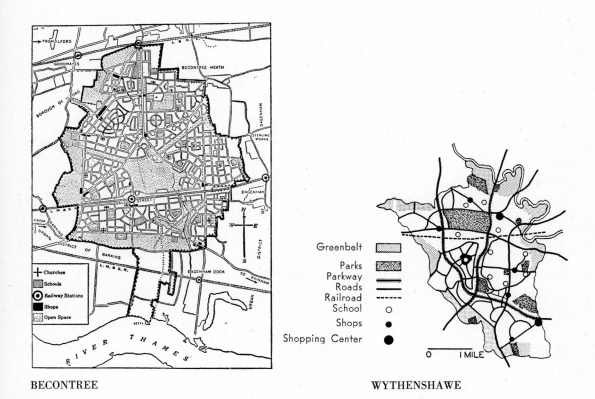

Greenbelt

Parks

Parkway

Roads

Railroad

School   ○

Shops   ●

Shopping Center   ●

BECONTREE

WYTHENSHAWE

0   1 MILE

THE GARDEN CITY AND THE SATELLITE TOWN

Reflecting the ideas of Ebenezer Howard, the Garden City of Letchworth was begun near London in 1903 and Welwyn soon followed. Limited in their initial planning to an ultimate maximum population, the garden cities were surrounded by agricultural fields similar to the original proposal by Robert Owen. The satellite towns of Wythenshawe and Becontree are similar to the garden cities with the primary exception that the latter are self-contained, each having its own industry, whereas the former are dependent upon the larger industrial cities, to which they are attached, for industrial employment.

close to the heart of the Englishman. The most successful housing developments were, consequently, those in which this type predominated.

The Satellite Garden Town. Two great projects were undertaken in this period —Becontree, a satellite community for 25,000 families on 2,770 acres near London, and Wythenshawe, adjacent to Manchester.

Sir Ernest Simon has called Wythenshawe a satellite garden town in contrast to a garden city such as Letchworth and Welwyn. The two have similar characteristics: a residential area of low density of not more than twelve families per acre, factory and shopping areas, parks, schools, and other civic buildings, and protective buffers of permanent agricultural belts on the periphery. However, a garden city is intended to be a self-contained and self-sustaining community whereas the satellite garden town is situated close to a large city in which the residents of the garden town may have their work and places of business.

The city council of Manchester appointed a Housing Committee in 1926 to consider the possibility of a satellite garden town to relieve the congested slums in the city. An estate of about 2,500 acres in single ownership adjacent to the city on the Mersey River was recommended as the site. It was later increased to 5,500 acres, and after some opposition locally and in Parliament the entire area was incorporated in the city in 1930, most of the land being finally purchased at agricultural value. Mr. Barry Parker, Architect, was invited to prepare plans for the estate. An agricultural belt of 1,000 acres was reserved, and the original grounds of the estate were retained as a 250-acre park. A golf course of 100 acres was also provided. Two broad parkways run through the town connecting with the city. The residential areas which border these parkways are separated from the roadways by an open space 150 feet wide. Side roads give access and ingress to abutting property and the main road has been confined to through-traffic with limited access. The residential area is 3,000 acres with a maximum density of 12 houses per acre; 25,000 houses are planned with an ultimate population of 100,000.

The land on which Wythenshawe is built remains in the ownership of the city of Manchester. Both the city and private enterprise may build on the estate and by 1935 a total of about 4,800 dwellings had been completed. Of these the city built some 4,600. It is planned that about two-thirds of the residential area will be used for municipal housing, and one-third for private housing. About 500 acres are reserved for industrial, commercial, and civic buildings.

Some criticism was leveled at the city council of Manchester for extravagance in purchasing a large tract of land and reserving large areas for permanent open space. Sir Ernest Simon, a staunch leader for improved housing in England, has defended the policy of the city with a comparison of the method pursued in the usual procedure:

Let us consider first the question of the bulk purchase of land. The question is whether the City Council has been wise to purchase so large a block of land straight off, or whether it would have been more economical to continue its previous policy of purchasing relatively small plots of land as and when required. It has in fact, since the War, purchased nearly 2,000 acres at a cost which has been gradually rising, but which must average about 400 pounds an acre, giving a total of about 800,000 pounds. In Wythenshawe, on the other hand, the original purchase of 2,500 acres was at 80 pounds an acre. Since then prices have gradually increased. As development has proceeded and as it has become known that the Corporation was in the market for more land, the prices have been put up, and the average price paid for the whole 3,500 acres is perhaps in the neighborhood of about 100 pounds an acre, or a total of say 350,000 pounds.

If at Wythenshawe the Corporation had pursued its old policy, first of all developing main roads and main drainage, then gradually buying pieces of land as they were required for housing and became ripe for building, there is not the least doubt that they would have had to pay a similar average price to that paid in the rest of Manchester; that is to say about 400 pounds an acre.

The effect of the bulk purchase therefore is that the land has been purchased at an average price of 100 pounds per acre as against an average of 400 pounds. So far as the 2,000 acres are concerned which are to be used for municipal housing, nobody denies that this land was needed for housing, and that it would, at some time, have had to be bought for that purpose. The economy through buying in bulk has therefore been 300 pounds an acre, or a total of 600,000 pounds for the 2,000 acres. Against this saving must of course be set the annual loss in owning the land up to the time of development; say 4 per cent for interest charges. This amounts to 8,000 pounds per annum. From this must be deducted the rents receivable from the agricultural land (less cost of management) which would bring the net burden down to a figure of say 6,000 pounds per annum, that is to say, against a total saving of 600,000 pounds there is an annual charge, so long as the land is wholly undeveloped, of 6,000 pounds. The period of delay before full development is, of course, uncertain, but if Manchester proceeds with its programme of building 3,000 houses a year, most of them being necessarily built at Wythenshawe, the estate will be fully developed in less than ten years. Assuming, however, that twenty years were required, the burden of interest, beginning at 6,000 pounds per annum and gradually falling to nothing, would amount in the whole period to 60,000 pounds. The net saving on the housing estate owing to the early purchase would therefore be no less than 540,000 pounds.

Let us now turn to consider the 1,500 acres purchased for factories, shops, public buildings and private enterprise houses. Development is still in its early stages, and no particulars have been published as regards the terms on which this land is being leased for these different purposes. We are informed, however, that the ground rents which are being obtained are such that they represent on the average a capital value of at least 300 pounds per acre above the bare cost of the land. When these 1,500 acres are fully developed there will therefore be a profit on the capitalized value of the land of at least 300 pounds an acre, or 450,000 pounds on the whole area. Against this item also there will be a set-off representing the interest charges during the period of development, which on the assumptions previously made should certainly not exceed 50,000 pounds, leaving a net gain of 400,000 pounds.

Taking the landlord account as a whole (covering the 3,500 acres) we come, therefore, to the following conclusion: that the bulk purchase of 3,500 acres by the Corporation as against the old policy of hand-to-mouth buying of the land required for housing, and not buying any land for other purposes, will, if the estate is fully developed in twenty years or less, show a capital advantage to the Corporation of approximately 1,000,000 pounds.

Accusations of extravagance against the City Council for the bulk purchase of land are, therefore, the exact reverse of the truth. The fact is that the City Council has shown a high degree of business foresight in making the purchase, which will ultimately be of great benefit to the ratepayers.

There is only one other aspect of the Wythenshawe development which has been called extravagant: the generous reservation which has been made in the plans for the agricultural belt, parks, parkways and the preservation of spinneys. Admittedly, the area reserved is an advance on what has previously been done; but the difference between the normal practice of reserving 10 per cent of the area for parks, on the one hand, and what has been done at Wythenshawe on the other, is not great. The total expenditure on open spaces in the whole three parishes of Wythenshawe, even if the whole agricultural belt is actually purchased by the City Council, will certainly not reach 200,000 pounds; it must be admitted that the necessary open spaces could have been provided for perhaps 50,000 pounds less. But this extra expenditure will make a big difference to the amenity of the estate. Can anybody seriously call this extravagance when it is set off against the 1,000,000 pounds which will be gained on the landlord account?[1]

Sweden. Mature policies of land acquisition by cities in the Scandinavian countries resulted in aggressive participation in the supply of housing by private enterprise via the public utility societies and housing co-operatives. Copenhagen in Denmark, Stockholm in Sweden, and Oslo in Norway made outstanding progress in both urban and rural housing, and standards were maintained at a relatively high level. It is estimated that 10 per cent of the population in Stockholm live in housing produced by the co-operative societies alone, and a fifth of the people in Copenhagen and Oslo are accommodated in co-operative and public utility housing.

The industrial revolution did not reach Swedish cities until electric power had been developed as a major power source. As a consequence congestion did not afflict Swedish cities to the extent suffered by other cities on the continent. Decentralization was feasible —power was brought to the people rather than the people congregating at the source of power. While migration to cities during the nineteenth century had increased ten- to twentyfold elsewhere, the increase of population in town and country was stable in Sweden. During the nineteenth century rural population increased from 1,000,000 to 2,000,000, and urban population increased from 2,000,000 to 4,000,000.

The central district of Stockholm contained its share of slums, but they did not constitute the relatively large problem prevailing in continental cities. The principal problem in Sweden was overcrowding within dwellings, undoubtedly due to the rigorous climate and the heating problem it created. More than 50 per cent of the families occupied apartments of one and two rooms.

Since Sweden was a neutral country during World War I the economy had not only escaped suffering but had fared quite well. A shortage of housing occurred because construction had lagged, but the government was in a satisfactory financial position to render all needed assistance to correct it. From 1917 to 1920 municipalities subsidized public utility societies and co-operative groups that were building low-cost housing to the extent of one-third the cost. In 1920 this subsidy was reduced to 15 per cent of the cost because of increased wages and resulting capacity to pay higher rents. With stability generally restored by 1923 the subsidies were discontinued. Interest rates on mortgage money were high, and the State Dwelling Loan Fund was set up to make loans for second mortgages at low interest rates to offset the high first mortgage costs.

It was a tradition in Sweden for citizens to have the greatest possible freedom from government aid or interference. This tradition had not only been strengthened by, but was largely due to, the vigorous and aggressive co-operative movement. It became an effective and progressive instrument for the maintenance of democratic procedures and economic freedom. In order to remove itself from housing operations as much as possible, the government created an independent agency in 1929 to

[1] *The Rebuilding of Manchester*, Sir E. D. Simon, Longmans Green & Company, 1935.

administer the Swedish Housing Loan Fund. This agency loaned government funds at low interest and long terms to continue the building of housing for low-income families. The successful operation of co-operatives soon obviated any need for these loans, and financial responsibility was shifted to the co-operative societies. By 1934, 10 per cent of the people in Stockholm lived in housing developments sponsored by the co-operative societies.

The co-operatives were of two major types. The S.K.B. (*Stockholm Kooperativa Forbundet*, or Stockholm Co-operative Society) was engaged in the production of various consumer goods. Housing built by this society was primarily for its member employees. The H.S.B. (*Hyresgasternas Sparkassa och Byggnads-forening*, or Tenant Savings Bank and Building Society) was an organization specifically organized to build dwellings for members of the society, and membership was not restricted to any particular occupation. Careful research in planning was carried on by this society, and the projects it developed introduced advanced techniques in planning, equipment, and community facilities.

Since 1904 the city of Stockholm had purchased 20,000 acres of land surrounding the city. This land was incorporated and planned for "garden suburbs." The city installed streets and utilities, and sponsored a program for working families to lease lots and build their own dwellings. Loans were available from the municipality up to 90 per cent of the value of each unit. The loans were in the form of materials purchased by the city, the balance (10 per cent) being the owner's contribution in labor. Standard plans for the dwellings, ranging from 700 square feet to 1,000 square feet in floor area, were prepared by the city, and skilled supervision was provided during construction. It was a popular and successful program, offering an opportunity for low-income families to leave the congested slums.

Rebuilding of cities was aided by the Town Planning Act of 1931 which required all urban communities, regardless of size, to prepare a rebuilding plan. All improvements thereafter were obliged to conform to the plan.

In 1935 encouragement was given to rehousing slum dwellers by means of rent rebates ranging from 30 per cent of economic rents according to family size. There were other forms of housing improvement such as joint rehabilitation of substandard buildings by owners of contiguous property for which the municipality advanced loans. Housing for the aged and for single women were also included within the scope of municipal programs.

The methods employed in Sweden to maintain good housing were varied. Public policy was always flexible enough to be adjusted as changing conditions warranted, and private enterprise, through the co-operatives and housing societies, was courageous and astute with its investments.

France. Epidemics of cholera generated some activity in the nineteenth century to correct substandard housing in France, and the threat of mob violence moved Napoleon III to build wide avenues through the slums as a means to control them. But it was not until 1894 that serious legislation was enacted. The Act passed at that time was similar to the Belgian Law of 1889 which made funds available from the government

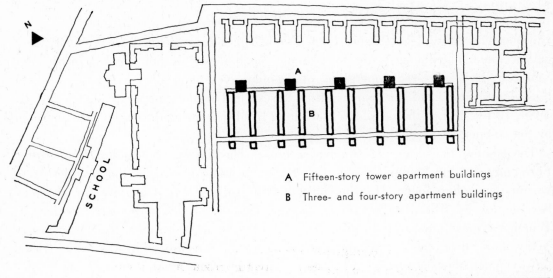

A   Fifteen-story tower apartment buildings

B   Three- and four-story apartment buildings

LA CITE DE LA MUETTE

Beaudoin & Lods, Architects

The first stage of development at Drancy, near Paris. One of the large housing projects built by the Department of the Seine in the outlying districts around Paris. This unusual project shows the usual difficulties that arise when urban expansion proceeds independently of adequate plans for the extension of utilities and transportation facilities. It was largely vacant because these facilities were lacking until World War II when it was converted into a military barracks.

Marcel Lods

at low interest rates for houses to be sold exclusively to industrial employees. In 1912 the *Office Public d'Habitations à Bon Marché* (Public Office for Low-cost Housing), an organization of local authorities, was empowered to loan funds for, and subsidize, low-cost housing. It was augmented several times later until the Loucheur Act of 1928, which concentrated further upon production of housing for low-income families and expanded financing through public authorities and private enterprise. Nearly half the dwellings provided by the Public Office after World War I were concentrated about Paris.

Despite ambitious plans to rebuild the congested slums—the *ilots insalubre*—a blot was dropped on the housing program in Paris. When the city walls were razed, it was expected that the open space would be reserved and the surrounding slum belt cleared and rebuilt with appropriate standards of planning. It was another idle dream. When the fortifications were leveled, the land was leased to speculative enterprise in 1930 and some 20,000 dwellings crowded into tightly planned tenements eight stories high were built in the open space. The adjacent slums remained.

There was some encouragement in the late thirties. The Department of the Seine planned a series of *cité jardins* in the outlying areas of Paris. While literally translated as "garden cities," these developments were designed as satellite garden villages somewhat similar to Wythenshawe in England. In the words of M. Henri Sellier, Administrator of the Housing Office of the Department of the Seine, the *cité jardins* were planned as "essential elements of the City of Greater Paris."

Another blow befell the program. The necessity for co-operation from public utility agencies in the successful development of the city was amply demonstrated. Lack of proper arrangements for transportation meant failure for some of the *cité jardins* outside Paris and near failure for others. The interesting project at Drancy La Muette remained vacant because transportation was not provided. Chatenay Malabry, planned for 20,000 people, and Plessis Robinson were partly occupied, but transportation was not completed.

The post-war housing program in France hardly set a standard to serve as a guide for urban development. The plan for the *cité jardins* about Paris was courageous, but, as indicated above, it was not enough for success. Urban planning is complex, and the variety of public services makes the difference between success and failure.

Germany. Certain policies had been well established in Germany prior to World War I. Public utility societies and trade union co-operatives were recognized as effective instruments in the housing field. State financial aid was an accepted method; during the last half of the nineteenth century Bismarck had inaugurated social insurance, and this source supplied funds for housing loans for many years. Local governments had also assumed responsibility for housing government workers and financing public utility societies.

During his tenure of office in 1902, Mayor Adickes of Frankfurt obtained passage of a law (*Lex Adickes*), permitting the city government to pool private property, rearrange it to conform to the city plan, and redistribute such land for redevelopment. In this process the city was further authorized to retain 40 per cent of the land, without compensation to the owners, for streets, parks, and other public uses. Pursuant to this enactment in Frankfurt, a policy was adopted in numerous German cities to acquire outlying vacant land on the periphery. The purpose of this policy was protection from the inevitable speculation and resulting boom in land prices which accompanied the rapid increase in urban population.

This policy was fully rewarded after World War I when the need for housing, production of which had come to an abrupt halt, became most acute. The cities were then in a position to lease large quantities of these public lands to private and co-operative organizations for the construction of housing without the penalty of excessive land costs. In seventy German towns with more than 50,000 population, more than 6,000 acres of city-owned land were leased between 1926 and the rise of Hitler. Similar policies were adopted in other countries, Austria, Switzerland, Holland, and Denmark, and 15,000 acres outlying Prague in Czechoslovakia were made available for housing.

The first world war left Germany impoverished. Inflation upset the monetary system, an inactive building industry left a serious housing shortage, and the country was undergoing transition from imperial to republican government. High financing costs rendered it difficult for private enterprise to cope with the housing problem. Interest on mortgage money had more than doubled, moving from 4 per cent to as high as 10 per cent. Rents had quadrupled while wages had increased only 50 per cent. It became imperative for state and local governments to finance a large part of the housing program.

Property owners had become beneficiaries of the inflation which had the effect of liquidating all previous mortgages. As a consequence the *Hauszinsteuer* (House Rent Tax) was adopted in 1921. Prewar rents were used as the base for a tax levy ranging from 10 to 50 per cent of the rents, and the funds thus derived were used to finance second mortgages at a very low interest rate (generally 1 per cent) to compensate for the high cost of first mortgage money. Administered by local government, these funds were loaned to public utility societies and co-operatives for housing. The effectiveness of this policy is evident in the production of some 3,000,000 dwellings between the war and the rise of Hitler. More than three-quarters of these dwellings received financial aid from the government. The housing problem was not solved, a sufficient supply of dwellings was not provided and the slums remained, but the program represents a remarkable achievement for what it did accomplish.

German cities had suffered the same kind of chaotic growth experienced by other cities on the continent during the nineteenth century. It was obviously necessary to reconsider land utilization and planning if the tremendous housing program were to result in a permanent asset to the communities in which it was built. It is a significant contrast with our own experience in the United States. Emergencies have been the excuse to postpone urban planning in our country; the emergency in republican Germany was considered the sound reason to engage in the most serious planning.

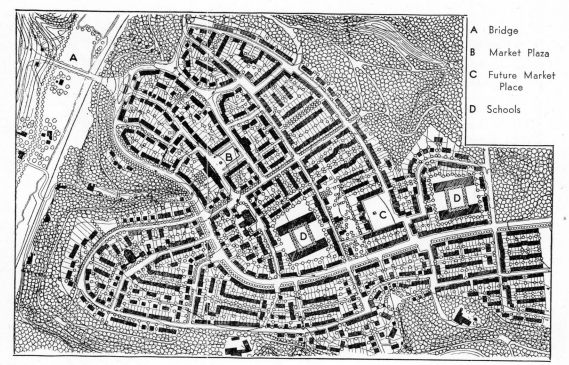

A	Bridge
B	Market Plaza
C	Future Market Place
D	Schools

MARGARETHEN-HOHE, Essen

George Metzendorf, Architect

Emerging from the Garden City movement, this village was developed in 1912 by the Krupp family for workers in the industrial steel plants in Essen. The community was planned for 2,000–2,500 dwellings (12,000–16,000 population) and the first stage is shown in black. It illustrates a number of planning features. Surrounded by forest, the principal connection with the city is by way of the bridge (A) on the north boundary. Rather than bisecting the plan in the usual manner, the main traffic street swings around the village and by-passes the market plaza (B). This shopping center and the future principal market place (C) are conveniently located within the dwelling area rather than upon the periphery. The schools (D) are situated within blocks of dwellings rather than upon the traffic roads. The road system is designed to fit the topography of the site but is arranged to avoid through-traffic on any but the main roadway. It will also be observed that buildings are generally set back at road intersections to avoid obstruction of traffic vision at the corners.

It is a curious paradox that this development to improve the living environment of the working people of Essen was dedicated to the same member of the Krupp family for which the powerful military cannon "Big Bertha" was named a few years later.

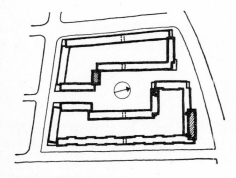

POSSMORWEG, Hamburg

Built in 1927–'28 on plans by Schneider, Elingius, and Schramm. A variation of the "hollow square" planning characteristic of the early housing program in Germany. Under the direction of the city architect, Fritz Schumacher, this type of planning continued in Hamburg. The large space in interior courts was a vast improvement over high land coverage, but orientation of the dwellings was compromised.

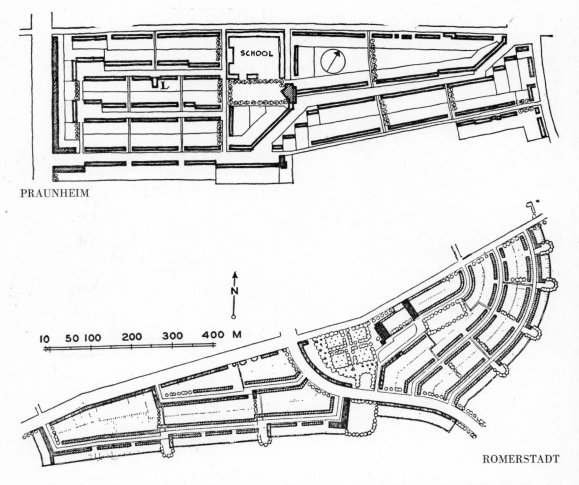

PRAUNHEIM

10   50 100   200   300   400 M

ROMERSTADT

Praunheim and Romerstadt were among the early developments in the extensive program under the direction of Ernst May in Frankfurt am Main. Praunheim with 1,441 dwellings was begun in 1926 and extended through 1930; Romerstadt with 1,220 dwellings was built in 1927–28. The architects were May, H. Boehm, Bangert, and E. Kaufmann.

Two-story row-houses predominated in these developments, although some three-story apartment buildings were included. Orientation was not dealt with as insistently as in subsequent planning, but the houses were planned somewhat differently on each side of the street. The ample open space is noteworthy, and community facilities were well considered because of the isolated site location. Schools and play areas, guest houses, shopping, and a theater were planned.

The unit plans show a dwelling for the north side of a street with the living room to the south, or street side. In this case, it will be seen on the plot plan that these dwellings are set back from the street line. In the dwelling for the south side of the street, the living room is placed on the opposite side from the street, facing south. The third unit plan shows the type of minimum dwelling developed in Frankfurt am Main for an outside corridor giving entrance to the dwellings.

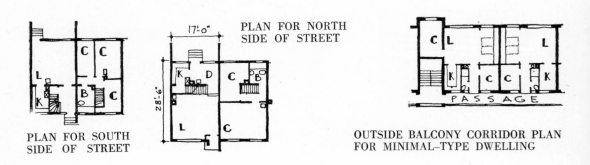

PLAN FOR SOUTH
SIDE OF STREET

PLAN FOR NORTH
SIDE OF STREET

OUTSIDE BALCONY CORRIDOR PLAN
FOR MINIMAL–TYPE DWELLING

ROMERSTADT

European Picture Service

Private living gardens are provided for the dwellings and there are allotment gardens for vegetables in some areas.

Despite the shadows cast over that country since Hitler's rise to power and the national frustration it brought, the housing program of the 1920–30 decade looms as an example of aggressive, though immature, democracy in action.

The pressing demand for new dwellings gave neither the time nor the funds for a real program to clear the slums; this was necessarily postponed until an adequate supply of dwellings could be built. Two effective means were brought into play in the early twenties: the public utility society (limited-dividend company) and the co-operative society. The public utility society, though comparable to the limited dividend company in this country, was subject to careful supervision by the state and was eligible to receive the benefits of several forms of subsidies found necessary to implement a large supply of new housing. They were formed for the purpose of building low-cost housing and, in spite of state supervision, exercised a high degree of initiative and ingenuity in the planning of their projects. The co-operatives, or self-aid societies, were largely organized by trade unions as a means to supply housing for their members. These companies enjoyed privileges similar to public utility societies and assumed the same obligations. The effectiveness of these groups is demonstrated by the extensive operations of the three largest which built 71,000 dwellings up to 1929. These three, known as "Dewog," "Gagfah," and "Heimat," were among some 4,300 co-operative societies in operation.

In addition to large organizations there were a number of smaller private companies engaged in the program, but they contributed to a much less degree than the above-mentioned companies. The government created various agencies under jurisdiction of the several provinces and municipalities, for research in the technical phases of planning, construction, and financing. The results of this research were made available to all private and public organizations in the housing field.

With few exceptions, planning prior to 1925 had been confined to the usual city blocks. Inadequate building regulations had permitted an excessive density of population and building coverage within these confines. The first step away from high density in the postwar program was the arrangement of buildings about the perimeter of the usual city block with building coverage reduced within the center of the block. This "hollow square" form enclosed recreation and service areas, the buildings being mainly apartments of three and four stories in height. Many large-scale developments were placed upon tracts of vacant land. Here freedom from the subdivision of the gridiron system led to more informal planning and the "row house" was adopted where density was not a prerequisite. Main traffic streets were confined to the periphery of the projects, and the internal residential roads were bordered by parallel rows of dwellings. Apartments of three and four stories were also included along the marginal areas of the site.

Research in planning techniques soon led to a rational consideration of orientation. Sunlight in every room was a rule, and the orientation of all buildings to provide east and west exposure became mandatory. The preferable exposure was west light for living rooms and east light for bedrooms. The attention devoted to the proper

PAPPELHOF, Chemnitz, 1929

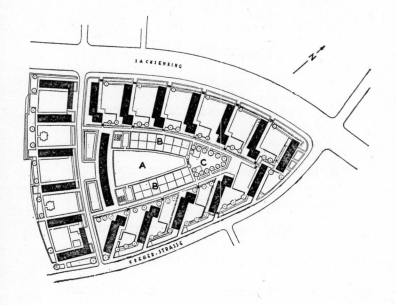

This project of 521 dwellings in three-story apartment buildings illustrates a well-organized allocation of land uses. Uniform orientation is provided all dwellings, and the buildings are placed perpendicular to the boundary streets. Access to the park, the gardens, and the playground is convenient from most of the dwellings. Six stores are provided along the transverse service road.

A Park

B Allotment Gardens

C Children's Playground

NIDDA VALLEY, Frankfurt-am-Main

When the post-World War I housing program was begun in Germany, Ernst May was the architect-planner engaged to direct the program in Frankfurt-am-Main. Because of the shortage of dwellings the clearance of slums within the central city was necessarily postponed until an adequate supply was available. May planned a series of satellite housing developments about the periphery of the city, and the Nidda Valley district is an illustration. Ample open space was retained about the housing areas which were planned in a manner similar to Romerstadt and Praunheim located in the Nidda Valley.

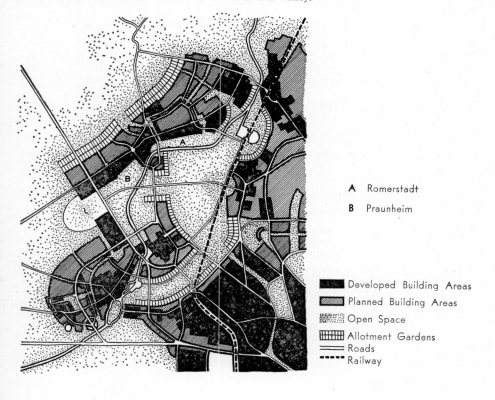

A Romerstadt

B Praunheim

Developed Building Areas
Planned Building Areas
Open Space
Allotment Gardens
Roads
Railway

DAMMERSTOCK, Karlsruhe
1929

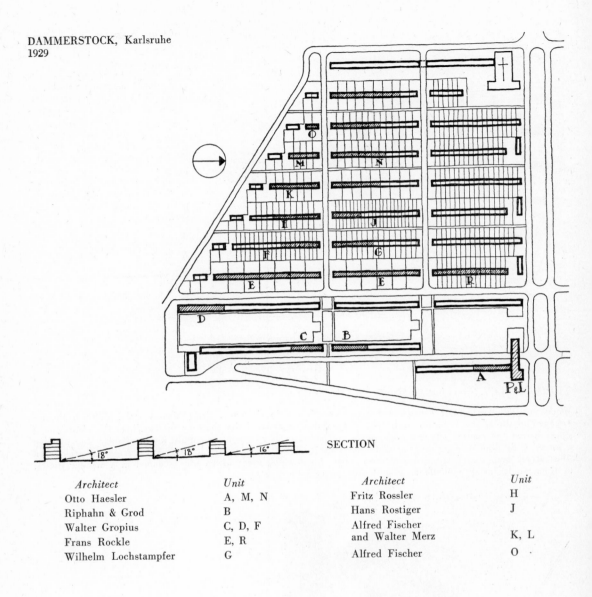

SECTION

Architect	Unit		Architect	Unit
Otto Haesler	A, M, N		Fritz Rossler	H
Riphahn & Grod	B		Hans Rostiger	J
Walter Gropius	C, D, F		Alfred Fischer and Walter Merz	K, L
Frans Rockle	E, R			
Wilhelm Lochstampfer	G		Alfred Fischer	O

This project, 750 dwelling units, demonstrates the rigid formula for site planning that emerged in the German program:

1. Uniform orientation for all dwellings.
2. Elimination of traffic between buildings.
3. Open space in proportion to building height.

All dwellings were two rooms in depth and the alignment of all buildings in the north-south direction admitted sunlight in every room of every dwelling. Buildings were placed perpendicular to the streets, and a maximum number of the dwellings thereby faced upon free open space on both sides of the buildings. Streets were reduced to a minimum and treated as service lanes. As building heights increased, the angle between the roof line of one row and the ground line of the next remained constant, as seen in the section.

The project was planned under the direction of Walter Gropius, but a number of architects were engaged in the design and a wide variety of dwellings resulted. In most of these the relation of dwellings to exterior space was the same. Living areas faced upon private gardens opposite the entrance side. Apartments were confined to one row of three-story and one row of four-story buildings located at the east side of the site; the rest of the units were two-story row houses.

Utility services—heat and laundry—were contained in the individual row houses, and a central heating plant and laundry (P&L) was provided for the apartments. As in most of the German developments, the small ownership of automobiles is reflected in the absence of parking space for vehicles.

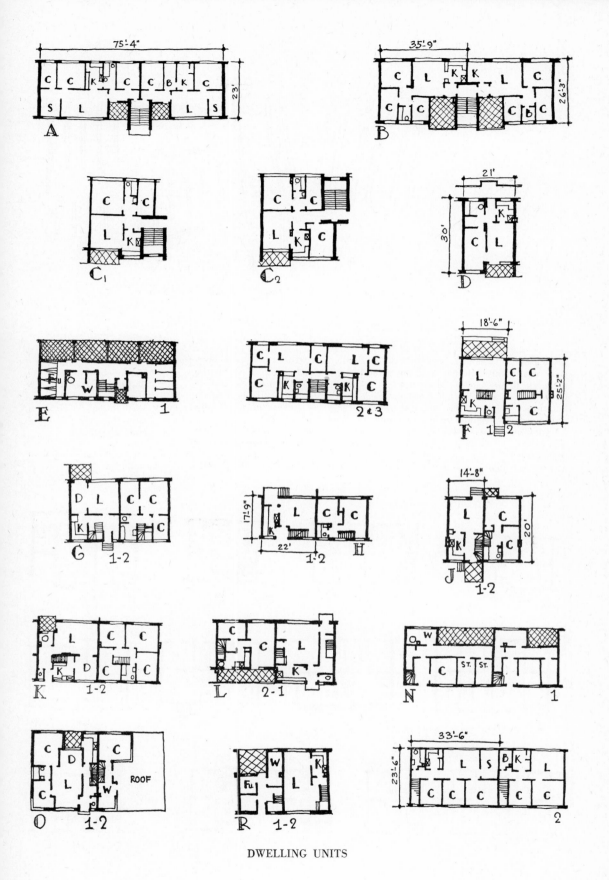

DWELLING UNITS

SIEMENSTADT, Berlin

1929–31

PARK

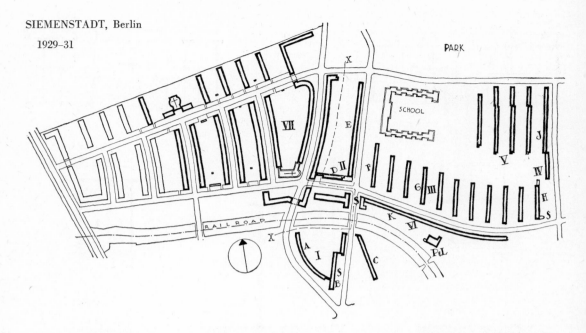

Siemenstadt, developed in a suburb of Berlin, comprises three- and four-story apartment buildings built by several housing companies. It shows the tendency to arrange building rows in a north-south alignment to provide uniform orientation for all dwellings, and the elimination of streets between buildings to avoid traffic interference. A large school, churches, and shops (S), a central heating plant and laundry (P&L) are provided.

The project was designed by a number of architects and includes a variety of dwelling plans, but all have been planned with similar consideration for orientation of the rooms. Unit J is adaptable to different room arrangements, and Unit K, being situated in a building running east and west, places all living and sleeping rooms with south exposure.

Group	Architect	Unit
I	Hans Scharoun	A, B, C
II	Walter Gropius	D, E, F
III	Hugo Haring	G
IV, V	Fred Forbat	H, J
VI	Otto Bartning	K
VII	Hans Hertlein	

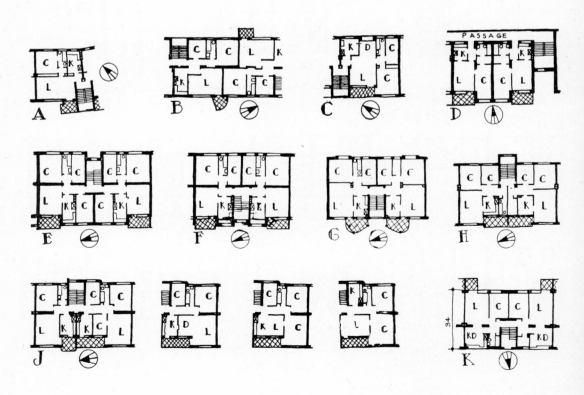

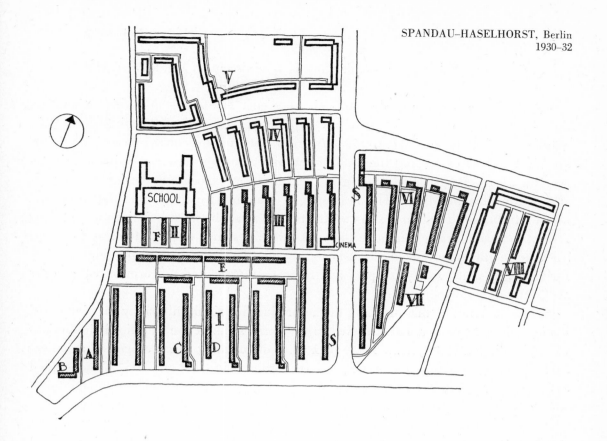

This project represents the final development in the technique of site planning. Uniform orientation is obtained for substantially all dwellings. Traffic is confined to streets laid perpendicular to the building rows, and space between buildings is completely free. A school, cinema, and shops (S) are incorporated. It will be observed that the dwellings are generally small units, conforming to the tendency to meet the growing need for housing of the increasing number of small families.

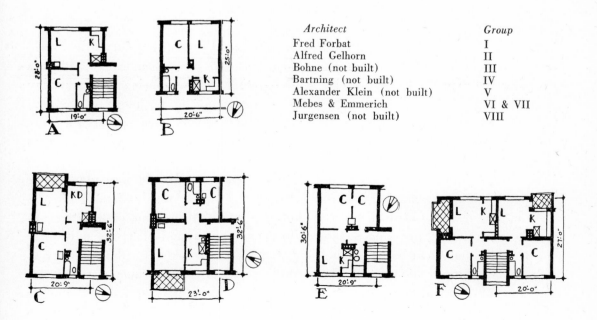

Architect	Group
Fred Forbat	I
Alfred Gelhorn	II
Bohne (not built)	III
Bartning (not built)	IV
Alexander Klein (not built)	V
Mebes & Emmerich	VI & VII
Jurgensen (not built)	VIII

orientation for all dwellings at this time is reminiscent of the fifth century B.C. in Greece.

The process was like a modern planning hygiene. The final step in this rationalization was directed to the relation of the buildings to the streets. Buildings located in parallel lines along each side of a street did not provide equal privacy for living areas nor quiet for sleeping rooms. The new site planning produced uniform orientation for all dwellings but did not give them uniform exposure upon the open spaces surrounding the buildings. The next step in planning technique was the placement of all buildings at right angles to the streets. The space between buildings was thereby free of vehicular traffic, although the walks were designed to permit access for small trucks to facilitate movement of goods and service. This arrangement provided privacy for all living units, safety for play and recreation areas, and uniform orientation for all dwellings.

Strict adherence to this planning theme produced a rigid uniformity that increased during the late twenties, but it served to overcome some of the traditional inhibitions of the gridiron street system. These principles of planning were recognized as guides to challenge the designer, and some projects developed in 1931 and 1932 demonstrated some liberation from the previous regimentation. A more plastic and flexible treatment was emerging, but progress was interrupted by the political domination of Nazism.

Recreation space for children and adults, shops, meeting rooms for common use, and kindergartens were provided in the housing developments. Home laundry was customarily performed by the housewife. In early projects laundry facilities were placed upon the roof of two-story buildings, one-half being roofed and one-half open drying space. This practice carried over to apartment buildings until the adoption of central heating systems encouraged central laundries or "washeries" in conjunction with them. Private gardens were provided to the extent that space permitted but were usually confined to the single-family row houses. Some subsistence plots were included in a few of the large developments.

Probably the most outstanding example of integrated planning occurred in Frankfurt-am-Main. Ernst May, the architect-in-charge, and his associates undertook a comprehensive plan for the entire city in preparation for the housing program. May subscribed to the principle of satellite communities about the periphery of the city. The housing developments were surrounded by permanent open spaces but were planned as part of the city expansion rather than detached and self-contained garden cities.

The best and most enlightened professional talent was brought into play in the program. Planning techniques were subjected to a complete revaluation. While this was a natural result of critical material shortages and high building costs, it encouraged the evolution of planning methods which had a profound effect not only upon housing alone but on urban planning and architecture. Stirred by the necessity to reach basic solutions of social and economic problems, there came a renascence of architectural and planning thought. It can be said that a new concept of the urban environment emerged. A new sense of freedom was expressed. It had not yet reached maturity when it was halted by the insidious spread of Nazism and suppression.

Holland. At the turn of the century, the Act of 1901 in Holland required that every city with a population of 10,000 or more prepare a comprehensive town plan, in which new areas for housing were to be allocated. Housing standards were to be established by the local authorities who were charged with responsibility to ascertain compliance with them, exercising the power of condemnation where necessary. The local authorities were also empowered to build low-cost housing. Government funds were made available to public utility societies at low interest rates and limited dividends.

During and following World War I these powers were extended and the housing program was accelerated. In the ten years after the war some 500,000 dwellings were built in Holland. Because careful attention was directed throughout the program to meet the needs of the various income levels, it was possible to confine the "public" housing primarily to the problem of direct slum clearance.

Russia. Since the revolution of 1917 planning and housing in Russia have been treated with vigor. The contrast between Imperial Russia and the Soviet Union is apparent. Vast plans for industrial development were made and many were carried out. New cities were built and portions of old cities rebuilt.

There appears to be a distinction, however, between the tremendous activity and the standards of planning adopted by the Soviets. The latter does not measure up to expectations suggested by the former. A city plan like that proposed for Stalingrad, a linear city, suggests hopeful prospects for the reorganization of the urban pattern. The executed housing developments, on the other hand, are extensive, but the standards, the small apartments in multistoried buildings, leave much to be desired and offer little to warrant particular attention.

The form of government in the Soviet Union and the economic structure are so different from governments in the western world that comparisons are ineffective. The political processes occupy such an integral part of urban development that experience and accomplishments in planning in the Soviet Union are not subject to satisfactory appraisal.

Italy. As early as 1865 in Italy powers were vested in public authorities to expropriate land for streets and roads. The severe cholera epidemic in Naples in 1885 forced these powers to be extended to control insanitary dwellings. In 1919 the same powers were extended throughout the country. This Act, being directed at the clearance of slums, permitted local authorities to transfer land acquired by condemnation to other appropriate uses such as parks. In 1928 cities were required to prepare plans for their extension and rehabilitation.

With the advent of Fascism the state undertook aggressive steps in city rebuilding. Every effort was directed to the emulation of ancient Roman glory. Extensive clearance was undertaken in the central areas of Rome, and open spaces were preserved to enhance the ancient monuments.

Families displaced by these clearance projects were encouraged to move to the outskirts. The government developed large tracts of residential suburbs on the city periphery. Migration to the city was offset by reclamation of the Pontine marshes for agricultural enterprise and the establishment of decentralized administrative and market centers surrounded by farm groups. To eliminate the substandard shacks on the edge of the city, loans and grants were available to owners for rebuilding. A law of 1908, which provided loans to public utility societies, was revived, and the *Instituti per le Casa Popolari* were accorded low-interest loans and tax exemption for twenty-five years for "limited-dividend" housing for the working classes.

Austria. Austria emerged from the Empire period and World War I financially bankrupt. Inflation had reduced to a minimum the capacity of private capital to produce housing. Municipal government was forced to take the major role and Vienna undertook an energetic program. Public funds were not available, and it was necessary to obtain them by a tax on rents. This was inaugurated in 1923 and launched an active program, approximately a quarter of the revenues from taxes being devoted to housing in 1928.

Switzerland. Switzerland had a housing shortage following World War I, and local governments rendered financial assistance to co-operative organizations as encouragement to produce an adequate supply. However the situation in Switzerland did not present as serious a problem as most countries because of stable policies of private finance that prevailed during most of its history. The advantages of democratic capitalism had always been more evenly distributed in Switzerland, and the excesses suffered in many countries had been absent to a marked degree. The result was that this little country had not sunk to such low depths that violent action was required to restore balance.

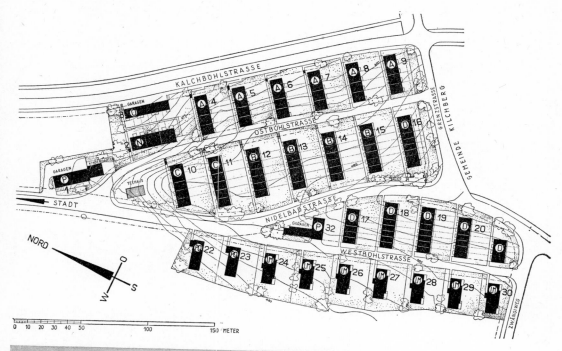

NEUBUHL, Zurich

Architects Artaria and Schmidt, Hubacher and Steiger, M. E. Haefeli, W. M. Moser, Alfred Roth.

This development of about 200 dwellings was built in 1930 and contains most of the basic planning elements of contemporary site organization. Most of the dwellings are two-story group houses. Uniform orientation is applied throughout the project, but it will be observed that the south exposure is favored rather than east and west as in most German projects. Living rooms of all dwellings are located opposite the entrance and face directly upon a private garden with southern exposure. The buildings are placed at right angles to the streets, and no dwelling faces upon them.

Garages are located at three points (P-1, P-32, and O-3). Shops and a kindergarten are provided in unit P-1.

Designed by a group of young architects, the architectural quality of this relatively small development has a refreshing clarity not frequently apparent in low-cost housing.

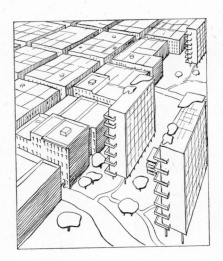

CHAPTER 8

TRANSITION

The Speculative Instinct. The development of real estate in the United States has not been distinguished for its attention to the amenities of a living environment. Speculation was the moving spirit as the frontiers widened and pushed forward. This was not a singular characteristic reserved to enterprising Americans alone. It rather points a difference between the opportunities open to the people of this land and those of countries elsewhere. It reflects the desires that caused the people to seek this land. Freedom from oppression and tyranny implied certain rights, and among them was the right for a man to have a piece of land upon which to build a home for his family. The search for that right was itself something of a speculation and abuse of the privilege was not a newly cultivated characteristic of mankind.

During the colonial period it was customary to obtain grants of land from the mother country, and it was considered a just reward due the leaders of colonization. The subdivision and sale of the land so acquired were common practice. However, it was not always a lucrative one, and some of the heaviest dealers in land met with financial failure. Some of the large land-estates were preserved through the English system of long-term leases rather than sale.

Speculation in land offered strong temptation in the latter half of the nineteenth century. Whole towns were used as a speculative medium, and they sprung up almost at random along the railroads that stretched across the land. Some of these towns have become cities, many have vanished, and others remain as ghosts of the speculative orgy in gold and silver.

Land Subdivision. The promoter entered upon the stage of this flourishing enterprise. He was a super-salesman with highly cultivated powers of persuasion. For him the land was a commodity for sale or trade. He was not a developer, he was a dealer. Success depended upon the rate at which this commodity changed hands. With a little cash and much credit, he would option a piece of land, mark it off in "lots," and place them upon the auction block. In most cases the purchasers of these lots were themselves engaged in a similar, though somewhat milder, form of speculation.

Hope ran high as these "deals" were transacted. There were occasions, however, when the turnover was not as rapid as the promoter had anticipated. He then unwittingly became a "developer." To stimulate response to the opportunities he was offering the public, he found it helpful to "improve" the property. The term "improvement" was at first a rather exaggerated description since it implied hardly more than scraping the earth's surface and calling the scar a road with a romantic name. The promoter sometimes embellished his subdivision with a fancy real estate office. Later it became more customary to install a few utilities and build a house or two as an inducement to the homeseeker to buy in an "established" neighborhood.

The above description may appear as a caricature, but there are those who still remember the heydays of speculation it depicts. Exploitation and promotion were not always accompanied by the most reliable business tactics, but the growing necessity to improve the property exerted a salutary influence upon the subdivision of land. It was necessary to apply more serious consideration to the soundness of a venture that required this degree of financial investment, and it led to the practice of subdivision control exercised by most cities today.

The Suburban Community. Although the history of speculation in land has not been of the most savory variety, there were those who chose this medium as an instrument for the improvement of land development. This choice was not motivated by the high purpose of the Garden City movement in England, for instance, nor was it prompted by deep concern for the nature of the city or its social and economic welfare. It was rather the natural result of competitive necessity prodded, no doubt, by that satisfaction of the creative impulse which achievement invariably delivers. There were accomplishments, and they altered the future prospects for our cities in a manner hardly suggested by the subdivision practices employed then and, still too frequently, now.

With the dawn of the twentieth century high land costs squeezed the single-family dwelling farther and farther to the outskirts. The swelling city forced these outskirts to such distances that community facilities which one time served the urban population were no longer readily accessible. The development of extensive facilities in the suburbs gave to them the character of satellite communities. Decentralization was in progress.

Only the surveyor had been associated in the layout of subdivisions. With the development of independent residential communities, however, the planner became a more active participant. One of the earliest large-scale residential subdivisions was a 1,600-acre tract to be known as Riverside, near Chicago. It was designed by Frederick Law Olmsted and Calvert Vaux in 1869. Garden City, Long Island, was another such development and it has since become substantially a self-contained community.

The gridiron street system offered the subdivider the most convenient pattern for surveying and recording deeds. It was typical of real estate development but offered little in return as a living environment. The exceptions are, therefore, the more noteworthy for the progress in planning they demonstrated.

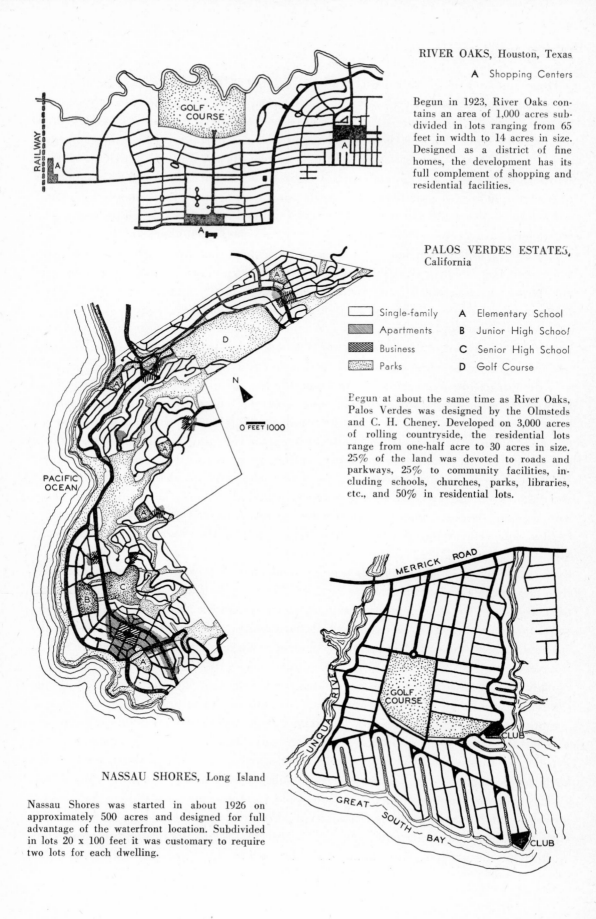

RIVER OAKS, Houston, Texas

A Shopping Centers

Begun in 1923, River Oaks contains an area of 1,000 acres subdivided in lots ranging from 65 feet in width to 14 acres in size. Designed as a district of fine homes, the development has its full complement of shopping and residential facilities.

PALOS VERDES ESTATES, California

	Single-family	A	Elementary School
	Apartments	B	Junior High School
	Business	C	Senior High School
	Parks	D	Golf Course

Begun at about the same time as River Oaks, Palos Verdes was designed by the Olmsteds and C. H. Cheney. Developed on 3,000 acres of rolling countryside, the residential lots range from one-half acre to 30 acres in size. 25% of the land was devoted to roads and parkways, 25% to community facilities, including schools, churches, parks, libraries, etc., and 50% in residential lots.

NASSAU SHORES, Long Island

Nassau Shores was started in about 1926 on approximately 500 acres and designed for full advantage of the waterfront location. Subdivided in lots 20 x 100 feet it was customary to require two lots for each dwelling.

Roland Park, in Baltimore, was a subdivision begun in 1891. It was distinguished for singularly high standards of physical development. It was designed for fine residences, but there were few suburbs not so intended. Another pioneer development was Forest Hills, Long Island. It was one of the earliest planned residential suburbs, started in 1913, and the development company undertook the construction of many of the homes, apartments, and shopping facilities.

After World War I a number of well-planned communities were initiated. Mariemont, Ohio, designed by John Nolen in 1921, became a satellite of Cincinnati. It was devoted primarily to single-family homes with a density of six or seven units per acre, although apartments were included in connection with the principal shopping center.

About this time two other distinguished developments were begun in widely different sections of the country. River Oaks in Houston, Texas, occupies an area of 1,000 acres and was planned with a full complement of community facilities including a golf course and market center. In 1923 the Palos Verdes Estates was planned on a dramatic site overlooking the Pacific Ocean south of Los Angeles. The site covered 3,000 acres, and residential lots ranged in size from one-half acre to 30 acres. About one-quarter of the total area was allocated to schools, parks, churches, libraries, shopping, and recreation. A few apartment areas were proposed about the various shopping centers, but one-half the area was given over to residences restricted to single-family dwellings. The remainder was in roads and landscaped parkways.

Numbered among other notable subdivisions in this country are Shaker Heights in Cleveland, the Country Club District in Kansas City, St. Francis Woods in San Francisco, Nassau Shores, Long Island, and Westwood Village in Los Angeles. Each of these developments marks a high level of planning a living environment. There was no serious intention on the part of subdividers to cope with adequate housing for families of low income in these communities. They were intended for the upper income group and were promoted accordingly.

The contrast between these developments and the average subdivision is the more apparent when we observe the rank and file of urban expansion. It was not planned; it simply oozed over the edges of the growing metropolis. A minimum of improvements in streets, walks, sewers, water, electricity, and gas distribution was installed. The unaware purchaser was left to foot the bill at some later date or shift the burden to the urban taxpayer.

Local governments gradually awoke to the havoc being wrought in the suburbs, and legislation was enacted to require subdividers to make certain improvements as a condition to approval of the development. These early regulations were feeble, but they were an acknowledgment that some measure of control was necessary to protect the city for the people who live in it.

The Mobile Population. Suburban expansion was encouraged by the growing urban population but it did not drain off the excess population from the center of cities. People responded to their natural desire to live near their work, and employ-

QUEENS, New York City   *Fairchild Aerial Surveys, Inc.*

The typical living environment of the early twentieth century city. The type of subdivision which Sir Raymond Unwin and Henry Wright sought to improve in their searching studies of urban planning and housing.

ment opportunities were concentrated in the city center. Then the nature of these opportunities changed from the pre-factory system. Stable industrial employment was uncertain. With expanding commercial enterprise the tendency to shift from job to job extended to movement from city to city. Mobility of the family offered advantages over fixed tenure.

The urban population thus became transient in character. Freedom to move was not desirable but it was necessary. The rental apartment satisfied this requirement and it became popular. The familiar tenement of the nineteenth century remained for the poor, but the multi-family building was no longer confined to the low-income family. It achieved a new dignity as a form of urban living. Park Avenue, the Gold Coast, and Nob Hill were as popular among the well-to-do as the Lower East Side for the immigrant family.

Oddly enough, the standards of planning did not change with the range of income groups who found the apartment popular. Lots of 40 and 50 feet in width were more common than the 25-foot lot of the nineteenth century and the "dumbbell" tenement of New York was outlawed, but the internal planning, the size and number of rooms in "high-class" apartments made up for much of the additional lot area. There was little difference between the open space about the building, whether for the "swank" trade, the "efficiency-apartment" for the middle-income white collar clerk, or the low-income industrial worker. Narrow interior courts and side yards and little or no set-backs at front or rear prevailed as standard practice.

The city was having growing pains. The industrial economy had thrown out of gear all previous concepts of what a city should be. The traditional dwelling for the average American family was the single-family house. It had fulfilled the desires and living habits since early colonial times. Then the village of homes was engulfed by the industrial metropolis. Instead of a place to live, the city became a place to make a living. The family no longer dwelt in its home; it hired apartment space for temporary occupancy. The speculative opportunities for profit in this form of building enterprise were obvious, and full advantage was taken of them, but the apartment as a form of *investment* for capital was not yet fully realized. Adjustment to the new kind of city was, and still is, slow. But there were signs of improvement.

World War I. During World War I it fell to the lot of the Federal government in the United States to assume responsibility for housing of workers in war industries. Two agencies were created to implement this program: The Housing Division of the Emergency Fleet Corporation, and the United States Housing Corporation. The Emergency Fleet Corporation, through loans to shipbuilding companies, completed some 9,000 family dwellings and 7,500 single-person accommodations. The United States Housing Corporation had planned some 25,000 units in 60 projects, but completed about 6,000 family units in 27 projects, none of which were ready before the war came to an end.

Services of the most talented professional men in architecture and planning were enlisted for the program. Among the large-scale projects were Yorkship Village at

CRANE TRACT
HOUSING PROJECT AT
· BRIDGEPORT· CONNECTICUT·
· U·S·DEPARTMENT·OF·LABOR·
· BUREAU OF INDUSTRIAL·HOUSING·&·TRANSPORTATION·
· U·S·HOUSING·CORPORATION·
· R·CLIPSTON·STURGIS·ARCHITECT·
· A·H·HEPBURN· ASSOCIATE ARCHITECT·
· ARTHUR·A·SHURTLEFF·TOWN·PLANNER·
· A·H·TERRY·ENGINEER·
0   50   100   150

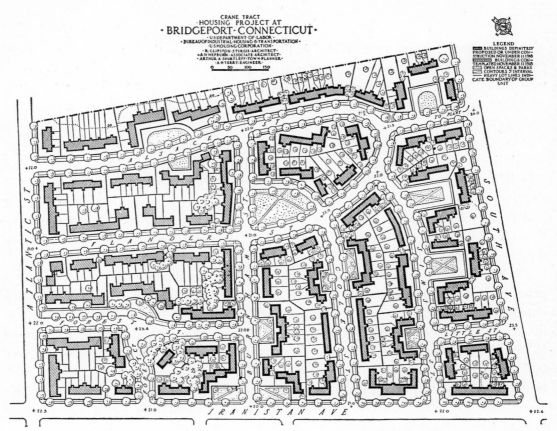

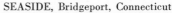

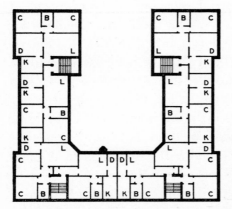

SEASIDE, Bridgeport, Connecticut

One of the World War I housing developments
undertaken by the Federal Government, it included
flats and single family residences at a density of
about seventeen dwellings per acre and demonstrated
the advantage of large-scale planning.

METROPOLITAN PROJECT, New York City
Andrew J. Thomas, Architect

One of the earliest large-scale apartment projects in this country.
The strong habit of the single lot is revealed in the series of
individual buildings repeated upon the large site.

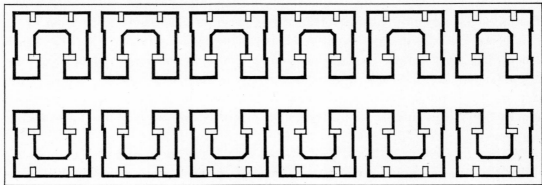

Camden, New Jersey, Alantic Heights in Portsmouth, New Hampshire, Buchman in Chester, Pennsylvania, Union Gardens at Wilmington, Delaware, and a number of developments at Bridgeport, Connecticut. It was a statutory requirement that projects built by these war agencies be sold immediately upon termination of the war. To implement this provision of the law the projects followed the general pattern of subdivision practice. Superblocks and common open spaces for recreation were absent, but the studied layout of residential streets and design of shopping centers offered a decided contrast with the practices to which most people had grown accustomed in their living environment. A distinct characteristic of the planning of all dwellings was a unit only two rooms in depth in contrast with the narrow, deep building typical of the usual restricted lot in the ordinary urban subdivision. The planning of these projects exerted a strong influence in the decade following the war.

The Garden Apartment. Mr. Andrew J. Thomas, an architect who participated in the war program, was active in the postwar period. One of the early projects designed by him was a large-scale development built by the Metropolitan Life Insurance Company in Long Island City. In this project Mr. Thomas applied the simple principle of "two-room" deep dwelling units, with stairways serving two dwellings per floor. The units were grouped in a series of U-shaped buildings with a ground coverage of about 50 per cent of the lot area. The open courts faced the garden. It was a vast improvement over the small, enclosed light courts of the single lot but retained the characteristic narrow space between buildings.

Thomas carried this simple planning technique further in the development of buildings with various forms, using a basic unit of two and three dwelling units per stair. The essential contrast with previous planning was the relation of the buildings to the streets. Planning on the single narrow lot under the Tenement House Act of 1901 and before caused the building to be placed at right angles to the street—a narrow front and long depth. This forced all but the dwellings on the street front to face into a small courtyard, light-well, or narrow rear yard. With removal of the restrictions imposed by the narrow lot, large-scale planning permitted the arrangement of buildings with a broad front and shallow depth. The interior of the lot was opened up with improved exposure of all dwelling units toward the street and expanded interior court. This planning was henceforth known as the "garden apartment."

Henry Wright. In 1926 the City Housing Corporation built Sunnyside Gardens, a large project planned by Henry Wright and Clarence Stein, on a 10-block site in Long Island. The architects applied the "garden apartment" in a simple perimeter form surrounding the interior garden. They also introduced the row, or group, house and the two-story flat—one dwelling above another with separate private entrances. The ground coverage was less than 30 per cent of the lot area.

Studies by Henry Wright about this time demonstrated the importance of comparative analysis in planning. He emphasized the necessity for a complete analysis of the costs that enter into housing. The planner and architect had been prone to detach their functions from that of management. Wright made clear that these functions could not

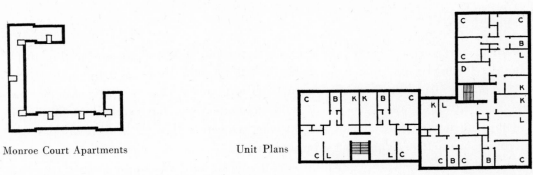

Monroe Court Apartments   Unit Plans

Interior Garden Court

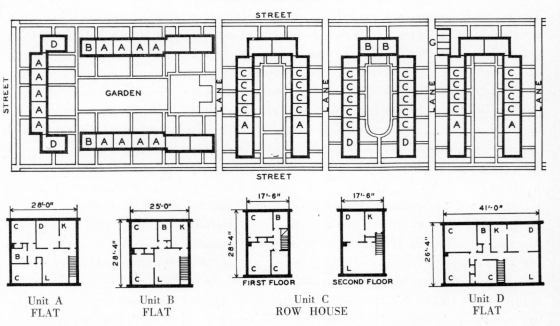

Unit A   Unit B   Unit C   Unit D
FLAT   FLAT   ROW HOUSE   FLAT

SUNNYSIDE, Long Island

An early large-scale development within the framework of typical city blocks. This project, planned by Henry Wright and Clarence Stein, provided further evidence of the advantages of low density and large-scale planning.

be isolated and produce satisfactory housing; that improvement could not be expected unless plan-analysis was merged with experience in the management and maintenance of housing.

During this period much speculative building was producing the dreary, monotonous rows of cheap and poorly planned single-family and flat buildings which still curse so many of our cities. Henry Wright insisted upon the advantages of the group house, used at Sunnyside, to improve the planning of both dwellings and the space about them. The row, or group, house was not a revolutionary dwelling type. It was prevalent in all eastern cities. Baltimore and Philadelphia are famous for their row houses with clean, stone entrance stoops. But Wright demonstrated the principle of planning dwellings two rooms in depth rather than the tandem arrangement of rooms to which the usual row house had degenerated. He showed the improvement in land planning with the group house in comparison with detached units and their wasteful and useless side yards. Wright contributed much to the enlightenment that emerged in the 1920 decade and early thirties.

Radburn. Inspired by the "garden city" idea, the City Housing Corporation acquired a vacant site in New Jersey within commuting distance of New York City. On this site Henry Wright and Clarence Stein planned the community of Radburn. This plan introduced the "super-block." In these blocks, ranging from 30 to 50 acres in size, through traffic was eliminated. Traffic streets surrounded rather than traversed the areas. Within them, single-family dwellings were grouped about cul-de-sac roads.

The houses were oriented in reverse of the conventional placement on the lot. Kitchens and garages faced the road, and living rooms turned toward the garden. Pathways provided uninterrupted pedestrian access to a continuous park strip, leading to large, common open spaces within the center of the super-block. Underpasses separated pedestrian walks from traffic roadways. The community earned the name of "The Town for the Motor Age."

Radburn allocated space for industry, shopping, and apartments, but permanent green space surrounding the town, typical of the English garden cities, was not incorporated. The development is not yet complete, but the residential character has been a prototype of sound community planning ever since.

Housing—An Investment. Subsidy was a means to encourage the colonial expansion of this country, push railroads across the land, and smooth out the peaks and valleys of economic inequalities. It was used whenever necessity dictated. In 1926 it was introduced to housing with passage of the New York Housing Law which established the State Board of Housing. This Act granted the privilege of tax exemption for a twenty-year period to limited-dividend companies engaged in housing within reach of the lower middle-class. The statutory ceiling on rents was $12.50 per room per month in the borough of Manhattan and $11.00 per room elsewhere. Investment in apartment development was encouraged by this legislation.

Fourteen projects, providing a total of nearly 6,000 dwellings, were undertaken in this program. The best known were three co-operative developments of the Amalga-

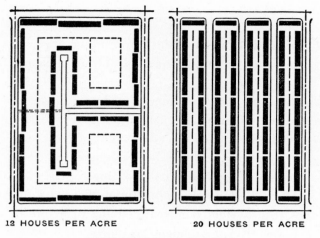

12 HOUSES PER ACRE   20 HOUSES PER ACRE

DEVELOPMENT OF 20 ACRES

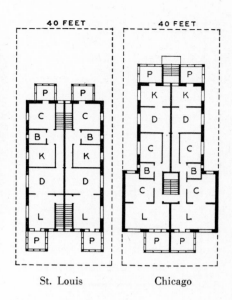

St. Louis   Chicago

	12 Houses to Acre	20 Houses to Acre
AVERAGE FRONTAGE PER HOUSE	21 ft.	21 ft.
Cost of raw land per acre	$1,000	$1,000
Cost of 40 ft. roads per yd.	$51.25	$51.25
Cost of 30 ft. roads per yd.	$41.25	—
NUMBER OF HOUSES	240	400
Gross area	20 acres	20 acres
Area of roads	2.46 acres	4.76 acres
Net area	17.54 acres	15.24 acres
AVERAGE SIZE OF PLOT	353 sq. yds.	184 sq. yds.
Road frontage:		
40 ft. road	3,732 ft.	10,370 ft.
34 ft. road	2,162 ft.	—
AVERAGE ROAD FRONTAGE PER HOUSE	24.54 ft.	25.9 ft.
Total cost of land	$20,000	$20,000
Total cost of roads	$46,740	$88,575
Ave. cost of land per house	$83	$50
Ave. cost of roads per house	$195	$221
Ave. cost of roads and land per house	$278	$271
Cost per sq. yd. of plot	$.79	$1.47
GROUND RENT PER PLOT PER WEEK, AT 6%	$.32	$.31

(From *Modern Housing*, by Catherine Bauer)

"NOTHING GAINED FROM OVERCROWDING"

TYPICAL FLAT PLANS DURING THE FIRST QUARTER OF THE TWENTIETH CENTURY

Early in the century Raymond Unwin wrote his treatise *Nothing Gained from Overcrowding*, in which he compared the typical subdivision street system with a more open development using the cul-de-sac street. In the United States, real estate development was taking the form shown in the photograph—a monotonous row of houses along street after street—and the single lot persisted with the building of individual "flat" buildings in the Middle-Western cities. These two-story buildings, with one apartment above the other and with most rooms facing a narrow side yard between the buildings, were reminiscent of the "dumbbell" tenements of New York.

JAMAICA, Long Island

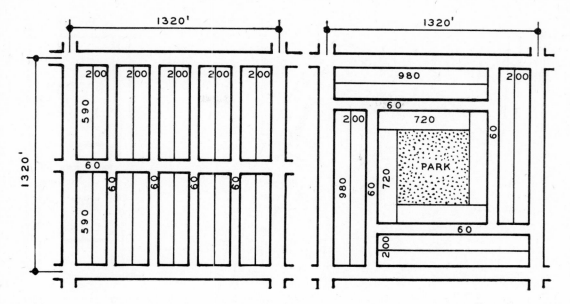

Above is a comparative study by Henry Wright to demonstrate the improvement which a modification in the typical gridiron street and block layout might provide. The sketch on the left is the usual street plan, that on the right the proposed replanning. With but slight loss of street frontage for subdivision of residential lots (the usual plan has 11,800 lineal feet of streets while the modified plan has 10,720 lineal feet), an interior park is gained and through traffic on all interior streets is eliminated.

Wright developed his "Case for the Row House" with studies like the one illustrated below. In this study the typical block layout with two-story flat buildings facing the street is compared with a revised plan using continuous rows of two-story flat units; the alley is eliminated, garage courts are consolidated at the end of each block, and a park space is gained in the center of the block accessible from all dwellings. In the typical plan some of the rooms in the dwellings face on the narrow side yards between buildings (lower sketch). The revised plan (upper sketch), however, eliminates these side yards resulting in an improved plan of the dwelling units, all of which face upon ample open space to the front and rear of the buildings.

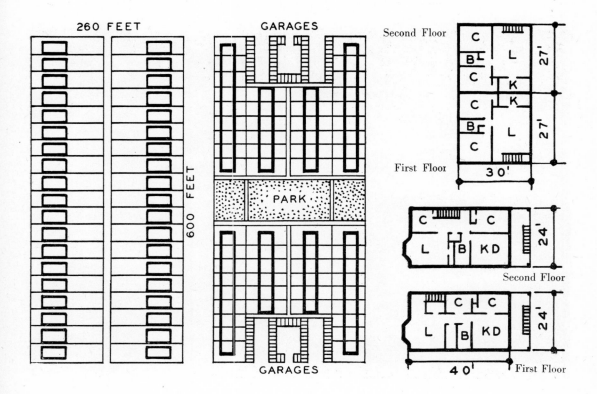

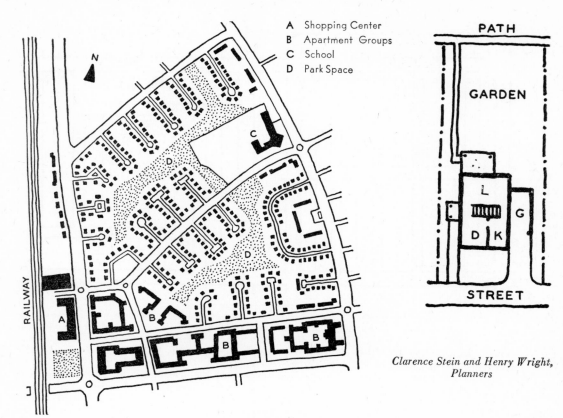

A Shopping Center
B Apartment Groups
C School
D Park Space

PATH

GARDEN

STREET

L
D K
G

Clarence Stein and Henry Wright,
Planners

RADBURN, New Jersey

The Radburn plan became synonymous with "the town of the motor age." In this plan the cul-de-sac (dead-end) residential streets became service roads rather than traffic ways, the house being reversed so that the living rooms face on the rear gardens with pedestrian paths leading to the continuous park space.

PROJECTS APPROVED BY THE NEW YORK STATE BOARD OF HOUSING*

Project	No. Apts.	Bldg. Coverage (%)	Density (families per acre)	Height (stories)
Academy Housing Corporation	476	43.9	149	6 (elevator)
Amalgamated Dwellings, Inc.	232	59.7	166	6 (elevator)
Amalgamated Housing Corp. First Group Second Group Third Group	625	50.2	114 (av.)	5 (walk-up) 6 (elevator) 6 (elevator)
Boulevard Gardens Housing Corp.	958	24.8	83	6 (elevator)
Brooklyn Gardens Apts., Inc. Fourth Ave. Project Navy Yard Project	165 140	52.5 59	181 230	5 (walk-up) 5 (walk-up)
Farband Housing Corp.	129	69.1	172	6 (elevator)
Hillside Housing Corp.	1,405	34	88	4 and 6 (walk-up and elevator)
Knickerbocker Village, Inc.	1,585	46	317	13 (elevator)
Manhattan Housing Corp.	44	69.4	184	6 (elevator)
Stanton Housing Corp.	44	68.8	191	6 (elevator)
Stuyvesant Housing Corp.	93	72.4	216	6 (elevator)
TOTAL	5,896			

* Report of the State Board of Housing to the Secretary of State of the State of New York, 1937.

mated Clothing Workers, providing 625 apartments. In addition to the Housing Board projects in New York City, other limited-dividend and semi-philanthropic developments were undertaken. Phipps Houses, Inc., a veteran housing organization, built 344 apartments in four- and six-story walk-up and elevator buildings near Sunnyside Gardens in New York. In 1930 John D. Rockefeller, Jr., built the Paul Laurence Dunbar apartments in Harlem, 513 apartments designed for acquisition of the dwellings by the tenants. About this time the Julius Rosenwald Foundation built the Michigan Boulevard Gardens, also for Negroes, on the south side of Chicago, and the Marshall Field Estate built Marshall Field Apartments on the near north side of Chicago. Chatham Village in Pittsburgh, built by the Buhl Foundation, was a two-story group house development planned by Henry Wright.

These projects did not produce speculative profits but were sound investments that served a high social purpose. This purpose is not nourished by irresponsible interests

PHIPPS HOUSES, New York City

Clarence Stein, Architect

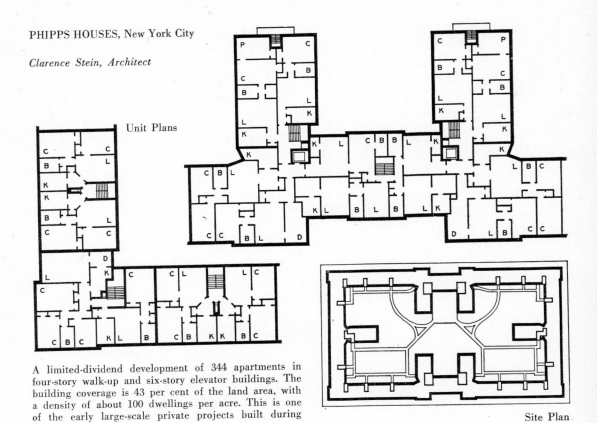

Unit Plans

Site Plan

A limited-dividend development of 344 apartments in four-story walk-up and six-story elevator buildings. The building coverage is 43 per cent of the land area, with a density of about 100 dwellings per acre. This is one of the early large-scale private projects built during the late twenties.

Site Plan

Unit Plans

DUNBAR APARTMENTS

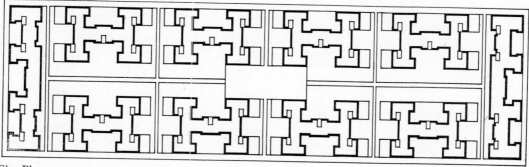

Site Plan

MARSHALL FIELD GARDEN
APARTMENTS, Chicago

Andrew J. Thomas, Architect

These projects of four- and five-story apartment developments during the 1920 period
illustrate the transition in planning from
the concept of separate buildings on single
lots of the typical subdivision (Metropolitan, Dunbar, Marshall Field), to continuous
indented rows of buildings arranged about
the periphery of a large site (Phipps, Michigan Boulevard Gardens, Amalgamated).
This trend from smaller building units to
larger and longer buildings was characteristic of large scale planning during this
period, but we will observe in later developments that, as familiarity with large scale
planning progressed, the trend is reversed
by a more frequent use of smaller building
units. The essential difference represented

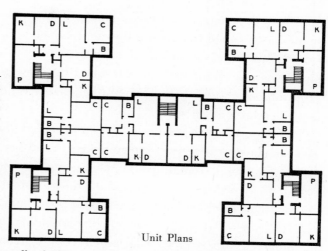

Unit Plans

by this change was the tendency to group smaller buildings *within* the open space which large sites made
possible rather than *enclose* the open space with continuous buildings. Freedom from the single small lot and
the restrictive pattern of the usual gridiron street
system made it unnecessary to protect the interior
garden space from the surrounding streets and permitted greater latitude in planning the buildings
within the open space.

Unit Plans

MICHIGAN BOULEVARD GARDENS, Chicago

Klaber & Grunsfeld, Architects

Site Plan

concerned with quick turn-over of capital and unlimited profits, nor does it thrive on exploitation and speculation in land, buildings, and people.

During this period good planning was demonstrated to be economical planning. Twenty-five years prior, the typical tenement covered 85 per cent of a narrow, deep lot. More than half the rooms either had no light or peered into dingy light-wells. Open space about the dwelling was either the paved traffic street or a shabby refuse-ridden rear yard. The energetic talents of such architects as Ernest Flagg, Grosvenor Atterbury, Andrew Thomas, Henry Wright, Clarence Stein, and Frederick Ackerman served to bring a vast change in all this. Land coverage was reduced to 50 per cent or less, and space was planned to enhance the environment and provide room for recreation. Careful planning and better interior arrangement of rooms reduced waste space within buildings and eliminated unnecessary corridors and halls. Attention was given to appropriate size and use of rooms rather than the greatest number of people that could be loaded on a given site.

The importance of the period we have been discussing is not the quality of planning as a standard to which we aspire today, but rather as a comparison with the unwholesome planning it replaced and the processes which brought it about. Complete disregard for housing standards and the desire for profit regardless of the exploitation it entailed had produced high density, excessive land coverage, and decidedly bad housing. The theory that these evils were essentially good business was exploded. Good planning was discovered to be an effective instrument to compete with bad planning. When laws were enacted to curb irresponsible building of slums, the road was cleared for good planning with financial benefits as well as the restoration of social values.

The period of activity during the twenties and early thirties did not solve our urban housing ills but it did provide a foundation upon which future progress could be continued. Building companies became conscious of the advantages of investment in housing. Large-scale planning opened the opportunity for arranging buildings on land so that all dwellings were well located on the site. As a permanent investment such factors were important. Good planning was becoming a good investment. Release from the long, narrow lot permitted greater efficiency in planning, lower land coverage, better dwelling units, more space for light, air, and recreation, and safer investment. Permanent values were built in by good planning.

Mr. Charles F. Lewis, Director of the Buhl Foundation which built and is managing Chatham Village in Pittsburgh, said in 1937:

Capital is frankly challenged by this unusual opportunity for sound and productive use of its funds.

Essentially this will be an investment and not a speculative use of capital. . . .

No less has it been demonstrated by the so-called limited dividend companies, from Boston in 1871 to Pittsburgh in 1934, that limited dividends pay. I refer you specifically to the remarkable success of the City and Suburban Homes Company of New York, founded in 1896 by Mr. R. Fulton Cutting and associates. After years of operation, in 1933 in the midst of the depression, this company could boast assets of nearly $10,000,000, a surplus of more than $1,380,000, and net earnings of from $263,000 to $445,000 per year through four depression years. Its average

Unit Plans

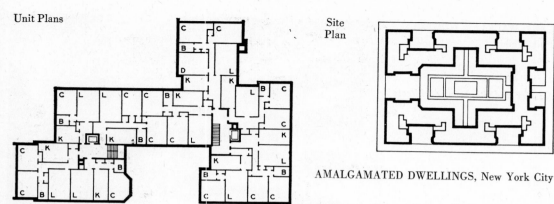

Site Plan

AMALGAMATED DWELLINGS, New York City

This project, built in 1930 on plans by Springsteen and Goldhammer, was one of the first undertaken under the program of the State Board of Housing. It is one of three built by the Amalgamated Clothing Workers trade union as a co-operative enterprise. The buildings are six stories high with automatic elevators. The land cost was $5.61 per square foot.

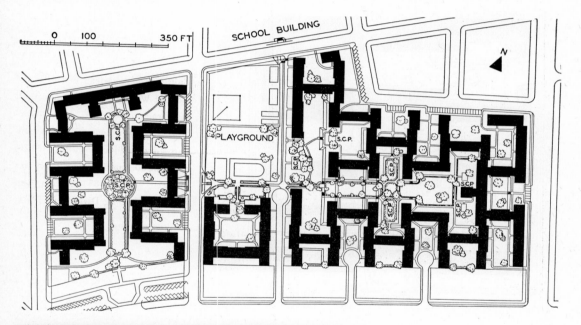

SCHOOL BUILDING

0   100   350 FT

PLAYGROUND

Fairchild Aerial Surveys, Inc.

HILLSIDE HOMES, New York City

This project of 1,405 apartments, designed by Clarence Stein, was approved by the New York State Board of Housing and is one of the seven that received loans from the Housing Division of PWA. While the land cost was about 70 cents per square foot, the land coverage is one of the lowest in the New York area—about 32 per cent—and the density is about 88 families per acre. The typical city street plan is replaced by continuous garden courts surrounded by four-story walk-up and six-story elevator apartment buildings. Play areas for children are distributed in this open space and traffic is confined to the peripheral streets.

CARL MACKLEY HOUSES,
Philadelphia

Kastner and Stonorov, Architects

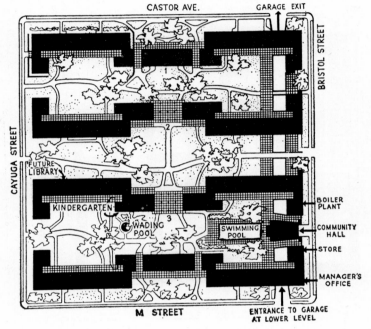

CASTOR AVE.
GARAGE EXIT
BRISTOL STREET
CAYUGA STREET
FUTURE LIBRARY
KINDERGARTEN
WADING POOL
SWIMMING POOL
BOILER PLANT
COMMUNITY HALL
STORE
MANAGER'S OFFICE
M STREET
ENTRANCE TO GARAGE AT LOWER LEVEL

Built by the American Federation of Hosiery Workers for the members of that trade union, this project contains 284 apartments in three- and four-story buildings, with a density of about 50 families per acre. It was financed with an 85 per cent loan from the Housing Division of PWA.

Dallin Aerial Surveys

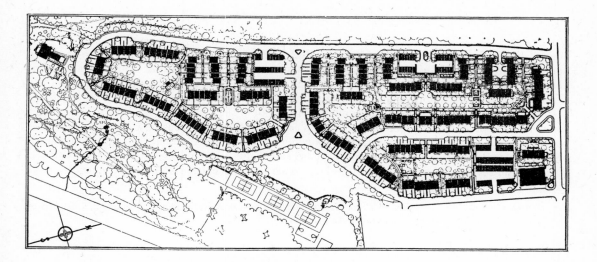

CHATHAM VILLAGE, Pittsburgh
Ingham and Boyd, Architects

A limited-dividend project originally planned for 300 units within reach of the $2,200-3,600 per year income group. The first stage of development was 128 dwellings. The density is about 12 families per acre in two-story group houses, demonstrating the theory of Henry Wright who espoused the cause of the group house on urban land which had not yet reached the high levels of many areas. This project was built as an investment by the Buhl Foundation.

BUCKINGHAM, Virginia

One of the earliest large-scale rental developments undertaken in the FHA program, Buckingham is located just outside Washington, D.C., for "white collar" workers in the nation's crowded capital. Designed by Henry Wright, Allan Kamstra, and Albert Lueders, it was planned for 2,000 units on a 100-acre site. The first stage (shown in detail) comprised 622 dwellings on 30 acres. The land cost was 25 cents per square foot and permitted low density —about 20 families per acre—with a building coverage of about 20 per cent of the land area. Approximately 13% of the area is in streets. Dwellings are two-story group houses and flats.

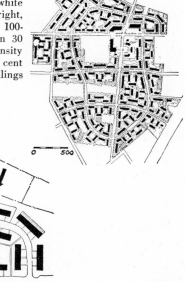

SCP = SMALL CHILDRENS PLAYGROUND

annual dividend rate, from 1899 to 1939, was 4.65 per cent. Or let us take six non-co-operative apartment projects built in New York City under the New York State Housing Board. All have been consistent dividend payers in good times and bad. Or let us take, in the city of Washington, the Washington Sanitary Improvement Company, which with assets of nearly $1,500,000 can boast that from 1897 to 1923 it paid an annual dividend of 5 per cent, and from then on straight through the depression, of 6 per cent. Or the Washington Sanitary Housing Company which has paid 5 per cent per annum without interruption since 1927. While Chatham Village in Pittsburgh has not yet published earnings statements, those statements when released will give further evidence of the investment soundness of the large-scale housing enterprise on the limited-dividend basis.[1]

[1] *Opportunities for Building Rental Properties.* Conference on Local Residential Construction, Chamber of Commerce of U.S., Washington, D.C., November 17, 1937.

CHAPTER 9

ISSUES IN FOCUS

The Great Depression. On the heels of the building boom during the prosperity decade of the twenties came the crash of 1929 and the decade of depression that followed. Financial credit dried up, building stopped abruptly, and unemployment brought widespread privation to millions of families. As the depression gained momentum, economic and social chaos followed in its wake. Marginal investments in stocks evaporated into thin air. The "water" that had been poured into building investments during the craze of the boom was drained off, and "ownership" changed hands in rapid succession as the level lowered. Homes on farms and in the cities were foreclosed at an alarming rate. Real estate foreclosures jumped from 68,100 in 1926 to 248,700 in 1932.

The complete state of despair made it imperative for the government to act. In an effort to stem the tide, President Hoover called his Conference of Home Building and Home Ownership in 1931. This conference revealed many of the problems that beset the nation and laid the groundwork for action which ensued in subsequent years. Some 28 states enacted moratoria on mortgage foreclosures in 1931 and 1932. This device relieved the hysteria but only postponed the solution. The Emergency Relief and Construction Act of 1932 created the Reconstruction Finance Corporation. This agency was empowered to loan government funds to bolster the faltering economy.

The tide of national collapse forced the government to assume increased responsibility for the helpless economy, and, beginning in 1933, the Congress created a series of agencies in rapid succession. These acts brought into focus a fact that had been almost unwittingly overlooked: the people of the United States had no inventory of the national welfare, the assets and liabilities of a going concern dealing in democratic enterprise. The blessing of abundant natural resources, the accident of favorable geographic location, and the aggressive enterprise of a free people had brought fortune and a position of world leadership to this country. This achievement had blinded the people to the corollary of great industrial and financial empires—the precipitation of social and economic hardships that filter into the lives of many in society. The Great Depression lifted the veil on this scene and disclosed the gap which had formed between fortune and stability. It was apparent that the country must take stock of its resources in order to measure the future prospects for its enterprise.

Inventory. The necessity for improvement in the physical condition of our cities had been recognized. The presence of slums and blight, and the sporadic attempts to correct the situation, attested to that. As had been fully demonstrated in the successful business enterprise of this country, however, a factual knowledge of current inventory on hand, the kind of stock it represents, and a study of the market to be supplied are essential to the conduct of democratic government as well as individual welfare. The government therefore undertook the Real Property Survey of 1934 as a comprehensive inventory of the supply and condition of housing in this country. It was learned that nearly one-third of the urban dwellings were in need of major repairs and lacked indoor bathing and toilet facilities. In the 64 cities surveyed 2.3 per cent of all dwellings were found to be unfit for human habitation, 15.6 per cent were in need of major structural repairs, and only 37.7 per cent were considered in good condition. Only 34 per cent of the dwellings had hot and cold running water, 8 per cent had no water supply in the dwelling, 17.1 per cent no private indoor toilet facility, and 25 per cent had no bathing facilities. The only fuel for cooking in one-third of all the dwellings was coal or wood.

Unemployment and the depression had produced alarming economic hardships for millions; it was estimated that the annual income of 37 per cent of all urban families in 1934 was $800 or less. Further investigations, however, revealed even more significant facts about the economic status of the people. Studies by the Brookings Institution showed that a broad segment of American families had surprisingly low incomes before the depression had engulfed the nation. In 1929, 21 per cent of the families in cities had incomes of less than $1,000 a year, 21 per cent were between $1,000 and $1,500, and 17 per cent were between $1,500 and $2,000 per year.[1]

It was apparent that a major reason for the housing problem was a lack of sufficient income to pay the price of a decent home. The lowest rents were generally in the areas of substandard housing; it was estimated that rents of $20 per month or less were concentrated in the substandard category, and more than 50 per cent of all rental dwellings rented for less than this amount. The large cities presented a more complex picture. In Cincinnati, for example, 41 per cent of the families were paying a rent of $28 per month for dwellings which had only a cold-water sink.

The depths to which the national morale had sunk caused investigations into many of our economic ills. Studies were made of the costs of urban maintenance. These studies produced evidence of the economic burden that decaying sections of cities were heaping upon the taxpayer.

The cost to maintain blighted districts and slums was many times the revenue the cities collected in taxes from these areas. A relatively small section of Cleveland containing 2.37 per cent of the population showed a net loss to the city of $1,750,000 in the year 1932; one square mile of blighted area in Chicago cost the city $3,200,000

[1] *America's Capacity to Consume*, Maurice Levén, Harold G. Moulton, and Clark Warburton, The Brookings Institution, Washington, D.C., 1934.

in services as compared to the tax levy of $1,191,352 and an actual tax collection of only $586,061. The low rent areas of Boston cost the city $92.30 per capita but paid the city only $13.30 per capita in taxes. The high rent areas paid into the city treasury $312.80 per capita but cost the city only $73.80 to maintain. In Indianapolis the blighted areas cost $27.29 per person while the maintenance of other areas cost but $4.00 per person.

The wholesale foreclosure of mortgages on homes and stoppage of home-building made it imperative to examine the status of home-ownership. It was the general policy of financial institutions to loan about two-thirds of the construction cost or appraised value of homes. It was necessary for the prospective home-owner to invest the balance of one-third as his "equity." When costs were high during the boom of the twenties, the number of families who had managed to accumulate, in savings, this proportion of the dwelling cost was relatively small. Because the urge for home-ownership was strong, the device of the "second mortgage" came into use. This provided the prospective owner with a source for supplementary financing and reduced the amount of equity needed. Lenders of second mortgages held only a secondary right in the property mortgaged and the length of such loans was usually short and interest charges high.

This device expanded the number of home-owners, however. It appeared easier to make high monthly payments to finance a home than to accumulate the savings for the equity required for a first mortgage only. As long as incomes remained stable the home-owner paid his monthly installment with the knowledge that he would some day have title to the home and then be relieved of the burden of rent. But the depression violently altered this situation. The earning capacity was not only lowered, but millions of families had no incomes at all. The foreclosures in the early depression years demonstrated that numerous families had assumed financial obligations they simply could not carry.

"Priming the Pump." All of the conditions described in the foregoing paragraphs were obviously not the result of the depression alone. They were aggravated by the economic plight into which the nation had been plummeted, but they were the result of decades of indifference and neglect for the economic health of the nation. Furthermore, they were conditions for which there could be no quick and immediate cure. Government action was therefore devised as a "pump-priming" process. It was immediately necessary to stall the wave of foreclosures on homes, and the Home Owners Loan Corporation was created.

Although too late to save one and one-half million homes, this agency was able to hold the line for more than a million with direct loans to threatened home-owners. Loans were made for a period of 15 years at an interest rate of 5 per cent, with the principal amortized in regular monthly payments. By June 1936, the HOLC had made 1,017,948 loans on urban dwellings in a total amount of $3,093,450,641. Between 1937 and 1940, 12 per cent of the outstanding mortgages in the country were held by HOLC. More than 500,000 loans were advanced to distressed farm owners by the Federal Land Bank (originally created in 1917) and the Farm Mortgage Corporation.

According to the 1941 Statistical Abstract of the United States, the number of foreclosures on urban real estate ran the following course:

1926	68,100	1934	230,350
1927	91,000	1935	228,713
1928	116,000	1936	185,439
1929	134,900	1937	151,366
1930	150,000	1938	118,505
1931	193,800	1939	100,961
1932	248,700	1940	75,310
1933	252,400		

There were nearly as many homes foreclosed during the ten-year period between 1930–
39 as the number of new homes built. An average of 180,033 homes were foreclosed
annually, whereas an average of about 270,000 new homes were built per year.

In 1934 the National Housing Act created the Federal Housing Administration. It
was the purpose of this agency to encourage credit for home financing and to revive a
badly beaten house-building industry. FHA was a Federal government insurance agency.
Its function was the insurance of loans by private lending institutions for construction
of housing, and it tackled the problem on three fronts. Loans were insured for construction of new single-family homes, for alterations and repairs of existing dwellings,
and for rental housing.

Restoration of the home-ownership principle was not enough to revive the industry.
Construction had bogged down so badly and credit channels were so clogged that a
gross broadening of the whole market for home-ownership was necessary. Whereas
financial agencies had previously loaned some two-thirds of the cost of dwellings, FHA
guaranteed mortgages up to 90 per cent of the cost. Under Title II of the Act, 90 per
cent loans were insured for dwellings costing $6,000 or less, including house and lot,
and 80 per cent loans were insured for dwellings not exceeding $16,000 in cost. This
was later modified to provide insurance of 90 per cent of the first $6,000 and 80 per
cent of the balance for homes not exceeding $10,000 in cost. Prior to our entry into
World War II in 1941, FHA-insured loans for new housing under Title II amounted
to $3.11 billions for 725,000 mortgages, and nearly all dwellings built during the
depression decade enjoyed the benefits of this program. Insurance of loans was also
extended by FHA (Title I) for repairs and alterations to existing houses. This program
reached $1.24 billions of insured loans.

Another feature of the Act was directed at the encouragement of rental housing. The
depression had nipped in the bud the fruitful prospects for investment housing begun
early in the century and sponsored by such agencies as the New York State Board of
Housing. The National Housing Act was intended to renew this program and provided
for insurance by FHA of 80 per cent loans for limited-dividend large-scale housing
developments. Despite the broad market and the urgent need for rental housing in this

country, the popularity of the home-ownership program had sapped the incentive to engage in this phase of the program to the extent warranted by the market and investment opportunities. Although there were 335 projects undertaken, there were only about 35,000 dwellings produced.

The FHA program was government insurance against loss by financial institutions for loans they extended for home-building. There were some who observed the novelty of the Federal government guaranteeing lending agencies against the risk of loss, but this inconsistency with the traditional operation of our economic system was overlooked because the application of a "hypodermic" had become essential to stimulate the building industry. Being welcomed by financial institutions, it was an effective instrument.

Accompanying this treatment for home-building was an improvement in financing residential construction. The second mortgage practice was eliminated, systematic repayment of loans—regular amortization—was introduced, and interest charges for borrowed money were reduced, the FHA interest being $4\frac{1}{2}$ per cent plus $\frac{1}{2}$ per cent for insurance.

FHA established minimum standards for construction and planning as a condition of its mortgage insurance. The fact that this policy brought about an improvement in the quality of residential construction is a sad commentary upon the standards of local building regulations and the laxity of their enforcement.

Experiments. "Pump-priming" assumed a variety of forms. Huge sums were spent for public works, highways, dams, bridges, public buildings, and relief. Cities benefited through projects for new sewers, drainage, streets, schools, recreation centers, but there were no essential changes in the character of the city. The emergency created by the unemployment of millions of people left no time, or so it seemed, to deliberate the possible reformation of the urban framework.

On the other hand, the vast displacement of workers in paralyzed industrial plants disturbed many serious reformers. Some inclined to the theory of subsistence homesteads located near decentralized factories as an effective antidote to periodic unemployment. There ensued a series of experiments with the forms of urban and rural patterns.

The National Industrial Recovery Act of 1933 established the Subsistence Homesteads Division in the Department of the Interior. This Division built rural projects in which part-time industrial workers could acquire a house and subsistence plot. No down payment was required, and long-term loans were made by the government to eligible homesteaders.

A key to recovery was rehabilitation of the agricultural economy of the country. In 1935 the Congress created the Resettlement Administration and there began a program of soil conservation and agricultural adjustment the country had long found wanting.

The subsistence homesteads were transferred to the jurisdiction of the Resettlement Administration and merged with the rural resettlement program engaged primarily

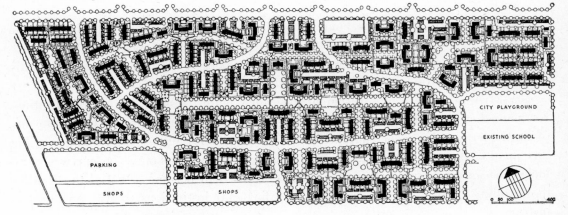

WYVERNWOOD, Los Angeles   *Witmer and Watson, Architects*

This FHA-insured rental project for "white collar" workers is composed of 1,100 two-story apartments on a 72-acre site with a coverage of about 25 per cent of the land area.

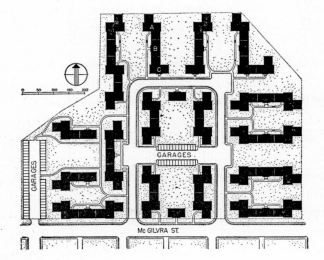

EDGEWATER PARK, Seattle

Graham and Painter, Architects

A 305-dwelling, FHA-insured development on the shore of Lake Washington, it comprises two-story apartments and flats.

INTERLAKEN GARDEN APARTMENTS, Westchester County, New York

Young and Moscowitz, Architects

This project, planned for 3,500 units, is one of the largest approved for FHA insurance. The first stage was 525 dwellings of two stories with a building coverage of only 14 per cent of the land area.

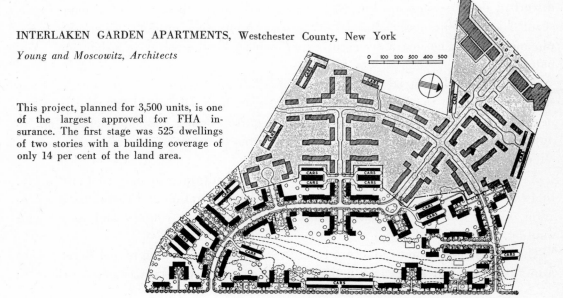

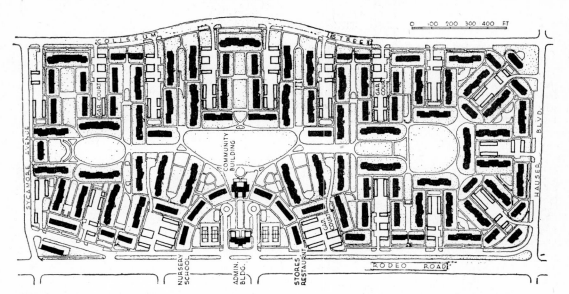

BALDWIN HILLS VILLAGE, Los Angeles

Reginald Johnson, Lewis Wilson, Edwin E. Merrill, and Robert Alexander, Architects

One of the latest and most attractive of the large-scale rental developments, this project consists of 627 dwellings in one- and two-story group houses and flats on an outlying 80-acre tract. The low land price, $2,300 per acre, permits low density, about 8 families per acre, and a coverage of only 7.3 per cent of the land. A feature of this project is the private patio for about two-thirds of all the dwellings. It will be noticed in the plan that the boulevard along the north boundary (bottom of plan) is separated from the project by a park-strip and a service road from which the various garage courts are accessible. Additional parking space is provided by indented parking areas along the service drive and along minor boundary streets. Small playgrounds for children are distributed about the development in addition to the "village green" in the center.

Vic Stein

THE GREENBELT TOWNS

As a component part of the Federal government's search for ways and means to cope with the modern city and its living environment, the Resettlement Administration planned four "greenbelt towns" beginning in 1935. They were satellite communities near large cities. The designs were inspired by Howard's Garden City idea, but they were not planned as self-contained towns; they were more like dormitory villages, the sources of employment for the residents being in the near-by cities. Each was surrounded by a belt of permanent open space, part of which could be farmed or gardened. A full complement of community facilities was included in each town—shopping, schools, and recreation space.

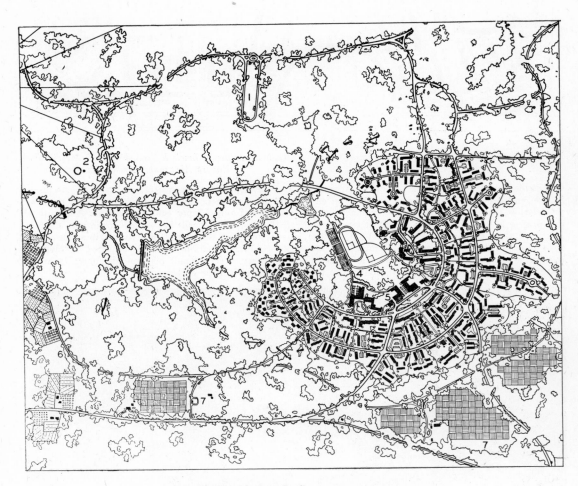

GREENBELT, Maryland

1 Water Tower

2 Disposal Plant and Incinerator

3 Picnic Center and Lake

4 Community Center

5 Store Group

6 Rural Homesteads

7 Allotment Gardens

This development is on a 2,100-acre site about 25 minutes' drive by automobile from Washington, D.C., and includes 712 dwellings in group houses and 288 in apartments, a total of 1,000 units occupying an area of 250 acres. There are 500 garages. The sixteen-room elementary school is jointly used as a community center, and the shopping center includes space for a post office, food stores, a drug store, a dentist's and a doctor's offices, a 600-seat theater, and such service shops as shoe repair, laundry, tailor, barber, and beauty shops. There are a bus terminal, a garage and repair shop, a fire station, and a gas station. The recreation facilities include an athletic field, picnic grounds, and an artificial lake. The super-block is used, each block containing about 120 dwellings with interior play areas. Underpasses provide continuous pedestrian circulation without crossing main roads. The commercial and community center, in the approximate center of the plan, reduces to a minimum the walking distance from all dwellings.

GREENBELT, Maryland

A semi-rural residential character was retained within the urban environment of the "greenbelt" towns.

GREENHILLS, Ohio. This development is a satellite of Cincinnati, about 11 miles from the central district. The entire site is 5,930 acres. Planned for 3,000 dwellings, 1,000 comprised the first stage of building. Twenty per cent are single- and two-family units, nearly half the units are in group houses containing three to six units per building, the rest—about one-third—are apartments. Garages are available for 17 per cent of the dwellings, although space is arranged to provide them for all dwellings if necessary. A total of 168 acres is used for housing, 12 acres for the community center, and 35 acres in roads; 50 acres are for allotment gardens, community parks, and playgrounds. Protective open space occupies about 695 acres. The remaining 4,970 acres in the site are devoted to farms and wooded and wildlife areas. In this, as in Greenbelt, the super-block is the basic element, each averaging about 25 acres and housing between 400 and 500 persons per block. The community center contains the shopping district and the combined grade and high school for 1,000 pupils and auditorium-gymnasium to seat 1,100 people.

1 Town Common
2 Commercial Center
3 Community Building
4 Athletic Field
5 Interior Park
6 Swimming Pool
7 Sites for Future Resi-
    dential Development
8 Greenbelt

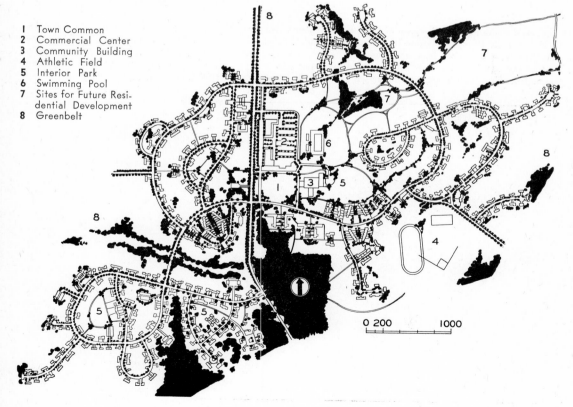

0 200   1000

GREENDALE, Wisconsin

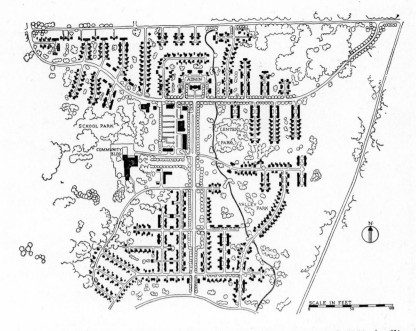

This site of 3,500 acres is about one-half hour from Milwaukee. Planned for 3,000 units, only 750 dwellings have been built. The single-family detached house predominates, 380 units being of this type, 370 being twin houses. Most dwellings have attached garages. The community center and school and the shopping area at the center of the plan are within one-half mile of all dwellings. Generous park spaces are adjacent to the central part of the town, and permanent open agricultural space surrounds the built-up area.

This project was not built because of legal entanglements. The proposed site, between 3,800 and 4,200 acres, was within one-half hour travel time of a number of industrial centers between Philadelphia and New York City. The ultimate plan would have accommodated some 4,000 families, but the initial development was intended to be 750 units. A few single detached houses and apartments were proposed, but the row or group house predominated. The super-block and cul-de-sac roads, with large interior recreation space, were featured.

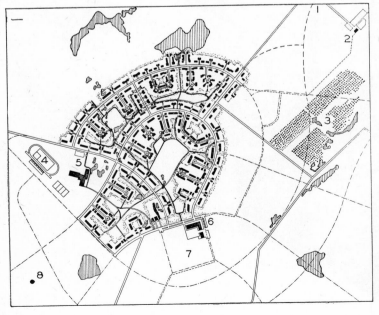

GREENBROOK, New Jersey

1 Pumping Station
2 Sewage Treatment Plant
3 Gardens
4 Athletic Field
5 Community Building
6 Shops and Garage
7 Future Town Center
8 Water Tower

in the removal of rural families from submarginal lands, of which there were an appalling number, to good farm land. The Resettlement Administration assisted the financing of these families with long-term amortized loans for land, buildings, and operating capital. Included within this broad program were rural projects for migratory workers in the western states. This combined the subsistence principle with part-time agricultural employment and its attendant quasi-industrial operations.

In addition to its rural operations, the Resettlement Administration engaged in an experiment with "greenbelt" towns. Four projects were planned, three of which were built: Greenbelt near Washington, D.C., Greenhills near Cincinnati, and Greendale near Milwaukee. The idea of a permanent belt of agricultural land surrounding these communities was borrowed from the Garden City pattern of Ebenezer Howard. The resemblance stops there, however, since the Resettlement suburban projects otherwise functioned largely as residential "dormitory" satellites for the near-by metropolis similar to any other suburban development.

In 1936 the Resettlement Administration became the Farm Security Administration which continued the rural program, with the addition of aid in the acquisition of farms by tenant farmers provided in the Farm Tenant Purchase Act of 1937. All these functions were subsequently transferred to the Department of Agriculture where they now reside.

Slum Clearance Begins. The depressing environment of the urban dweller in the slums was aggravated by the poverty of unemployment and public relief. When the National Industrial Recovery Act was drafted in 1933, a policy expressed by President Hoover's Conference on Home Building and Home Ownership was remembered. That policy referred to the problem of the slums. It read: "Unless this problem can be met by private enterprise, there should be public participation, at least to the extent of the exercise of the power of eminent domain. If the interest of business groups cannot be aroused to the point where they will work out a satisfactory solution of these problems through adequate measures for equity financing and large-scale operations, a further exercise of some form of government powers may be necessary in order to prevent these slums from resulting in serious detriment to the health and character of our citizens."

The reminder of this policy appeared in the NIRA with the following slender clause: ". . . construction, reconstruction, alteration, or repair under public regulation or control of low-rent housing and slum-clearance. . . ."[2] As a result of this provision the Housing Division of the Public Works Administration was created.

It was the intention of this agency to loan funds to private enterprise for slum clearance and construction of large-scale low-rent housing projects. The Reconstruction Finance Corporation had been empowered, in 1932, to make loans up to 85 per cent of the cost of similar developments by limited-dividend companies operating under the jurisdiction of state legislation. New York was the only state prepared with adequate

[2] Title II, Sec. 202.

KNICKERBOCKER VILLAGE,
New York City

Knickerbocker Village is a slum-clearance project built by the Fred F. French Company with financial assistance from the Reconstruction Finance Corporation. Situated on the site of the notorious "lung block" on the lower east side of Manhattan, the land cost was extremely high. According to the 1935 Report of the State Board of Housing the average cost per square foot was $14.06. No form of subsidy was available from the RFC, although the interest rate was only 4 per cent on the borrowed funds. The State Board of Housing required that rentals not exceed $12.50 per room per month ($11.00 p.r.p.m. in areas other than Manhattan) to receive the benefit of tax exemption. Despite the advantage of this financing arrangement, it was necessary to produce a very high population density on the site to support the investment. Although the land area covered by buildings is less than the surrounding slums, the buildings are thirteen stories high and house 1,593 families. This is 50 per cent more than originally occupied the site.

Fairchild Aerial Surveys, Inc.

WILLIAMSBURG
HOUSES, New York City

Board of Design: R. H. Shreve, M. W. Del Gaudio, A. C. Holden, William Lescaze, Samuel Goldstein, Paul Trapani, G. H. Gurney, H. L. Walker, J. W. Ingle

One hundred years ago the site of this project was a country village. When the project was built in 1936, the site was occupied by 1,279 families at a popula-

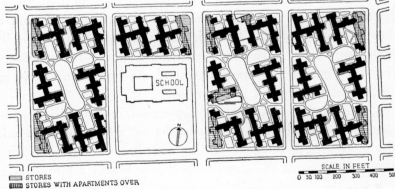

STORES
STORES WITH APARTMENTS OVER

SCALE IN FEET
0 50 100 200 300 400 500

tion density of 166 persons per acre. Two-thirds of the buildings were two- and three-story frame structures. More than one-half the number of dwellings had no running hot water, two-thirds had no private toilets, and three-quarters were without baths. The area was a fire hazard and refuse-ridden. This is the slum that had grown from a farm land within a period of 100 years. Williamsburg Houses is a development of four-story walk-up apartment buildings of fireproof construction. The site covers 25 acres and the project provides 1,622 dwellings. The total cost per unit was about $7,700 of which about $2,500 was the cost of the land and "improvements" demolished. It was the largest project built by the Housing Division of PWA.

The Original Site

WILLIAMSBURG HOUSES

The Finished Project

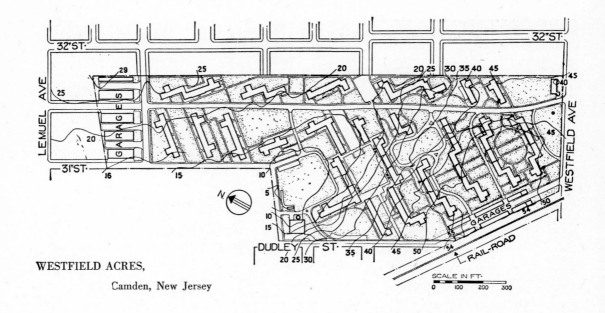

WESTFIELD ACRES,

Camden, New Jersey

Architects—J. N. Hettel, C. L. MacNelly, F. H. Radey, A. B. Gill, Oscar Stonorov, H. N. Moffett, H. E. Hall,
J. C. Jefferis, G. L. J. Neutze

A project by the Housing Division of PWA of 514 apartments in three-story buildings. The site was a vacant area of 25 acres, the area of buildings covering only 15 per cent of the land. The cost was about $5,300 per dwelling. No through-traffic bisects the site, and garage compounds are located on the periphery. In this project we again observe the advantages of large-scale planning over the usual city street system and lot subdivision. The original planning of streets indicated outside the project area is replaced by interior roads designed only for service access to the buildings. Large open spaces flow throughout the site and provide safe recreational areas and gardens for adults and children.

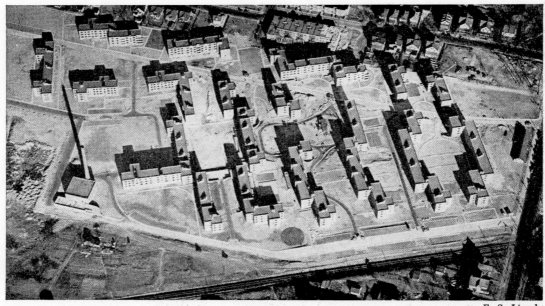

F. S. Lincoln

legislation and only one project was financed by RFC: Knickerbocker Village, a slum clearance project approved by the New York State Board of Housing.

The Housing Division of PWA embarked upon such a program, loaning 85 per cent of the project cost to limited-dividend corporations whose applications demonstrated satisfactory evidence of the 15 per cent equity required of the applicant. Only seven projects could be approved and the necessity for a broader construction program caused the Housing Division to alter its course. It launched a program of direct construction of low-rent slum-clearance projects.

Coupled with the objective of creating employment in the building industry was the social aim of adequate housing for families of low income living under substandard housing conditions. Although there had been experience in European countries as far back as the nineteenth century, government in the United States had not ventured into the field of housing prior to 1933. Touching, as it did, upon most of the social and economic ills of our urban communities, it is needless to say that the Housing Division was beginning a stormy career.

The Housing Division met with numerous set-backs in its short career of about 4 years, but finally completed some 22,000 dwellings. The right of eminent domain for the acquisition of sites divided into multiple ownerships was denied by the courts in connection with a slum clearance project in Louisville in 1935.[3] This right was denied on the premise that condemnation of land for housing was not a "public purpose" within the domain of the Federal government. Thenceforth the Housing Division was forced to select sites which could be acquired without recourse to condemnation. This forced, in turn, the use of vacant land for many projects. Despite this apparent handicap, twenty-seven of the fifty-one projects were built on sites which had been previously occupied by slums.

Construction costs were higher than seemed warranted. To claim this to be the result of waste and inefficiency is to beg the real issues that confronted the Housing Division and the entire recovery program. The chaos of emergency had filtered into every nook and cranny of our economic and social life. This entailed a degree of waste in human and material resources beyond any possible measurement. Recovery was neither expected nor claimed by way of economy and efficiency, and the housing program of the Housing Division was construed as one means to accomplish this recovery. It is to the credit of the agency that enduring standards of decent housing and constructive principles of urban planning were treated as integral parts of a program intended primarily as an instrument for economic recovery and creation of employment.

The United States Housing Act. The aggregate accumulation of substandard housing in this country adds up to a national problem of no small proportions. To that extent it is in the public interest for the national government to assume responsibility for assistance in improvement of housing conditions. However the direct impact

[3] Decision by District Court of U.S. for Western District of Kentucky, January 4, 1935, upheld by U.S. Circuit Court of Appeals for the Sixth Circuit, 2 to 1 vote, July 15, 1935.

of bad housing occurs at the local level, the community we define as the city. Direct responsibility for maintenance of adequate housing standards rests with the local government.

Recognizing the essential need for local responsibility and administration of housing affairs, and the necessity for assistance to families of low income in obtaining decent housing within their capacity to pay, the United States Housing Act was passed by the Congress in 1937. This Act created the United States Housing Authority charged with the power to loan funds to local housing authorities established by state law to build low-rent public housing for families otherwise unable to obtain decent housing they could afford. The USHA was empowered to make annual contributions to these local authorities to bring rents within the range of low-income families. According to the Act the purpose of the law was "to assist the several states and their political subdivisions to alleviate present and recurring unemployment and to remedy the unsafe and insanitary housing conditions and the acute shortage of decent, safe, and sanitary dwellings for families of low income, in rural or urban communities, that are injurious to the health, safety, and morals of the citizens of the United States."

When the Act became law there were only fifteen states with legislation creating local housing authorities eligible to receive loans from USHA. There were forty-six local authorities in these states. The necessary legislation was enacted in rapid sequence and when the United States entered the postwar era, there was legislation in forty-one states, the District of Columbia, Hawaii, Puerto Rico, and the Virgin Islands, with a total of 448 authorities in cities and 368 in counties.

The foundation of the Housing Act was decentralized control, with local initiative and responsibility. USHA may be considered analogous to a banker who loans funds to build houses; the local authority is the borrower; the purpose is building a project for rent to families in a community who, because of their low income, can afford only substandard housing facilities. The need for public housing arises from the fact that the low-income families cannot afford to pay an "economic rent." The USHA therefore makes annual contributions to the local authority, in addition to its function as a "banker," to offset the difference between an economic rent and the rent the low-income families can afford.

In conducting this program full responsibility rested with the local authority to determine the need for public housing, the location of projects, the planning, construction, and management of the developments. These projects are the property of the local authority. USHA loans 90 per cent of the total cost of a project at a low interest rate (about $2\frac{1}{2}$ per cent) for a period up to 60 years. The remaining 10 per cent is borrowed by the local authority through the sale of its bonds to other lending institutions. The annual contributions from USHA are fixed by the Act at not more than 1 per cent above the current rate of interest on the loans (about $3\frac{1}{2}$ per cent) and, in practice, the maximum contributions are substantially equal to the annual interest and amortization charges for the entire loan. However, they may be adjusted annually as the income levels and operating costs in a community fluctuate.

It becomes the obligation of the local authority to ascertain that the rents are maintained at a level which meets the needs of the lowest income families who could not otherwise find decent housing facilities. The Housing Act provided that rents could not exceed one-fifth of the income for families with less than three dependents and not more than one-sixth of the income for families with three or more dependents. By administrative ruling only families living in substandard dwellings were eligible to become tenants.

The local authorities, being created by the states, derive their powers from the states. They are vested with the right of eminent domain in order to assure the acquisition of sites for projects. According to the Housing Act it was required that one substandard dwelling be eliminated for each new dwelling built by the local authority. This requirement could be fulfilled either on the site of a project or, if the site was vacant or more dwellings were placed upon it than prior to demolition, the remainder could be eliminated by the city through the exercise of its police powers.

The program has been fraught with heated criticism and support. Proponents were often overzealous; opponents frequently socially unaware. The former claimed that housing should become a political issue but alienated the politicians. The latter insisted it should remain free from politics and proceeded to make their opposition a major political program. Early debate was focused upon the question of whether USHA was remaining within the area of housing for the low-income families and was clearing slums; more recently it has become popular to identify public housing with socialism and un-American activities, alleging it to be contrary to the interests of free enterprise. These are issues that remain thus far unresolved in terms of national policy.

Meeting the Need. The depression uncovered convincing evidence of poor housing conditions and the economic burden of blight on the urban community. Vast unemployment emphasized the plight of millions of families with insufficient incomes to buy or rent decent dwellings. Financial assistance from the Federal government was not only accepted, it was invited by local governments and enterprise generally. Public works contributed much to the physical wealth of the country. The Federal Housing Administration was welcomed by financial institutions, the construction trades and businesses, and prospective home-owners. The public housing program was too small to make a dent in the slum problem of cities; a total of 168,000 dwellings were built by local authorities with USHA loans in the 4 years of the program before the war, but the housing problem of the urban population was only revealed, it was not solved.

According to the Final Report of the Executive-Secretary to the Temporary National Economic Committee on Concentration of Economic Power in the United States in 1938, less than one-fifth of the new housing was in the market for three-quarters of the population with incomes under $2,000 a year. The lower third of the income group, below $1,000 per year, could only afford 1 per cent of the new houses; the income group between $1,000 and $1,500, being 24 per cent of the urban families, could afford only 3.7 per cent of the new houses; and the $1,500–$2,000 income

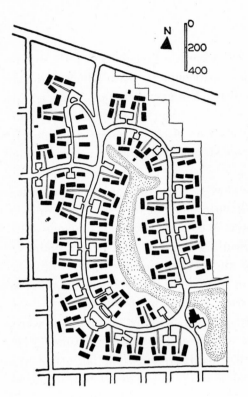

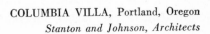

COLUMBIA VILLA, Portland, Oregon
Stanton and Johnson, Architects

A project of 400 dwellings built by the Housing Authority of the City of Portland, Oregon, with financial assistance of USHA. This project has an unusually low density and comprises one-story twin houses and one- and two-story four-unit buildings. Designed as a series of dwelling courts, the dwellings face upon free open space. Parking spaces are combined with each court and laundry buildings are distributed about the site for convenient tenant use.

Although the public housing projects, of which this is one, were financed and owned by the local housing authorities and built for rent to families of low income who were otherwise unable to afford the cost of decent housing in their community, the standards of planning the projects were similar to those financed as private investments insured by the Federal Housing Administration. The distinctions between the private and public housing developments were therefore less in the amenities of the living environment they provided than in the methods of financing to cope with the various economic levels of the people in the community.

Being permanent improvements in the community, just as all other housing developments, the public housing projects were built to standards of planning considered adequate for a permanent neighborhood environment. The type of project varied with the characteristics of the community in which they were built and ranged from those of low density and ample open space, such as the one illustrated here, to tall apartments with high density in the more crowded large cities in the country.

Leonard Delano

group, representing 15 per cent of the population, could afford only 15 per cent of the new houses. The rest of all houses, 81 per cent of the total production, was available to only 24 per cent of the families in the income range above $2,000 per year.

This ratio of incomes to the cost of new houses was not a phenomenon; it was not a new development in the housing market. It was more or less typical, but the depression made it more apparent. It was customary to assume that second-hand houses would filter down to successive income groups as production of new houses supplied the upper-income brackets. This process is rather natural but it has one distinct weakness: it encourages the accumulation of substandard houses. This will be treated later at more length since it presents an obstruction in the path of full production to meet the wide range of income groups in the housing market. This situation, however, must be recognized in appraising the combined efforts to supply housing through the normal channels of private enterprise, through government guarantee of private lending institutions against loss on loans for housing, and through public housing for low-income families.

The issues have not remained in clear focus. The program was new in this country; there had been little previous attention to housing for families in the slums with the exception of social settlement and charity organizations. Criticism of public housing diverted attention from the problem of housing for families of the lower income brackets and the rehabilitation of the decaying city. This criticism was not always accurate. Frequent claims were made that public housing did not reach the families for which it was intended.

Nathan Straus, former Administrator of USHA, reported the following income groups housed in the public housing projects sponsored by USHA prior to the war:

Annual Income per Family	Percentage of Families Housed
Less than $500	7.7
$500–749	32.8
$750–999	33.4
$1,000–1,249	21.4
$1,250–1,499	4.8
Over $1,500	0.1

According to Mr. Straus in his book, *Seven Myths of Housing,* the average shelter rent, that is, the rent for an unfurnished dwelling but including the mechanical equipment such as refrigerator and cooking range, was an average of $12.79 per dwelling per month in USHA-aided projects over the entire country. The rent including the cost of utilities—electricity, heat, water, and cooking fuel, was an average of $17.98 per dwelling per month. The average income of tenants was $832 per family per year.

The average construction cost for the dwelling, exclusive of land, site improvements, and overhead, was $2,700 per unit in USHA-aided projects; the average cost of FHA-insured dwellings was $3,601 between 1938–40. The total cost including land, site improvements, such as roads, walks, utilities, landscaping, and community facilities, commissions, and administration, was an average of $4,307 per dwelling unit in USHA-aided projects; and $5,332 per dwelling in FHA-insured houses in the same period.

In evaluating the USHA program there was reference to alleged high costs. Some confusion prevailed because USHA inherited the projects built by the Housing Division of PWA; these latter had cost in excess of USHA-aided developments, as indicated in the following comparisons where both types of projects were built:

Place	Average Construction Cost	Average Monthly Rent	Average Family Income
Charleston, S. C.			
PWA	$3,732	$19.33	$1,349
USHA	2,939	12.26	765
Jacksonville, Fla.			
PWA	2,746	15.32	850
USHA	2,667	10.58	750
Toledo, Ohio			
PWA	4,328	16.64	1,208
USHA	2,996	14.25	839

The principal issue that emerged from the public housing program was the dual character of its avowed purpose: to clear slums and rehouse families who, by force of their economic status, could not afford the full cost of decent housing. The causes of physical decay in our cities and the economic level of a large segment of the people who live in slums and blighted areas are interwoven. It is necessary, however, that they be untangled if we are to see clearly a program designed to rehouse urban America.

The most obvious reason to separate these two phases of the problem is the fact that slums and blight cannot be remedied without displacing the people who occupy them. If the cleared areas are to be rebuilt with housing—low-rent housing—the displaced people must find a place to live during the operation. The shortage of decent dwellings at low enough rents is a chronic condition. To force people out of one blighted area into another simply lends credence to the oft-quoted statement that people make the slums.

Slum clearance is a popular phrase and an essential objective, but it is necessary that the sequence of *clear slums and rehouse* be reversed to *rehouse and clear slums.* This later sequence has been followed in other countries where intelligent steps have been taken to improve urban housing conditions and remove blighted areas from the city. Housing estates were built on the periphery of English cities, garden towns in the suburbs of Swedish cities, and Holland and Germany planned town extension programs.

Slum clearance is more than pulling down old houses or tenements. It drives straight to the heart of urban rehabilitation. It immediately becomes part and parcel of urban planning for commercial and industrial land uses, and transportation as well as housing. In a word, it implies the planning of our cities. Slum clearance should be treated as urban redevelopment. Much of the misunderstanding that arose from the public housing program was due to the confusion between a program to clear the slums and blight from our cities and a program to build decent housing for low-income families.

Housing is a part of the whole urban complex. It proceeds independently of slum clearance and, to the extent that city planning produces a pattern for the appropriate locations of new housing, it precedes rather than follows the clearance of slums. This is not to suggest that families should not be rehoused in the areas cleared of slums. Many blighted areas are particularly well suited for housing; many blighted areas would become desirable locations for income groups that can well afford housing requiring no suggestion of public subsidy. But the issue of the public housing program was the appropriate use of urban land in our cities, and it was not—probably could not have been—resolved for want of adequate planning preparation.

It was quite natural to suppose that a "slum clearance" project would be located in a "slum." It was likewise natural to assume the worst slum would be the best place for such a project. These assumptions pressed heavily upon the prewar program because they are not necessarily true. In many instances they led to completely erroneous conclusions with respect to the selection of sites.

Mixed land uses have induced blight. Dwellings intermingled with industrial and commercial surroundings are utterly incompatible. They lack the essential ingredients for stability; they create an environment in which blight is built-in and slums are inevitable. It would seem to be normal logic that an area zoned for business or industry is no place for housing. However, blighted residential property is, with few exceptions, found in just such zones of land use. To replace slums with good housing in these areas is not appropriate land use, it is not good investment for the city, and it is due to a lack of planning.

The absence of local planning, added to the popular zeal to get rid of ugly slums, presented the major dilemma of the prewar program to begin a comprehensive program for slum clearance and low-rent housing in this country. The experience demonstrated that a housing program cannot be carried on in our cities, whether by private enterprise or the public, until it is preceded or accompanied by appropriate urban planning.

The Planning Dilemma. At no other time had there been a more pressing need for the benefit of city planning than the years of the Great Depression. Nor could there have been more convincing evidence of its absence. Much lip-service had been rendered the cause of planning in previous years, and a small but vocal profession had grown up around this theme. Yet cities were unprepared for action when the time was ripe.

The state of the Union was desperate at the beginning of the thirties. A program for action was imperative. There was encouragement when the Administrator of Public Works appointed the National Planning Board in July, 1933. For the first time in the history of this country the advantages of research and analysis of our great natural resources were available for the general welfare. Prior to this time it was customary for separate offices of the government to collect facts; it was now provided that these facts should be correlated and thus become the pattern for appropriate action by the respective agencies of government.

The National Planning Board became the National Resources Board by executive order of President Roosevelt in June 1934. It was the purpose of the Board "to prepare and present to the President a program and plan of procedure dealing with the physical, social, governmental, and economic aspects of public policies for the development and use of land, water, and other national resources and such related subjects as may from time to time be referred to the Board by the President." The National Resources Committee succeeded the Board in 1935, and in July 1939 all these functions were transferred to the National Resources Planning Board.

The Board and its predecessors were organized on a regional basis. Probably the most significant work was performed by way of encouragement of planning at local levels and technical assistance to local planning agencies. Regional, state, and city planning was reviewed and organized, comprehensive reports on the state of natural resources and recommended plans for appropriate conservation and use were made, developments and the relative importance of technological changes were recorded, and valuable data were assembled on urban growth and population.[4]

In 1943 the National Resources Planning Board was discontinued and its functions have since been performed by various committees of Congress.

The work of the National Resources Planning Board and its predecessors was directed at issues of national scope. The resistance to planning these agencies confronted was reflected at the local level. Cities were unprepared when the depression struck, the few exceptions emphasizing the general absence of plans. Faced with an immediate opportunity to establish permanent improvements in their environment, there was little evidence that the people had concerned themselves with the question of their future urban development.

The issues of emergency and sound planning were confused. Building and maintaining the city constitute a complex and a vital problem. It requires planning to cope with this problem. The housing program during the depression demonstrated the tragic results of its absence. Subdivisions sprawled across the city without consideration of a plan into which the urban development could be integrated with the future use of land and become an effective means for improvement of community welfare. The public housing program was too frequently interpreted as an opportunity to get rid of some isolated eyesore or festering slum that pricked the civic pride.

By the time that cities had become aware of their plight, the economic cost of blight, and the social hazard of slums, there was no time to plan. That would have to wait until the depression had spent itself and prosperity had returned. Had civic leadership glanced back upon the history of city development it would have been abundantly clear that planning can never wait. The course of human affairs marches steadily on and the

4 See Bibliography, Part II, for partial list of publications.

direction of its course is determined by the degree of planning which precedes it. When goals are set, they can be reached; when they are absent, the urban community drifts like a ship without a compass. The goals have not yet been considered, and our cities are still adrift.

War Begins a New Decade. Then came war, and another stroke of irony marked the affairs of human conduct. Planning assumed proportions never before conceived in history. With destruction of civilization a grim prospect, the scale of planning was gargantuan, staggering the imagination, even in retrospect. However, it was military planning.

When the ominous spread of Nazi domination engulfed central Europe and threatened another world war, Congress enacted the National Defense Bill of June 1940. Industry turned its attention to production of war materials, and the Lanham Act authorized funds for housing workers in the defense plants. Numerous government agencies entered the housing program. In July 1940, the Office of Housing Co-ordinator was established to determine the need in places of acute shortage and allocate Federal funds to the various agencies.

New construction by private enterprise insured by FHA was stepped up, HOLC assisted in the conversion of existing facilities, the low-rent program under USHA was stopped, and 100 per cent loans were extended to local housing authorities to build defense housing. The Public Buildings Administration, Defense Homes Corporation, and Maritime Commission undertook construction of large-scale permanent government housing, and the Federal Works Agency launched a large program of prefabricated temporary dwellings.

With the attack on Pearl Harbor on December 7, 1941, all the energy of the nation was directed to the successful prosecution of the war. Peacetime and defense housing was supplanted by a vast program of war housing, and huge plants were constructed to build ships, airplanes, and armaments.

In February 1942, all Federal housing agencies were consolidated in the National Housing Agency. The National Housing Act was amended to include Title VI, providing insurance by FHA of 90 per cent loans, amortized in 25 years, for housing built by "operative" builders for sale or rent to war workers. The necessity to conserve materials was critical. The floor area of dwellings and the critical materials used in them were rigidly restricted. The Lanham Act was amended to provide for the construction of temporary dwellings by the Federal government.

More than 800,000 new dwellings were built and about 200,000 existing units converted by private enterprise, for a total estimated cost of $4,000,000,000. Nearly 550,000 family dwellings and 170,000 dormitory units were built, and 50,000 existing structures converted into family dwellings, through the direct operations of the Federal government. There were, in addition, about 80,000 "stop-gap" shelters provided in the form of trailers to permit mobility for shifts as changing needs dictated. The cost of this program was some $2,300,000,000 for a total of 850,000 living units.

It has been estimated that migration of industrial workers to man war jobs created

WAR HOUSING, San Francisco

Within the range of this aerial photograph are five of the war housing projects built in San Francisco for workers engaged in shipbuilding and allied industries during World War II. They were planned and built by the Federal government as temporary dwellings intended, according to the Lanham Act authorizing their construction, to be removed within two years after the President declared a termination of the war emergency. Being temporary dwellings and built during a period when the conservation of critical materials was of paramount urgency, they were planned with consideration for economy in cost, space, quantity and quality of materials, and construction time.

Since the end of the war these dwellings, and thousands of others built in a similar manner and for the same purpose in many localities, have been the subject of criticism for their "substandard" planning and construction. The criticism is justified and the dwellings should be removed as soon as production of housing with adequate standards of planning and construction absorbs the housing shortage.

An examination of the photograph, however, causes one to ponder the criticism of this "substandard" character attributed to these projects. The fact that they are readily distinguishable in the picture suggests a reason to raise this question. Among the criteria for appraisal of the quality of a living environment is that of appropriate planning of the streets, their relation to the topography of the site, and the resulting harmony between the dwellings, circulation about them, and the shape of the land upon which they are built.

San Francisco is a series of hills and valleys, and the picture casts some doubt on the validity of an assumption that the war projects are below the standard of the more permanent development about them. Laid in a gridiron, the street system of the city ignores the geographic nature of the beautiful site of this great city. The hills, on which the war projects were built, had been platted for this same gridiron street pattern. The war projects, however, demonstrated a standard of urban planning that cannot be ignored in an appraisal of their value. The contrast between them and the "rectilinear habit" is too apparent to be overlooked. This contrast is further enhanced by the development of the central shopping centers and parking facilities within the war projects in comparison with the inorganic spotting of retail business strung along the streets of the permanent residential districts throughout the city.

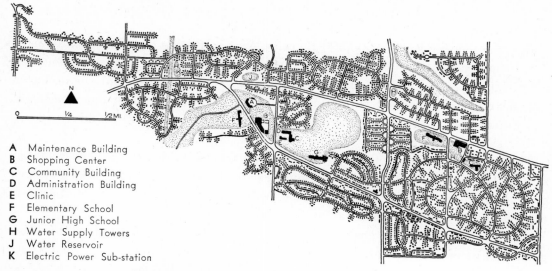

A   Maintenance Building
B   Shopping Center
C   Community Building
D   Administration Building
E   Clinic
F   Elementary School
G   Junior High School
H   Water Supply Towers
J   Water Reservoir
K   Electric Power Sub-station

McLOUGHLIN HEIGHTS, Vancouver, Washington

This was one of the largest single World War II housing assignments by the National Housing Agency—about 5,000 dwelling units. The initial project of 1,000 acres required facilities for a population substantially the same as the city of Vancouver itself. Seven groups of architects were assigned areas for planning in the entire development, being co-ordinated by the local housing authority.

The plan has been criticized for an absence of a single over-all pattern. This criticism exposes the usual nostalgia for monumental uniformity to which we became accustomed during the eclectic nineteenth and early twentieth centuries. Although the project reflects a lack of mature study because of its emergency nature, the plan is nevertheless fairly well organized. The principal highway from Vancouver, situated to the west of the site, splits into two major traffic routes with transverse arteries crossing at points between ½ and 1 mile apart.

The long buildings indicated in the plan were added at a later date and interspersed among the initial units along the highways and remaining open space. Except for these later additions, an examination of the plan shows that most of the dwellings were arranged about minor residential roads, the main highways being largely left free from frequent intersections.

The site is a plateau above the Columbia River, the source of employment for war workers having been located along the river to the south of the project.

a need for housing some 9,000,000 families. War work was distributed in all parts of the country, but the most pressing need was in large centers for the tremendous new industrial plants. Individual projects of 5,000 units were built in such places as Willow Run near Detroit; Norfolk, Virginia; Vancouver, Washington; and San Diego and San Francisco, California. The largest single operation was 10,000 dwellings for the Kaiser shipyards at Portland, Oregon.

The influx of great numbers of workers and their families strained every urban service. Housing was not complete without new streets, utility systems, parks and playgrounds, theaters, shops and markets, and restaurants. Whole new communities were created in a few months, and war production was sustained.

The war was won. The goal had been clear—the survival of freedom. Planning guided the campaign. The production and distribution of goods, materials, food, weapons, and man power were planned. It was necessary, and well done.

Thus ended another paradox in the course of human events. While military planning was winning a great campaign, planning for the peace to come was abandoned. It will be remembered that the National Resources Planning Board died during the conflict, and the planning process, with which our institutions were saved in war, has since been denounced as an enemy of freedom. We have need to learn from yesterday so as to prepare today for a better tomorrow.

PART III

THE CITY
OF TODAY

This is not inflaming or exaggerating
matters, but trying them by those
feelings and affections which nature
justifies, and without which we
should be incapable of discharging
the social duties of life, or enjoying
the felicities of it.
—Thomas Paine, *Common Sense*

CHAPTER 10

AN AGE OF
URBAN ANARCHY

Liberty or License? A century before the Golden Age of Athens, a Greek philosopher, Heraclitus, said the problem of human society is to combine that degree of liberty without which law is tyranny with that degree of law without which liberty becomes license. The democracy of Athens and the Constitution of the United States were wrought from the same precepts. An organized society was formed about a group of laws, a set of rules to guide the people in their conduct. The purpose was to guarantee liberty and justice for all.

Inspired by this freedom the people of America created a vast domain of commercial and industrial enterprise. And they built great cities.

Today we see these cities scarred by congestion and decay, speculation and ugliness. We see the science and invention of our remarkable age snarled in a tangle of the urban network. The mediocrity of our cities is a travesty on the productive genius and creative energy of America.

It is not the desire of the people that their cities should be so built. It is rather their ambition to create fine cities, else the forward strides that have been taken would not have been attempted. It is the essence of democracy that the people shall be masters of their destiny, that their behavior shall be guided by the precepts of law and order. Yet our cities suffer disorder and confusion as though born of anarchy. The most frantic antidotes of regulation appear inept and futile. The reasons for this state of urban affairs may be apparent upon examination.

The City Builders. Who are the city builders? They are the multitude of city people who invest in urban property and improvements. All the people participate. Some share by their investments of capital in physical improvements for conduct of profitable enterprise; others invest in municipal revenue bonds which pay for public improvements. All participate through their payment of taxes for the public services that make urban investment feasible.

Forty per cent of the city area is public property: the streets, parks, schools, and a variety of public improvements. Within this area local government may shape the streets, traffic arteries, and open spaces according to the designs of official planners. But the bulk of city building, 60 per cent of the total urban area, proceeds parcel by parcel as industry, business, and home-seekers find opportunity for investment.

Those who invest for personal profit are guided by the "market" for improvements. The measure of this "market" is double-barreled. Investment in a city implies stability of values. By its nature the city is a permanent institution whose purpose is to shelter the continuing activities of people. It is not a natural speculative medium. An immediate "market" induces investment, but a continuing "market" makes of it a sound investment.

Stability depends upon the quality of the improvement itself. It also depends upon the quality of the other improvements that have preceded and those that will follow. It depends upon the standards at which a community maintains itself, the maintenance of existing facilities, and the standards it demands for future improvements. These standards determine the difference between environmental degeneration or stability, and upon them rests the difference between speculation and sound urban development.

Nor is it the physical improvements on private land that alone affect the health of urban investment. The warp of the community pattern is the network of streets, utilities, and transportation. The city functions through the circulation of goods and services; the strength of the urban pattern is measured by the adequacy and convenience of the circulatory system, the stability of investments by the level at which the community maintains itself.

Urban growth is, in some respects, analogous to processes in nature. The soil of fertile and prosperous citizenship is tilled, the seeds of investment are planted, and the garden is cultivated with urban management and maintenance, both public and private. All urban activities and functions are inseparable. The only area in which they may be isolated is that of speculation, and, for that reason, speculation is damaging.

Speculation—quick turn-over for quick profit—contributes in large measure to building a city, but the speculator assumes no responsibility for his product since he is not concerned with the use of the improvement. That responsibility and the obligation for maintaining it are shifted to others when he transfers ownership. The motive of speculation consequently induces inferior quality; it is concerned only with the least possible initial cost.

Speculative improvements are none the less an investment in the city. They are investments in which the public participates. Public services must be made available to all property, and the cost of these services is paid by taxes and public utility rates. These costs are measured to a large degree by the quality of the improvements that comprise the city. High quality holds stable values, resists spotty shifts in urban land use, and wasteful extension and duplication of public services.

Rules of Democracy. What determines the physical form of the city? It emerges from the initiative and enterprise of many people, acting individually and in groups. However, the people are guided by a set of standards and not from some preconceived model of the future city, however brilliant or inspired. This set of standards is the *law*.

The real plans for our cities are the standards prescribed by law—the codes and ordinances that regulate the development of urban property.

It is a cardinal point of our constitutional form of political organization that ours is a government of laws—the rules by which our democratic "game" is played. City building is guided by the maximum quantity and minimum quality the law allows. Laws form an integral part of the whole planning process, and it is appropriate to the democratic process that the people who design and invest in urban building shall find free expression and action *within the limits prescribed by law.*

That this process imposes a singular responsibility upon the citizen must be self-evident. It is the obligation of the people to determine the standards they deem appropriate for their city and translate these standards into effective rules and regulations. It can be fairly stated that this responsibility has not been discharged with the intelligence and devotion demanded of citizenship in a democracy. Our cities bear violent testimony to that fact. If we are to bring improvement to the urban environment it devolves upon the people, civic leaders in business, industry, the arts, and public office, to assume this responsibility with vision, integrity, and an unflinching will to serve the public interest. In the final analysis it is only the few who reap profitable reward through violation of the general welfare.

Urban development implies a continuing responsibility, all forces acting together and interdependently. The degree to which these forces are integrated reflects the aspirations, ambitions, and convictions of a community, and the initiative and responsibility of the citizenship in whole and in each of its parts. When the forces that contribute to city building are unbalanced, inequities develop and the city declines. The energy is sapped, the city no longer provides a field for sound and continuing business investment, and the environment degenerates.

Since the laws applying to the physical development of the city set the standards for that development, it is important to examine the effect of these regulations and the prospects for improvement in them. It is important for those who invest their capital for profitable return and for those who pay the taxes that maintain the community. The cities themselves bear testimony to the ineffective nature of many of our laws. The legal framework that molds the urban pattern provides some advantages, but cities appear to have drifted into a state approaching anarchy.

CHAPTER 11

THE ZONING FANTASY

Exaggerated Standards. Nearly 1,300 cities have adopted zoning ordinances since the first comprehensive act of 1916 in New York, and about three-quarters of the urban population are living in communities with this form of regulation. About half of the municipalities in the country are still without zoning ordinances, but the popular acceptance of this form of control for urban development represents considerable progress. It is significant that the broad range of interests in so many communities recognize the advantages accruing to all concerned through the character of regulations embodied in zoning. With this recognition so strongly rooted in our urban conduct, it is a paradox that cities continue to deteriorate, that congestion increases, and uncontrolled obsolescence spreads. The anachronism may be explained if we inquire into the limitations—the standards—these laws prescribe.

With the enthusiastic reception of zoning regulation in this country came fantastic predictions for the future growth of American cities. Statistical data were culled from many sources to support gross estimates of future urban development. These data were undoubtedly further encouraged by the optimism and speculative urge that accompanied expansion of the industrial city and concentration of the commercial city. The incongruous results reflected in zoning ordinances are not surprising, but these results provide the reason for the congestion and blight that beset cities today. Mr. Harland Bartholomew has said:

Zoning had come about partly through the desire of certain residential districts to obtain a protection which is difficult, if not impossible, to secure by private initiative, and partly through municipal authorities to seek to curtail the enormous losses brought about by uncontrolled growth. Zoning as now practiced, however, has scarcely succeeded in attaining either of these objectives. The same forces of speculation that have warped city growth in the past continue to do so through distortion of zoning ordinances.[1]

[1] *Urban Land Uses*, Harland Bartholomew, Harvard City Planning Series, Harvard University Press, Cambridge, 1932.

We have zoning laws and building regulations predicated upon good principles of urban land control, but they fail to establish standards of urban development that produce good cities. The anachronism is an integral one—it exists within the laws themselves. Cities have well-nigh created a Frankenstein out of a sound policy of land control.

In New York City the zoning laws permit a building volume sufficient to house a population of 77,000,000 people.[2] If the city of Chicago were built to the maximum of the zoning limits prevailing until recently, it could have housed the entire population of the United States.[3] Translated in terms of population density it would be possible, according to law, to house 1600 persons or 460 families, per acre in New York City, and 2200 persons, or 630 families, per acre in Chicago.[4] These figures seem preposterous, but they represent a basic reason for the congestion of our cities. Nor are these two great cities unique in this respect. Data collected by Harold Buttenheim indicated that the same density, or greater, would be possible in Buffalo, Cleveland, El Paso, Minneapolis, Providence, Washington, D.C., Milwaukee, and Nashville. As many as 200 families per acre could be accommodated in Cincinnati, Denver, Duluth, Yonkers, and, until a recent modification, in Los Angeles.

Actual conditions in our cities have not reached the terrific pitch these laws permit. According to the study by Harland Bartholomew in *Urban Land Uses,* some 90 per cent of the people in the average American city live in single- and two-family dwellings, and about 10 per cent in apartments. The density of population is seven or eight families (thirty persons) per acre in single dwellings; twenty families (seventy persons) per acre in two-family dwellings; and about thirty families (105 persons) per acre in apartments. The average population density in all residential districts of the small city ranges between twelve and fifteen families per acre.

Even in large cities the average density of population does not present an apparently congested picture. Homer Hoyt estimated the density in residential areas of Chicago in 1923 was 100 persons, about thirty-three families, per acre. In 1930 half the population lived in multiple dwellings, 30 per cent in two-family flats, and 20 per cent in single houses.[5] On the island of Manhattan 25 per cent of the residential buildings are single-family dwellings.[6] According to the 1940 Census, 67.9 per cent of all structures in urban communities were single-family dwellings and 17.9 per cent were two- and three-family buildings.

High population density is generally considered most acute in New York City. It is an average of about 190 persons, or some fifty-five families, per acre in the residential areas. However, the most restricted residential districts in Brooklyn and

[2] *City Planning-Housing,* Werner Hegemann, Architectural Book Publishing Company, Inc., New York, 1936.
[3] *100 Years of Land Values in Chicago,* Homer Hoyt, University of Chicago Press, Chicago, 1933, p. 440.
[4] Calculations made from data presented by Harold Buttenheim in "Planning for City, State, Region and Nation," American Society of Planning Officials, 1936.
[5] *100 Years of Land Values in Chicago,* Homer Hoyt, University of Chicago Press, Chicago, 1933, p. 292.
[6] "The Structure and Growth of Residential Neighborhoods in American Cities," Federal Housing Administration, Washington, D.C., 1939.

Queens would house 539 persons, or 150 families, per acre if built to the maximum limits of the zoning law in these areas.[7]

The congestion we daily observe in all large cities and some small ones belies these statistics. Why? The answer is in the population density the law allows. The "highest and best use" of property is that prescribed by zoning laws, and property values are established accordingly. When land is developed to the maximum density permitted by law, a saturation point is reached before all properties have been so developed and the value of unbuilt or underbuilt property is drained off by the over-built neighbors. Congestion thus injures the overbuilt and the underbuilt properties alike; excessive density is undesirable for the property so developed and injurious to the property that cannot be developed at all. But the average is struck, and the fact that it is not bad enough to appear alarming does not reduce the harm done to urban investments by the fantastic limits the laws allow.

Horse-and-Buggy Shopping. The design of commercial zoning persists in retaining horse-and-buggy characteristics. It is standard practice to line a highway with business frontage. In early days of the village the road led to the door of the shop. The horse was tied to the hitching post in front and "parked at an angle." This form of curb parking has lingered on while the automobile replaced the horse and buggy, while the number of cars leaped from 8,000 at the turn of the century to 32,000,000 in 1940, and while the electric tram and motor bus have made the horse-car extinct.

The shopping promenade of yesterday has become the traffic artery of today, but the design of business zoning remains unchanged. Mile upon mile of highways are "stripped" with excessive zoning for commercial use. "Strip" zoning with its curb parking has become a curse upon the urban environment. Through-traffic on highway arteries does not mix with the ready ingress and egress for the parking and service needed for shopping districts. Submarginal business enterprises, blighted houses, acres of weed patches on unimproved lots stretch along the streets zoned for business and have created a state of built-in blight from which we can hardly recover for generations. Even though corrective zoning measures were undertaken at once, it would require a long time for transition; zoning is not retroactive and the investments based upon current practice must run their course before effective improvement can be realized.

Mixed Land Uses. Protection to property expected of zoning has been largely limited to single-family districts. It is a peculiarity of current zoning that as the economic intensity of land use increases toward the center of the city, each lesser economic classification is also permitted therein. Single-family dwellings are permitted in two-family zones, both types in multiple-dwelling areas, all residential uses are permitted in commercial zones, and all residential and commercial uses are permitted in industrial zones. As a result the only zone restricted to the use for which it is designed is the single-family zone; in this zone no other use is permitted.

[7] *New York Plans for the Future*, Cleveland Rodgers, Harper & Brothers, New York, 1943; and *City Planning-Housing*, Werner Hegemann; First Volume of Text: Historical and Sociological, Architectural Book Publishing Company, New York, 1936.

Development of site as permitted
by the zoning ordinance.

PARKCHESTER, New York City

*Board of Design: R. H. Shreve, A. J. Eken,
R. W. Dowling, H. C. Meyers, Jr., Gilmore
Clarke, Irwin Clavan, George Gove.*

Courtesy The Architectural Forum

Development of site as built by the Metropolitan Life
Insurance Company.

The problem of current zoning regulations is demonstrated in this illustration. Zoning not only establishes the uses to which land may be put, that is, industrial, commercial, residential, but it sets the standards by which improvements upon the land may be developed. In residential districts the zoning regulations set the standards of maximum density—the maximum number of people for which building space may be provided—through the building volume resulting from restrictions on the front, rear, and side yards, building heights and setbacks. The standard of maximum density permitted in zoning ordinances for most cities is so excessive that the normal market for building space is usually accommodated at an average density considerably below that permitted by law. As a result, the individual properties improved to the maximum permissible density drain the values from adjacent unimproved or under-improved properties and create unstable land values which effect incalculable damage to investments in, as well as the physical environment of the urban community.

It has become customary to associate the subdivision of land in small parcels with this unstable community character and suggest that large-scale development is the appropriate solution. This suggestion reveals an awareness of current unstable trends, but it overlooks the real source of the evil—the serious deficiency in the legal standards established by zoning and building regulations. Mistakenly diagnosing an effect for the cause invariably leads to prescriptions that weaken the patient, and the antidote of large-scale development for our urban ills tends to stigmatize small-scale enterprise and discourage opportunities for moderate capital investment in urban development and rebuilding.

On the other hand, when the standards for urban development provided in our various regulations over the use of land—primarily the zoning ordinances—are so defined that the resulting improvements will preserve an appropriate relation between open space and building space, whether the plots of land are large or small, it will become unnecessary to rely solely upon large-scale development as the salvation of our contemporary urban environment. Participation in urban building may proceed, then, with assurance of a satisfactory aggregate effect on the living and working environment regardless of the size or scope of the enterprise.

The plans presented here illustrate, in part, the difficulty in maintaining adequate standards of land improvement under current zoning practices. The site is that of Parkchester, the largest single housing development in the United States. It was financed completely by the Metropolitan Life Insurance Company, an institution that has invested in housing as a matter of policy since the early twenties. Located in the Bronx, New York City, the site contains 129 acres and cost about $31,000 per acre, an average of 71 cents per square foot. In planning the project (*right above*), it was intended that the advantages of large-scale planning should be adopted: through streets were reduced to a minimum, ample open spaces for recreation were included, and shopping facilities were appropriately situated. 12,273 dwellings were placed upon the site in buildings ranging in height from seven to thirteen stories. Some 200 stores and a 2,000-seat theater are a part of the community plan, and garage space for about 4,000 cars and parking space for 1,300 cars are provided.

The resulting density in the project is 95 families per acre—about 320 persons per acre—and the building coverage is 27.4 per cent of the land area. This density is higher than seems warranted in view of the relatively low land cost, but it is the comparison of this density and land coverage with that permitted by the zoning law which exposes the real problem of normal urban development.

The sketch (*left above*) indicates the coverage of buildings on the land that would have been possible under the zoning ordinance and which, under normal circumstances of small scale building on individual lots, is the manner in which land in this section of the city is improved. According to the provisions of the zoning ordinance 24,800 families could have been loaded on the site at a density of 183 families, or 640 persons, per acre. Even though the executed project resorted to seven and thirteen story apartment buildings to achieve the open space within the site, it is built to only one-half the population density the zoning ordinance would have allowed.

It is hardly feasible to expect urban development to follow a sane pattern of population density when the laws that regulate the use of land encourage excessively intense use, and it is not satisfactory to rely exclusively upon tremendous large-scale building ventures—this single project cost about $50,000,000—as the only means to restore decent standards of land improvement to the living environment.

SINGLE–FAMILY DWELLING AREAS

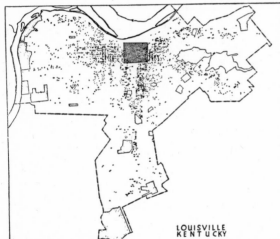

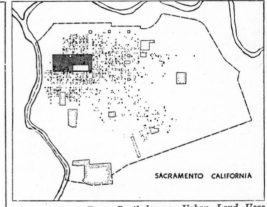

From Bartholomew, Urban Land Uses,
Harvard University Press

TWO–FAMILY DWELLING AREAS

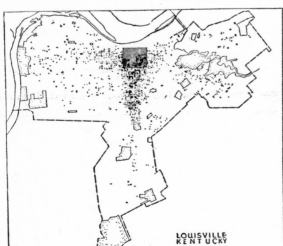

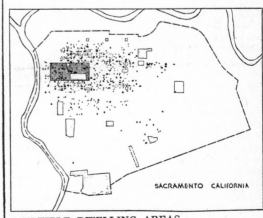

MULTIPLE DWELLING AREAS

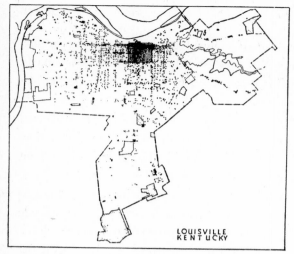

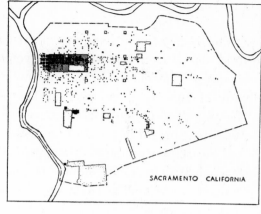

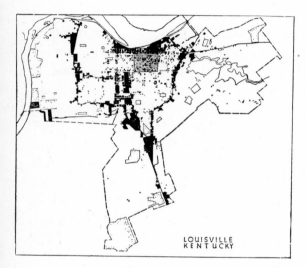

COMMERCIAL AREAS

From H. Bartholomew, *Urban Land Uses,*
Harvard University Press

INDUSTRIAL AND RAILROAD AREAS

MIXED LAND USES

The mixture of various land uses prevailing in our cities is clearly shown in these illustrations. While some uses, such as industry and commercial, tend to concentrate in certain areas, the same uses also filter throughout residential areas. Apartments—multiple dwellings—are heavier near the city center but they are also distributed over areas otherwise predominately occupied by single family dwellings. Single family homes receive protection in zones reserved for that use only but the varying standards of density and land improvement in areas of mixed uses removes from the community any semblance of a desirable and harmonious pattern of living. Reduction of excess zoning for each of the "higher economic" uses, a common standard of population density for residential development (see Chapter 25), and elimination of "strip" commercial zoning along highways by consolidation of retail business in shopping centers would materially improve the situation. A major cause for mixed land uses is the current practice of zoning in American cities. This practice is the permission of "lesser economic" land uses within areas of "higher economic" uses. Thus residential development, being classified as a "lesser economic" use, is permitted in commercial and industrial zones which are classified as "higher economic" uses. Similarly, commercial uses, interpreted as a "lesser economic" use than industrial, is permitted in areas zoned for the latter use. When we recognize that industrial districts are decidedly undesirable as a residential environment, the absence of logic in current zoning practices seems quite apparent but, paradoxically, it likewise seems quite difficult to impress local government authorities and civic leaders with, not only the sinister effect upon the living conditions of the people which the resulting mixture of residential, business and industrial uses create, but the serious resistance which these inappropriate uses offer to the natural expansion of commercial and industrial development in districts appropriately situated for these more intensive uses. It does not seem unreasonable to assume that a well-planned community would establish areas of adequate size and appropriate location for the various land uses and limit development in these zones to the uses for which they are designated. Thus, only industries would be permitted in industrial zones, only business uses in commercial zones, apartments in multiple-dwelling zones, etc., just as only single-family dwellings are now permitted in zones of that classification.

Zoning is invariably based upon this pattern of concentric rings, receding in suc-ceeding stages from industrial and commercial uses at the center to single-family dwellings on the outer circle. The inner ring consequently becomes a hodge-podge mixture of houses, apartments, business buildings, and industrial plants.

The practice of "spot" zoning, individual parcels of land zoned for a different use than that prevailing in an established area, has become almost standard practice. The filling station or the "corner grocery" spotted in a residential district is not an unusual sight, but it undermines the stability of neighborhoods.

The amount of land zoned for business development has been estimated at three to ten times the area that will ever be needed in the locations it is provided. Economic soundness is not a feature of excess commercial zoning. There was a time when busi-ness zoning in Milwaukee was three times as large as the area actually developed for business while 10 per cent of the existing stores were vacant.[8] New York City has enough area zoned for business to accommodate a business population of 344,000,000, a working population five times as great as the potential capacity of dwelling accom-modations in the city.[9] Nearly 2,400 persons per acre could be accommodated in hotels according to the zoning ordinance. Fifteen thousand people work in the Empire State Building alone. Add to this horde of people, the absence of vehicular parking and we gain some idea of the reason for congestion in the city.

Yet reluctance to relieve this congestion is strong. Robert Moses, Construction Co-ordinator for New York City, proposed a change in the zoning ordinance in 1946. It was proposed to restrict the lot coverage to 65 per cent of an interior lot area and 80 per cent of a corner lot, unless off-street parking and loading facilities were pro-vided. Opposition to the change was supported by the claim that one-third of the esti-mated $4,000,000,000 in real estate value in central Manhattan would be sacrificed.[10] The zoning was not changed.

The ever-present prospect for turning to a profit any land zoned for business has built strong active and potential resistance to any modification for a lesser economic use. It is strong temptation to engage in some form of commercial enterprise without consideration of the qualifications for it, the market demand, adequate financial support, or appropriate location. Submarginal businesses degenerate into blight for want of a sufficient income to maintain the physical structure. There are about 1,750,000 retail stores in the United States, and the annual mortality ranges from 250,000 to 450,000. Half the stores did less than 9 per cent of the total business in 1929; in 1940, 35 per cent of all the retail stores did only 3.2 per cent of the total business.[11] Blighted buildings, vacant lots zoned for business, and run-down dwell-ings interspersed among them create an unhealthy environment for existing busi-ness enterprise, but it occurs in every city and town. Excess commercial land use

[8] *Urban Land Uses*, Harland Bartholomew, Harvard City Planning Series, Harvard University Press, Cam-bridge, 1932.
[9] *City Planning-Housing*, Werner Hegemann, First Volume of Text: Historical and Sociological, Architectural Book Publishing Company, New York, 1936.
[10] *Architectural Forum*, September 1946.
[11] *Planning Neighborhood Shopping Centers*, Marcel Villanueva, National Committee on Housing, Inc., 1945.

and "strip" business zoning along traffic streets do not produce orderly or useful communities.

Congestion has encouraged the high land values attached to property within the city, and determination of land use classifications in zoning ordinances has been guided by these values. With this concept of urban land use firmly rooted, it has been inevitable that less and less land per family unit is required as the zones of multiple dwellings move toward the center of the city. Open space per family constantly shrinks: a minimum lot size of 5,000 square feet may be required in single-family zones while the area of land per family in multiple-dwelling districts may diminish to 250 square feet.

With this combination of mixed land uses and open space shrinking toward the center of the city, it is not surprising that the present aspect of the inner districts is one of mediocrity, if not utter banality. Add to these the inevitable hope of realizing a higher sale price for residence property located in a commercial or industrial zone, the tendency toward blight through neglect of maintenance pending realization of that fond hope, and the reluctance of lending agencies to make residential loans in a business or industrial area nipped with blight, and we have a rather dismal picture of the effectiveness of our current zoning practices.

Ceiling Unlimited! The Wall Street district in New York City bristles with the most dramatic display of skyscrapers the world has ever seen. Bond clerks and stockbrokers creep between the cracks and crevices of their cavernous walls. The tallest structures ever built by man are held in the palm of uptown Manhattan. People can neither comprehend nor even see these giant masses, although they live and work in their long dark shadows. The capacity of man to build such immense structures has amazed the world, but the source of wonderment to thinking persons is man's oblivious willingness to trap himself in their vicious jaws.

Each of these huge monsters has made derelicts of its neighbors, but each has been built within the law. By the grace of law their builders themselves may become the derelicts one day. This grotesque spectacle, this display of apparent insensate greed and rank disdain for human values, is all within the law. Congestion has reached such proportions that the right to light and air is legally sold as a commodity.

Yet the Regional Survey of New York and Its Environs showed that within the 8½ square mile area between 59th Street and the Battery, on the island of Manhattan, the average height of buildings is only six stories covering 60 per cent of the land. The average height in the Wall Street district is less than eleven stories covering less than 50 per cent of the ground area. In uptown Manhattan the average height is but seven floors with a ground coverage of 60 per cent. The prospect of all property being built to the maximum legal limits gives one a shocking pause.

Regulations requiring set-backs for tall buildings in New York City were hailed as a revolutionary advance in zoning. In reality they did little more than force a more picturesque silhouette in the design of skyscrapers, a design which was then "typed" and imitated over the nation as a "new" architecture. There is little common

New York City   *Berenice Abbott*

WALL STREET CANYON

United Airlines   *Chicago*

Chicago

American Airlines   *New York City*

CEILING UNLIMITED!

sense in lifting open space six or sixty stories into the air and planting gardens on the roofs when the earth surface is crowded beyond reason. The only "gain" is a few more cubic feet of building into which more, and then more, people can be packed.

Laws that permit such absurd conditions are not only obsolete, but they are dangerous instruments with which to guide the shape of the environment of our homes and workshops. They are unsafe. They permit just about anything anyone wants to to do, and such a process is not democracy in an organized society—it approaches anarchy. "Until land use is rationalized and zoning inspired by a working city plan, the economic brake of mortgage collapse will continue to be a more effective check for overbuilding than the public brake of zoning control."[12]

[12] *Architectural Forum*, January 1945.

CHAPTER **12**

WEEDS IN THE GARDEN

The Curse of Blight. We have been discussing the standards of zoning that affect new building enterprise. Let us now consider the existing urban structure and the problems it presents.

The most sordid ill that besets cities is the scourge of blight. Unchecked obsolescence stretches its withering fingers over the urban environment and brings degeneration to the city. Irresponsible civic management invites, and negligent urban housekeeping permits, it to spread. It menaces health, it breeds crime and delinquency, and it brings traffic death and injury. It undermines civic pride, it threatens municipal bankruptcy, and it gnaws at the human mind and nerves.

Blight casts its sinister shadow across the face of the city. It decays the core of the central business and industrial districts, and it disintegrates the outskirts. It is not confined to the "slums," but it is there most apparent; it is there that we have failed to maintain decent standards of living.

Accumulation of Substandard Housing. It is conservatively estimated that one-fifth of all urban dwellings in the United States are substandard, and some authorities place the number as high as one-third. The Real Property Inventory of 64 cities in 1934 and the U.S. Census of 1940 showed approximately 15 per cent of all non-farm dwellings were in need of major repairs and nearly one-third were in need of major repairs and lacked indoor bathing and toilet facilities. The National Housing Agency estimated that 7,000,000 substandard dwellings existed in use in the United States in 1940.[1]

This is a social and economic cancer. A doctor maintains accurate records of each patient under his care; little semblance of a record is kept of what is being done to rid ourselves of the wretched disease of urban disintegration. From such information we have, it is apparent that substandard housing is multiplying five times as fast as it is being eliminated. The present accumulation of 7,000,000 deteriorated dwellings is growing at a rate of 173,000 each year while only one-fifth of this number is being removed.

Accurate and consistent data on the elimination of substandard housing are scarce,

[1] *Housing Needs,* National Housing Agency, 1944.

WEEDS IN THE GARDEN

Some of the weeds in the garden of
our urban environment. Derelicts in
the business district force retreat from
the urban center, and housing slums
blight the lives of people. Keeping
their eyes steadily aloft to hopeful
visions of the future is almost too
much to expect of our young people
in the midst of such surroundings.
Mixed land uses—houses in the midst
of business and industrial areas—do
not and cannot produce decent living
conditions and they block appropriate
expansion of commercial districts and
industrial development. The resulting
blight within these areas of our cities
is neither economically sound for the
city tax payer or private investor in
good city development, nor does it
create decent human values.

but estimates have been attempted. David L. Wickens[2] estimated that 415,000 non-farm dwellings were demolished during the decade 1920–29. M. H. Naigles[3] estimated that 397,000 dwelling units were torn down or destroyed by catastrophe between 1930 and 1940. It is further estimated that during this latter period approximately half the total units were demolished through natural catastrophe so they were not confined to substandard units alone.

The results of these estimates indicate rather clearly that the elimination of substandard housing is proceeding at a yearly rate of no more than one-tenth of one per cent of the total supply of urban housing, whereas the National Housing Agency estimated that dwellings are becoming substandard at an annual rate of about 173,000 units, or one-half of one per cent of the total housing supply.

Demolition of Substandard Housing, published by the National Association of Housing Officials, 1936, gave data on eight cities: Boston, Cincinnati, Cleveland, Detroit, Milwaukee, Philadelphia, Pittsburgh, and St. Louis, from which the following deductions can be made:

The number of housing units demolished per year by permit (voluntary) during the period 1929–35 was 3,065, the number demolished per year by condemnation during 1933–36 was 3,200, or a total of 6,265 units per year. Compared with the aggregate size of these eight cities (1,860,000 families), the number of units demolished each year was one-third of one per cent of the total number of existing dwellings. Undoubtedly the percentage of units demolished in these large cities is considerably above the average for the country and would tend to support rather than conflict with the estimates set forth above.

This picture has two sides. The familiar face is the social disgrace of inadequate housing for "one-third of a nation." We have laws that define the minimum standards acceptable to Americans. We have police powers vested in local officials to enforce these laws. The standards may not be as high as they should be, but their lack of enforcement is appalling. Our tradition of property rights has created certain barriers to effective enforcement. Exercise of police power invokes the power of condemnation without compensation to owners. To rally popular support for prosecution on such terms is not easy until structures have sunk to such revolting depths of degradation that they may be classed as "unfit for human habitation." About 2 per cent of all urban dwellings fall in this category, although eight to ten times this number are below the standards presently prescribed by law. It is therefore the dwelling which has just reached the state of "unfit for human habitation" that marks the actual minimum standard of housing, despite the various and sundry laws which presume to set acceptable standards. The oft-quoted "American standard of living" is left dangling in something of a vacuum. As Harold Buttenheim, editor of *The American City*, has said: "We not only need to defend our standard of living, we need to achieve it."[4]

The other side of the picture is a Hydra-headed monster. It is the economic menace

[2] *Residential Real Estate*, 1941.
[3] *Housing and the Increase of Population*, U.S. Department of Labor, 1941.
[4] *Architectural Forum*, January 1945.

of obsolescence. It wanders in the dark shadows of indifference, and its prey is every citizen.

An Economic Loss. The disintegrating city is not, in its present condition, a good financial risk for the taxpayer: blight costs too much. Blight cost the people of Indianapolis $50.64 per capita in excess of revenue. The people of Cleveland paid $1,131,953 more than the tax revenue in an area that occupied three-fourths of 1 per cent of the city area and contained less than 3 per cent of the population.[5] The low-rent sections of Boston cost $92.30 per capita and paid $13.30 per capita in taxes; the high-rent areas paid $312.80 in taxes but cost only $73.80 to maintain. The suburbs did not help carry this burden. They paid $41.80 in taxes but cost $62.30 per capita.[6] The population of San Francisco was less in 1940 than in 1930, but the municipal budget was 34 per cent higher.[7] In 1943 a 3-mile area in Los Angeles paid $207,825 in property taxes; it cost the city $488,511.[8] In the pamphlet *Blighted*, published in 1946, the California Reconstruction and Re-employment Commission presented the situation in succinct terms:

Although slum and blighted districts make up 20 per cent of metropolitan residential areas in the United States they account for 33 per cent of the population, 45 per cent of the major crimes, 55 per cent of the juvenile delinquency, 50 per cent of the arrests, 60 per cent of the tuberculosis victims, 50 per cent of the disease, 35 per cent of the fires, 45 per cent of the city service costs— and only 6 per cent of the real estate tax revenue.

Interference with Production. There is another head on this ugly monster. It is more readily concealed. It is fraught with mingled pride and prejudice, a complex mixture of community welfare and property rights. It is the "no-man's-land" in the field of production.

Estimates of housing needs for the decade after World War II have ranged from an average of 1,260,000 urban dwellings per year, according to the National Housing Agency, to as high as 2,000,000 per year. Compared with the average annual production of 700,000 houses per year during the prosperity decade of 1920–30 and 270,000 per year for the depression decade of 1930–40, this is an impressive demand for production. The highest production achieved in a single prior year was 937,000 dwellings in 1925.

Money is the grease for our economic machinery. Unless it circulates the machinery grinds to a halt. It is investment for production that keeps the wheels turning. Except for periods of distortion, such as the immediate years following the war, when balance between supply and demand is tipped off scale by excessive prices, consumer demand spurs production, and fair and free competition supplies equilibrium for the economy.

There is unfair competition with the production of an adequate supply of new

[5] Slums and Blighted Areas in the U.S., Bulletin No. 1, Edith Elmer Wood, Housing Division, Federal Emergency Administration of Public Works, 1935, Washington, D.C.
[6] What Do Slums Cost?, William Stanley Parker, *Architectural Record*, February 1935.
[7] *San Francisco Chronicle*, November 10, 1940.
[8] City Planning Commission, Los Angeles, California.

dwellings. It is the pool of 7,000,000 substandard houses now in use in this country, a reserve of obsolescence which the National Housing Agency estimates is growing at the rate of 173,000 dwellings each year. It is the "hand-me-down" house, the supply of which is depreciating in value at the rate of 350,000 units each year, calculated at the conservative depreciation rate of only 1 per cent per year. Though it is obscure, the most insidious competition with the production of new houses is the "hand-me-down" which has long since been paid for, outlived its economic usefulness, and attained its obsolescent old-age.

One-half of the estimated need for dwelling production during the post-war decade depends upon our capacity to replace obsolete housing. The probable increase in the number of new families in the next 10 years will require some 600,000 houses per year in addition to the present supply.[9] Dr. Robinson Newcomb's estimate is between 560,000 and 640,000 new families per year and the National Housing Agency estimated a need for 620,000 dwellings for new families and relief for doubled households. Housing in excess of this number must be for rehousing existing households, and this drives straight to the heart of the replacement market.

The inordinate housing shortage and price inflation following World War II may suggest that these broad estimates are no longer valid. That they represent, however, a rather typical and continuing long-range picture of the effect of replacement on housing production has been indicated by Miles Colean[10] in his remarks on the future housing demand. Mr. Colean cites the decline in formation of new families which may be anticipated in the postwar period; having reached a peak of 1,050,000 new families in 1947, the annual rate of new families formed is expected to drop to some 400,000 in 1949 with the prospect that this rate will continue through 1955. At the 1947–48 production rate of some 900,000 dwelling units per year it is therefore probable that the market represented by formation of new families and the "undoubling" of families sharing housing may be absorbed by about 1952. His conclusion that the market demand until 1960 may consequently average 667,000 units per year created by new families, "undoubling," and the usual low rate of demolition, tends to support rather than alter the above picture. Calling particular attention to the disproportionate relation between the immediate postwar demand, the production rate, and the probable average demand over a long period, Mr. Colean suggests that the demand may be reduced to about 400,000 units per year during the latter part of the 1950–60 decade, and he then directs attention to the necessity for looking to the replacement market as an important factor in the maintenance of new dwelling production.

New dwellings have been limited to the relatively high-income market; during the twenties three-quarters of all the houses built were for one-third of the population with the highest incomes. At the 1940 price and income levels the National Housing Agency estimated that two-thirds of the housing need was for dwellings costing less than $5,000 or renting for $50 per month. The postwar inflation boomed the

9 *Architectural Record*, July 1943.
10 *Future Housing Demand*, Miles Colean, Building Contractor of California, September 1948.

price and cost structure to new record levels and, while income levels followed in the wake of this surge, the relative effect of these changes from prewar conditions may show an even wider margin in the measurement of production costs and income distribution. These economic shifts serve to emphasize a very real question: Can production of new houses within the range of cost and rental limits forming the greatest segment of the housing market be sustained in the face of competition from the accumulated mass of "hand-me-downs" which need only pay for successively lower standards of maintenance and diminishing taxes year by year? Here is the real and ever-present threat of unfair competition with effective, essential, and healthy expansion of the house-building industry. It is not surprising that production of new houses is confined to the "safe" market; competition forces production for those who can readily afford new houses and are certain of paying the costs.

Obsolescence is not only crunching decent living between its grizzly fingers; it is stifling the field of production upon which our continued prosperity and economic freedom depend.

Downtown Declines. The story is the same in the commercial districts; they are blighted too. Whole districts have become derelicts, snarled and ugly tangles where teeming throngs of people gather to conduct the business of great cities. Worn and haggard and with shredded nerves, the urbanite bears effective testimony to the disintegration of the city.

"Downtown" is under an economic oxygen tent and the breathing is coming shorter and shorter. Old buildings choke the circulation. Out of 140 business blocks in Detroit, 105 had obsolete buildings more than fifty years old. Land is more valuable vacant than improved. In three years preceding 1940, ninety-six buildings in Detroit's central business district were demolished. In 1936 vacant lots on the lower east side of New York had increased to 646,653 square feet from 200,000 square feet two years earlier. With the exception of 75,000 square feet used for parking, these lots were unused. Another 1,000,000 square feet were occupied by obsolete buildings, boarded-up and unused.[11]

The path to delinquency is evident in the trend of assessed values. An old area in Sacramento, California, for example, was assessed at $1,785,945 in 1937. In 1944 it had declined to $1,233,710 and the land value was higher than the improvements. Between 1932 and 1942 the assessed value of land in a downtown section of Los Angeles decreased more than one-half and the improvements lowered one-third. The land value was still 50 per cent more than the buildings.[12]

These distortions offer little encouragement for improvement. The city needs to be released from congestion. A survey of 200 cities by the National Association of Real Estate Boards showed that the gross volume of retail sales lost as much as 25 per cent to the neighborhood centers. Retail sales in downtown Los Angeles shrank

[11] Economics of the Parking Lot, Walter Blucher, _The Planners' Journal,_ Vol. 2, No. 5, quoting Joseph Platzker, Secretary, East Side Chamber of Commerce, New York City.

[12] _Blighted,_ Pamphlet 10, California State Reconstruction and Re-employment Commission, Sacramento, California, January 1946.

from nearly one-half the total for the city in 1925 to one-third in 1935. Meanwhile Hollywood increased 20 per cent, Wilshire nearly doubled, and Westwood grew 300 per cent.[13]

The seeds of blight are nourished in the soil of civic irresponsibility. Unless it is checked, a healthy urban structure cannot survive. Cities will continue to decay until obsolescence is controlled. Accumulation of obsolescence not only produces physical blight but strangles the economic system, a system that thrives only when production is kept in motion. Production requires more than the introduction of new products into the economic stream; it must be sustained through replacement of obsolescence as well.

[13] *Ibid.*

CHAPTER 13

EXPANSION

Escape! The wanton neglect of the congested centers of our cities has been equaled only by the wastefulness of its sprawling expansion. People are fleeing from the city in search of relief from the ugly evils of congestion in their living and working environment. This does not raise the question of decentralization versus rebuilding. It is fruitless to debate that issue. Cities are being continuously rebuilt, after a fashion, and decentralization is not only coming, it is already here. The central problem is to turn the current exodus from a rout into an orderly expansion by way of planning and effective legislation to implement the execution of the plans.

Thus far, expansion has amounted to a scattering of homes over the available outlying countryside. This has provided a means to escape from the outmoded living environment within cities rather than a means to accommodate gracefully the growing urban population. It has not been guided by the foresight of planners, enlightened civic leadership in business and government, nor wisdom in urban economics and finance. Credit for meeting the demand for better living must go to that aggressive group of patent medicine men of real estate we have identified as "lot hawkers." Only they were prepared for the call and they made a contribution to improved urban living. Of those who could afford to escape, there are few not living in some subdivision promoted by the early hawkers of real estate or their more recent offspring. The process was chaotic, unplanned, and it created more problems for the future than it solved at the present. But the people were temporarily served.

Henry Ford said, "Plainly, so it seems to some of us, that the ultimate solution will be the abolition of the City, its abandonment as a blunder. . . . We shall solve the City problem by leaving the City."[1] This thesis reflects the underlying discontent with cities, but can it be a mile-post on the way to reaching a decent environment?

People Need Cities. Seeking an alternative to periodic unemployment, in the early years of the 1930–40 depression, many subscribed to the theory of decentralized industrial plants. Near these plants the workers would have their homes on subsistence

[1] *The Modern City—A Pestiferous Growth*, pp. 156–157; Ford Ideals, being a Selection from "Mr. Ford's Page" in the *Dearborn Independent*, The Dearborn Publishing Company, Dearborn, Michigan, 1922.

LONDON (The shaded portion shows what is now the County of London)

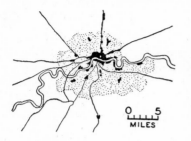

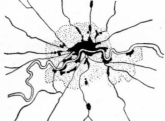

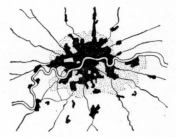

Mid-17th Century   Mid-18th Century   Mid-19th Century

THE EXPANDING METROPOLIS

The growing city has become the metropolis sprawling unplanned over the countryside. Whether it is Chicago, London, or Kansas City, cities everywhere are moving with disorder along the same pattern. The sketches illustrate the city of today in dotted lines or shaded portions, the areas in black the urban growth.

Today

KANSAS CITY

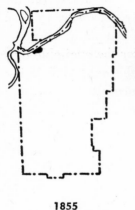

1855   **1895**   **1917**   **1930**

Located at the crossroads of old Roman roads on the Thames River, medieval London was extending beyond its walls before the great fire; the population was then less than one-half million. Destroyed by the fire, medieval London was rebuilt in the classic style. An important port city in the eighteenth century new roads were built and the city was growing—population three-quarters million. The industrial city of the nineteenth century with the greatest port in the world, factories, and railroads expanded rapidly beyond its internal slums. The population of the County of London was 2,808,000 and greater London held 3,222,000 people. The city of today, a center of finance and commerce for a great empire, sprawls into the adjoining countryside and obliterates the road system. Population, County of London—4,397,000, Greater London—8,204,000.

Kansas City, Missouri, a great inland city of some 400,000 people today, was a town of hardly more than 4,000 persons in 1855. At the turn of the century it had grown to 165,000 and 20 years later had a population of more than 330,000. The area contained in the city of today is 60 square miles.

Founded as a town in 1833 on the Chicago River near the shore of Lake Michigan, Chicago had a population of more than 300,000 by 1875. By the dawn of the twentieth century it had reached 2,000,000, and 25 years later it was 3,000,000. In 1940 the population was 3,396,000 in the area of 211 square miles. Having consumed the land along Lake Michigan, it was necessary to restore open space along the shore by "making" land through a stupendous undertaking of filling-in the lake front to form the great system of parks and traffic arteries known as the Outer Drive.

New York City, with a population of less than 200 persons in the early seventeenth century and not more than 14,000 in the middle of the eighteenth century, today has a population of 7,455,000.

Zurich, the site of an early lake village and the Roman town of Turicum, moved through its stormy political history of the Middle Ages and as late as the early nineteenth century had no more than about 10,000 population. Today it has extended its boundaries to include its suburbs with a total population of some 344,000 persons. Also an early Roman town and, having a strategic site on the Mediterranean, an important port and trading center in the Middle Ages, Barcelona remained a relatively small city. Today its population is 1,000,000.

CHICAGO

Before 1850   1875   1900   1925

NEW YORK CITY

1760   1800   1930

BARCELONA

18th Century   19th Century   20th Century

ZURICH

1633   1833   1933

RICHMOND, Virginia

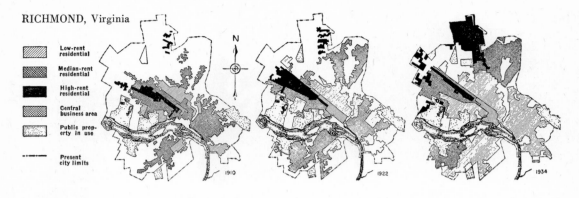

- Low-rent residential
- Median-rent residential
- High-rent residential
- Central business area
- Public property in use
- Present city limits

1910   1922   1934

ST. LOUIS, Missouri

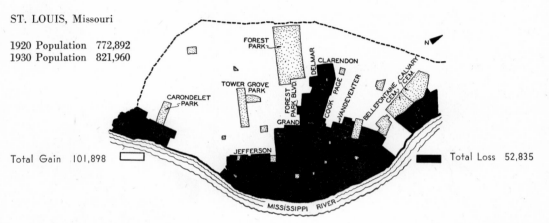

1920 Population 772,892
1930 Population 821,960

FOREST PARK
CLARENDON
DELMAR
FOREST PARK BLVD
COOK
PAGE
VANDEVENTER
BELLEFONTAINE CEM.
CALVARY CEM.
TOWER GROVE PARK
CARONDELET PARK
GRAND
JEFFERSON

Total Gain 101,898

Total Loss 52,835

MISSISSIPPI RIVER

PEOPLE NEED CITIES

People are retreating from the congested city; they are on the move, but not to the country. They are moving to the suburbs where they may find relief and still retain the advantages of the urban environment. Cities are decentralizing. These population movements within the metropolitan area are indicated in the sketches.

NEW YORK CITY

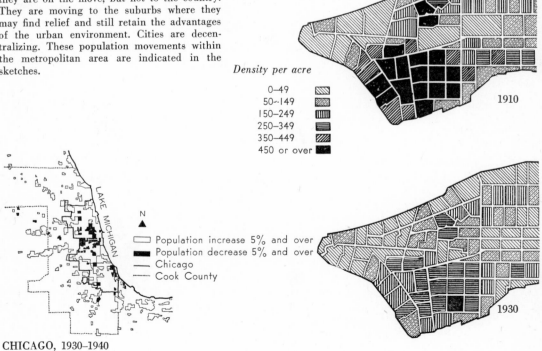

Density per acre

- 0–49
- 50–149
- 150–249
- 250–349
- 350–449
- 450 or over

1910

1930

N

Population increase 5% and over
Population decrease 5% and over
Chicago
Cook County

LAKE MICHIGAN

CHICAGO, 1930–1940

plots and, so it was supposed, they could weather a storm of reduced employment or augment their incomes in times of fair production. This movement gave the impression that cities were losing their places as industrial centers.

It is in the cities where people find their work. According to a study by Daniel B. Creamer,[2] in 1935, three-quarters of all industrial jobs are within the major industrial centers, and these centers are in but 200 of the 3,000 counties of the United States. More than one-third of all jobs are in the large cities, and one-fifth in the peripheral areas and satellite communities contiguous to them.

People have congregated in cities for their mutual welfare. This is an industrial age, and the urban framework forms the basic pattern of our economic and social system. Nearly two-thirds of the people live in cities. The number of urban communities in this country increased from a half-dozen in 1790 to more than 3,400 in 1940; the urban population climbed from 3 per cent of the total population in 1790 to 56 per cent in 1940.

Decentralization is on the march. Industrial expansion is dodging the fictitious speculative land values that are ruining all urban activities, but it is not disappearing from the urban pattern. The apparent movement from cities in the depression was not a rural migration. The greater proportion of this population remained in the metropolitan area of the larger cities.

The suburban districts of metropolitan areas under 1,000,000 population gained twice as fast as the central cities themselves, with a similar trend in areas over 1,000,000. The suburban and satellite areas of Detroit and San Francisco-Oakland increased twice as fast as the central urban districts; the suburban and satellite communities around Chicago, New York, and Pittsburgh gained three times as fast as the central cities; around Philadelphia they gained six times as fast; St. Louis more than ten times; and around Cleveland nearly eleven times.[3]

People are retreating from congestion, but they want and are retaining, the advantages of an urban environment. Despite the desirable characteristics of refuge in rural surroundings, the urban framework forms the basic employment pattern of our industrial society. The role of cities is more vital today than ever before. They provide the range and diversification of employment essential to a free existence of the people. Our task is not destruction of the city, it is to build a better one.

The Burden of Expansion. In the mad scramble to have the advantages of the city but be free from the curse of its environment, the people willingly fed the wild expansion to the suburbs. Spreading at random about the metropolitan area, excess subdivisions have inflicted a heavy toll upon the city and those who invest in it. Extension of public services—utilities, streets, schools, transportation, police and fire protection—over sparsely occupied sections has heaped a heavy burden upon the city exchequer.

Financing the urban community has become a lingering illness. Debt hovers

[2] *Is Industry Decentralizing?*, Daniel B. Creamer, University of Pennsylvania Press, 1935.
[3] *Population and Industrial Trends*, Ladislas Segoe, American Society of Planning Officials, 1935.

over property and improvements until a fateful day when it is either paid up in full or foreclosed. It hangs over the City Hall and drains the taxpayer. Investments are unplanned; lending institutions compete for loans in the expanding suburbs, mushrooming over the countryside and sapping the values in the central urban districts. As Miles Colean said "Lenders thus find themselves in the unpleasant situation of financing their own funeral."[4] In its zeal to become the biggest city or display its popularity, the city invites chaos, and awaits a day when the Federal government must be summoned to bolster the crumbling local economy.

Vacant Lots and Delinquency. Undoubtedly moved by the same spirit that caused excessive zoning, subdivisions reached fantastic figures. In the State of New Jersey 60 per cent of the subdivided property in 1938 was vacant and the State Planning Board estimated it would take fifty to one hundred years to absorb. In 1928 more than one-half the subdivided lots were vacant in Cook County, exclusive of Chicago, and one township had enough vacant subdivided lots to accommodate a population twenty times the current population. The City of Chicago had a total of 1,227,000 lots in 1928, and only 668,000 of these were used. In Grand Rapids there were 51,000 lots in use while 40,000 were vacant in 1931. Milwaukee had 36 lots per 100 persons in 1927, only about two-thirds of these being used. Within the metropolitan area of Cleveland in 1929, 47 per cent of the subdivided lots were vacant, and in 1931 there were enough vacant lots in Los Angeles to accommodate a population increase of 83 per cent.[5] There is as much area in vacant lots in New York City as the land actually developed for residential use, and the total of undeveloped property and unopened streets is 25 per cent of the city area.[6] In 1941 the developed area of Chicago was 24.1 per cent of the entire city while 21.4 per cent was still vacant.[7] A survey of twenty-two cities showed an average of 44.7 per cent of the area was vacant.

There is vacant land in cities but it is disorganized almost to the point of uselessness. The effects of this extravagance and excessive subdivisions are not alone felt by the city through the high cost of public services and disorderly growth. It shows up in tax delinquency which has its impact upon the property owners themselves. In 1938, 98 per cent of the tax delinquent property in Michigan comprised vacant lots, and these vacant lots were 66.5 per cent of all the subdivided lots. It has been estimated that 30–40 per cent of the subdivided lots in the average city are tax delinquent.[8] The delay in putting to use premature subdivisions places a heavy burden of "carrying charges" upon purchasers and the taxpayers alike.

The artificial political boundaries that divide cities from the adjoining communities create insidious competition. Unincorporated areas incline to lesser standards for physical improvements than their more populous neighbors. Invited by the prospects for cheaper development, uninspired builders surge to the outskirts, create the slums

[4] Speech before Mortgage Bankers Association, New York City, reported by *Architectural Forum*, February 1943.
[5] *Local Planning Administration*, Ladislas Segoe, International City Managers' Association, Chicago, 1941.
[6] Urban Economics and Land Values, Edwin Spengler, *New Pencil Points*, April 1943.
[7] What Are Cities For?, Charles Ascher, *The Annals*, November 1945.
[8] Local Planning Administration, Ladislas Segoe, International City Managers' Association, Chicago, 1941.

of tomorrow, and retreat to other equally fruitful fields. Consistent standards of land use, zoning controls, and subdivision practices are as badly needed as building regulations. Co-operation between adjoining political subdivisions may one day become a reality. Until that time there is little prospect for improvement in the character of urban expansion.

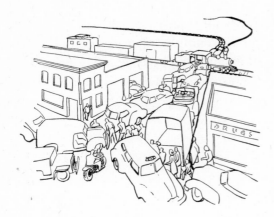

TRAFFIC AND
TRANSPORTATION

From Boulevard to Gridiron. Of all the amazing products of a remarkable age none has made more striking progress than the vehicles of transportation. On the land, the sea, and in the air, speed, comfort, and economy are accomplished realities. For 3,000 years the horse provided the only means of transportation. Then came mechanization and in the brief period of one hundred years we have seen steam, electricity, gasoline, and oil develop power and speed of which our ancestors never dreamed.

From the meandering path came the sweeping curves and broad straight ribbons of the modern highway. But all the vehicles of our mechanized age move into the jaws of a gargantuan trap when they enter the city—the network of urban streets. The problem of urban transportation is the archaic pattern of its streets. The automobile, the airplane, the Diesel locomotive, and electric power have introduced a new dimension so sweeping that cities will experience a complete metamorphosis or perish.

Out of the maze of lanes and roads of the medieval town were carved the monumental avenues of the Renaissance. The fortified walls of the old cities were leveled, and it was expected they would remain as open spaces about the crowded towns. Avenues built in these spaces were intended as promenades. These boulevards were not intended to be traffic arteries. The famous Ringstrasse of Vienna retained some of the character of the original boulevard and became the setting for stately buildings which enhanced the civic nature of the city. In Paris much of the space created by leveling the walls was devoured by speculation in the name of accommodating the crowded populace. The boulevards carved out of the slums of Paris by Baron Haussmann were caught in the conflict between the concept of a promenade and that of a traffic thoroughfare. The promenade that gave civic grandeur to the avenues of the seventeenth-century city has degenerated with misuse and abuse at the careless hands of mercantilism in the last century. For all practical purposes the wide streets built in our cities today are simply nostalgic recollections of the promenade of yesterday and used for an entirely different purpose—a traffic artery—for which they were neither designed nor adaptable. Superimposed over these avenues is an overlay of

192

gridiron streets which originated for convenience of subdivision and easy description and record of sale.

It is this inept pattern of streets which we have inherited and are trying desperately but hopelessly to use for modern traffic. It is against this background that we must project the characteristics of the new vehicles produced in our industrial age.

The Horseless Buggy. The horse and buggy and horse-car served the people well. In the latter part of the nineteenth century electric power replaced the horse, and the street car came into use. The early vehicles were not such a far cry from many of the cars seen on the rails today. It became the dominant means of transportation.

At the turn of the century came the horseless buggy. As soon as it earned its true identity as the automobile, a new era of transportation was born. In forty years there were 32,000,000 of them in this country. But the street system of our cities did not change in all these years of revolutionary developments. Today the system is archaic.

It is sometimes claimed that the motor vehicle created the congestion of cities. The opposite is true. The extent of the city was only 2 or 2½ miles in radius in the days of the horse-car. The electric street car expanded the radius to 5 miles with a travel time of about one-half hour each way. The automobile stretched this radius to 15 miles in the same travel time. The only relief from congestion has been possible because of the motor vehicle. It is an unplanned and obsolete street and transportation system and excessive population density that have caused congestion. The city is strangling itself with the congestion of vehicles that are themselves choked in the tangle of the city streets.

What Good Is Speed? In 1847 the *Messageries Nationales* coach line in France traveled at 6 miles an hour and 56 miles a day. With the introduction of asphalt about 1860 the improved roadways brought an increase in the speed of travel. The *Malles-Poste* coaches traveled at a rate of 9 to 12 miles an hour and made 75 miles a day.[1] The Regional Survey of New York and Its Environs reported the average speed automobiles could make in New York City business area was 5 miles per hour, and a report by the Automobile Club of Southern California compared the effectiveness of the modern automobile with the horse and buggy. The latter traveled from First Street to Tenth Street on Broadway in Los Angeles, in 10 minutes and 21 seconds, sixty years ago. Today it takes the automobile 14 minutes and 12 seconds.[2] In its study of traffic conditions in Washington, D.C., the Public Roads Administration found auto drivers could make an average speed of 14.2 miles per hour from their homes to town, but by the time they had found a parking place and walked to work the average speed was reduced to 8½ miles per hour.[3]

We are aware of a very simple rule but seem helpless to apply it. The rule is that every type of vehicle has a specific use and roadways must be designed to fit them.

[1] *Can Our Cities Survive?*, José Sert, Harvard University Press, Cambridge, 1942.
[2] Out of the Noose, Ed Ainsworth, *Los Angeles Times*, June 12–18, 1938, republished by Automobile Club of Southern California, 1938.
[3] Intangible Economics of Highway Transportation, Public Roads Administration, 1933, *Annual Proceedings*, Highway Research Board.

Dave Packwood

THE PARKING PROBLEM AND TRAFFIC CONGESTION

Dave Packwood

TRAFFIC JAM

WHEELS OF DEATH

Dave Packwood

Until this rule is applied, congestion will itself remain the impediment that denies relief.

Wheels of Death. If urban traffic were confined solely to the irritation of traffic jams we might withdraw to a point of vantage and view the scene as a stupid farce. But it has indeed become a weapon of murder. We shuddered at the horror of the early robot bombs hurled across the English Channel by the Nazis. But news that automobiles kill the same number of people in this country at the same rate year in and year out is greeted with normal complacency. We clamored for punishment of our enemies in war, but tolerate the killing and injuring of 50,000 children in our city streets each year. Between December 7, 1941, and August 14, 1945, our war casualties were: *killed*—261,608; *wounded*—651,911; *missing*—32,811; *prisoners*—124,194; a *total* of 1,070,524. During this same period casualties from traffic reported by the Institute of Traffic Engineers, November 1945, were: *killed*—94,000; *injured*—3,300,000; a *total* of 3,394,000.

Traffic Jam. The mass movement of people has broken under the strain of congestion in the obsolete street system. Electric street cars that carried 85 per cent of the passengers in 1922 carried less than half the passenger traffic in 1940. The automobile had taken over, and in so doing the delinquency of urban congestion was further aggravated. The elevated railway and subway did not provide relief. The electric interurban replaced the steam railroad service to the suburbs early in this century, and now the autobus is replacing the electric train.

These shifts and changes have not been made because greater economy, convenience, safety, speed, or comfort accrued to the urban dweller. Each has been a measure of expedience forced by the breakdown of the street system. The essential function of transportation—the movement of people—has been lost in the deluge of vehicles in city streets and the overwhelming problem of disentangling the jam of vehicles and pedestrians. Urban transportation presents a series of contradictions. The cost of operation and storage of the private automobile is the highest of all forms of transportation; electric rapid transit is the most economical. Yet the automobile is on a steady increase.

Public transportation is grinding human dignity beneath its wheels. Jammed and packed with their human cargo, the honking busses and clanging trolley cars wind their tortuous way through the maze of city traffic. In desperation, rapid transit in some cities has burrowed underground. In New York City 57 per cent of the passenger travel is in the subway.[4] Downtown traffic in Chicago became so acute that nearly 40 per cent of the people were traveling on elevated trains. Now that city boasts an underground system. As a solution of the traffic problem these devices are pure deception. Aside from the outrageous expense to build such systems, common sense and experience inform us that congestion on the surface of the earth is only further aggravated when the hordes are disgorged. Concentration is encouraged,

[4] Regional Survey of New York and Its Environs, 1931.

congestion is exaggerated, and then more subways are needed. The endless circle begins all over again.

The pedestrian is a human jumping-jack, dodging all manner of vehicles in his frantic struggle for his place on the sidewalk. In the report of the Regional Plan of New York and Its Environs, Mr. Lawson Purdy estimated that sidewalk areas should be calculated at the ratio of 5 square feet per person. He used an average of 100 square feet of building per occupant and based his estimate on the assumption that one-half to one-third of building occupants use the sidewalks at one time. It was then discovered that, according to the zoning law, so much building space could be built in the business district of New York City that pedestrians would have less than $3\frac{1}{2}$ square feet per person in the combined area of both streets and sidewalks. This is little more than half enough space for sidewalks alone, to say nothing of the streets for vehicular traffic.

Experience has amply demonstrated that vehicles of different types and traveling in opposite directions must be segregated to move with economy, speed, and safety. In 47,000,000 miles of traffic through the Holland Tunnel only one death occurred. Norman Bel Geddes[5] pointed out that, at this rate, the death toll could be reduced to less than one-fifth the present number.

Outworn "First-Aid". The vehicles of today can hardly be expected to function under the handicap of such feeble devices as the policeman's whistle and "stop-and-go" signals. Speed "limits," "slow-down" signs, and "safety zones" are reduced to an absurdity when traffic cannot reach one-half the limit permitted by law on some streets, and other streets invite danger to pedestrians and drivers alike, regardless of speed. Painted white lines to "channel" vehicles traveling in opposite directions at 30, 40, or 60 miles an hour are not only ludicrous, but a serious hazard to life and limb. The confused muddle of passenger automobiles, motor-buses, trucks, motorcycles, pedestrians, and the old-fashioned conveyances that pass for rapid-transit street cars, is the ridiculous spectacle of inept urban management.

Each mode of transportation available to us today has its own respective advantages and limitations. The city of tomorrow must adapt its street system and urban land uses to these characteristics. They become the elements of urban design with which the city is to be formed.

Parking. The impact of the private automobile upon the urban pattern is hardly manifest more impressively than in the parking problem. In his lectures on "Housing and Town Planning" at Columbia University in 1946, Sir Raymond Unwin estimated that the number of automobiles that come each day into the 3 square miles between Forty-second Street and Central Park in New York City, if placed end to end, would be 1,045 miles long. J. L. Sert has estimated that the entire city of New York with an area 100 times this portion of the city has only $5\frac{1}{2}$ times this length of streets.[6] Sir

---

[5] *Magic Motorways*, Norman Bel Geddes, Random House, 1940.
[6] *Can Our Cities Survive?*, José Sert, Harvard University Press, Cambridge, 1942

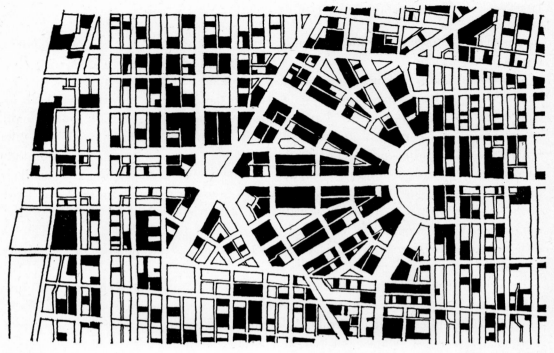

Detroit

OPENING UP THE CITY

The congestion of traffic in the heart of the city is a serious problem that has grown out of the crowded space in which the daily population is concentrated. Pedestrians have difficulty making their way through the maze of streets to the shops and offices they patronize, mass transportation vehicles struggle through traffic jams and automobiles crawl through the streets.

The result of this traffic stalemate in the city center is nourishing the decentralization of business enterprise to serve the hordes of urban dwellers seeking relief in the suburbs. Obsolescence is overtaking the city center and the demand for terminal parking space is gradually restoring some semblance of openness in the congested city. The street system is a hangover from the horse and buggy days and the spotty location of open space and complexity of ingress and egress between traffic streets and parking lots obscures the reality of this space, but the cities are nevertheless opening up. Some suggestion of this phenomenon is indicated in the accompanying sketches.

If all the obsolete buildings were removed from the downtown district of Detroit the resulting combination of this space with the existing vacant lots and streets would present the contrast between built-up and open areas shown in the sketch of that city. The black areas show the modern buildings in the central business district and the extent of present and potential open space is shown in white. This hardly suggests a planned organization of the space for efficient or economical use but it reveals the actual situation in the central district.

A similar trend is indicated in the sketch of a portion of the downtown area of Los Angeles, another city in which the private automobile is breaking open the seams of the archaic street and land use pattern. The areas in black show existing buildings, the white spaces indicate streets and vacant lots most of which are used for parking. Many of the present buildings could be classified as obsolete and their removal would add materially to the vacant areas. The street system is the usual gridiron plan and all streets are used for circulation of private automobiles, trucks, mass transportation and pedestrians, which is a combination use that does not work in the modern city. The vacant space used for parking is greater than the casual observer is customarily aware, but it is ineffective because of the conflict between ingress and egress of vehicles into and from parking lots and the stream of traffic. Furthermore it is hardly appropriate to apply the term of "open space" to these vacant lots and crowded streets; they could be more accurately described as cluttered areas which only add to the congestion and confusion in the business district. It is through streets like these in the heart of the city which 40% of the automobiles must travel to reach destinations clear outside the central district and on which almost a third of the traffic in the average city is caused by roving automobiles searching for places to park.

In an effort to provide for terminal parking space serving the downtown district, the Planning Commission of Pasadena proposed a plan in 1947 (unexecuted) for the progressive development of parking areas. In the section of the business district illustrated only 14% of the area is occupied by commercial buildings and 18% is already devoted to parking lots. These lots provide 2,648 parking spaces but even though the ground area covered by business buildings is relatively small, there are some 2,700 employees and 38,000 patrons of shops and business who daily enter this area. Being a major satellite city in the Los Angeles metropolitan area and served

Los Angeles   Pasadena

■ Existing Buildings

□ Parking Space up to 1947

▨ Parking Space Added in 1947

◱ Additional Parking by 1960

inadequately by mass transportation facilities, the vast majority of those who visit the business district need parking space for private automobiles.

Another effect of the population movement within cities suggested in the sketches and the diagrams which indicate the retreat of people from the central areas to outlying sections of the city is the trend in land values. The shift from depressing values in the city center to increasing values on the outskirts is illustrated in the Baltimore diagram.

We cannot put these various conditions together, observe the pattern they present and the relation which each has to the other, without recognizing the crying need for a careful examination of urban growth which may lead to a new attitude toward the organization of the city of tomorrow.

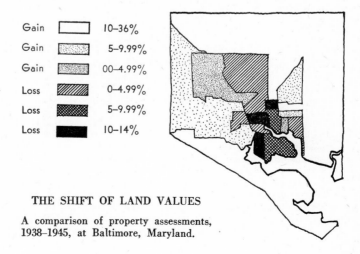

Gain		10–36%
Gain		5–9.99%
Gain		00–4.99%
Loss		0–4.99%
Loss		5–9.99%
Loss		10–14%

THE SHIFT OF LAND VALUES

A comparison of property assessments, 1938–1945, at Baltimore, Maryland.

Raymond calculated that space to park all the automobiles using the streets of New York every day would take more than one-third of Manhattan Island.

There is not sufficient room in cities for automobiles to move about. A report by the Automobile Club of Southern California indicated that 50 per cent of the ground area in the "downtown" district of Los Angeles is in parking lots.[7] In this city, with more "space" than any other, traffic is jammed. There is not enough land area in the whole business center to park all the cars that enter this section each day. Parking space increased in downtown Detroit from 110 lots in 1927, with a capacity of 7,720 cars, to 265 lots in 1933, accommodating 17,251 cars. Walter Blucher[8] also reported that open-lot parking in Milwaukee increased from 3,080 cars in 1927 to 9,009 in 1935. Bridgeport, Connecticut, a typical city, had 17 lots with a capacity of 1,279 cars in 1928; in 1939 the number of lots was 43 with parking capacity for 3,146 cars.[9] James B. Steep, economist-engineer, estimated that parking facilities in Detroit will have to be doubled, yet parking lots earn only one-third of their taxes.[10] A bus terminal proposed for New York City was intended to move 30,000 persons per hour in 735 motor-buses. If terminal parking facilities were to be provided for this many people in private autos, they would require four-story buildings covering 9 blocks 660 by 250 feet in area, and the time for entrance and departure of cars would span hours of time.[11]

The Economic Enigma. The lack of parking facilities imposes an economic loss upon cities. According to Thomas C. Desmond, the Philadelphia main shopping district loses an estimated $10,000,000 in sales each year because parking is inadequate. In Baltimore downtown property values lowered $60,000,000 in 15 years. The probable loss in property values for the entire country is close to $5,000,000,000 a year.[12]

The physical and fiscal problem presented by the parking requirements and devices cannot be ignored much longer. Congested use of land for buildings has forced parking underground as it has rail lines in subways. These magnificent construction feats will no more solve the parking problem than subways provide a solution for the mass transportation problem. It has been proposed to build such a "garage" in Los Angeles. According to the most recent published estimates of the capital cost—$4,000,000 to park 2,500 cars—a price of $8.00 per square foot could be paid for land and accommodate the same number of cars; the equivalent of $5.00 per square foot could be paid and allow enough space per car to permit "driver-parking" and reduce the parking charge. In all probability the above-mentioned capital cost is considerably below the actual cost to build such a facility; to the extent that the cost exceeds this figure, the price that could be afforded for land on the sur-

[7] Out of the Noose, Ed Ainsworth, *Los Angeles Times*, June 12–18, 1938, republished by Automobile Club of Southern California, 1938.

[8] The Economics of the Parking Lot, Walter Blucher, *The Planners' Journal*, Vol. 2, No. 5.

[9] *Architectural Forum*, February 1939.

[10] *Architectural Forum*, January 1940.

[11] Transit and Urban Expressways, Leslie Williams, The 2nd Annual Conference of the Eno Foundation for Traffic Control, Inc.

[12] No Parking, Thomas C. Desmond, City Expert for the New York State Senate, *Los Angeles Times*, Sept. 7, 1947.

face of the earth would increase. The city of Pasadena proposes to increase the amount of ground level parking space to serve the central business district.[13] The estimated cost per car space is $800—one-half the estimated cost per car in the Los Angeles underground garage.

Congestion is aggravated by underground facilities. It would be relieved if parking were provided on the surface, and this would lead to a gradual balance between building floor space and open ground space. It would also lead to a gradual removal of physically blighted structures which have become dregs on the market for commercial floor space. Both these results would serve the ultimate objective of decongesting the city.

Making surveys of the traffic problem is almost habit-forming. The fifty-first survey of traffic in New York City since 1907 was completed in 1946, the report "Selected Measures for the Partial Relief of Traffic Congestion in New York City" costing $80,000. It recommended a program estimated to cost $132,000,000 for *partial* relief, and only a small part of it was looked upon with favor by the authorities.[14]

Surveys add more statistics to the overflowing stock already collected. But until effective remedies are adopted and executed, this knowledge of the problem serves no purpose; it only adds to the burden of rising costs of local government, lends more confusion to the traffic dilemma, and produces no results.

[13] *Pasadena Star News*, November 23, 1947.
[14] *Architectural Forum*, December 1946.

CHAPTER 15

PLATITUDES

Plans Must Be Flexible. Planning is plagued with platitudes. A number of familiar expressions have almost reached the stature of symbols, the mere mention of which presumably being sufficient to convey a significant message. It would be well to examine some of these phrases in order to recognize their meaning.

We frequently hear reference to the necessity for "flexibility" in city planning. It is suggested that city plans must be adjustable to changing conditions, that cities grow like "living cells." These are convenient terms and contain much truth. Unfortunately they too generally become picturesque phrases. There are some very specific limitations upon their value and application.

A city is more than buildings, streets, utilities, steel, concrete, and glass. Nevertheless, these are the materials of which the physical structure is made. They are inert. They have chemical properties, but they are not elastic. Once in place they cannot be shifted about to suit either fancy or "changing conditions." They are static. The width of a street does not pulsate with the intensity of traffic flow, nor can a building flex its beams and columns.

In these important particulars the analogy of city building to a "living organism" is literary confection. The pictorial similarity between a medieval town plan and the cross section of a tree or the veins in the human arm becomes pure poetry. Lifted out of the rarified atmosphere of romantic fantasy, "flexibility" means enough space to bring the products of industrial genius into useful service in the city structure.

Cities are inflexible because they are so crowded there is no room for the various elements to "work." They are frozen into congestion, and flexibility will be attained only through the establishment of adequate standards to guide those who participate in building the city.

There comes a moment when decisions must be made. When that moment arrives, there is a degree of finality implied by the act of decision. The structure of the city does not float; it cannot be tugged or pushed about. When a building or other civic improvement is erected, it is there to stay. Flexibility in the plan of a city will be accomplished by standards for city building that preserve enough space for all improvements without overcrowding.

Trends or Escape? In nearly every walk of business enterprise there is reference to "trends." New conditions, scientific development, and social improvement require adjustments in the conduct of enterprise. They likewise require adjustments in the city. Shifts in the growth of cities prompted by such changes and accompanied by some degree of orderly direction serve as a measure of trends in healthy city development.

But these shifts are confused with quite another sort of change: the urge to escape from the contagious disease of obsolescence and unrestrained speculation. Healthy enterprise shuns association with derelict neighbors; unbridled physical deterioration repels improvement. Shifts in the urban pattern compelled by these desultory forces do not mark *trends*. They report a rout, a desperate and disorderly retreat. Diagnosing this disease as a trend is to spread the contagion further, and ignore or misinterpret the only value that observation of trends can provide: a guide to the natural and appropriate use of land in the growing city.

Economy and Efficiency. Economy is a familiar slogan. It is also a worthy aim. In practice, however, it has unfortunately been too frequently reduced to a fiction. Expenditures for civic improvements are generally decided upon by their budget appeal, not their adequacy. Patchwork improvements display such an appeal; they appear to be "economical." The question of whether they may actually solve any particular problem is usually overlooked or avoided. Economy may really be, and usually is, quite another matter. We have seen a street widening prove inadequate almost upon the day it was completed. We have seen the immediate need for another improvement added. We have seen the value of adjacent land enhanced with each such piecemeal improvement, and new buildings erected about it. We have then seen the public forced to pay the added increment of land and building "value" each of these improvements has induced. This process is characteristic of urban "economy," but it is not economical.

Each new or improved utility service introduced to a city crowds some equally needed service. The utility system—sewers, water, gas, electricity—distributes the energy to operate a city of a million people. Yet these vital veins are, with some rare exceptions, buried beneath, or suspended above, the arteries that carry the stream of daily traffic. The conflict between these services is experienced day in and day out. A utility line breaks down and the repair job stops the circulation of automobiles and street cars. These conflicts choke an already congested city and it is not economical. It has been estimated that congestion in New York City costs the city $1,000,000 a year. In Boston, it was estimated that the trucking business loses $20,000,000 a year because of traffic congestion.

"Efficiency" is another ingrown term. Efficiency obviously has virtue; that virtue is the elimination of waste. In the name of "efficient" planning, however, there are examples of the creation of waste. We have observed acres of subdivisions, planned with alleged efficiency, which are actually a waste of the urban resources. We have seen the width of a street, the size of a house, or the lot it occupies squeezed to an efficient minimum so low it is reduced to nothing more than a cheap commodity.

Recalling the studies by Sir Raymond Unwin and Henry Wright, efficient planning is more than an obsession to save; it is also a method to *improve*. Standards are the measurements by which we must be guided rather than remain content with what Elizabeth Denby called "the intellectual pleasure which the architect got from a triumphant arrangement of inadequate space."[1]

What Is Adequate? It must be clear that space in a city must first and foremost provide for *adequacy;* it must be ample.

The measure of adequacy will be the capacity of the space to receive the buildings of a city without itself being lost completely. It means enough space so that buildings may stand alone or together without violating the sensibilities of those who see and use them. It means that cities will provide space into which the buildings are built rather than a solid mass of buildings through which the fissures we call streets are carved.

The concept of space means a relatively constant limitation on population density regardless of the heights that structures may reach. The prospect of squeezing more people into the same space creates instability, not only in land value, but in urban services. It imposes an extravagance on the installation of service facilities. Water, sewers, gas and electric distribution, telephones, streets, walks, transportation, fire, health, educational and recreational facilities cannot be estimated with any possible degree of economy. These services must be installed of sufficient size and quantity to meet unlimited future requirements, or be repeatedly removed, altered, and replaced as the demand may fluctuate. Either course is an extravagant venture as city budgets and utility bills attest.

Within a reasonable concept of space in the urban environment is the room for the vehicles of transportation to circulate with ease and safety. This means enough room to separate the different types of vehicles and the direction of their travel; room enough to move about on the surface of the earth rather than burrow into the ground with subways. This means the city will no longer be a maze of streets and alleys slicing through a solid bulk of buildings.

This concept means that parking space for the free-moving vehicles of our contemporary age shall be a component part of all floor space provided within or adjacent to, buildings, and it means that this integration will bring the relation between open space and building floor area into some degree of balance.

There will be enough room for all the essential utility conduits, a network of vital service arteries so aligned within their respective rights-of-way that interference is avoided at all times.

This concept of space means room enough for people to walk in safety and some

[1] *Europe Rehoused*, Elizabeth Denby, W. W. Norton and Company, Inc., New York, 1938.

degree of beauty; trees would not be unwelcome. Finally it means an environment in which the human spirit can rise above mediocrity; it means relief from the din and the danger that fray the human nerves and dull the human mind.

On Being Practical. It may be suggested that the concept of space within the city described above is not a "practical" one. The planning of cities is rather cluttered with bromides, but hardly is any so overworked as the "practical." Compromise is the inevitable road to satisfactory human relationships. The capacity to compromise is a requisite to accomplishment. It implies, however, that an objective is clearly defined. The objective of planning is the solution of a problem; in city planning the problem is that of an environment that is rapidly disintegrating under the spell of congestion and ugliness.

Opinions may vary as to the way in which to arrive at the objective of decent cities, but no purpose is served until some area of agreement can be reached about the nature of the objective itself. Solutions call for ideas. They deal in ideas. Ideas are the tools with which we shape an objective, and they cannot be dismissed only because they may at first appear "impractical." We see about us the results of thus being "practical"; we see these results repeated time and again: more congestion, more traffic problems, more deterioration, more expense, and boundless confusion and bewilderment. If we peer behind this scene, we may well find the reason: the process of planning *began* with a compromise. The ideas that are the stuff of progress never reach the surface where they may be observed and tested for their validity.

Nor is this approach really practical. The first test of practicality is whether a thing "works." Can it be claimed that our cities work? Is traffic congestion practical? Or the crowded business centers? Or the blighted areas and slums? Are the extravagant devices for parking automobiles—overhead and underground—practical? Is the mediocrity of the living and working environment, and the obsolete transportation in our cities really practical? Is it practical to spend huge sums on surveys, consultation, and plans, then ignore them all? The urban malady of congestion is like the itch: scratching produces a sensation of relief. But common sense tells us the only practical treatment is a cure, not more irritation.

Must it be considered impractical to propose standards which have as their sole purpose a restoration of permanent values in the urban environment? Ample space for London was rebuked by F. J. Forty, Chief Planner for the rebuilding program, with the words, "I want it [London] to be the leading place of commerce in the world and not—as some planners suggest—a park."[2] Must this be the interpretation of the need for adequate space within our cities? The original plan proposed for the City of London, a plan that offered little improvement over the city that was destroyed, was commented upon by Donald Tyerman in the *Observer* as "timid rebuilding proposals." He said, "The makers of this plan are not planners but pessimists."[3]

We might hark to the words of Lewis Mumford:

[2] *Architectural Forum*, September 1944.
[3] *Ibid.* The plan to which Mr. Tyerman referred was that proposed for the mile-square "City" of London by the Improvement and Town Planning Committee.

As so often has happened during the last quarter century, the self-styled practical men turned out to be the weak irresponsible dreamers, afraid to face unpleasant facts, while those of us who were called dreamers have, perhaps, some little right now to be accepted—at least belatedly—as practical men. By now history has caught up with our most dire prophecies. That is at once the justification of our thinking and the proof of its tragic failure to influence our contemporaries.[4]

[4] *Architectural Forum*, May 1945.

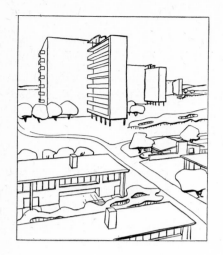

CHAPTER **16**

HOUSING

Policies and Problems. The housing problem remains unsolved, but certain policies have taken shape during the past two decades. The necessity for government to render assistance in some form has been recognized. It is apparent that private enterprise, unaided, is not able to provide an adequate supply of housing of satisfactory standards to meet the wide variation in the income levels of all the people. This is evident in the generally popular program of assistance by the Federal Housing Administration in its mortgage insurance plan, the programs of the Federal Home Loan Bank Administration to provide a national credit reserve, and the Federal Savings and Loan Insurance Corporation to insure investors in home financing institutions. Acceptance of government assistance through public housing for the low wage earners is still an issue before the people, but the history of housing in Europe and the situation which faces the United States indicate that the issue revolves about the extent to which public housing shall become an integral part of our economic and social machinery, rather than complete rejection of such a program.

In 1940 there were 37,300,000 dwelling units in the United States. Of this number about 29,700,000 were urban dwellings and 7,600,000 were rural. The U.S. Census of 1940 confirmed the Real Property Inventory of 1934, from which surveys it has been estimated that between 20 per cent and 30 per cent of the urban dwellings are physically substandard. The rate at which housing is growing obsolete exceeds the rate at which substandard housing is being eliminated, and there has accumulated a quantity of substandard housing estimated by the National Housing Agency to have been 7,000,000 in 1940. The program of the United States Housing Authority was so relatively small that its effect upon the total housing supply was practically negligible.

Practically every city is vested with the police power to require maintenance of adequate housing standards, but the enforcement of these powers is not only so lax as to be ineffective but the nature of the problem has moved clear beyond the scope of these devices. Lack of planning, poor subdivision practices, excessive land values, ineffectual zoning, archaic streets, and inadequate transportation have created a condition of congestion, mixed land uses, and economic distortions that render whole sections of the city in a process of built-in physical decay and social disintegration. The problem has transcended piecemeal treatment for improvement and has reached the stage of large-scale rehabilitation as the only feasible procedure. Such a procedure implies the co-ordination and participation of all forces at the command of the urban population.

Capacity to Pay. The capacity of people to pay the costs of housing presents an issue of paramount importance in a consideration of the housing problem. Studies by USHA in 1940 indicated that one-third of all families had incomes of less than $1,200 a year while only 1.2 per cent of the housing built by private enterprise, including the assistance of mortgage insurance by FHA, was available within these income limits. One-sixth of the families had incomes ranging between $1,200 and $1,600, with 4.9 per cent of the housing available within these limits, and one-sixth had incomes between $1,600 and $2,100 with 17.7 per cent of the housing in this range. One-third of the families were in the highest income group with more than $2,100 per year, and 76.2 per cent of the housing was built in this range. Substantially three-quarters of all housing produced was within the means of only the upper income third of the people, whereas all but a fraction of the balance of one-quarter was confined to the middle income third. The lower income third were able to afford practically no new housing.

The National Housing Agency has estimated that an average annual total production of 1,260,000 dwelling units will be required during the 10 years following World War II (Table A).

TABLE A. ORIGIN OF NEED FOR CONSTRUCTION OF NONFARM DWELLING UNITS, 1946–55*

Character of Need	No. of Units
Increase in number of families:	
Increase in families and migration from farms	4,100,000
Servicemen's households to be established or re-established	1,400,000
Undoubling of married couples living with another head of family	700,000
Total	6,200,000
Balance of units required to bring total number of vacancies up to 5 per cent of total supply of dwelling units in 1955	100,000
Total new need	6,300,000
Replacement of units destroyed by fire, storm and flood	200,000
Replacement of substandard units demolished	6,100,000
Total replacement need	6,300,000
Grand total	12,600,000

* *Housing Needs, A Preliminary Estimate,* National Housing Bulletin 1, National Housing Agency, Washington, D.C., November 1944.

Analysis by NHA was carried further to ascertain how this estimated supply should be distributed in order to meet the range of need. Adjustments were made to accommodate changes in costs which had occurred between 1940 and 1944 when the estimates were made (Table B).

TABLE B. NEED FOR CONSTRUCTION OF NONFARM DWELLING UNITS, 1946–55, BY MONTHLY RENTAL AND APPROXIMATELY EQUIVALENT SALES PRICE, AT THE 1944 PRICE LEVEL*

Monthly Rental	Approximately Equivalent Sales Price	Estimated Units Needed (Percentage of Total)
Under $10		10
$10–$19		12
$20–$29		14
$30–$39		15
$40–$49	$3,000–$3,999	15
$50–$59	$4,000–$4,999	16
$60–$74	$5,000–$5,999	14
$75 and over	$6,000–$7,499	7
	$7,500 and over	12
		100

* Ibid.

Since the termination of armed hostilities, costs have advanced greatly. It becomes difficult to make further adjustments until some degree of stability in wages and prices is restored. The effect of the inflationary spiral by the end of the year 1947 is suggested in a study by Miles Colean in which the costs of new single family housing produced are compared with the new level of incomes prevailing at that time.[1]

These statistics include all families and all dwellings, farm and nonfarm, and in Table D Mr. Colean estimates the price range of single family houses in industrial

TABLE C

Estimated Price Brackets	Per Cent of Total New Dwellings in Each Bracket	Family Income Brackets	Per Cent of Total Families in Each Bracket
Under $4322	20	Under $1000	13
$4322–6981	23	$2000–2999	20
$6982–9641	25	$3000–3999	18
$9642–12,301	18	$4000–4999	13
$12,302 and over	14	$5000 and over	21

[1] Who Can Afford Our New Housing?, Miles Colean, Building Contractor of California, April 1948. It is rather difficult to reconcile the "price brackets" estimated by Mr. Colean with recent experience in the inflated housing market. These estimates indicate that more than 50 per cent of the new dwellings in industrial centers were below the $10,000 price bracket although few buyers seem to find them available. However the tables indicate the upward trend.

areas including New York, Boston, Chicago, Philadelphia, Cleveland, San Francisco, and Los Angeles.

TABLE D

Estimated Price Brackets	Per Cent of New Houses
Under $4322	12
$4322–6981	19
$6982–9641	26
$9642–12,301	24
$12,302 and over	19

The postwar trend in incomes and costs presents economic distortions which offer little foundation for conclusions. Whether a balance between incomes and the cost of living should stabilize at a new plateau or return to a lower level, the foregoing data convey some measure of the *relative* nature of the housing problem, although the latter course may accentuate the burden of long-range housing investments incurred during the inflationary period.

The Second-Hand House. It is frequently assumed that *new* housing is not expected to reach all the people; that low-income families should logically accept second-hand dwellings which they can afford. This point of view reflects a policy that the benefits of our society should naturally "filter down" to each successive income level. Opposed to this policy is the theory that our economy thrives to the extent that all economic levels are directly served with new products. The public housing program grows out of the latter policy; it derives from the theory that low-income families should be "siphoned out" of substandard housing by the positive process of providing standard housing within their means.

Past experience brings into focus the distinction between the "filter-down" and the "siphon-out" theories. The "hand-me-down" dwelling is not confined to any particular income level. High-cost as well as low-cost housing is transferred from one owner to another, and rental housing in all brackets is occupied by successive tenants. The weakness of the "filtering down" process is the *accumulation of substandard second-hand housing* which is retained on the market and in use. According to National Housing Agency estimates this accounted for some 7,000,000 urban dwellings in 1940. Exercise of police power to enforce the maintenance of housing standards prescribed by law is confined to an infinitesimal number of obsolete dwellings which have reached the last stages of physical decay, dwellings which may be classified as "unfit for human habitation." This is only a fraction of the number which are substandard when measured either by existing laws or improved planning and construction standards. Effective removal of obsolete housing from the market must consequently result from operation of the normal channels of competitive enterprise. As has been previously discussed, the competition of obsolete housing works in reverse: obsolescence backs up and creates a dam against the production of new housing in the low-cost field. Privileged, as it is, with a system of progressively decreasing taxation and declining attention to maintenance permitted by ineffective police powers, obsolescent dwellings present a form of competition which offers little inducement for active production of new low-cost housing. Undoubtedly this is a major, though obscure, reason why the construction industry has not been more successful in reaching the middle- and low-income housing market. The "filtering-down" process is therefore a deterrent to production and employment in the construction industry, a deterrent which, in periods of low employment, has required the intervention of government through the medium of public works or underpinning the financial structure by such means as insurance of risk provided by the Federal Housing Administration.

A Man's Castle. Home-ownership has always been a cherished ambition of the average American family; "a man's home is his castle," is a well-known phrase in the annals of housing. Stable social values growing from a sense of personal proprietorship in the community are an essential asset claimed for home-ownership. This valid quality warrants encouragement of home-ownership by every sound economic means. The history of home-ownership, however, has not demonstrated convincing evidence that this principle of soundness has prevailed in practice. An unduly wide gap exists between the desirability and the reality of home-ownership.

The industrial age itself has produced certain limitations on home-ownership. Uncertainty of stable employment has made mobility frequently advisable and sometimes necessary. The obligation of ownership often becomes a burden rather than a benefit. The disorganized and handicraft nature of the building "industry" presents a curious contrast with the assembly-line technique of the present industrial system. The complex character of building construction breeds high prices. The cost to borrow money for the purchase of a home on the installment plan has imposed a heavy burden on the average home-owner and is beyond the means of many families.

Since the turn of the century about 40 per cent of all urban dwellings have been owner-occupied. They have ranged from 37 per cent in 1900 to 46 per cent in 1930, dropping to 41 per cent in 1940.[2] Small cities have been favored with a higher percentage of owner-occupied homes than large cities, being about equally divided with rental housing. In large cities the percentage of owner-occupied homes increased from 20 per cent in 1900 to 30 per cent in 1930, dropping to 25 per cent in 1940.

The Financing Chain. Previous reference has been made to the ability of people to pay for shelter. Annual income of a family is one factor that measures that capacity. Another is the capital which a family must have for purchase of a home. The capital an owner invests from his savings is known as his *equity*. He must borrow the balance of the cost of a dwelling. Borrowed capital is obtained from lending institutions by pledging the home as security for repayment of the loan. The instrument by which this pledge is made is known as a *mortgage*. It is apparent that the ability to own a home depends a great deal upon the lending policies prevailing among financial institutions. In the last decade of the nineteenth century the value of the owner's equity in a home was an average of about 78 per cent of the value of the home. Between

[2] *American Housing, Problems and Prospects,* The Twentieth Century Fund, 1944.

1930 and 1934 it was only 47 per cent.[3] In other words it was necessary to have about three-quarters of the cost of a dwelling in order to own a home before the turn of the century; in 1930 less than half the cost was needed in order to receive a loan to finance a home.

During periods of "boom" and their apparent prosperity, when costs are high, it is usual practice for home buyers to finance their dwellings by borrowing as much as possible on a "first" mortgage, this mortgage giving the lender a prior lien upon the property in the event the borrower fails to meet his obligation for repayment. During the prosperous twenties it was the general practice of lending institutions to loan about 60 per cent of the cost of a home. Because of high land and building costs which also prevail in these periods, prospective home-owners having inadequate reserves to pay the balance of 40 per cent of the costs, must find additional financing. The practice of "second" and "third" mortgages came into popular use. Individuals or institutions lending funds on second mortgages have only a secondary call upon the proceeds of a property in the event of foreclosure to recover payment. To compensate for this risk, the interest rate was high, and the time for repayment of the loan was short.

Mortgage practices became so complicated under these various circumstances that ownership of a home generally was more a fiction than a fact. The actual equity an owner had in his dwelling was considerably lower than the records of the first mortgage market indicated. A home-owner seldom enjoyed possession of his home; the legal documents representing the transaction were rather a record of a continuing debt than evidence of *title* to a home.

The terms of a mortgage generally established a fixed obligation for repayment with interest. In times of depression earning power of owners may drop below their capacity to discharge an obligation contracted during periods of prosperity and high costs. Refinancing has been one instrument to meet such conditions. It provides for a modification of a mortgage agreement by extending the time for repayment, or partial repayment to reduce the principal. But this process invariably entails additional costs to the owner for the services of redrawing new legal instruments. The alternative is foreclosure of the mortgage, the lending institution taking possession of the property and selling it to recover the loan. There is usually a period of redemption in most states, during which the owner has the opportunity to pay his debts and recover the property.

Financial Reform. The boom of the twenties saw much home financing via first and second mortgages and at high-cost levels. During the depression years of the thirties ability to meet these obligations decreased materially. Millions of homes were threatened with foreclosure, and about one and one-half million were lost. While the many and diverse Federal agencies created during this period reduced the burdens of home-ownership already contracted, they did not lift these burdens completely.

The Federal Housing Administration instituted the practice of regular amortization

[3] *Ibid.*

of home loans and diminished some of the chaos in home financing by elimination of the second mortgage practice. But the disparity remains between the *fixed* financial obligation and the *variable* ability to discharge it. Dwellings built or purchased in periods of high prices are lost in periods of depression prices, whereas dwellings built or purchased at low economic levels only transfer to others the burden of inflated costs during periods of boom.

Interest rates were reduced by the FHA program. During the twenties interest rates were 8 per cent and above. Under FHA they were reduced to $4\frac{1}{2}$ per cent plus a service charge of $\frac{1}{2}$ per cent. This improved the prospect for home-ownership but extended the period for repayment, thereby continuing the financial obligation for a longer time. These two factors, longer repayment periods and lower interest rates, have broadened the market for home-ownership but have not overcome the uncertain financial burdens in the future.

The decrease in the amount of owner's equity increases the opportunity for apparent ownership among the lower income group. It also increases the risk of the owner's equity being "washed out" in depression periods. This danger is evident in the policies of lending institutions which restrict the amount of loans to about 60 per cent of the dwelling cost. To reduce the required equity it has been necessary for the government to insure mortgages in greater amounts. This insurance under the FHA program guarantees the financial institutions against loss but offers no protection for the owner's equity. That the systematic amortization of debt does not offer a sweeping solution to all our problems of financing is suggested in the following words of Mr. Ernest M. Fisher, as Deputy Manager of the American Bankers Association:

It is commonly supposed that FHA insurance eliminates the risk involved in a mortgage loan. . . . . One of the fundamental tests of the soundness of any home financing program is whether it facilitates the payment of indebtedness. To be sound it must promote the liquidation, not the perpetuation of debt. . . . . To attain debt-free home-ownership is a worthy motive. But it is not easy; and it is an error closely akin to crime to minimize the difficulty. The undue extension of the term of the mortgage may serve to contribute to the delusion that home ownership is easy to attain. It can be demonstrated that little is to be gained by the borrower and much is to be hazarded, by the extension of the term beyond 20 or 25 years. For every penny saved in monthly payments by such an extension, the borrower obligates himself to pay tens of dollars in interest charges. . . . . The smaller the margin of equity the more likely it is to be erased by market fluctuations.[4]

Many Want to Rent. It is generally agreed by most reliable authorities that a larger supply of rental housing is necessary to serve the large proportion of the population whose tenure must remain mobile and who do not care to assume the responsibility of home-ownership, or those persons with incomes or savings inadequate to finance home-ownership. It has already been pointed out that some 60 per cent of the population is in the rental market, yet rental housing constituted only one-third of the dwellings built during 1920–30, reaching a peak of nearly 40 per cent in one year

[4] *Architectural Record*, April 1944.

only; less than one-fifth of all units built during 1930–39; and one-sixth of all units in 1940. Of all rental housing built in 1939, 60 per cent was concentrated in five large cities—New York City, Washington, D.C., Philadelphia, Chicago, and Los Angeles.[5]

Undoubtedly the financing promoted by FHA made home-ownership appear much more feasible than in previous history, and it accounts, in part, for the decline in the rental housing field. There is, nevertheless, an undersupply of dwellings for rent and this forces an increased dependence upon older dwellings to meet the demand. This has tended to widen the gap of social distinction between home-ownership and rental status among the middle-class and low-income groups. Such distinctions lead to the gradual breakdown of communities, having the effect of classifying rental dwellings on a lower plane than owner-occupied. This situation does not prevail in very high rental dwellings since they provide a profitable field for new building. New construction is not prevalent in areas characterized by physical decline and yet these are the areas in which the majority of middle- and low-rent housing is situated. When new developments of rental housing have been undertaken, they have become popular and valuable assets to a community, but so long as the supply of rental housing is completely limited to old buildings stability of a community is extremely uncertain.

How Much Does It Cost? If every family enjoyed a sufficiently high income to afford the cost of good housing, there would hardly be a housing problem. It is outside the scope of this subject to deal with the wide range of conditions affecting family income and the variety of economic issues and theories they present. We should, however, consider the elements which make up the cost of housing.

These costs fall into two main categories: (1) the capital cost and (2) the operating cost. These elements are interrelated but can be treated separately for purposes of definition.

Capital costs include the initial investment in land and its improvements, and the building with its appurtenances.

1. *Land*

The first element is the land upon which the dwelling rests. Many items affect the value and cost of land: (a) the kind and quality of the neighborhood and the location of the property within it; (b) the income groups residing therein; (c) proximity of community facilities, schools, and shopping; (d) zoning laws and building codes, and the protection they afford the neighborhood from encroachment of land uses inimical to the maintenance of a satisfactory living environment. This form of protection sometimes presents curious inconsistencies. The potential for other than residential use may be the cause for an increase in land value rather than stability of land use, but this is an ever-present threat to the stability of a residential environment. The pressure of speculation for modification of land use can be overcome only by the most vigorous insistence of residents that a stable community pattern either be maintained or restored to their neighborhood; (e) the extent and quality of the utility improvements—the kind of pavements and sidewalks, availability of sanitary and storm

[5] *American Housing, Problems and Prospects*, The Twentieth Century Fund, 1944.

sewers, water, electricity, and gas distribution being among these; (f) topography, soil conditions, and natural drainage; (g) availability of urban services, including fire and police protection, building inspection, etc.; (h) property assessment and the tax rate; (i) the fees for appraisal, real estate commissions, title insurance, etc.; (j) the general market conditions aside from speculation in potential change of land use. Periods of prosperity and depression have a major effect upon the price of land, frequently exerting a stronger influence on prices than all other factors combined.

2. Building Construction

This is the largest single item of capital investment in a home. It is the shelter, the floor space, and its arrangement. It includes: (a) labor and materials; (b) utility equipment and services for heating, lighting, cooking, refrigeration, and sanitation; (c) profits of contractors for materials, equipment, and labor; (d) architectural services for the design and supervision of construction; (e) landscaping; (f) market conditions, which, as with land, strongly influence the cost according to the degree of scarcity or abundance. But the greatest element is the chaotic nature of the building enterprise. Mr. Raymond V. Parsons[6] has estimated that a small five-room house in the prewar cost bracket of $5,000 contains more than 80,000 separate parts which must be installed to complete the dwelling, with methods which cling to the age of handcraft operations. The contrast with assembly-line production is apparent.

Operating costs include the periodic charges which continue during the useful life of the dwelling.

1. Financing

The cost of financing a home is a component part of the capital cost enumerated above. However, it is not alone affected by these costs, depending also upon mortgage policies of lending institutions. These factors, which may be completely independent of the capital costs, often mark the difference between the possibility of owning a home and the inability to afford it. The cost of financing is divided into two parts: (a) the charges for repayment of the principal of the loan with interest, and (b) the interest which an owner would be receiving on his equity if this capital were otherwise invested. Modifications in the practice of mortgage policies for home financing, encouraged by the FHA program, have led to the amortization of home loans in regular and systematic payments for a specified period of time. Whereas loans were previously made for short terms and high interest rates, subject to renewal at the option of the lender, the FHA program has induced long-term loans (between 20 and 25 years) at lower interest rates.

2. Maintenance

Repairs for the physical structure of the building and grounds, replacement of the mechanical parts of the dwelling, and redecorating are usually undertaken by the home-owner in a sporadic manner and when the necessity forces him into action. It would be preferable and to his advantage if he were to consider these costs as he does in his business enterprise, by establishing a depreciation fund upon which to draw for these expenses. They vary considerably with the quality of the construction and equipment, and the standard of upkeep the owner chooses to maintain. It is usually estimated that the value of a dwelling will depreciate annually at a rate of 1 per cent or 2 per

[6] *Survey Graphic*, February 1940.

The following tables give the monthly costs for residence loans and estimates of taxes and maintenance which may serve as a guide in evaluating housing costs. The material is based upon the mortgage insurance program of FHA and appeared in the September 1938 issue of the *Architectural Forum* and costs must be adjusted to postwar II in inflation levels.

TABLE A. MONTHLY MORTGAGE COSTS

HOUSE AND LOT	MAXIMUM MORTGAGE	AMORTIZATION PERIOD IN YEARS					
		10	15	17	19	20	25
. . . . . .	$ 1,000	$ 10.59	$ 7.88	$ 7.26	$ 6.77	$ 6.57	$ 5.81
$ 3,000	2,700	28.59	21.28	19.60	18.28	17.74	15.69
3,500	3,100	32.83	24.43	22.51	20.99	20.37	18.01
4,000	3,600	38.12	28.37	26.14	24.37	23.65	20.92
4,200	3,700	39.18	29.16	26.86	25.05	24.31	21.50
4,400	3,900	41.30	30.73	28.31	26.40	25.62	22.66
4,600	4,100	43.42	32.31	29.77	27.76	26.94	23.82
4,800	4,300	45.54	33.88	31.22	29.11	28.25	24.98
5,000	4,500	47.66	35.46	32.67	30.47	29.57	26.15
5,200	4,600	48.71	36.25	33.40	31.14	30.22	26.73
5,400	4,800	50.83	37.82	34.85	32.50	31.54	27.89
5,600	5,000	52.95	39.40	36.30	33.85	32.85	29.05
5,800	5,200	55.07	40.98	37.75	35.20	34.16	30.21
6,000	5,400	57.19	42.55	39.20	36.56	35.48	31.37
$ 6,200	$ 5,500	$ 58.25	$ 43.34	$ 39.93	$ 37.24	$ 36.14	
6,400	5,700	60.36	44.92	41.38	38.59	37.45	
6,600	5,800	61.42	45.70	42.11	39.27	38.11	
6,800	6,000	63.54	47.28	43.56	40.62	39.42	
7,000	6,200	65.66	48.86	45.01	41.97	40.73	
7,200	6,300	66.72	49.64	45.74	42.65	41.39	
7,400	6,500	68.84	51.22	47.19	44.01	42.71	
7,600	6,600	69.89	52.01	47.92	44.68	43.46	
7,800	6,800	72.01	53.58	49.37	46.04	44.68	
8,000	7,000	74.13	55.16	50.82	47.39	45.99	
8,200	7,100	75.19	55.95	51.55	48.07	46.65	
8,400	7,300	77.31	57.52	53.00	49.42	47.96	
8,600	7,400	78.37	58.31	53.72	50.10	48.62	
8,800	7,600	80.48	59.89	55.18	51.45	49.93	
9,000	7,800	82.60	61.46	56.63	52.81	51.25	
9,200	7,900	83.66	62.25	57.35	53.48	51.90	
9,400	8,100	85.78	63.83	58.81	54.84	53.22	
9,600	8,200	86.84	64.62	59.53	55.51	53.87	
9,800	8,400	88.96	66.19	60.98	56.87	55.19	
10,000	8,600	91.07	67.77	62.44	58.22	56.50	
$11,000	$ 8,800	$ 93.19	$ 69.34	$ 63.89	$ 59.58	$ 57.82	
12,000	9,600	101.66	75.65	69.70	64.99	63.07	
13,000	10,400	110.14	81.95	75.50	70.41	68.33	
14,000	11,200	118.61	88.36	81.31	75.82	73.58	
15,000	12,000	127.08	94.56	87.12	81.24	78.84	
16,000	12,800	135.55	100.86	92.93	86.66	84.10	
17,000	13,600	144.02	107.17	98.74	92.08	89.35	
18,000	14,400	152.50	113.47	104.54	97.49	94.61	
19,000	15,200	160.97	119.78	110.35	102.90	99.86	
20,000	16,000	169.44	126.08	116.16	108.32	105.12	

cent of the capital costs (or replacement cost), depending upon the care which has been given it. This is a reasonable allowance for the cost of upkeep.

3. *Taxes*

Taxes are a periodic charge upon real estate. They include the taxes for, and are allocated among, the local political subdivisions and departments for administration, fire and police, schools, sanitary disposal, water, and other urban services. Taxation is one of the largest single items in the regular expenses for maintenance of a dwelling, ranging between 25 per cent and 50 per cent of the periodic financing costs for the capital investment. Whereas there is a tendency for assessed values of property to be reduced as time passes, and thereby reduce the annual tax bill, taxation continues for the duration of the life of the building and is not terminated upon a future date as with the charges for financing of the capital cost.

4. *Insurance*

This includes insurance protection against loss from fire and storm damage, etc.

5. *Utilities*

The costs for cooking and heating, lighting, water, and refrigeration are essential items in the operating costs.

Most authorities consider that the cost of shelter should not exceed one-fifth of the income of a family of moderate means in order to maintain a reasonable balance of the family budget. The cost of shelter, including the utility services, should approximate one-quarter of the income. As a simple illustration, let us assume we wish to build a home which costs $5,000 including the equipment, contractor's profits, architect's fees, and landscaping on a lot which has cost us $1,000, including real estate commissions. Under the FHA program it is necessary that we have 10 per cent of this total cost of $6,000, or $600 in cash, as our equity. The insured mortgage is 90 per cent, or $5,400. Interest on the loan is 4½ per cent, plus ½ per cent service charge for the insurance. Our loan must be repaid, or amortized, in regular monthly installments over a period of 25 years. Table A shows the monthly installments which repay loans of different amounts, with the interest prescribed by FHA.

If we were to invest the $600 equity in some revenue-producing enterprise we would receive an income from it. Assuming such an investment would earn 5 per cent interest, we are obliged to consider this as part of our cost for shelter since we have elected to invest it in our home. We also have expenses for taxes, insurance, maintenance, and utilities. Table B shows the estimated costs for these items. While they vary considerably in various parts of the country and under different conditions, they will serve to illustrate the method of calculating the cost of housing.

A financial statement of the monthly costs for our $6,000 dwelling will appear as follows:

Financing Costs

Interest and amortization on $5,400, being 90% of the cost, for 25 years.. $31.37
Interest on owner's equity, being 5% per year on $600.................. $ 2.50

$33.87

Operating Costs

Taxes, estimated as an average.. $13.98

Insurance..   1.03

Maintenance, estimated at 2% of the capital cost to maintain a satisfactory
standard of upkeep...   8.33

                                                                       ————————
                                                                        $23.34

Total monthly costs (excluding utilities).......................... $57.21

Utilities

Heat, light, cooking fuel, water, refrigeration........................ $10.00
                                                                       ————————
TOTAL MONTHLY COST..................................... $67.21

Applying the "rule of thumb" that the average family budget should not exceed one-fifth of the income for shelter, nor one-fourth of the income for shelter including the cost of utility services, our income should range from $3,200 to $3,400 per year in order to afford the $6,000 dwelling described in the foregoing illustration.

TABLE B. OTHER MONTHLY COSTS

| HOUSE AND LOT | TAXES | | | | HEAT | | MAINTENANCE AND DEPRECIATION | | FIRE INSUR-ANCE |
	Average Low	Average	Average High	Average South	Average	Average North	1%	2%	
$ 3,000	$ 3.51	$ 6.99	$12.24	$1.66	$3.33	$ 5.00	$ 2.08	$ 4.17	$0.53
3,500	4.10	8.16	14.28	1.73	3.44	5.15	2.42	4.83	.61
4,000	4.68	9.32	16.32	1.80	3.55	5.30	2.75	5.50	.69
4,500	5.27	10.49	18.36	1.87	3.66	5.45	3.08	6.17	.78
5,000	5.85	11.65	20.40	1.94	3.77	5.60	3.42	6.83	.86
5,500	6.44	12.82	22.44	2.01	3.88	5.75	3.75	7.50	.95
6,000	7.02	13.98	24.48	2.08	3.99	5.90	4.08	8.17	1.03
6,500	7.61	15.15	26.52	2.15	4.10	6.05	4.42	8.83	1.11
7,000	8.19	16.31	28.56	2.22	4.21	6.20	4.75	9.50	1.20
7,500	8.78	17.48	30.60	2.29	4.32	6.35	5.08	10.17	1.28
8,000	9.36	18.64	32.64	2.36	4.43	6.50	5.42	10.83	1.37
8,500	9.95	19.81	34.68	2.43	4.54	6.65	5.75	11.50	1.45
9,000	10.53	20.97	36.72	2.50	4.65	6.80	6.08	12.17	1.53
9,500	11.12	22.14	38.76	2.57	4.76	6.95	6.42	12.83	1.62
10,000	11.70	23.30	40.80	2.64	4.87	7.10	6.75	13.50	1.70
11,000	12.87	25.63	44.88	2.78	5.09	7.40	7.42	14.83	1.87
12,000	14.04	27.96	48.96	2.92	5.31	7.70	8.08	16.17	2.04
13,000	15.21	30.29	53.04	3.06	5.53	8.00	8.75	17.50	2.21
14,000	16.38	32.62	57.12	3.20	5.75	8.30	9.42	18.83	2.37
15,000	17.55	34.95	61.20	3.34	5.97	8.60	10.08	20.17	2.54
16,000	18.72	37.28	65.28	3.48	6.19	8.90	10.75	21.50	2.71
17,000	19.89	39.61	69.36	3.62	6.41	9.20	11.42	22.83	2.88
18,000	21.06	41.94	73.44	3.76	6.63	9.50	12.08	24.17	3.05
19,000	22.23	44.27	77.52	3.90	6.85	9.80	12.75	25.50	3.21
20,000	23.40	46.60	81.60	4.04	7.07	10.10	13.42	26.83	3.38

Let us now observe the housing costs in a project of dwellings for rent. They are similar, in principle, to the costs of home-ownership but require a more businesslike operation than the average home-owner sees fit to consider. Management of a home is absorbed in the normal domestic duties; in rental dwellings it constitutes a specific item of cost which must be calculated as a part of the rent.

As an illustration, we will assume a development of thirty apartments to be located upon an acre of land. The cost of the land is $20,000, to which we must add the cost of real estate commissions of 5 per cent, or $1,000. In order to reach low rentals we intend to build low-cost dwellings of simple design. Let us assume a construction cost of $3,000 per unit including contractor's profits. The installation of utilities—sewers, water, gas, and electricity—and landscaping are assumed to cost $300 per apartment. The fees for architectural and engineering services are assumed to cost 6 per cent of the building and site improvement costs. Initial capital will be needed to purchase the land and meet the periodic payments for construction during the period prior to completion and occupancy of the project. Interest on this "working capital" is the charge for carrying the development until it is completed and returning revenue in rent. We will assume we require one-half the full estimated cost of the project for one year during the planning and construction period. The interest rate for this working capital is 6 per cent. Administration of the business affairs, clerical work, and overhead during development of the project must also be included in the cost. We will allow an amount of 5 per cent of the total estimated project cost for these expenses.

The estimated capital cost of the proposed development will appear as follows:

Land

One acre at $20,000	$20,000	
Commission at 5%	1,000	
		$21,000

Buildings

Thirty apartments at $3,000	$90,000	
Equipment at $100 per unit	3,000	
Site improvements at $300 per unit	9,000	
Fees at 6% (Buildings and site improvements—$99,000)	5,940	
		$107,940

Carrying Charges

3% for one year on $128,940	$ 3,840

Administration

5% for one year on $128,940	$ 6,400
TOTAL CAPITAL COST	$139,180

The average cost per apartment is $4,637. It is now necessary to estimate the rental we must charge in order to undertake this investment as a business enterprise.

Under the terms of the FHA program it would be possible to obtain an insured loan in the amount of 80 per cent of this estimated cost. We must have the balance of 20 per cent, or $927 per unit, as our equity to invest in the project. On this equity we wish to receive an interest of 6 per cent. The 80 per cent loan of $3,710 per unit will cost 5 per cent interest and must be repaid in 20 years. The regular amortization of this loan in equal payments each year is $301.99, or $25.17 per unit per month. This figure is obtained by consulting an "amortization table" available and in use by financial institutions. These tables are mathematically calculated according to the interest rate and amount of loan to show the equal payments per year which will repay a total obligation within a specified period of years. This cost for financing is sometimes calculated in two parts, one being the interest on the loan, the other as a depreciation fund set aside for the purpose of repaying the loan in installments. The amortization plan for regular predetermined payments is coming into popular use since the advent of FHA.

The tax rate varies in each community, but we will assume it to be 5 per cent of the assessed value, being based upon 50 per cent of the appraised value of the property. This is equivalent to a cost for taxes of $2\frac{1}{2}$ per cent of the full estimated cost of the project, exclusive of the fees, carrying charges and administration. We will also assume that the insurance costs are $5.00 per unit per year.

The above costs are classified as fixed charges; they are continuing costs each year and are independent of the management costs which may vary according to the standards we wish to maintain.

The operating costs include management and maintenance, repairs and replacements, and a reserve for vacancies. These costs vary widely with the methods of management, the size of the development, and the standards of maintenance. It is an example of the essential co-ordination of many talents in the housing field and requires the most careful consultation with qualified experts in property management. This cost has ranged in various rental projects from $100 to $200, and higher, per dwelling per year. For the purpose of illustrating a method rather than the accuracy of the respective items, let us assume a management and maintenance cost for our project of $175 per dwelling per year. We will also calculate the average number of vacancies to be 5 per cent of all units.

The financial statement for the project will appear as follows:

Fixed Charges

Interest and amortization on 80% loan ($3,710 at 8.24%)	$301.99
Interest on 20% equity ($927 at 6%)	55.62
Taxes (2½% of $4,088)	102.20

$459.81

Operating Costs

Management and maintenance ($175 per apartment per year)	$175.00
Insurance at $5.00 per unit.....................................	5.00
Vacancies at 5% (of $639.81)	31.99

$671.80

TOTAL EXPENSE PER APARTMENT PER YEAR..........................	$671.80
TOTAL EXPENSE PER APARTMENT PER MONTH.......................	$ 55.98

In the foregoing financial statement we will observe that an allowance has been made for interest on the owner's equity invested in the development. No other item for "profit" has been included. The estimated rent of $55.98 per unit per month is consequently the minimum revenue which may be charged and provide a "sound" business venture. In the event the rental market warrants a rental in excess of this minimum, the amount of this excess will constitute a profit in addition to the 6 per cent dividend we have included for the equity invested in the project.

Every individual in the city has a home. Some may be rooms in a lodging-house or a hotel, others fine houses on large estates. Some are slums. Whether the home is a hovel or a mansion, every person has one. Dwellings of the people occupy nearly three-quarters of the urban area. The economic equation by which the people acquire and maintain a place to live measures the social and physical health of a community. The economics of housing is the base upon which cities rest. It is the foundation on which the social superstructure is built.

If we want to see the real city, we do not confine our view to the great skyscrapers, the shopping promenade, or the park and boulevard. To see the city, we look at the dwellings of the people. We see how people live, their streets of homes, the environment in which they raise their families, the children who will be the fellow-countrymen and neighbors of our children a generation hence.

It is this view that gives us direction toward the city of the future. When we comprehend this aspect of the city, we can guide more accurately the tools with which we shape the urban environment.

PART IV

THE PLANNING

PROCESS

If we could first know where we are,
and whither we are tending, we could
better judge what to do, and how to
do it.

— *Abraham Lincoln*

CHAPTER **17**

THE LEGAL
FOUNDATION

Until recently public contact with city planning has been limited; even today most people have little knowledge about planning, its practices, its limitations, or its significance to their daily living. First contact usually comes when a building permit is sought and the aspirant is either granted a permit or informed that he may not proceed with the improvement as he desired. If the permit is granted, the relationship of the individual and planning is a fleeting one and his lack of knowledge continues. If, however, the permit is denied, the citizen may inquire the reason. When informed that the *law* denies him that right because it is inconsistent with the welfare of the community, the citizen may depart from the planning office, accepting this interpretation of the law. Or he may have the temerity to ask: What law? How does a community come by the right to restrain him from the free exercise of his will in developing a parcel of property he owns? Is this not the confiscation of private property without due process of law and without just compensation, both of which are violations of the Constitution of the United States?[1] What can be done to circumvent the law? This citizen may also ask: What is the racket?

It is in the interest of the people that they be informed on these questions; they are the foundation of planning in democracy.

When Official Planning Began. The time when land was first allocated to specific uses is, of course, shrouded in prehistoric mystery. The failure of land to respond to cultivation demonstrated that certain land was not adapted to agricultural use but, since there were few ways of passing this information on to others, it was probably necessary for successive users to learn by trial and error what marginal areas were unfit.[2]

[1] Federal Constitution, 14th Amendment, 1868, Section I: "No State shall make or enforce any law which shall abridge the privileges or immunities of citizens of the United States; nor shall any State deprive any person of life, liberty or property without due process of law, nor deny to any person within its jurisdiction the equal protection of the laws."

[2] "Because the ground is chapt, for there was no rain in the earth, the plowmen were ashamed, they covered their heads. Yea, the hind also calved in the field and forsook it, because there was no grass. And the wild

225

Tribal experience indicated that certain land was suitable for raising crops, other land was better for grazing animals, and some was unproductive. When these experiences were transmitted from generation to generation by word of mouth and tribal custom, we had the first haphazard land-use plan. Certainly enforcement was effective; struggle for survival in a not too friendly world left the line between life and death too thin for a man to cultivate land a second time after it had refused to give him food the first time. Thus land was identified as either agricultural or nonagricultural and, if the latter, it had little value. Since there was much land and the people were few in number, man, living a nomadic life, found little need to fight for or limit himself to any single area. In those regions where the land gave bountiful harvest from the seeds planted, the wanderers settled down and formed the first permanent agrarian communities.

The customs of land use in the earliest days defined the planting seasons, the harvesting seasons, the first descriptions of crop rotation, and the idea of resting the land after a number of years of use. The priesthood wielded tremendous persuasive powers, and many codes of land use were incorporated in religious doctrines, some of which are still part of religious observations today.

With the development of civilization, the building of cities, and the growth of population, land took on other values than that attached to agricultural use. The fixed marketplace became a land use of great value, the public open space, the forum, and the commons being the important center of the town. Special places were designated for the storage of explosives, for the slaughter of animals, and for the residential developments of the aristocracy. It did not take rulers long to recognize that the relationship between land uses was of paramount importance, that the slaughterhouses had no proper place on the windward side of their palaces. In our present-day cities we have taken far less care in locating smoke- and dust-producing industries. It is true, of course, that protection of a few homes from obnoxious conditions was a far simpler task than controlling industrial development in relation to the mushrooming residential areas that crowd our urban landscape today, but some application of this principle might have given us a far less objectionable environment in our urban communities.[3]

While the storage of powder in a convenient place was important to the people's defense, it was soon recognized as a menace when stored too near their homes. With these early concepts of danger and discomfiture began the first official designation of areas within which certain uses were segregated as a matter of protection to the people in a community.

In ancient cities people were themselves regulated as to where they might live.

---

asses did stand in high places, they snuffed up the wind like dragons; their eyes did fail, because there was no grass." Jeremiah 14, 4–6.

[3] Decrees of King Philip of Spain, 1573; *Ex parte Shrader*, 33 California 279, 1876: "Habeas Corpus to review judgement of conviction for violating order of the Board of Supervisors of the City and County of San Francisco prohibiting the maintenance of slaughter houses, the keeping of swine, the curing of hides or the carrying on of any business or occupation 'offensive' to the senses or prejudicial to the public health or comfort, in certain portions of the city." The courts held this to be a valid use of the police power.

Workers were restricted to areas outside the fortress walls and were called within when required to protect the interests of rulers. As cities grew in size and power, certain minority groups were restricted to areas commonly called "ghettos." These minority groups differed in various periods and in different parts of the world, but history repeatedly records their plight, their misery, and deprivation. These ghettos were always the overcrowded slums and the center of poverty, and when disease struck the city the people in these areas suffered most. Fear of these plague-ridden spots generated hatred and conflict, and confinement of living quarters was extended to restrictions on the work the inhabitants might perform and the places they might travel. Seldom did such imposed regulations have legal foundation, but since they were enforced by the police and with public sanction they were accepted as equivalent to legal control.

To assume that such conditions are confined to history or remote places would be unrealistic since there remains today considerable regulation over minority groups; the areas in which they live are not called ghettos but they retain many historic characteristics.

The Police Power. Use of the police power to carry out the official aims of a group in power has always been considered proper, but abuse of the power by ruling governments in the past gave rise to actions by the people to curtail that power. Anglo-Saxon and French legal procedures are the outgrowth of the struggle of the people against the autocratic, whimsical, and sometimes frivolous use of powers by the heads of states and nations. The Constitution of the United States and the Bill of Rights were created to guarantee that there would be no punitive action by an individual or government against persons without just cause and with full and open trial in the courts of law.

Today it is a widely accepted principle that the source of all power lies in the hands of the majority of the people. This implies that the people of a city or town, through the governing body, have the right to enact laws and regulations that support their ideas of what is best for their community. The distinction between this principle and the exercise of power in the past, whether by a minority or a majority, is our recognition that regulations of law today apply to all the people, and no class is expected to be immune. The principal restraint upon law is that it shall not contradict the Constitution of the United States or the constitution of the state in which it is enacted.

The power to pass laws to protect the welfare of all the people, whether they be enacted at a local or a national level, is called the exercise of the police power.[4] Enforcement of the legislation enacted by the people or their representatives generally rests with the police department, which apprehends persons accused of law violation.

[4] Police power was expressed in ancient law as: "Due regulation of domestic order of the kingdom where members of the state, like a family, are bound to conform their behavior in good propriety . . . to be good members and an orderly part of the community"; and later: "Police Power . . . is the name given to the inherent sovereignty which is the right and duty to exercise when the public policy demands enforcement of such regulations for the general welfare as are necessary for the regulation of economic conditions to provide for adequate community life." *Parker* v. *Otis*, 130 California 322.

The police department is required to explain the charges preferred and turn the accused over to the courts for a decision on innocence or guilt and the terms of punishment prescribed by the law. The United States Constitution assures that the punishment meted out shall not be cruel and unusual, or arbitrary.

It is necessary that the police power be exercised for a worthy purpose and with definitely stated objectives. In cases where police power is used to deny the use of property without compensation, it must be clearly shown that the continued use of that property would be inimical to the best interests of the community. A house that is structurally unsound or badly infested with rats may be dangerous to the public in general as well as the persons living in it, and it is thus subject to being closed under the police power without compensation to the owner. The equity for such actions rests upon the assumption that the people are obliged to maintain their property at standards which will not impose a nuisance upon the community and the necessity to exercise the police power to abate such a nuisance does not warrant compensation to the owners of the affected property.

Taking land for a public purpose when the owner does not want to sell is known as exercise of *eminent domain*. Condemnation of the property is instituted in the courts which then establish a fair price based upon testimony from witnesses representing the owner, the community, and impartial appraisers. Use of the right of eminent domain is not to be confused with use of the police power: the principal difference between the two powers lies in the matter of compensation to the owner; under the police power the state does not "take" the property from its owner—it denies the owner the right of use because of conditions of the property which are contrary to the public welfare.

The police power of a community is limited to the area within its political boundaries. Thus the state laws may be enforced within any part of the state unless otherwise provided in the laws, the county laws only within the county, and city or township laws only within their limits.

The police power was retained by the sovereign states at the time of formation of the Federal government. Only when the national welfare is involved and when the local government is unable to cope with a situation does the state deem it necessary to call for assistance from the Federal government. Federal laws, however, do affect the relationships between the states; we have an Interstate Commerce Commission to regulate rates on railroads dealing in interstate commerce, and the national labor laws regulate wages and hours of persons employed in industries which sell their products through interstate commerce. These instances are uses of the police power by the Federal government.

Some states give the police power to cities and counties by specific legislative acts; others grant this right to communities in their state constitutions.[5] The purpose of the police power is to protect the health, safety, and general welfare of its citizens, but the manner in which the power is granted differs in the various states. The power to

[5] Article II, Section II, Constitution of the State of California.

make laws and regulations dealing with the activities of the citizens of a community
and the property they possess is a key to the planning process and particularly to that
phase called zoning.

Zoning—The First Step. The first steps in the direction of modern city planning
can be traced to practices of establishing districts within which certain rights of citizens were legally curbed. King Philip of Spain,[6] in outlining the procedure for establishing communities in the New World, instructed his explorers that streets were to
be oriented in such a manner as not to be windswept, and that slaughtering places
for cattle were to be located on the outskirts of town so odors would not prove offensive to the townspeople. In Boston the segregation of the storage place for gunpowder
from the center of the city was one of America's first recorded acts of zoning. In
1810 certain Napoleonic decrees and the Prussian codes of 1845 contained land-use
regulations.

Most early laws were concerned only with those uses considered a menace to life
itself, and regulations against most of these uses were based on presentation of evidence in court that the uses were existing and had proven themselves dangerous. This
proof was possible, in most instances, only after some great loss of life directly trace-
able to the specific use. In most cases, such as the tenement house fire disasters in
New York City, continued construction of the dangerous buildings was prohibited
but little was done to eliminate the danger that hung over the thousands of people who
continued to live in "outlawed" fire-traps. It was considered a critical point in all
zoning law that the establishment of dangerous uses could be prevented, but that such
laws could not be retroactive. Uses not conforming with the law could not be eliminated
unless each was proved in a court of law to be in such a condition that its continuance
would be a menace to the people as a whole. It was construed by the courts that zoning
investment in land and improvements thereon, when incurred in accordance with prevailing law or in the absence of legal regulation, deserved protection even though
subsequent regulations clearly indicated them to be inappropriate.[7]

Legal action on zoning affairs passed through two stages of development before
it arrived at the place it enjoys today. The first stage included a group of court cases
which actually preceded zoning and served to establish the base for zoning law and
gained its recognition as a legal use of the police power. These cases dealt with
"nuisance uses" which the courts treated as separate and individual matters, the court
deciding in each specific case whether a use was detrimental to the health, safety, and
public welfare. As time passed, the courts required more evidence as a base for reference, evidence "indicating the character of a community," before it was willing to rule
upon the validity of a use. This call by the courts for a comprehensive city plan is
now answered in the Master Plan of land use.[8]

[6] Law of the Indies, King Philip of Spain, 1573.

[7] *In re Kelso*, 147 California 609, 1905. Ordinance prohibiting the quarrying within certain areas of the city
of San Francisco. Held invalid as being arbitrary and unwarranted interference with rights of private property.
Mode of quarrying may be regulated to prevent nuisance, but absolute prohibition of right to take rock is invalid
use of the police power; also *Miller* v. *Board of Public Works*, 195 California 477, 1925.

[8] *Oklahoma in re Dawson*, 136 Oklahoma 277; 277 Pacific 266: "If no effort is made to continue zoning, then
comprehensiveness of zoning could be reasonably challenged."

In California[9] an ordinance which prohibited a slaughter house, hog storage, and hide curing in certain districts of the city was upheld in the courts. In Los Angeles,[10] in 1895, an ordinance which prohibited the operation of a steam shoddying plant within 100 feet of a church was upheld; in this latter case the court passed not only upon the nature of the specific use but upon the relationship between uses.

The legality of the establishment of fire districts has been upheld in most courts, the structural nature of buildings and their relation to space being admitted as an important factor in determining the uses permitted within a structure. In San Francisco, because of the great number of wooden buildings with party walls, certain districts were established by ordinance within which hand laundries were prohibited; wood fires were burned in the stoves upon which the laundry was boiled and several serious fires resulted. This ordinance was taken to the state Supreme Court[11] and was held unconstitutional and invalid because it was a breach of the 14th Amendment of the Constitution of the United States to empower a man or group of men at his or their absolute and unrestrained discretion to give or withhold permission to carry on a lawful business in any place. It was pointed out that the washing of clothes was not opposed to good public morals nor was it subversive of public decency, but the court cited the fact that all but one of the non-Oriental applicants were issued permits in a similar business in like areas and were permitted to continue in business whereas the petitioner and two hundred others of his race were denied permits. The court held that the ordinance was not unreasonable since it did not tend to regulate business, but that its application was arbitrary class legislation discriminating against one group in favor of another. It thus violated the 14th Amendment of the United States Constitution, and the ordinance was declared to be invalid. The fair administration of a law is integral with the provisions of the law in the eyes of the courts.

One of the earliest decisions in this country upholding an ordinance in the nature of a zoning regulation was made by the courts in 1920.[12] In sustaining a town plan before it, the court stated: "It betters the health and the safety of the community; it betters the transportation facilities; and it adds to the appearance and the wholesomeness of the place, and as a consequence it reacts upon the moral and spiritual power of the people who live under such surroundings."

Changing Interpretation of the Law. The series of laws which establish the right to plan and enforce plans is like a chain linking all the powers of government with the needs and desires of the people. As in all other legal procedures in a democracy, there is always available to individuals and groups of people the final recourse to the courts for determination of the reasonableness of a law or the fairness with which it has been applied.

Some very significant changes have taken place in the interpretation by the courts of laws regulating the use of property. The growth of communities into large cities

[9] *Ex parte Shrader*, San Francisco, 1867.
[10] *Ex parte Lacey*, 108 California 326.
[11] *Yick Wo* v. *Hopkins*, 118 U. S. 356, 1885.
[12] *Windsor* v. *Whitney*, 95 Connecticut 357, 363.

has necessitated more detailed and involved legislation governing self-discipline in human relations. What may have passed unnoticed in a small community may be viewed as dangerous in cities. Thus the keeping of pigs, horses, and chickens would be considered as an accepted right in a farm town, but would be looked upon with horror on Manhattan Island. What may be tolerated in a small community as a necessary nuisance is contested and actively combated in a metropolis. The maintenance of open privies in backyards may be accepted practice in nonurban areas with no funds for sewage disposal, whereas the same condition in any large city would have the entire population declaring it a menace to the health and life of all the people.

There has been in the eyes of the court a necessity for recognizing the problems created by the concentration of people in our cities. The dangers of disease, crime, delinquency, fire, and injury from traffic are rapidly multiplied as the housing, commerce, and industry of the large city absorb the open space which formerly insulated people against these dangers. Thus there came into being the concept that people have the right to protect themselves against these and other hazards by planning an environment which will meet the requirements of urban living. Where we would have relied in the past upon the police power to prohibit acts which the courts determined to be a violation of a law, today we enact laws which tend to discourage in advance those acts which can be prevented.

Our philosophy of urban conduct is no longer confined to the public health, safety, and general welfare but has extended to the use of the police power for the maintenance of such matters as "public convenience and comfort." The Supreme Court of the United States has said:[13] "The police power of a state embraces regulations designed to promote the public convenience or the general prosperity as well as regulations designed to promote the public health, the public morals, or the public safety." Traffic laws which prohibit parking on certain streets are justified on the grounds that they make access to important areas a matter of greater convenience as well as assure the safety of people. Laws which prohibit dangerous or obnoxious uses from residential areas are considered to protect property values from depreciation and, in this manner, protect the general prosperity.

Some efforts have been made to incorporate in zoning laws such matters as architectural control, seeking thus to protect the esthetic feeling of people, but the courts have not yet given much comfort to the prospect for wide acceptance of the enforcement of this device through the police power.[14] Restrictive covenants to enforce discrimination against minority groups by race restrictive provisions in zoning ordinances were declared unconstitutional by the United States Supreme Court in 1927.[15]

[13] *Chicago B. & Q. Ry. Co.* v. *Drainage Commissioners*, 200 U. S. 561, 592.
[14] *Soho Park and Land Co.*, 142 Atlantic 548.
[15] *Buchanan* v. *Worley*, Louisville, Kentucky, 245 U. S. 60; 62 Law Edition, 149. Ordinance regulated occupancy of blocks of city; colored people could not occupy buildings in blocks where greater number of dwellings were occupied by whites and vice versa.
The United States Supreme Court, *38 Supreme Ct. Report, 16,* ruled this ordinance unconstitutional because it forbade the sale of property to a person because of his color . . . this was not a proper use of the police power, even though the City of Louisville claimed that mixing of the races (colors, *Ed. comment*) would create riots. This use of the police power was a violation of the 14th Amendment of the Federal Constitution, for it prevented the use of property and deprived its owner of use without due process of law.

The Public Welfare. The courts were called upon to rule on some mighty problems in the early days of zoning. What was the public welfare? When was public health or life endangered? What was an obnoxious use? At what point is the establishment of a district reasonable and at what point does it become arbitrary? Was it proper for the court to substitute its judgment for that of the legislative body on matters of the "substance" of a zoning ordinance? When can a community permit a use in one area and deny it in another?

A series of court decisions records the differences of opinion held within the courts themselves, but filtering through them all are decisions accepted today as a sound precedent for interpretation of the community's right to establish zoning districts and regulate the use of property. The Hadacheck case[16] in Los Angeles, 1913, cites one of the basic considerations in all zoning law. Although it preceded recognized zoning statutes, it dealt with the violation of a city ordinance prohibiting the maintenance of brickyards and kilns within a designated residential district of some three square miles. The court ruled that this use of property must cease and desist since the smoke, dust, and fumes emanating from the plant were damaging to the health of the people living near by. In this case the brickyard was located and operating in the area before it was occupied by residences, but the court did not consider the property right claimed by the owner to be as important as the health and welfare of the people. The claim of discrimination was raised by the owner since brickyards and kilns were permitted in other areas near residential developments, but it was disallowed on the grounds that "it is no objection to the validity of the ordinance that in other districts similarly situated brick kilns are not prohibited. It is for the council to say whether the prohibition should be extended to such other districts."

In another case[17] the city of South Pasadena attempted to restrict the operation of a rock-crusher in a high-class residential district. This district was then sparsely developed, whereas similar operations were permitted in other and more heavily populated residential districts. The ordinance was declared unreasonable and void. It was ruled unreasonable to prohibit such use in a sparsely settled district when the same use was permitted in a densely populated district. The court made much of the fact that the poorer class of homes surrounding the industrial district are entitled to the same protection as the fine homes. The courts held in the Throop case, and in others dealing with the mining of natural resources, that these minerals must be extracted where they are found, and if this use is denied there would be no material for construction.

Recently a new controversy has gone to the courts; it deals with the relative value of natural resources. In the Roscoe area within the limits of Los Angeles rock has been quarried for many years and each pit has been abandoned when the supply became exhausted; the area of mining is then extended to a new site for extraction. In this same area, because of the excellent climatic conditions, great numbers of

[16] *Ex parte Hadacheck,* 165 California 416, 1913; *Hadacheck* v. *Sebastian,* 2390 Supreme Court, 394; 60 Law Edition, 348.
[17] *Matter of Throop,* 169 California 93 (1915).

health-seeking individuals have established their homes. The expansion of rock-quarrying has, it is contended, undermined the value of the climatic resource to the point that the lives of the people are jeopardized. The residents point out that the air is filled with dust particles, that the unfenced and abandoned pits are dangerous, and that children have been killed and injured. The Planning Commission of the community upheld the contention of the residents, whereas the City Council reversed this stand. The lower courts have upheld the legislative body, refusing to substitute its judgment for that of the council on matters of "substance."

The interpretation of the general welfare clause is fundamental to all zoning, and planning rests upon the thesis that regulation of property use will secure to the community numerous benefits. Among others it will lessen congestion on streets, secure greater safety from fire, panic, and similar dangers, promote health by requiring adequate light and air, prevent overcrowding of the land, avoid undue concentrations of population, facilitate the provision of adequate transportation, water supply, sewage disposal and other basic necessities such as schools, parks, playgrounds, and civic and cultural amenities. The preservation and stabilization of property values are also important to both individual and community; the more these values are conserved, the greater will be the city's income from taxation, and the lower will be the tax rate to supply the required services. Blight, obsolescence, and slums are discouraged, the city retains a good "character and appearance," and improvement in the physical and moral fiber of the community reduces the need for, and cost of, many social services.

Maintenance of the "general welfare and prosperity" as a reason for imposing race restrictions by means of zoning was termed an illegal use of the police powers by the U. S. Supreme Court. The property owners sought to prove that the intrusion of "nonwhite" families into a "white" district caused a loss of property values and thus endangered the prosperity of the community. The court held that the agencies of government could not be used to enforce a law which specifically violated the 14th Amendment of the Constitution. The courts in many other cases have ruled that financial gains or losses are not, in themselves, sufficient to decide the validity or constitutionality of a law.[18]

Tests of the community's right to prescribe the manner of development within its boundaries "spread-eagled" the courts during the 1920's. In these early days decisions were more likely to support the individual against the community welfare, the courts being reluctant to take action which would infringe upon property rights. Inexperience in the framing of zoning laws was reflected in some phrasing which suggested discrimination to the courts. The courts hammered at a thesis which has become a cornerstone of zoning: to be valid the law must be reasonable and fairly applied.

As zoning received wider acceptance as a proper use of the police power, a variety of features were incorporated in the ordinances. There were efforts to use the law

---

[18] *Smith* v. *Collison*, 119 California Appellate 180, 1931. Depreciation in value of property is not fatal to the validity of the ordinance.

as a device to protect the property of the few while permitting the remainder of the city to continue unprotected. Occasionally, in concert with the land speculator, property was zoned for a use which would bring the highest price at the moment; whether the use was commercial, residential, or industrial was of little concern. A weird pattern of "spot" zoning covered the land like a crazy quilt. Purchasers of vacant land were informed they could use the land for any purpose they willed, and their neighbors were helpless to protect their investments. Efforts of public officials to maintain conformance with the "character" of a neighborhood when called upon to issue building permits were hotly contested. "Interim Ordinances" were sometimes enacted to forbid encroachments upon "fine" residential districts and, although some of these were sustained, the courts generally found them invalid because of the arbitrary nature of their boundaries; the courts viewed the guarantee of a special area from detrimental uses as a discriminatory act since the same encroachments were permitted unchecked elsewhere.

In all these decisions the courts were actually leading the way toward the planning of cities; the courts were appealing for a "comprehensive plan" which would provide a foundation for zoning acts and decisions of equity in the shaping and administration of these acts.

Zoning and Community Character. One of the most important legal decisions in the history of zoning was the Euclid case[19] in 1926. In his decision, Justice Sutherland of the United States Supreme Court pointed out that each community had the right and the responsibility to determine its own character, and, as long as that determination did not disturb the orderly growth of the region or the nation, it was a valid use of the police power. Justice Sutherland stated:

Point is raised by the appellees that the Village of Euclid was a mere suburb of Cleveland, and that the industrial development of the latter had extended to the village, and that in the obvious course of things would soon absorb the entire area for industrial enterprise, and that the effect of the ordinance was to divert such natural development or expansion elsewhere, to the consequent loss of increased values to the owners of land within the village. But this village, though physically a suburb of Cleveland, is a separate municipality, with powers of its own and authority to govern itself as it sees fit within the organic laws of its creation and the state and federal constitutions. The will of its people determines, not that industrial development shall cease at its boundaries, but that such development shall proceed between fixed lines. If therefore it is proper exercise of the police power to regulate industrial establishments to localities separated from residential sections, it is not easy to find sufficient reason for denying the power because its effect would be to divert an industrial flow from a course which would result in injury to their residential public to another course where such injury would be obviated. This should not exclude the possibility of cases where the general interest so far outweighs the interest of the municipality, that the latter should not be allowed to stand in its way.

This decision made it abundantly clear that a community may determine the nature of development within its boundaries; it may plan and regulate the use of land as the people of the community may consider it to be in the public interest. Justice Sutherland also enunciated another principle: a community is obliged to relate its plans

[19] *Village of Euclid, Ohio* v. *Ambler Realty Company*, 272 U. S. 365 (1926).

to the area outside its boundaries. Again the courts anticipate the planning process. Cities are not surrounded by walls, they are each a part of their region and each is obliged to plan the spaces within its boundaries as an integral part of the plan for spaces outside its boundaries. This suggests, for instance, that a highway plan prepared without consideration for the routes of major importance within the regional plan would constitute an improper use of the police power. A community has both the right to determine its character and the obligation to relate its plan to its regional environs.

Enabling Legislation for Planning. The grant of police power by the states to the cities and counties vests these political subdivisions with the power to regulate their affairs and enforce the regulations. It is nevertheless found necessary on occasion for the state to enact legislation for the specific use of that power and such legislation is generally termed "enabling acts." Its purpose may be twofold. It may be for the purpose of affirming the state policy in matters of vital interest to the people at any given time and thereby encourage local communities to act, or the special legislation may be for the purpose of removing doubt that the police power was intended for the specific subject of the act. Such enabling acts are drawn to establish clearly the relation between the use for which the police power is granted and the public health, safety, convenience, and general welfare, and the preamble states in detail the purposes of the legislation.

Zoning enabling acts are sometimes passed by the state even though cities and counties have been previously delegated the police power but are reluctant to exercise it until the state has specifically signified that it be so used. These special enabling acts are usually written in greater detail than the general grant of the police power. In the case of zoning they define the scope of zoning, the procedure for adoption of the ordinance, the composition of the zoning board and its powers and functions, the methods for modification or exceptions to the ordinance.

State Planning Acts are a form of special enabling legislation, although they generally establish a state agency to co-ordinate planning functions at the state level in addition to the specification for local planning activities. Such acts describe the functions of a state planning board and prescribe the process for each city and county to accomplish a complete planning job for itself. These laws usually call for the preparation of a Master Plan, list the scope of the Master Plan, and specify the methods for its adoption and enforcement. Power is sometimes given to the local planning commission to levy a tax upon the general public for funds to administer the law, but this power is seldom invoked; planning commissions prefer to work within the departmental family of the city government and draw their support from the general tax funds.

Another form of enabling legislation is that which creates new agencies in the state, cities, or counties to cope with problems of a particular nature. Housing and urban redevelopment acts are of this type, local agencies being created with powers conferred upon the city or county to engage in the program prescribed in the state statute.

Just as specific enabling legislation is created at the state level to cover certain fields of urban activity, so special ordinances are drawn at the local level to define in detail the manner in which city charter provisions are to be executed. In cities where there is no "freeholders' charter"[20] the state laws are in effect, whereas in cities having charters which define the exercise of the police power in stricter terms than the state, the local law takes precedence.[21] Thus, if a state speed limit in a school zone is 20 miles per hour and the city law restricts the speed to 15 miles per hour, the city law is enforceable. If, on the other hand, the city has a limit of 25 miles per hour or no regulation at all for those specific areas, the state law is then enforceable. City charters often define in terms almost identical to the state enabling legislation the functions of a planning commission, and as long as all the duties included in the state law are included in terms not less restrictive, the city charter provisions apply.

Too frequently there is no provision for a penalty for failure to abide by the requirements of state legislation. An example would be the case in which states call for all counties to have planning commissions[22] and many small counties ignore the requirement. Since there are few ways to compel the local government to conform, great resources are sometimes dissipated without control. In some states the local governments are restricted from the benefits of funds appropriated by the state for public improvements until they conform with state laws. There are occasions when funds for the state highway system are withheld until the counties adopt Master Plans of highways which show the relationship between the state routes and local roads.

Transition. Since the inception of action against the use of property deemed a menace to health and life of neighbors, zoning has passed from the stage of regulating land uses for the preservation of property values to the present position of accepting responsibility, not only for protection of the *status quo,* but for the creation of a better city, better state, and more prosperous nation. It is true that, as zoning becomes a more effective instrument for improvement of the good city, it becomes less like the traditional instrument called "zoning" and more like the act of planning the city, for many other factors than those usually identified with zoning enter the scene.

Recently zoning has become a means for both conservation and planning; the narrow concept of zoning is extended to the broadest interpretation of the use of the police power for the protection of the public welfare. In these instances zoning law anticipates the future and guides the development of areas through planned uses rather than waiting until the die is cast and merely fixing land uses that already exist. In the cut-over areas of Michigan, Wisconsin, and Minnesota, where erosion threatened to rip the growing heart out of the soil and create "dust-bowl" conditions, steps have been taken legally to label as submarginal the worst of the land. In this way use of rural land was discouraged until such time as the top-soil can be replaced and refertilized. Further "mining" of trees in the areas not entirely destroyed was

---

[20] An act of municipal incorporation, provided for in the constitutions of the individual states.
[21] *Brougher* v. *Board of Public Works,* 205 California 426, 1928. A charter city need not follow the procedures of the State Zoning Enabling Act.
[22] State Conservation and Planning Act, California, 1947.

forbidden and a reforestation program, under the guidance and with the assistance of the Federal government, now assures the people of a continuing supply of lumber for future generations. Thus the priceless possession of fertile land will not be wantonly wasted.

J. H. Bradley, in his *Autobiography of Earth*, has stated: "The fabric of human life has been woven on earthen looms." We must use every device in our legal system to protect our land and devote it to its highest and best uses for we cannot escape to new frontiers after abusing and ruining what we have. Almost two centuries ago George Washington observed: "Our lands . . . were originally very good; but use and abuse have made them quite otherwise. . . . We ruin the lands that are already cleared, and either cut down more wood, if we have it, or emigrate into Western country."[23] The use of the police power—zoning—to insure our future seems neither arbitrary nor in contradiction of any freedom assured to the people by the Constitution.

An attempt to preserve a large and important agricultural district from premature subdivision into small urban lots is embodied in the recent zoning ordinance for Los Angeles.[24] Agricultural zones are established within which the land may be subdivided in parcels of not less than 5 acres. Had this extension of the police power been exercised twenty-five years ago, mutilation of this area of beautiful orange groves would not have taken the toll it represents in many parts today. Over much of the 212 square miles of the San Fernando Valley, now covered in part by this agricultural zone, the land was subdivided into small lots. Prematurely developed, the paved streets, curbs, and gutters are overgrown with grass and weeds; land was removed from circulation and no longer contributed to the support of the people. It stands as a monument to enterprise without vision, named "land speculation." The use of police power to restrain this reckless wasting of resources seems to be clearly within the legal right of a community.

Through the instrument of planning supported by the decisions of the courts, the city can determine in advance a rational pattern of land use to which the people may aspire with a reasonable prospect of reaching their goal. In setting their objectives, the experience from past errors could aid in avoiding the same pitfalls. Some profit might be gleaned from the San Fernando Valley example; there the city fathers have viewed the zoning as hardly more than postponement of an inevitable further subdivision. With some vision and more courage, some agricultural zones might become permanent reservations of open space—the open space so essential to a restoration of decent living in our urban environment. This suggests shades of Ebenezer Howard's garden city but, in contrast, this form of zoning could be classified generally as delayed-action rather than a plan.

The Planning Commission. The planning commission is the legal agency of the city through which most public planning is performed. In many cities the official family is few in number and the planning commission may have no staff, the city

[23] To Hold This Soil, Publication No. 321, U. S. Department of Agriculture, 1938 (U. S. Government Printing Office, Washington, D.C.).

[24] Comprehensive Zoning Plan, City of Los Angeles Ordinance No. 90,500 (1948).

engineer or clerk being largely responsible for the preparation of all plans; larger cities, however, usually have well-staffed organizations of qualified personnel.

The commission is a group of private citizens appointed by the mayor and approved by the city council. These commissioners are leaders in local enterprises, real estate, banking, chamber of commerce, or attorneys, architects, doctors, labor representatives, and social workers. It might be assumed that some commissioners, by the nature of their background and personal interests, would be devoted to preservation of property values rather than the general community welfare. Although it cannot be denied that such has been the case in some instances, it is not infrequently found that men with experience in the private business of city building are well qualified to serve the public interest and respond accordingly when given positions of genuine public responsibility.

New commissioners are not always adequately informed about the planning process, its purposes or objectives, and they may require some time for training and familiarity with the nature of their responsibility. Some cities appoint *ex officio* members to the board of the planning commission to assist the commissioners in their tasks. These members may be the heads of various departments of the local government, the city engineer, the road commissioner, the county surveyor, city attorney, the public works officer, health officer, or members of the legislative body. They advise the commission on matters in which they have special knowledge, but they seldom enjoy the privilege of voting upon the proceedings before the commission.

Exclusive of *ex officio* members, the commission varies between five and nine in number according to the provisions of local charter regulations or the state legislation which creates the planning commission; the civic interest and qualifications of the members are more important than the numerical quantity. Frequency of commission meetings depends upon the extent of the planning program which, in some large cities, is sufficiently active to warrant the establishment of a separate commission to administer the zoning ordinance.

The planning commission usually serves in an advisory capacity to the legislative body, the council and the mayor referring matters of planning to the commission for reports and recommendations which the legislative body may accept or reject. As a rule the preparation of the Master Plan and other plans for civic development are specified in the enabling legislation which creates the commission, and in such activities the commission requires no specific instructions from the legislative body although these functions require legislative appropriation of funds for an adequate staff and, unless the council is sympathetic to the planning program, it can effectively delay the commission's performance.

Being an advisory rather than an executive agency of the local government, the planning commission recommends plans to the legislative body after it has held public hearings to ascertain the response and opinions of citizen groups.[25] When a plan is

---

[25] The State Planning Act, in California, requires both the Planning Commission and the Legislative Body to hold public hearings. However each body may act as it sees fit, regardless of the expressed public sentiment or prejudice.

adopted by the legislative body, it becomes a law which governs the actions of all the people in the community including local governmental agencies. Consequently, all city departments are required to refer their plans for specific improvements to the planning commission for review and approval. The service performed in the general public interest by this co-ordination avoids duplication of services and cross-purposes which can readily occur in the wide range of urban activities.

Matters which generally fall within the legal responsibility of planning commissions are the Master Plan, zoning ordinances and subdivision codes, but the co-ordinating functions are becoming a more important service as the city grows. While the planning commission administers the zoning ordinance in most small cities, some large cities have a separate zoning administrator and board of appeals. This board is respon sible for interpretation of the zoning law and such variances from the ordinance as unforeseen conditions may warrant. The planning commission prepares the ordinance, and the zoning administrator, or local building and safety department enforces it.

Relief from the requirements of the planning policies established by law is provided every citizen if the law deprives him of property without just compensation or if it is applied in a discriminatory manner. This relief may be obtained by appeal to the planning commission and the legislative body. In the event that these appeals fail to bring a satisfactory resolution of the case, it may be referred to the courts for decision. It is from such cases that the great fund of judicial opinions on the planning process have emerged.

CHAPTER 18

THE MASTER PLAN

A Comprehensive Plan Is Needed. After the early adventures in zoning property for specific uses it became increasingly apparent that this use of the police
power to safeguard the public welfare could not stand by itself. The courts had upheld
the right of a community to exercise the police power in legislating regulations governing the use of land. They had granted that a community has the right to determine
its own character. Great conservative minds like Justice Sutherland had supported this
right of the citizens, and there was a growing popular acceptance of zoning as a means
to protect the interests of a community.

But the courts perceived the necessity for a community to appraise the use of all
land within its political jurisdiction and give consideration to conditions in areas contiguous to it in order to determine properly the appropriate uses and provide a firm
basis for the control of land use prescribed in zoning ordinances. The courts had found
good reason for this view.

They had observed numerous abuses of the police power to establish arbitrary and
discriminatory districts. In addition to the abuses previously described, there was a
tendency to establish many small districts as a means to restrain the construction of
some particular improvement or deny a use deemed undesirable in some existing
structure. There are also cases in which a zoning ordinance was intended to create or
protect a monopoly. This was illustrated in the small community of Atherton, California. With an area of 2,500 acres and 1,000 population, the entire community was
zoned for residential use with the exception of 1.1 acres which was improved with
existing business and remained unrestricted. The court held the ordinance to be unreasonable since the town council, through its act of zoning, offered no evidence that the
area was adequate to provide the needs of the community and allow for future population growth.[1] It was therefore construed that the ordinance conferred special rights
by establishing a monopoly for existing enterprise.

In order for the courts to have assurance that zoning districts were not arbitrarily

[1] *In re White*, 195 California 516 (1925).

determined, they required evidence that the various districts were related to an over-all evaluation of land use in the city. There was a growing insistence upon a "comprehensive plan" for land use to form a foundation for zoning ordinances, and the opinion of Justice Sutherland in the Euclid case clearly expressed the need for this evidence. In the fulfillment of this need the process of the Master Plan was evolved.

Seeking techniques with which to satisfy the requirement for a *comprehensive plan*, some communities willfully avoided the issue by employing specious devices. One of these was the zoning of all land in a community to the least restrictive use with the exception of certain limited "refined" districts. A community could thus allege in court that it had enacted a comprehensive zoning ordinance since every parcel of land in the city was within a zoning district. Although the statement was true, it was not a plan. The other technique was to zone all land not specifically zoned for other purposes, as a residential district with the provision for variances from the residential use; in the administration of the ordinance each variation was then interpreted as an act of making more "precise" the original plan. Neither of these techniques could have stood the test for long since they were evasions of the basic principles of planning.

Too frequently zoning practices resolved themselves into a process of "freezing" the existing land uses including all the misuses which had previously established themselves. In some communities, an inventory and classification of all existing land uses were adopted as the "Plan" of the city. Travesties on planning, these practices are gradually being replaced by a more enlightened concept of planning and its advantages to civic growth and development. As a means to provide a pattern for future development of the city, the Master Plan has become a generally accepted instrument.[2]

Inventory of the Physical Structure. Before any plan can be made, the physical structure of the community must be known and understood—its rivers, its mountains, its plains, and prairies, its hills, its climate, the direction of its winds. Is the land suited for agriculture, is it good for grazing? Are there oil or mineral deposits, is it subject to floods, are there natural or historic features to be preserved? The geology, hydrography, meteorology, and geography must be rediscovered beneath the blanket of the built-up city. Thus we can comprehend the three primary elements of nature without which there is no life; land, water, and air.

The constant relationship of land, water, and air is necessary to the support of human life. One can imagine controlled air conditions, and we know that water can be transported from distant mountain sources to semi-arid regions, but the land is where you find it. Perhaps it can be built up, the marshes drained, fertility improved, and water can increase its growing yield, but land itself must have the basic capacity for response to man's treatment and we classify it as good or bad according to its fitness to provide life for mankind.

Because a parcel of land may be suitable for a variety of uses, it is the relationship between these uses which becomes the problem of planning. Some uses are favorable

[2] *The Master Plan*, Edward M. Bassett, Russell Sage Foundation.

to each other, whereas some are not only detrimental but dangerous. Recognizing that land may have many uses and that the relationship between them is the most important consideration, the plan begins with a definition of land uses and the appropriate location within the topographic, geologic, and geographic structure of the city. Upon these the city pattern should be developed.

Inventory and Classification of Land Use. Regardless of the high aspirations a people may share for the future of their city or the distant range over which they prepare their plans for its development, the planning process must obviously begin with the city as it exists. It is consequently necessary to know the way in which the land is used and maintain the inventory as a current record. From this inventory the physical characteristics of the city are discernible, those which warrant change or necessitate retention in the Master Plan may be determined, and some existing uses may become key controls over the pattern of future land use.

This prospect is particularly marked by the fact that zoning laws are not retroactive, and the transition from an existing land use to another classification may span a great number of years. According to Anglo-Saxon theory, if land has never been used for a particular purpose it does not constitute a deprivation of property rights to deny the right to so use it in the future. On the other hand, it is assumed that zoning ordinances must not restrict property to uses considered less liberal than the existing use. The courts have held that zoning may not be retroactive, that existing land uses may not be "zoned out of existence." They must be permitted to continue as "nonconforming" uses if they are inconsistent with the use the zoning ordinance prescribes.

This may appear to permit the continuation of a nonconforming use which would prove to be a detriment to the surrounding development, like an obnoxious industry in a residential zone. The courts have pointed out that other means are available for relief from such intrusions; proof that a nonconforming use is a nuisance and dangerous to the life and health of the inhabitants and the public welfare may be sufficient reason for the courts to deny a use to continue.

Nonconforming uses may not be renewed if destroyed by fire or act of God. In such cases the new structure must conform to the provisions of the current zoning. In some ordinances a nonconforming structure may be repaired or slightly altered, but it may not be modified to the extent that the space or facilities are enlarged, nor may a different nonconforming use replace that which is removed.

Some zoning ordinances specify a period during which a nonconforming use shall be retired. This time is equivalent to an amortization period with an established date for removal of the structure, the period being related to the years of use already experienced in the structure and the investment in it. In this way property values and human values may be reasonably balanced, and intruding uses gradually removed to be replaced by conforming uses. The logic and equity of such a method would seem enough to impel cities to adopt it in the public interest.

Most cities classify their land in four major categories: agricultural, residential, commercial, and industrial. Each of these broad groups is subdivided into uses ranging from the most to the least obnoxious, from the most to the least restricted, from the most concentrated to the most open. This is generally identified as "step-down" classification as it is applied within each of the four broad groups. Thus the general industrial classification contains heavy industry and light industry, expressing the difference between a boiler works and a tin shop, for example. A large department store would be classified in heavy commercial, whereas a neighborhood grocery store would be placed in the lightest commerical zone. Likewise, a multistory apartment building would be in the least restricted residential zone, whereas a single-family detached house is in the most restricted area.

The number of intermediate steps between the most intense use and the least intense will vary in different communities as the complexity of the community may warrant. In a very large city there may be as many as fifteen classes of land use, whereas in a small town there may only be nine. This difference in the number of classifications does not suggest less accuracy in determining the classifications; it indicates that the manner in which the land is used in a small town is less complex than a large city. The number of classifications should be as few as possible consistent with a complete coverage of the various uses of land and an accurate description of each.

A city should have a record of the way in which the land within its boundaries is used, as well as the quantity of space and structures which comprise it. A periodic inventory of these assets should be undertaken just as a well-organized and well-administered business maintains an inventory of its stock and the value of it. During the depression of 1930–40, land-use surveys in a number of cities were conducted under auspices of the Works Progress Administration of the Federal government. These data were of immeasurable value to the planning commissions in the respective cities, and yet there are few instances in which the records were subsequently maintained in current form.

A continuous record may be maintained by reference to building permits and the tax assessor of the city. Other sources of reference are The Sanborn Insurance Atlas; the Building and Safety Department of the city, which records changes in building occupancy and alterations that indicate a change in the use of existing structures; the Health Department, which maintains data on substandard structures, pest infestation, lack of sanitation facilities; and the local housing authority from which information may generally be obtained on the physical condition of housing. Banking and lending institutions frequently maintain valid information on new building activity.

The record of urban land use is not for the purpose of only ascertaining the condition of the physical structure. It provides the information necessary to observe the rate at which the city is increasing or decreasing its physical plant in the various classifications of land use. It offers a basis for measuring the amount of land to be reserved in zoning for future developments of the city, the quantity of land, and the most appropriate location for the various uses.

The land-use inventory is good urban business and should be maintained of current record. It is not a plan; it is part of the vital data from which plans may be made.

Inventory of Social and Economic Factors. If the data on the nature of the physical character of the city seem to be a complicated process, the social and economic facts are even more so. People are not inclined to conceal the manner in which they use the land unless an evasion of the law is involved, but they are reluctant to divulge their ages, incomes, or personal health; such information is naturally considered to be of a personal nature. To plan for the community welfare, however, it is important to know about the people who make it and for whom it is intended.

The principal source of economic and social data is the U. S. Census;[3] included in the census of 1940 were data on family incomes, family sizes, dwelling rent, condition of structures, owner and tenant occupancy of structures, years of schooling, age composition, occupation of the wage earner, and other information. Based upon these data, the Bureau of the Census analyzes the spending habits of the various income groups which indicate the amount in each income group spent for rent, clothes, food, amusement, and other living necessities. Much of the latter data is given for the whole city and is therefore difficult to relate to the census tracts which are the units in which urban statistics are usually tabulated. Housing data in the census are listed by blocks and provide a source of information for the land-use survey.

Although most public and private local agencies normally assemble only the information on the social and economic structure of the community in which they are directly interested, the planning agency may obtain and correlate this special information to form an over-all picture. Since the various agencies may interpret similar data in different ways, these differences must be resolved by the planners on the basis of the best available known facts.

It is a well known cliché that anything can be proved with statistics; the corollary is that statistics may not prove anything. It is important that they not be misleading. As an illustration, the increase in the number of families and the number of houses built may be substantially identical and thereby indicate no shortage of dwellings. These "pure" numbers mean little as an evaluation of the housing supply in relation to the housing need. The number of families formerly "doubled-up," the cost brackets of the new residences, the absence of a normal vacancy factor, and the occupancy of substandard housing facilities are among the statistics to be evaluated with those on the number of families and the housing supply.

Juvenile delinquency and crime data in the local police and probation department files record the location of the incidents and the residences of offenders. Other social statistics support as well as guide the preparation of the Master Plan and the building of a good city. Data on disease and health can be obtained from the health departments of the cities, counties, and state, as well as the tuberculosis and health associations. Many other private agencies, such as foundations, service clubs, veterans' organizations, universities and charitable groups have valuable data. Material on the birth rate, death rate, infant mortality, marriage and divorce rates are other social factors, and the rate of population immigration and emigration, the years of schooling, occupa-

---

[3] U. S. Census, Department of Commerce, Washington D. C., 1940.

tions of the working force, the cultural inclinations are among the data which the planning commission must necessarily correlate objectively.

Information on the economic development and prospects of the community is usually available through the Chamber of Commerce, and these data can be cross-referenced with reports by Dun and Bradstreet and the U. S. Department of Commerce. Trends in industrialization and increases in the working force can be traced through the U. S. Department of Labor, the State Employment Services, and local industries. The trends in the industrial population will have a decided effect on the planning process. Data on the earning capacity, the average years of employment, the social security structure, types and diversification of employment, and the income groups represented in the working population are necessary to calculate the purchasing power of the community and the ability to pay rents and taxes. These statistics are important as a basis for the Master Plan.

Changing Character of Cities. With the assembly of the data previously suggested—that part of the planning process identified as research—we learn the nature of the existing city. This is the knowledge needed for analysis of the city; from it we learn why the city was begun, how it grew, and why it prospered.

There are reasons why cities are located where they are; they were important reasons in the history of the city and they bear upon its future. They may be important as a pattern for the continuous development of the city or they may reveal what changes have overtaken the city and thus indicate the new directions for which the city must be planned. The reasons for the founding of a city may have multiplied, or they may have vanished. There may be entirely new purposes for the city than those which moved its original settlement.

The sleepy village of the eighteenth century has apparently little in common with the metropolis of today. There may remain reminiscent marks of its historical origin, but the functions may have altered completely. As the city grew in size, as the population increased, and as new enterprises developed, the character of the city may have altered. Perhaps the quality of community living deteriorated as the city grew from a small, intimate town to the unfriendly metropolitan machine it now seems to be. Much may have been lost in this process, enough to question whether the city can recover the human values by which the living standards of people are measured.

The changes in urban character reflected in the growth and the deterioration of neighborhood life are illustrated in all our cities. It is apparent in a growing metropolis like Los Angeles. Hardly more than twenty years ago this community was reputed for its climate, its recreational opportunities, its beaches, and the grandeur of its mountains. The quality of its living environment and the pleasant mildness of its atmosphere made this city a haven for travelers from all parts of the world.

The population of Los Angeles was 500,000 in 1920; in 1946 it was 1,805,000 and the city had spread thin over the 452 square miles of its area. From its beginning as the center of a predominantly agricultural area it has developed an important industrial economy. Industrial plants have sprung up with little or no attention to their probable effect upon the living conditions of the region and its inhabitants. Water was brought more than 250 miles to supply the growing population. Congestion overtook this city of "open space," blight and slums are taking their toll, and smoke and fumes taint the air.

This story differs only in degree and detail in all our cities; it is the tale of the metropolis. The native advantages of our urban communities have not been respected by the people who built them; in the name of a bigger and more prosperous city, they have been desecrated and the people are retreating. The people are fleeing the city and it remains neglected, but the same indifference is guiding development on the outskirts. Rather than make capital of the native characteristics of a region, exploitation of the urban community is undermining its own investments.

Thus, it is toward a double-barreled objective that the Master Plan of a city or region is directed: forestalling the drift into chaos in the yet undeveloped areas of the city and the gradual reconstruction of the developed area of the city with particular attention to blighted sections and improved circulation. The present chaotic development of the city is a trend and it may be corrected and redirected to the benefit of all the people when the advantages are appropriately exploited through planning.

The changing nature of the city must be appraised, and the natural character defined. Shifts in the emphasis of the urban economy and the services and functions it performs require adjustments in the living habits of the people, the land use, and the transportation, if they are to continue as favorable environments in which to live and work. The Master Plan will reflect these adjustments and thereby become a guide for the future growth and development of the community. This demands inquiry into every facet of urban existence; it calls for the co-ordination of a team of trained people and enlightened and enthusiastic citizens.

The Plan Is Teamwork. Knowledge of the physical structure of the city will reveal certain natural uses for the land and existing uses which deserve particular respect in the plan. There may be well-established industrial areas, commercial centers, residential developments, a great park, waterways, railroads, and historical and natural features. This knowledge will also indicate some apparent maladjustments in current land use for which corrective measures are obviously necessary. It will also indicate an appropriate relation between industrial and residential areas. With these broad strokes the Master Plan is begun.

The city is linked with its neighbor cities and towns and its environs by the highways, railroads, and mass transportation facilities; these form the main arteries of circulation about the city and they will form the boundaries of the neighborhood units. The freeways, parkways, rapid transit and railroads will establish the relation between the sources of employment in commerce and industry, and the residential neighborhoods.

Laid upon this general plan will be the reservations of open spaces, the areas adapted for natural parks, or the submarginal lands unsuited for active urban development. In this process the Master Plan begins to take shape.

The Master Plan will reflect the policies on the density of population desirable and consistent with the character of the city in its residential areas, and it will indicate the standards for the relation of building bulk and open space in these areas and in the commercial districts. Within the broad land-use plan and guided by these standards, the precise plans for the various areas of the city may be refined as the time for their development approaches. The schools and playgrounds may be located within the neighborhood units, and requirements for the local shopping centers may be determined. Space may be reserved for the freeways and rapid transit rights-of-way. Detailed plans for the improvement of the "downtown" business center may be formulated, and the reconstruction of blighted areas in the central sections of the city may be planned and executed. The Master Plan will set forth the appropriate use to which the land in the city should be devoted so that the enterprise of city building may have a tangible guide in its determinations for investment.

It takes teamwork to produce the Master Plan, a plan that contains the inspired will of a people bent upon building a decent and fine city. The decisions emerge from the co-ordinated teamwork of sociologists and economists, statisticians and engineers, finance advisors and lawyers, politicians and architects, health authorities and public administrators, and public-spirited businessmen and consumers. It takes boundless enthusiasm and enlightened civic interest, and it takes a competent staff of trained planners to perform the job of co-ordination and translation.

The Master Plan is the projection of this teamwork into a city form which serves as a common objective, a form in which urban development may proceed with order as the city grows, prospers, and expands. The plan consists of two general patterns: the *Plan for Land Use* and the *Plan for Circulation.*

The Plan for Land Use. This plan designates the areas of the city adapted to development for the various urban land uses: residential, commercial, industrial, and open space. It sets forth the restrictions on density of land use in terms of population or building bulk; it specifies the areas for multiple-housing and single dwellings; it defines the areas to be reserved for recreation, conservation, and agriculture.

This plan will establish the allocation of neighborhood units with their several facilities. It is the plan which sets the standards to guide the city builders in their various enterprises, and a complete plan will be more than a single map of the city. It will be the compilation of all the data from which the estimates of required areas were calculated and the standards determined; it will become a reference for all who are engaged in urban development.

This plan will chart the relation of the city to the region and indicate its integration with its satellite communities, and the plan will define the areas and standards for subdivision of new land. This is the plan which forms the foundation for zoning ordinances, and the precise plans for parks and recreation, the location of schools and other public buildings, the civic center, cultural and sports centers. It is the plan which will guide the city in the design of utilities—sewers, gas, water, electric distribution, and street lighting. And this is the plan to which all can refer for guidance in determining their investments in the city.

The Plan for Circulation. This is the plan for major highways and streets, routes for mass transportation, railroads, airfields, and waterways. It will define the through-traffic arteries, freeways, parkways and their intersections; it will chart the course of rail and bus routes for mass transportation about the city and its environs. It is in this plan that all lines of communication will be integrated for the circulation of the people in and about the urban area.

This system of circulation will define the boundaries of neighborhood units. The internal street system within this broad framework need be determined to the extent that it impinges upon the through-traffic arteries or mass transportation routes. The internal design of the streets could remain until development is imminent and then be made more precise.

As the city develops, this plan will become the reference for improvements and extensions of the circulation system. Precise plans may be made for railroad passenger and freight lines, yards, terminals and stations, air terminals and fields, and internal helicopter connections. Harbor and waterway development may be guided by this plan as improvements are proposed.

The Plan for Circulation and the Land-use plan require complete integration, and they may require occasional modification, but there is no development within one category which can remain unrelated to all others.

The Plan Is a Process. The preparation of a Master Plan for all cities and counties is required in many states, and a passage from the California law illustrates that little doubt is intended; it reads in part:

It shall be the function and duty of the planning commission to prepare and adopt a comprehensive, long term, general plan for the physical development of the city, county, or region, and of any land outside the boundaries thereof which in the commission's judgment bears relation to the planning thereof. Such plan shall be known as the MASTER PLAN and shall be so prepared that all or portions thereof may be adopted by the legislative body. . . .[4]

As indicated in the foregoing passage, a part of a Master Plan may be prepared and adopted independently of other parts when the planning commission and the legislative body deem it in the interest of the community to do so. The public hearings attend these actions and provide the opportunity for the people to familiarize themselves with the plan and to suggest changes and improvements. In some cities, representatives of the planning commission appear before local citizen groups to describe the plan and its effects upon them and the development of their property and environment. The Master Plan may thus assume a reality for the people, a realization that the plan is theirs.

After the Master Plan has been adopted by the legislative body ". . . no road, street, highway, square, park, or other public way, ground or open space shall be

---

[4] Compilation of laws relating to Subdivisions and State and Local Planning, State of California, p. 6, Section 4. Supervisor of Documents, Sacramento, California, 1937.

acquired by dedication or otherwise, and no street, road, highway or public way shall be closed or abandoned, and no public building or structure shall be constructed or authorized in the area . . . until the location, character, and extent thereof shall be submitted to and shall have been reported on by the planning commission."[5] It is such statements of official policy that establish the planning process in our cities, and it is such statements which have been upheld by the courts of our land because they recognize the necessity for a city plan.

Ladislas Segoe describes the Master Plan in the following terms:

> The comprehensive city plan or master plan, while it must be thoroughly practical and sound economically, must give expression also to other than the purely materialistic aspirations of the people of a community. Only then will the plan possess—in addition to its influence toward a more convenient, efficient economical development—the inspirational force that will force civic interest, devotion and loyalty essential for building better cities.
>
> The comprehensive city plan or master plan must therefore be—first, a balanced and otherwise attractive general design best suited to present and probable future needs; second, in scale with the population and economic prospects of the community; and third, in scale with its financial resources, present and prospective. The satisfying of the above criteria calls for the application of scientific as well as artistic effort, in order to produce a city plan of attractive form, pleasing balance and detail, attuned to the economic and social activities of the community. . . .[6]

It is probably more accurate to define a Master Plan as a process rather than a conclusive statement. It is a pattern for the physical development of the city, a pattern to guide the city builders in locating their investments and measuring the prospect for success. It is a design for the physical, social, economic, and political framework for the city; it welds the sociological, economic, and geographic properties of the city into a structure.

To suggest that the plan is a fluid process may imply that decisions are not represented in it. The plan for a city will be modified as conditions may alter the affairs of people from time to time, but a Master Plan represents certain decisions of vital importance to the welfare of the people and their city. It represents a decision on the number of people the city may be built to accommodate; it represents the standards by which the city will be developed. It represents decisions on the appropriate relation between the uses of land, the relation between the land to be developed for residential, commercial, and industrial enterprise. It calls for decisions on the lines of communication that link these areas—the circulation system. And it represents decisions on the plan for reservation of open space throughout the city.

These are broad decisions, but they are essential to the formulation of a pattern for city building. It is upon these decisions that the health of urban development rests for they express the aspirations of a community and set the goals toward which the city may advance.

Yes, the Master Plan represents a set of ideals, the aims and ambitions an enlightened people hold aloft as standards of civic welfare. These are not easy words to utter—

[5] *Ibid.*
[6] *Local Planning Administration*, Ladislas Segoe, International City Managers' Association, Chicago, 1941.

they have been so frequently ground into grains of dust which settle promiscuously upon the motives of men. Yet ideals move people toward deeds of human welfare, and it is upon such deeds that good cities will depend. If we choose to set aside ideals in city building because they have been often branded visionary, we are choosing the course of nihilism. If the standards of city building are not founded upon a set of ideals for our cities, we will pursue the process of anarchy. It is not therefore amiss to acknowledge that ideals shall guide the decisions represented in the Master Plan.

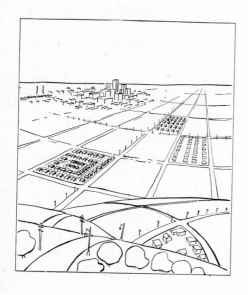

CHAPTER **19**

SUBDIVISION
OF LAND

The Use of Land. The earth is our primary resource. Millions of years in time created the few inches of soil that supports humanity. The greed and neglect of man have often destroyed what took nature an infinite time to develop, and the story of man's improvidence with the land is suggested by Walter Havighurst[1]:

In 1823 a little Norwegian wanderer, named Cleng Peerson, walked overland from New York to the western territories. At Chicago he turned north. For six days he printed his steps in the blank sands of Lake Michigan. At evening he boiled his kettle at the lake's edge. He slept under the soothing drones of water. At the site of Milwaukee (three log huts, one of them empty) he found a tall man, naked to the waist, beside a cabin hung with traps and snowshoes.
"What will I find if I continue north from here?" Cleng Peerson asked.
Solomon Juneau was a fur trader. He knew the great twilight of the forests.
"Woods to the world's end," he replied.
It was literally true. Woods for 600 miles. In that day six-sevenths of Wisconsin was forest. Two-thirds of Minnesota was forest. The upper peninsula of Michigan was all forest. And the forest began beyond Lake Superior, stretching away toward Hudson Bay. A country as big as France and every mile of it mysterious with forest twilight and haunted with the sound of running water. . . . Cedar, hemlock, tamarack and pine. A forest rich and vast enough for the needs of a nation forever.
Try to find that forest now. . . .
The timber cruisers came, walked through the country. . . . Behind them came the lumber kings and the great corporations. They logged off the forest in a furious assault. "Come and get it" was the cry of the lumber camp. . . . "Come and get it" was the slogan of the corporations. . . .
How did the big corporations get hold of all of the timber? There was the Stone and Timber Act of Congress, designed to safeguard national resources. But the corporations found the loopholes, and they got the timber. . . .
Following the mining of timber came the fires that swept not only the fallen timber but the seeds as well . . . so there was no second growth. Conservation of this forest preserve came 50 years too late.

This is so with all of our resources. In our desire to provide a maximum of opportunity and a minimum of regulation, we are prone to pass on a heritage of poverty

[1] The Land and the People, Walter Havighurst, *Land Policy Review,* June 1941.

251

in natural resources. So often our willingness to protect our resources emerges only after irreparable damage has been done. The control of land subdivision has been similar to that of soil conservation. It is accepted only after most of the urban land has already been butchered into pieces that render our city the unhappy affair we now experience. Carol Aronovicci said: "Wisdom is knowing what to do. Virtue is the doing it. . . ." In the subdivision of land as in many other affairs, our virtue precedes our wisdom and, it might be observed, the "doing" of many subdivisions is without much virtue.

Private Property in Land. The history of land-ownership commenced when men grouped into tribes. Living on wild food and game, primitive tribes appropriated the territory they occupied. Like the American Indian or the pastoral people of the Asiatic steppes, the primitives guarded their territory from intrusion by other tribes, but equality of use was open to all the members of their own community. Remnants of these ancient customs survive; in territorial waters all have the right to fish, and in our national forests the birds and beasts are stalked during hunting seasons.

The land belonged to the tribe and not to the individual; in this we detect a precedent for the sovereign state as the true owner of all land. As the tribes grew in size and acquired territory by conquest or peaceful consolidation, they subdivided into villages. A degree of local autonomy was tolerated, but the land remained as a community holding.

This ancient tradition that the land is vested primarily in the community, with rights to its use being granted to individuals, has persisted despite the forms which these rights have assumed from time to time. This concept of land ownership, derived from tribal possession of the land, was later reflected in the feudal system when land was vested in the king as the head of the state.

In the feudal system land was "granted" by the king to his lords for their pledge of military support. The lords in turn allocated rights to the use of land to their serfs and villeins, these rights becoming an integral part of the social and political caste system. As the feudal system dissolved, the privileges of the lords were transformed into a form of ownership, and the landlord was born. In England the system of leasing land estates to tenants reached a stage in which the tenants were assured rights to the land even more firm than those of the landlord-owner; the tenants' intimate association with the land and its use warranted secure protection against unfair eviction and assurance of full compensation for improvements he might effect in the land.

The character of land tenure is complicated and has varied in different countries at different periods of history. While the landlord-tenant system prevails in some countries, the peasant proprietorship is predominant in others. The concept of land-ownership has gradually moved from that of possession—the act of presence on the land as a place to live and to cultivate or capture food for survival—to that of land as property; in this latter concept the land becomes a commodity and we associate it with private land-ownership.

Because of this identification it is necessary to recognize the relation between private ownership and the interest retained by the community in the land. The legal rule has been expressed that there is no absolute private right to land in our system, the state alone being vested with that right which it concedes to the individual possessor only as a strictly defined subordinate right, subject to conditions enacted by the community from time to time.[2] Quoting from the *Encyclopaedia Britannica:*

> Land tenure, throughout the world shows that it has pursued one unvarying course, commencing in the community of tribal possession, land has everywhere by degrees been appropriated to the village, to the families and to the individuals. But in every stage the condition of its enjoyment and use have been absolutely regulated by the community in reference to the general welfare. . . . Those who refuse to admit the right of the state to impose such conditions on private property as it deems for the general benefit, may be dismissed with brevity. Not only do they show entire ignorance of the history of land tenure at all times, but they belie the daily action of the British legislature. Parliament seldom lets a session pass without making some laws which assert the right of the state to take possession of property for private or public benefit, to tax it, and to restrain or regulate the rights of its owners over it. Nor is there any theory of the basis of property which does not tacitly admit that it is subject to the authority of the community.[3]

Land in the United States was originally vested in the Crown of the country which colonized the area. The British king made grants of land to the trading companies, and they in turn transferred the grants to individuals or groups of settlers. It was customary for these settlers to establish compact villages in the New England country with each family receiving a holding of 20 acres. Outside the area of these individual holdings, the land remained in custody of the community for use by all members of the group. In the South, however, large tracts were granted for agricultural development.

The King of Spain held absolute title to the land in the Spanish colonies. His subjects were dispatched to those areas the Crown desired to be populated, and the land was leased for cultivation. The crops were specified, and, if for any reason the settler neglected to cultivate the land, he was deported from the colony. Provisional grants of huge estates were made to favorites of the Crown in the western country which later became California. The first of these was in 1784, and *ranchos* like those of José Verdugo in the San Fernando Valley and Manuel Nietos between the Santa Ana and San Gabriel Rivers occupied areas of 68 leagues or 390,000 acres stretching from the mountains to the sea. These great holdings were roughly measured; the *vara,* the measurement of distance, was calculated on horseback, and the later problems of untangling disputed claims may well have originated with the relative spryness of some caballero's horse.

Like the Roman *praesidium,* the German *marktplatz,* and the New England Common, the plaza occupied the center of the Spanish colonial pueblos. House lots were grouped about the plaza, with the planting fields and public pasture land lying beyond them. Although this form was originally adopted for protection from attack by hostile tribes, the social advantages were later realized, and the Spaniards used this pueblo form in all the cities they founded in North and South America.[4]

[2] *The Encyclopaedia Britannica,* The Werner Company, Chicago, 1893, Vol. 14, p. 259. (American Revision.)
[3] *Ibid.*
[4] El Pueblo, Security Trust and Savings Bank, Equitable Branch, Los Angeles, California, 1948.

Founded in 1781 the town of Los Angeles illustrates the typical village plan. Eleven families traveled overland to settle this new town, and history records what was probably the first of the "super-colossal premiers" for which Hollywood later was to become famous. The Indians and the garrison joined with the settlers in a gay fiesta marking the establishment of the town.

Each of the settlers was permitted to cultivate 14 acres of land outside the residential area, and an equal allowance of stock and equipment was given to each family. He had free range for his stock on the pueblo lands lying outside the land designated for cultivation.

The first subdivision of the City of Los Angeles was quite simple. It covered an area of 4 square leagues or about 36 square miles centered about the plaza which measured 275 by 180 feet. In accordance with de Neve's instructions, the old plaza lay with its corners to the cardinal points of the compass, the streets extending at right angles so that "no street would be swept by the wind." Upon three sides of the plaza were the house lots, 55 feet in width. One-half of the remaining side was reserved for public buildings, the other half was for open space.[5]

After the American Revolution, land formerly held by the Crown of England went to the respective states and, in order to resolve the conflicting interests of the states in this land, much of it was made a public domain under the Federal government. The United States thereby became proprietor of the great frontier areas. Because the government of the new nation needed revenue for its operation and the expansion of the vast country, settlement was encouraged by the sale of land at nominal prices, and grants were offered in return for development. The Homestead Act was one such method, entitling the citizen to 160 acres of land on the condition that he bring it under cultivation within a period of 5 years. Huge grants were made to the railroads as encouragement to extend their rails across the western territories, about 10 per cent of the public domain in 1867 being turned over to the several railroad companies.

These policies overlooked the possible dissipation of natural resources in forests and minerals that later took place, and it has been subsequently necessary to devote much legislation to the restoration and protection of these domains. In urban communities the abuse of land through speculative excesses has paralleled the dissipation of the natural resources in rural areas.

Land Subdivision and Speculation. As our nation grew in size and the urban centers became large metropolitan areas, there was increased competition for land for all purposes. Great estates were broken up and sold in parcels of varying size. Land was still considered, for the most part, as a base for some economic or social use. Not until recent years did it become a speculative commodity, to be bought and sold, like stocks and bonds, for a profit and, not infrequently, a loss.

Some of the wildest exploits in land sales occurred in Florida and California during the early 1920's. Reality was beyond dreams in those fabulous days. Florida land was sold at fantastic prices to people in New York and the New England states, and

[5] *Ibid.*

much of the land was under water. When the boom broke, thousands of people found themselves with worthless property and their life savings lost.

Real estate speculation in California was somewhat reminiscent of the exploits of the *Americanos* following the Spanish occupation when tales of fantasy colored the accretion of large land holdings. One such tale cites a case in which all land was to be registered in the land office at a specified time or be declared free for claim by anyone desiring it. Various tricks were employed to deceive the Spanish *rancheros:* some notices were never published, or they were "lost"; some were phrased in language not understood by the Spanish landowners; or, as a last resort, owners were terrorized to keep them from the registry office until the deadline had expired.

In later days of speculation, land was subdivided and sold in flood areas and on precipitous hillsides; in one area the gridiron platting of streets rendered the lots so useless that 90 per cent of the land has since reverted to the state for failure to pay taxes. A multitude of 25 by 100 foot lots were laid out and sold for "a dollar down and a dollar a week." There were no sewers and no paved streets, and heavy rains washed out roads and water pipes. These subdivisions were not only poor investments for the purchasers, but they were wanton wastes of the urban land resources.

As lots in these scattered "wildcat" subdivisions were sold off, there followed the demand for urban services and facilities and for transportation which could not be supported. When the boom died in California as in Florida, thousands of lots, some improved and some devoid of pavements or utilities, remained as evidence of premature and irresponsible subdivision. Assessment districts, which had been formed to pay for the improvements promised by the subdivider, defaulted on their bonds and the scene was one of economic desperation.

The depths to which abuse of urban land subdivision sank is best illustrated by the contrast of fine residential suburbs which were begun during the same period. Such developments as the Palos Verdes Estates near Los Angeles, St. Francis Woods in San Francisco, Roland Park in Baltimore, Forest Hills on Long Island, River Oaks in Houston, and the Country Club District in Kansas City are among a number in which the best techniques in land division and development were employed. These exclusive residential areas were the forerunners of the high standards which now regulate subdivision practice.

Subdivision Regulations. The questionable practices of the 1920's placed the subdivider of land in an extremely poor light, and the able practitioner was unavoidably identified with the unscrupulous. Reforms were overdue, and the necessity for regulations over the subdivision of urban land was urgent. These controls are based upon the principle that the use and development of land constitute a right bestowed by the community upon the individual and this right may be withdrawn or withheld when and if the individual violates the conditions upon which it is vested in him. The power of eminent domain, the police power, the power to tax real estate, and the power to regulate the use of land are expressions of this principle and it provides the structure upon which the development of urban land is built.

A subdivision may be defined as: "Any land, or portion thereof, shown on the last preceding tax rolls as a unit or as contiguous units which is divided for purposes of sale, either immediate or future, by any subdivider into five or more parcels within any one year shall be considered to be a subdivision and requires the filing of a map for the approval of the planning commission and the legislative body."[6] Such a definition, or one of similar form, is usually contained in state laws which vest in cities and counties the right of police power for the regulation of land subdivision, or in planning acts which outline the procedure for preparation of the Master Plan.

The definition of a subdivision like the foregoing does not preclude the sale of a portion of an individual lot; this right is retained by the individual property owner. A parcel of land may be sold in whole or in part at the discretion of the owner without the necessity to follow the subdivision procedures. It is only necessary to inform the tax assessor of the sale so that the official records may be adjusted and the taxes reassigned. The regulations applying to the development of individual parcels of land are the zoning laws and the housing, health, and sanitation laws. The division of property falls within the classification of subdivision regulations when (according to a definition like the preceding illustration) a piece of land is divided into at least five separate parcels each of which is to be separately sold within a period of one year.

There are many interests involved in the subdivision of land including those of the original owner, the developer, the prospective buyer, and the city as a whole. Ladislas Segoe states:

To the land developer the subdividing of land is primarily a matter of profit. He is chiefly interested in realizing as much money as he can from the sale of his land in the shortest possible time. To the community the subdivision of land is a matter of serious public concern. The activities of the developers shape the future of the community and condition in a considerable measure the quality of the living and working conditions of its inhabitants. Where such activities are uncontrolled or inadequately controlled they also may place an undue burden on the public treasury by reason of excessive cost of public improvements and maintenance, unnecessarily high operating costs of public services, and through the participation of the community in the financing of improvements in premature subdivisions.[7]

One of the first steps taken in some states for the control of subdivisions was the licensing of the subdivider. To obtain a license some education was necessary in the principles and practices of land sales as well as a knowledge of state and local laws pertaining to the subdivision of land. In both state and local laws it was generally necessary for the owner of land to employ a licensed engineer to prepare the subdivision map for recording. This was an effort to ensure the accuracy of the subdivision maps and avoid alteration in the development after it was recorded. In more recent years it has been frequently mandatory to record on the subdivision maps any unusual or hazardous conditions such as the danger of floods in low areas. Such land has not been necessarily precluded from sale, but the purchaser was warned of what

[6] Subdivisions Map Act, California, Article 3, Section 11535 (1943).
[7] Local Planning Administration, Ladislas Segoe, International City Managers' Association, Chicago, 1941, p. 495.

he was purchasing. If life was endangered, however, the public body could deny the right to subdivide and sell the land.

Subdivision of land is the method of transforming a city plan into a reality. Many elements in the over-all plan are realized at the time the land is developed. Highways are dedicated, streets and alleys are paved, sewer and water lines and electric power are installed, new schools are constructed, transportation lines are extended, and police and fire protection is expanded. The city plan is either realized or it is lost in the subdivision of land. The control a community retains over land subdivision is the means by which the elements of the Master Plan are enforced.

Having sovereign rights over the land within their boundaries, state laws govern the ownership, transfer, and use of private property, and they vest in cities and counties the right of police power to regulate the subdivision of land. Some states establish the procedures for subdividing land and have real estate commissions which ensure compliance with these procedures. The real estate commission operates in a manner similar to corporation commissions which regulate the sale of stocks and bonds. They check the legitimacy of sales organizations, the quality of the lots offered for sale, and ascertain that the required improvements are either installed or assured by a bond posted by the subdivider prior to approval of the subdivision and sale of the land.

The design of subdivisions is the responsibility of the local government of the community in which the land is situated. Under the provisions of the Master Plan, the local planning agency is generally charged with the responsibility for decisions on the "community design" of subdivisions, the shape and size of lots, the size and length of streets, the spaces to be reserved for community facilities, schools, and recreation.

In effect, the community reserves an equity in the land and vests in the individual the right to own and use land subject to the requirements for the general welfare of the community. Thus the city may require the subdivider to dedicate certain streets for access to property and it may demand that sewer lines be installed. If this facility is not available, the city may require larger lots to avoid the possibility of water and soil contamination by effluent from cesspools or septic tanks. The city may require service roads where land abuts a principal traffic way to control the ingress and egress to property, and it may require the installation of specific utilities and roads, walks and curbs, street lighting, electric distribution, or require the subdivider to post a bond to cover the cost of such improvements before the final map of the subdivision is approved. The subdivider may be required to conform with a major highway plan for the community and the grades and proposed alignment of city streets.

The local planning agency aids the subdivider in planning his land, suggests improved methods of site planning, and recommends to the legislative body exceptions to established regulations which may be warranted by peculiar characteristics of the various sites. Material assistance has been rendered by the Federal Housing Administration in the improvement of subdivision design; this Federal agency has performed a service in raising the quality of subdivision design in communities where local laws are ineffectual or no trained planning officials are active.

One of the primary deficiencies in subdivision practice today is the difference in standards which prevail in adjoining communities. These differences are apparent in the strange street alignments, blocked roadways, alternately wide and narrow streets, and differences in type of pavements we frequently observe as we move from one community to another. Less discernible, perhaps, but more disastrous to the general community welfare and regional development are the differences in standards for the design and construction of real estate subdivisions, some communities willfully lowering their standards below those of their neighboring areas to invite the subdivision and development of land within their boundaries only to suffer the pain of a degenerated community at some later date. Many cities have made agreements to co-operate in matters of subdivision where the developments are within a certain distance of their respective boundaries. Where regional planning agencies are active, they have co-ordinated the subdivisions of the various cities within their jurisdiction and here is a field ripe for significant service and progress.

A method for the exercise of quantitative control over land subdivision is yet unresolved, but it is urgently needed as a means to restrain excessive and premature expansion of subdivisions. Repetition of the economically disastrous practices of the 1920's, many of which are recurring today, need to be forestalled, but the method of legally accomplishing this purpose has not been developed. There were suggestions for issuing "certificates of necessity" during the 1930 decade when the effects of "wildcat" operations became painfully obvious. These certificates were to allow subdivision of land only when the developer could demonstrate the need for developing his property and produce some evidence of bona fide purchasers for it.

The most effective means to cope with excessive subdivision thus far has been the requirement that a subdivider install all utilities and improvements, including streets and walks, in conformance with the standards established by the community. The subdivider must thus install, at his expense and prior to sale, all the required improvements. This transforms the subdivider from the usual position of a land speculator to that of a land developer. When required to meet the full capital costs of a complete improvement, it is likely that the developer will consider more thoroughly the financial soundness of his development in terms of its timeliness before he ventures willfully upon a highly speculative enterprise.

Subdivision Procedure. Our conception of land has changed from that of the soil we cultivate for food and the earth from which we extract the minerals and materials to sustain our civilization. The change has come about almost imperceptibly, but nonetheless surely. Land is still used for the same primary purposes. However, it is not only used for the goods it produces; it itself is treated as a good to be bartered for trade. As such a commodity, trading in urban land is frequently conducted independently of its productive usefulness in the traditional sense. Ostensibly the value of land is linked with the manner in which it may be used, but possession is quite generally acquired for the purpose of exchanging it as a commodity rather than for its natural productive use.

As a result of this gradual shift in emphasis upon land, we have grown unaware of the vital impact which the process of transforming raw acreage into improved urban lots exerts upon the community welfare. It is to assure the protection of the general welfare that subdivision regulations have been devised, with the knowledge that, in the final analysis, it is the general welfare that protects sound investment in urban development.

Although procedures vary in different localities, the following steps may serve as a description of the general sequence from an unimproved site to the development of parcels available for sale:

1. The land is surveyed to ascertain the precise description of its boundaries, the abutting streets, local drainage conditions, contours of the land, and the special features or structures that may occupy the site.

2. Official records are consulted to define the location of special easements or rights-of-way that must be retained in developing the land. There may be a proposed highway passing across the site or easements for sewers or power lines to serve the site or adjoining land. All restrictions on the use of the property must be determined: deed restrictions and zoning, the location of existing sewers or other requirements for sanitation, the height of the water table, the type of soil. The data on orientation and wind directions may affect the layout of streets and building sites. The surrounding land uses, both existing and permitted, require investigation.

3. Schools, parks, playgrounds, and other cultural and social facilities are located, and availability of transportation and shopping facilities is evaluated in reference to the services they may provide to the residents in the proposed development.

4. The subdivision ordinances are consulted for restrictions which may apply to the size and shape of lots, the width and grade of streets, the set-back lines to be observed, and the methods for presentation of the maps required by the local government agency: the planning department, real estate commission, or city engineer.

5. The developer should employ a planner or engineer to prepare the tentative or preliminary plan for the development of the property. This map should show, with reasonable accuracy, the manner in which the land is to be subdivided: the approximate size, shape, and the number of lots, the location of streets, their radii or curvature and grades, the method for providing drainage in all areas, and the utilities to be installed. The zoning and proposed land use—open space to be reserved or developed for recreation, shopping, or other community facilities—should also be indicated.

6. An estimate is then prepared to show the probable total cost for development of the site and indicate the minimum selling price for the lots to defray the cost of the land, the improvements, and the overhead for subdivision commissions and profits.

7. Before filing the tentative map with the local agency, planning department, or city engineer, it is generally considered good practice to consult with the Federal Housing Administration land planning officials and lending agencies. This is particularly important if approval for mortgage insurance by FHA is expected to be ultimately sought by purchasers of the lots.

8. The tentative map is then filed with the local agency, planning commission, or engineer, and this agency submits it to the various city departments for advice on engineering, health, schools, fire and police protection, and recreation. The suggestions and requirements of each department are co-ordinated by the planning commission, and the specific conditions for approval of the proposed subdivision are then issued, these conditions being based upon the public health, safety, or the general welfare of the community. On many occasions the planning staff will prepare a revised plan to suggest improvements in the design of the site or indicate the manner in which the plan may better conform to the Master Plan for the city.

9. After approval by the planning department and the legislative body, the developer proceeds with the preparation of the final or "precise" engineering map for the land. The street improvements and utilities are shown, the lots are staked on the ground, and minor changes which may be dictated by peculiarities in the site, such as hilly areas, are recorded. The final map is then filed with the city authorities who check it for conformity with the approved tentative map. If compliance is apparent, the final map is submitted to the local legislative body and the mayor for final approval. It is then officially recorded.

10. Before sale of the land may be undertaken the final recorded map must usually be filed with the state real estate commission and approval of sale obtained from that government agency.

Modern Subdivision Trends. The subdivision of land is responding to the techniques of large-scale planning, and the magic words of mass production and prefabrication are having their effect. Jerry-building persists, to be sure, and the city faces a struggle to combat the insidious effect of the cheap product of unprincipled, speculative developers. Pressure to retreat from decent standards of land development is strong, and resistance is difficult in a period when an acute housing shortage and high costs create a social as well as an economic problem for city dwellers. A commentary on the vigilance required by a community to maintain adequate standards is revealed by the following excerpt from a newspaper editorial:

According to a recent statement by the local Home Builders' Institute a good way to get more low-cost homes is to inaugurate a program aimed at reducing land development and subdivision costs.

Here are some of the things the Home Builders say they would like to do in developing future low-priced residential areas:

(1) Eliminate cement sidewalks and gutters and install macadam rolled gutters (and presumably "tow-path" sidewalks); (2) lay out 40-foot lots instead of the prevailing 50-to-60-foot residential plots; (3) increase block lengths from the present city and county 1000-foot limit to 1800–2000 feet; (4) reduce street widths to 24–26 feet instead of the present requirement of 32–34 feet; (5) reduce paving requirements for these streets; (6) eliminate presently required FHA soil tests and grading plans for drainage.

Chew this up and what you have, say the Home Builders, is a means of cutting the costs for low-income homes in Los Angeles County approximately $1289 per acre.

Significantly, however, the Home Builders halt their arithmetic with this figure. A little long division and you find out that all these "savings" add up to just about $147.84 per lot per home.

So what you have is a sort of straining at a gnat and swallowing a camel. To reduce the price of the average low-cost dwelling less than $150 here are a group of so-called "builders" who would wish upon the city and its environs some pretty sloppy, backward-looking neighborhoods.[8]

City building is not, nor can it become, a short-range process. There is a permanence about the city which cannot be avoided, and the standards by which it is built have a lasting effect upon the health, safety, and general welfare of the community. There must be ways and means to cope with temporary economic maladjustments other than lowering the standards for city building if the health and decency of the city are to be preserved and improved.

The growing acceptance of the principles of *community* planning is one of the encouraging signs of an improvement in standards. Land in the heart of cities is already subdivided and built up. Improvement in city planning within these huge areas of the city must necessarily emerge with techniques of urban redevelopment. The major activities have been consequently taking place on the outskirts of the cities and will undoubtedly continue until urban redevelopment becomes an effective instrument for rebuilding the central areas.

In the outlying areas there is increasing evidence that land developers are consciously directing their operations toward the creation of neighborhoods of homes rather than the customary surveyor's gridiron chopped into diminutive lots. These new housing developments have their prototype in the fine residential subdivisions of exclusive suburbs begun during the 1920's, but they are not confined to the high-income clientele that marked those early developments.

Large-scale production and enlightened land planning techniques are being directed to the development of well-designed homes—the integration of the house and the land of which it is a part—in neighborhoods equipped with conveniently located schools and playgrounds and balanced shopping centers. With the further development of mass-production methods, the "package unit" of land, house, landscaping, and community facilities may reach the broader range of the middle-income families who, in the past, have found only the well-worn, second-hand house or the cheap, jerry-built, speculative subdivision their only sources for a home.

Attention to the amenities of good community planning is apparent in the standards espoused by such organizations as the Community Builders Council of the Urban Land Institute. The members of this organization include some of the pioneers in the development of subdivisions and the planning and building of residential communities. That good planning may also be good business is attested to by the appeal of such men and organizations for an improvement in subdivision development.

Consumer groups are also seeking the advantages of co-operative action to obtain the environment of a good neighborhood, community facilities, and lower costs. Through such ventures, the emphasis upon the quality of the living environment supersedes the attention to profit. The mediocre product of speculative ventures has succeeded in the past and will continue to succeed so long as it remains a profitable enter-

---

[8] "Plans for City Building," Editorial by R.E.G.H., *Daily News*, Los Angeles, California, Friday, August 6, 1948.

prise. As the initiative of creative enterprise in community building produces better standards in the living environment, the ventures in speculative practices will be reduced to a diminishing level of investment; by this form of competition and the maintenance of decent standards of land subdivision—land planning—our cities may gradually improve as an environment for the people.

PART V

CONTEMPORARY

STANDARDS

Zoning in its best sense looks not
only backward to protect districts
already established but forward to
aid in the development of new districts according to a comprehensive
plan having as its basis the welfare
of the city as a whole.
— *California Supreme Court*

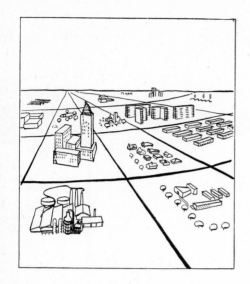

CHAPTER 20

THE ZONING PLAN

The Precise Plans. The Master Plan sets the basic policies for development of the city, the general relation between the various land uses—residential, commercial, and industrial—and forms the framework of the urban structure. From time to time this general framework is translated into *precise* plans which specify the zoning for land use, streets and highways, mass transit, recreation and conservation, subdivision expansion, utilities, railways and airports, civic centers, schools, and urban redevelopment. The precise plans interpret the basic policies for urban development reflected in the Master Plan and serve to adjust the Plan to new situations and conditions as they arise.

The precise plans serve a dual function. On one hand, they define the standards for development of the city, the standards of population density, the design of the circulation system, and the amount and location of open space and physical facilities for business and residence. On the other hand, the precise plans provide a *program* for development, a basis for timing proposed improvements in the city, the location, design, and installation of utilities, schools, parks, the extension of subdivision development, and the redevelopment of blighted areas. Thus, the need for public improvements may be geared with the ability to finance such improvements and maintain a co-ordinated pace with expansion of private development.

These functions presume continuous attention to the process of urban planning. A Master Plan which collects dust in the archives of the city hall is a monument on the grave of lost opportunities in urban improvement. Planning is a *process* which anticipates the needs of a community, proposes ways and means for the satisfaction of these needs, and relates these proposals to the orderly development of the city and realization of the Master Plan. The precise plans are the instruments with which these functions are performed.

Zoning Districts. In the zoning or land-use plan the community is divided into districts in which the land is restricted to certain specified uses. The size, shape, and location of these districts reflect the major uses indicated by the Master Plan and should be formed to invite the natural development of neighborhoods. The Master Plan may indicate an area to be appropriate for single-family dwellings, whereas the zoning plan may permit a commercial use within specified limits to be developed as a shopping center and contribute to the neighborhood quality of the area. A site for a school and a park may also be provided within such an area. Such developments of the precise plans are refinements of the Master Plan, their purpose being the creation of balanced community design.

Most zoning ordinances provide for different densities of population in different areas of residential and commercial districts. One residential district may permit only single-family houses with a density of five families or eighteen persons per acre, whereas another district may permit "unlimited multiple residential" use in which the density can reach hundreds of people per acre. These variations in population density must be reflected in other precise plans for the city since they affect the provisions of all community facilities and services. The size and location of schools, commercial land use and transportation, police and fire protection, and the size of utility services vary considerably with the number of people to be served.

The following description of land uses indicates the variety of districts which may appear in the zoning ordinance. The classification of these districts will differ in various communities, and local customs and requirements will determine the definition of each classification:

Agricultural districts permit the use of land consistent with economically feasible agricultural enterprise, the subdivision of land being governed by the type of agriculture normal to the area. Agricultural districts about some urban areas may establish a minimum lot area of 5 acres, another, 2 acres, while some include one-acre lots in this classification. Uses considered generally permissible in this type of district include farming, poultry-raising, dairying, and cattle and horse grazing. Restricted residential uses may also be permitted in this zone provided that the permissible agricultural uses are not of an obnoxious character. Hog raising may not be permitted in an agricultural zone because it is generally interpreted as an obnoxious use within an urban area. There are usually provisions in the zoning ordinance for exceptions by special permit if an investigation of the particular situation demonstrates no prospect of endangering the general welfare.

Estate districts are sometimes created to provide property owners the opportunity to establish a character of residential development measured primarily in terms of large-size lots. In some suburban areas it is desired to develop a rural quality, and the estate zone is for such a purpose. This is generally the most restricted residential zone, the minimum lot sizes ranging from 20,000 to 40,000 square feet in area. Some "agricultural" uses are frequently permitted in this zone, like poultry for domestic consumption or saddle horses. Estate zones are usually established at the behest of the property owners or developers who desire to attract clientele wishing reasonably large tracts protected from the infiltration of small-lot subdivision. Other factors sometimes warrant the establishment of estate zones; when facilities for sewage disposal are absent or limited, or police and fire protection are not readily available, or community facilities such as schools or commercial districts are remotely situated, it may be advisable to limit the population an area is permitted to accommodate.

Single-family districts are zones in which the land use is restricted to a single dwelling unit per lot. The zoning ordinance establishes a minimum lot area permitted in these zones and frequently specifies the minimum lot width. The standards vary considerably, some cities still permitting lot widths of 25 feet street frontage, but a width of 50 feet or more is being accepted in most communities as the minimum, with a minimum lot area of 5,000 square feet. Such restrictions are not retroactive, and property owners are not obliged to comply with regulations enacted subsequent to the recording of subdivisions with lesser restrictions.

Two-family districts permit the erection of either two single-family dwellings or a duplex on a single lot. Some communities now deny the right to build two separate dwellings on a lot, requiring that they be attached and under one roof structure. This zone permits twice the density of the single-family zone, although some ordinances require minimum lot sizes in excess of those in single-family districts.

Apartment house districts are the zones in which four-family buildings may be built on a single lot and, unless the minimum lot area is adjusted upward in size, these zones permit four times the density of the single-family zone. The two-story "walk-up" apartment or "flat" buildings are typical in this zone, although the height limits may permit building in excess of two stories.

Multiple-residence districts are usually several in number, each district in this classification being related to the type and height of structure and population density permitted on an individual lot. Some ordinances establish the differences in the classification of multiple-residence districts by permitting double the population density in each successive classification. When there are two or three classifications of this type of dwelling, the least restricted may result in an unlimited population density, subject to other restrictions such as side, rear, and front yards.

Hotel districts are usually considered the least restricted of the "residential" zones, although they may be identified with a commercial classification. Seldom is there a control of population density in these districts other than limitations imposed by side, rear, and front yards.

Commercial districts are regulated according to the enterprise conducted upon the premises, the zones ranging from the most restricted business, like the "corner grocery" or gasoline filling station, to the "heavy commercial" uses in which some light and nonobnoxious industrial pursuits are tolerated.

Industrial districts also range from the most restricted uses for "light" industry in which either electric power only may be employed or smoke, odors, and sound are rigidly controlled, to the unrestricted "heavy" industrial areas in which any type of manufacturing enterprise or process is permitted. Certain industrial uses which may endanger the public are frequently restricted to specified areas, whereas still others may require special permits by legislative action to conduct business. The manufacture of fireworks or fertilizer or the dumping of refuse and garbage may be restricted to the least restricted industrial zones with a further provision that they must be confined to areas at least 500 feet from a more restricted zone.

Special uses. In some communities there may be special uses to which land may be subject, such as drilling for oil and mining for rock or minerals. It is customary to control the use of land for uses of such a special nature by requiring individual action by the planning commission and issuance of permits by official action of the city council. The establishment of cemeteries may also come within this category and be subject to a similar control.

In addition to the uses prescribed in the various restricted districts, there are other provisions in the zoning ordinance to regulate adequately the use of land:

Height. Each district prescribes limitations upon the height to which structures in that district may be built. In restricted residential zones the height limit is generally two stories; in the multiple-residential zones it may be three or four stories for the most restricted classification to an unlimited height in the least restricted classification. The limitation of height in terms of floors may be augmented by a height in feet, such as 35 feet for the three-story district, or 150 feet for a thirteen-story district. Height limits are also prescribed for commercial and industrial districts, and any similar regulations appearing in other codes, such as structural or mechanical requirements, should be consistent with the zoning ordinance.

Density. Regulation of population density in residential districts is usually accomplished by prescribing the minimum area of land for each family dwelling unit built thereon. The standards for this requirement vary violently since each successive district from the most restrictive to the least permits a greater population density; a single-family district requiring 5,000 square feet of lot area for each dwelling while an area of only 300 square feet of lot area per dwelling unit may be the only requirement in a multiple-residential district.

Building bulk. It is not enough to define the building height in a zoning ordinance; the lot "coverage" must accompany this control in order to regulate the volume of building. The ordinance therefore specifies the space between buildings, the side, rear, and front yards, or other set-backs which may be necessary, and these distances are usually increased with the height of the structure. Some communities further require that buildings may cover only a specified percentage of the area of the lot. This relation of open space to covered space is not proportionate and, as prevails in the limitation on heights, the result is an ever-increasing population density as buildings rise higher into the air. This inconsistency in standards of open space is probably the most serious problem facing the future development of our cities. The inequitable distribution of space, the effect upon land values, resistance to rehabilitation created by these values, and the maladjustment of community services are heaping an increasing burden upon the city and its people.

Automobile Parking. In order to obtain some relief from congestion, some cities have amended their zoning ordinances to require the provision of parking space in connection with all building enterprise. These provisions vary from the requirement of a relatively small amount of space to rather ample space for some businesses. The requirements likewise vary as to location for the space: some provisions permit the space to be located upon property other than that being improved, others require that the space be contained within the limits of the lot being improved. Faced with the urgency to protect the future of the central district, large cities over 100,000 population have been the most inclined to adopt such provisions. LeCraw and Smith, of the Eno Foundation, estimate that some 23 per cent of the cities in this population group have some form of zoning for parking. Cities of lesser size with these provisions are: 3 per cent of those between 10,000 and 25,000; 7 per cent between 25,000 and 50,000; and 18 per cent between 50,000 and 100,000.[1]

The most common variety of parking control has been the regulation against street parking between 2:00 A.M. and 6:00 A.M., with the ostensible purpose of keeping the streets clear for cleaning and snow removal. Such a provision practically forces off-street parking, but it is not a direct and effective manner to achieve the positive purpose, and more cities are now inclined to adopt a positive method.

Most cities with zoning ordinances for parking require one car space for each dwelling unit in multiple dwellings, and some have adopted the stringent requirement of 1½ space per dwelling. Provisions are likewise made for off-street parking in connection with other building types. These are either less popular or of fairly recent origin, although places of public assembly, stores, and office buildings are being required to provide facilities in an ever-increasing number.

The majority of cities require one car space per three rooms in hotels, and some require one space per room. One space per room in hospitals is the favored ratio; a ratio of one space per four seats and one per ten seats appears to be the range for theaters; requirements for public assembly range from one space per five seats to one space per ten seats. For restaurants, several cities require parking space equal to the floor area.[2]

Public parking facilities for retail stores have received less attention than seems warranted, more emphasis having been given the provisions for service loading and unloading. Some cities require one space in public parking per 200 square feet of floor area, and others specify space equal to the floor in the building. Service facilities are specified in terms of reservation for loading, such as one truck space for each 5,000 to 20,000 square feet of floor area, a minimum of one space for every 2,000 square feet of lot area, or a reservation between the service alley and loading area, such as a space equal to one-half the width of the alley but not less than 14 feet between the alley and the building line.

Most cities that have zoning provisions for off-street parking applicable to office buildings require one space per 200 square feet of building floor area. These pro-

[1] Zoning for Parking, Charles S. LeCraw and Wilbur S. Smith, *Traffic Quarterly*, The Eno Foundation for Highway Traffic Control, Connecticut, January 1947.
[2] *Ibid.*

visions range to one space per 1,000 square feet in buildings having more than 7,500 square feet floor area, as in the recent Los Angeles ordinance. There are few ordinances requiring parking for industrial buildings except those for loading facilities. The latter are frequently similar to the requirements for retail stores, but some specify one loading space for industrial and wholesale buildings for each 8,000 square feet of floor area ranging to as high as each 20,000 square feet area.

The definitions of a "parking space" vary considerably, ranging from an area of 125 square feet to 400 square feet. The majority of the ordinances have adopted an area of 200 square feet as the appropriate space. Many have provided for off-street parking by stipulating that the space shall be "adequate," a term not recommended since it leaves the issue open to arbitrary administrative decisions and potential abuses.

A majority of the cities with parking ordinances require that the space shall be provided on the same lot as the building. There are variations in this, however, some cities permitting the space to be located some distance away. A distance of 200 to 300 feet is the most frequent provision, although it ranges up to 1,500 feet. The distance from the lot on which the building is located varies with the size of the city and intensity of development; small cities require less distance. An average of some 275 feet is usual for cities of 10,000–25,000 population and ranges up to an average of 700 feet in cities with more than 100,000.

Without provisions in the zoning ordinance that make off-street parking mandatory for each building improvement and in a quantity which will cope with the parking problems created by commercial enterprise, it will become necessary to develop such facilities as independent ventures. These are less certain of maintaining a balance between commercial floor area and parking space, but there have been demonstrations which enjoyed some success, such as the merchant association in Oakland, California. It seems only reasonable that the enterprise which creates the problem should assume responsibility for solving it. If this is not required by law, it must be undertaken by the city, or authority be granted to private corporations under state enabling legislation.

Provisions for parking facilities in zoning ordinances do not measure up to standards adopted and deemed essential by some business concerns. Chain markets have been most concerned with the provision of an adequate space for car parking. They generally plan upon parking space twice the sales floor area of the store, and on the West coast it is not uncommon for some of the large retail markets to seek sites of sufficient size to provide parking space four times the floor area.

Some Conventional Faults. Zoning is the instrument with which regulation over the use of land may be administered in the interest of the general welfare by protecting the interests of each individual who invests in the development of the urban community. Because it is such a vital instrument, the inadequacies to which reference has been made elsewhere in this book deserve serious consideration by all who profess a genuine interest in the future welfare of the city. Some of these faults have become matters only of habit, and some are unwittingly espoused by "authorities" on planning. That correction of faulty practices is overdue may be apparent in the cities themselves.

One such fault is the convention of "transition zoning." It is customary to view the pattern of a city as a pyramid; the greatest density of people, buildings, and land values lies at the center of the city and gradually diminishes as the outer edges are approached. Except for some areas of completely unrestricted and obnoxious industrial uses, the transition from one zone to the next proceeds from the least restricted to the more restricted in successive stages, heavy commercial uses are adjacent to industrial uses, light commercial next to heavy commercial, unrestricted multiple-residential next to light commercial, restricted multiple-residential next to unrestricted, and so forth through the various zones to single-family dwelling districts on the fringes of the city pattern.

The logic of this sequence is more apparent than real; it breaks down at the juncture between the zones of high density residential and the zones of heavy commercial, industrial, and railroad property. Because the single-family dwelling is associated with desirable land use in contrast with the multiple dwelling as a less desirable use, it is a paradox that transition zoning should force the greatest population density contiguous to the land uses which provide the least desirable qualities for a living environment. There appears little logic to support the exposure of the greatest number of people to environmental conditions deemed undesirable for a lesser number.

This paradox would not be corrected by the simple device of establishing single-family districts instead of multiple-residential contiguous to commercial and industrial zones, although it would carry with it more logic. It rather points to the necessity for more attention to the location of open spaces—parks and recreation—as buffers between the areas in which the land uses are definitely separated in character and function. This is not a short-range program in the development of cities, but the zoning of *space* between areas of widely separate character would probably provide a means to the gradual redevelopment of these areas for permanent open space. Seldom is there provision of a *zone* for *permanent open space* which assures the city of immediate or ultimate retention of land for this purpose.

Another serious fault in the habit of zoning is the "strip-zoning" for commercial and "income" residential uses along all the principal and secondary highways throughout the city. This creates traffic congestion which cannot be corrected by the use of any device for traffic signals or channeling. Every foot of street frontage along such a highway must be accessible from the street if it is to be of value for its zoned use. This requires that one traffic lane on each side of the street must be reserved for ingress and egress if not parking. If the street functions with reasonable satisfaction as a through-traffic artery, the speed of the vehicles and the necessity for attention to their safe operation detracts from the advertising advantages of the street for commercial purposes. The result is a plan which is impractical as a traffic artery and undesirable as a shopping street.

In a similar category is the custom of commercial zoning on all four corners about the intersection of two important traffic thoroughfares. This usually results in one or two of the four corners having the most strategic location for business but none enjoying a position convenient to the people who patronize them. It would be preferable if corners where traffic movement is vital were designed for the least distracting uses, with provision for selected *centers* for business enterprise which depend upon the most regular flow of pedestrian patronage.

The serious fault of mixed land uses common to zoning practice has received comment elsewhere in this book. Zoning is predicated upon the exclusion of the least restricted land uses from areas of greater restriction, but it does not provide for the exclusion of the more restricted uses from areas of less restricted uses; residences may be built in industrial zones but industries may not be built in residential zones. An industry in a residential zone need be no more detrimental than a dwelling in an industrial area. On the contrary, it is conceivable that the former might be far more desirable when it is not an obnoxious variety, but a dwelling in an industrial area cannot withstand the effect of blight.

Mixed land uses are not economically sound; land occupied by dwellings in an industrial zone is removed from its highest and best use for industrial improvement, and expansion is forced elsewhere. Consolidation of industrial development with the circulation and transportation appropriate for it is nullified, whereas the families living within the area are subjected to all the characteristics of an inferior living environment. This situation repeats itself, only by diminishing degree, in each of the successive stages of land use through commercial and multiple-residential zones.

The intermixture of land uses renders it practically impossible for the community to estimate the needs of the people and provide the necessary services. Obsolescence and blight are apparent on all sides and the healthy expansion of industry, commerce, and residential uses is seriously retarded. This condition leads to the suggestion that only the use for which a district is designated should be permitted in it; just as the single-family dwelling is the only use permitted in a district so zoned, only commercial uses would be permitted in a commercial zone, and industrial districts would be restricted to industrial development. A plan to accomplish such a policy might be comparable to the amortization policy in effect in some cities for the gradual removal of uses which do not conform to the adopted zoning plan for land use.

The history of zoning has demonstrated the importance of avoiding restrictions or requirements in the zoning ordinances which are impossible to enforce clearly. Not only does such a course subject an ordinance to unreasonable administration, but it breeds disrespect for the basic intentions for which the rules were formulated; it further provides selfish interests with their most valuable weapon to defeat the purposes of these essential regulations over urban development. Prejudices should no more be written into the zoning ordinance than they should be employed to defeat its purpose.

The Quantity of Land Uses. The location of various uses designated on the

Master Plan is one important factor in planning; the quantity of land and building bulk allocated to these uses in the zoning plan is the other. Whereas determinations on both these elements of land use are subject to a variety of local conditions, it must be recognized that the excessive areas devoted to the least restricted land uses in the zoning of our cities—multiple-residential, commercial, and industrial—are so common, and the impact of resulting mixed land uses has had such a tragic impact upon their development, a revaluation of zoning is long overdue. The deterioration of the urban enviroment has taken its toll in social values and is telling on the economic stability at an increasing rate. Reconsideration of excessive zoning could possibly do more than any other urban enterprise to restore stability to investments in capital as well as the welfare of the people in our cities.

The land area allocated to the various uses in the zoning ordinance compared with a map of existing uses in almost any city reveals little relation between them. Industrial zoning cuts huge paths across the city along railroad rights-of-way and waterfronts, the central business district is a great rectangle in the heart of the city with fingers of "strip" commercial zoning stretching and criss-crossing along every highway as far as the city limits, and multiple-residential zoning occupies a large proportion of the remainder. Single-family zones are distributed about the outskirts.

A map of the existing land uses, on the other hand, shows little resemblance to this pattern of zoning; the spotty character reveals the effect of mixed land uses while no area is devoted in quantity comparable to those provided on the zoning map. There is little purpose served by a zoning map which presents an orderly pattern of land use when the city for which it is designed shows no resemblance to it and little apparent prospect of ever achieving such a pattern. It may be suggested that zoned land uses must allow adequate space into which the various urban activities may grow. Such is the case, to be sure, but greater is the necessity, therefore, to establish in the zoning ordinance the standards for this development which will provide a balance in the land uses, the standards of population density and building bulk which bear a reasonable relation to each other.

As has been observed before in this book, these balances are quite absent in the current practices of planning and zoning cities. Current standards permit unlimited congestion and excessive land uses in the less restricted areas and this situation actuates the appeal for reconsideration of the standards of land use.

While it is obviously necessary to apply statistics with utmost care, data on the actual uses of land in cities may provide a more valid measurement of space needs than the land uses allocated in current zoning ordinances. A study by Harland Bartholomew, *Urban Land Uses*, in 1932, records a series of surveys in a number of small "self-contained" cities and satellite towns. The "self-contained" cities range in size from 5,000 to 300,000 population, the satellite towns are less than 25,000 population, and the data on land uses should be helpful in evaluating the actual need for space in the various classifications of land.

ACTUAL LAND USES
Based on *Urban Land Uses*

Areas below exclude vacant undeveloped land. Vacant land averages 6.8 acres per 100 persons in self-contained cities and 8.3 acres per 100 persons in satellite cities.

	No. Acres per 100 Persons		Percentage of Developed Area	
	Self-contained Cities	Satellite Towns	Self-contained Cities	Satellite Towns
Single-family dwellings	2.935	4.68	36.0	44.5
Two-family dwellings	.143	.18	2.1	2.0
Multi-family dwellings	.076	.12	1.0	1.7
Commercial	.179	.13	2.3	1.4
Light industrial	.236		3.2	
Heavy industrial	.217	1.17	2.6	10.3
Railroad property	.463		5.4	
Streets	2.82	3.01	33.5	29.7
Parks and playgrounds	.479	.11	6.3	1.3
Public space	.622	1.01	7.6	9.1
	8.170	10.41	100.0	100.0

LAND USE REQUIREMENTS IN AMERICAN CITIES*

Net Acres/100 Persons		*Percentage of Developed Area*
Residential	3.0	40
Commercial	.3	3
Industrial	.5	7
Railroads	.4	4
Streets	2.7	30
Parks and playgrounds	.6	6
Other public uses	.5	6
Semi-public uses	.3	4
	8.3	100

* *Local Planning Administration*, Ladislas Segoe, International City Managers' Association, Chicago, 1941.

The total land area in the survey cities[3] was approximately 15 acres per 100 population. Of this area an average of 6 to 7½ acres per 100 persons in the "self-contained" cities was actually developed, whereas about 11 acres per 100 persons were developed in the satellite communities. The rest was undeveloped land within the city limits, an area ranging from 22 to 66 per cent of the total in larger cities and amounting to an average of about 40 per cent of the total area in both types of communities. This conveys some idea of the latitude which still remains for our urban communities to control their future development.

The extent of mixed land uses is apparent in the accompanying maps, and it was observed in the surveys of 14 cities that nearly 6,000 apartment buildings were spotted over an area of 3,500 city blocks—an average of 1.7 apartment buildings per block. Were the population density in apartments and single dwellings somewhat similar, this mixture of dwelling types might not prove the undesirable environment it now represents, but the unfavorable effect is evident in the difference in lot area per family prevailing in these two types of dwellings. The lot area for single-family houses is between 5,000 and 7,000 square feet, whereas it reduces to 1,350 square feet per family when developed for apartments.[4] So long as this difference in population density is an accepted practice in urban zoning, the overzoned multiple-dwelling areas and their widespread mixture with single-family dwellings offer little actual protection for the latter type of dwelling.

Nearly 80 per cent of the urban population is housed in single-family dwellings, and this type occupies 36 per cent of the developed area of cities compared with two-family and multiple dwellings housing the remainder, 20 per cent of the people, and occupying but 3 per cent of the developed urban area. The excessive zoning for apartment development cannot provide the protection to single-family development when apartments filter through great segments of the city actually occupied largely by single-family houses. Large metropolitan cities undoubtedly need a greater ratio of multiple-residential zoning than the smaller cities, but the percentage of families occupying single-family houses is considerably greater than the superficial observation of our cities suggests.

The Bartholomew survey revealed that larger cities have a greater proportion of their areas allocated to parks and playgrounds than the satellite communities. This condition is probably due to the lesser density of residential development in the satellite towns; about 45 per cent of the developed area, or nearly 5 acres per 100 persons, is occupied by single-family dwellings in the satellite towns compared with 36 per cent of the developed area, or 3 acres per 100 persons, in the larger cities.

Some cities are primarily trading and distribution centers for a wide agricultural area, some may be resort centers in recreational localities, but the economic backbone of most cities is industrial enterprise.

Zoning for industry, like commercial zoning, is in excess of the required demand.

[3] *Urban Land Uses*, Harland Bartholomew, Harvard University Press, Cambridge, 1932.
[4] *Ibid.*

Most small cities have about 10 per cent of their developed area occupied by combined light and heavy industry and railroad property. The area zoned for these uses is three times this area or more in some cases. As in commercial zones, this excess industrial zoning contributes seriously to the blight of a city. Within these zones there is permitted every variety of structure from single-family dwellings to heavy manufacturing plants and railroads. The environment is decidedly unhealthy for residential development; residential improvements are not encouraged because of the potential use of the land for industrial development, and lending institutions are reluctant to risk loans for new buildings. The inevitable result is blight, mixed land uses, and then slums and all that goes with them.

"Strip" zoning for industrial use is too frequently practiced. This is particularly true along railroad rights-of-way which are invariably considered ripe for location of new industry. This is an insidious practice which could be greatly improved by some degree of consolidation of industrial areas reached by spur tracks and separated from other land uses by belts of open space to serve as buffers between industrial areas and residential development. Such a pattern would establish an appropriate relation between the location of employment and the dwellings of the workers, with a reduction in the transportation that now clogs the cities.

The area of land needed for industrial uses of all kinds depends upon the types of industry located in a city, or for which a city may be particularly adapted. Light manufacturing plants, which use automatic machine processes, may occupy space in multistory loft buildings and require less ground space than heavy industry, such as steel mills, which process raw materials and require extensive space for storage and movement of materials and products. Prevailing density ranges from 20 to 240 employees per acre in the environs of New York City and New Jersey industrial areas. The highest density is obviously in Manhattan where industry is located mostly in loft buildings of several stories. In New York City and environs the industrial uses average about 40 employees per acre, and this is also the basis for estimating industrial space requirements in Los Angeles. Space occupied by industrial uses in New York City itself is a little more than twice this density, or about 88 workers per acre.

Heavy industry prefers a location unplatted and without street improvements. The site may thus be planned for the specific requirements of the plant operations. Access by spur railroad tracks to main transportation lines is important, and some heavy industries need port facilities. Light industry generally uses motor truck transportation, and their locations are considerably more flexible.

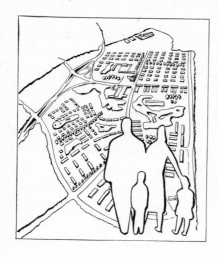

CHAPTER 21

THE NEIGHBORHOOD UNIT

A Unit of Urban Design. When prehistoric men found land which would support them in relative safety and comparative permanence, they formed towns. Mutual aid in times of danger and co-operation toward a general improvement in their living conditions encouraged the development of the city; people realized they could create more things for themselves by working together than they could individually. Being a social entity man seeks the companionship of his fellowmen. Generally desiring the association of others as much like themselves as possible, people with common interests assembled in groups to secure for themselves protection and the maximum amenities of life.

As the city grew in size, some areas within it assumed certain homogeneous qualities which we have identified as neighborhoods. People who came to America frequently grouped together with those who spoke their common language, shared their particular religious tenets, or stemmed from similar racial backgrounds. When some of their number became richer than the rest and enjoyed the greater mobility provided by a fine brace of horses and a carriage, they moved their residences to near-by hills and formed more exclusive neighborhoods founded on differences in social and economic status. Different environmental standards were established and people who desired and could afford them gathered there to secure these amenities.

Some neighborhoods developed, as in ancient times, more from compulsion than native choice; restrictions of prejudice, limitations of language, or economic pressures often forced the cultivation of neighborhoods identified by class distinctions.

As open space in the growing city was built up, some neighborhoods were unable to retain their original identity, the economic level of the people living within them being inadequate to maintain a standard of physical maintenance or community services. Decay set in and slums were on the way toward formation. Residents of formerly exclusive areas moved to new districts beyond the reach of this influence. The metropolis created by the industrial revolution completely dissipated whatever urban unity remained from the medieval town and, except for exclusive residential districts which escaped from the sprawling industrial city, the distinctions between neighborhoods gradually merged into a common mediocrity. It was necessary to restore some semblance of human identity to the urban scene and, prodded by the social evils that enveloped the factory town, social workers emerged with the settlement house. Probably the settlement house movement which began in London about 1885 was the first conscious recognition of the neighborhood as a basic element in the urban structure; it served as a nucleus for the restoration of human values which had dissolved within the indistinguishable mass of the industrial metropolis.

The dissolution of these values has created among urban dwellers a detachment from each other. Opinions among social scientists differ on the effectiveness of the neighborhood principle as a means to overcome this detachment. Some contend it is imperative to re-establish a "face-to-face" relationship through neighborhood association, others expect that people will seek their friends no matter what distances may separate them, even while they remain only chance acquaintances and even strangers with their next door neighbors, and some oppose the neighborhood with the claim that it leads to a grouping of people that inevitably results in compulsory class distinctions.

These conflicting opinions notwithstanding, it has become a practical necessity to employ the neighborhood unit, or its counterpart, as a means to restore a recognizable form in the physical organization of the city. However large or small the city may be, there must be a workable unit of human scale with which to weave the urban pattern into a workable whole. Dissolution of human scale has allowed the industrial and commercial metropolis to become socially stagnant and physically flabby. As Benton McKaye said, "Mankind has cleared the jungle and replaced it with a labyrinth."[1]

The Neighborhood Unit Defined. The neighborhood unit is not some sociological phenomenon; it embraces no particular theories of social science. It is simply a physical environment in which a mother knows that her child will have no traffic streets to cross on his way to school, a school which is within easy walking distance from the home. It is an environment in which the housewife may have an easy walk to the shopping center where she may obtain the daily household goods, and the man of the house may find convenient transportation to and from his work. It is an environment in which a well-equipped playground is located near the home where the children may play in safety with their friends; the parents may not care to maintain intimate friendship with their neighbors, but children are so inclined and they need the facilities of recreation for the healthy development of their minds and spirit.

The unit of measurement for space in urban society is the individual; the common denominator for the arrangement of that space is the family. To satisfy their relatively simple social wants, it is natural for families to seek the advantages which appropriately planned neighborhoods provide. The functions of a neighborhood have been described by C. J. Bushnell[2] as: maintenance, learning, control, and play. One of the

[1] *The New Exploration: A Philosophy of Regional Planning*, Benton McKaye, Harcourt, Brace & Co., New York, 1928.
[2] Community Center Movement as a Moral Force, *International Journal of Ethics*, Vol. XXX, April 1920.

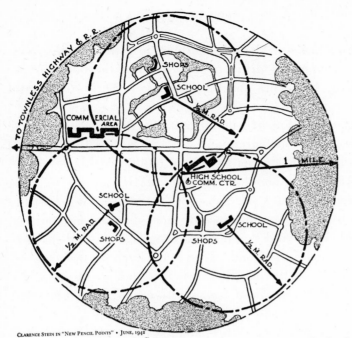

CLARENCE STEIN IN "NEW PENCIL POINTS" • JUNE, 1942

Clarence Stein's determinations of the proper areas to be included in the Neighborhood Unit.

In the upper-right diagram the elementary school is the center of the unit and within a one-half mile radius of all residents in the neighborhood. A small shopping center for daily needs is located near the school. Most residential streets are suggested as cul-de-sac or "dead-end" roads to eliminate through traffic, and park space flows through the neighborhood in a manner reminiscent of the Radburn plan.

The upper-left diagram shows the grouping of three neighborhood units served by a high school and one or two major commercial centers, the radius for walking distance to these facilities being one mile.

THE NEIGHBORHOOD UNIT

The Neighborhood Unit

as seen by

Clarence A. Perry

Perry was one of the first to give some consideration to the physical form of the neighborhood unit. It is substantially the same as that in the diagram by Stein but suggests that the maximum radius for walking distance from the home to the community center should be only one-quarter mile. Accepting the practice which was then, and still is, generally prevalent, shopping areas are situated at intersecting traffic streets on the outside corners rather than at the center of the unit.

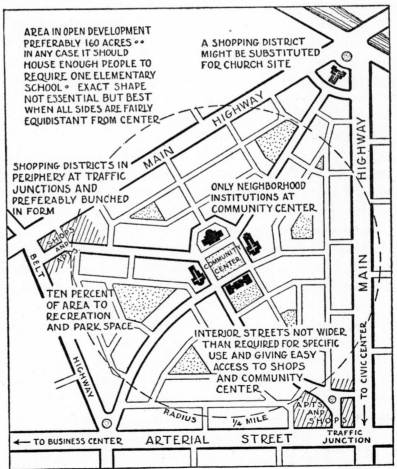

Reproduced from New York Regional Survey

earliest authorities to attempt a definition of the neighborhood in fairly specific terms was Clarence A. Perry. Although opinions differ to some degree, the definition he set forth in the Regional Survey of New York and Its Environs, 1929, is still a valid statement.

Perry described the neighborhood unit as that populated area which would require and support an elementary school with an enrollment of between 1,000 and 1,200 pupils. This would mean a population of between 5,000 and 6,000 people. Developed as a single-family dwelling district with a population density of 10 families per acre, the neighborhood unit would occupy about 160 acres and have a shape which would render it unnecessary for any child to walk a distance of more than one-half mile to school. About 10 per cent of the area would be allocated to recreation, and through-traffic arteries would be confined to the surrounding streets, internal streets being limited to service access for residents of the neighborhood. The unit would be served by shopping facilities, churches, a library, and a community center, the latter being located in conjunction with the school.

The neighborhood unit, or some equivalent of this unit, is repeatedly referred to in proposals for urban reorganization.[3] The suggested form varies widely, but the essential characteristics are fairly consistent. The suggested population appropriate for a unit has ranged between 3,000 and 12,000 people. In the plans for Chicago in 1942 the range was from 4,000 to 12,000; in the Greater London Plan, 1944, by Abercrombie and Forshaw, the unit size is 6,000 to 10,000. Some authorities have expressed a desire for units of smaller size than a school district, believing the nature of the neighborhood requires a relatively small size—generally 1,000 and not to exceed 1,500 families. Despite the variations, the principle of the neighborhood unit runs through all considerations for social, physical, and political organization of the city; it represents a unit of the population with basic common needs for educational, recreational, and maintenance facilities, and it is the standards for these facilities from which the size and design of a neighborhood emerge.

N. L. Engelhardt, Jr., has presented a comprehensive pattern of the neighborhood as a component of the successively larger segments in a city structure. The neighborhood unit includes the elementary school, a small shopping district, and a playground. These facilities are grouped near the center of the unit so that the walking distance between them and the home does not exceed one-half mile. An elementary school with a standard enrollment of between 600 and 800 pupils will represent a population of about 1,700 families in the neighborhood unit.[4]

Two such units (3,400 families) will support a junior high school with a recreation center in conjunction; the walking distance does not exceed one mile from the center to the most remote home. Four units (6,800 families) will require a senior high school and a commercial center. It will also be an appropriate size for a major park and recreation area. This grouping of four neighborhood units forms a "community"

[3] See Chapter 27, Part VI.
[4] The School-Neighborhood Nucleus, N. L. Engelhardt, Jr., *Architectural Forum*, October 1943.

with a population of about 24,000 people. The component parts of this community pattern are integrated, and such communities may be arranged in whatever combinations the sources of employment and communications to and from them may require.

Open Space. To suggest that American communities are deficient in recreational facilities is only to repeat what has been often said by many authorities. The reasons for the deficiency are manifold, but one of the most glaring is ill-planned land uses. Our present zoning practices provide extravagant areas for commercial and industrial uses, and the result is an urban pattern riddled with mixed land uses and an absence of stability in residential improvements. Consequently, we are faced with two predicaments: either excessive land values render it too expensive to allot adequate open space for recreation, or existing parks are swallowed by commercial and industrial areas from which the people are trying desperately to escape to a better living environment.

A similar situation prevails with our schools. Because of unfortunate site selection, miscalculated population shifts, or lack of planning at the outset, schools are found languishing in the midst of business and factory areas, stranded between main traffic arteries, or situated in lagging subdivisions too remote to serve the people. Recreation and education are linked with all other phases of urban development, whether they are planned or unplanned. Statistically, parks and playgrounds are deficient in amount, but the maldistribution of available facilities is even more striking. This combination of circumstances makes it imperative to establish neighborhood units in city planning.

As has been suggested in previous pages of this book, the absence of open space is an urban curse. One of the most vital aspects of community living, and the one which has been too frequently avoided, is adequate space for recreation. Open space would have been available if it had been so planned and reserved when land was inexpensive. But urban growth has been a mad scramble to subdivide and sell every parcel of property that could receive a building, and many which were not so fit.

As the machine has produced more and more with less and less manpower, and with the organization of labor, the work week has been reduced from 60 hours to the 8-hour day and the 6-day week; then, during the 1930's it was further reduced to 40 hours and in some trades to 35 hours. Not only has this change made more leisure time available, but the intensified nature of modern production has rendered the necessity for relaxation and recreation the more important.

Uncontrolled spread of blight hastened the flight to the suburbs, the process we usually identify as decentralization, and the absorption of open space within the central areas of our cities was a major factor in creating this blight. The combination of mixed land uses, physical deterioration, and lack of open space has created a situation which can hardly be cured by the injection of occasional playgrounds into these areas. They will improve the amenities within the hard and bare confines of blighted areas, but such devices will not remedy the condition; replanning and rebuilding will be needed in the great areas of our blighted and congested urban core. This process of rebuilding will necessarily be predicated upon the provision of ample open space, but there is another important and urgent problem of open space which our cities are facing: the reservation of space within all the subdivisions spreading out across the urban landscape. Standards—adequate standards—of open space are urgently necessary to avoid a repetition of the identical problem presented by the blighted city centers.

Open space in the city is usually considered as the area for recreation, and appropriately so. However, this space falls into a number of categories. There is space devoted primarily to active playgrounds for children, youths, and adults; there is also space arranged for the more passive relaxation of adults. These spaces are those to which reference is generally made in a consideration of recreational facilities. Another classification should not be overlooked: the conservation of natural areas within as well as without the city. This conservation may take the form of greenbelts to serve as buffers between different land uses—between residential and industrial areas—or it may become a reservation of places of particular historic or geographic interest, or spaces which are topographically unsuited for satisfactory development in other urban improvements.

The standards of open space cannot adequately specify the required areas in a city for all these classifications; part of the distinction of cities derives from the way in which the natural site is shaped and planned. The specified spaces for defined recreational uses are not the full measure of adequacy of a recreational program under any circumstances; an abstract area of land in proportion to the population is but a part of the planning for recreation space in the city. It is the distribution of this space which measures the adequacy, not the amount alone.

Neighborhood Recreation. There are three categories of recreation space for which the distribution as well as the amount of land is an important factor. They are identified by different terms in various localities, but the National Recreation Association has classified them as (1) the Playlot, (2) the Children's Playground, and (3) the Playfield. Each type fulfills a specific function in the design of neighborhoods and groups of neighborhoods.[5]

The first category, the Playlot, is for small children under 8 years of age. It is the equivalent of the "back-yard" of homes in sparsely settled residential districts, and in single-family districts the function is generally fulfilled by the usual open space about the homes. This is usually adequate when the street system is so designed that through traffic is discouraged or eliminated. In densely built apartment districts, however, the Playlot assumes an important function and there should be one Playlot available for each group of families ranging from 30 to 60 in number. The size of each lot should range from 1,500 to 2,500 square feet in area, and each should be located within a clear view of all the dwellings it serves. If a Playground is more distant than several blocks or is separated from the residential district by a busy traffic street,

[5] *Play Space in New Neighborhoods*, A Committee Report on Standards of Outdoor Recreation Areas in Housing Developments, National Recreation Association, New York 1939.

the area of the Playlots should be increased to 2,000 to 4,000 square feet. The Play-lots should be equipped with such devices as low swings, slide, sand-box, jungle gyms, and space for running and circle games; a portion of the lot should be paved. All equipment should be designed and arranged for small children, and authorities have pointed out the fascination of tots for objects like low walls, logs, and other common forms like shallow trenches and small hills. Some form of enclosure—a hedge or fence—about the Playlot is advisable, and a pergola and benches for mothers should be included.

The second category is the Children's Playground. Designed for children whose ages range from 5 to 15, this Playground is the center of recreation activities for a neighborhood. Most authorities contend that a Playground should be within one-quarter mile walking distance of the dwelling area it serves; this distance is particu-larly important in densely built districts, and it should not exceed one-half mile in the most sparsely settled residential areas. A study of five large cities surveyed a total of nearly 35,000 children; of this number two-thirds went to a Playground within three blocks of their home and three-quarters lived within four blocks.

The preferable location for a Playground is adjacent to a community center or ele-mentary school, where supervised recreation is possible. The National Recreation Association recommends an average of one acre per 1,000 population for Playgrounds, but some cities have a standard of one-half acre per 1,000 population. In these latter cases, however, it is generally assumed that the Playground will be augmented by some of the play space usually provided about the elementary school. The following schedule of suggested space allowances indicates a comparison between the National Recrea-tion Association recommendations and those of the Community Builders Council of the Urban Land Institute:[6]

Population	Number Children	National Recreation Association (Acres)	Community Builders Council (Acres)
1,000......	200	2.3	....
1,500......	300	2.55	....
2,000......	450	3.05	3.25
3,000......	600	3.5	4.0
4,000......	800	4.45	5.0
5,000......	1,000	5.35	6.0
6,000......	1,200	6.25	

As a rule a playground for fewer than 200 children is impracticable for operation, and more than 1,200 children require two or more separate playgrounds. The National Recreation Association recommends a minimum of 3 to 5 acres for a Playground; the Community Builders suggest the minimum be 2 to 2½ acres.

The Playground should provide an area for apparatus and an open space for informal

[6] *Community Builders' Handbook*, Community Builders' Council, Urban Land Institute, 1947.

play. There should be courts for various games such as soccer, soft-ball, tennis, hand-ball, and volleyball. Space is also needed for the quiet activities such as crafts, dramatics, and story-telling. A wading pool is desirable in warm climates, and there should be a Playlot with its facilities included. The lot should be near a shelter and rest area for adults. Lighting for evening use is desirable. Because economy in the operation and maintenance of recreation space in a community is highly important, it is impracticable to substitute a number of small play spaces throughout a residential development. The recommended sizes and design of spaces are more economical and avoid the confusion between the various age groups who use the facilities.

The Playfield is intended for young people and adults and provides a variety of recreational activities. A single Playfield may serve four or five neighborhoods; the walking distance should not exceed one mile, one-half mile radius being preferred. The National Recreation Association recommends a size of one acre per 800 population served by it, with a minimum size of 10 acres and a preferred minimum of 20 acres. Here again the standards vary, some cities holding to a minimum average area of one-

MINIMUM STANDARDS FOR PUBLIC RECREATIONAL AREAS
CITY PLANNING DEPARTMENT—LOS ANGELES, CALIFORNIA*

Nature of Recreation	Operational Agency	Ages Served	Minimum Acres	Service Radius	1 Acre Serves	1 Site Serves	Desirable Features Minimum Facilities
1 PLAYLOT	Group Housing	Pre-school	⅛	1 block	—	136 tots	Housing projects only
2 NEIGHBORHOOD PLAYGROUND WITH PARK FACILITIES	Elementary or junior high school or recreation dept.	5 to 14 and aged persons	Active area—3	¼ to ⅜ miles	218 children	600–800 children	Space for juvenile tag and athletic games, crafts bldg., table games, rest area and boundary planting
			Passive area—2	Same	2000 tot. pop.	3000–10,000 tot. pop.	
3 DISTRICT PLAYGROUND AND PARK	Senior high school or recreation dept. and park dept.	15–20 and adults	Active area—10	¾ to 1½ miles	290 youth	1,000–4,000 youth	Swimming pool, athletic field, all-purpose building, facilities for large group activities
			Passive area—5	Same	2,000 to 6,000 pop.	10,000 to 50,000 pop.	
4 SPORTS CENTER	Recreation dept.	Youth and adults	30	5–10 miles	Variable	500,000 pop.	Multiple facilities for field games, field house
5 URBAN PARK	Park dept.	All	30	5 miles	2,000 tot. pop.	50,000 to 100,000 pop.	Shade, lawn and water
6 REGIONAL PARK	Park dept.	All	No limit	No limit	Variable	Variable	Outstanding scenic or recr'l attractions
7 BEACH	Recreation dept.	All	No limit	No limit	Variable	Variable	Multiple recreation facilities
8 CAMP	Recreation dept. or school board	Various	20	No limit	Variable	Variable	Isolated location in primitive area
9 SPECIALIZED PARK	Park dept.	Various	No limit	No limit	Variable	Variable	Golf course, or other special uses
10 CULTURAL SITE	Semi-public or public	All	No limit	No limit	Variable	Variable	Historical, scientific, or educational interest
11 MISCELLANEOUS OPEN SPACES	Any government agency	All	No limit	Local	Variable	Variable	Planted strips, squares, public bldg. grounds
12 PRESERVE OR RESERVATION	Any government agency	All	No limit	Local	Variable	Variable	Protection of primitive or scenic areas

* APRIL 1948.

half acre per 1,000 population for this type of recreation space. The N. R. A. suggests one Playfield for each group of 20,000 population, and the space should be designed for the same facilities as a Children's Playground with the addition of space for sports like football, baseball, hockey, archery, a swimming pool, outdoor theater, bandshell, and a recreation building. Night lighting should be provided.

Urban Conservation. The three types of recreation spaces—Playlot, Children's Playground, and Playfield—require the greatest attention with regard to their distribution in the community, the adequacy of space allotted to them, and their relation to the traffic arteries, community facilities, and accessibility from the homes. The total space for recreation is not confined to these categories, however. There are, in addition, the large city parks which supply the main facilities for city-wide recreation, organized sports, public golf courses, open-air entertainment, and the zoological and botanical gardens. These parks usually retain or reintroduce natural surroundings to the city and, where the sites are so adapted, they maintain the native wildlife as far as possible. They vary greatly in size, but they are usually of considerable area. Fairmount Park in Philadelphia and Griffith Park in Los Angeles each contains nearly 4,000 acres; Forest Park in St. Louis with its famous outdoor amphitheater has 1,380 acres, and Golden Gate Park in San Francisco contains about 1,000 acres. In addition to well-known Central Park which has only 840 acres, New York City has five other parks, ranging from those of 1,000 acres to the nearly 2,000 acres each.

Another type closely akin to the large park is the familiar "city" park which serves as a breather in the built-up urban areas. Their frequency depends a great deal upon the degree of population density, 5 miles apart being an average distance in congested areas and 10 miles being a standard in a highly decentralized city like Los Angeles. It is preferable that these parks be not smaller than about 30 acres in size, with a standard of about one acre per 2,000 people as a minimum area. This type of park is somewhat reminiscent of the Boston Commons (44 acres), but it is not intended to resemble a village green like the diminutive 6-acre public squares located in each quadrant of the original plan by Penn for Philadelphia. Such "squares" are little more than open space upon which some buildings may front. The city park should provide a natural atmosphere which may induce relaxation and some degree of repose.

The broadest reach of open space may be identified as the regional parks or park reserves. They comprise great areas of space, most of which is maintained in its natural state. Cook County Forest Preserve near Chicago is one of the greatest of these spaces devoted to conservation; it contains more than 30,000 acres. Others are the South Mountain Park of 15,000 acres near Phoenix, Arizona, the 10,000 acre reserve near Denver, Tilden Regional parks in Oakland, California, and the Westchester Park System in New York.

It is the great stretches of open spaces represented by these reserves or regional parks for conservation purposes, and also some of the large city parks, that stir the vision of greenbelts many of these spaces might have become had they been formed as an integral part of the city plan. These parks are frequently the transition between the urban development and the rural countryside, being situated beyond the center of population. They might have been formed as green buffers to separate the different land uses within the city and have been even more accessible to the people than their present location offers.

There are many recreational spaces of a special nature: cultural centers including the museums and art galleries, beaches, amusement parks, sports centers including athletic fields, swimming pools, and stadiums. There are also the grand sweeps of broad parkways in which recreation areas are developed; the Outer Drive along the lake front of Chicago is a magnificent illustration of this latter facility.

The over-all minimum urban space devoted to the total of the foregoing recreational spaces ranges from about 3 acres per 1,000 population in the city to a desirable standard recommended by the National Recreation Association and other authorities of 10 acres per 1,000 population. It is further recommended that the urban area be planned for a reservation of about 10 per cent of the gross area of the city to accommodate the space for an increase in population growth. In the vigorous replanning of London in preparation for the rebuilding program which must move forward as a result of war devastation, the standard of open space in the outlying areas of the county is 7 acres per 1,000 population, while the density of land use within the city boundaries has forced a standard of no more than 4 acres per 1,000 persons.

The absence of open space within our cities may serve as the signal for tomorrow's direction in planning. It will be a sad commentary, indeed, if 20 or 30 years hence our suburbs present the plight of the central city today. Now is the time to prepare the open space within the growing subdivisions for we cannot forget that the slums of today were the subdivisions of yesterday.

Schools. The School Board in each community has its policy for extension and design of the public school plant, but there are a few simple standards which are being generally adopted as a key to the allocation of space for the school system. These standards link closely with recreational space since the elementary school is the focal point within the neighborhood unit, and the junior and senior high schools within the group of neighborhoods we have identified as a "community." The open space for recreation should become therefore an integral part of the school location and thereby provide the type of adult supervision and youth leadership necessary to guide the development of young people.

N. L. Engelhardt, Jr., has estimated one-half child of elementary school age (grades one through six) in the average family. The average for families among the low-income group is about .7 children per family and .4 children per family in the high-income group.[7] Since most communities favor elementary schools with an enrollment between 600 and 800 pupils in the first six grades, a neighborhood designed about such a school would have a population of between 1,500 and 1,700 families, or between 5,000 and 6,000 people.

[7] The School-Neighborhood Nucleus, N. L. Engelhardt, Jr., *Architectural Forum*, October 1943.

Two such neighborhoods would support a junior high school with enrollments between 1,000 and 1,200, and four neighborhoods would support a senior high school of about 1,500 enrollment. The walking distance for a junior high school (grades seven through nine) should not exceed one mile, and the Senior High School (grades ten through twelve) should be a distance of not more than $1\frac{1}{2}$ miles.

Although the public school system in most communities does not support nursery schools, it would be desirable to establish them by private means. The size recommended by Engelhardt is 25 children for each school within a radius not to exceed one-quarter mile from the most distant home served. The average is .1 child of nursery school age per family, and a nursery school would serve about 400 families.

It has been considered necessary too frequently in the past to select a school site after the population has arrived and the land has been absorbed for other uses than education or recreation. Consequently, standards of adequate area for these facilities have been overshadowed by expedient decisions based upon the cheapest price for such land that might still be available. It is being generally agreed, however, that a minimum standard for the three types of schools is: elementary—5 acres; junior high—10 acres; and senior high—20 acres.

The Neighborhood Is People. The neighborhood is necessary as a unit with which the city may be reconstructed, but it is not a physical element alone. It is the people who really make the neighborhood, and whether or not they participate in community affairs as personal friends need not be the thread upon which their welfare hangs. People are obliged to act in unison with their fellowmen for the continued maintenance of standards for schools, recreation, utility improvements, zoning, and such other civic enterprise as the community may embrace. This responsibility is shared by all regardless of where they live and under whatever conditions. It is the act of citizenship, and the neighborhood is the smallest denominator within the city for effective expression of civic consciousness. In the process of discharging these obligations the people grow to know each other and they form group activities which generate civic interest; clubs for social, political, or intellectual discussion, as well as recreation, are formed, and through these media local problems are aired and common resistance to undesirable trends is generated or greater amenities encouraged.

The people thus will find means to retain the neighborhood identity and character. They will insist upon adequate zoning and ascertain that the will of the majority be not violated by a selfish few. They will find ways to change with an ever-changing world and yet maintain the community integrity and character. The airplane and the automobile will produce profound changes in the city, but the neighborhood must retain the basic, the elementary, physical characteristics which mark it as a unit for service to the people who live within it.

The neighborhood must stem the insidious growth of obsolescence within its confines and aid adjacent communities to do the same. While an improvement can increase value, deterioration can cause a slum. Blocking the road to decay is a primary task before a neighborhood and wise planning is the first step; planning and

THE NEIGHBORHOOD UNIT

The organization of neighborhood elements suggested by N. L. Engelhardt, Jr. A more complete diagram of neighborhood units grouped in relation to the various levels of school facilities. It will be noted that a radius of one-half mile is adopted as the maximum walking distance to the elementary school but playgrounds and nursery schools for small children are proposed with a radius of one-quarter mile walking distance for the families in the neighborhood.

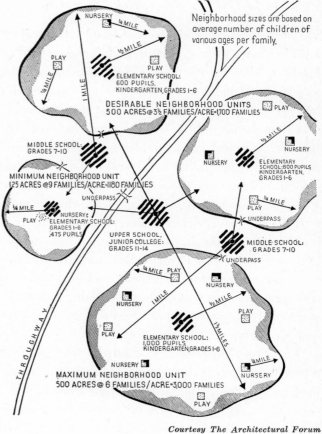

Courtesy The Architectural Forum

A TYPICAL FAMILY'S DAILY ACTIVITIES

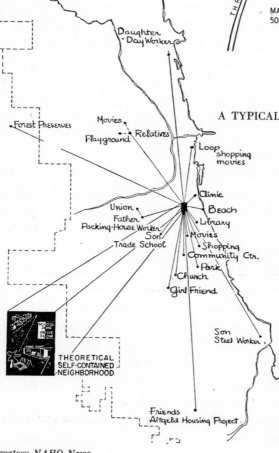

Courtesy NAHO News

The distribution of a family's daily activities in Chicago is interestingly portrayed in this map and illustrates two salient facts:

1. The advantages which might well accrue to the family by the assembly of neighborhood facilities within convenient distance from the home: shopping, school, recreation, community center, movies, library, church, clinic, etc. Such a physical organization of neighborhood facilities would not fulfil the social requirements of all the families living in the neighborhood, but their convenient presence would avoid the necessity to travel inordinate distances for many who are not so inclined.

2. The necessity for adequate transportation—circulation—about the urban framework, to relieve the time and strain now imposed upon the urban dweller in his daily travel to and from his work, his friends, and the less frequent, though not less necessary, cultural facilities a city makes available.

The physical organization of neighborhood units and community groups, integrated with the transportation system of the city, is intended to accomplish these objectives and thereby remove the necessity for the range of travel currently imposed and illustrated in this map.

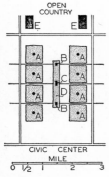

KEY

SECONDARY SCHOOL	◉
SENIOR "	
JUNIOR "	●
INFANT "	
SHOPPING CENTRE	⬚⬚⬚
TRAFFIC ROADS	══
RAILWAY	═
RAILWAY STATIONS	⊖
OPEN SPACES	▱

Population Per Unit

1	4500	5	3000
2	4500	6	2500
3	6500	7	3000
4	4000	8	1600
	9	5500	

Courtesy Carter and Goldfinger, London

THE COUNTY OF LONDON PLAN

The neighborhood unit was the primary planning unit in the development of this city plan. The sketch on the right is the diagrammatic organization of neighborhood units; the sketch on the left shows the application of this general scheme to a specific district of the city.

A NEIGHBORHOOD UNIT by José Sert

A Neighborhood Unit
B Junior High School
C Senior High School
D Township Center
E Light Industry

This diagram illustrates an organization of neighborhood units suggested by José Sert. While some authorities have stated that the maximum walking distance from home to the elementary school should be one-half mile, this diagram indicates a maximum distance of about one-quarter mile, which is the standard accepted by a number of communities. In contrast to a population density of 20–25 persons assumed as a desirable average in many communities, Sert assumes a density of two or three times this number, which may account for the shorter walking distances he proposes from homes to the several schools in his scheme.

The elementary school occupies a central position in the neighborhood unit, and a group of these units—six to eight in number—constitute a "township" with a population of between 56,000 and 80,000 people. A junior high school serves four neighborhoods; a senior high school serves the eight units; these facilities are situated within a "township center" surrounded by a "greenbelt." The neighborhood unit includes the elementary school, pre-school play-lots, playground, church, shopping center, library, and emergency clinic. The "township center" includes the junior and senior high schools, community auditorium and meeting rooms, concert hall, theaters, main shopping center, recreation and administrative center.

Traffic ways by-pass the neighborhood units and connect them with the "civic center," which includes the regional facilities for administration, education, hotels, trade and recreation, and transportation stations on one side, and on the other side are the locations for light industrial plants. All these elements are separated from each other by "greenbelts," and the open countryside is accessible to all the people.

YORKSHIP SQUARE, Yorkship Village

Electus D. Litchfield was the architect of this shopping center in a housing community for war workers in World War I. This is reminiscent of the early village square rather than recent developments for neighborhood shopping. Vehicular and pedestrian traffic are not separated, but the facilities are consolidated about a central space rather than being strung along a traffic way in the manner to which we have become generally accustomed in our cities.

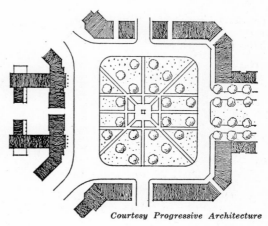

Courtesy Progressive Architecture

constant community vigilance are the tools with which the urban community may become a desirable place in which people may live and work rather than merely a commodity to be sold or traded for a profit. The common objective of a neighborhood is the maintenance of a living environment suited to the nature and desires of the people who are a part of it.

The neighborhood unit we have been describing is not a strange or a new element in the city. Each of us has referred at one time or another to "our neighborhood." It means to us something not quite specific but nonetheless real. It means the area in which we live, our house and those of our neighbors, the stores where we shop for our daily necessities, our school and its playground, and our local park. It is not only meaningful as the place we live and the street we traverse to and from our work, it is also the key to a sound investment in a home. Property values are sustained in proportion to the standards of maintenance a community insists upon—the quality it itself expects to maintain. This quality is achieved only through vigorous attention to neighborhood standards and these standards are established through the planning process.

CHAPTER 22

COMMERCIAL CENTERS

The New Market Places. The market place has always been the focal point of the city, a center for the exchange of goods. In ancient times it was the open space to which farmers and craftsmen brought their products for barter. The development of transportation and money systems implemented the transfer of goods, and the barter system shifted to a form of retail enterprise. Expansion of commerce created a merchant class dealing in the exchange of goods produced by others than themselves. The importance of cities increased as centers of wholesale and retail trade.

As with so many other activities of man, the industrial system brought more changes in the nature of the market place. Not only did the transportation of goods quicken, but the systems of communications accelerated the exchange of goods. The great cities became the trading centers in which world commerce was concentrated. With the growth of urban population the city continued to expand its wholesale and retail functions, but emphasis in the great business centers of the city has shifted from the commodities being exchanged to the methods and processes for trading in them. The goods are replaced by pieces of paper—documents—which purport to represent them, and transactions for the transfer of commodities are consummated by an exchange of these documents. Negotiations for the sale and payment of goods transferred from a merchant in Montevideo to a merchant in Buenos Aires are transacted in a London banking house, or the exchange of grain and meat between the producer on the farm and the consumer in the city next door is arranged through the trading centers of New York or Chicago. The industrial system has introduced a variety of commercial functions to the city never present in the simple market place of the ancient town, and four recognizable types of commercial districts have emerged in the modern city.

"Downtown" of the large metropolitan city is familiar to every urban dweller. It is the financial and administrative center of its region and, in some cities, it has become the center of business for the nation. New York has its Wall Street, Chicago its LaSalle Street, Paris its Bourse and London its Exchange district, but every city has its financial center even though it may serve as a satellite of a greater center. "Downtown" includes the wholesale and retail centers for service to the satellite districts within the city proper or its region. These centers have not been planned; they have simply crept outward and upward within the network of obsolete and confining streets as the fortune of cities and nations fluctuated. Degeneration of the central business district is an urban tragedy. Serving a vital and useful purpose as the heart of the city, it presents a challenge to business and civic enterprise. Marked by intolerable congestion, noise, fumes, exorbitant land values and overcrowding, it has apparently grown impotent to regenerate itself. Shifting restlessly away from the blight which time imposes upon helpless commercial districts, disintegration eats further into the urban core over the years and leaves the outlying areas of the city the only haven of refuge for healthy enterprise.

A second type of commercial area is the small, central business district of the satellite community. Dependent upon the metropolitan center for major administrative and wholesale functions, the small commercial center contains the chain retail stores, professional offices, service supply enterprises, motion picture theaters, branch banks, and stock exchanges. In the small self-contained city, this district will also provide wholesale facilities and include the necessary administrative and transportation centers.

The third type of commercial district is the community center for outlying sections of the city. It may overlap with, or be the counterpart of, the commercial center of the satellite community, but it contains the large-scale service facilities which do not lend themselves to further subdivision and distribution. Among these facilities are the large food market, chain stores of various types, branch banks, and telegraph, telephone, and postal district offices, motion picture theaters, branch library, and medical and dental professions.

The smallest commercial unit is the neighborhood shopping center. The modern counterpart of the "corner grocery store," the neighborhood shopping center provides the day-by-day commodities for the direct convenience of a limited population. Here, the housewife may perform her regular shopping for the staple goods, and it may have an independent grocery store and meat market, radio and electric shop, shoe repair shop, hardware store, a bakery, drug and stationery store, and barber and beauty shop.

Overzoning. The amount of urban land zoned for commercial uses is excessive beyond reason. When communities were small and served a vast outlying area, commercial uses were permitted along both sides of principal traffic routes. When a highway passed through the center of a town, it became the axis for the central business district, and "shoestring" business developed at random along its route. As the population of the community expanded, additional traffic routes were provided and more business stretched along them. It was then presumed that successful business on the highway proved them to be the proper location for commercial enterprise and, with little further examination of the amount of business a community could support, all existing and proposed street highway frontage was zoned for commercial use. It is now impossible to classify any business areas as shopping "centers."

About one-quarter of the streets in our cities are used as main thoroughfares with the property fronting upon them zoned for business use. This supports the estimate by Harland Bartholomew that some 25 per cent of the total area of the average city is occupied by commercial zoning, whereas the area actually used by retail business is only about 3 per cent of the total developed area of a city. This contrast gives some measure of the degree to which cities have been overzoned for business development along the traffic arteries.

The gross excess of commercial zoning weighs heavily upon the city. Despite the relatively small proportion of commercial zoning which is actually developed for business, much of this enterprise operates on a marginal basis. The mortality rate of retail business is extremely high, between 15 and 25 per cent of the retail stores going out of business each year. About one-third of all retail stores have a life-span of a year or less, one-half remain in business no longer than two years, and less than one-quarter remain as long as 10 years. Mr. Robert Dowling, a prominent real estate counsellor in New York City, estimated that four or five times as many stores are in business as the need demands.

Inducement to engage in uneconomic ventures is apparently strong, and the impact spreads far beyond the failure of an individual entrepreneur. Unstable business enterprise breeds physical blight; the "shoestring" investments in retail business are analogous to the "shoestring" character of zoning. In some cities fully half the property zoned for business is used for residences and these mixed land uses not only create an undesirable residential environment but remove the prospect for consolidation of shopping facilities for convenient access.

The key to the appropriate amount of space for commercial development is the purchasing power of the people who patronize the business, the anticipated volume of sales, the density of population, income levels of the people, and the proximity and the type of services available in adjoining business districts. Techniques for analysis of purchasing power have been developed by authorities in this field, but they are usually applied to the consideration of single enterprises rather than an entire commercial district. With the development of new planned communities the neighborhood shopping center is receiving more attention as an economic unit. Here, however, we again find a contrast with excessive zoning. Desiring to induce prospective retail enterprise, the developer of shopping centers must offer reasonable assurance of a stable and continuing market and, as a result, he usually provides a minimum of space for competitive enterprise. These "controlled" shopping centers may unduly restrict competition to assure a safe market for investors, but this necessity points up a salient reason for the blight of unsound business enterprise that floods the areas of excessive commercial zoning in our cities at large; it gives force to the fact that zoning for business use must be reduced to a reasonable compromise between the tendency toward monopoly and the excesses present in current zoning practices.

How Much Land for Commercial Use. Each community has some peculiar local conditions and practices which will bear upon estimates of the amount of land required for commercial purposes, but investigations in a number of cities shed some light upon the relation between population and the land area for business as a point of departure in developing appropriate standards for the allocation of space for commercial districts. The familiar "rule of thumb" for allocating space for commercial development is 50 feet of street frontage for each 100 persons in the area to be served. According to the survey by Harland Bartholomew in *Urban Land Uses,* an average of 63.7 feet of street frontage per 100 people was actually developed for retail trade of all types in small, self-contained cities.

That the "over-all" amount of space devoted to business is an inadequate measure is evident from observation of cities as well as further statistics of land use. The distribution of the space is equally important, if not more vital, to the welfare and service of a city than the total area allocated for commercial development. Thus the Bartholomew survey showed that 44 per cent of the total commercial area—about 28 feet of street frontage per 100 people—was in the central business district, and 56 per cent —35 feet of street frontage per 100 people—was distributed in the residential neighborhoods.

A survey by the Los Angeles Regional Planning Commission showed a further breakdown in the types of commercial districts.[1] The combined commercial uses amounted to 2.72 acres of land per 1,000 persons throughout the County of Los Angeles. Of this area 1.19 acres was in neighborhood shopping districts, while local or community business districts occupied .92 acre, and the balance, .46 acre per 1,000 persons, was in the satellite commercial centers. An additional .15 acre per 1,000 persons was contained in the main "downtown" business center of the city of Los Angeles. These classifications of districts correspond to the four types described at the beginning of this chapter. The Los Angeles County survey included a great variety of communities, ranging from the great metropolitan area of the city of Los Angeles through the small towns surrounding this city to semi-rural areas served by village centers. The Bartholomew survey, however, covered small cities and indicated an average of 1.79 acres per 1,000 persons in the total commercial development, of which .79 acre was in the central business district and the remaining one acre in the outlying or residential districts. The land area devoted to all commercial uses in four large urban centers in proportion to the population is shown below:

Acres per 1,000 Population

Detroit 3.50
San Francisco 1.75
St. Louis 2.15
Los Angeles (City) 3.30

The areas which are set forth in the foregoing table do not include any provision for

[1] *Master Plan of Land Use (Inventory and Classification),* Regional Planning Commission, County of Los Angeles, California, p. 38.

automobile parking, which has become an imperative necessity in commercial districts, but the quoted areas do include all business uses regardless of their financial soundness.

Neighborhood Shopping Centers. The present excessive zoning for commercial land uses is out of control and it is difficult to exercise reason in a consideration of standards of appropriate space in the central business districts. The development of neighborhood shopping districts, however, offers more encouraging prospects. Developers of planned residential communities are beginning to recognize the desirability of establishing local shopping centers, not only for the convenience of the residents but as profitable business ventures. Although competition is a stimulus to retail business, it is natural for commercial enterprise to seek a stable and continuing market. Developers of business property consequently incline to restrict the amount of space they provide in a shopping center as an inducement to, and protection for, the enterprises invited to establish their businesses within the center. As previously suggested, this restriction may shade toward monopoly in effect, but reasonable competition is a recognized advantage to entrepreneurs, and the increased volume of business it induces leads to an invitation to competition rather than elimination. In developing shopping centers, therefore, emphasis shifts from the prospect for speculation in land, which promotes the overzoning for commercial use, to the more vital element of the purchasing power of the population within the radius of service. Studies in this field lead to a more rational allocation of urban land for business use than can be otherwise expected.

TABLE A. NEIGHBORHOOD SHOPPING FACILITIES
(*Based on estimates by Robert Dowling*)

No. Families	Floor Area (sq. ft.)	Type
50	3,500	One general store
250	9,500	Market, drugs, bar and grill
500	12,000	Same as above with stationer, laundry, cleaner
1,000	17,000	Same as above with specialty shops, delicatessen, beauty shop, bakery
2,500	35,000	Same as above with addition of market, drugs, stationer and laundry, also restaurant, barber, florist, bowling (8 alleys)
5,000	90,000	Same as above with addition of market and drug store, also theater (1,200 seats), variety shops, post office, professional offices, doctors, etc.
10,000	290,000 (3,500 second fl.)	Same as above with library, three theaters

Note: The above calculations appeared in the *Architectural Forum*, October 1943.

Using the average expenditures per capita for various goods and services reported in the U. S. Census for 1940, Marcel Villanueva[2] arrived at an area of .73 acre of floor space per 1,000 people in a community of 2,500 population, and .86 acre per 1,000 people in a community of 5,000 population. These areas are equivalent to approximately 23 and 26 front feet per 100 persons, respectively, and do not include space for auto parking. The Community Builders' Council[3] suggests a street frontage of 20–30 feet per 100 people or a floor space of about one acre per 1,000 people. The report on "Present and Future Land Uses" for San Francisco noted that:

An analysis of the acreage devoted to business uses other than that of a metropolitan character shows that the requirements for local business varies from .75 acre to 1.5 acres per 1,000 people, averaging about 1.2 acres but running more often at about .8 acre in areas containing only neighborhood service establishments.[4]

When community developers provide shopping centers as an investment, however, the allocation of space for these facilities is more conservative than the above estimates. A proposal by Mr. Robert Dowling (Table A) estimated a street frontage of 11 feet per 100 people for a population of 250 families or about 875 people. For a community of 500 families (1,750 people) the street frontage drops to 8 feet per 100 people, and the commercial frontage for a population of 1,000 families (3,500 people), and more, is between 5 and 6 feet per 100 persons.[5] This is equivalent to a floor space of only about 1/10 acre per 1,000 persons for populations more than 1,750 persons, and 1/4 acre per 1,000 people for smaller communities of about 875 people.

While the Community Builders' Council suggests an average of one acre per 1,000 persons as a desirable allocation of commercial space, the examples cited by that organization range from one-half to three-fourths acre per 1,000 persons. The proposed floor space for a population between 700 and 1,000 families is as low as one-third acre per 1,000 persons, an average of about 15 feet of frontage per 100 people.[6] Hugh Potter, who developed River Oaks in Houston, Texas, suggests 2 front feet per 100 people with a maximum of 10 feet.

The space requirements cited in the foregoing estimates provide no allowance for auto parking. In developments by the David Bohannon organization in the San Francisco Bay area, three-quarters acre of land per 1,000 people has been designated for commercial shopping and this area includes parking space. Assuming a 2:1 ratio of parking space to floor space, this area is equivalent to about one-fourth acre of building floor space per 1,000 persons.

In appraising the variations between estimates of space for shopping it is necessary to account for differences in the basic assumptions or in local situations. Previous reference has been made to the tendency to restrict space in facilities developed as

[2] *Planning Neighborhood Shopping Centers*, Marcel Villanueva, National Committee on Housing, Inc., New York, 1945.

[3] *Community Builders' Handbook*, Community Builders' Council, Urban Land Institute, 1947.

[4] *Present and Future Land Use (Budgeting the Land)*, The Master Plan of San Francisco, San Francisco City Planning Commission, November 1944.

[5] Neighborhood Shopping Centers, Robert Dowling, *Architectural Forum*, October 1943.

[6] *Community Builders' Handbook*, Community Builders' Council, Urban Land Institute, 1947.

SHOPPING CENTER, RIVER OAKS, Houston, Texas (*Stayton Nunn and Milton McGinty, Architects*)

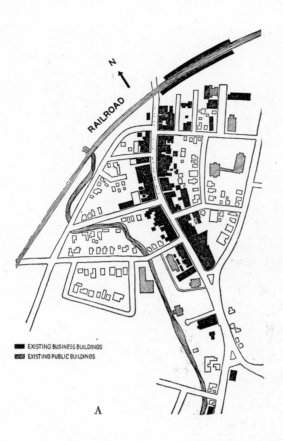

EXISTING BUSINESS BUILDINGS
EXISTING PUBLIC BUILDINGS

A

EXISTING BUSINESS BUILDINGS
NEW BUSINESS BUILDINGS
EXISTING PUBLIC BUILDINGS
NEW PUBLIC ARCADE
RESIDENTIAL BUILDINGS
PARKING AREAS
• BUS STOP

B

Courtesy The Architectural Forum

C

SHOPPING CENTER, RYE, New York
(Ketchum, Gina and Sharp, Architects)

A proposal for gradual reorganization of the business center for Rye. This community business district is characteristic of most commercial districts in small and large cities: stores line a street that is also the principal traffic artery, and parking facilities are lacking. Figure A shows a plan of the existing conditions and Figures B and C show the plans for redevelopment in two stages. Traffic is rerouted, the present main street becomes a pedestrian mall and parking and service are distributed about the periphery of the shopping center.

To accomplish the redevelopment of urban centers in a manner such as that suggested in this plan requires the whole-hearted co-operation of those who own and control property in the commercial districts of our cities. It is generally assumed that such co-operation is of a singular nature, but it is identical with the kind of co-operation that must be demonstrated by all citizens if our urban communities are to keep pace with the industrial and technical development in our time. The building of our cities is essentially a co-operative venture; without co-operative spirit and action the democratic procedures of our society are rendered ineffective.

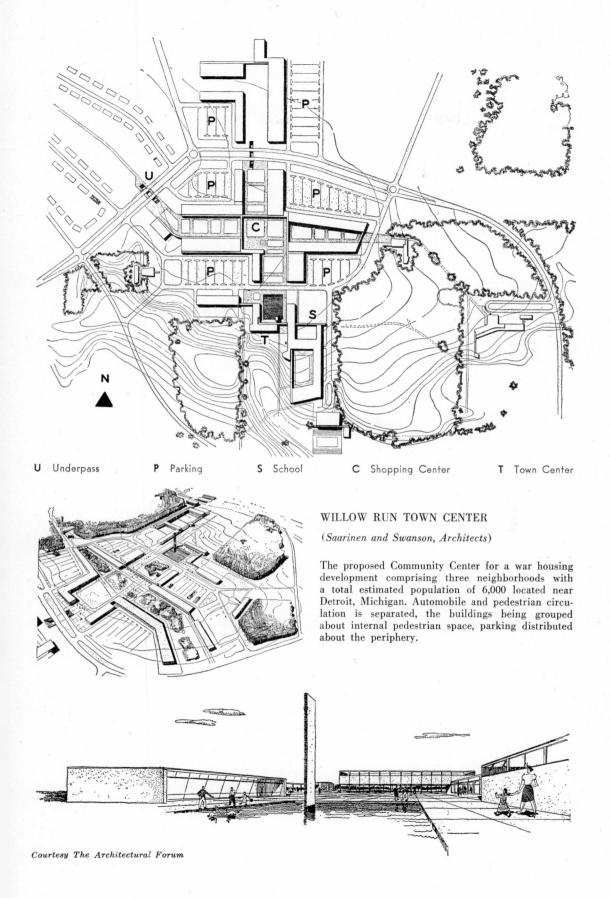

U Underpass   P Parking   S School   C Shopping Center   T Town Center

WILLOW RUN TOWN CENTER

(Saarinen and Swanson, Architects)

The proposed Community Center for a war housing development comprising three neighborhoods with a total estimated population of 6,000 located near Detroit, Michigan. Automobile and pedestrian circulation is separated, the buildings being grouped about internal pedestrian space, parking distributed about the periphery.

Courtesy The Architectural Forum

Theoretical Area Requirements for a Typical Neighborhood Shopping Center for 2,500 Population (625 Families). The center is to serve a residential unit covering one square mile and located at least two miles away from any other shopping center. Figures are based on the national average per capita expenditures, according to the census of 1940. (Source: *Planning Neighborhood Shopping Centers*, Marcel Villanueva, National Committee on Housing, Inc.)

Per Capita Sales		Types of Stores in Neighborhood Center	Size of Stores Adjuncts	Area Sq. Ft. Per Store	Estimated Sales	Prevailing	
Basic[1]	Total					Rents	Per Cent
Food		**Food**					
Food.........$83.36	$208,400	1 Grocery (package liquor, no meats).	20 x 60	1,200	$60,000	$1,560	2.6
		1 Grocery (with Meats) Self-Service.	25 x 70	1,750	90,000	2,340	2.6
		1 General Store, Meats.............	20 x 60	1,200	58,400	1,518	2.6
				4,150	208,400	5,418	
		Alternate (In place of 3 Stores).............	40 x 100	4,000	208,400	5,418	2.6
		Automotive					
Filling Station.. 16.57	41,425	2 Filling and Service Stations......	120 x 200	24,000	20,712	890.5	4.3
			120 x 200	24,000	20,713	890.5	4.3
					41,425	1,781	
Repair Garage.. 3.35	8,375	1 General Service-Repair Garage including yard (combination)...	100 x 110	11,000	8,375	837	10.0
19.92	49.800			59,000	49,800	2,618	
		Drug and Stationery Store					
Drugstore...... 9.15	22,875						
Cigars......... 1.58	3,950	1 Store including Fountain, Cigars, Books, and Varieties.........	25 x 100	2,500	29,325	1,407	4.8
Stationery..... .45	1,125						
News......... .55	1,375						
11.73	29,325						
		Laundry-Dry Cleaning and Shoe Repair					
Laundry....... 3.80	9,500						
Dry-Cleaning... 2.49	6,225	(Pick-up Service)...............	20 x 81	1,620	17,900	1,432	8.0
Shoe Repair.... .87	2,175						
7.16	17,900						
		Eating and Drinking Places					
Lunchroom ... ⎰16.21	40,525	1 Lunchroom and Counter.........	50 x 100	5,000	20,000	1,380	6.9
Restaurant&Bar⎱		1 Restaurant and Bar.............	50 x 100	5,000	20,525	1,212	5.9
				10,000	40,525	2,592	
		Barber Shop and Beauty Parlor					
Barber Shop and Beauty Parlor 3.65	9,125	1 Combination Store with Alcove...	20 x 70	1,400	9,125	780	8.55
		Real Estate and Insurance 1 Office.........................	15 x 60	900		900	
Totals............	**$355,075**			79,570	$355,075	$15,147	

SUMMARY OF AREA REQUIREMENTS:
- Store Buildings and Adjuncts — 79,570 Sq. Ft.=1.82 acres or .73 acres per 1,000 population
- Off-Street Parking — (1.82 ac. x 2)=3.64 acres or 1.45 acres per 1,000 population
- Total: (Exclusive of provisions for future growth) = 5.46 acres or 2.18 acres per 1,000 population

[1] The basic per capita sales indicated are national averages subject to local adjustments, according to regional variations.

investments for commercial rental income. The income levels and consequent purchasing power of the people to be served by a shopping center will affect the quantity and type of these facilities. Mr. Dowling's suggested areas were based upon a district with families having an average income of $2,500 per year, although he undoubtedly calculated conservatively to compensate for the quantity of established business enterprise existing in the surrounding area. Villanueva assumed a neighborhood of families with an average annual income below that in the Dowling estimates, but he assumed no other facilities within a 2-mile radius. The differences between the ratio of commercial space to population in the Los Angeles County survey and the average self-contained small city surveyed by Bartholomew may be explained by the low density and

Theoretical Area Requirements for a Typical Neighborhood Shopping Center for 5,000 Population (1,250 Families). Other conditions are identical to those of the 2,500-population center on the opposite page. (Source: *Planning Neighborhood Shopping Centers*, Marcel Villanueva, National Committee on Housing, Inc.)

Per Capita Sales		Types of Stores in Neighborhood Center	Size Buildings and Adjuncts	Area Sq. Ft.	Estimated Sales	Prevailing	
Basic	Total					Rents	Per Cent
		FOOD (Arbitrary Distribution) 1 Delicatessen..............	20 x 60	1,200	$60,000	$ 1,560	2.6
		1 Grocery, package liquor; no meats.....................	25 x 70	1,750	90,000	2,340	2.6
		1 General store; meats..........	20 x 60	1,200	58,400	1,518	2.6
Food Total.....$83.36	$416,800	1 Market for all foods..........	40 x 100	4,000	208,400	5,418	2.6
		Alternate in place of 3 stores and a market (One Super-Market in place of 4 stores).....	50 x 100	5,000	416,800	10,836	2.6
Variety Store... $7.42	37,100	GENERAL MERCHANDISE 1 Variety Store.............	40 x 80	3,200	37,100	1,892	5.1
Clothing Store.. 3.26	16,300	APPAREL GROUP 1 Clothing Store (family)........	25 x 70	1,750	16,300	766	4.7
Filling Stations. 16.57	82,850	AUTOMOTIVE GROUP 4 Filling and Service Stations (each)	120 x 200	24,000	20,712.5	890.5	4.3
			120 x 200	24,000	20,712.5	890.5	4.3
			120 x 200	24,000	20,712.5	890.5	4.3
			120 x 200	24,000	20,712.5	890.5	4.3
				96,000	82,850	3,562	
Auto Repair... 3.35	16,750 99,600	1 Auto Repair Garage and Yard............	100 x 115	11,500	16,750	1,675	10.0
Drug Store, Fountain..... 9.15	45,750	DRUG STORES 1 Drug Store, Fountain.........	30 x 100	3,000	45,750	2,196	4.8
Stationery..... .45 Cigars........ 1.58 Fountain ...... 3.22 News.......... .55 5.80	29,000	STATIONERY STORES 1 Corner-store Type, Fountain...	20 x 60	1,200	29,000	1,653	5.7
Eating & Drinking Places.... 16.21	81,050	Arbitrary Distribution) 1 Luncheon and Counter.......	50 x 100	5,000	25,000	1,725	6.9
		1 Restaurant (Tearoom)........	50 x 100	5,000	25,000	1,725	6.9
		1 Bar-Grill..................	50 x 100	5,000	31,050	1,832	5.9
Shoe Repair.... .87	4,350	1 Repair and Bootblack.........	10 x 57	570	4,350	391	9.0
Barbershop.... 1.82	9,100	1 Barbershop.................	15 x 60	900	9,100	910	10.0
Beauty Parlor.. 1.83	9,150	1 Beauty Parlor..............	20 x 70	1,400	9,150	915	10.0
Liquor Store... 4.45	22,250	1 Package Liquor Store.........	15 x 100	1,500	22,250	667	3.0
Dry-Cleaner.... 2.49	12,450	1 Store (Independent Operator)..	15 x 60	900	12,450	996	8.0
Laundry....... 3.80	19,000	1 Store (Independent Operator)..	15 x 75	1,125	19,000	1,520	8.0
		Real Estate 1 Office.....................	15 x 60	900		960	
		& Insurance 1 Office.....................	15 x 60	900		960	
TOTALS............	$801,900			147,995	801,900	35,181	
Fuel......... 7.70 Bldg. Materials. 2.14 Lumber & Misc. 5.00 14.84	38,500 10,700 25,000 74,200	FUEL AND BUILDING SUPPLY YARD 1 Building and Yard...........	200 x 200	40,000	74,200	1,781	2.4
GRAND TOTALS....	$876,100			187,995	$876,100	$36,962	

SUMMARY OF AREA REQUIREMENTS:
    STORE BUILDINGS AND ADJUNCTS   187,995 Sq. Ft.= 4.3 acres or .86 acres per 1,000 population
    OFF-STREET PARKING   (4.3 ac. x 2)= 8.6 acres or 1.72 acres per 1,000 population
    TOTAL: (Exclusive of provisions for future growth)   12.9 acres or 2.58 acres per 1,000 population

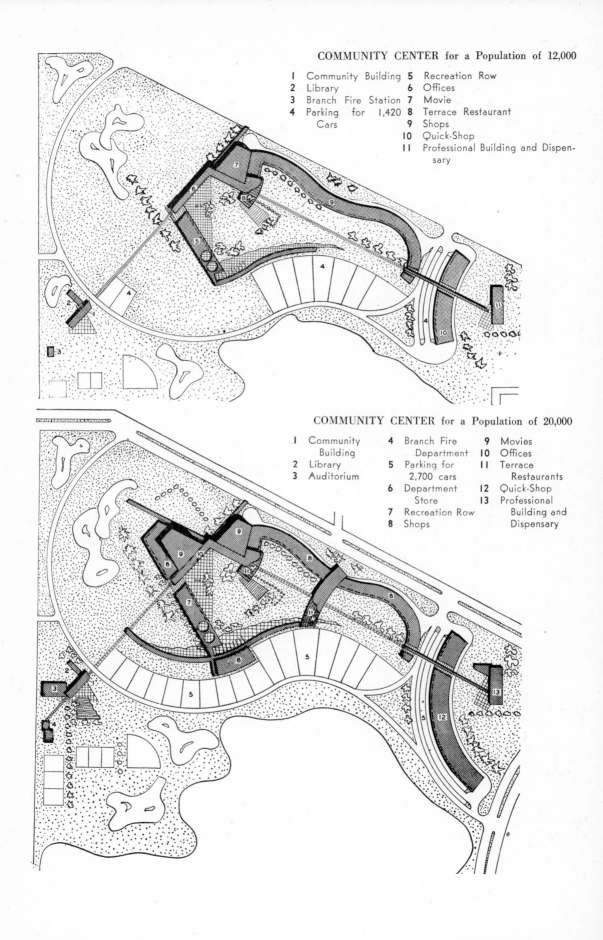

COMMUNITY CENTER for a Population of 12,000

1 Community Building
2 Library
3 Branch Fire Station
4 Parking for 1,420 Cars
5 Recreation Row
6 Offices
7 Movie
8 Terrace Restaurant
9 Shops
10 Quick-Shop
11 Professional Building and Dispensary

COMMUNITY CENTER for a Population of 20,000

1 Community Building
2 Library
3 Auditorium
4 Branch Fire Department
5 Parking for 2,700 cars
6 Department Store
7 Recreation Row
8 Shops
9 Movies
10 Offices
11 Terrace Restaurants
12 Quick-Shop
13 Professional Building and Dispensary

1 Community Building (Administrative Offices and Meeting Rooms)
2 Library
3 Auditorium
4 Branch Police and Fire Station
5 High School (Play Facilities Used Jointly with Adults)
6 Churches
7 Elementary School

8 Parking for 4,500 Cars
9 Department Store
10 Shops (Includes Telegraph, Banks, Post Office)
11 Recreation Row (Bowling, Billiards, Skating, Refreshments)
12 Movies
13 Offices (Includes Rental and Insurance Agencies, Dancing Schools, etc., Pick-up, Shoe Repair, Drugs, etc.)
14 Terrace Restaurants
15 Quick-Shop (Markets, Cleaning and Laundry)
16 Professional Building (Doctor, Lawyer, Dentist, Dispensary)
17 Clubs
18 Heliport (Taxi Service to Municipal Airport)

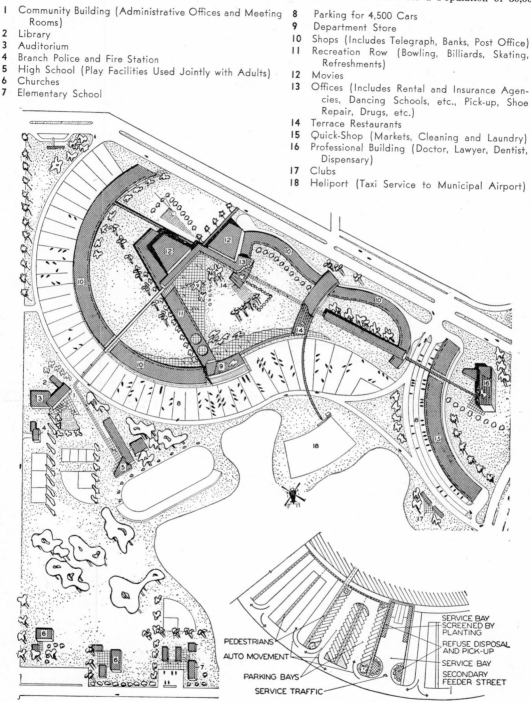

PEDESTRIANS
AUTO MOVEMENT
PARKING BAYS
SERVICE TRAFFIC

SERVICE BAY SCREENED BY PLANTING
REFUSE DISPOSAL AND PICK-UP
SERVICE BAY
SECONDARY FEEDER STREET

TARZANA, California

A progressive plan for development of a shopping and community center for a small town. The sketches show the anticipated development at various stages in the city growth—12,000, 20,000 and 30,000 population respectively. The informal arrangement of the plan accommodates minor or major improvements at any time and permits some variations in the space for facilities without removing the general pattern of the development. Parking would be provided as the center grows, the sketch showing the arrangement for patron and service access and parking.

(Thesis by Allan Walter, School of Architecture, Universtiy of Southern California)

numerous satellite communities spread over the area of 1,200 square miles in Los Angeles County in contrast to the compact nature of the small city.

Each community has characteristics which form the basis for judgment of the appropriate relation between the population and the space required for the commercial facilities to serve it; it is the restoration of a balance between them in our zoning ordinances upon which the health of city development, in part, depends.

Parking for Shopping Centers. The future stability of commercial enterprise will depend in large measure on the adequacy and convenience of space for automobile parking available to customers and employees and the arrangement for service facilities. The effect of deficient parking and service facilities may be measured by the shift of retail business to outlying areas and the relative decline of property values in the central business district.

It is generally estimated that the space provided for automobile parking in commercial districts should be equal to the floor space in buildings, but this "rule of thumb" can only be applied roughly to office and wholesale facilities. Centers devoted primarily to retail business require as much as 3 and 4 square feet of parking space for each square foot of floor space in the buildings occupied by such uses. These requirements are more fully treated in Chapters 20 and 23, but the appropriate ratio depends upon the type of service offered in the shopping center, the area served, the availability of mass transportation, and the travel habits of the patrons. It has become abundantly apparent, however, that adequate parking space is an essential ingredient of the space allocated to commercial enterprise. Chain markets, mail-order houses, restaurants, and entertainment centers have initiated the practice of providing their own parking facilities, and the space requirements for some of the more enterprising of these business concerns range as high as 4 square feet of parking for each square foot of building floor space, but it is evident that the city will be forced to enact legislation for adequate space in order to maintain some order in the redevelopment of the central areas.

Planning the Commercial Center. The only rules that need apply to the planning for commercial enterprise are those which likewise apply to all other activities in the city: circulation about the business district must be safe and convenient; and pedestrian, vehicular, and service traffic should be separate each from the other, with ample parking facilities distributed within reasonable walking distance from the shops. This walking distance may well increase when the physical environment of the commercial district is made attractive; until then we may expect the current habits of shoppers, who desire the closest possible parking place, and the trend to shopping in the outlying areas to continue unabated.

A metropolitan business district may have an effective service radius of 50 or 100 miles, or it may be a center for tourist trade ranging over the entire nation, but the neighborhood shopping center should be within one-quarter to one-half mile walking distance from the homes served by it. The neighborhood shopping center is an integral part of the neighborhood center and should be accessible without crossing major traffic ways. The district or community shopping center will be within a 1½-mile radius of the community in which it is located and may be designed as a minor civic and educational center.

Since it has been estimated that less than 4 per cent of retail business is attracted from those who pass by on the through-traffic artery, there is little to support the retention of commercial development along the highway. Consolidation of commercial facilities is urgently needed; it is needed to restore stability to property values and convenience for the multitude who daily patronize the variety of business enterprise in our cities. It is also needed to stem the insidious spread of blight which is gnawing at the core of cities. This consolidation will come by way of recreating "centers" of business connected but not traversed by traffic arteries and the rejection of "strip" or "shoestring" zoning along the highways which retain the long-departed horse-and-buggy form and tempo of the village.

CHAPTER 23

THE CIRCULATION SYSTEM

The Strait Jacket. The space in cities devoted to the movement of people—the street system—occupies about 30 per cent of the urban area. With the advent of the motor car, use of the streets changed radically from the days of the horse and buggy. The network of narrow city streets created a bottleneck of traffic congestion and, in the 1920's, the traffic problem was the dynamic subject at city planning conferences. About this time engineers and planners undertook the design and classification of major streets and highways. That the process was marked by little imagination is apparent in our street system today.

In pioneer days the surveyor had laid out the land in huge sections of one mile square, and road building followed these section lines. Each section was a handy parcel of land in which to criss-cross a gridiron of streets—a big square divided into little rectangles. The chance of mechanical error was practically eliminated in this system, but a dead-level standard of mediocrity thrust the road system into a strait jacket. Precise as logic, the streets were uniformly set at a width of 60 feet and spaced 330 feet apart in one direction and 660 feet apart in the other.

As automobile travel increased, the system of Major and Secondary Highways was contrived. The Major Highways were established along the principal section lines one mile apart, and the right-of-way was widened to 100 feet. At the quarter-section lines, the right-of-way was widened to 80 feet and the street was designated as the Secondary Highway. The ingenuity exposed in this system was further enhanced by naming most of these highways "boulevards."

With the designation of these Major and Secondary Highways, and spurred by the conviction that relief from traffic congestion would come by way of wider streets, there followed a rash of street-widening projects along the newly established rights-of-way. Such was not the fortunate outcome, however. More traffic was invited onto these streets, slow-moving and short-haul traffic mixed with vehicles destined for more distant points, left turns occurred at all intersections, truck and passenger vehicles vied

306

for parking and loading space along the curbs, vehicular and pedestrian traffic conflicted, unlimited ingress and egress flowed from abutting property into the traffic lanes, frequent intersections impeded movement, and the multitude of commercial distractions along the streets brought chaos to the city.

Negative Control—Traffic Engineering. Because the street plan of cities is impotent to cope with the traffic upon them, there have been various methods devised to control the operation of vehicles. It might be more accurate to describe these as measures of control by default, but they are essential to maintain any movement of vehicles through the city streets. The calculation and administration of these controls are known as "traffic engineering."

The traffic engineer finds himself in the rather awkward position of responsibility for forcing the movement of the irresistible force of traffic through the impenetrable obstacle of congestion. Perched upon the horns of this dilemma, the traffic engineer is a repair man rather than a builder, a deviser rather than a planner, a first-aid traffic "corpsman" rather than a surgeon. Traffic engineering is necessary because the planning of the city circulation system has been neglected.

Traffic engineering embraces the host of devices with which the city-dweller is familiar: stop-and-go signs at street intersections, slow-down warnings and speed limits, parking limits and prohibitions, the policeman's whistle, the "safety islands" at points of boarding street cars and busses, the white and yellow lines painted upon the pavements to "channel" moving vehicles and the mechanical divisions which are sometimes employed for this purpose, and the one-way street. The list of these "solutions" is long, but none has singly, nor in combination, brought any genuine relief of the traffic problem. The devices are more appropriately described as stunts rather than solutions; they are expedient measures to cope with immediate traffic problems in the form of "first-aid" treatment and offer no real improvement in the capacity of the transportation system to move people.

The automobile travels at a reasonably rapid speed with relative ease, comfort, and convenience. Interruption of the flow of travel conflicts with the effectiveness of the machine as a means for the mass transportation of people, and this interruption also creates hazards to safety. The synchronization of "stop-lights" has improved the continuity of movement, but the effect of these interruptions remains. The average cycle for change of the traffic signal is one minute; cars traveling in one direction are stopped for 30 seconds and move for 30 seconds. The effect of this interruption is a reduction to 40 per cent of the number of cars which could pass a given point if the flow were uninterrupted. In other words, a street intersection controlled by traffic-lights can accommodate only two-fifths the number of cars a free flow of traffic will carry.

The conversion of streets from two-way to one-way travel is a familiar system traffic engineering is frequently forced to employ. It is a method for channeling traffic and avoids the conflict of left-hand turns across lanes moving from the opposite direction, but the traffic signal is still necessary to permit the passage of pedestrians, and traffic flow continues to suffer periodic interruptions.

There is a reluctance to design streets for peak traffic loads because of the alleged wasteful space during the periods of less intensive use. The alternative is conversion of six-lane trunk streets to four lanes in the direction of heavy flow and two lanes for the opposite direction during the morning rush and reversal of this process for the evening peak. While the painted channel lines are usually the only means for marking these lanes, some cities have mechanical barriers which may be raised and lowered from continuous slots along the channel separations.

The traffic engineer maintains data on the movement of people and vehicles, he measures the service of commercial centers by traffic counts of registered automobiles that park there, he measures the capacity of sidewalks by counts of pedestrians who traverse them, and the probable effectiveness of street widening or new streets and freeways is estimated by counts of local and through traffic. The need for and effectiveness of traffic signals, prohibitions on left turns and curb parking, and special lanes for traffic flow, are calculated by the traffic engineer from the variety of traffic counts and data he compiles, and he aids the public transit companies in the routing of mass transportation vehicles.

The traffic engineer is maintaining a gallant struggle to cope with the imponderable traffic tangles he confronts and, until the urban street system is designed for the vehicles which traverse it, his devices will remain essential ingredients of our city circulation. It is a choice between two traffic evils: no control and complete chaos or negative control to avoid paralysis.

The Street System. The amazing attachment which man has for the wheel of his car results in the automobile being used for a trip to the corner grocery only two blocks from home. This has impelled the subdivider of lots for sale to assume that streets must go in all directions, for he was never quite sure on which corner the stores might be built. With some reasonable planning preceding the subdivision of land today, the street system may be simplified and restoration of the walking habit has some prospects for fulfillment. Internal walks through the sites of large-scale housing developments, like the Greenbelt towns, provide safe and pleasant circulation to the various community facilities.

The most economical, convenient, and maneuverable means of movement is locomotion on foot. Its use is decreasing because the automobile is handy; it is also decreasing because the environment is not planned for it and is unattractive as a place in which to walk. Yet the pedestrian way is still an essential element in the circulation system of our cities. Harking from the days of the horse and buggy is the habit of interpreting the vehicular street as the promenade for pedestrians. It no longer serves that function, but the sidewalks are still designed as an adjunct of the streets. The Garden City plan, the Greenbelt towns, as well as the community of Radburn, planned internal circulation for pedestrians, and the "arcades" in business blocks and neighborhood shopping centers suggest a similar treatment in the commercial centers, but they are uncommon. With an improvement in planning for terminal parking facilities for cars and simplification of vehicular circulation in both

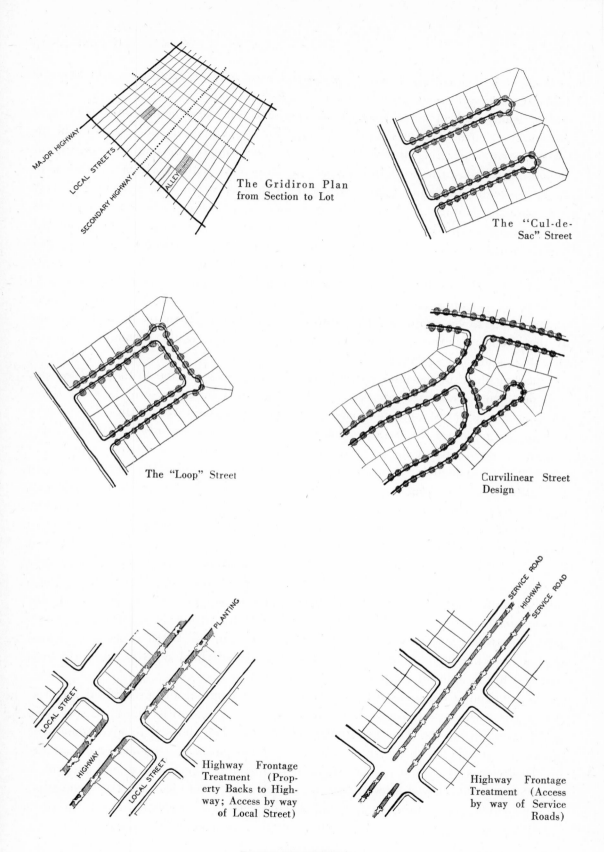

The Gridiron Plan from Section to Lot

The "Cul-de-Sac" Street

The "Loop" Street

Curvilinear Street Design

Highway Frontage Treatment (Property Backs to Highway; Access by way of Local Street)

Highway Frontage Treatment (Access by way of Service Roads)

TYPES OF STREETS

business and residential areas, the pedestrian way may be returned as an effective and attractive element of circulation.

The usual width of a residential walk is 4 or 5 feet. Designed as an integral part of the street curb, it allows adequate space for street planting not available in the "park" strip separating the walk and curb. The integral design, however, needs sloped, or rolled, curbs to permit access into driveways without a repetition of steps along the walk. In commercial districts the sidewalk width ranges from 10 to 20 feet, with an average of 15 feet being a generally accepted standard for a walk traversed by "window-shoppers" in the main business center. The estimate by Lawson Purdy of 5 square feet of sidewalk area per person suggests the necessity to calculate the area of pedestrian ways according to the population density of the area served; Mr. Purdy estimated that the sidewalks would be used by one-half to one-third of the building occupants at any one time.[1] Were the maze of "downtown" traffic streets to be simplified by substitution of pedestrian malls through portions of the shopping centers, the circulation of pedestrians could become convenient, attractive, and far less dangerous.

Since one-third of the land in the urban community is devoted to the road system, it is pertinent to observe how this land came into public ownership. In early times travel over the safest and most easily traversed routes created "public" roadways through usage. Since the basic ownership of all land was the sovereign right of the state, it was normal for the ruler to designate "post" roads and highways to assure protection for channels of communication between communities. When ownership was granted to individuals, the head of the state provided for a means of access to property, although some passageways remained toll roads until a very late date. In cities the subdivision of land into individual parcels was regulated by decree to maintain certain open spaces for travel and safety against fire. This practice is reflected in modern subdivision design whereby the state, in granting the right to individuals to subdivide land, requires that the roadways which give access to property be dedicated to public use. Streets thus dedicated to public use and accepted by the city for maintenance may either remain as public easements for such time as they are required as streets or they may be deeded to the city in "fee simple." When streets are vacated by the city, the land occupied by them is usually divided equally and title to it returned to the abutting property owners.

The gridiron street plan formed a pattern of rectangular blocks divided into rectangular lots which were usually very narrow to conserve on utility lines and very deep to conserve on streets. The curvilinear design was then devised to give some semblance of "character" to the subdivision, or subdue the deadly monotony of parallel streets stretching to infinity. The alternative soon developed into a curved grid, a series of parallel curved streets, with no more living amenities than the rectangular grid provided. The more exaggerated of the "designs" assumed the form of a violently swirling street system in which orientation was completely obscured.

[1] *Regional Survey of New York and Its Environs,* 1931.

It is customary to maintain the narrowest practicable width for local residential streets which serve only the abutting property. When parking is desired on each side of the street, the right-of-way is between 54 feet and 64 feet wide, with a pavement width of 36 feet. The paved surface may be as narrow as 30 feet, but this suggests parking on one side only since the traffic lanes should not be less than 9 feet wide. Although local streets of narrow width are more economical in their initial cost, the weaving of automobiles about parked cars is a hazard to the safety of children in the neighborhood.

Economy of street design has been more rationally approached through the effort to reduce the total length of streets rather than their width. Care in site planning brought about an abandoning of the artificial picturesqueness of the arbitrary street system and led to the use of the cul-de-sac and the loop street.

The cul-de-sac, or dead-end street, came into use to eliminate in a positive manner through-traffic. They terminate in a circular or hammer-head "turn-around," and, to retain their inherent advantages, they should be short—a maximum length of 250 feet is recommended. The advantages are dissipated in long cul-de-sacs since they induce accelerated traffic speeds and render access for service and fire-protection facilities more complicated. Probably the most renowned example of the cul-de-sac street system is the community of Radburn, New Jersey. In this development the system is fully exploited by the consolidation of open space and reduction of street crossings, the separation between vehicular and pedestrian circulation being enhanced by the use of pedestrian underpasses beneath the major streets. Although this separation of traffic is desirable, the narrow tunnel-shape of the usual pedestrian underpass tends to accumulate refuse and dirt, and presents dangers which may be avoided by convenient pedestrian overpasses above slightly depressed streets.

The loop street is a variation of the cul-de-sac and is employed in substantially the same manner. However, it eliminates the necessity for the "turn-around" and provides continuous circulation required by some communities to assure no interference with accessibility for fire protection and other services. While it does not offer complete separation between vehicular and pedestrian traffic, it is as effective as the cul-de-sac in eliminating through-traffic. The length of the loop street is not as important as that of the cul-de-sac, since the movement of traffic is continuous, but, like the cul-de-sac, traffic is normally confined to vehicles of the residents or for service and delivery within the block.

There are some disadvantages in the cul-de-sac and the loop street, but careful planning can reduce these to a minimum. It is sometimes alleged that circulation about a community becomes confusing, although a simple plan can overcome much of this objection. House-numbering and street-naming require attention since they vary from the customary pattern for which the usual systems have been devised.

The collector street is, as the name suggests, the street into which the local residential streets feed. It may be designed to flow into the secondary or major traffic arteries, in which case the right-of-way is usually 60 feet wide with a pavement 36 feet in width. Frequently, however, the collector streets are comparable in traffic load to a secondary highway and must be so designed.

The traffic load from the local residential streets and their collector roadways is carried by the secondary and major highways and, although a difference in function is suggested by this terminology, there is often little real distinction between the traffic they carry. The secondary highway is intended to serve areas intermediate between the major traffic streets and thence connect to the major highway. However, major highways have grown so congested that much traffic escapes along the secondary and collector streets, thus rendering each the equivalent of a major traffic artery.

Secondary highways are usually 80 or 84 feet in width of right-of-way, with a pavement width of 64 feet having four lanes for traffic and two for parking. The major highways are customarily 100 feet in width with a pavement width of about 76 feet having six lanes for moving traffic and two for parking.

It is gradually becoming apparent that access from abutting property to major and secondary highways must be denied. The movement of traffic cannot be maintained when it is repeatedly interrupted by the ingress or egress of vehicles from side streets. Frontage along these main traffic routes must obtain their service access from either alleys or minor service roads parallel to the highway. A service road is generally 28 feet in width, allowing parking on one side only, and the usual width of alleys is 20 feet with parking prohibited. Service roads may be screened from the highways with a planting strip; the highway is thus enhanced while the abutting property is shielded from it, an asset to the development of residential neighborhoods contiguous to highways.

Authorities generally agree upon three standard elements in the street plan of a city with the typical concentric form.

1. The first element is the radial street, designed as six- or eight-lane arteries connecting roadways entering the city with the central business area. These streets carry the heaviest traffic load and some would become freeways or expressways.

2. The second element is the belt street, designed to by-pass the central area and distribute heavy traffic about the circumference of the city. Surveys have shown that nearly half of all vehicles traversing the central business district in most cities are destined for other points. These vehicles travel through the downtown area because the traffic arteries all lead through it. Belt streets would remove this traffic before it reaches the central area.

3. The third element is the cross-town street, designed to distribute heavy traffic from the radials and belts. They serve as principal circulation arteries in east-west and north-south directions through the city and would be six- and eight-lane streets about one mile apart in each direction. They would distribute traffic to the industrial and shopping areas and become the boundaries which define "neighborhood units" within the city.

This framework of streets would be variously designed as freeways and expressways, combining automobile and mass transportation. Cross-town streets would carry the feeder lines to rapid transit lines on the radial and belt expressways. Within this framework are the circulation streets which serve the neighborhood units. These streets would be the usual four-lane roadways, and provide the additional local mass transportation required in the neighborhood.

The Freeway. One means of relieving traffic congestion is the relatively new form of traffic artery—the freeway. The freeway is essentially a pair of parallel roadways, each of which carries one-way traffic in opposite directions, with complete separation from each other and free from all cross-traffic. Ingress and egress in either direction flows into or from the channel of travel via accelerating and decelerating lanes. Traffic moves unimpeded by any interruptions from light signals or stop signs. All cross-traffic is carried over or under the freeway, and access from abutting property is closed from the freeway right-of-way.

The freeway appeared on the American scene during the early 1930's, with the construction of the Downtown expressway parallel to the Hudson River in New York City, the Pulaski Skyway from Newark, New Jersey, to New York, and the commencement of the great Chicago Outer Drive. Later developments soon followed in New Jersey, Pennsylvania, New York, Connecticut, Delaware, California, and in the vicinity of Washington, D.C.

Many of these early routes were limited in scope, but they were designed for the unimpeded movement of vehicles by the shortest feasible route between two or more points. The freeway may parallel existing streets or cut across their present pattern. It marks the beginning of a new form of artery which may aid in solution of the traffic problem and create the huge cells that will ultimately frame the groups of neighborhood units as the city grows and is rebuilt. With the freeway a new urban form is emerging.

The right-of-way for a freeway is necessarily broad; it must provide adequate space to be depressed or raised without adversely affecting abutting property. Limitations on the width vary with circumstances. Land cost may be one obvious prospect for forcing economy in land area, but another may appear in state laws which restrict the acquisition of property for public improvements to that required for the principal function of the facility. Such restrictions would limit the right-of-way to the area required only for the traffic lanes and adjacent walkways, the acquisition for contiguous buffer spaces being considered excessive. To cope with such a situation in New York City, the routes were acquired by the Park Department as park strips and the traffic ways were built within them; the term Parkway is consequently applied to them. Some states have enacted statutes to permit the acquisition of ample space for the freeway right-of-way; in California a space 150 feet on each side of the centerline of the roadway may be acquired, thus providing for purchase of marginal property to avoid the creation of small remnants of land otherwise unusable for development.

The freeway is usually designed for three lanes of traffic in each direction, and rarely more than four lanes. These are intended for the free movement of vehicles, and the greater the number of lanes, the greater is the interference from vehicles weaving between them seeking a satisfactory channel of speed or access to the decel-

The proposed West Route, Congress Street Expressway in Chicago. A four-track electric rapid-transit railway runs in the central mall.

TYPES OF FREEWAYS

The sketches on the opposite page illustrate various types of freeways at the junction of a major or secondary highway from which changes to lateral transportation may be provided. The "right-of-way" in each scheme—building-line to building-line—is 300 feet in width.

Type 1 is a double three-lane expressway providing for buses in the outside lane. Pavement is widened to four lanes for loading and unloading at the underpass to eliminate interference with continuous auto travel. A width of 144 feet, not including the marginal streets, will accommodate an expressway of this type. It represents the usual freeway with the addition of the extra width for bus platform. The center mall is 12 feet in width.

Type 2 is for buses in the outside lane, as in Type 1, except that bus lane is separated from the freeway where it turns out to the platform. A minimum width of 170 feet between the marginal streets is necessary for this type.

Type 3 is an expressway for bus mass transportation in which the separate lanes for bus station platforms are located between the freeway lanes. This center station is accommodated in a width of 170 feet between marginal streets by curving the outer freeway lanes with a radius of at least 4,000 feet. The center mall is 30 feet wide.

Type 4 is a double three-lane auto freeway with rapid transit (electric train) in the center mall. For two tracks—one in each direction—a 50-foot wide mall is required. The center platform for trains provides access to the upper level highway. A minimum of 150 feet between marginal streets will accommodate this type.

Type 5 is a combination of three-lane auto freeway with separate outside bus lanes for loading and unloading and double rapid-transit tracks in the center mall. A width of 220 feet between marginal streets is needed.

Type 6 shows three-lane freeways with separate inside bus lanes for loading and unloading and a double rapid-transit track in the center mall. The width between marginal streets is 220 feet, the mall 50 feet.

Schemes 4, 5 and 6 could accommodate two rapid-transit tracks in each direction—one local, one express—by a small increase in the width of the mall. While auto lanes for ingress and egress are not shown in 5 and 6, they could be incorporated. The grade for these lanes should not exceed 4 per cent in the case of elevated or depressed freeways.

TYPES OF FREEWAYS

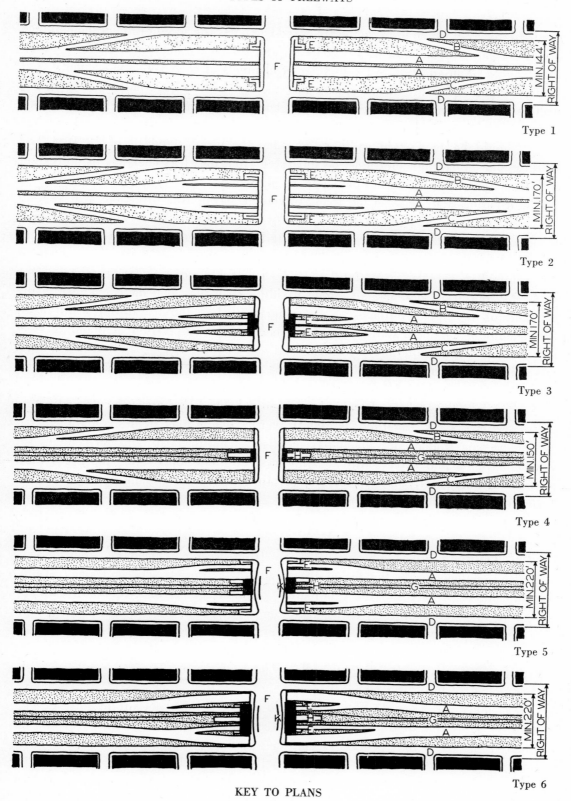

Type 1

Type 2

Type 3

Type 4

Type 5

Type 6

KEY TO PLANS

A. Through-traffic lanes
B. Departure lanes
C. Entrance lanes
D. Marginal streets
E. Bus loading lanes
F. Lateral feeder highway
G. Railway tracks
H. Railway station
K. Feeder bus stations

erating lane from which to leave the freeway. The lanes for acceleration at the entrance and deceleration at the exit of the freeway, and for emergency parking for disabled cars, should be in addition to the number of channels of clear traffic movement.

Ingress and egress are at infrequent intervals, not less than one-half mile apart and preferably at one-mile distances; this frequency will permit adequate stops for bus connections if they are permitted on the freeway system. Lanes for truck or bus travel should be 15 feet in width rather than the usual standard of 12 feet, and loading and unloading zones must be separated from the clear channels of movement with transition lanes leading to the stopping places.

The dividing strip between the roads traversing in opposite directions will vary in width according to the nature of the right-of-way. Some separations are broad enough to permit service stations, emergency parking bays, and fully landscaped spaces, but the usual width is between 10 and 20 feet. Because the freeway, presently intended for automotive vehicles, may later provide a logical and appropriate channel for mass transportation vehicles, an ample dividing strip may one day demonstrate the economy of its original purchase; a minimum of 30 feet and a desirable width of 50 feet should be planned. Oversight, indifference, or lack of vision in planning freeways will cost the people much in money as well as time, confusion, and discouragement; it is demonstrated today in some cities where the freeway and mass transportation plans failed to be integrated.

Safety and efficient flow of traffic have been enhanced by improvements in lighting and directional signs. Lighting for night travel has made long strides, some highways having become ribbons of lighted pavement requiring no headlights on vehicles for adequate vision and safety. Although not yet fully developed and employed, color may be advantageously used to identify certain lanes for speeds and points of departure from the roadway. The scale of letters and placement of signs which indicate directions, places, and distances are important factors in the design of traffic-ways for smooth and safe circulation.

The Traffic Lane. Traffic hazards arise from excessive speed, but they may be due also to deficiencies in the design of roadways. Separations between traffic traveling in opposite directions and the elimination of intersections are essential. The provision of off-street parking so curb parking may be prohibited is necessary; only one disabled car can reduce a three-lane roadway to a two-lane street and add the hazard of rapid accumulation of vehicles at this bottleneck. Given the free flow of traffic which these improvements offer, the effectiveness of the motor car depends upon the shape of the roadway over which it travels.

Traffic lanes vary from 8 feet to 15 feet and this variation is not a fault until it occurs within the same line of travel. The local street may have a width of 10 feet and the through-traffic artery may be 12 feet, but the width should be constant for each. Local streets serving residential areas are customarily designed for a lane of 10 feet, being 4 feet wider than the standard automobile and none too great a separation between two moving vehicles passing at a rate of 25 miles per hour. On highways and freeways the

CITIES ARE PLANNING SYSTEMS OF FREEWAY ROUTES

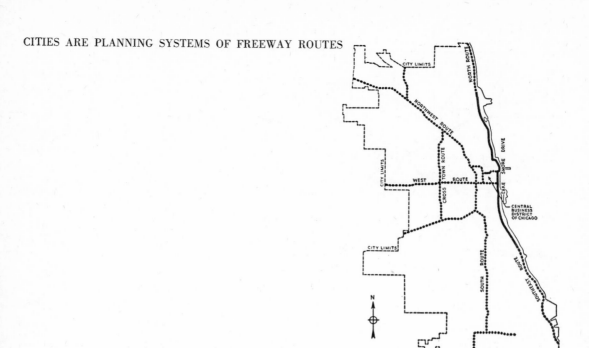

CITY OF CHICAGO
COMPREHENSIVE SUPERHIGHWAY SYSTEM
GENERAL PLAN

EXISTING EXPRESSWAYS
PROPOSED EXPRESSWAYS

Courtesy Concrete Highways and Public Improvements

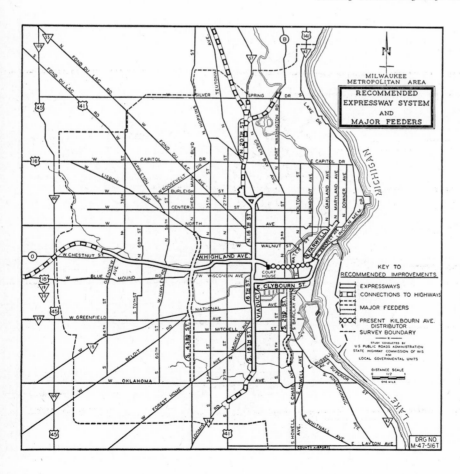

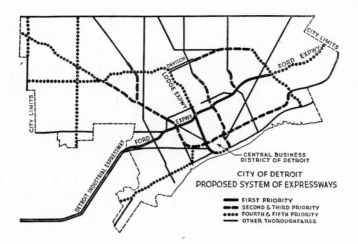

CITY OF DETROIT
PROPOSED SYSTEM OF EXPRESSWAYS

━━━━━ FIRST PRIORITY
━ ━ ━ SECOND & THIRD PRIORITY
• • • • FOURTH & FIFTH PRIORITY
───── OTHER THOROUGHFARES

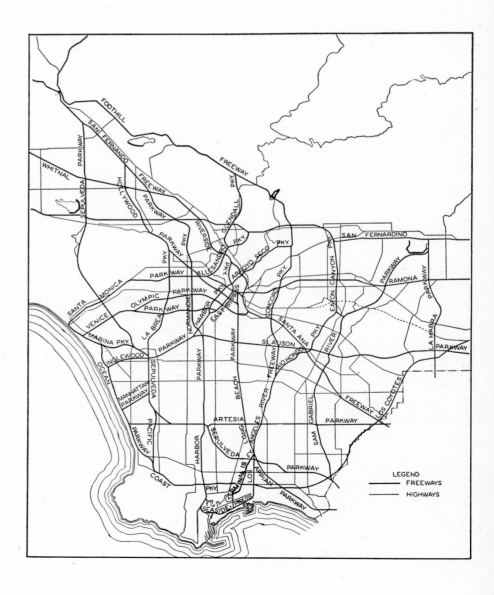

LEGEND
━━━━━ FREEWAYS
───── HIGHWAYS

Los Angeles

width is generally 12 feet, increased to 13 or 14 feet on the curves.[2] When the free-way or highway is designed for the operation of trucks and busses, a lane of 15 feet in width should be provided.

The width of the lane intended for parking vehicles is usually 8 feet; this assumes the wheels will be one foot from the curb and allow 3 feet between it and a vehicle passing along the centerline of the adjacent moving lane. If the parked vehicle is a truck, it will project into the adjacent lane, creating a hazard of side-swiping. It seems more sensible to make no distinction between the width of a lane for parking and one for moving vehicles; in peak hours when curb parking is prohibited, this lane adds a traffic way to the otherwise overcrowded street.

One-third of all trips by motor vehicles of all types are within the city limits, and 90 per cent of the rest are within a radius of 30 miles. The automobile is adapted to use for local travel and is readily maneuverable and quick-starting. However, it can achieve high, comfortable and relatively safe speed, depending upon the roadbed and the driver at the wheel.

The appropriate roadway is an uninterrupted straight run or sweeping curve. A car traveling at 10 miles per hour requires a turning radius of about 40 feet with a level roadbed and 30 feet if the road has a 10 per cent slope. When the speed reaches 30 miles per hour, the curve should be 400 feet on a level road and 230 feet with a 10 per cent slope. At 60 miles per hour the radius of the curve should be 1,400 feet if level, and 900 feet with a 10 per cent bank.[3] Since the average critical speed of automobiles has been between 30 and 35 miles per hour, it would appear that road curves of some 250 feet, well banked, would be adequate, but it is necessary to provide for the far more rapid travel which will continue to occur upon our freeways, a free flow needing a radius of at least 1,000 feet.

The combined factors of human response and the mechanical action in bringing a car to a halt make clear visibility at street intersections mandatory. The driver of an automobile traveling at a speed of 10 miles per hour quickly perceives a necessity to stop the car, but by the time he has translated this perception into the action of applying the brakes the car has traveled a distance of 8 feet. Another 8 feet will be traveled before the brakes bring the vehicle to a stop. Traveling at 30 miles per hour a car will go 20 feet between the time the driver detects the need to stop and has translated this perception into action against the brakes. The car will travel another 60 feet before it is stopped. At 60 miles per hour the car will have moved 45 feet between perception and action on the brakes, the braking distance being another 230 feet.[4]

Previous reference has been made to the effect of weaving on the flow of traffic. This injects both a hazard and a deterrent to speed. The absence of left-hand turns

[2] *Vocation and Function of Urban Freeways, Post-War Patterns of City Growth*, Frank H. Malley, American Transit Association, New York.

[3] Comprehensive Planning for the City: Market and Dwelling Place, Part I: Traffic Design, Hermann Herrey, *Pencil Points*, April 1944.

[4] *Ibid.*

reduces the problem to some degree since autos entering a roadway have no necessity to move out of the traffic stream to the left. The weaving action is nevertheless present in a street of more than one lane in width since cars in the left lane will have to leave the traffic stream on the right. A car traveling in a traffic stream moving at a speed of 10 miles per hour will need only 170 feet to weave from left to right in a two-lane highway and 320 feet in a three-lane road. When the traffic stream is moving at 30 miles per hour, however, the weaving distance in a two-lane road increases to 750 feet and 1,230 feet in a three-lane road. At 50 miles per hour the weaving distance is 1,890 feet in two lanes and 2,900 feet in three lanes.[5]

Elimination of grade intersections removes stop-and-go signals and increases both the speed and the safety of vehicles. A comparative survey in Milwaukee revealed the average speed of traffic on the usual street is 13.4 miles per hour while the average speed on a section of freeway, free from intersections, is 31.8 miles per hour. The average speed on all the streets in the city is 16.8 miles per hour during the rush-hour traffic and 18.2 miles per hour for normal traffic. The comparison is further accentuated by the improvement in rates of accidents, the ratio being one to twenty between the freeway and ordinary street intersection with an injury ratio of one to twenty-seven.[6]

Not only is safety improved by the elimination of street intersections, but economy in time and money is effected. Estimates by the Automobile Club of Southern California indicate the freeway is seven times as safe as the normal street system, saves 50 per cent in driving time, and is 30 per cent cheaper in operating costs of the automobile.

These statistics indicate the nature of the horizontal space dimensions the auto has introduced to the urban traffic pattern and emphasize the basic fact that streets intended for smooth and safe traffic flow cannot have frequent intersections without destroying the effectiveness of the vehicle.

Adjustment to the new character of modern vehicular travel has been slow and the change in approach to the design of roadways has probably been most apparent at the points of intersection. Traffic circles were the first attempts to merge traffic flow and avoid the conflicts of left turns. While traffic was light, the circle was adequate, but the increase in number of vehicles recreated congestion at these points.

The "cloverleaf" was the next step toward a solution of traffic interchange, but it has a weakness. The driver of a vehicle intending to turn left must cross beyond the intersecting street for which he is destined, and then make a right turn into a curve which leads back to the cross street he seeks. It is confusing for a driver, traveling at a fair rate of speed, to find himself passing beyond the intersection he seeks and then turn right for a left-hand direction. Familiarity with a roadway offsets this sort of confusion, but it is not assurance of the safest form of traffic artery.

Other types of interchange structures have been designed for the purpose of over-

[5] *Ibid.*

[6] *Milwaukee Origin-Destination Survey,* Concrete Highways and Public Improvements, Portland Cement Association, Spring 1947.

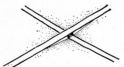

Simple Grade Separation between
Two Highways

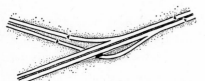

Braided or "T" Interchange

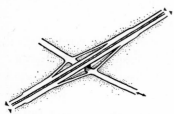

Simple Interchange of Freeway with Highway

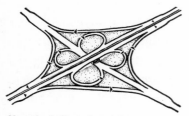

Cloverleaf Interchange

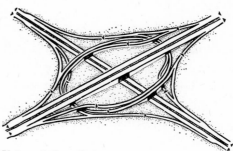

Universal Interchange

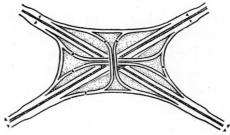

Four-level Interchange

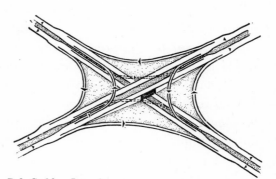

Bel Geddes Interchange

TYPES OF FREEWAY INTERSECTIONS

Aerial Photograph Co., Chicago

coming the weaknesses of the circle and cloverleaf, and most have incorporated the best features of each. However, all designs assume that slow vehicles remain on the right-hand side of the roadway and, because left-hand turns on level roads are a handicap to speed and safety, movement from the freeway is channeled to the right regardless of the destination of the vehicle. In the General Motors Exhibit at the New York World's Fair in 1939, Norman Bel Geddes presented a highway design in which a driver would turn left from the left-hand lane, and this turn would have the same radius of curvature as the right-hand turn. He observed that the term "slow lane" is a contradiction of the freeway system and that the speed of vehicles would probably be similar in all lanes. Bel Geddes proposed that the number of through-lanes continue undiminished regardless of the left and right turns, and he provided a lane for transition into the left-hand turn as was customary for the right-hand turn. Similarly the transition lanes for entrance to the freeway would be from both left and right sides of the roadway.

The adoption of this logic is rather slow since it suggests some changes in the normal habits of drivers accustomed to the present formula for turning right out of a freeway no matter what direction may be the ultimate destination. It also necessitates some changes in the habits of the engineers who design the highway system. Meanwhile, the knotty problem of the smooth and safe intersection of traffic is met by some rather fantastic combinations of the circle, the universal, and the cloverleaf.

Movement of People. The function of the circulation system is the movement of people about the city and in the performance of this function every form of mass transportation, except railways and subways, is routed on a street system originally laid out for the easy subdivision of land and in the time when the horse and buggy was the common mode of conveyance. The result is a paradox: the automobile receives the most attention in plans for the improvement of urban traffic but is the least efficient form of urban transport, whereas the autobus is replacing the electric train, although the latter is essentially the most efficient form of rapid transit for the mass movement of people. That the development of effective rapid transit is the most economical, as well as the most efficient means for the mass transportation of the urban population, may be apparent by comparison of the characteristics of vehicles and the roadways they use.

A typical traffic street with the usual intersecting streets will accommodate 700–800 private passenger automobiles per lane per hour passing a given point. It will carry about 180 autobusses and 150 street-cars per lane per hour. Since it is the movement of people rather than the movement of vehicles with which we are concerned, the capacity of the street must be translated into the number of people these vehicles will transport. Studies have demonstrated that private autos carry an average of 1.75 persons per car. An autobus will carry about 40 persons seated and a street-car about 50 seated persons. The single lane of the typical trunk street will therefore accommodate about 1,200 passengers per hour in private autos while the bus carries 7,200 and the street-car 9,000. The capacity of the bus and street-car may be further increased with standing passengers, raising the capacity of the bus to 9,000 and the street-car to 13,500 per hour.[7]

These figures apply to the capacity of a single lane for each type of vehicle. A proportionate increase in the capacity would occur by the addition of lanes if they could be retained as clear channels. Painted white lines demarking the lanes are of some aid in the typical street, but they do not prohibit the weaving of vehicles from one lane to another, and the effect of weaving measurably reduces the efficiency of the street. Surveys have shown that weaving reduces the capacity of the second lane of traffic to 75 per cent of the single lane, the capacity of a third lane is 56 per cent of the single lane, and a fourth lane is only 26 per cent of the single lane.[8] Three lanes in one direction with unrestricted weaving have a capacity of only 2⅓ lanes of clear channels with no weaving.

Studies by the American Transit Association demonstrate the increase in movement of people by the addition of mass transportation facilities on the city streets. A typical city street with a pavement width of 60 feet and no curb parking provides three lanes of traffic in each direction. This street will accommodate about 2,100 private autos in three lanes, assuming reasonable restrictions on weaving, and carry 3,700 passengers per hour. If one lane of autos is replaced by a bus, the number of autos is decreased to 1,200 and their passenger load to 2,100, but the bus line carries 7,200 seated passengers and 9,000 including standees, increasing the total capacity of the street to 9,300 seated and 11,100 including standing passengers. If the bus line is replaced by a street-car, with a capacity of 9,000 seated passengers and 13,500 seated and standing, the total load of the street is 11,100 seated and 15,600 passengers seated and standing.[9] In each case the standing passenger load is assumed to be 25 per cent of the seated passengers in autobusses and 50 per cent of the seated passengers in street-cars.

This study shows that the substitution of a bus line for a lane of autos on the ordinary trunk street will carry two and one-half times the number of people carried by three lanes of autos alone, and the substitution of a street-car line for one lane of autos will carry three times the number of people. In both cases all passengers are seated. When standing passengers are included, the capacity of the street is increased to three times the number of people in busses and nearly four times the number in street-cars.

A limited access roadway with no grade crossings materially increases the capacity of private automobiles, but this capacity is not increased proportionately with the speed which autos can reach with uninterrupted flow. Studies show that the theoretical maximum number of vehicles is accommodated at a speed of about 32 miles per hour, and that the theoretical maximum number of cars is about 2,060 per hour per lane. The practical maximum number of cars that can be carried at this speed, however, is only about 75 per cent of this number, or 1,500 cars per hour per lane, the capacity decreasing above and below this critical speed.[10]

[7] *Moving People in the Modern City*, American Transit Association, New York City.
[8] *Ibid.*
[9] *Ibid.*
[10] *Ibid.*

A freeway carrying 1,500 cars per hour will move 2,500 people in a single lane as compared with 1,200 passengers on the ordinary city street. The number of seated passengers carried by an autobus increases from 7,200 to 10,000 per hour and 13,000 including standees. The capacity of the electric street-car is likewise increased when interference of other traffic is removed; it increases from 9,000 seated passengers and 13,500 including standees on the ordinary street to 13,500 seated and 20,000 including standees per track per hour with uninterrupted movement. The free flow of uninterrupted rail lines further permits the effective use of multiple trains which carry 27,000 seated and 40,000 including standees per hour on a single track, while two tracks in the same direction, with one local and one express train, can increase the total capacity per hour to 70,000 seated and 100,000 or more including standing passengers.[11]

A six-lane freeway—three lanes in each direction—will reduce the capacity per lane for automobiles from 1,500 cars per hour for a single lane to about 2,700 cars for two lanes and 3,500 cars in three lanes. Three lanes will carry about 6,000 passengers per hour in private automobiles compared with one autobus lane carrying 7,200 seated and 9,000 including standees.[12] Autobusses operating on a three-lane freeway would probably also be reduced in efficiency because of the inevitable conflict with automobiles. If the same decrease as automobiles were applied to the autobus, the latter would still carry 8,000 seated persons and more than 11,000 including standees.

Freeway costs vary with the cost index at any time, the locality, and the cost of site acquisition, but they have generally ranged between $2,000,000 and $4,000,000 per mile for a six-lane roadway in metropolitan areas. In its report "Toll Roads and Free Roads," the Public Roads Administration estimated the cost at $633,000 per mile in rural areas and $1,158,000 in urban areas, including land cost, before the Second World War. The East River Parkway in New York City cost $2,000,000 per mile, and the limited ways along the Outer Drive of Chicago were about $1,500,000 per mile. The Hendrik Hudson elevated roadway in New York, built in 1934, cost $3,000,000 a mile compared with the Arroyo Seco freeway in Los Angeles, built in 1939–40 and requiring little land acquisition at a cost of $840,000 per mile.

Use of the freeway has been confined, with few exceptions, to the private passenger automobile and represents a high capital cost per passenger carried by autos alone. The average cost of a freeway is about $500 per mile per passenger carried in autos, but an increase of 50 feet in the width would accommodate a double track for rapid transit or separate lanes for autobusses.[13] The extra cost has been estimated at approximately 15 per cent of the total freeway cost and the average cost per mile would be reduced to about $50 per passenger.[14]

The freeway incorporating rapid transit lines—the expressway—or some form of overhead train system—the "elevated train" or monorail—requires a fairly com-

[11] *Ibid.*
[12] *Ibid.*
[13] *Postwar Transit and Highway Plans, Postwar Patterns of City Growth*, Charles E. Deleuw, American Transit Association.
[14] *Transit and Urban Expressways*, Leslie Williams, 2nd Annual Conference of the Eno Foundation for Traffic Control, Inc.

modious right-of-way for protection to abutting property. Because there is a firm reluctance to retire any of the land surface from present or potential use for commercial development in the urban centers, there is resistance to either of these surface forms of transportation into the heart of the city. Distracted by the overwhelming congestion on city streets and the inadequacy of rapid transit systems to move the people with convenience, comfort, or speed, the subway is the natural alternative.

Unfortunately the subway marks the final evidence that the city has succumbed to strangulation by urban congestion. By comparison with the expressway, in which mass transportation facilities are incorporated, the cost of subways has ranged between $6,000,000 and $14,000,000 per mile for a double-track line. An uninterrupted flow of travel for multiple-electric trains is accomplished, but at a cost that exceeds every other form of mass transportation. Only the private automobile exceeds the cost of subways and it is four or five times the cost per passenger mile.

The Impasse—Terminal Parking. When the horse and carriage was the common mode of conveyance, stopping places along the road customarily provided a service for the care of teams while the traveler lodged or conducted his business. The horses were "put up and baited." Because there was sometimes abusive obstruction of the roads, curbs against the random tethering of animals were found necessary in those early days.

Then the automobile entered the city with a vengeance. In cities with a population over 500,000, the number of people who enter the downtown business center in automobiles ranges from 40–50 per cent of the total. Exceptions are New York City and Chicago; in the former, the percentage is near 15 per cent and in Chicago it is about 30 per cent. In cities between 100,000 and 500,000 population 60–75 per cent of the total number of people entering the business district travel in automobiles, and in smaller cities, under 100,000 population, the percentage jumps to 70–90 per cent, with an average of about 80 per cent.

Ways and means to accommodate this wave of automobiles in the business districts have run the gamut of ingenious arrangements. Parking lots, basement garages, multi-story elevator garages, roof parking, and curb parking with and without parking meters are among the devices being used in varying amounts and effectiveness.

Probably the most novel and elaborate device thus far is the Union Square Garage in San Francisco. The land for this project, a city park one square block in size, was leased from the city. The garage was built in four separate levels beneath the surface of the park, provides 10 acres of floor space and ramps, and has a capacity of 1,700 cars. This is equal to 125 blocks of curb parking.

The total cost of the development was $1,500,000 which was financed with 6,800 shares of 6 per cent cumulative preferred stock sold at $100 per share. The balance of the capital was obtained through an $850,000 loan from the Reconstruction Finance Corporation. It is reported that the enterprise pays some $16,000 a year in taxes to the city in addition to an annual land rental of $5,000. Title to the project will transfer to the city when the financial obligation has been paid off. Mr. Andrew Pansini, who

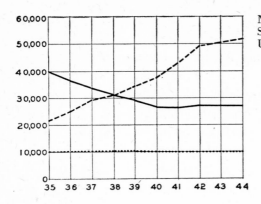

NUMBER AND TYPE OF TRANSIT PAS–
SENGER VEHICLES OPERATING IN THE
UNITED STATES, 1935–1944

----- Motor Buses and Trolley Coaches
——— Surface Railway
·········· Subway

CAPACITY OF A SINGLE TRAFFIC LANE

Passengers Carried per Hour

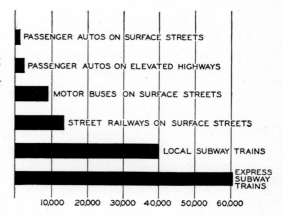

PASSENGER AUTOS ON SURFACE STREETS
PASSENGER AUTOS ON ELEVATED HIGHWAYS
MOTOR BUSES ON SURFACE STREETS
STREET RAILWAYS ON SURFACE STREETS
LOCAL SUBWAY TRAINS
EXPRESS SUBWAY TRAINS

10,000 20,000 30,000 40,000 50,000 60,000

Underground Parking Garage in Union Square, San Francisco

operates the garage, believes that any city with a population of 200,000 or more, could support a similar venture.

The motorist wishes to park as near his destination as possible, and surveys have indicated that he will accomplish this, in many instances, at the expense of illegal curb parking. Surveys have also indicated that the motorist entering the downtown district for business or shopping does not wish to walk from his parking place a distance of more than 1,000 feet. In a midwestern city, Rockford, Illinois, the following desires were indicated by motorists:[15] Of those who parked for one-half hour or less, 41% would walk one block, 36% would walk 2 blocks, and 14% would walk 3 blocks, 4% would walk 4 blocks; of those who parked for one hour, 15% would walk one block, 37% two blocks, 28% three blocks, and 12% four blocks, 4% five blocks; of those who parked up to two hours, 6% would walk one block, 28% two blocks, 29% three blocks, 23% four blocks, 6% five blocks, and 5% six blocks; of those who parked for more than two hours, 20% would walk two blocks, 33% three blocks, 20% four blocks, 13% five blocks, 8% six blocks, and 4% more than six blocks. If we assume the city block to be 400 feet long, it is apparent that those who wish to park for a short time—one-half hour or less—wish to be within 500–600 feet of their destination; those who park for about one hour wish to be no farther than about 1,000 feet from their destination, and those who intend to remain for a longer time would wish to be no farther than about 1,200 feet from their destination.[16]

It must be granted that these surveys deserve qualification. Consider the environment through which the urbanite must travel; it is little wonder the shopper dislikes to walk in the downtown district, or in many other sections of the contemporary metropolis. Ugliness is abhorrent and it repels a human being; it can hardly be expected that people will wish to walk about a business district fraught with every disagreeable feature and lacking convenient shopping and business facilities. When the cities acquire the self-respect which comes with pride in the physical beauty of an environment, the willingness of motorists to walk through these surroundings will probably reveal quite a different set of statistics.

About 80 per cent of the parkers in the central business district remain for one hour or less, the number ranging from 60 to 90 per cent. When curb parking is permitted, the average time is about 30 minutes because of the preponderance of people who enter the business district for brief periods. Relating these several factors, the parking facilities for the downtown business district could be consolidated in areas ranging between 500 feet and 1,000 feet in radius from the center of a well-planned group of stores and office buildings. Convenience would be enhanced by the elimination of congestion, discomfort, and hazard caused by the conflict between pedestrian and vehicular traffic, and it is possible that this new element of convenience might encourage pedestrians to walk more and further increase business.

Requirements for parking vary considerably, but experience has divulged some

[15] Parking in Downtown Rockford, Illinois, Chicago Motor Club, January 1942, from *Parking*, Wilbur S. Smith and Charles S. LeCraw, The Eno Foundation for Highway Control, Inc., December 1946.
[16] *Ibid.*

factors which assist in estimating the requirements. The average space per occupant in commercial buildings—office space—is approximately 150 square feet in floor area. If all regular occupants in these business structures were to use private automobiles for their transportation, an area of 150 square feet per person would be required in parking, the equivalent of one square foot of parking for each square foot of building floor space.

This space does not provide for people who patronize the business enterprise and it may be estimated that an equal number enter the commercial district for this purpose as those who occupy the commercial buildings. In the average city, however, about 50 per cent of the people entering the downtown district use the available means for mass transportation—rail or bus. This results in a required space for parking equal to the building floor area, a figure generally confirmed by authorities.

Market and retail shopping imposes a considerably heavier burden upon parking space. It is a policy of many enterprises, food markets particularly, to provide an area for automobile parking between three and four times the floor area of the market. Mr. Hugh Potter, who has successfully developed such neighborhood shopping areas as River Oaks in Houston, estimates that 3 square feet of parking space should be provided for each square foot of floor space in a market building or shopping group. It is therefore necessary to adjust the required area for parking in central business districts according to the estimated uses to which the land will be put. These estimates will likewise warrant adjustment as mass transportation is improved and becomes capable of adequately moving the largest possible number of people who enter and leave the business district.

Railroads. Builders of the railroads sought level terrain or followed the easy grades along water courses. As cities sprung up along these routes industry developed on the lines of transportation. The passenger station was the entrance to the town and the center of the city grew about it. Providing convenient commutation to the suburbs, the commercial district expanded about this hub.

With the passing of time and the neglect of orderly urban development, industry continued to creep along the railways and waterfronts. The city grew and new railroads entered to help build the metropolis. These lines of transportation were vital to the economic development of the city, and industries were accorded preferential sites along the rights-of-way as encouragement to locate in the city. Blocked by spur tracks and sidings, the street system was interrupted, and traffic problems and hazards were created.

Replacement of the various independent and scattered stations by the "union station" improved the reception, dispatch, and interchange of passengers and freight, but the city still suffers from the chaotic network of separate rail lines that stretch like tentacles in all directions. Consolidation of the various competing lines is slow because of complicated joint agreements, the abandonment of rights-of-way, the high cost of building new facilities for roads already equipped with terminals, and the necessity for co-ordination which would tend to reduce possibilities for independent expansion. Reduction in the duplication of facilities which would result from such consolidation, however, would be of immeasurable profit to the city. Simplification of the street system, traffic routes, and grade crossings would alone vastly improve urban circulation and reduce the present hazards and disorderly pattern.

The shipping of freight comprises a far larger part of railroad business than passenger traffic and presents the more complicated planning problems. Except for some terminal locations, a large part of the freight business is "through" shipping, that is, freight destined for points beyond the city. As the city grew up and spread away from the railroad, the "yards" remained a no-man's-land within the heart of the urban core. Occupying valuable land and disrupting the circulation system of the city, the "yards" are generally too cramped for the efficient handling of the tremendous operations involved in the classification, assortment, and redistribution of freight, as well as storage, switching, and make-up of trains.

Studies for the City of Detroit[17] suggest the appropriate rearrangement of the rail-road lines for the metropolis of today. Designating many of the present rights-of-way as future routes for freeways, the railroads are consolidated upon an integrated system of trackage. A great belt line intercepts the incoming roads about the circumference of the city; along this belt line the "yards" and freight stations are located. From this circumferential belt line the freight is assorted and distributed to the industrial and commercial areas of the city or sent on its way to other points. A sub-belt system may be necessary to serve industrial areas in many cities, from which spurs would provide access to the individual plants.

Replanning of the railroad lines, consolidation of trackage, development of union stations where practicable, removal of "yards," and distribution along belt lines will facilitate the operation of this vital system of transportation and release the city from another of the bonds which now strangle circulation.

The Third Dimension. Man's ability to free himself from the face of the earth created new problems; as a means of transportation for great numbers of people the airplane is no longer theory. While the airplane was an experiment, terminal facilities were located as far as possible from people. With millions of people now flying each year, location of the airport in urban centers and rapid delivery of passengers to their destination are the joint concern of air line operators and the public. Connections from the airport to the destination in the city have become a greater problem than the flying time between cities.

Airport planning is a component part of the Master Plan for the city. It requires a complete analysis of the market comparable to the research conducted for other forms of transportation: an analysis of the present and potential passenger, cargo, and mail business which may be expected in the community; meteorological data; the present and planned land use within and about the city; extent of training program proposed by operators; the local traffic—inter-city and state; transcontinental and international air routes; and prospects for development of private fields.

[17] *Proposed Generalized Land Use Plan,* City of Detroit Master Plan, City Plan Commission, May 1947.

Air transportation is in a state of flux, developments in the type of equipment continuing to change and policies of air line operators being subject to modification with experience. The attitude of the urban population also varies, some desiring complete immunity from proximity to flying fields and lanes, others inclining to the development of residential communities designed about the airplane as a vehicle for commutation.

Planning for air transportation must be conceived at a regional scale, the distribution of airports being arranged for convenient and rapid connections to the strategic parts of the city and by a variety of means which have not yet been settled. Downtown feeder airports to which light ships may bring passengers into the heart of the city are being considered, helicopter flights from the major port to landing space in the city center is a possibility, and air mail service, like that established in Los Angeles from the municipal airport to the main post office less than a quarter of a mile from the city hall, is already in operation. Air transport is an integral part of the transportation of the city, both passenger and cargo, and must be, like the railroad, a component part of the city plan.

Integration or Disintegration. How may these various and diverse characteristics of contemporary vehicles be merged into an effective transportation system?

It is apparent that a change must be made in the present street system and this change may affect other aspects of land use. The freeway is hailed as an instrument with which to create a new framework for the community of tomorrow. The freeway can aid in relief of congestion in the central areas of the city, but the rebuilding of these areas to provide ample parking space and an environment as attractive as the outlying areas of the city must be created; otherwise, the freeways may become the arteries which carry the people past the outmoded central districts to the shopping districts which have their stakes in a well-planned, convenient, and pleasant environment of this day.

Adequate parking space and planned open space and commercial development may be substituted for the futile "strip" zoning along traffic arteries which themselves will be replaced by the freeways. Removed from traffic congestion, replanning will obtain ingress and egress to the business district for vehicles and pedestrians. Curb parking may become a thing of the past; with some exceptions the space along the curbs in central areas is less than one-fifth the amount of parking provided in lots and garages, and yet it is all hopelessly inadequate. Traffic flow is reduced about one-half by curb parking on the average street, and being a serious obstruction to traffic movement, the courts have held that streets are for the movement of traffic and not places for storage of vehicles. Being separate functions, terminal parking space for cars, the traffic arteries, and the space for circulation of pedestrians with their access to shopping and commercial enterprise, will be planned as separate elements.

There must be a plan for transportation and this plan must become a guide for each improvement in the city. During the long and arduous period in which the plan is being formulated, first-aid remedies will be necessary. Traffic bandages and tourniquets, splints and casts will be needed. It is necessary, however, that the distinction between the expedient nature of these first-aid measures and permanent solutions be continuously recognized. The breakdown represented by traffic congestion must be treated in the most infectious spots to keep the urban traffic stream flowing, but these devices of traffic engineering must not be confused with basic improvements in the street pattern and mass transportation. Too frequently they are interpreted as one and the same with the result that the prospect of a solution to the urban traffic and transportation dilemma is given up as hopeless. Students of the problem realize that disintegration will eat deeper into the core of the urban environment and lead gradually, though eventually, to a complete loss of values, unless basic changes are made.

The evidence is already present in cities. We see the decay at its worst in the movement or, to put it more accurately, the retreat of sound business from the blight that has consumed one-time "high-class" districts. We also see the creation of entirely new business centers and we see them growing temporarily prosperous at the expense of the older established areas. Finally we see the first-aid methods being repeatedly used in the vain attempt to revive the dying areas.

Undoubtedly, cities will continue to have a hub we call "downtown." There is reason in the grouping of certain enterprises—civic administration, retail and wholesale business, financial interests, amusement, recreation and cultural centers. And there is an air of activity of "downtown" that satisfies a deep-seated human desire; the bright lights offer a genuine attraction and a characteristic appeal of urban life. But none of these reasons provides any excuse for the rank congestion that results from the high density of people and buildings that currently curse cities. These qualities can be present without appalling overcrowding.

Modern motor transportation has extended the convenient radius of the urban area to some 15 miles. This represents an area of 700 square miles. While we are accustomed to consider the large city as typical, there were, in 1940, only ten metropolitan areas in the United States which reached this area. Only fourteen cities exceeded a population of 500,000 people, and there were seventy-nine between a population of 100,000 and 500,000 while two hundred and fifty were between 30,000 and 100,000.

According to Mr. Charles E. Deleuw, rapid transit is necessary when the volume of persons moving in one direction reaches 15,000 per hour.[18] With effective rapid transit the urban population could be reasonably distributed about the city and eliminate congestion. Mr. Bartholomew suggests that transit service with headways of about 20-minute intervals could be provided when the population in an area served is ten persons or more per acre.[19] The average density of population in Chicago was 16,000 persons per square mile in 1940, or about 25 persons per acre. In the much smaller city of Richmond, Virginia, the population density was an average of less

[18] *Postwar Transit and Highway Plans, Postwar Patterns of City Growth,* Charles E. Deleuw, American Transit Association.

[19] Modern Transit—Key to Community Planning, Harland Bartholomew, *Tomorrow's Cities,* American Transit Association.

than 10 persons per acre—5,000 per square mile. The uneven distribution of the people over the area of the city produces congestion in some sections and unduly sparse settlement in others, but there is space within even the largest of our cities to accommodate a greater population than they now boast without the congestion that prevails. Congestion is not necessary to accommodate the concentration of population within the metropolitan areas of our industrial urban age; five or six million people could be accommodated at the relatively low density of six families per acre within a 700-square mile area of a great city and preserve ample open spaces throughout the environment.

It is quite useless to expect solutions to the traffic problem so long as commercialism suffocates decent growth and improvement by retaining built-in congestion. The time may come when special interests and civic leaders will recognize that some of the land now held for high density commercial and residential use must be relinquished for other more appropriate use, such as open space for adequate circulation.

It may be argued that this suggestion is both impractical and uneconomical; yet the present means of urban transportation are not economically sound nor do they satisfactorily move the urban population. Adequacy is among the major criteria for the measurement of practicality and economy, and persistence in the provision of inadequate transportation facilities can be classified in no other category than sheer extravagance, an unmitigated waste of public and private resources.

Not a single urban inhabitant is immune to these matters. The condition of cities is shattering the human nerves, paralyzing the human body, twisting the human mind, and breaking the human spirit. And the state of civilization today is showing the results.

PART VI

NEW HORIZONS

Slowly but surely humanity achieves
what its wise men have dreamed.
—*Anatole France*

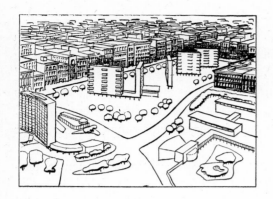

CHAPTER **24**

REBUILDING
OUR CITIES

Misuse of Land. Physical decay has eaten deeply into the urban environment. Blight, congestion, and sprawling suburbs are a burden upon the taxpayer and a social disease evident in juvenile delinquency, crime, ill-health, and degenerated morale. Our cities have not been blasted by bombs; their foundations are undermined by neglect and indifference. Physical disintegration is wearing the urban fabric threadbare and transformation is no longer a repair job. Patching and minor alterations can only prolong what we have. Creation of adequate traffic circulation and transportation, open space, and decongestion of population density are not face-lifting, they call for a series of major operations.

Nor is it a matter of law enforcement. It must be abundantly clear that the current legislative framework which molds the physical structure of cities permits "criminal" use of urban land. The laws underwrite congestion, and police powers have lost their sting. It is futile to protest the license of urban conduct with recriminations against developers of urban property; all are acting within standards prescribed by law. Time and generations of real estate turnover have obliterated tangible evidence of responsibility for creation of these standards. Responsibility now rests with the public—the people in whose hands the process of democracy rests.

Harland Bartholomew has said, "Too often is the American city considered an unlimited speculation in real estate."[1] Stimulated by the almost anarchic nature of laws governing urban development, speculation has enjoyed a violent career. Inflation bubbles are blown up, then burst; credit structures crumble and land prices puff a little but rise again to unprecedented heights.

Land is a natural resource; it is not a product of men's toil. Value which may be attached to it is essentially a by-product, a value not of the land itself but of the way in which the land may be used. Stable values for land can be maintained only through social controls, controls cast in the form of laws prescribing the limits within which it may be used. Because the laws have failed to establish reasonable limitations, restraint upon speculation has been absent from the urban scene.

Congestion created high land values and congestion now threatens to destroy them. To ward off this impending disaster, the compelling motive for improvement in the

[1] *Urban Land Uses,* Harland Bartholomew, Harvard City Planning Series, Harvard University Press, Cambridge, 1932, Introduction.

urban environment is the protection of land values. But misuse of land is like an itch: relief seems to come from more scratching. So congestion begets more congestion and we find any essential or permanent improvements emerging rather as "windfalls," welcome but not intended. Such is the nature of the usual "practical" measures proposed for treatment of urban ills. The process is not marked with economic sanity, as the rotting core of cities and the "decentralizing" forces, reaching madly for cheaper and cheaper land, fairly attest.

Sound business thrives on production and distribution; it creates investment opportunities. Speculation travels in the wake, clinging like a leech and eating away its solvency. The effect is apparent in the urban pattern. Industrial and commercial expansion was expected to continue horizontally and outward from the center. As speculation set in and land prices boomed, industrial enterprise eluded the trap by hurdling to the outskirts. Commercial enterprise expanded vertically via the skyscraper or skipped to the expanding market in the suburb. It was a battle of business trying to avert strangulation by land speculation.

What havoc has been wrought by this economic warfare! In its wake lies a mass of industrial, commercial, and residential derelicts hemmed in by a network of obsolete streets and alleys. It has left land values so inflated they substantially defy self-improvement through normal enterprise. It has heaped a relentlessly increasing burden of taxation upon the people, and it encourages the persistent exodus of the population to the periphery of cities, and beyond.

City government is in partnership with this process. As the city deteriorates the cost of upkeep increases. Revenue to pay the bills comes from taxes, and about 80 per cent of local taxes comes from real estate. If land values were not increased, the tax rate would have to be. That truth does not provide particular comfort for entrenched politicians; the tax rate is one device which measures their popularity. The effect is illustrated in the sequence reported by the *San Francisco Chronicle* of May 24, 1945. In 1940 the tax rate in San Francisco had increased gradually to $4.295. It went to $4.396 in 1941 and $4.48 in 1942. 1943 was an election year for local officials and the rate curiously decreased to $4.36 in that year. In 1944 it bounced up to $4.69 to make up for the reduction conveniently found possible in the preceding year.

The city is practically forced to promote the upward spiral of fictitious land values in order to maintain its income from tax assessment, and the borrowing capacity of municipalities is measured by the assessed valuation of urban property. As municipal debt grows, assessed values must be sustained or increased to support bond issues for capital improvements. It is a rather swift-twisting vortex into which the urban machinery is drawn.

Indecision! A Chinese wall surrounds the city. Within these walls we hear resounding lip-service to the welfare of people and the protection of property. There are occasional spurts of activity in planning the city, but when we see them on review they appear as though the Pied Piper had returned. The plans are made for

SAN FRANCISCO

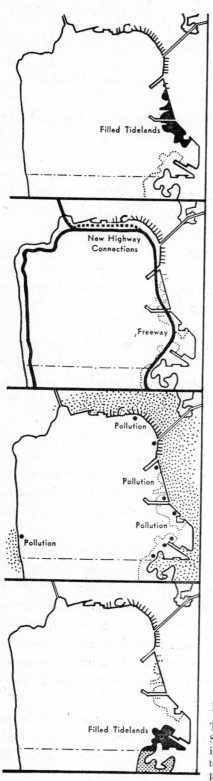

Beach Erosion

Land Slippage

Sand Accretion

Beach Erosion

Filled Tidelands

New Highway
Connections

Freeway

Pollution

Pollution

Pollution

Pollution

Unified Marina and
Aquatic Parks

Enlarged Beach

Picnic Areas

New Parking Areas

Improved
Bayview Park

New Park

Aquatic Park

Ferry Building

Filled Tidelands

Yacht Harbor

FRINGE PLANNING

The proposed plans for San Francisco in 1943 illustrate the tendency to concentrate upon the periphery of our cities while the central areas remain untouched. Meanwhile the people are invited away from the city as escape from congestion. The fringes need planning, but they are integral with the redevelopment of the central core and its environs where the urban ills are most acute. These areas have since been tackled by the Planning Commission in San Francisco, used here only as a typical illustration.

Courtesy The Architect and Engineer

escape from the city. Broad highways, freeways, bridges, and beaches entice the crowded urban dweller through the gates. Green belts adorn the countryside, and "model" subdivisions are dressed in a variety of charming architectural robes from Monterey to Cape Cod.

But within the walls all seems to remain the same. Charts, graphs, and maps depict the course of urban change and decay. Numerous "experts" are consulted, and voluminous reports are issued. There may be some daring new proposal to widen a street a few feet or boldly change some two-way alley into a one-way street. The congestion, the chaos, and the ugliness, however, are untouched. The foundations of the vital urban core are crumbling, the physical and financial welfare of the city is jeopardized, and civic leadership hesitates to face the issue.

There are some encouraging signs visible through these shrouds. It was not long ago that the prospect of an orderly rehabilitation of the decaying city structure was treated as a visionary scheme of radical dreamers. It is now slowly but surely becoming a popular subject and has been dignified by the title of "Urban Redevelopment."

The overwhelming statistical record of disintegration requires no further repetition to confirm the necessity for positive corrective action, but the advocates of urban redevelopment are divided into two camps. Mixed emotions of suspicion, jealousy, and self-interest divide the forces, cloud the issues, and obstruct action. On the one hand are those who, comprehending the social and economic evils rooted in our cities, recoil at the prospect of saving the financial souls of those who allegedly made and profited from the slums. On the other hand are those who, confessing the evils, are reluctant to admit the inability of conventional enterprise to cope with them. If the advocates in both camps would permit the issues to remain in focus and observe them steadily, much of the controversy might be dispelled. But suspicion moves them to sidle cautiously up and then stealthily amble away.

Cities are for the people. They are not objects to be coddled by zealots nor commodities to satisfy speculative greed. The philosophy of escape from the city is a retreat from reality; within this philosophy are the seeds of our own destruction. To deny the place of the city in our industrial age is to invite economic slavery and social suicide. Our proper course is not the destruction of urban life; it is to build a better one, and it is time that the people exercise their democratic powers to correct the evils of urban disintegration. The survival of our democratic processes depends upon the bold and intelligent use of the power it vests in the people themselves.

Land Costs Too Much. The central problem of urban rebuilding will be the cost of land. Measured by any standard of appropriate land use the land will cost too much; it will be out of all proportion to the economic value for redevelopment on acceptable terms, and any other terms will make the venture worthless.

The cost of land in a slum area in Cincinnati was approximately $2.00 per square foot, and the estimated cost of buildings demolished was about $400.00 per room, this cost of existing improvements being a total financial loss.[2] The Detroit City Planning Commission made a comprehensive study of a blighted area in Detroit, an area of approximately 78 acres. The study indicated that the average cost of the land was 91 cents per square foot including existing structures. A plan was prepared for the redevelopment of the area. It provided a density of 13 dwellings per acre, a room rental of $14.50 per month, a tax rate of 3.3%, mortgage interest at 3.5%, and amortization at 1.5%. A dividend rate of 6% on the invested capital of a prospective building company, and vacancy at 10%, resulted in a financial set-up which could support a land cost of not more than 10 cents per square foot.[3]

If we are to restore decency to the urban scene, the excess cost of land must be liquidated—written off the books as a loss. No magic will make it vanish. There are but two sources—private philanthropy and public aid—and it is hardly feasible to predicate the rebuilding of our cities upon the magnanimity of private philanthropy.

Some suggest we wait until cities become so sick land prices will fall to a reasonable level—"let them stew in their own juice." It is the policy which has prevailed thus far, and we find the real victims of such a course are the multitude who are forced to tolerate blight, decay, and hazard of the present urban existence because they can afford no better; it is the multitude whose roots are in the city, its life, and its economy.

It was Thomas Jefferson who said that that government is best which governs least. Our traditions, our political form of democracy, and our economic form of capitalism are woven about this principle. It follows that voluntary action by owners of urban property would be the course most acceptable to the American people. Co-operation among owners in blighted areas has been frequently suggested and could become an effective instrument. Mr. Arthur Holden and others have proposed the pooling of equities in property as one method, but positive results from such programs are wanting.[4] The problem of land values consistent with appropriate standards of development persistently raises its ugly head. Owners are reluctant to "write-down" the valuation of their property, and voluntary liquidation of excess value is essential. When these circumstances can be combined into effective action, every encouragement should be afforded by way of legislation and administrative policy. Voluntary action by individuals and co-operative action between them constitute a "right" to be jealously guarded; there are forever trespassers whose lust for power and appetite for profit would swallow individual freedom.

Lacking concerted willingness or ability on the part of those who own urban property to check the disintegration of cities, it falls to the lot of the public through the instrument of government. "The legitimate object of government," said Abraham

[2] Conference on Planning Problems, Ladislas Segoe, American Society of Planning Officials, Chicago, February 13–14, 1941.

[3] Report by Mr. Emery, Conference on Planning Problems, American Society of Planning Officials, Chicago, February 13–14, 1941.

[4] Gabriel Over Block 326–A, Arthur Holden, *Architectural Forum*, January, 1935; A Basis for Procedure in Slum Clearance, *Architectural Record*, March 1933. Also refer to the suggestion for land "revaluation" in *The City* by Eliel Saarinen, Reinhold Publishing Co., N. Y., 1943.

Lincoln, "is to do for a community of people whatever they need to have done but cannot do at all or cannot do so well for themselves in their separate and individual capacities."

Redevelopment on the Horizon. Concern over the degeneration of cities was confined, for a time, to social reformers in the field of housing and a few Utopians who envisioned the potential capacity of our age to produce a totally new environment. Interest expanded, however, to include business, financial, and industrial enterprise as the dangers to our people and their institutions have become more apparent. Interest on the part of some has been stimulated by an aversion to the sole participation of public housing as an instrument for rebuilding, some by their outright opposition to public housing in any form, and others who are genuinely disturbed by the downward trend in the physical environment and convinced that broad steps must be taken to stem the tide. As these various forces move into the center the issues are gradually coming into clearer focus and positive action has begun. The extent of this action is described in the following report prepared in 1946 by Mr. Hugh Pomeroy, then Executive Director of the National Association of Housing Officials:[5]

Within the past five years, 20 states have adopted urban redevelopment laws for the purpose of facilitating the clearance and rehabilitation of slum and blighted areas in their cities. The statutes thus far enacted are of two types: private corporation and public agency (five states have adopted legislation of both types). The earlier laws were designed to encourage private enterprise, through the operations of private urban redevelopment corporations, to accomplish the two basic phases of urban redevelopment: (1) land assembly and clearance, and (2) construction of housing and appurtenant community facilities. The newer laws, all of them enacted during 1945, place the responsibility for land assembly and clearance upon local public bodies, leaving the actual redevelopment of the area to private enterprise.

Exercise of the power of eminent domain in site assembly is a basic feature in all urban redevelopment legislation. In about half of the earlier corporation laws this power is delegated under certain conditions to the private redevelopment corporations; in the others, the city retains the power for use at the request of the corporations. All of the newer laws retain this power in the municipality, authorizing its use by the public redevelopment agency.

Urban redevelopment legislation is distinct from and supplementary to local housing authority enabling legislation, now in effect in 40 states, whereby cities are authorized to create local housing authorities and invest them with the power of eminent domain for use in clearing slums and constructing low-rent public housing. Such local authorities may accept federal or state aid for these purposes. However, under three of the 1945 urban redevelopment laws, local housing authorities are also the redevelopment agencies; under two more 1945 urban redevelopment laws, local authorities may be so designated. In only one state—Alabama—is the redevelopment law intended as a substitute for the low-rent housing law, construction of additional public housing by the local authority being expressly prohibited.

One immediate advantage in the 1945 public agency type legislation is that it enables the community through a public agency to replan redevelopment areas on a broad scale, parceling out particular sections to private operators for redevelopment and retaining other sections for public use. Under the private corporation approach there is no reference to a redevelopment plan, but only to the plan of the project of the individual corporation. Piecemeal redevelopment through such a method could very well stifle further redevelopment once the most economically favorable sites had been rebuilt.

[5] Analysis of Urban Redevelopment Laws, Summary of the 1945 Housing Year, *Bibliography of 1945 Housing Literature*, National Association of Housing Officials, Chicago, May 1946.

Private Urban Redevelopment Corporation Laws. Eleven states have adopted urban redevelopment corporation laws, authorizing the creation of private corporations with the power to accomplish the entire job of land assembly and redevelopment. Such corporations are given all necessary general corporate powers, including the power to borrow money and issue bonds. In addition, they are given the assistance of certain public powers, privileges, and exemptions in the use of which, however, it is required that detailed plans for the location, construction, financing, and operation of redevelopment projects must be approved by one or more designated agencies of the municipality and, in some cases, the state. The detailed plans of the project must usually include a description of the land and buildings to be acquired; the dwelling, recreational, and other structures and open spaces to be provided; anticipated costs and method of financing; a statement of the approximate rentals to be charged; and data to show that the project will not cause undue hardship to families then living on the site. Additional public controls are provided by all the laws, including usually a limitation on the amount of dividends a redevelopment corporation may pay each year and restrictions designed to prevent the transfer of the project for a use not intended by law. Financial aid by the locality is not uniformly provided for in the laws; the principal aids provided are tax concessions and the furnishing of streets, parks, and other public works.

Public Agency Urban Redevelopment Laws. Fourteen states have enacted urban redevelopment agency laws authorizing local public bodies to act as redevelopment agencies in accomplishing the initial phase of urban redevelopment—land assembly and clearance. In some cases, existing public bodies, such as the municipal corporation itself or the local housing authority, are designated for this purpose; in others, new redevelopment agencies are created. Actual redevelopment of the cleared areas is left either to private enterprise, with private firms or individuals purchasing or leasing the land from the redevelopment agency, or to public agencies for public use.

A basic factor in these laws is the authority granted to the redevelopment agency to acquire property in the redevelopment area at its present value and to make the land available for redevelopment at its use value, the loss to be absorbed in most cases by a combined federal-local subsidy. Another basic feature is that no tax concessions are granted to private purchasers or lessees of the property.

All of these laws authorize the redevelopment agencies to exercise the power of eminent domain in the acquisition of redevelopment areas. Most of them expressly grant power to the redevelopment agency to exercise continuing controls over the property after it is sold or leased to private redevelopers, in order to assure compliance with the provisions of the law and the redevelopment plan as to future uses of the property. However, because the essentially public powers involved in urban redevelopment are retained in public hands, these laws do not provide for detailed supervision, particularly over the finances, of private redevelopers.

On the national level, the Wagner-Ellender-Taft Bill (S. 1592) was introduced to the Congress in 1946. Known as the General Housing Bill, it was not acted upon by the 79th Congress. A similar bill, identified as the Taft-Ellender-Wagner Bill (S. 866), was introduced in the 80th session of the Congress. This bill provided a broad legislative base for a national housing and urban redevelopment program, extended and broadened the private housing program of the Federal Housing Administration, provided for continuation of the public housing program, and implemented urban redevelopment through loans to local agencies for land acquisition and subsidies to assist in writing off the excess land cost. The bill provided the basis for a national housing policy, but it did not receive action by the 80th Congress. This inaction was reversed by the 81st Congress when in the spring of 1949 housing legislation was enacted. It contained the principal features of previously considered bills with particular reference to appropriations for loans by the Federal Government to local redevelopment agencies for acquisition of land in blighted areas for its subsequent sale or lease for redevelopment by public or private enterprise, loans by the Federal Government to local housing authorities for the construction of low rent housing developments and improvement of farm housing conditions.

Liquidating the Excess Cost. Searching for ways and means to revive cities without recourse to subsidy, Mr. Alfred Reinstein of New York City proposed a plan for the city to acquire land for redevelopment and sell it at auction. Assuming that the bid prices would represent the increased value of improved community planning whereas the cost of acquisition would reflect the depressed values of a deteriorated neighborhood, it is expected that such a procedure would provide a "new way for private enterprise profitably to develop deteriorated areas in urban communities without government subsidies and with full taxes paid to the city."[6]

It is generally agreed that the elimination of subsidy is a desirable objective. Such a purpose, however, forces a choice between continuation of the congestion of high population density with which we are now familiar and the cost, by way of subsidy, to reduce the density and restore more ample open space within cities. Without subsidies to liquidate high land costs it is difficult to imagine the form that projects might assume. Even such projects as Knickerbocker Village and Stuyvesant Town in New York City are the beneficiaries of subsidy—tax exemption and a cheap price for vacated streets. The former development replaced a slum of 5 acres on the lower East Side of New York City with a population of 1,085 families; it was then known as the lung block. The reported cost of land was $14.06 per square foot so the new project crowded 1,593 families on the same site.[7] Plans for Stuyvesant Town by the Metropolitan Life Insurance Company creates a "town" of 8,800 families on eighteen city blocks with a density of 445 persons (about 160 families) per acre. The buildings will be thirteen stories high and cover 28 per cent of the land. No schools are contemplated in this "town" of 24,000 with an estimated number of 6,600 children.

Acknowledgment of the disparity between the cost of land, inflated by congestion and speculation, and the economic value for redevelopment, has dispelled much of the controversy about the necessity for subsidy to liquidate the excess cost.

In 1939, Mr. Arthur Binns, a prominent realtor in Philadelphia, insisted before the National Association of Real Estate Boards that "private capital and private enterprise may yet cause the occasion for government subsidy to disappear." In 1943, however, Mr. Binns told the Denver Real Estate Exchange that "for good or evil, the time has passed when unassisted private enterprise can possibly rebuild the old cities of the country."[8]

Mr. Thomas Holden gave expression to the issue of subsidy when he asked: "Why should we bail out insolvent real estate with government money, any more than we bail out insolvent shoeshine parlors, grocery stores, manufacturing enterprises, or railroads?" He further adds that "the city is one of the principal creditors of the insolvent

[6] *Architectural Record*, June 1944.
[7] Report of State Board of Housing, State of New York, 1935.
[8] *NAHO News*, National Association of Housing Officials, February 12, 1944.

property" and "can afford to make concessions in order to help the enterprise get back in the black."[9]

The apparent contradictions reflected in these statements give the reason why government is concerned with urban redevelopment. It may be recalled that railroads have been the beneficiary of government subsidy, that pure food laws and regulations of corporations protect the people from abuses by a wide variety of enterprises, and that the "city" itself is "government." It is hardly probable that government money would be needed to bail out insolvent real estate if the laws had established adequate standards for the maintenance of a decent environment, and if government itself had not "contributed to the insolvency."

There has emerged an assortment of propositions intended to avoid the direct implication of subsidy. They have taken the forms of low-interest credit from the government, tax-exemption, rent certificates, and tax "incentive." Mr. Herbert U. Nelson of the National Association of Real Estate Boards has proposed exemptions in calculating income taxes as a stimulus for production, and it has been argued that such devices are not subsidies.

Subsidies have been frequently debated in the annals of our economic history. They have been supported and attacked with equal vehemence in the halls of representative government. It has been alleged that undue advantage is accorded privileged groups or the dispensation of public funds is extravagance. Paradoxically, however, subsidy has become an accepted instrument with which wrinkles in our economic fabric have been traditionally ironed out. There are no mathematical gymnastics which can repair the broken financial machinery of the urban structure and absorb the excessive cost without cost to the taxpayer. Taxes in such amounts and for such purposes as may be determined through the processes of representative government become an obligation upon the people. Any exemption from this obligation, in whatever amount and for whatever purpose it may be accorded, is a form of subsidy. If incentives are necessary to improve the urban environment and the incentives are offered by granting exemption from taxes in any form, the extent of such tax exemption is a subsidy, and the issue of subsidy can be resolved only by an appraisal of the most equitable distribution of the cost it entails.

The Penalty for Neglect. The cost of rebuilding our cities is the price that must be paid to restore a decent standard of city building. It is the price that must be paid to liquidate the error of permitting such congestion that rebuilding is not otherwise an economic possibility. Responsibility for this mistake rests with every community in which it has been permitted. While much lip-service is given to local responsibility, it has been customary for city and state governments to side-step the issue of subsidies by transferring that responsibility to the Federal government.

The reason for this is fairly clear. The cost of maintaining obsolete cities has already exacted heavy demands upon the taxpayer. To meet these demands high land values have been promoted as a foundation for high tax revenue and extended bond issues. If

[9] Practical Urban Redevelopment, Thomas S. Holden, *Architectural Record*, November 1943.

the city is to assume the responsibility for liquidating the excessive values thus created, the burden will rest upon the local taxpayers; the tax rate will have to be increased to "write off" the excess value that has accumulated—a contradiction that is difficult for the electorate to comprehend.

The taxpayer has a financial stake in the physical plant of the city which he cannot lightly wave aside. This is illustrated in a study by Alex L. Trout, "Desert in a Housing Swamp."[10] It was estimated that the taxpayers of Detroit had accumulated a capital investment of $1,534 per dwelling in the municipal plant, these assets being allocated as follows:

Water supply and distribution	$ 287
Sewers	267
Pavements, streets, exclusive of land value	235
Schools, libraries, and museums	235
Parks, boulevards, recreation, zoo	173
Street railways	144
Lighting	87
Fire, police, health	75
Miscellaneous	31
	$1,534

For every family living in the city there was invested in these facilities an amount equal to or greater than the assessed value per dwelling in the blighted areas. As much as four-fifths of this investment is wasted every time a family moves to the suburbs and additional facilities must be duplicated there.

This presents a double-barreled dilemma. The people have substantially made urban disintegration a legitimate enterprise; meanwhile they have contracted a huge investment in the city. Now they are obliged to pay the price to recover a decent urban environment.

The Indianapolis Plan. An enlightening, though rare, demonstration of positive local initiative is the action taken in Indianapolis. A singular feature of the Redevelopment Act of 1945 in the State of Indiana is the power it grants to levy local taxes for urban redevelopment purposes. This is the key to the assumption of genuine local responsibility; it is the instrument with which a community assumes the obligation to foot a bill it itself has contracted.

The Indianapolis Redevelopment Commission was empowered to levy and collect a tax within the corporate limits of the city for the purpose of executing a redevelopment program. Its powers and duties are otherwise similar to those prescribed in redevelopment legislation in a number of other states; they investigate the problem of blighted areas in their city and may acquire by purchase, gift, grant, condemnation, or lease, real estate or personal property necessary to their purpose, and they may sell or lease property they so acquire for such purpose. The Redevelopment Commission is an agency for the assembly of land required for redevelopment; it is not an agency which under-

[10] *Real Estate and Building*, September 1939.

STUYVESANT TOWN, New York City

Thomas Airviews

This project, undertaken by the Metropolitan Life Insurance Company as an investment, is a slum clearance development for which the power of eminent domain was exercised by the city to assemble the 18-block site. The New York State law grants tax exemption as a subsidy to reduce the rents. There are 8,800 apartments in 13-story buildings covering about 28% of the land. It is estimated that 24,000 people will be accommodated in the project, the size of a small city. The project is designed for an average family size of only 2.75 persons and represents about 6,000 children. The investment company could not afford to provide space for schools or other community facilities such as libraries and churches, and less than one-third acre per 1,000 persons is planned for recreation. This poses the question of the standards for the redevelopment of urban areas. The value of rebuilding the blighted districts of our cities will be measured by the degree to which a balance between population density and the amenities of urban services and well-planned land use are recaptured. Since the subsidy of tax exemption and vacation of streets is not adequate to provide the necessary community facilities in a project like Stuyvesant Town, the equivalent of further subsidy will be necessary for the city to establish them outside the development.

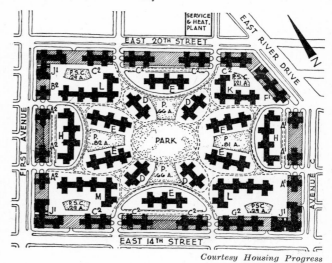

Courtesy Housing Progress

THE INDIANAPOLIS PLAN

Fall Creek, the initial project proposed by the Redevelopment Commission for Indianapolis, is a tract of some 160 acres which became a blighted area with a population of 1,400 persons. The Commission will co-ordinate the work of several public agencies to provide flood control along the creek, the improvement of streets, park spaces, and the enlargement of the school. The land will be sold to private enterprise for improvement of the housing area to conform with standards prescribed by the Redevelopment Commission and the City Planning Commission. The assembly of the site will be financed with funds obtained from a local tax.

MICHAEL REESE HOSPITAL REDEVELOP-
MENT PLAN, Chicago, Illinois

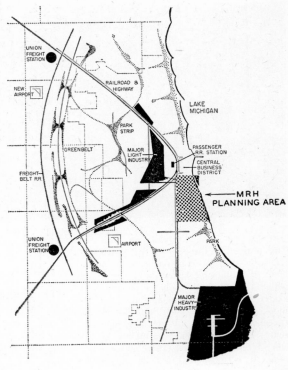

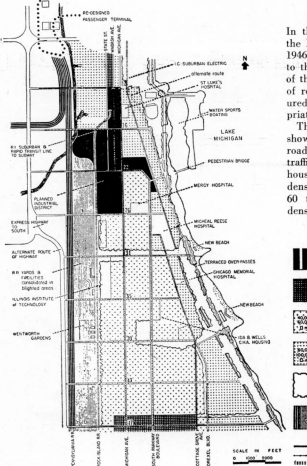

In the plans for redeveloping the area surrounding
the Michael Reese Hospital in Chicago, proposed in
1946 (*left*), attention was directed by the planners
to the possible reorganization of the larger elements
of the city (*above*). With such studies the feasibility
of redevelopment of the central areas may be measured and their replanning integrated with appropriate development of the city.

The plan for redevelopment of the Hospital area
shows the allocation of land for industry and railroads, main shopping center, parks and principal
traffic arteries, and housing. It is proposed that the
housing will be redeveloped in areas of different
densities: one area having a density ranging from
60 to 100 persons per acre, the other having a
density of 100 to 150 persons per acre.

Courtesy The
Architectural Forum

INDUSTRIAL AREA

MAJOR SHOPPING & CULTURE

LOW DENSITY HOUSING

HIGH DENSITY HOUSING

PARKS & RECREATION

RAILROADS & YARDS

————— STREET CAR LINES
- - - - - BUS LINES
∷∷∷∷∷ RAPID TRANSIT LINES

Before
Redevelopment

PALMOLIVE

WATER TOWER

ALLERTON

Courtesy The Architectural Forum

"THE MAGNIFICENT MILE,"
Chicago, Illinois

A proposal for the commercial redevelopment of the north Michigan Avenue district in Chicago stretching between the Chicago River and Lake Shore Drive.

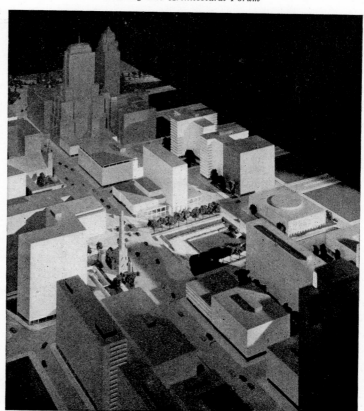

After
Redevelopment
*Holabird and Root
Architects*

Hedrich-Blessing Studio, Chicago

takes the rebuilding program. This latter function is performed by either private enterprise or other appropriate public agency. The Commission has the responsibility, however, for determining the appropriate use of land in co-operation with the City Planning Commission and may require that the land be redeveloped according to an accepted redevelopment plan.

Success of the Indianapolis program hinges upon the Special Tax Levy permitted in the Act. The Commission is empowered to levy a special tax up to 10 cents on each $100 of taxable valuation for the first two periods of taxation, and up to 5 cents on each $100 of taxable valuation for each subsequent taxable period. The first tax levied by the Commission amounted to $550,000, and it launched its program with these funds. The first project by the Commission involves a blighted section of the city, for which it is estimated the cost of acquisition would be $874,515, and it is proposed to sell or lease the site for development by private enterprise in accordance with a redevelopment plan it has prepared.

The Power of Eminent Domain. Cities will have to make plans—great and bold plans—for rebuilding. These plans must chart a dual course. One course will trace the legal standards establishing the volume and space limitations for all building, the other will define public improvement—the streets and traffic arteries, parks, and recreation areas, and public facilities. These plans will entail major operations within the congested core as well as the less densely built sections. These operations will drastically alter the shape of the environment and will require adjustment of present urban conduct, not the least of these adjustments being the crazy-quilt pattern of land subdivision.

Urban property has been divided among a multitude of owners. As transportation arteries, boulevards, and parks are carved out of the present tangled disorder, property lines will be thoroughly chopped to pieces, and consolidation of much of the property will unquestionably be the only manner in which this land can be redeveloped. To implement this consolidation of land parcels and assure the assembly of properties for redevelopment by public agencies or private enterprise, there are few who do not acknowledge the necessity for exercise of the right of eminent domain.

It is therefore vital to the maintenance of democracy that the nature of this power be fully realized. The right of eminent domain—the power of condemnation—is a public power. It is a power vested in the people to be employed when the public interest is served thereby. Exercise of the power of condemnation is necessary today because the people have allowed their cities to degenerate into places of speculation, decay, and hazard. This social and economic mistake of permitting congestion will cost the people a great deal to liquidate the excessive land values it has created. It is the people who must assume responsibility for this state of affairs and it is the power of the people which must be invoked to correct it.

Rebuilding our cities calls for broad and courageous planning; it also demands restraint in the use of public powers to execute these plans. In their urban redevelopment legislation five states have already transferred the public power of eminent domain, in part, to private corporations. We cannot be unmindful that corporate business may be as ready as the corporate state to engulf the individual rights of the people, and immensity of the job of rebuilding our cities cannot become a means to escort big business alone into the field of urban investment. The large-scale formula must be applied to replanning, but it is not the sole panacea for rebuilding. As sweeping moves are made, and they must be made, the wave of excitement to get results must not be allowed to submerge the rights of individuals and small business enterprise.

The Scale of Planning. Large-scale planning and building has struck a popular note as the salvation of our cities. Before we are carried away by this hopeful prospect, it would be advisable to shed some light of reality upon it.

A city is built in a series of individual "projects": some in old sections, some in new, some large, some small. Some projects are no more than single homes, others may be a group of dwellings, a subdivision, a small store, a shopping center, or a huge skyscraper. No city in history was conceived and built in one fell swoop, no matter how powerful a dictator ruled the people. But plans have been laid, and today it is more urgent that they be laid than at any time in history.

There have been days when rulers needed not to plan for the people; their planning was for themselves. The great monumental avenues, plazas, and palaces were memorials to their vanity and glorious power. Then democracy, a government of the people, by the people, and for the people, changed this. Planning was no longer a tool of monarchs; planning in democracy is a program of action for the general welfare. We saw such plans in the democracy of Athens. Such is also the stuff of which the plans for our city of tomorrow must be made.

Our industrial and commercial system of today renders planning an essential process. Organization of the complex facilities in our world *is* planning, and the integrated arrangement of these facilities calls for far more preparation than ever before. Only through the process of preparation—planning—can the aggregate of all the projects that make our cities be undertaken for the mutual benefit of the people who build them and the people who use them.

To this end, large-scale planning is essential. It is essential to the building of a modern community environment. It is essential to assure that communities will be so built. Planning is now an instrument which the people may use in their own interest. The primary unit in the structure of our form of government is the city, and the city becomes the common denominator for organized planning operations. It is city planning that becomes the essence of large-scale planning.

The size of the projects undertaken for civic improvement is incidental to the main premise: planning is an instrument wielded by the people in the public interest. The scale of that planning is relative. A highway may cut across city, regional, and state boundaries, or a single neighborhood may have the characteristics which lend it to treatment as a planning unit. In either case the basic planning decisions stem from considerations of the general welfare of the community and the integration of all parts of the physical framework. These planning operations must then become specific in their decisions and be rendered effective and binding by law.

The Scale of Building. The process of *building* a city is quite another matter. Large-scale building operations have advantages: they may be profitable to those undertaking them, or they may be necessary for the proper rebuilding of certain areas of a city. But to make plans for which large-scale building operations become the only feasible means of development is to bait the trap of "bigness." The implication is clear in a statement by Mr. Thomas Holden:[11] "By common consent, the first necessity for reorganizing insolvent properties in blighted neighborhoods is to consolidate properties under unified ownership and management; in other words, property must be assembled in order to make up units large enough for modern economic development and use."

This illustrates a process of thinking which presumes that "modern economic development and use" must be big to survive, a contradiction of the conception so frequently expressed that free enterprise depends upon the continued vigor and prosperity of "small" business. Nearly one-half of the construction industry is devoted to home-building and most of the houses are produced by small builders. More than two-thirds of all houses produced in 1938 were by builders who built less than thirty homes a year. A Congressional Committee headed by Senator James E. Murray reported that 87 per cent of the 215,000 building organizations in 1939 were doing less than $5,000 business annually. Planning which denies active and prominent participation by small business and industry does not seem consistent with the tenets of freedom of enterprise, which is a basic concept of our democracy.

To Sell or Lease? Negligence and abuse have sapped some of the vitality of our traditional practices. The public power of eminent domain is summoned to force adjustment, and public funds will undoubtedly be drawn upon to aid in purging the economic congestion. The power of condemnation and public credit now receive general acceptance as necessary instruments for urban rebuilding. These are not measures to be taken as temporary sedatives. The high cost should produce a cure; it is reasonable to expect them to prevent a recurrence of the same ills. Is that goal prescribed in recent legislation?

Every state law for urban redevelopment enacted to date provides that land acquired by condemnation may be resold. It is generally provided that the new use to which the land is put shall conform to standards of use which conform to a Master Plan for redevelopment.

Public financial assistance for urban rehabilitation serves a dual purpose. It implements rebuilding at standards of land use that will restore a decent environment, and it provides unlimited opportunities for sound and profitable investment by private enterprise. The investment of public funds, as subsidies, is warranted on the condition that the resulting improvement is permanent, and there must be assurance that the same investment to cure the same ills will not be repeated every generation. It is of

[11] Practical Urban Redevelopment, Thomas S. Holden, *Architectural Record*, November 1943.

vital importance therefore to ascertain that the new standards of land use are of a permanent nature.

To determine this it is necessary to refer to the laws that apply to urban building. A Master Plan is not a permanent document, nor are the "administrative decisions" which emanate from a planning agency preparing that document. A Master Plan is only part of a series of legislative acts controlling the development of cities. An immediate improvement may conform to the new standards administratively determined within the scope of a Master Plan, but subsequent use of land will depend entirely upon later revisions and modifications which may emerge. Reliance upon administrative policy, no matter how inspired, is to invite inevitable chaos and abuse.

Adequate protection is afforded only by the laws that set the standards, and there is little evidence that reasonable legal standards are yet remotely intended. Referring to the proposed zoning revisions in New York City, Henry Churchill, in *The City Is the People,* remarks that the revision would reduce the possible population from 77,000,000 to a "mere" 60,000,000, and "this drastic blow to real estate is being viewed with much alarm." Some cities, where traffic is paralyzed, are considering only one-quarter the needed amount of parking space. In reality no solutions to the standards of urban development are being considered, and until the time arrives that solutions are written into law there is no assurance of permanence.

This raises a decided question as to the advisability of delivering land, acquired by the public power of condemnation, back to the same abuses that have made it necessary to exercise that power. The question may be elaborated by inquiring if justice is served by taking land from some private owners and selling it to other private interests at a reduced price. The use of public funds is for the purpose of bringing land costs down to an economic value for redevelopment at standards of decent land use. To that extent the public interest is served and to that extent it must be protected. To sell land at a subsidized price is to make a gift of public funds as an inducement to engage in urban rebuilding for a profit. Such a policy is somewhat a distortion of the high purpose for which it is designed.

In 1942 a Royal Commission reported its recommendations for a reconstruction program in England.[12] The chairman was the Honorable Augustus Andrewe Uthwatt, a member of the House of Lords. That report said in part:

We recommend, therefore, that once any interest in land has passed into public ownership it should be disposed of by way of lease only and not by way of sale, and that the authority should have the power to impose such covenants in the lease as planning requirements make desirable, breach of such covenants to be enforceable by re-entry.

Building on leased land is by no means novel. It is common practice in commercial enterprise and offers no deterrent to sound investment. It need offer no obstruction to the sale of improvements on the land. Nor would tax revenue be affected since a lease value would return revenue to the city and the usual taxes could be assessed

---

[12] Report of the Expert Committee on Compensation and Betterment presented to Parliament by Minister of Works and Planning, September 1942.

against the improvement. Objection to local bureaucracy could be avoided by obtaining the services of competent and established firms in property management.

We are confronted with a situation in which public powers must be called into action to restore the productive enterprise of our cities and the initiative of private enterprise in our urban economy, and, in so doing, create an urban environment consistent with our contemporary capacities and skills. The fact that land values obstruct the path to this goal becomes a matter of concern to the people—a public responsibility—and the gains made at the expense of the people must be retained by them.

As the prospects for orderly rebuilding of our cities loom brighter on the horizon of the future we cannot be unmindful of its underlying purpose: re-creation of an urban environment in which the functions of the contemporary city can be performed with order. Other advantages will accrue, but we may be guided by the definition by Aristotle: "A city should be built to give its inhabitants security and happiness."

Urban rebuilding is not for the purpose of restoring stability to real estate values, although this will result. It is not for the purpose of bailing out the bad investments of landed gentry, since much of the decaying city still pays dividends to its absentee owners. It is not intended to recover speculative losses, since the curse of blight has fallen upon the property of those who cannot afford to join the flight to better places. It is not for the purpose of reinforcing government bureaucracy, although the public which these bureaus represent has a heavy stake in the problem. It is not for the purpose of providing ripe opportunities for investment and profit, although it will open this fertile field. It is not for the purpose of providing employment, although it will create unlimited opportunities for labor in field and factory. Urban rebuilding is for none of these things specifically, but each is a part serving the main objective: building a decent city for the people.

The "New Towns" in England. England suffered heavy casualties to its cities during World War II. One-third of its 13,000,000 dwellings were damaged by bombs, and there was practically no new building. With devastation all about them, the necessity for rebuilding caused the people to consider plans for recovery when the holocaust was over. The 1944 Town and Country Planning Act extended government financial aid to local authorities for the purchase of land when rebuilding was possible. The destruction of large urban areas, however, impressed many thoughtful people with the possibility of recapturing some open space within their congested urban centers.

While agriculture in England can support only about half of the population, and a large proportion of the people live in urban communities, there are only seven major industrial cities. Congestion in these cities is acute, but it is still the British habit to live in "cottages." At any rate, such is their desire. A density of twelve families per acre has become almost a British ideal. It was the density suggested by Ebenezer Howard, it became the density for the Garden Cities, and Sir Raymond Unwin dwelt at length upon it as a desirable standard. It remains today the standard toward which enlightened planners strive. Nevertheless, the population density in large cities is high, and the necessity for large-scale postwar rebuilding was considered a propitious time to begin a program for the decongestion of the cities.

In preparation for this a number of commissions were appointed by the Churchill government to investigate the various problems and recommend basic national policies. Among these was the Royal Commission under the chairmanship of the Honorable Augustus Andrewe Uthwatt of the House of Lords. The Uthwatt report, completed in 1942, was a penetrating examination of the problem of land tenure and its effect upon urban development.[13] It provided a foundation for subsequent national policies pertaining to city building.

Out of the welter of their history, the British have cultivated a remarkable ability for political common sense. With this political astuteness they somehow realize their aims and ambitions. Anticipating the huge rebuilding of devastated areas, it is not surprising to find the British embracing a new concept of the urban structure. It may hardly be accurate to call the postwar program new since it is novel only in certain devices they employ.

The elements of the Garden City hold a strong appeal to the average citizen; the characteristics of the village, in contrast to the metropolis, attract them. Proximity to the beautiful countryside is a natural desire. They look upon the bicycle with more favor than the subway. They enjoy walking, probably more than motoring. The two successful Garden Cities, Letchworth and Welwyn, are before them for comparison with the huge and congested cities. The English people have seen the advantages of the smaller community as a better way of life. They have always been justly proud of their delightful rural country, and preservation of the countryside has occupied the aggressive attention of the most influential peers of England.

The New Towns Act of 1946 is therefore less novel than might be supposed. It is rather an instrument with which the people intend to achieve the better way of living for which they yearn.

The rebuilding plan of 1944 for Greater London and the London County Council Plan, both of which were prepared by Professor Patrick Ambercrombie and F. J. Forshaw, were based upon a dual objective: decongestion of the metropolis and preservation of green areas about the periphery. While some authorities desired a standard of population density near the twelve-family-per-acre ideal even in the city center, it was considered necessary to compromise with this standard in the congested areas.

The County of London has an area of 117 square miles with a population of about 4,000,000, and it contains the city of London, one mile square, which has a population of 10,000 people. The density preferred by the planners in areas reserved for residential use in the County was 100 persons per acre. Because the existing density was very great, an average density of 136 persons per acre was selected and this requires a 39 per cent reduction in the present population, the removal of about 618,000

13 *Ibid.*

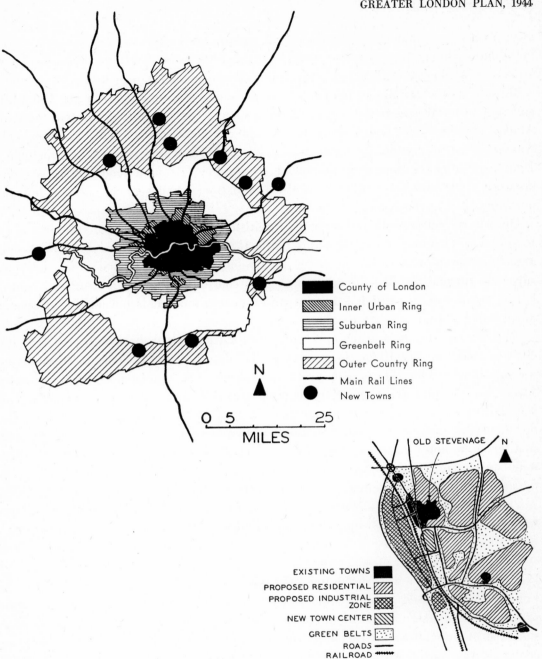

Preparing for decentralization the 2,600 square mile area of Greater London has been planned in four rings surrounding the County of London. The density of population within the County will be reduced to a maximum of 136 persons per acre; the density within the Inner Ring to between 75 and 100. These areas comprise the present heavily urbanized parts of London. This reduction will decrease the present population by 1,033,000 people who will be dispersed within the Suburban Ring at a maximum density of 50 persons per acre and the Outer Country Ring at a maximum density of 20 persons per acre. The Greenbelt Ring will be held as open space primarily for recreation, only the existing towns being permitted to increase their population on present unimproved platted lots.

The New Towns located generally within the Outer Country Ring will aid in the decentralization of industry as well as the population. Stevenage is the first of these proposed new towns and is planned upon theories similar to the Garden City: largely a self-contained city with reservation of ample open spaces to serve as greenbelts within the town and to separate the industrial zone from the residential development.

people. Greater London comprises 700 square miles and has a total population of 8,000,000. The area outside the County is planned for a density of 75 persons per acre in some parts and 100 persons in others; the effect is a reduction of 415,000 persons in addition to the reduction in the County, a total reduction in population of 1,033,000 persons to be decentralized. The replanning will permit redevelopment of the County area with 60 per cent single-family houses and 40 per cent apartments. Retention of the "greenbelt" surrounding the urban area is an integral part of the plans, so it is necessary to provide for the excess population elsewhere. The New Towns Act of August, 1946, was the result.

Under this Act it is proposed to build about twenty new towns ranging in size from 30,000 to 60,000 population. Although the sites thus far selected are within some 50 miles of London, the towns are not to be designed as satellite communities; they will be independent, self-contained cities. A government corporation will purchase the sites and develop the basic town facilities—streets and utilities. This corporation will retain ownership of all land in the town and lease to private enterprise for development of industry, commerce, and dwellings.

The local government will be the governing authority, and, when the community is well established, it will operate as any other town. The only distinction will be the ownership of the land, but this will not alter the normal development of private enterprise. The prospect of success with the new towns did not rest with the experience at the Garden Cities; there was considerable interest on the part of industry. By 1946, 1,500 industrial firms had expressed interest in moving to new sites within the Greater London area, and 200 of these desired sites in the proposed new towns located within a radius of 20–50 miles from London.

The total cost of an average new town, with a population of about 50,000, is estimated to be about $15,000,000 per year for a ten-year period. About half of this cost will be borne by the government, the balance through development by private enterprise. The first approved town is Stevenage, in Hertfordshire, intended for a population of 60,000 on a 6,000-acre site.

The size of the towns reflects the desires of the British people. They prefer to be near enough to their work so they may walk from and to their homes. Two or three miles was the maximum desirable diameter and would place all families within reach of the permanent green space about the town and remove the complicated problems of mass transportation. Railroads will carry them to the larger cities when and if they wish.

British Land Policy. The low ebb of the British economy following the war caused the enactment of the Town and Country Planning Act of 1947 in which a policy of planned use for all land, rural and urban, was adopted. Each local authority is required to prepare a comprehensive land-use plan which shall establish appropriate locations for industries, urban and agricultural development, and permanent open space. The policy stems from recommendations of the Uthwatt report of 1942, predicated upon the principle that the value of land is primarily created by the community and increase in value belongs and shall accrue to the community.

The Act continues the powers of the government to acquire land and sell or lease for development by private enterprise, but it is necessary for enterprise to conform to the new land-use plan. This plan will entail some considerable modification in land use; some areas will necessarily be reduced in value by the change from industrial to residential use or from residential use to open space, while other areas may increase in value.

Recognizing that a market value for land has already been established for the use permitted prior to adoption of the new plan, the government determined to compensate owners for the loss they might thus suffer. The compensation is to be measured by the difference between the current market value and the value represented by the new land use. It was estimated that the aggregate reduction in value for all land affected in the country was 300,000,000 pounds, or approximately $1,200,000,000, and this sum was appropriated.

A property owner who receives payment for this depreciated value is then able to sell his land for the new use, stipulated in the plan, at a lesser price appropriate to that use. In so doing he does not incur a loss to himself nor does he inflict upon the purchaser the penalty of a price in excess of the value commensurate with the new land use. The change in use permitted by the plan for some land will increase its value, and it is provided for the government to recover the increment of this increased value. An enterprise desiring to improve land according to its new use is required to obtain a permit from the government authority. At that time the original market value and the increase in value are determined; the improvement company then purchases the land from the owner at the previous market price and deposits with the government the amount of the determined increase in value.

This procedure has been called the reservation of "development rights." The government compensates the owners who suffer loss in land values because of the new land-use plan, but it retains the benefits of increased increments created by the plan by charging the developer with the amount of the increase. There is no financial loss to landowners or to the developers: landowners are compensated for any decreases in the value of their land imposed by the plan and developers pay the price consistent with the new use. The policy introduces no change in the normal effect upon business enterprise; the new features of the program are: (1) Land is improved in accordance with a comprehensive plan for land use, and (2) the speculative value which may be anticipated in some uncertain amount at some indefinite future is removed. It is a program which culminates after many years of serious attention to the problems of land and its use in England.

CHAPTER 25

POPULATION DENSITY

The Deficiency of Zoning. City building is in very large measure guided by the laws that define the rules of conduct in our organized society. It is a typical process in democracy that the people enjoy freedom to act within limits established by the laws enacted through representative government. Independent accomplishments by enlightened individuals are indispensable; they serve as healthy examples of good citizenship. But the collective behavior which produces the city is necessarily conditioned by what the "law will allow."

We have observed the effect of the principal type of legislative framework—zoning —upon our cities. This review demonstrated a basic deficiency: the excessive volume of building which can be placed upon the available space in our cities. The zoning laws that set the standards of urban development permit a crowding of people and buildings that is strangling cities to death. In order for a modern metropolis to live it must have the space for the manifold facilities within it.

The congestion of people, buildings, and the services of transportation and utilities within the city is convincing evidence that the minimum standards of zoning are quite inadequate. Zoning, as practiced, is deficient in two respects: (1) the inadequacy of minimum standards, and (2) the varying application of these standards. It is essential that these two deficiencies be corrected in the interest of establishing some stability in land values and municipal budgets and of restoring to the city a semblance of workability it now lacks.

The balance between freedom and order is the delicate thread upon which democracy hangs. It is needed in city building as completely as it is needed in every other phase of our social and economic existence. An appraisal of urban development shows this balance has not been attained. But it gives us some direction toward a formula which would produce a measure of equilibrium.

We are impressed by the overcrowding and congestion in some parts of the city and the underdevelopment in others. This has given rise to the idea, for example, that an apartment is an undesirable neighbor for a single-family dwelling. Such a notion is entirely justified when we observe the difference in the standards of density between these two types of dwellings. There is little reason for a requirement of 5,000 square feet of land per dwelling unit in some residential zones when other zones in the same city permit as low a standard as 250 square feet per dwelling unit in an apartment building.

The Unit of Measurement. The genuine unit of measurement in society is the individual human being, and it is the unit by which we are obliged to calculate the requirements of our cities. It is frequently assumed that the needs of individuals vary. Such is the case, to be sure, but this fact does not preclude the definition of certain requirements common to all, that is, minimum space standards. This is recognized in current laws: building ordinances prescribe minimum areas for rooms in dwellings, minimum ceiling heights, minimum space about buildings—side yards, rear yards, and front yards—and maximum building heights. Those who want and can afford standards in excess of these are free to have them, but current regulations accept the theory of common standards.

There are almost violent inconsistencies in the variations of standards of space for uses which are presumably identical. The small area of land required for an apartment in one zone compared with a larger area of land per apartment in another zone bears no apparent reference to differences in the sizes of dwellings or the families that might occupy them. A dwelling large enough to accommodate a family with several children may be located in a zone requiring no more than 500 square feet of land per dwelling, while small dwelling units may be located in a zone requiring 5,000 square feet of land. These are poor excuses for standards, but their acceptance is acknowledgment of certain requirements common to all people, even though the variable application contradicts their value as standards.

The fact that many people have little space on the earth while others enjoy an abundance does not support a claim that basic human needs greatly vary. Family composition and characteristics vary, and so do personal desires, but the variations should be measured in terms of individuals. Children need ample space for active recreation and education not required by adults; families need space in proportion to the number of children they comprise, but the nature of relaxation desired by elderly people and the sports engaged in by adults demand large spaces per person, and it can hardly be accurately assumed that the area for adult passive recreation suggests much less space *per person* than that for children. If all the plus and minus factors in measuring the relative need for space were added up, it is doubtful that the net difference would amount to more than 10 per cent of the total urban land area. This variation is more than absorbed by the range of individual choice exercised by people and the "psychological elbow room" people need and now find lacking in their urban environment.

Allowing for freedom of choice among individuals we are justified in the conclusion that the essential need for space in our cities is substantially similar for all people. While our zoning laws place the concentration of population near the business and industrial centers, we find a large proportion of the people who work in these areas have families who need the advantages of low density. By the same token, many single and elderly people who can adapt themselves to concentration have the least necessity for proximity to the central areas where concentration exists.

The concentric rings of receding concentration in our cities constitute a paradox. Zoning adopts this pattern and perpetuates the paradox by legalizing it. It is commonly accepted because of a fallacious basic assumption that high population density and its component—the tall building—are economical. Current zoning practice bears no relation to a balance between concentration and dispersion of people, their homes, or their workshops. Zoning is the direct outcome of the price of land and the improvements thereon; these factors, and not human values, are the accepted units of measurement in determining the zoning plans of our cities.

A Single Standard. If the basic needs of people were translated into a common standard of population density, the apartment dwelling and the single house, the tall building and the low building, would approach equal acceptability. They would become equally desirable as neighbors, as standards of habitation, and places in which to work. A variety of dwelling types is necessary to the satisfaction of the wide range of desires and family needs in a city. But they all serve the same essential function— habitations for people. As human shelter they would be expected to share common minimum standards of living amenity. Space on the earth is one of these amenities, and the facilities of the city can be calculated only by reference to the common unit, the human being.

We seek a formula for urban development which recognizes this common denominator. That formula will establish a volume envelope for buildings derived from a single standard of population density acceptable to a community. It would provide a single standard for each type of land use rather than the double, triple, and sometimes quadruple standard that has become the habit of current zoning regulations. Such a formula would be translated into a constant relation between the amount of floor space and the ground area it occupies.

The formula we desire is one in which buildings may be high or low, broad or slender, while the floor space they contain remains substantially the same; a formula which rejects the proposition that more people may be added in less space by the simple device of piling floor upon floor. The higher a building may be built, according to the formula we seek, the more would be the open space surrounding it.

We are searching for a formula in which investors in urban property may determine for themselves the form of the improvements they believe best serves the market for their capital; a freedom of choice which can be made within a standard that assures no injury to one's neighbors or the investments they may have. We wish to find a formula in which the variety of development in our cities would be limited only by the ingenuity of the planner working within an envelope of adequate space; working with standards which may become the maximum or the minimum without freezing the urban environment into a rigid and inflexible mold.

A Formula. We are accustomed to the appearance of an unlimited concentration of people permitted in apartment districts of some of our larger cities and, as a result, it has almost become a habit to associate congestion of population with normal city development. While this impression is confirmed by the heavy concentration in relatively small areas of such great cities as New York City, Chicago, or Philadelphia, the average actual density, even in these urban behemoths, does not bear out an assumption that high density either exists or is essential to healthy urban growth and development. The average density in relatively small cities is between twelve and fifteen families per acre (Chapter 11, Part III), including all types of dwellings from single homes to multiple-family buildings. It is a standard of twelve families per acre—forty to forty-five persons—in residential areas which we shall adopt for the purpose of illustrating the formula we seek.

This is a standard which could be uniformly applied to all residential development. It is relatively high for single-family homes, six to seven dwellings per acre being the usual subdivision practice, but it is possible to obtain fair open space if skill is applied to the planning of street circulation and the shape of lots, and we are concerned, at this point, with a minimum permissible density as distinguished from the standards of development which many land developers would desire in the best subdivision practice. By the same token, a density of twelve families per acre seems low for apartment development. It is our premise, however, to avoid a series of variable standards for urban development and seek a relatively uniform single standard of density. Several million people, at a density of forty-five persons per acre, could be served with efficient rapid transit within a radius of 15 miles and a maximum traveling time of one-half hour, and there are few cities of more than one million population. Mr. Bartholomew has suggested that rapid transit could be provided at 20-minute intervals for a density of ten persons or more per acre.

For commercial districts we have assumed a density of 150 persons per acre as a standard of occupancy in business structures, but, since pedestrian traffic is particularly heavy at the ground level in commercial areas, the density is reduced to slightly more than half this number.

In both residential and commercial areas the *Space Control Chart* indicates an ascending curve, a sliding scale, as building height increases. This provides for the additional floor space for horizontal and vertical circulation and service facilities required in high buildings. It also gives some advantages to high buildings in the proportion of permissible floor space to ground area since the effectiveness of open space increases with the height of buildings. The range of increase in permissible floor space is some 10 to 15 per cent between two-story and thirty- or forty-story buildings and this variation is not enough to distort the formula; utilities, community facilities, and transportation would not be materially affected by this degree of difference.

In the application of this formula we need not be concerned with the type or shape of structure an investor may choose to build; the only conditions which would be placed upon the development of property would be the maximum square feet of enclosed floor space permitted on the property, as indicated by the *Chart*, and the setbacks for front, rear, and side yards contained in current ordinances. No other limitations, like building height or profiles, would be imposed; the governing standard for development of the property would be the proportion of total floor area in relation to the total "lot" area upon which a building was to be erected.

Since it is the relation of floor space to permanent open space upon which this formula is based, it is necessary to recognize that the subdivided "lot" is only a portion of the larger area of the city—the streets, parks, and other public spaces which provide permanent open space in a city. It is logical to include these spaces in arriving at the permissible floor space on a "lot" and it is consequently assumed that the area of abutting streets, alleys, parks, and other adjacent public space would be included in calculating the permissible floor area on a property. Thus the "lot area" could be measured to the centerline of abutting streets and other permanent open space; the wider a street or the greater the size of an adjacent park, the greater would be the ratio of permissible building floor space since the standard of population density would remain relatively constant.

It is further proposed that terminal parking facilities shall become an integral requirement in the development of the land. In residential areas the parking space would be equal to one-quarter of the permissible floor space, being the equivalent of about one car space per family; in commercial districts parking space would be equal to the floor area plus twice the ground floor space in the structure. This space could be provided in whatever form the investor might elect, but it would be required within the property lines of the development.

There would no longer be any necessity for height limits in either residential or commercial zones; the choice would remain with those who invest in and build the city. As building height increased, the space about the building would also increase; a constant relation between floor area and ground area would be maintained whether the building were high or low.

By contrast with current legal limits the densities suggested in this formula are low. In evaluating density, however, two facts cannot be overlooked: (1) Because current standards bear no relation to the human scale in urban development, cities are now so congested they no longer function for the people, and (2) the actual population density in residential areas distributed over the average city today does not vary considerably from the standard suggested in this formula.

The formula is at wide variance with the exorbitant densities in congested sections of large cities. It is directed at these outrageous densities. It pleads for a reasonable density of people on the land, whether in their homes or workplaces. It accepts the fact that there must be space for the movement of the people and the facilities that render a city useful and convenient. It rejects the thesis, represented by current practice, that an ever-increasing density of population can be loaded on the land.

The density standards used as illustrations of the formula are based upon present

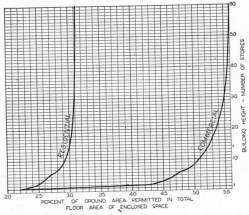

The accompanying graph illustrates a formula for application of a relatively uniform standard of population density for two types of urban development—residential and commercial. It is predicated upon the theme described in the text—that the variable standards employed in current zoning practice are ineffective instruments for orderly urban growth. The existence of variable standards creates constant pressures for the change from a zone of low density to a zone of higher density. The differences in standards of population density or, as interpreted in this formula, the standards of permissible floor space in relation to lot area, create variations in land values which are likewise arbitrary, variations in values resulting from an arbitrary decision that one lot may be used to house a small number of people while a lot of a similar size nearby may be used to house more people.

The formula is also based upon the premise that the standards of population density currently permitted in various zones are excessive, but the standards illustrated in the graph are not proposed as representing the only standards which should apply, although they are not considered unreasonable. It is essential that standards to be adopted in shaping a formula such as this reflect the local characteristics of a community. The issue upon which this suggested formula focuses is the necessity for a constant and reasonable proportion of enclosed building space and the land occupied by this enclosed space.

The calculations for this graph have been based upon a unit of about 200 square feet of enclosed floor area per person, and a population density of some 45 persons per acre, in residential buildings. A density of about 150 persons per acre and an area of about 125 square feet per person of enclosed building space has been used for commercial structures. Because the pedestrian traffic at the ground level is generally far in excess of that at floors above this level, the density in commercial districts has been reduced to less than 100 persons per acre for one-story structures and the ground floor of higher structures. These densities have been translated into a proportion of permissible enclosed floor space to ground space, the formula being expressed in terms of permissible floor space as a percentage of "lot" area. It is further assumed that the "lot" area will extend to the centerline of all permanent open public spaces which may abut the "lot," such as streets, alleys, and parks.

To compensate for the increased floor space required for horizontal and vertical circulation and services as buildings rise into the air, the proportion of floor space to ground area assumes a gradually ascending curve. Such a curve may be adjusted to reflect a nominal advantage in the ratio of floor space to ground area in high buildings. This advantage is reasonable since the effect of free ground space increases with building height and, if the proportion of the increased floor space is maintained within a reasonable range—say 10 to 15 per cent difference between the heights of two stories and thirty or forty stories—the possible increase in population accommodated is not enough to throw the general equation out of balance; the size of utility distribution systems, amount of community facilities and transportation, for example, would not be materially affected by this differential.

In addition to the proportion of floor space to ground area reflected in this chart, space for the terminal storage of vehicles would be required. It is suggested that this parking space in residential development should be one-quarter of the total permissible building floor area with the condition that this space should be provided within the property occupied by the building. In commercial development the suggested parking space provided within the property lines is equal to the total permissible floor area plus twice the ground floor area of the structure to be placed upon the lot.

Application of the formula may be illustrated by the following example:

Assume a residential lot with a street frontage of 100 feet and a depth of 170 feet, facing a street of 60 feet in width. Measuring to the centerline of the street increases the equivalent "lot" area to 20,000 square feet (100 x 200 feet). Referring to the chart, we find that the permissible floor space is 23 per cent of a lot of this size for one-story buildings or 4,600 square floor area. For a two-story building the allowable floor area is 24 per cent of the lot size, or 4,800 square feet. A building three stories high may be 25 per cent of the lot area, or 5,000 square feet, and a four-story building, 26 per cent of the lot area, or 5,200 square feet, etc.

Assuming the building code restricts the setbacks to 30 feet front yard, 20 feet rear yard, and 5 feet side yards—a net area of 10,800 square feet—the building coverage on the balance of the lot is limited only by the above-mentioned floor space for the various heights, with the further condition that parking space must be also provided in an amount of 1,150 square feet for one-story buildings—one-quarter the area of the floor space—1,200 square feet for two stories, 1,250 square feet for three stories, 1,300 square feet for four stories, etc. This parking space may be provided in any form desired—at ground level or in multi-level—but it shall be contained within the area of the property.

As a practical matter a natural height limit will be reached for a building on this lot when the space per floor diminishes to an unworkable area; it is hardly feasible, for instance, to plan a satisfactory and usable space within an area of 1,000 square feet per floor in a five-story building, which would be the average permissible floor space in a building of that height on this lot. There need be no limits on the shape of a building in the application of this formula; some floors may be greater than others, the limitation being confined to the total floor space permitted for the various building heights that may be considered feasible for this lot.

conditions in residential areas in average American cities, cities in which congestion has not yet smothered human values. The density standard in commercial districts would allow ample space for circulation, parking space, and the manifold services required by business enterprise. However, the precise numerical ceiling on densities is not the real issue posed by this formula. The issue is the urgent need for a reasonable ceiling on density in our cities, a density determined by each community which reflects the aims, ideals, desires of the people, the characteristics of the community, the qualities it desires to preserve or achieve, and the local color and individuality. Perhaps some habits will have to be broken, some practices uprooted. If this be so, the challenge will demand resolute leadership. These are decisions within the control of the local citizenry; if they are not made, cities are doomed to continued mediocrity and some to utter sordidness.

There could be an alternative to the single standard suggested by our formula—a triple standard which would recognize a *maximum* desirable density for single-family dwellings, a *minimum* building height for high density, and an intermediate density comparable to or somewhat greater than the single standard proposed in our formula. This alternative would operate for single-family areas in a manner similar to present zoning practices in which only single-family dwellings are permitted in zones so classified; the density might then be limited to five homes per acre. Our formula might then be increased to a density of some sixty persons per acre, translated into a relation between permissible floor space and "lot" area with a minimum building height of two or three stories prescribed in order to preserve adequate open space. The third classification—a minimum building height to accommodate a high density—would be consistent with the frequent assertion that high buildings offer the advantage of population concentration desirable in the great city in order to reduce the time consumed in travel about the metropolis.

There is merit in the contention that high buildings serve a significant role in the modern city, but the advantages must be real rather than fictitious. Height as a desirable form of urban improvement in its present application is not only a fiction but a delusion. Height now means nothing more than exploitation of land and congestion. To bring high buildings and high population density into the useful service which they can perform in today's urban pattern, our rules for urban land use require a drastic alteration. High population density does not work until buildings are so high that the open space about them is commodious. This is the foundation of the dramatic theories enunciated by Le Corbusier (Chapter 27, Part VI), and it is the key to an effective use of high buildings in our cities. If we are to capitalize on this advantage, it is necessary to frame our rules for urban development accordingly; to permit the intense use of land, now customary and regardless of the open space that may result, is to invite a continuance of present congestion and extravagance in urban services.

High population density will be effective when the proportion of land covered by tall buildings is highly restricted; Le Corbusier has been so bold as to suggest that

ALDEN PARK

Philadelphia

Tall apartment buildings in open space—
a desirable living environment that might
have been lifted out of the city of tomorrow by Le Corbusier.

NEW YORK CITY

The spacing of skyscraper towers
in the Wall Street district.

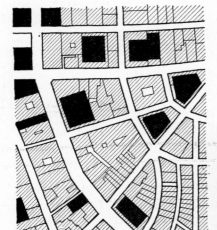

Setbacks that begin too late and
too far above the man in the
street.

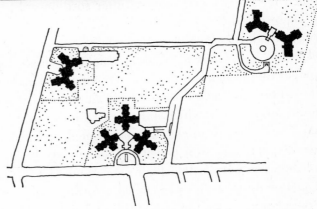

American Airlines

Apartment Towers on the
Lake Front of Chicago

POPULATION DENSITY

The excessive and sometimes intolerable intensity of population density induced by the absence of standards in current zoning regulations has obscured the desirable quality of a physical environment in which a variety of types and sizes of buildings are possible and now present. A single standard of density—translated into a ratio of floor space to land area—would remove the necessity for "height limits" and other artificial restraints on land improvement. It would also remove the exploitation of land and congestion which, it must be acknowledged, will have to be decreased before an improvement in our urban environment may be anticipated.

The variety which would be induced by such a method of regulation is suggested by the skyscrapers of New York. These dramatic spectacles are superimposed upon a pedestal of excessive building bulk covering the land, but it is this over-intensity near the ground, not the height of skyscrapers, that curses city development.

A single standard of population density would also remove the necessity for restricting certain zones to specific types of residential development: open space would be the foil for harmonizing the differences between multiple dwellings in high buildings and single-family homes. That such a proposal is not essentially novel is apparent in the development of Alden Park near Philadelphia. Built many years ago, these huge apartment buildings, set within ample open space, provide the aspect of a park, and become even more attractive neighbors for single-family homes than many a monotonous subdivision of single dwellings we find today.

Force of circumstances rather than planning or the acceptance of adequate space standards caused the apartment towers on the lake front of Chicago, but they also suggest the advantages of space. They tell the story of how overdevelopment within the law on some lots siphoned away the investment opportunities for their neighbors on adjacent lots. But this same story lends some credence to the suggestion for a single standard, even though that standard produced a much lower average population density than now provided in current zoning regulations.

this coverage should be 5 per cent of the land. The formula which has been described herein seeks a single standard of density by which urban services can be measured and open space retained without imposing restrictions on building height or form. A restriction on the proportion of land covered by tall buildings with high density would produce comparable results, but this implies the acceptance of a *minimum building height* to accommodate such densities. This alternative offers a choice, but it also raises a question as to whether such a proposition would receive as favorable acceptance as the single standard or would produce better cities.

It may be assumed that the whole question of population density which has been raised in this chapter is so highly theoretical as to render it purely academic in its application to realistic city building. It may also be claimed that the formula that has been suggested is utterly visionary. Let us assume for a moment, however, that our cities intend to recover from the disease of congestion they now suffer. It must be evident that prevailing treatments for this disease are no more than "first aid" for the temporary relief of pain. No cure is implicit in current measures, and those who prescribe them are generally aware that they simply postpone the inevitable operation.

When we diagnose the urban malady, we invariably return to the basic cause—excessive population density and its component of intense land use. We then arrive at a basic prescription—a limitation on the ratio of floor space in buildings to the ground area they occupy. This is the alleged purpose of zoning, and to that extent the formula is not new. The difference occurs at the point where the intent of zoning is obscured by the excessive building bulk it permits upon the land.

The formula accepts the single-family dwelling and the towering skyscraper alike, but it rejects the overloaded coverage imposed by high density and contends that these excesses are neither desirable, nor workable, nor necessary. A further distinction between the formula and current practice is the contention that a single standard of density for a specified land use—residential or commercial—would provide the range of freedom to city builders consistent with democratic processes. The identical standard of open space for all buildings would make of them good neighbors whether they were high or low, broad or slender, and the common standard of open space would, of itself, become the harmonious foil for the variety of urban expression that is typical and good for a democratic environment. Finally, it is not enough to claim an idea to be impractical and brush it aside; it is because our cities today are impractical that we seek ways and means to bring them into democratic balance.

CHAPTER **26**

CONTROL OF
OBSOLESCENCE

Taxation in Reverse. There is not now available to us a single instrument with which to control the spread of obsolescence. The police power to restrain the "nuisance" of blight is limited to such an extent that it is ineffective. Obsolescence itself is an obstruction to full production of housing. Normal competitive enterprise does not and cannot cope with it, as the accumulation of huge areas of blighted districts testifies. The only device now employed is zoning, and it is an illusion that petrifies urban improvement.

When blight sets in, it is considered ripe for a more intense land use. As single-family districts, some being the "fine old sections," begin to run down, their only salvation seems to be a change to apartment development. Intensity of land use moves relentlessly from the city center, and the "old" areas are drawn into this ever-widening vortex. The greater density permitted in apartment zoning then swiftly moves to reinforce a claim to higher land values. Thenceforth only multiple-dwelling development can be afforded. Old residences are converted to apartments and the district further declines. Strip zoning for business use is soon permitted, and stores are spotted in the neighborhood. After that, "light" industrial uses seep in. The "salvation" of revised zoning is dissipated among mixed land uses, and the community environment is decayed.

Pressure is ever present to "save" obsolescent areas of our cities by permitting a greater intensity of land use. There are few instances where this insidious process has restored to blighted areas a decent standard of residential or commercial development. The mixture of land uses leaves a series of derelicts in its wake. Land values increase rather than decrease as blight eats its way from the central core of the city, and they defy recovery of neighborhood values. Good development retreats from these damaging blows and seeks protection of "new" and more economical land at a safe distance. Disorderly expansion continues.

We may continue this futile process, but it cannot deliver healthy city development.

It is not a satisfactory substitute for planning an orderly arrangement of appropriate land uses, nor can it overcome the spread of obsolescence. The illusion actually induces deterioration of the urban environment. Obsolescence is a disease, and decay will continue to gnaw at the core of cities until it is brought under permanent control. Physical and social self-maintenance is the urgent need—a form of preventive treatment that will build resistance to decay and render major operations less necessary. It is such a form of control we now seek.

Buildings are built to provide space in which to live or conduct business. Taxes are collected to support the public services that make these building ventures possible and profitable. Today taxes are measured by the assessed value of land and buildings. The value of land may increase. The value of physical improvements, on the other hand, depreciates with age and use. At the same time the cost of public services increases as physical deterioration continues. Yet the present assessment of taxation actually works in reverse of this: *tax revenue goes down as the cost of urban maintenance goes up.*

There is little inducement for an owner to remove obsolete buildings so long as it is possible to derive a profit from them. The present order of real property taxation penalizes new construction and encourages the retention of old buildings until they have reached the last stages of decay. It retards sound real estate development and management, it makes unhealthy communities, and it adds to the burden of the taxpayer. This trend must be checked and then reversed.

Taxation is our traditional instrument for maintaining economic and social equilibrium. Our system of enterprise is intended to give the individual full freedom of choice and initiative. Devices employed by government to reinforce the public welfare should remain consistent with this pattern. It is up to the individual to measure his opportunity for investment; he must determine the extent to which he, in his own interest, will take part in the building of a community. But his interest cannot be served when a system of taxation imposes the penalty of high taxes on new building while it encourages competition from old buildings. Yet that is our current method of *ad valorem* taxation, and it is inimical to the full use of our productive resources.

Take a leaf from the experience with income taxation. In computing the tax base on business enterprise the cost of improvements necessary to carry on the business may be deducted from gross income. There have been many illustrations of improvements induced by this advantage. Application of the same principle to real property taxation would establish a logical order: as buildings deteriorate with age, contribute to the spread of blight, and retard the production of new building, taxes would increase rather than decrease. Taxation would assume an effective role as an instrument for encouragement of expanding production, protection against blight, and revenue to the community for public services. This instrument is the more effective because real property taxes are levied primarily by local government and are thereby readily subject to such periodic adjustments as changing local conditions may warrant.

Natural Elimination. The control of obsolescence has a twofold purpose: we are concerned with the maintenance of both a stable economy through continuing full production and adequate standards through continuous improvement. The FHA program introduced the repayment of loans for urban construction in regular installments over a predetermined period—amortization. This helped to stabilize financing, but more than that it has recognized the vital part that *time* plays in our economic machinery. It acknowledges that buildings have an "economic life," a period of economic usefulness in our system. The wheels of the system are kept turning by the circulation of money, and the time required to pay for buildings marks the frequency of the circulation of money. Unless the demand for building continues to exceed the existing supply, circulation of building money diminishes or ceases. The building industry then subsides or stops.

If the physical life of buildings were linked to the economic life, building money would continue to flow into the production of new buildings. Improved methods for doing things would find normal reception and application. But so long as old and obsolete buildings remain on the market they suffocate new building production. Run-down and worn-out buildings sustain themselves too long on no-maintenance and low-rents. It is that type of competition that sucks the lifeblood from productive enterprise; it is that type of competition that must be weeded out. Control of obsolescence would maintain the economic flow of goods and services, and a higher level of decency in the urban environment. Taxation could be effectively used to establish this control if the rate were related to the economic life of buildings.

In *Building Height, Bulk and Form*,[1] George B. Ford pointed out that the average life of skyscraper buildings was calculated at between twenty-five and thirty years. According to the Real Property Inventory of 1934 only 15 per cent of all dwellings were more than thirty-five years old. The period of residential financing ranges between fifteen and twenty-five years. Except for commercial and dwelling structures that have become a sordid blight on a community, few acceptable buildings remain in use for more than thirty-five years, without such major alterations that they become the equivalent of new buildings. It is the old and obsolete buildings which need to be weeded out of the urban environment.

It would be practicable to establish a tax base for new buildings and thereafter increase the tax rate from year to year. During the early life of a building—about ten years—the increase would be moderate. Thereafter it would gradually accelerate for the succeeding fifteen to twenty years. After that the increase would move rapidly upward at such a rate that a major improvement to sustain a profitable income on the building or a complete removal to make way for a new structure more suitable to the market and the community would be induced by the time the age of the structure had reached thirty-five years. A major improvement would cause a building to revert to a proportionately lower tax bracket rather than be penalized by an increased assessment according to current policy. Improved construction standards would be encouraged because they would benefit by lower tax brackets rather than be discouraged by the present *ad valorem* system.

[1] Harvard City Planning Series, Vol. II.

This suggestion rejects the traditional supposition that a building may remain so long as it produces a revenue satisfactory to its owner. It may seem to be bitter medicine, but the accelerating degeneration of our cities has amply demonstrated that neither the public welfare nor sound private enterprise is served by current methods. This proposal does not presume to solve the broad problem of taxation, but it would place our current tax system in a logical order without which regulations accepted today offer no prospect for correcting the insidious evil of obsolescence.

No surgeon ever performed an operation without destroying some live tissue. His aim is to save the patient, knowing that time will heal the wounds and restore the living cells. Our economy as well as our social well-being depends upon our capacity to carve out the parasite of decay with the destruction of as little useful tissue as practically possible. But we cannot continue to rely upon the vagaries of chance. It must become a matter of law in an organized society.

This proposition presents problems, to be sure. Not the least of these is the one faced by home-owners of low income who depend solely upon their dwelling as a place to live. It may be alleged that this order of taxation would impose an undue hardship on these families. While the most articulate protests to this apparent injustice will undoubtedly come from those who profit most from blighted property, each community will have to face, sooner or later, this question: How long can the accumulation of obsolete buildings and improvements, that deface the environment and eat away the civic solvency, be tolerated? Each community is obliged to address itself to that question and deliberate the problems—all the problems—it poses. When the answer has been decided, and only then, will cities begin the long road out of the sordid morass that the anarchy of urban development has wrought.

The Justement Plan. Louis Justement[2] suggests a "retirement plan for buildings" in which the life of buildings would be limited to a period of fifty years. In support of his plan Mr. Justement says:

The owners of commercial, industrial and residential property are generally aware of the declining value of their "improvements" due to the factor of obsolescence. Sound accounting methods require and our income-tax laws permit annual depreciation charges for improvements. Unfortunately, buildings which have been depreciated to zero, on paper, are not thereby destroyed; they continue to exert their blighting influence on the city. The long-term mortgage, which is becoming increasingly popular, provides for the *complete* amortization of a loan within the term of the mortgage, which rarely exceeds thirty-three years and is limited to twenty-five years in the case of dwellings. A limitation of fifty years on the life of the building would permit the owner during the life of the mortgage to secure exactly the same income he would now secure. At the end of that time he would still have another seventeen to twenty-five years in which to enjoy the revenue from unencumbered property—assuming that the original financing had worked out according to plan.

It will be observed that Mr. Justement's reasoning is substantially in accord with that which has been previously set forth except for the difference in the estimated "life" of buildings; Mr. Justement has adopted the span of fifty years, whereas the period

[2] *New Cities for Old*, Louis Justement, McGraw-Hill Book Company, Inc., New York, 1946.

established in the foregoing proposal is approximately thirty-five years. It is evident that Mr. Justement has extended the life span to fifty years to permit an owner a period of "grace" beyond the economic life, during which time the building will be producing revenue free and clear of debt upon the property.

As has been indicated heretofore, it is this period that tends to create a vacuum in the continuous flow of production because of the element of competition between old buildings free of obligation and new buildings burdened with the debt which is essential to construction financing. It may be that this period of "grace" is for the purpose of inducing the adoption of such a proposal, but dealing with the problem in theory, as we are, it does not seem desirable to acknowledge such a compromise at the outset. Beginning with a compromise too frequently beclouds issues and forsakes the principles upon which a proposal is predicated. It is furthermore quite possible that the proposition to limit the life span of urban buildings would find its greatest support from that segment of productive enterprise which would recognize the distinct advantages in a closer relation between the physical and economic life of structures.

As a further inducement for the adoption of the retirement plan, Mr. Justement proposes a reduction in the assessed valuation of buildings at the rate of 2 per cent per year. Local real estate taxation would therefore be based upon a gradually decreasing assessed valuation, which would, in turn, reduce the revenue to the city. It is this feature which we have endeavored to avoid in the method suggested heretofore; it is the advantage of progressively lower taxation which has induced the retention of old buildings on the market and rendered a satisfactory standard of maintenance practically impossible to sustain.

The Justement plan tends to freeze the life of buildings rather than to create a flexible arrangement which would place the burden of decision upon the owner of property. An owner would have the option of adjusting his property to such changes as the market might warrant during the fifty-year period, but it is probable that the benefit of decreasing rather than increasing obligation to the community would act as it now does—contrary to the public interest—until the fifty-year period had elapsed. With a system of increasing taxation the owner is caused to be constantly aware of his responsibility to the community while he retains the freedom to determine the use and disposition of his property as he may see fit.

All things grow obsolete with time and change. That is inevitable. But obsolescence must be brought under control, as weeds are kept out of a prosperous garden. Degeneration of the urban environment is an epidemic feeding upon lack of attention. Production, essential to freedom of enterprise and the general welfare, suffocates. No amount of temporary welfare or occasional reform will compensate for continued indifference to the insidious spread of obsolescence. Absence of public control and treatment is like the underwriting of obsolescence by law. It has become a public liability. It is consequently a public responsibility to devise machinery to put its house in order, and keep it in order by progressive regulation of obsolescence.

CHAPTER 27

THE NEW UTOPIANS

The Atom Bomb. World War II produced the atom bomb. The blast at Hiroshima forced upon people a realization of the tremendous destructive power science had loosed upon the world. The shock of atomic power shattered the nerves and morale of the world, leaving people with a fear for their future. Uncertainty has engulfed humanity.

There can be no definite calculation of the effect which atomic power will have upon the shape of our cities, but theories have been numerous. The milder variety propose positive decentralization; many suggest cities be built completely underground. There could hardly be more startling testimony to the appalling fear that has gripped the people.

In May 1947 the President's Advisory Commission reported on Universal Military Training. It recommended the dispersion of industry and the location of some plants underground. *Life* magazine, June 16, 1947, carried a commentary on the hideous prospects science has plummeted upon the world. A group of scientists described their solution. The habitable areas of the United States would be divided into 25-mile squares. The population density would be 600 persons, 160 dwellings, per mile along each side of these squares. Dwellings would be located about the periphery of the square, the factories in the center. It is estimated that this scheme would result in "only" 2,000 persons killed and 500 houses destroyed if an atom bomb hit. The more desirable dispersion would be twelve families per mile, in which case the number of destroyed dwellings would be reduced to 100. The compromise is proposed, however, because the complete dispersion would become *too costly!* Safety would nevertheless be improved: while 2,000 would be lost in the proposed dispersion, the authors estimate a bomb would kill 50,000 in present cities. In the Hiroshima blast there were 135,000 casualties and 60,000 buildings destroyed.

The sinister implications must surely be clear. The world today has at its command energy so powerful that protection from self-destruction has become too costly to afford. It must be apparent that the essential qualities which render a city less vulnerable from the air and long-range missiles are the same qualities we desire in a decent environment in peace. Congestion is no more desirable in time of peace than it is in war.

A major question is posed before the people: Must we lose, through threat of uncontrolled atomic energy, the living and working environment we desire in peace, only to substitute one less desirable and much more costly in war? This is the prospect as we look toward the future.

The Early Pioneers. Men in all walks of life have raised their voices against the inequities, the ugliness, and the congestion of the city. William Morris, Ruskin, Geddes, and Jacob Riis early perceived the evils and protested them. Many turned the light of critical analysis upon the city, testing the forces of disintegration in the laboratories of their keen minds, and dared to describe cities that men could build when they acquired the will.

Nor were they all cries in the wilderness. Housing, the most appalling testimonial to neglect in the urban scene, received attention. Planning agencies were formed; zoning and building laws enacted. But all these efforts remained a step behind the improvement of which society was capable; they never quite caught up with technological and scientific development.

There were those who indulged their vision of the cities that could be built. They were the New Utopians on the cultural scene. They were not all dreamers, among them being numbered men with a keen practical sense.

In 1882 Soria y Mata, in Spain, propounded the theory of the linear city—*La Ciudad Linear*. It was his theory that the highway should be the spine of communications which would provide access to industry and housing bordering upon it. The scheme was like a continuous artery feeding a series of cul-de-sac road systems. This urban organization differs from the concentric growth of large cities. The village spreads along a roadway in the linear fashion, but, as it expands beyond a rural community, it moves in all directions from the center.

It was this concentric form with which most theorists worked. Raymond Unwin, a pioneer in housing in England, espoused the cause of decentralization about the concentric basic plan. He visualized the creation of satellite communities, ranging in population from 12,000 to 18,000, with community facilities and some industry, and requiring no vehicular transport within them. Each community would be connected to the central city by rapid transportation.

Men like Unwin and Ebenezer Howard were absorbed with the basic city structure and living amenities. We must also count among the New Utopians Daniel H. Burnham, who viewed the city from another vantage point. Burnham, it is true, missed the issues upon which Unwin dwelt persistently and patiently. The "City Beautiful" was Burnham's haven—the classic form and the monumental avenue and plaza. But to him we are indebted for an inspiring message, not written in stone or steel, but in words. It has goaded many later travelers to better deeds; it has been a light shining through many a dark cloud hanging over the environment of man:

Make no little plans; they have no magic to stir men's blood and probably will not be realized. Make big plans; aim high in hope and work, remembering that a noble, logical diagram once recorded will never die, but long after we are gone will be a living thing, asserting itself with ever-growing insistency. Remember that our sons and grandsons are going to do things that would stagger us. Let your watchword be order and your beacon beauty.[1]

As the twentieth century drew on, many opportunists became articulate. Congestion inspired a variety of panaceas, and some of the most fantastic proposals were suggested by otherwise practical men. Probably the most popular theme was the double- and triple-deck street. High land cost was so firmly rooted in the urban state of mind that its effect was accepted as the normal course of "land economics." Nevertheless the traffic problem had to be solved, and piling layers of streets upon each other had the appearance of plausibility. As the roofs of skyscrapers moved upward so did proposals for multiple-level streets.

The Urban Complex. Beneath, on the surface of the earth, darkness pervaded man's environment. A complex gripped the people; there was a growing apprehension of the light. Man was building so broad and so high that the more there was light the deeper were the shadows. They engulfed humanity, and a phobia against the light was generated. People cultivated a preference for the darkness; it veiled the contrasts of their daily existence. The artificial glow of night-life became popular, and the people found release from the realities about them. With the dawn they scurried into their shells of office cubicles or apartment cells.

The art of walking was all but discarded. A subway train brought the people to the heart of the city; the least time in the open air and daylight, the more readily was the conscience of man assuaged. Escape from reality was sought in the brilliant shadows of the motion pictures; into this world of fantasy and make-believe all could retreat momentarily.

The metropolis laid heavily upon its inhabitants. The problem of the underprivileged increased, social welfare expanded, and more and more of the tax income was directed to charity.

In his Ford Ideals, the great industrialist said what was in the minds of many people: "Nothing will finally work more effectively to undo the fateful grip which the city has taken upon the people than the destruction of the fictitious land values which the city traditions have set up and maintained."[2] Coming from a leader of industry it is rather perplexing that Henry Ford did not suggest how land values might be "destroyed," but he pointed his words at the major obstacle to improvement of the urban environment: spiraling land values.

All who have protested the congestion and ugliness of the city reveal the anachronism of our industrial age—the inability of society to muster the forces of technological progress in the cause of urban organization. Directed toward the same objective—improvement of the urban environment—theories conflict and opinions vary. It is inevitable

---

[1] *Daniel Burnham: Architect, Planner of Cities*, Charles Moore, Boston, 1921.
[2] *The Modern City—A Pestiferous Growth*, pp. 156–157; Ford Ideals, being a Selection from "Mr. Ford's Page" in the *Dearborn Independent*, The Dearborn Publishing Company, Dearborn, Michigan, 1922.

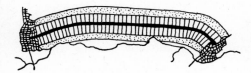

The Linear City
of Soria y Mata, 1882

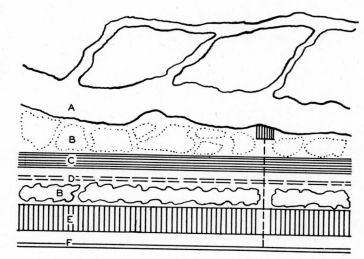

Linear City Plan for Stalingrad
by N. A. Milyutin, 1930

A Volga River

B Greenbelt

C Residential

D Highway

E Industrial

F Railroad

THE LINEAR AND THE CONCENTRIC CITY

The linear city is as old as the village. It began with the roadside town, but in 1882 Soria y Mata proposed it as a conscious form for urban development. This was before the automobile had entered the urban scene. Milyutin carried the idea further, adapting it to an industrial city and incorporating the "greenbelt" as a separation between the elements—housing, circulation, and industry. This type is shown as applied to the city of Stalingrad.

In contrast to the linear form, or ribbon development, is the concentric form which is more or less typical of the metropolis of today. It is the form represented in the diagram of the scheme suggested by Sir Raymond Unwin, a group of satellite communities surrounding the central city and connected to it with rail lines.

It is a combination of these forms which will probably emerge in the city of tomorrow, the advantage of clear circulation and orderly expansion offered by the linear city combined with the integrated form of the small, concentric community. A comparison of these two forms is suggested in the photograph below. The usual and undesirable characteristic of the linear or ribbon town is demonstrated on both sides of the highway in the lower portion of the picture; each property facing upon and having direct access to the highway. The organized plan of a separate community with adequate access to the highway but removed from it except for one or two entrances, is suggested in the portion in the upper right.

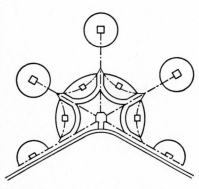

Diagrammatic Scheme of Central City with Satellite Towns by Raymond Unwin.

Desirable and Undesirable Planning along the Highway.

Courtesy The Architectural Forum

and it reflects the enigma of the age. The tremendous advance of science and invention thrusts forward the horns of a dilemma and civilization is perched upon them.

Le Corbusier. In 1922 there was displayed in a Paris exposition a vision of *La Ville Contemporaine* by the architect Le Corbusier. His utopian scheme was a city of magnificent skyscraper towers surrounded by a broad and sweeping open space. The city was a huge park. Sixty-story office buildings accommodating 1,200 people per acre and covering but 5 per cent of the ground area were grouped in the heart of the city. The transportation center, rail and airfield, was the hub. Surrounding the skyscrapers was the apartment district, eight-story buildings arranged in zigzag rows with broad open spaces about them, the density of population being 120 persons per acre. Lying about the outskirts were the *cité jardins*, the garden cities of single houses. The city was designed for a population of 3,000,000.

The beautifully delineated plans and succinct reasoning with which they were described created a sensation, and in 1925 Le Corbusier adapted his *La Ville Contemporaine* to the center of Paris.[3] The contrast with the old city was dramatic and the architect hammered at his theme, pointing his finger of scorn at the feeble but still undesirable population density in Paris—an average of 146 persons per acre, and 213 persons in the overcrowded sections—spread thin over the city.

Le Corbusier followed this conception with his *Ville Radieuse*, the Radiant City, a city of continuous rows of tall buildings woven in zigzag form across landscaped space. A prolific writer and indefatigable reformist, he prepared his visionary schemes for Algiers, Nemours, Antwerp, and Stockholm. He was enamored of the skyscrapers of America and the energy of the industrial processes. His "shock" value was tremendous and those who waved aside his proposals as another wild dream were themselves quite blind to the wilderness which had overtaken the city in which they themselves were trapped.

The American Contrast. Le Corbusier has dreamed of his city from within the medieval environment of the European city. He dramatizes the skyscraper and the ingenuity, the daring, the courage, the skill which have made it. His desire for the machine, conditioned air, push-buttons, swift elevators, is like a romance with science. It is the contrast with the European city he sees in the

tonic spectacle, stimulating, cheering, radiant, which from each office, appears through the transparent glass walls leading into space. Space! That response to the aspiration of the human being, that relaxation for breathing and for the beating heart, that outpouring of self in looking far, from a height, over a vast, infinite, unlimited expanse. Every bit of sun and fresh, pure air furnished mechanically. Do you try to maintain the fraud of hypocritical affirmations, to throw discredit on these radiant facts, to argue, to demand the "good old window," open on the stenches of the city and street, the noise, air currents, and the company of flies and mosquitoes? For thirty years I have known the offices of Paris: conversations cut to pieces by the uproar, suffocating atmosphere, the view broken thirty feet away by the walls of houses, dark corners, half-light, etc. . . . Impostors should no longer deny the gains of our period and by their fright

[3] This was known as the *Plan Voisin*.

prevent changing from one thing to another, keeping the city or cities in general from going their joyously destined way.[4]

Thus Le Corbusier compares the skyscraper with the city of Europe not yet out-grown its medieval scale—the narrow twisting roads which the boulevards exaggerate. The towers of Manhattan, rising straight and free into the air, are common to the American; the tall building in Europe is still the thirteenth-century cathedral tower. The gridiron plan is straight and clear to the European eye, the hygiene of plumbing so inviting, the brilliance by night so thrilling. It is a fascination not reserved to Europeans alone; Americans like it too.

Let us examine the proposition posed by Le Corbusier. He argues "concentration" versus "congestion." He demonstrates his city will concentrate the people, conserve the daily hours they consume in horizontal travel, and direct this time into productive effort and leisure. He contends the American skyscraper is *too small* and proposes a residential population of 6,000,000 on Manhattan, a density of 400 persons per acre, and 88 per cent of the ground area free and open; and he is confident it can be done.

There are none who know this better than Americans. Several times the density proposed by Le Corbusier has been housed in the huge apartment buildings of America. In his City of Tomorrow, Le Corbusier suggested a density of 1,200 persons per acre in sixty-story skyscrapers, but the density in Radio City is more than twice as much and it can be nearly three times in downtown Los Angeles. Nearly 10,000 people per acre work in the Empire State Building. Americans have built the tallest structures ever built by man and they have housed more people on an acre of land than any time in the history of mankind. Concentration is an accomplished fact in America.

Undoubtedly Le Corbusier would point out that cities are not built to these amazing densities everywhere. He is aware that the average height of buildings in New York City is only four and one-half stories and he proposes the floor space be enclosed in skyscrapers which would thus leave great open space about them. This implies that *only* skyscrapers could be built, that low buildings would not be permitted since they would cover the ground as it is now covered. The magnificence of his conception cannot be denied, but there is a blind spot in his vision.

The values that make the cities show the differences between them. Congestion in Europe is still a medieval form—flat, horizontal, crowded within a net of feudal streets, population density of 200 persons per acre. Congestion of the American city is new under the sun; the congestion of too many people heaped upon too small an area of land, with zoning laws that prescribe it shall be so.

Le Corbusier pleads for concentration and deplores the sprawling city that has lost its space under a blanket of building bulk. The singular fate of the American city is that we have both in one—the concentration of unbearable density *and* the sprawling city. We call it the metropolis and it too has forsaken its space. With a density of 400 persons per acre housed in residential skyscrapers on Manhattan, Le

[4] *When the Cathedrals Were White*, Le Corbusier, Reynal and Hitchcock, 1947.

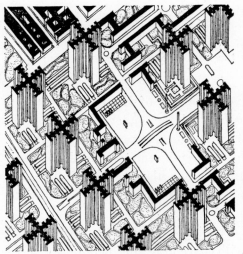

"PLAN VOISIN" by Le Corbusier, Paris, 1925

CONTRAST Between Old and New in "Plan Voisin"

After the introduction in 1922 of his plan for an ideal city of 3,000,000, Le Corbusier applied the same theories to a section of Paris. Known as the "Voisin" plan, the sixty-story skyscraper office buildings are set in vast open space, main traffic highways are clearly defined with complete separation of traffic, and ample parking space for vehicles is provided. The plan is a rectangular arrangement of streets but local and through traffic are distinctly separated, and the large open spaces are treated with informal pedestrian circulation and landscaped. The difference in scale of open space and building coverage is indicated in the plan sketch.

"LA VILLE RADIEUSE" by Le Corbusier

The plan submitted in the international competition of 1933 for the replanning of Nedre Normalm in Stockholm was an adaptation of Le Corbusier's scheme for continuous "staggered" rows of high buildings (shown in black) set upon piers within broad open space. This plan also shows the clear distinction between the various types of roadways: the encircling "freeway" raised above the ground level, the secondary traffic ways uninterrupted by the building forms, and the informal system of local traffic and pedestrian ways which likewise circulate freely beneath the buildings which are open at the ground level. The existing or new proposed low buildings (cross-hatched) are provided settings within ample landscaped open space.

A Railroad Station   **B** City Hall   **C** Concert Hall   **D** Palace

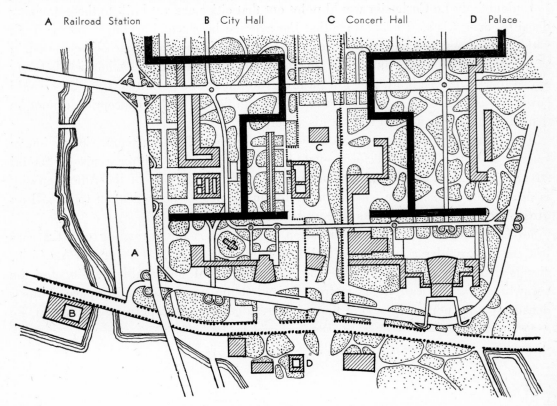

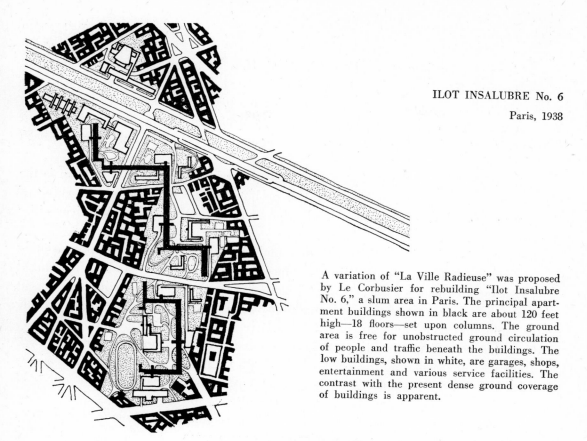

ILOT INSALUBRE No. 6

Paris, 1938

A variation of "La Ville Radieuse" was proposed by Le Corbusier for rebuilding "Ilot Insalubre No. 6," a slum area in Paris. The principal apartment buildings shown in black are about 120 feet high—18 floors—set upon columns. The ground area is free for unobstructed ground circulation of people and traffic beneath the buildings. The low buildings, shown in white, are garages, shops, entertainment and various service facilities. The contrast with the present dense ground coverage of buildings is apparent.

The drama of the Skyscraper, RADIO CITY, New York

Paul J. Woolf Photo

Corbusier suggests the costs could be absorbed. How little the European can conceive the values of American urban soil: $10, $100, $1,000 per square foot with the prospect for an advance in the market price on the morrow. Stuyvesant Town in New York City has been built to the density proposed by Le Corbusier, and it was necessary to overcome the high cost of land in an area so blighted it has been losing population for 20 years.

In America, whether it be New York, Chicago, or Los Angeles, the problem is the reduction of density, not an increase. The problem is one of reducing the value of land, a value high density created, land value that has been rooted in American cities *by law*.

When we view the city in that light, the number of people that can be appropriately accommodated upon an acre of land to balance the economics of urban land is reduced to an academic theory rather than a practical equation. The principle of decent standards for decent city building is obscured by the urgency of protecting the feeble gains zoning has made thus far. Land values have been established by the zoning laws and resistance to change is adamant. The proposed revision of the law for New York in 1946 was unacceptable, the effect of the 1945 ordinance upon land value in Los Angeles has drawn heavy fire, and the prospect of restoring reasonable standards of land use and population density fades into the deep shadows.

The Skyscraper—Is It the Answer? Let us assume for a moment that population density permitted by law in American cities were compromised to the level of that suggested by Le Corbusier. What then are the implications? If concentration is an organic necessity of the metropolis, is every man destined to live in an apartment cubicle, in thirty- or sixty-story buildings? Is this the way every man desires to live? Again we find the shades of the European. There it is either the apartment or the castle; only peasants and the very wealthy live in houses.

Is man to be conditioned by science and economics? Or are these the servants of man? Are they creatures of man or is man their slave? Does not man so mold his economics that it may distribute the goods of this world for his use, and does he not invent so that his wants may be better served? If these be true, are we not obliged to evaluate first our desires and define our wants so as to employ science and economics to our advantage?

The city performs a far greater variety of services today than ever before. Its functions are more complex. Yet the same forces that have made this so are those which now render congestion unnecessary. Science, commerce, and industry have intensified the functions of the city. They have also created the instruments to neutralize its effect. The heavy concentration of people is no longer necessary for the conduct of business or for convenient and comfortable living. Methods of transportation, power, and communications invalidate the crowded concentration we unwittingly accept as a necessary evil of urban existence. Crowding of people and buildings is a negation of every contemporary means of communication and transportation at our command. Congestion denies them the chance to serve to their full capacity.

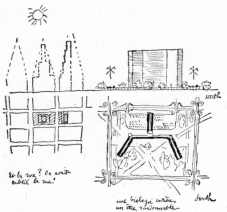

re-formation cellulaire:
le logis

Cellular reorganization,
apartment buildings

And the street?
The street was forgotten

A complete biology, a
reasonable existence

re-formation cellulaire de la ville

Cellular reorganization of the city

MANHATTAN

These sketches illustrate Le Corbusier's theories applied to the island of Manhattan. He says the skyscrapers of Manhattan are "too small" and proposes that the island be developed in huge blocks in which large and tall buildings may be placed in adequate surrounding open space, only 12 per cent of the ground being covered by buildings, 88 per cent remaining free for circulation and landscaped space.

The three sketches at the left contrast the street system of today with the large cells proposed by Le Corbusier; below, the present coverage of the diminutive blocks is contrasted with the open space provided in the large cellular block; and, above, the building coverages over a number of blocks are contrasted.

The validity of Le Corbusier's proposition is proved by the American skyscraper, but it is defeated by the exploitation of land for which the skyscraper has been employed. This question also remains to be reflected upon: Are we to capture the advantages of high density in tall buildings in ample open space and require that every building must be tall in order to have it thus? This question is important since high density *plus* broad open space is only feasible when buildings are *very* tall and if the same density is also permitted in low buildings we return directly to the congested form of city we have today. (See Chapter 25.) In the photograph at the bottom, one can vaguely perceive the city of Le Corbusier emerging obscurely through the haze of reality.

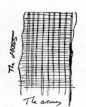

au temps du cheval

au temps de l'auto
(re-formation cellulaire)

Aspect de la deuxième
Métamorphose de New-York

Troisième métamorphose

For the horse age

For the automobile age
(cellular reorganization)

New York in its
second metamorphosis

The third
metamorphosis

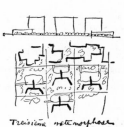

Courtesy The American Architect

There is stimulation in great distances seen from the skyscraper. Conditioned air has its advantages. The elevator rising 1,000 feet a minute is rapid vertical transit. But do these render the human desire for a house on its land a phenomenon or a whim? Horizontal space means much to the human being. Contact with the earth is not a choice reserved to the agrarian, the tiller of the soil, alone. There is a sense of freedom, human freedom, in traversing the space of the earth under one's own power —on foot. There is a healthy sensation when interior and exterior living space merge into unity, with no more visual separation than a crystal sheet of glass. There is mental freedom and a quiet repose in horizontal space.

Because the "economy" of ownership is often a fiction or because the people are frequently tenants does not alter the essential desire for the horizontal space for living. This is not a question of politics, economics, or social reform. It is a matter of human aims, aspirations, desires, and the mental repose in physical reality. It is not a theory of esthetics, nor is it romantic nonsense that people desire a home and garden. It is not enough to substitute air-conditioned cells in multistory buildings because we have the technical know-how to create them.

It is the fundamental desires that beat in the human breast which must shape the city. The skyscraper holds its head aloft with an air of plausibility; it can absorb high land cost and save utilities and transportation time. But it also can create congestion and high land values that nullify its advantages and remove all choice for another form of habitation from the hope of the urban dweller. If we are concerned with economy, it is not the skyscraper that produces it; the skyscraper is not built because it is economical—it is not so. It is built because the cost of land is *extravagant*, and continuing this process without restraint only adds fuel to the flames of urban congestion, blight, and disintegration.

Return to Space. Where, then, do the desires of the people and the theories of Le Corbusier meet? He is a very human architect and planner. It is a sense of human needs that has fired his driving energy. His designs have emerged from the warp and woof of people. The two shall probably meet in the open spaces for which the people of the city yearn and Le Corbusier pleads, plans, and ponders. We can plan our cities unafraid of horizontal space. The skill and enthusiasm, so admired by Le Corbusier, the same capacity which could build the towering city of concentration he has envisioned, could produce the transportation and communications to connect the people at a horizontal level.

The liberation of space from the limitations of structure is a basic theory Le Corbusier has espoused. He has stressed the freedom in the form of space which the technology of modern frame construction affords. It is the primary characteristic of contemporary building plan and design, and Le Corbusier has translated it into his theories on city planning. He lifted his buildings above interference with the ground surface and left horizontal space free from the obstruction of traditional building masses. This same liberation is open to us by way of science and invention in transportation and communications. It can free us from the concentration that now restricts the type of habitations available to us just as it can reduce congestion by the concentration of the skyscraper Le Corbusier suggests.

The people may have tall buildings and low buildings, open space and convenient communications. The people may have the amenities of living in the proportions they desire. They may have these things in city life when congestion is outlawed, when the tendency to crowd more people on the land and create distorted land values has been dissipated. They may have good cities when we learn to exploit the manifold frontiers of our future civilization—the frontiers of the new organization of urban functions.

Urban Reorganization for Space. The overgrown metropolis feeds upon its inhabitants. Gnawing at the physical, mental and spiritual fabric of the people the city repels improvement, and no inhabitant can escape the heavy weight of urban living regardless of fortune or social status. The insidious course of urban disintegration forces an examination of the basic nature of the urban structure and it is to this task that the New Utopians have set themselves.

Decentralization is the theme running through all studies of the New Utopians. Whether it is referred to as re-centralization or as sub-centralization, the theme reveals the typical search for escape from congestion but, in contrast to the chaos of expansion now contributing to the breakdown of the city, it is directed to an organic reorganization of the urban functions. It is significant that most proposals cling to the essential idea of the city as an organism; the complex and diverse facilities of the city are not forsaken. The desirability of close proximity between the dwelling and the workshop has urged concentration in the great city and it has turned into congestion, but the independent self-contained "garden city" is seldom proposed as an antidote by the New Utopians. Space, free and open space, is urgently sought, and the constituent parts of the metropolis are subjected to major reorganization; and even those who, like Le Corbusier, espouse "concentration" are in reality seeking a form of decentralization.

It is this quest for space that lends unity to otherwise apparently divergent views on the future of the urban structure, a divergence which may be illustrated by the distinctions usually drawn between the "linear" city and the "concentric" city forms.

The linear city of Soria y Mata was an early proposal (1882) for decentralization of the concentric city. Essentially a magnification of the village form, the extension of urban development along an arterial highway may have appeared to be a way out of the congestion of old cities before the automobile came upon the scene. Violent changes in the forms of transportation have since demonstrated the ineffectiveness of such "strip" development, but the linear city struck at a singular evil of the concentric city—the gradual absorption of open space, through persistent expansion about the periphery, removes the countryside farther and farther from the urban population. Adapting the advantage of the linear city—constant nearness of open space—to the new forms of transportation and industry, later proponents, like Milyutin, proposed continuous zones of industry and dwellings parallel with the railroad and highway, each zone separated by belts of open park and recreation space.

An advantage claimed for the linear city is the opportunity it affords for limitless expansion along each of the ribbon zones. This is an asset likewise attributed to the concentric city. Reflection upon this, however, suggests it is a weakness rather than a virtue. The unchallenged assumption that the city should accommodate an unlimited population has created of it the medium for speculation it is today. When we conceive of the city as a desirable environment for people, we are obliged to acknowledge human scale as a criterion of urban design, and human scale is maintained in proportion to the degree to which the physical form retains an identification of its individual parts. The almost brutal quality of the great city is due largely to the absence of human scale; all sense of community recognition is lost in the common grayness of the industrial metropolis. The limitless centrifugal expansion of the concentric city obscures this identity and forfeits human scale.

While the ribbon form of the linear city restores open space within the city, it, like the concentric city, retains the ingrown deficiency of unlimited expansion. To recover a semblance of identity and recapture open space near the people, the "garden city" and the satellite town emerged. The disorderly process of current decentralization spreads suburbs about the countryside for the same purpose. Merging these qualities—community identity and open space—we find the linear city and concentric city converge upon a common pattern as a basic urban form.

The "garden city" and typical satellite town rely upon their relatively small size to maintain a balance between urban development and surrounding open space, whereas the linear city employs open space as buffers between different land uses. In his plan for "La Cité Industrielle" in 1917, Tony Garnier united these elements of a self-contained city and segregated land uses by separating the residential areas from the factory district, highway, and railroad, with the equivalent of a "greenbelt."

A series of satellite communities, each planned along the lines of "La Cité Industrielle" and linked by transportation routes, suggests a form of linear city composed of a series of community cells, a hint of this cellular organization being contained in the "ribbon" plan for Stalingrad. If we then recognize the function of central commercial, cultural, and administrative facilities to serve the large population within the orbit of metropolitan industrial areas, the desirable characteristics of both the linear and concentric forms may emerge as a *regional* city. It is such a reorganization of urban space, in which the advantages of regional facilities may be restored without sacrificing the people in the cauldron of congestion, that the New Utopians are attempting to bring into clearer focus.

Search for Form. The International Congress of Modern Architects (CIAM) subjected the city to re-examination and posed four basic elements of the urban biology: (1) *sun*, (2) *space*, (3) *vegetation*, (4) *steel and concrete*. Le Corbusier assumed a leading role in CIAM and organized the Assembly of Constructors for an Architectural Renovation (ASCORAL) to extend the investigations into the character of the city.

ASCORAL set forth the "Three Human Establishments"[5]: the *farming unit*, the *radioconcentric city,* and the *linear industrial city.* The farming unit is the space for agriculture and the villages that serve it; the radioconcentric city is the existing urban area in which the theory of concentration evolved. Although the third "human establishment"—the linear industrial city—stems from earlier Utopians, it is a new element in the theories espoused by Le Corbusier. Leaving the "evils of the sprawling town," the studies of ASCORAL move into the country, and new industrial communities are located along the main arteries of transportation—water, rail, and highway—connecting the existing cities. Factories—the "green" factories—are placed along the main transportation routes, separated from the residential section by the auto highway and green strips. The residential area includes the "horizontal garden town" of single houses and a vertical apartment building with its complement of communal facilities. Sports, entertainment, shopping, and office facilities are distributed in this district, and all the facilities of the community are placed within ample open space enhanced with natural verdure. These industrial groups are placed at intervals along the highway and railway linking the existing cities, the latter remaining as administrative, commercial, and cultural centers.

The evolution of urban research has been shared by many students and it is a singular characteristic of this research that the big city is not, of itself, the point of attack. It is not a return to the village size or the breakdown of the big city which is usually sought. On the contrary, the great city has induced cultural advantages and a scale of commerce by which the benefits of the industrial world may be distributed. That these advantages have been abused, misused, or allowed to lie dormant does not deny their presence or potential development. The search is for an organic form for the city, and it is emerging as a regional city having as component parts the units we identify as neighborhoods. This regional city in contrast to the concentrated metropolis is the key to the reorganization of the urban structure.

José Sert proposes the grouping of several neighborhood units, six or eight in number, to form a township having a population of between 56,000 and 80,000 people. Each neighborhood has an elementary school, and the center of the township contains the high schools and principal shopping facilities. Light industry is contiguous to the township, and open space separates the townships from the light industrial areas. The city consists of a number of townships connected with the "civic center" in which the cultural, sports, and administrative facilities are located. Heavy industry stretches along the principal transportation routes which by-pass the city. Greenbelts surround the whole group and separate the various land uses. The scale and organization of the neighborhoods and townships give ready access to open space and natural surroundings. Removal of the urban population from open space is the terrible curse of the metropolis, and recreation space within walking distance of the home and greenbelts of natural landscape as protective "buffers" separating the various land uses are common features of all the New Utopians' plans.

[5] *Les Trois Éstablissements Humains,* ASCORAL, Denoël, 19, Rue Amelie, Paris, 1945.

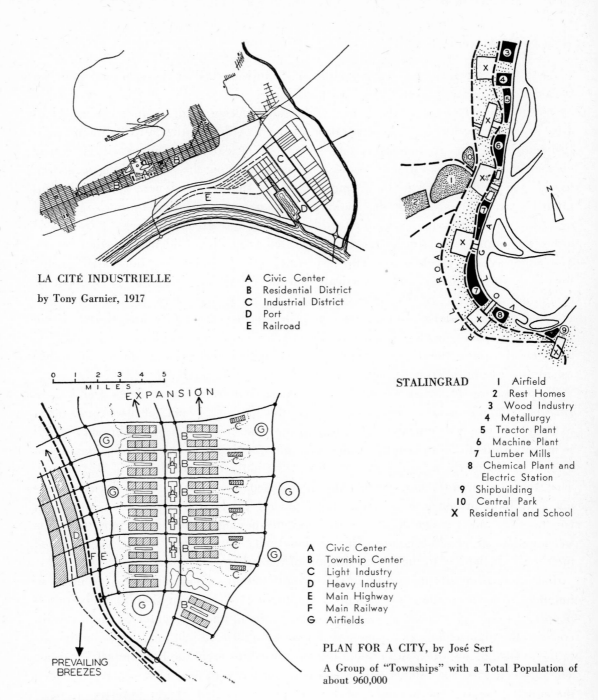

LA CITÉ INDUSTRIELLE

by Tony Garnier, 1917

A Civic Center
B Residential District
C Industrial District
D Port
E Railroad

STALINGRAD

1 Airfield
2 Rest Homes
3 Wood Industry
4 Metallurgy
5 Tractor Plant
6 Machine Plant
7 Lumber Mills
8 Chemical Plant and
   Electric Station
9 Shipbuilding
10 Central Park
X Residential and School

A Civic Center
B Township Center
C Light Industry
D Heavy Industry
E Main Highway
F Main Railway
G Airfields

PLAN FOR A CITY, by José Sert

A Group of "Townships" with a Total Population of
about 960,000

URBAN REORGANIZATION

Searching for an urban form appropriate to the metropolis of the industrial age, the New Utopians have produced some principles which may guide a reorganization of the city of tomorrow. These principles merge the
common characteristics of the "linear" and the "concentric" city forms; they accept the physical properties
of the neighborhood unit in favor of the basic needs of the family and regain the prospect for identity of
the individual parts of the great city now lost within the dreary grayness of the present metropolis. Because
the city form must change if it is to survive and because it must survive as an integral element of the
industrial age, the proposals of the New Utopians are essential ingredients of urban thought and action.

As Garnier's "La Cité Industrielle" used the greenbelt for separation between the factory and the home not
present in Howard's "garden city," and the plan for Stalingrad suggests a cellular organization of residential
and industrial units not present in the linear city of Soria y Mata, so the Ascoral plans by Le Corbusier syn-
thesize the essential characteristics of a new urban form.

The variety of this synthesis is further expressed in the diagrammatic presentation of other proposals.

PLAN FOR LONDON

by the M.A.R.S. Group

A Residential Units
B Main Shopping Center
C Administrative and Cultural Center
D Heavy Industry
E Local Industry
F Main Railway and Passenger Stations
G Belt Rail Line

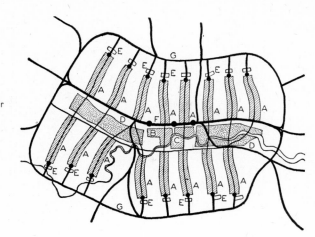

Using the neighborhood unit to form "townships" (Chap. 21), José Sert suggests their assembly along transportation routes. In this plan as in other plans, transportation assumes its natural role of connecting the individual functional elements of a city in contrast to the present action of traffic and transportation, that of spewing people, business, and factories indiscriminately about the urban scene. Organic recentralization rather than random decentralization is the theme in this and other plans, and Sert has emphasized the necessity for a relation between the "organization of space" and the organization of the movement of people about and between these spaces. He suggests a 15-minute period as the measurement of distance between the home and the workshop. The townships offer convenient access to civic and cultural centers, to employment sources in light industrial areas, and natural open space surrounding them.

Believing that the destruction by war offered an opportunity for a radical reformation of London, a number of British architects, who identified themselves as the M.A.R.S. group, suggested a general plan for space reorganization. A series of residential units connected by mass transportation to the industrial, commercial and transportation spine along the Thames River, the plan provides for broad greenbelts separating all elements of the city. A rail belt-line encircles the city for distribution to sub-centers and local industries.

Defining his theories, Ludwig Hilberseimer suggests an alternate space organization for London. Heavy smoke- and gas-producing industries are removed from the commercial and administrative districts. The plan is arranged with the intention that the residential units would be closely related to the various sources of employment; dwelling districts are related to each of these sources: heavy industry, light industry, commerce, trade and administration. As in the M.A.R.S. plan, these land uses are generally retained in their present location with the exception of heavy industry in the Hilberseimer plan. Rather than a belt-line as proposed in the M.A.R.S. plan, Hilberseimer suggests the advantage to expansion by the use of spur lines extending from the central rail spine for distribution of goods and people. The relation between dwelling areas and light industry or commercial land uses is illustrated in a manner reminiscent of the Sert plan; another illustration demonstrates the relation between dwelling areas and heavy industry, residential development being located within areas lying leeward of winds that carry obnoxious smoke and fumes.

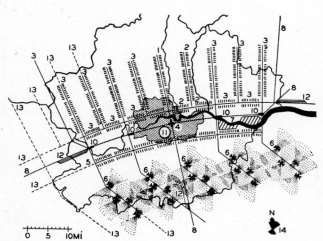

0 5 10Mi

From *The New City*, L. Hilberseimer, published by Paul Theobald

DIAGRAMMATIC SKETCH FOR LONDON, by Hilberseimer, 1941

1 Political Administration
2 Financial Administration
3 Commercial Administration
4 Central Station
5 Smokeless Industry
6 Smoke-producing Industry
7 Port of London
8 Long-distance Railroad
10 Main Railroad Station
11 Airport
12 Railroad Yards
13 Possible Extensions
14 Wind Diagram

Areas 1, 2, 3, 5, and 6 include Residential Districts

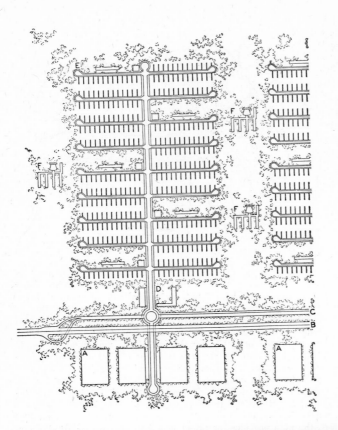

Relationship of Residential Areas to Light Industrial and Commercial Areas, as Proposed by Hilberseimer.

A Industry

B Main Highway

C Local Highway

D Commercial Area

E Residential Area

F Schools in Park Area

Hilberseimer's Wind Diagram for Smoke-producing Industry and Residential Areas.

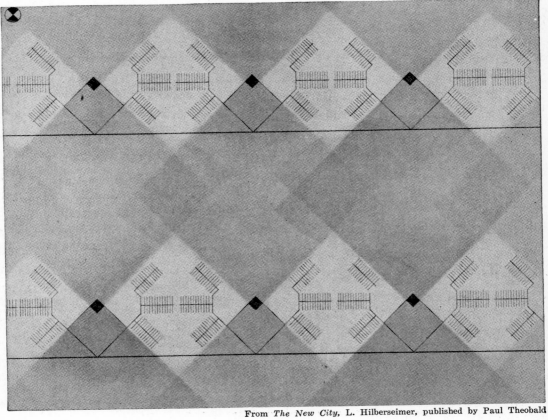

From *The New City*, L. Hilberseimer, published by Paul Theobald

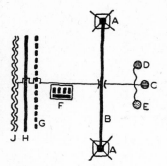

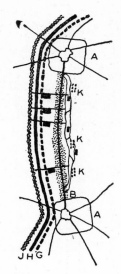

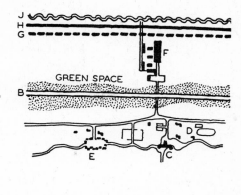

LA CITÉ INDUSTRIELLE

by Le Corbusier

A   Existing Central City
B   Auto Highway
C   Vertical Residences
D   Community Facilities
E   Horizontal Residences

F   Factories
G   Railroad
H   Service Highway
J   River
K   Industrial Communities

In 1945 ASCORAL, under the leadership of Le Corbusier, shifted attention from the existing urban center to a consideration of the basic organization of urban settlement in this industrial age. In the studies by this group, we find a fusion between the concentric form of the "garden city" and the ribbon form of the "linear city." The principal forms of circulation—water, rail, air and highway—become the arteries along which self-contained industrial cities are distributed. Although it is assumed that open space surrounding these industrial clusters would be maintained, the "greenbelt" is here used as a buffer between the various and separate land uses: housing, highway, and factories.

The basic organization is shown in the left-hand sketch, the passenger highway connecting the great existing cities, and between it and the river, rail line, and service highway are the groups of "green factories." Opposite are the housing areas which contain the administrative, shopping, sports, and educational facilities for the immediate population. The existing metropolis remains the principal administrative, commercial, and cultural center.

The sketch at the center indicates the distribution of industrial "cities" between the great cities, and the one on the right indicates the separation of traffic forms: the distinction between through traffic and local traffic, and the separation between them. Le Corbusier retains the tall building—the vertical residence—for apartments near the civic center while he places the community of single-family homes away from this center for the greater freedom for families.

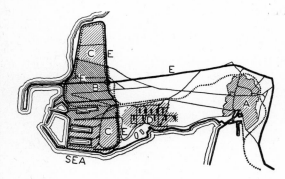

LA ROCHELLE–PALLICE

A   Old City of La Rochelle
B   Old Industrial Area of La Pallice
C   Extension of Industrial Area
D   New Vertical City
E   Highways
Dotted Lines Show Railroads

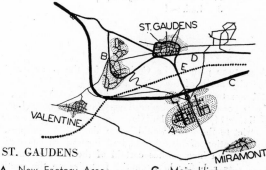

ST. GAUDENS LA ROCHELLE–PALLICE

In addition to St. Dié, Le Corbusier prepared plans for the reconstruction of these two cities, the application of the "industrial city" theory being even more apparent in the separation of rail and highway traffic from the housing areas, and the removal of new residential development from the existing city.

ST. GAUDENS

A   New Factory Area
B   New Residential Area with Community Facilities
C   Main Highway
D   Secondary Highways
E   Railroad

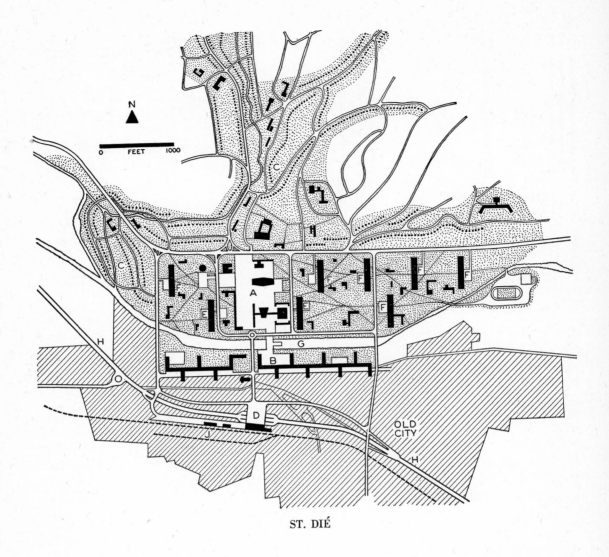

ST. DIÉ

A Civic and Cultural Center
B Industry
C Single-Family Houses
D Railroad Station
E Tall Apartment Buildings (First Stage)
F Tall Apartment Buildings (Second Stage)
G Meurthe River
H Automobile Highway
J Railroad

A postwar plan by Le Corbusier for the reconstruction of St. Dié. Destroyed by bombs, the central part of the city north of the River Meurthe has been replanned as the civic, cultural, and residential section. Eight tall apartment buildings surround the civic center, each building being about 150 feet high and housing 1,500 persons. The displaced population numbered 10,000 people, and the initial development presupposes the building of four tall buildings—a "vertical garden city"—to accommodate 6,000 people, while the single-family district to the north would house about 4,000 persons. The large open space throughout the town plan permits the retention of historic old buildings which survived the fire of war.

The plan incorporates certain of the theories embraced in the "industrial city" scheme—the Meurthe River serves as a buffer between the factories on the south bank and the residential and civic area on the north. The large cells created by the major traffic arteries are developed as landscaped parks and informal pedestrian circulation.

Incorporating these same features, Ludwig Hilberseimer emphasizes the orientation of the city and the appropriate relation of industry to residential areas. The pollution of air is a nuisance beyond present control. Not only is it a hazard to the physical health of the people, but it is a detriment to stability of urban land use and values. Until the location of industry and the mechanical control of smoke and fumes are treated simultaneously there is little, if any, prospect for abatement of the industrial nuisance and its deleterious effect upon the urban environment.

Reformation of the urban structure suggested by the New Utopians received some impetus through the necessity for reconstruction after World War II. Le Corbusier, with his typical zeal, tackled the replanning of St. Dié, St. Gaudens, and La Rochelle-Pallice. In these projects he applied the theories which emerged in the ASCORAL research. The pattern of a unit of the linear industrial city was overlaid upon the ruins of St. Dié.

The River Meurthe bisects the town. A principal highway is planned through the south half; the industrial area occupies the space between this and the river. North of the river is the residential and cultural city. Eight skyscrapers set in broad space are planned, and houses are distributed about the periphery. Half the population affected by the devastation of bombing—about 10,500 people—will be housed in four skyscrapers, the other half in the garden city of single dwellings and gardens.

The plans for St. Gaudens and La Rochelle-Pallice leave the old cities intact. New areas are developed for industry and residence. The theoretical relation of the urban functions represented in the linear industrial city is applied. In St. Gaudens, the railway and a new highway separate the factory district from the old city. A vertical garden city is on one side of the old town, a horizontal city of single houses on the other. The old city of La Rochelle is protected by a broad "greenbelt," the present industrial city of Pallice is expanded along the waterfront, and between the two is the vertical city of tall buildings which also enjoy a site overlooking the sea.

On Common Ground. Implicit in the planning theories of the New Utopians is the basic assumption that land allocated for specific uses will be reserved for those purposes only. This seems a reasonable assumption; presumably it is the reason for planning land use, but it is quite contrary to our current practice of zoning.

It is our present concept of zoning that the intensity of land use recedes outwardly from the center of the city with the provision that land zoned for one use may also be devoted to other uses of lesser "economic" intensity. Thus all uses are permitted in an industrial zone, and only industry is excluded from commercial zones while all types of dwellings are permitted therein. This sequence ends with the single-family zone as the only area reserved solely for its specified use.

Mixed land uses, the characteristic of present urban development, would be excluded in the proposals of the New Utopians. Were this premise to be adopted in our cities today, the gap between them and the theoretical studies of the New Utopians would be far less than a casual comparison might suggest. Reorganization of the urban pattern suggested by the New Utopians is not essentially different from the current

BROADACRES
by Frank Lloyd Wright

Essentially a "linear" city form, Frank Lloyd Wright's proposal distributes industry, commerce, housing, social facilities, and agriculture along the railroad artery and has access to highways. The unit which dominates this plan is the minimum of one acre of land for each family rather than the neighborhood unit, although the various neighborhood facilities are provided.

A County Seat Administration

B Airport

C Sports

D Professional Offices

E Stadium

F Hotel

G Sanitarium

H Small Industry

J Small Farms

K Park

L Motor Inn

M Industry

N Merchandising

P Railroad

R Orchards

S Homes and Apartments

T Temple and Cemetery

U Research

V Zoo

W Schools

Area of Plan is
Two Square Miles

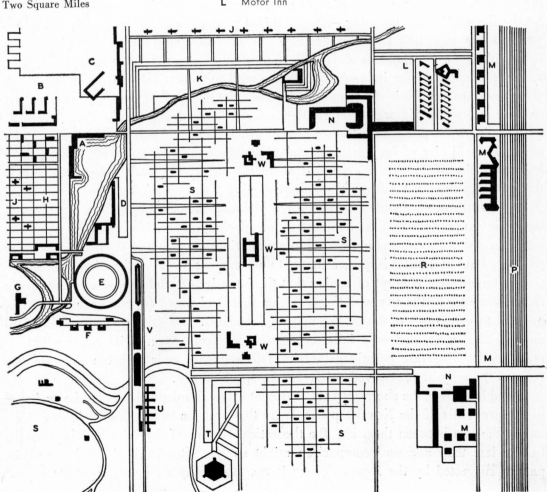

CITADE DES MOTORES near Rio de Janeiro

Paul Lester Wiener and José Sert

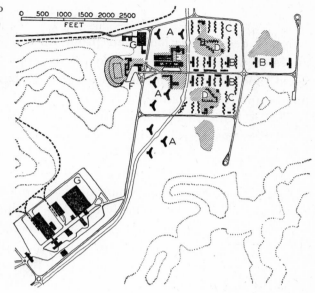

A Dormitories

B Tall Apartment Build-
   ings

C Low Dwellings

D Parks, Schools, Shop-
   ping

E Civic Center

F Sports Center

G Industry

Shaded Areas Are Com-
munity Space

A city planned for aircraft production was sponsored by the government of Brazil. Contemplating an ultimate population of 25,000, the plan provides four neighborhoods, each having a population of about 6,000 persons. Each neighborhood contains eight-story dormitory buildings, each accommodating 800 persons, located near the industrial areas; eight-story apartment buildings housing a total of about 1,200 persons; 2,600 people in three-story apartment buildings; and a school, and social facilities. A central business district and sports center are located near the residential section, the principal factory area being somewhat removed.

The major traffic arteries surround and demark the neighborhood units, by-passing, and not traversing, either the residential units or the commercial (civic) center.

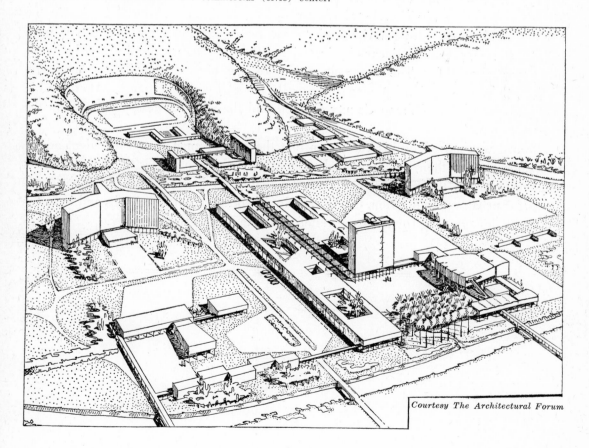

Courtesy The Architectural Forum

trend of decentralization; their proposition is that the use of urban land shall be allocated with reasonable attention to the appropriate purpose for which it is designated, and their designs acknowledge the characteristics of today's industry, commerce, and transportation.

This is a disarming thesis since mixed land uses permitted under current zoning regulations accelerate disintegration of the urban environment. Were the uses prescribed in the zoning plan for most of our cities today the only uses to which the land could be put, excess zoning for industry and business would be discouraged, zoning for multi-family buildings would diminish in areas where single-family dwellings are the predominant and admittedly desirable habitations, and the case for orderly urban growth would be more clearly established. Zoning which permits mixed land uses invites speculation on a future shift in value and, although this inducement may turn a profit for some, it becomes a deteriorating force in the community.

There is a perceptible line of continuity springing from the dismal factory town of the nineteenth century to the Garden City of Ebenezer Howard and thence to the linear industrial city of Le Corbusier. This line moves at a tangent to the city we know today, but there is an affinity with the decentralization that is drawing the lifeblood away from the overgrown, overzoned, and congested metropolis.

Howard espoused a return to the human scale of the neighborhood community, and Le Corbusier seeks an organic relation between home and workshop. Howard took his leave from the big city, Le Corbusier spaces his industrial communities in the country, and Frank Lloyd Wright rejects the metropolis with his suggestion for a county government and a linear city in which at least an acre of land would be available for every family. The greenbelt of Howard's garden city is likewise an ingredient of the New Utopians' plans; it is equally integral with the plan by Abercrombie and Forshaw for the London County Council and the more radical proposals by the MARS group.

Howard was moved by his conviction that the people must have convenient access to open space and their places of work. The same conviction guides the New Utopians and the plans for the English New Towns. Lagging far behind these forthright statements for urban reorganization, the disorderly decentralization of suburbs and industry is nevertheless groping for the same relief from the great cities of today.

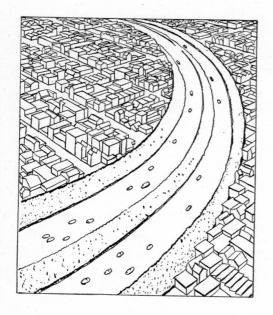

CHAPTER 28

METAMORPHOSIS

Symbols of Purpose. Freedom is a native characteristic of mankind. It has been sought and fought for from time immemorial. Transcending creature instinct for self-preservation, the human mind makes of man a social entity. The creature is conditioned by its environment, whereas man, through his intellect, has the capacity to mold his environment to his purpose. Purpose, then, lies at the vital core of human conduct.

Material progress marks peaks of civilization, but the culture of a people is measured by relative social values and the purpose that directs human progress. The cultivation of human sensibilities, the shaping of intuitive powers, and the spiritual content of social institutions elevate a people to the cultural plane. These processes are nurtured in the soil of freedom wherein people share responsibility for society and each man is an active collaborator with his fellowman in directing their mutual affairs.

The city is a laboratory in which the search for freedom is carried on and experiences are tested. The design of the city is the warp and woof of people's lives; the pattern is woven with the toil of mind and hand guided by a purpose. We cannot dissociate purpose from achievement in evaluating the affairs of men or charting a course toward human welfare. We detect symbols of that purpose in city building; symbols of the dominant will of a tyrant or the common weal of free men, the rigid formality of ruling authority or the plastic form of liberty, the sumptuous pretension of aristocracy or the humble simplicity of democracy.

The Pharaohs of Egypt created their symbol of unity—the pyramid. Forged with the toil of countless slaves, the pyramid is a symbol of the unity of uncontested power wielded by autocratic rulers over the lives of people. The Emperors of Rome built great fora, a series of huge projects dedicated to the glory of mighty rulers.

Each forum was designed about an axis, the arrangement of structures and spaces dictated by symmetry. Like a symbol of undaunted might the centerline dominated the cities built by emperors, and when their power waned there were no strong citizens to sustain the social order.

The monarchs of France built avenues and plazas designed about the symbolic axis of autocratic power. The liberated space of the baroque city was appropriated by the rulers rather than the ruled. Louis XIV built his palace and gardens at Versailles. Aloof from the motley crowd of the city, he transferred his court to these magnificent spaces and ordered the streets to focus upon them. *L'état, c'est moi.* . . . Louis XV built the Place de la Concorde and in the center of the formal square he placed a statue of himself. The city was a formless mass of slums on which the bloated forms of palaces and gardens, boulevards and plazas were grafted. The urban population lost its identity as the people and became the crowd. Uniform façades lined the avenues as a frame for royalty. The people receded to the borders of the boulevards and took their places as spectators of the stately display rather than participants.

The city of Hellenic democracy was planned for the people. The houses were designed for the amenities of living—each dwelling arranged as every other dwelling for appropriate orientation and privacy. The agora was the meeting place for people and the market place and center of urban activity designed as an outdoor room for the mingling of citizens. The axis was incidental, it was not a dominant feature. Hellenic builders composed rectilinear forms with subtle refinement, shifted the scene from major to minor squares, and surrounded them with the continuous rhythm of colonnades. Streets did not bisect and obstruct the open space reserved for public assembly, and sculpture adorned the public square about the periphery of the open space. Size itself was not the aim of Greek city builders. The agora was large enough to accommodate the citizen population; its space was commodious, but the urban population was small. A monumental quality in public spaces was obtained through a juxtaposition of small and large spaces, contrast between the shape of forms, and the rhythm of voids and solids. The distinction between space for the movement across and circulation within the simple rectangular forms produced an order of quiet dignity.

Human scale was the measure of design in the Hellenic city, and it likewise guided the builders of the medieval town. Emerging from the Dark Ages and unprotected by the broad reaches of empire, the feudal town huddled within the confines of its encircling walls. The church provided the new common bond for humanity and, in response to the spiritual need of the people, the cathedral dominated the town but was not set apart from its surroundings. Built against other buildings, it formed an integral part of the enclosing walls of the plaza. Town life centered upon this plaza and it was designed for the mingling of people intent upon exchanging the products of their labor and learning the news of their fellowmen. The urban facilities were designed for use and they were arranged accordingly. Roadways traversed the plaza but left open space free for the movement of people. Fountains served the vital

THE PYRAMIDS, Symbols of Totalitarian Might

A HUMAN SCALE

The scale of the space-forms in cities reflects in some measure the degree of participation a people enjoyed in their civic affairs. The agora of the Hellenic city (see page 21) was large enough to accommodate the citizen population; its space was commodious but the city population was small. Size itself was not the aim of Greek city builders; the human scale was a measure of design for their urban environment. A monumental quality was obtained through the juxtaposition of small and large spaces, the contrast between the shape of forms and the rhythm of voids and solids.

The self-reliance of ancient society produced the unity of solid horizontal forms, the positive rhythm of colonnades. Builders in the Middle Ages, less certain of their mortal destiny, directed their vertical forms toward infinity. Released from the limitations of the monolithic structure of ancient forms, the heavy walls of the Roman vault, a greater play of forms was introduced to the medieval town. The massive forms of the classic city were transformed into the pointed arch and the flying buttress thrust heavenward to the spiritual unity of Christendom.

There was harmony among these forms, but devices were employed to link the enclosing frame of the open spaces. The width of streets entering a plaza was pinched, or the openings were spanned with a portal. Adjacent roads were diverted to spread the effect of their opening entering the square; or they were joined to enter the plaza as a single opening. Building mass was increased to compensate for the gap created by two intersecting streets at a corner of the square. Irregular angles of entering streets distorted the perspective to subdue the apparent penetration of enclosing walls.

Intimate scale marked the church square and the marketplace of the medieval town (opposite). The great bulk of the cathedral was given scale by the variety of its structural forms and sculptural interstices. Its mass was fused with the scale of the open space. Its size dominated the town—such was the spiritual need of a people emerging from the Dark Ages—but it was not set apart from its surroundings. It was a part of them, built against other buildings on one or more sides, and becoming an integral part of the enclosing walls. When its size warranted, more than one plaza was created about its dominant features, a façade, a tower, or a transept.

Sculpture adorned the public spaces, but they were placed so as to avoid interference with the natural circulation about the marketplace.

Serving as the principal water supply, fountains were situated to one side of open spaces, accessible for use without obstructing circulation. The parts of the urban form were disposed in a manner natural to their function in the community and, although this description is not intended to encourage a return to or the adaptation of the "picturesque medieval town" in development of the industrial and commercial city of tomorrow, we might well compare the integral character of the ancient urban forms with the unrelated and useless ornamental centerpieces to which many features of the contemporary urban scene have degenerated.

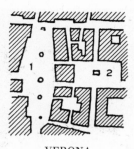

VERONA

1 Piazza d'Erbe
2 Piazza dei Signoria

San Michele
LUCCA

Cathedral Square
VERONA

Saint Louis Plaza
AUTUN

1 Fountain

MODENA

Cathedral Square
RAVENNA

San Fermo Maggiore
VERONA

Santa Anastasia
VERONA

Piazza del Santo
PADUA

1 Fountain and Statue

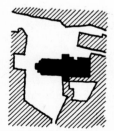

HILDESHEIM
Cathedral

WURZBURG
Cathedral

THE MEDIEVAL CITY

Piazza dei Signoria
FLORENCE

1 Fountain and Original Statue of David

function of water supply and they, like buildings and sculpture, were not isolated within the open space of the public squares.

City design is inextricably woven in the social order of people. The design reveals symbols of the dominant economic, social, political, and spiritual patterns of civilization. The city is a melting pot of cultural forces and its design is the expression.

Eclecticism. In the latter part of the eighteenth and early nineteenth centuries social upheaval burst the bonds of monarchical tyranny; the violent tensions of the industrial revolution broke the chain of cultural development. A new freedom was unleashed, but uncertainty of our cultural direction aroused emotional conflicts. An air of overconfidence concealed the indecision of society. The fancy of personal taste was the new right of every individual and it confused critical judgment. Taste sunk to mediocre levels, and ugliness settled upon the city.

Recoiling from the dread monotony of the industrial city, people sought escape from the ugly reality. They cloaked public edifices with an artificial pomposity and found retreat in dwellings that simulated sumptuous surroundings of a glorified ancestry. As though to insulate themselves from esthetic degradation, the arts donned the mantle of classic pedigree. A cultural veneer obscured the ugly environment of the "brown decades" and eclecticism engulfed society. Artificial taste flavored parlor conversation on the arts. Art became a commodity to be bought, sold, and collected; it moved from the streets of the people into the salon.

The muralist who once adorned the walls of buildings stepped down from his scaffold, retired to his studio, and painted pictures to be framed and hung in galleries. Works of art were no longer integral with the environment of people. The stained glass legends of the cathedral were replaced by book printing. Sculptured figures draped in Roman togas were fitted into the classic pediments of banks and court houses. Fountains no longer supplied water for the population; they dripped or spouted in memory of some event or person.

Civic design reflected the confusion and uncertainty about esthetics. Scholars studied the cities of old; they observed the assurance and strong centerline of imperialism and the picturesqueness of the Middle Ages. The past was like a vast storehouse of historic forms available for reproduction. New buildings, each with its historic prototype, were assembled about a whole complex of axes shooting off in all directions. Plazas were laced with major and minor axes, streets bisected open spaces at diagonals and at right angles, avenues focused upon pompous structures, and a galaxy of artificial features, statues, fountains, and formal landscape effects were arbitrarily distributed about these spaces. The variety of symmetrical effects interrupted the flow of traffic; both the utility and the scale of open spaces were lost to the people who traversed them.

The grandiose formality of open spaces was awe-inspiring, and the people were impressed. The grand planning of the World's Fairs "took." Like the great Mall in Washington, D.C., generous open space was admired but did not invite relaxation and rarely served as gathering places for the people. Their formal character was more like a picture to be observed rather than partaken of. The delightful quality of our capital city lies in the fine old elm trees that grace the residential streets and the quaint Georgian houses of the eighteenth century. Frederick Law Olmsted, the great landscape architect, strove to design open spaces for the people rather than an abstract feature in a grand plan, and Central Park in New York City is a case in point. While the people might be better served if this huge space had been more adequately distributed, it is nevertheless designed as a natural park for the people to use.

Eclecticism was a masquerade, and a veritable bazaar of planning forms appeared. The face of the city concealed the misshapen bulk behind the masque. Once functional features occupying a graceful place in the environment of people were now used as decorations on the false face of the city. The shopping street became the main variety show, but there were also special features. Forms of ancient Rome were frozen into civic centers, and plazas were carved out of slums to reveal a railroad station or open a traffic artery. New obstructions were then substituted: interrupting "squares" or "circles" as spots in which to isolate diminutive statues. The entire range of architectural and planning styles from the past were applied to the new city. Tastes were torn asunder in the process of selecting the appropriate garment or applying the right cosmetic. Inspired by the Gothic cathedral, the impressiveness of St. Peter's, the charm of the colonial meeting house, and the dignity of the Georgian mansion, the choice was not an easy one.

Cities Are Dated. Eclecticism with its parade of "styles" beclouded the tradition of city building, concealing the fact that urban forms in all great periods of culture were the contemporary expression of creative workers in their day. Neither order in our cities nor culture in our society can be expected without the creative expression of the contemporary character of our time.

There were undoubtedly accidental effects among the attractive features in cities of old, but we may be reasonably confident that the harmony is not due alone to the patina of age. There is an integrity of character in fine buildings and spaces that commands respect through the years. It is the integrity of creative effort, the quality of being *genuine*. It is the quality that gives harmony and continuity to creative works of all cultures. The process of reproducing the works from another period leaves a cultural void, and eclecticism is the expression of that void in our present stage of civilization.

When we observe the cities of old, we find little evidence of the eclecticism we suffer today. Cultures developed their own characteristics and it is by these characteristics that we identify them. When we detect signs of imitation we suspect a decline in civilization or a culture that is not yet mature. Cultures grew, expanded, evolved; just so did the forms of their cities. Changes in the style of buildings were reflected in the forms. A cathedral begun during the Romanesque period was built with heavy walls and small windows, round arches and vaults. Additions during the Gothic period were designed with pointed arches, refined tracery, and flying buttresses. The parts of a building were *dated*; we identify the time when they were built by the style in which they were built. The quality of thus speaking from the past is one we respect; it tells us of the character of the people; it has meaning for us.

Is it not significant that builders of today assume an opposite view of building design? How often we have observed objection to a design which would "date" a building. This contradiction marks a singular contrast with building of past ages and it is, in truth, the base following of fancy, the fashion of substituting artificial pedigree for creative expression. If we were to follow the tradition of great cultures of the past, we today would engage in the most powerful period of creative contemporary city building the world has ever seen. We have the people, the tools, the science, the industry, and the ingenuity to make the finest cities of all time.

Symmetry or Freedom? Democracy in city building is a framework in which the manifold functions of contemporary urban life may be accommodated with freedom of expression. Such freedom in organized society, as we are gradually coming to realize, implies self-discipline and respect for the dignity of our fellowmen.

Building laws not only permit but have actually forced an enormous bulk to be loaded on the land. Consequently, the city has been reduced to a network of street pavements lined with façades of unrelated buildings. Architectural banality and chaos are inevitable. The "right" to build as one wishes has approached a degree of license, and the ugliness has frequently provoked the panacea of architectural control.

In the name of democracy the proponents of architectural control suggest it will not interfere with free expression. Actually there is little else it can do. By its nature architectural control sets a form, usually in terms of some particular "style of architecture" or its equivalent, and the designer is henceforth bound by the capricious taste of a select few.

There are designers who produce a higher order of creative work than men of lesser talent, but should their genius deny the right of self-expression to those of lesser competence? Rare is the genius in the welter of men that can capture the sublime in steel, stone, and space. This is clear when we observe all the buildings of past ages rather than the isolated monuments alone. If talent to produce appropriate and beautiful buildings is limited, it is the task of society to raise the level of competence and widen the cultural horizon, not remove freedom of expression.

The city takes shape over the years through the enterprise of all the people. Moved by their desires, their opportunities, and the evolution of changing conditions, the city is in a continuous state of flux and its plan must accommodate a variety of forms. Eclecticism cultivated the impression that harmony of form is synonymous with symmetry, and planning assumed a rigid formality. Symmetry about an axis was assumed to produce a grand unity among the forms of the city. City building did not follow those plans, however, and the result was most discouraging if not a little puzzling; it seemed that planning was a futile enterprise and indeed the form it had acquired was futile.

There was reason for the failure of "grand" planning: boldly reminiscent of imperial domination over the lives of people, its forms were inimical to the tenets of democracy. Not only is the urge for free expression an integral characteristic of

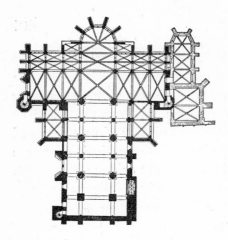

BUILDINGS ARE DATED

To be genuine is a characteristic of integrity
and this is a distinguishing feature of the cultures of past ages. When men built they did so
in the essential spirit of their times, and, in turn,
the builders served in the shaping of that spirit.
This is discernible in such a structure as the little
church of Saint Nazaire in Carcassonne. Begun
in the 12th century, the front and nave of the
church was in the Romanesque style. The apse
was not completed until late in the 13th and early
14th centuries and was built in the Gothic manner of the time. The differences are seen in the
photographs, and the heavy masonry of the
original portion is distinguishable in the plan
from the lighter structure of the Gothic addition.
The significance of ancient buildings and towns

is due in large part to the distinctive character they portray for us. It is this character that forms the real
tradition of culture—it is this tradition which has since vanished and needs restoration in city building of our
time—the tradition of solving problems and shaping an esthetic in contemporary terms.

PIAZZETTA OF
SAN MARCO,
VENICE

democratic society, it is a distinct right. There can be no "centerline" about which the city of democracy is built; it is a fluid, changing form. The rigid symmetry of formal planning is alien to democracy. An autocrat may decree a great plan and he has the power to draft the labor of people to execute it accordingly, but when that power transfers to the people a new concept of urban conduct emerges. It is then the people seek a set of standards we call laws adopted according to the will of the people as guides in the conduct of their mutual and independent affairs. A new concept of planning also emerges, not less compelling but more plastic and sensitive to the will and expression of individuals in society. The "grand" plan was conceived by a single mind to be imposed upon the future. Thenceforth skill in its execution was not the creative power of the individual to solve a problem, but the ingenuity with which the requirements of a later time could be warped into a precast mold. It was suggestive of a solution before the problem was stated.

That democracy imposes great responsibility upon the individual is self-evident; with the privilege of freedom goes responsibility. Harmony in the city of democracy calls for the exercise of individual responsibility and the mutual self-respect of a people. Since it was by means counter to democratic processes that a monarch carried out a vast venture like Versailles, so it is contrary to democratic behavior that individuals should ignore the works of others to memorialize their own vanity or expand the contents of their purses. Rivalry for "bigger and better" cities can do no more to open the way to creative civic design than can the stamp of classic planning.

The harmonious integration of various forms is the art of planning space, and the Piazza of St. Mark's in Venice is a classic illustration.

Building the Piazza of St. Mark's spanned five centuries. In it we find no sterile symmetry. It was an open space in which throngs of people could congregate. The ornate church of St. Mark's was erected in the eleventh century in the flourishing Byzantine style. The Palace of the Doges, built in the fourteenth and fifteenth centuries, was designed in the Gothic style of that period. It was a colorful building, but the façades were simple rectangles facing the sea and forming one side of the Piazzetta. The façade leading from the waterfront was set back to frame a view of the church from the canal. Detached from the church, the Campanile was a powerful accent in the group arrangement. When the Procuriatie buildings were built—late fifteenth and early sixteenth centuries—the Renaissance style was in flower. They were arranged about a long Piazza placed at right angles to the Piazzetta. Located at the intersection of these two plazas, the Campanile was visually linked with the long façades of the Procuriatie Vecchie and Library; the tower was not isolated in space like a centerpiece.

There was variety among the forms, each successive addition to the plaza built in the "style" of its period. The spaces were planned to harmonize these variations; no part was tacked on to complete an "original." The differences in architectural styles enhance the effect of this great plaza, the absence of axial symmetry impresses the observer. The flat façade of the Doges' Palace was not imitated elsewhere to conform to a preconceived "scheme"; the façades of the Procuriatie buildings were stretched into an oblong plan at an angle to the Piazzetta, and the contrasts in the forms and spaces were emphasized by slanting the buildings in plan. The plastic quality of this great plaza is eloquent refutation of the sterile process of symmetrical planning which has been frequently substituted for monumentality in our period of eclecticism.

Forms may be harmoniously integrated by appropriate contrasts—contrasts in plan forms adjusted to accommodate the contrasts in contemporary expression as it evolves in successive periods of culture. Michelangelo sought such a contrast when he selected the location for his sixteenth-century statue of David against the background of the rough-hewn walls of the fourteenth-century Palazzo Vecchio in Florence. Rather than becoming an unrelated centerpiece to which similar features have since degenerated, this statue was treated as an integral part of the design of the Piazza dei Signoria.

New Dimensions. With the abundant labor of slaves ancient cities were built of blocks of stone and wood, their heavy forms refined by sculpturing the structural members. Laying stone upon stone the medieval builders formed soaring arches, flying buttresses, and intricate tracery. During all these centuries all construction was wall-bearing; all structural stresses were in compression.

The industrial revolution brought a violent change. The massive construction of ancient cities was transformed to the lightness of steel in tension. Processed in the crucibles of smelting plants and testing laboratories, materials were refined, their basic qualities extracted and synthesized. A wide range of synthetic materials were assembled mechanically upon light structural frames. The dynamism of forces in tension replaced the static forms of compression, and the machine released a new freedom in the organization of space.

With the positive thrusts of railway, highway, and airway, new dimensions penetrated the twentieth-century city. Vehicles of transportation no longer mingle informally in the fashion of the Middle Ages. Seeking channels of uninterrupted directness, moving with uncompromising direction, straight ribbons stretch across level spaces and merge with irregular terrain in graceful sweeping curves. The highway is shaped to the contours of the land. Continuity is uninterrupted by natural obstacles; with almost defiant sureness bridges span chasms and tunnels pierce mountains. Unimpeded continuity is essential and insistent. Almost unnoticed, this new dimension has forced a new scale in city building.

The new scale appears in the Mount Vernon highway, the Westchester County Parkways, the New York City freeways, and the Outer Drive in Chicago. More rural than urban, the parkway combined with clear channel rapid transit for mass transportation is the salvation of the traffic dilemma in the heart of the city.

Matching the expanse of the parkway is the horizontal span of enclosed floor space. The city of today is a series of horizontal planes, one above the other, and the relatively constant floor heights retain the impression of human scale. Utility and economy are inconsistent with the inflated scale of eclecticism; excesses in scale that characterized the Baroque city are restrained. Scale is not absent in the volume of floor space enclosed in tall buildings; it has been lost in the congestion of these buildings upon the land—the absence of open space as a foil for their size. The skyscraper readily expresses the multiplicity of its floors, but the sense of scale has been destroyed by the depressive bulk of buildings in proportion to the open space about them. It is toward the restoration of adequate space that the new dimensions of the city are forcing urban development.

The Parkway. The parkway brooks no interference; freedom of movement is continuous. The futility of the usual network of streets is exposed. Like an irresistible force meeting an immovable object, the freeway meets the gridiron. The static form of the right angle meets the dynamic thrust of free form.

A rectilinear street arrangement has been generally interpreted as evidence of conscious planning. The assumption must be qualified by an appraisal of the purpose and functions for which the form was devised. The Roman city was patterned after the military camp, and agricultural and urban land has been subdivided into rectilinear plots, but it does not necessarily follow that the organization of a military camp or a convenient form for legal description and recording of deeds are keys to the conscious design of cities for the residence and commerce of people. On the other hand, Hippodamus adopted the checkerboard street arrangement for the purpose of allocating lots which would provide proper orientation of all the dwelling units erected upon them. Vehicular traffic was light, towns were small, and direct communication about them was of no particular import.

Today the city is the battleground between the right angle and the curve; the tight gridiron of the surveyor versus the swirling twists of our "planned" suburbia. The battle is being waged in a vacuum; chaos prevails in both, the monotony of one, the variety of disorder in the other. The process is one of dividing the land rather than forming spaces, laying out roads and lots rather than planning appropriate and related uses, and allocating parcels as merchandise tagged with a price rather than arranging space for living or business.

Planning circulation about the city implies a twofold purpose: the direct and natural connection between two or more points, and clear direction for those traversing the roadways. The gridiron provides the latter, but it is essentially a devious zigzag route between two points. Complete loss of orientation is the curse of curving roadways, and no amount of picturesqueness can compensate for the confusion it creates.

A test of planning is the order it produces, and the freeway is a new instrument for orderly space arrangement. Its horizontal expanse clearly defines it as an artery with positive direction in contrast to minor roadways. Reliance upon signs of nature or the rigid orientation of the gridiron in the old city is supplanted by the positive identification and direction of the sweeping freeway. A dominant feature of the modern city, it brings time and space into harmony. The parkway is destined to force an orderly development not yet apparent in the cluttered urban environment, or it will sweep the city clean.

The Penetration of Space. Just as the freeway has rendered obsolete the cor-

Proposed
Down-town Interchange
Buffalo, N.Y.

N. Y. D. P. U.

THE PENETRATION OF SPACE

Ignoring the present street system, the freeway slashes across the city, opening spaces hitherto strange to the urban dweller, and new housing of our day bears little resemblance, as a living environment, to the urban dwellings of a generation past. These pictures and those on the following pages do not illustrate the future urban environment, but they are the signs that mark the path to that future.

Aerial Photograph Co.

TRIBORO BRIDGE, New York City

THE PENETRATION OF SPACE   CALIFORNIA FREEWAYS

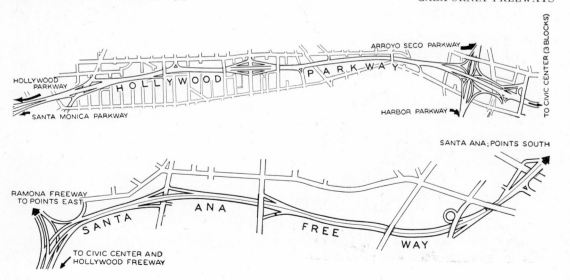

New York City Housing Authority

JAMES WELDON JOHNSON HOUSES, New
York City

SPACE IS RETURNING TO THE CITY

Parking Lots Open up the City

BALDWIN HILLS VILLAGE, Los Angeles

Margaret Lowe

ridor and gridiron street, a new relation between buildings and open space was introduced in the great housing developments during the 1920–30 decade. Park-like open space was incorporated in the eighteenth-century "terrace" dwellings of the Royal Crescent and Lansdowne Crescent in Bath and Regent's Park in London, and the "squares" of Bloomsbury introduced the garden to residential streets. However these developments were generally confined to the aristocratic classes, and the amenities were absent from the living environment of the majority of the urban population. Berlage in Holland and Otto Wagner in Vienna, during the early twentieth century, strove to treat the dwellings of the people as integral parts of civic design, but they retained the corridor street and uniform façades reminiscent of Baroque planning.

When the international housing crisis after World War I forced a widespread program of dwelling construction, the new dimensions pierced the archaic armor of the city. Large-scale planning, freed from the restrictions of single lots, completely altered the relation between dwelling and open space. The corridor street was abandoned, space between building façades was no longer devoted exclusively to vehicular circulation, and building units were arranged in orderly groups within free open space.

Space was designed for use, traffic arteries by-passed residential groups, and internal circulation was by way of service roadways and pedestrian walks. Recreation space was accessible from all dwellings, and buildings were planned so each dwelling unit enjoyed the same orientation as every other dwelling. For the first time since the building of Hellenic cities a common standard of amenities was applied uniformly to all dwellings in the community plan. There was an affinity between the continuity and breadth of space along the parkway and the flow of space through the developments of large-scale housing.

The infiltration of space in the center of the city is insistent although it expresses the anachronism of urban growth. While automobile parking lots expand and slums are cleared, adjacent lots are improved with a greater density than before and congestion persists round about; one ugly improvement is substituted for another. Nevertheless, space is forcing its way into the heart of the city.

Much land still lies vacant within the city and more lies fallow on the periphery. No pattern, no plan, and little thought have been directed to the future destiny of this land save outmoded zoning and ineffective building laws. Should we not profit by experience? The tragic results of chaotic expansion lie all about us, the heavy hand of public debt gropes frantically to support the crumbling environment, and all because we waited too long!

To pursue this course is to invite the same ills that now plague the central urban areas—and incur the same debt for blight and redevelopment again and again. It is a challenge to invest in the future.

Laws to prevent the abusive use of land is one step. Common sense suggests another: the reservation of space for public use—plan today our program for tomorrow. We will not save by waiting; now is the time for decision. Now is the time, not later, to decide upon the orderly expansion of the urban pattern, or abandon it to the termites of civic decay. If we intend to restore decency to the environment, now is the time to prepare.

The failure of inaction is written in the spectacle of present cities. The success of action is demonstrated in those rare instances when vision triumphed. What would Manhattan do without Central Park, Chicago without Lincoln Park, San Francisco without Golden Gate Park? In contrast, what a price the people have paid to "make" the land for Chicago's lake front, and the Moses parkways in New York. If ample space for public facilities is not reserved now, speculation will grip only more firmly—sink its roots deeper into the nourishment of urban expansion. To delay the day of reckoning will cost the future much too much.

Reservation of open space—"greenbelts" for recreation, broad thoroughfares, public services—is the least our urban program should include. It would make sense to plan regional park systems as permanent lungs and circulation to protect future expansion. It would make more sense for cities to acquire sections of outlying land as an antidote to the insidious effect of future speculative inflation.

There is need for civic enterprise to provide leadership for urban growth and development rather than remain forever a step behind. Our society requires such leadership—it represents the dominant will of the people. Civic enterprise is the joint participation of private and public initiative; it is neither one nor the other alone. The ultimate goal in our democracy—the general welfare—is approached when both act in unison. And it is then that profit becomes a healthy motive in our economic, social, and political system. This purpose can be well served by preventing urban ills from infecting new development while the cancer is being carved from the old city. Prevention will come by reservation of ample space before the cost renders adequate room too expensive.

The Habit of Congestion. Congestion has a strong grip upon the megalopolitan city. Excess upon excess of people and buildings are heaped upon the land. Size is an accretion of ever-increasing population; people are piled in a pyramid expanding at the base in proportion to the accumulation at the center. The heavy burden of building bulk has created a Frankenstein of land values, and the result is a paradox.

The value of land is a product of its use. Presumably the use is designed as a service to people, and the value of the land is measured by the income derived from performing that service. When, by increasing the intensity of land use, the income from it can be increased, the value of the land is likewise increased.

Following this logic with enthusiasm, city building proceeded according to the "highest and best use" to which urban land could be put. Absorbed with pursuit of this theory, attention to the basic concept that land value is derived from service to people shifted to the concept of land as a speculative commodity, and this is the status of urban land "economics" today.

It is not a new situation since exploitation of land has been common throughout history and its effect upon the development of cities has been one of degree, the extent

CHICAGO

As though struggling for light, air, and space, taller and taller buildings elbow their way toward the lake front and the broad open area of the Lakeshore Drive.

BEVERLY HILLS, California

The present plan of land coverage in this community is typical of the traditional assumption that all the land may be covered by buildings except for building regulations which may prescribe the side and rear yards to be provided in each improvement. The proposed plan of land coverage, suggested by Harland Bartholomew, reveals the change being wrought by the automobile. The freeway traverses Santa Monica boulevard and accommodates the rapid transit lines. Parking spaces surround the business center and penetrate the internal blocks within the district. The plan has not been officially adopted by the city nor does it suggest any particular change in the urban form, the relation of buildings to streets and the circulation system, but it shows that space will be returning to the city as the new dimensions are acknowledged.

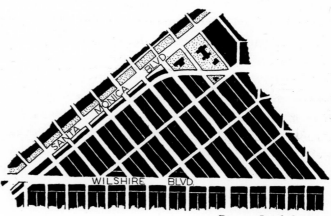

Present Land Coverage

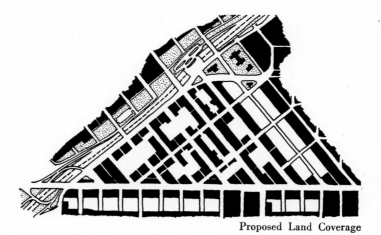

Proposed Land Coverage

to which urban growth in any period has been dominated by speculative excesses or implemented by tempered investment. The novel character of this process today is the self-consuming nature of land economics. The upward spiral of value has created congestion and, seeking to maintain an economic balance, more congestion is the usual antidote. As a result, value is not measured in terms of service to people; on the contrary, the people are now obliged to adjust themselves to congestion in order to maintain land values.

This paradox is at the root of the urban problem, but it is being resolved. Decentralization is gnawing at the values in congested areas, even though the unplanned and disorderly process has the effect of shifting the disease about the urban anatomy rather than curing the malady.

Congestion is a habit hard to break and we see it illustrated in some of the most courageous efforts to release the city from its shackles. The remarkable program of highways directed by Robert Moses in New York City may be fairly compared with achievements of the Roman Empire or Baron Haussmann in Paris. Yet the administrative prowess and engineering skill it represents are unconsciously tangled in the web of congestion.

Struggling to escape from congestion, the smooth freeways loosen themselves from one complicated intersection only to find themselves caught in another. High land cost is a challenge to engineering ingenuity and the results are triumphs of technical skill, but the capacity to build these structures is sometimes a delusion. The ready escape from congestion offered by the freeways is part of the formula for dissipation of excessive land values, but the highway design is threatened with early obsolescence when it is warped into complicated and extravagant intersections to avoid high land cost. Avoidance of high land cost is inadequate compensation if the civic improvement is a crippled rather than a permanent asset to the community. A full statement of the problem cannot omit the necessity for the most direct system of circulation integrated with redevelopment of congested areas.

A rare example of conscious civic design, Radio City in New York reaches for a new space freedom and its attractive plaza is a showplace of the city. In proportion to the tremendous building bulk that rises vertical above it, this forecourt is diminutive, but the illusion of space is a dramatic commentary on the overburdened physical congestion of the city. More apparent than real, the illusion is created not by its own spaciousness but by its contrast with the utter absence of space elsewhere about it.

In paying its compliments to a new order of horizontal space in urban design, this spectacular project focuses upon the habit of congestion. Utility and economy guided the design; the planning was directed by practical requirements. Yet it was found practical in this project to plan an area of six city blocks in contrast to the usual single lot or block. The buildings were planned to meet the practical requirements of space and construction, and yet it was also practical to allot an open space for a handsome plaza.

Do not these features pose a pertinent question as to just where practical planning

CIVIC ART

People respond to improvement in their community; they are affected and their pride is lifted by evidence of cultural energy in their city. They may not appraise these deeds with accuracy or identify them with discrimination, but they are moved by the existence of urban enterprise that transcends mediocrity. This is illustrated by the popular response to Radio City in New York City. In reality the "court" is a relatively diminutive space, but, in contrast with the absence of space within the environs, the appearance of size is exaggerated and the people are impressed. It is space for which the urbanite yearns and seeks and it is the design of space that presents the challenge to city building in the future.

Attention to the proportion of open spaces and building masses was an integral part of city building in the great cultural periods of the past. Studies by Camillo Sitte indicated that certain relationships between space and buildings were recognized in the medieval town. From these observations he estimated that the minimum dimension of a plaza should be equal to the height of the principal building facing upon it and the maximum distance should not exceed twice the height of the building. He considered that the length of a plaza should not exceed three times the width.

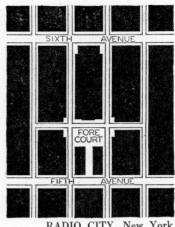

RADIO CITY, New York

Designers of the Renaissance were also apparently guided by rules of proportion between open spaces and building masses as well as the classic proportions of the buildings themselves. To obtain the effects they sought, the guides were more elaborate than those that appear in the medieval town. Studies by H. Maertens indicate that, to encompass the architectural detail within the height of a building, the spaces were arranged so that the distance from the observer to the building would be equal to the height. In order for an observer to contain properly within his vision an entire façade the distance was calculated at twice the height of the building. If the building façade was part of a group of buildings, the effect of the group arrangement required a distance between the observer and the building equal to three times its height. These general proportions seem to have been considered in creating the great plazas of the Renaissance and Baroque Periods and, as the scale of open spaces increased, the designers introduced sculptural forms—fountains, statues and monuments—at appropriate intermediate points within the spaces. The sketches give some key to the manner in which these devices were employed.

RENAISSANCE PROPORTIONS

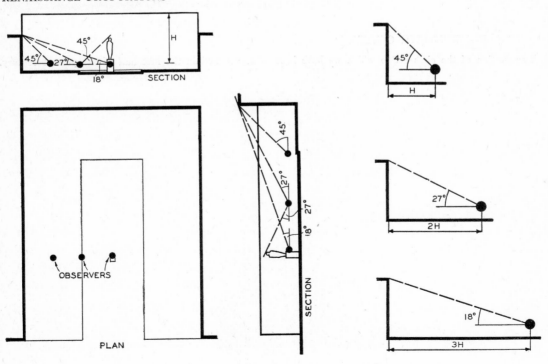

CIVIC ART—TWENTIETH CENTURY

A suggestion of the civic art to which we have become accustomed in the first half of the present century.

begins and where it ends? The rare features in Radio City were considered practical for this great commercial project; might it not be considered equally practical to plan even more adequate space in the city? This great venture demonstrated the practicality of planning forms hitherto adjudged impractical in our day; perhaps it is projects like Radio City that will break the habit of congestion in our cities.

The city needs space for the free flow of transportation and movement of people, space in which to create a desirable environment for living and for work, space in which the functions of the city and the esthetics of our time may be welded into an inseparable unity. Space in the city will encourage the inventive genius of mankind to fulfill the wants of people and free them from the wanton congestion that renders the city a detestable place in which to live and work.

The urban environment shrieks with the production of science and industry and the commodities of commercial enterprise. The city is like a cave in which a multitude of weird and raucous echoes create a psychological din. Self-discipline in organizing the advantages of our industrial age is lagging, and the city dweller is suffering distraction.

Reams of statistics show the habits of the urbanite. They reveal, for example, the short distance people will walk from their parking place to their shopping destination. This reluctance to walk is interpreted as a significant characteristic of the present-day shopper, but the fact that these statistics also measure the repellent character of the urban environment is overlooked. There is ample evidence of the response of the people to studied civic design and their hunger for open space. The diminutive plaza in Radio City evokes spontaneous response, and the success of planned residential communities and neighborhood shopping centers attests to the good business of adequate space. Statistics may show the characteristics of the urban population, but they may also reveal the deficiencies of the environment that induce those traits; they may tell the story of how rank congestion violates human sensibilities and how abhorrent are slums to the human spirit.

The Cultural Vacuum. City building is neglectful of human feeling; it is a cold, harsh enterprise devoid of the amenities for living. It explains the desire for escape which eclecticism provided, a refuge from reality in which the people could draw the walls of romanticism about themselves. It was not a real existence the people lived, but it showed that they could still dream, and it is dreams that will lead civilization out of the darkness—dreams of the future rather than the past.

The significance of freedom is not yet fully grasped; society is not yet adjusted to the democracy of our industrial age. Political rights have been won, and mechanical tools of phenomenal number and variety are at our disposal, but the significance of man's achievement is blurred in its whirling presence. It was entertaining and amusing fiction Jules Verne wrote about in the nineteenth century. Today reality so far surpasses his visionary anecdotes that society is bewildered. There is a strangeness about the powers science has thrust into the hands of man; his capacity to manipulate these powers and the responsibility it bestows cast a spell upon society. When we contemplate their effect upon our social and economic life, the stupendous possibilities are appalling. Imagination pulsates with the vibrating tempo of the modern world.

Evidence of technical progress is all about us. The material benefits of our age are delivered ready-made; gadgets are a part of our daily existence and we take for granted the marvelous developments of science. But the assimilation of these accomplishments into our cultural environment is coming hard. Forging a culture from the technology of our time is a complicated process. Ultimately adjustment of civilization to the reality of our age will generate the cultural climate in which the creative work of artists flourishes.

Meanwhile we are moving in a cultural vacuum, into which has been drawn the technological progress we misinterpret for culture itself. Eclecticism is a standard of mediocrity bred of materialism. Inured to this standard, we are hardly conscious of its reality and unaware of the cultural potentials present but undeveloped. Their development offers a whole new frontier in our world of progress—the cultural expression of democratic freedom in which the vitality of contemporary art will shape our physical environment.

Emotional intuition is necessary to creative expression, and the twentieth century has not yet recovered from the emotional confusion of eclecticism. Wavering between nineteenth-century romanticism and the functional utility of today's economy, the people harbor an uncertain fear about esthetics, and the art of building cities is suffering. In the absence of emotional stability a consciousness of esthetic values will have to be generated through an intellectual process. Application of the intellect, the logical analysis of our society, the problems to be solved, the materials and tools with which to work, all these may cultivate a capacity to reason about appropriate form and restore the psychological repose necessary to cultural maturity.

The tendency for some creative minds to shun esthetics is evidence of the distance we have to travel to the cultural horizon. Suggestive of eclectic sham, esthetics is wilfully avoided and reason substituted for emotional direction. In part because of this forced isolation from the false esthetic formula with which people have been imbued, there is a cultural energy stirring persistently within the framework of twentieth-century materialism. The arts are coming to life and a new esthetic is emerging, an esthetic of freedom, of space, and of release from the ancients. Cubism, sculptural mobiles, and photography experiment with a new integration of space, form, color, and motion; music moves to the tempo; architecture produces a new relation between space and structure, a liberation of enclosed space from structural limitations; and the scale of new dimensions is penetrating the city. The spectacular designs of Le Corbusier show horizontal ground space unencumbered, buildings raised upon "stilts," vehicles and pedestrians having uninterrupted freedom of movement.

There is resistance to the new esthetic, but it is more passive than active. The pursuit of material welfare distracts attention from cultural achievement as we bow low before the great god Mammon, but the result is indifference more than wilful denial. Economic distortions exert more convincing pressures for improvement of the urban

environment than does the creative urge for a fine city. The loss of land values due to
congestion and the economic burden of blight and social maladjustments are more
impressive than the esthetic and spiritual baseness to which the city has degenerated.

Unity of Purpose. The search for form in the urban environment would stagnate
without the imagination of fertile minds. It is the more regrettable that official planning
agencies are so timid in their leadership. The aspirations of city people are suffocating.
Some cities may have illusions of grandeur, others have ambitions for greatness, but
false pride obscures their decadence. We can hardly conclude that the ugliness of
our environment is due to a complete absence of civic pride, that nerve-racking
congestion and unhealthful overcrowding answer the natural desire for activity and
vitality, and that people have become so inured to their surroundings they prefer
mediocrity to an environment of decency and culture regardless of their social or
economic station in life.

What is there to stir the city-dweller in the prospect of nothing better than more
of the same? The people need to see new plans. Civic leadership needs to emerge
with standards of urban development that will convince the people it will be worth
the cost to restore decency to their cities.

Planning implies a goal to be reached. This, in turn, suggests some unity of purpose. Coventry, England, was devastated by war, and rebuilding was tragically needed.
Plans were drawn to make the city a better place than it had been. Yet reconstruction
waited. Why? The answer was in a report by B. J. McQuaid:[1] "Influential individuals
are showing signs of dissatisfaction over details. Some merchants oppose the idea, for
example, of parklike boulevards running through the shopping center. Community
merchants as a body appear convinced that traffic congestion is good business." Differences "over the degree to which rebuilding should be carried out along functional
lines of modern scientific city planning" delayed action. Sorely needed progress is
frustrated by disunity and unimaginative leadership. Unity of purpose—a conviction
about the form and character we desire for our cities—has been absent. Consequently,
planning has wandered aimlessly, frequently promising much but delivering little.

Cities have not yet reached the stage of crowding and congestion present laws
permit, and yet they are already pitifully overcrowded and congested. These legal
limits have induced a state of anarchy in city building. Feeble innovations for
improvement are not enough. Face-lifting will not do the job; it will take a major
operation. Our conception of unlimited exploitation of urban property and people will
need modification; the relation between the amount of space occupied by buildings and
the amount of land about them must be altered. An inspiring projection of the City
of Tomorrow by Le Corbusier, a studied group like Radio City, a well-planned subdivision like River Oaks, and the Parkways of New York and Chicago point the way.
If we expect our cities to be shaped in their images, however, we must look to the laws
that set the standards for that accomplishment.

Cities are breaking down. As they are rebuilt they must conform to standards which

[1] *Los Angeles Times* of July 1, 1945. Courtesy *Chicago Daily News.*

ensure they will not break down again. This will require major decisions, and we must be prepared to make them. Unless these decisions are made wisely, it would be far better and more economical to beat a hasty retreat from the congested urban centers and build new communities elsewhere. Bombs and shells have leveled Old World cities. We will soon be looking for the old cities in the New World.

We can build better cities when we quit gnawing at the fringe of the urban garment and accept some of the bitter with the sweet. We will replan our cities to provide a rational density of population, and from these plans we will lay a foundation of law that prohibits crowding and congestion of people and buildings. We will plan for such expansion and decentralization as the regions about our cities require, and we will plan for such rebuilding as obsolescence and decay demand. We will go about this as civilized human beings with due consideration for each other, rather than barbarians bent upon destruction or as creatures of greed and deception bent on personal power and profit.

The tragic impact of the great city upon human welfare aroused the search by the New Utopians, and their vision may light the way toward a metamorphosis of the city. Statistics, economic analyses, graphs, and charts urge a popular plea that planning must adopt scientific methods for the direction of future urban growth. The facts are essential; there can be no question about the necessity for full and complete information about our cities. But cities are. the creatures of people, built by people for people, and their form is subject to the will of the people. Scientific analysis may indicate trends, but it does not direct action.

Science is an invention—an instrument with which man reaches his objectives, the goals he may set for himself. The force that moves mankind in the selection of these goals is Morality, not science; it is a Morality rooted deep in his culture and sharpened by his intuitive capacity. Man has the power to control his environment; he can mold it to his purpose. He can observe trends, determine their direction, then reverse or shift them to suit his purpose. The course of human events is not some inevitable fate to which the people are destined; it is subject to their will. They can examine the facts and from them they can select their course. This is the power of man and it is the purpose of planning. Guided by a high moral sense, and acting with freedom, the people can plan their cities of tomorrow. And, in the words of John Ruskin, "Let it be as such work that our descendants will thank us for, . . . and that men will say, as they look upon the labor and the wrought substance of them, 'See this our fathers did for us.'"

BIBLIOGRAPHY

PART I

Adams, Thomas; *Outline of Town and City Planning*, Russell Sage Foundation, New York, 1935.

Aristotle; *Politics*.

Bannister, Turpin; *Early Town Planning in New York State*, American Society of Architectural Historians.

Bemis and Burchard; *The Evolving House*, Vol. I, A History of the Home, 1933–36.

Benson, Edwin; *Life in a Medieval City*, London, 1920.

Bosanquet, R. C.; *Greek and Roman Towns*, Town Planning Review, January, October 1915.

Breasted, James Henry; *Ancient Times: A History of the Early World*, Ginn & Co., 1914.

Bridgeport Brass Company; *History of Sanitation*, Bridgeport, 1930.

Churchill, Henry; *The City Is the People*, Reynal & Hitchcock, New York, 1945.

Gardner, Percy; *The Planning of Hellenistic Cities*.

Giedion, Sigfried; *Space, Time and Architecture*, Harvard University Press, Cambridge, 1943.

Glotz, Gustave; *The Greek City and Its Institutions*, Kegan Paul, Trench, Trubner and Co., Ltd., 1929.

——; *The Aegean Civilization*, Alfred A. Knopf, New York, 1925.

Green, Alice Stopford; *Town Life in the 15th Century*, 2 Vols., London, 1894.

Hamlin, Talbot; *Architecture Through the Ages*, G. P. Putnam's Sons, 1940.

Hammarstrand, Nils; *Cities Old and New*, Journal of the American Institute of Architects, New York, 1926.

Haverfield, Francis J.; *Ancient Town Planning*, Clarendon Press, Oxford, 1913.

——; *Town Planning in the Roman World*, Town Planning Conference, Transactions, R.I.B.A., London, 1910.

Hegemann, Werner and Elbert Peets; *Civic Art: The American Vitruvius*, Architectural Book Publishing Co., New York, 1922.

Hilberseimer, Ludwig; *The New City*, Paul Theobald, Chicago, 1944.

Lavedan, Pierre; *Histoire de l'Urbanisme*, Vol. I, Antiquité, Moyen Age, Paris, 1926.

Lloyd, Nathaniel; *A History of the English House, From Primitive Times to the Victorian Period*, London, 1931.

Marshall, Sir John; *Mohenjo-daro and the Indus Civilization*, published by Arthur Probsthain, London, 1931.

McDonald, William A.; *The Political Meeting Places of the Greeks*, Johns Hopkins Press, 1943.

Moses, Robert; *What Happened to Haussmann*, Architectural Forum, July 1942.

Mumford, Lewis; *The Culture of Cities*, Harcourt, Brace & Co., New York, 1938.

——; *The Condition of Man*, Harcourt, Brace & Co., New York, 1944.

Peets, Elbert; *The Genealogy of L'Enfants Washington*, Journal of the American Institute of Architects, April, May, June, 1927.

Pirenne, Henri; *Medieval Cities*, Translated from the French by Frank Halsey, Princeton University Press, 1925.

Plato; *The Republic*.

Poète, Marcel; *Introduction à l'Urbanisme; l'Evolution des Villes, La Leçon de l'Antiquité*, Paris, 1929.

Renard, Georges François; *Guilds in the Middle Ages*, London, 1919.

Robinson, David M.; *Excavations at Olynthus*, Part XII, Domestic and Public Architecture, Johns Hopkins Press, 1946.

—— and J. Walter Graham; *Excavations at Olynthus*, Part VIII, The Hellenic House, Johns Hopkins Press, 1938.

Rostovtzeff, M.; *A History of the Ancient World*, Vol. I, The Orient and Greece, Oxford Press.

Smithsonian Institution; *Bureau of Ethnology*, 8th Annual Report, Government Printing Office, 1891.
Town Planning Review; *Haussmann*, June 1927.
Triggs, H. I.; *Town Planning*, London, 1890.
Vitruvius; *The Ten Books on Architecture*, Harvard University Press, 1914.
Wallbank, T. Walter, and Alastair M. Taylor; *Civilization Past and Present*, Scott, Foresman & Co., 1942.
Williams, Henry Smith; *The Historian's History of the World*, The Outlook Co., 1904.
Wycherley, R. E., *How the Greeks Built Cities*, Macmillan & Co., New York, 1949.

PART II

Abrams, Charles; *The Future of Housing*, Harper & Brothers, 1946.
Alm, Ulla; *Cooperative Housing in Sweden*, published by The Royal Swedish Commission, Stockholm, 1939.
American Institute of Architects; *Reports of Committee on Community Planning*, New York, 1924, 1925, 1926, 1927.
Architectural Forum; *Limited Dividend Roll Call*, January 1935.
Augur, Tracy; *Planning Principles Applied in Wartime*, Architectural Record, January 1943.
Bassett, Edward M.; *Zoning*, Russell Sage Foundation, 1940.
Bauer, Catherine; *Modern Housing*, Houghton Mifflin Co., 1934.
Boardman, Philip; *Patrick Geddes: Maker of the Future*, University of North Carolina Press, Chapel Hill, 1944.
Boyd, John Taylor, Jr.; *Toward the Reconstruction of New York's Lower East Side*, Architectural Forum, January, August 1932.
Bridgeport Brass Co.; *History of Sanitation*, Bridgeport, 1930.
Buckingham, James Silk; *National Evils and Practical Remedies*, London, 1849.
Census of the U.S. (16th); *Census of Housing*, 1940, U.S. Department of Commerce, 1943.
Changes in Distribution of Manufacturing Wage Earners, 1899–1939; U.S. Departments of Commerce and Agriculture, Washington, D.C., 1942.
Childs, Marquis; *The Middle Way*, Yale University Press, 1936.
Churchill, Henry; *The City Is the People*, Reynal & Hitchcock, 1945.
Cobden-Sanderson, T. J.; *Art and Life, and the Building and Decoration of Cities*, London, 1897.
DeForest and Veiller; *The Tenement House Problem*, Vols. I and II, The Macmillan Co., 1903.
Denby, Elizabeth; *Europe Rehoused*, W. W. Norton & Co., 1938.
Dickens, Charles; *Hard Times*, London, 1854.
Eddy, H. P.; *Sewerage and Drainage of Towns*, Proceedings American Society of Civil Engineers, September 1927.
Engels, Friedrich; *The Condition of the Working-Class in England in 1844*, Leipzig, 1845, London, 1887.
Federal Emergency Administration of Public Works; *Homes for Workers*, Housing Division Bulletin No. 3, Washington, D.C., 1937.
Ford, James; *Slums and Housing*, Harvard University Press, 1936.
Fortune Editors; *Housing America*, Harcourt, Brace & Co., 1935.
Geddes, Patrick; *Cities in Evolution*, London, 1915.
——; *City Deterioration and the Need of City Survey*, The Annals of the American Academy of Political and Social Sciences, July 1909.
——; *Talks from My Outlook Tower*, Survey Graphic, February, April 1925.
Gray, George; *Housing and Citizenship*, Reinhold Publishing Corp., New York, 1946.
Graham, John; *Housing in Scandinavia*, University of North Carolina Press, Chapel Hill, 1940.
Hardy, Charles O., assisted by Robert R. Kucznzki; *The Housing Program of the City of Vienna*, The Brookings Institution, Washington, D.C., 1934.

Housing and Home Finance Agency; *War Housing in the U.S.*, Government Printing Office, Washington, D.C., 1945.

Housing and Public Health Committee; *London Housing*, London County Council, 1937.

Howard, Ebenezer; *Garden Cities of Tomorrow*, London, 1902; First Edition—*Tomorrow*—London, 1898.

Hoyt, Homer; *One Hundred Years of Land Values in Chicago*, University of Chicago Press, Chicago, 1933.

——; *Structure and Growth of Residential Neighborhoods in American Cities*, Federal Housing Administration, Washington, D.C., 1945.

Hurd, Richard M.; *Principle of City Land Values*, New York, 1903.

International Housing Association; *Housing and Building*, Julius Hoffman Verlag, Stuttgart, 1931 and 1932.

——; *Slum Clearance*, Vols. I and II, Julius Hoffman Verlag, Stuttgart, 1935.

Johansson, Alf, and Waldemar Svenson; *Swedish Housing Policy*, The Royal Swedish Commission, reprinted from the Annals of the American Academy of Political and Social Sciences, May 1938.

Leven, Maurice, Harold G. Moulton and Clark Warburton; *America's Capacity to Consume*, The Brookings Institution, Washington, D.C., 1934.

Lohmann, Karl B.; *Principles of City Planning*, McGraw-Hill Book Co., 1931.

McAllister, Gilbert, and Elizabeth Glen; *Town and Country Planning*, Faber & Faber, Ltd., London, 1941.

Merriam, Robert E.; *Subdivision of Land*, American Society of Planning Officials, 1313 E. 60th Street, Chicago, 1942.

Moore, Charles; *Daniel Burnham: Architect, Planner of Cities*, 2 Vols., Boston, 1921.

Mumford, Lewis; *The Story of the Utopias*, New York, 1922.

National Resources Board; *A Report on National Planning and Public Works in Relation to Natural Resources and Including Land Use and Water Resources with Findings and Recommendations*, Washington, D.C., December 1, 1934.

——; *State Planning: A Review of Activities and Progress*, Washington, D.C., June 1935.

National Resources Committee:

    Regional Factors in National Planning, December 1935.

    Regional Planning, Part I, Pacific Northwest, May 1936.

    Our Cities: Their Role in the National Economy, June 1937.

    Technological Trends and National Policy, June 1937.

    The Problems of a Changing Population, May 1938.

    Consumer Incomes in the United States, 1938.

    Residential Building, Housing Monograph, Series No. 1, Industrial Committee, 1939.

    Legal Problems in the Housing Field, Housing Monograph, Series No. 2, Industrial Committee, 1939.

    Consumer Expenditures in the United States, 1939.

    Urban Planning and Land Policies, Vol. II of the Supplementary Report of the Urbanism Committee, 1939.

    Urban Government, Vol. I of the Supplementary Report of the Urbanism Committee, 1940.

Nolen, John; *City Planning*, New York, 1929.

Olmsted, Frederick Law; *Public Works and the Enlargement of Towns*, Cambridge, Mass., 1870.

Owen, Robert; *A New View of Society*, London, 1813.

Post, Langdon W.; *The Challenge of Housing*, Farrar & Rinehart, Inc., New York, 1938.

President's Conference on Home Building and Home Ownership, Washington, D.C., 1931.

Purdom, Charles B.; *Building of Satellite Towns*, London, 1926.

——; *Town Theory and Practice*, London, 1921.

——; *The Garden City*, London, 1923.

Regional Survey of New York and Its Environs, Russell Sage Foundation, New York, 1927–31. See Bibliography, Part V.

Reiss, Richard L.; *British and American Housing*, National Public Housing Conference, Inc., 1937.

Riis, Jacob; *How the Other Half Lives*, Charles Scribner's Sons, New York, 1934. Original Edition, 1890.

Robinson, Charles Mulford; *City Planning*, New York, 1916.

Sennett, Alfred R.; *Garden Cities in Theory and Practice*, 2 Vols., London, 1905.

Sert, José; *Can Our Cities Survive?* Harvard University Press, Cambridge, 1942.

Simon, Sir E. D.; *Rebuilding Britain—A Twenty Year Plan*, Victor Gollancz, Ltd., 1945.

——; *The Rebuilding of Manchester*, Longmans, Green & Co., 1935.

Smith, Adam; *An Inquiry Into the Nature and Causes of the Wealth of Nations*, 2 Vols., London, 1776.

Steffens, Lincoln; *The Shame of Cities*, Collection from McClure's Magazine.

Stein, Clarence; *The Price of Slum Clearance*, Architectural Forum, February 1934.

Straus, Nathan; *The Seven Myths of Housing*, Alfred A. Knopf, 1944.

Survey Graphic; *Homes*, A Special Number, February 1940.

——; *The Case Against Home Ownership*, by Stuart Chase, May 1938.

Thoreau, Henry David; *Walden*, Boston, 1854.

Unwin, Raymond; *Town Planning in Practice*, London, 1909.

——; *Nothing Gained in Overcrowding*, Garden Cities and Town Planning Association, London, 1912.

Weimar, Arthur M., and Homer Hoyt; *Principles of Urban Real Estate*, Ronald Press Co., New York, 1939.

Wood, Edith Elmer; *Recent Trends in American Housing*, The Macmillan Co., New York, 1931.

——; *Introduction to Housing: Facts and Principles*, United States Housing Authority, Washington, D.C., 1939.

——; *Slums and Blighted Areas in the U.S.*, Housing Division, Federal Emergency Administration of Public Works, 1933.

Wright, Henry; *Rehousing Urban America*, Columbia University Press, 1935.

PART III

Abercrombie, Patrick; *Town and Country Planning*, New York, 1933.

Abrams, Charles; *The Future of Housing*, Harper & Brothers, 1946.

Ackerman, Frederick; *Controlling Factors in Slum Clearance and Housing*, Architectural Forum, February 1934.

——; *Debt as the Foundation for Houses*, Architectural Forum, April 1934.

Aronovici, Carol; *Housing the Masses*, John Wiley & Sons, New York, 1939.

Bartholomew, Harland; *Urban Land Uses*, Harvard University Press, Cambridge, 1932.

Census of the U.S. (16th); *Census of Housing*, 1940, U.S. Department of Commerce, Washington, D.C., 1943.

Churchill, Henry; *The City Is the People*, Reynal & Hitchcock, New York, 1945.

Craemer, Daniel B.; *Is Industry Decentralizing?* University of Pennsylvania Press, 1935.

Dean, John P.; *Home Ownership: Is It Sound?* Harper & Brothers, 1945.

Federal Housing Administration; *Planning Rental Housing Projects*, Washington, D.C., 1947.

Filene, Edward A.; *The Way Out*, New York, 1924.

Ford, Henry; *Ford Ideals*, being a selection from "Mr. Ford's Page" in the *Dearborn Independent*, The Dearborn Publishing Company, Dearborn, Michigan, 1922.

Gray, George; *Housing and Citizenship*, Reinhold Publishing Corp., New York, 1946.

Greater Boston Development Committee; *Surging Cities*, Theodore McCrosky, Charles Blessing, J. Ross McKeever, Boston, 1948.

Hegemann, Werner; *City Planning, Housing*, First Volume of Text: Historical and Sociological, Architectural Book Publishing Co., New York, 1936.

Home Loan Bank Board; *The Federal Home Loan Bank System*, Washington, D.C., August 1947.

Housing and Home Finance Agency; *Housing Costs*, Bulletin No. 2, National Housing Agency, Washington, D.C., 1944.

——; *Housing Needs*, National Housing Agency, Washington, D.C., 1944.

——; *Comparative Analysis of the Principal Provisions of State Housing Authority Laws Relating to Housing, Slum Clearance and Urban Redevelopment*, Washington, D.C., 1944.

Journal of Land and Public Utility Economics (Quarterly), University of Wisconsin, Madison, Wisconsin.

Kahn, Ernest; *The Economics of Housing in the U.S.*, Architectural Forum, August 1935.

——; *The Upkeep of Housing*, Architectural Forum, September 1935.

Law and Contemporary Problems, Housing Issue; Duke University Law School, Durham, N.C., Winter Issue, 1947.

Mumford, Lewis; *City Development*, Harcourt, Brace & Co., 1945.

National Resources Committee; *Our Cities: Their Role in the National Economy*, Washington, D.C., 1937.

Public Housing Administration; *Public Housing Design*, Washington, D.C., 1946.

Regional Survey of New York and Its Environs; Russell Sage Foundation, New York, 1927–31. *See* Bibliography, Part V.

Rosenman, Dorothy; *A Million Homes a Year*, Harcourt, Brace & Co., 1945.

Saarinen, Eliel; *The City, Its Growth, Its Decay, Its Future*, Reinhold Publishing Corp., New York, 1943.

Segoe, Ladislas; *Local Planning Administration*, International City Managers' Association, Chicago, 1941, Revised Ed. 1948.

Sert, José; *Can Our Cities Survive?* Harvard University Press, Cambridge, 1942.

Silk, Leonard; *Sweden Plans for Better Housing*, Duke University Press, Durham, N.C., 1948.

Straus, Nathan; *The Seven Myths of Housing*, Alfred Knopf, 1944.

Thompson, Tracy E.; *Location of Manufactures: 1899–1929*, Bureau of Census, Washington, D.C., 1933.

Thompson, Warren S.; *Population Problems*, New York, 1930.

Twentieth Century Fund; *American Housing*, New York, 1944.

Walker, Mabel L.; *Urban Blight and Slums*, Harvard University Press, Cambridge.

Wright, Frank Lloyd; *The Disappearing City*, William Farquhar Payson, New York, 1932.

——; *When Democracy Builds*, University of Chicago Press, 1945.

PART IV

Abrams, Charles; *Revolution in Land*, Harper & Brothers, New York, 1939.

A Standard State Zoning Enabling Act, Government Printing Office, Washington, D.C., 1926.

Action for Cities; A guide for community planning, American Municipal Association, Public Administration Service, Chicago, 1943.

Adams, Thomas; *Outline of Town and City Planning*, Russell Sage Foundation, New York, 1935.

Advisory Committee on Zoning, *City Planning Primer*, U.S. Chamber of Commerce, Washington, D.C., 1928.

American City Planning Institute; *Control of Land Subdivision and Building Development: City Planning*, July 1928.

American Society of Planning Officials; *A Program for Tax Abandoned Lands*, Chicago, 1942.

——; *A Model State Subdivision Control Act*, Chicago, 1947.

Architectural Forum; *Planning With You*, Reprint from August Issue, New York, 1943.

Ascher, Charles S.; *Better Cities*, National Resources Planning Board, Washington, D.C., 1942.

Bassett, Edward M.; *Model Laws for the Planning of Cities, Counties and States*, Harvard University Press, Cambridge, 1935.

——; *The Master Plan*, Russell Sage Foundation, New York, 1938.

——; *Zoning*, Russell Sage Foundation, New York, 1940.

Bettman, Alfred; *The Decisions of the Supreme Court of the U.S. in the Euclid Village Zoning Case*, University of Cincinnati Law Review, March 1927.

——; *City and Regional Papers*, Edited by Arthur C. Comey, Harvard University Press, Cambridge, 1946.

Black, Russell Van Nest; *Planning the Small American City*, Public Administration Service, Chicago, 1944.

———; *Building Lines*, Harvard University Press, Cambridge, 1935.

Bogardus, E. S.; *Fundamentals of Social Psychology*, D. Appleton-Century Co., New York, 1942.

Building New Neighborhoods, Subdivision Design and Standards, Chicago Plan Commission, Chicago, 1943.

California State Reconstruction and Reemployment Commission, *Forecasting a City's Future*, Sacramento, 1946.

Chase, Stuart; *What the New Census Means*, Public Affairs Committee, Inc., New York, 1941.

———; *Rich Land, Poor Land*, New York, 1936.

Cheney, Charles; *Architectural Control of Private Property*, Proceedings, National Conference on City Planning, 1927.

Cornick, Philip H.; *Premature Subdivision of Urban Areas in Selected Metropolitan Districts*, Division of State Planning, Albany, New York, 1938.

———; *Premature Subdivision and Its Consequences*, Institute of Public Administration, Columbia University, New York, 1938.

Crane, Jacob; *How to Make a City Plan*, National Real Estate Journal, April 14, 1930.

Dealey, G. B.; *The Newspaper as a City Builder*, American City, September 1930.

El Pueblo, Security Trust and Savings Bank, Los Angeles, 1928.

Encyclopaedia Britannica; *Land*, Vol. 14, R. S. Peale Edition, The Werner Co., Chicago, 1893.

Federal Highways Acts, Rules and Regulations, U.S. Department of Agriculture, Washington, D.C., 1922.

Federal Housing Administration; *Planning Profitable Neighborhoods*, Washington, D.C., 1938.

Fowlkes, John Guy; *Planning Schools for Tomorrow*, Committee on Planning for Education, Washington, D.C., 1942.

Hjelte, George; *The Administration of Public Recreation*, The Macmillan Co., New York, 1939.

Hoagland, Henry; *Real Estate Principles*, McGraw-Hill Book Co., New York, 1940.

Housing and Home Finance Agency; *Comparative Analysis of the Principal Provisions of State Urban Planning Laws Relating to Housing, Slum Clearance, and Urban Redevelopment*, Washington, D.C., 1944.

———; *Comparative Analysis of the Principal Provisions of State Subdivision Control Laws Relating to Housing and Urban Development*, Washington, D.C., 1945.

Hubbard, Theodora Kimball; *Manual of Information on City Planning and Zoning*, Harvard University Press, Cambridge, 1923.

Journal of Land and Public Utility Economics, Quarterly, University of Wisconsin, Madison.

Kingsley, S. C.; *Methods of Winning Public Support for a City Planning Program*, Proceedings, 14th National Conference on City Planning, 1922.

Land Subdivision; American Society of Civil Engineers, New York, 1939.

Land Use Survey, County of Los Angeles, Regional Planning Commission, Los Angeles, 1940.

Lautner, Harold W.; *Subdivision Regulations—An Analysis of Land Subdivision*, Public Administration Service, Chicago, 1941.

Lewis, Harold MacLean; *City Planning—Why and How*, Longmans, Green & Co., New York, 1939.

———; *Planning the Modern City*, 2 Vols., John Wiley & Sons, Inc., New York, 1949.

Lohmann, Karl; *Principles of City Planning*, McGraw-Hill Book Co., New York, 1931.

Los Angeles, A Preface to a Master Plan, Pacific Southwest Academy, Los Angeles, 1941.

Mayer, Albert; *Technique for Planning Complete Communities*, Architectural Forum, January and February, 1937.

McClenahan, Bessie Averne; *The Communality in the Postwar Social Order*, Sociology and Social Research, University of Southern California, January, February 1945.

———; *The Sociology of Planning*, Sociology and Social Research, University of Southern California.

Merriam, Robert E.; *The Subdivision of Land — A Guide for Municipal Officials in the Regulation of Land Subdivision*, American Society of Planning Officials, Chicago, 1942.

Metzenbaum, James; *The Law of Zoning*, Babser, Voorhis & Co., New York, 1930.

Moody, W. D.; *Wacker's Manual of the Plan of Chicago*, Chicago Plan Commission, Calumet Publishing Co., Chicago, 1916.

National Bureau of Standards; *Model Subdivision Regulations*, Advisory Committee on City Planning and Zoning, Department of Commerce, Washington, D.C., 1936.

National Housing Agency; *A Check List for the Review of Local Subdivision Controls*, Washington, D.C., 1947.

National Park Service; *A Study of the Park and Recreation Problem of the U.S.*, U.S. Department of the Interior, Washington, D.C., 1941.

National Resources Committee; *Regional Factors in National Planning and Development*, Washington, D.C., 1936.

——; *Our Cities: Their Role in the National Economy*, Washington, D.C., 1937.

——; *Suggested Procedure for Population Studies by State Planning Boards*, Washington, D.C., 1938.

——; *Urban Planning and Land Policies*, Vol. II of the Supplementary Report of the Committee on Urbanism, Washington, D.C., 1939.

——; *Industrial Location and National Resources*, Washington, D.C., 1943.

——; *The Problems of a Changing Population*, Washington, D.C., 1943.

National Resources Planning Board; *Human Conservation*, Washington, D.C., 1938.

——; *Progressive Planning Studies;* Tacoma, Washington; Salt Lake City, Utah; Corpus Christi, Texas; published in New Pencil Points, August 1943.

——; *Transportation and National Policy*, Washington, D.C., 1943.

Neighborhoods, Schools, Recreation and Parks, The Metropolitan Planning Committee and the Winnipeg Town Planning Commission, Manitoba, Canada, 1947.

Packard, Walter E.; *The Economic Implications of the Central Valley Project*, Adcraft, Los Angeles, 1942.

Person, H. S.; *Little Waters, Their Use and Relations to the Land*, for the Soil Conservation Service, Resettlement Administration, Rural Electrification Administration, November 1935, Revised April 1936, Washington, D.C.

Present and Future Uses of Land; Planning Commission of the City and County of San Francisco, California, 1944.

Proposed Generalized Land Use Plan, City of Detroit, City Plan Commission, Detroit, 1947.

Regional Survey of New York and Its Environs, Russell Sage Foundation, 1927–31. *See* Bibliography, Part V.

Robinson, W. W.; *Ranchos Become Cities*, San Pasqual Press, Pasadena, California, 1939.

Roterus, Victor; *The Economic Background for Local Planning*, Proceedings, Annual Meeting of American Society of Planning Officials, Chicago, 1946.

Scott, Mel; *Cities Are For People*, Pacific Southwest Academy, Los Angeles, 1942.

Segoe, Ladislas; *Local Planning Administration*, International City Managers' Association, Chicago, 1941, Rev. Ed. 1948.

So You Are Going to Plan a City, Fortune Magazine, N.Y., January 1944.

State Laws Related to "Freeways," Public Roads Administration, Federal Works Agency, Washington, D.C., 1940.

Stonorov, Oscar, and Louis I. Kahn; *You and Your Neighborhood*, Revere Copper and Brass, Inc., New York, 1944.

Sutherland, Robert L., and Julian L. Woodward; *Introductory Sociology*, J. B. Lippincott Co., New York, 1937.

The Preparation of Zoning Ordinances, Advisory Committee on City Planning and Zoning, U.S. Department of Commerce, Washington, D.C., 1931.

The Structure and Growth of Residential Neighborhoods in American Cities, Federal Housing Administration, Washington, D.C., 1939.

Thompson, Warren S.; *Population Problems*, McGraw-Hill Book Co., New York, 1942.

To Hold This Soil, U.S. Department of Agriculture, Washington, D.C., 1938.

United States Housing Authority; *Planning the Site*, Department of the Interior, Washington, D.C., 1939.

Wacker, C. H.; *Gaining Public Support for a City Planning Movement*, Proceedings, National Conference on City Planning, 1913.

Walker, Mabel; *Urban Blight and Slums*, Economic and Legal Factors in their Origin, Reclamation and Prevention, Harvard University Press, Cambridge, 1938.

Walker, R. A.; *The Planning Function in Urban Government*, University of Chicago Press, Chicago, 1941.

Waverly, A Study in Neighborhood Conservation, Federal Home Loan Bank Board, Washington, D.C., 1940.

Weimar, Arthur M., and Homer Hoyt; *Principles of Urban Real Estate*, Ronald Press, New York, 1939.

Whitten, R. A.; *Land Subdivision: The Effect of Density on Acreage Values and on Lot Values*, City Planning, October 1930.

Williams, Frank B.; *The Law of City Planning and Zoning*, The Macmillan Co., New York, 1922.

PART V

Zoning

Annals of the American Academy of Political and Social Sciences; *Building the Future City*, Philadelphia, November 1945.

Bartholomew, Harland; *Urban Land Uses*, Harvard University Press, Cambridge, 1932.

Bauer, John; *Postwar Planning for Metropolitan Utilities*, National Municipal League, New York, 1945.

Comey, Arthur C.; *Transition Zoning*, Harvard University Press, Cambridge, 1933.

Housing and Home Finance Agency; *Comparative Analysis of Principal State Zoning Law Provisions Relating to Housing, Slum Clearance, and Urban Redevelopment*, Washington, D.C., 1944.

Hubbard and Hubbard; *Our Cities of Today and Tomorrow*, Harvard University Press, Cambridge, 1929.

Lewis, Nelson P.; *Planning of the Modern City*, John Wiley & Sons, 1923.

Mumford, Lewis; *Human Problems of Dispersal*, Town and Country Planning, Summer, 1946.

Regional Survey of New York and Its Environs; Russell Sage Foundation, 1927–31.
    Vol. I. *Major Economic Factors in Metropolitan Growth and Arrangement.*
    Vol. II. *Population, Land Values and Government.*
    Vol. III. *Highway Traffic.*
    Vol. IV. *Transit and Transportation.*
    Vol. V. *Public Recreation.*
    Vol. VI. *Buildings: Their Uses and the Spaces About Them.*
    Vol. VII. *Neighborhood and Community Planning.*
    Vol. VIII. *Physical Conditions and Public Services.*
    Regional Plan, Vol. I, *The Graphic Plan.*
    Regional Plan, Vol. II, *The Building of the City.*

Sanders, S. E., and A. J. Rabuck; *New City Patterns; The Analysis and a Technique for Urban Reintegration*, Reinhold Publishing Corp., New York, 1946.

Segoe, Ladislas; *Local Planning Administration*, The International City Managers' Association, Chicago, 1941.

Stein, Clarence S.; *City Patterns, Past and Future*, New Pencil Points, June 1942.

Yeomans, Alfred; *City Residential Land Development*, University of Chicago Press, Chicago, 1916.

The Neighborhood Unit

Abercrombie, Patrick; *Greater London Plan 1944*, His Majesty's Stationery Office, London, 1945.

Adams, Thomas; *Design of Residential Areas,* Harvard University Press, Cambridge, 1934.

——; *What Proportion of Public Land and of Private Land Should be Reserved for Open Space,* American City, June 1928.

American Public Health Association; *Planning the Neighborhood,* Committee on the Hygiene of Housing published by Public Administration Service, 1948.

American Society of Planning Officials; *Preliminary Report of Committee on Park and Recreation Standards,* Herbert Hare, Chairman, S. R. DeBoer, Russell H. Riley; Proceedings, Annual Meeting, Chicago, 1943.

Anderson, Nels, and E. C. Lindeman; *Urban Sociology,* Alfred A. Knopf, Inc., 1928.

Augur, Tracy; *Planning Principles Applied in Wartime,* Architectural Record, January 1943.

Bogardus, E. S.; *Fundamentals of Social Psychology,* D. Appleton-Century Co., New York, 1942.

Brown, J. Lee; *Planning for Recreation Areas in Small Towns and Cities,* Office of Community War Services, Federal Security Agency, Washington, D.C., 1945.

Butler, George P.; *Introduction to Community Recreation,* McGraw-Hill Book Co., 1940.

Caudill, William; *Space for Teaching,* Texas Engineering Experiment Station, College Station, Texas, 1941.

Chicago Plan Commission; *Building New Neighborhoods, Subdivision Design and Standards,* Chicago, 1943.

Churchill, Henry, and Roslyn Ittleson; *Neighborhood Design and Control; An Analysis of the Problem of Planned Subdivisions,* National Committee on Housing, New York, 1944.

Dahir, James; *The Neighborhood Unit Plan,* Russell Sage Foundation, New York, 1947.

Deardoff, Neva R.; *Uniform Neighborhood Boundaries,* Architectural Forum, April 1944.

Engelhardt, N. L., and F. Engelhardt; *Planning School Building Programs,* Columbia University Press, 1930.

Fawcett, C. B.; *A Residential Unit for Town and Country Planning,* University of London Press, London, 1943.

Federal Housing Administration; *Planning Profitable Neighborhoods,* Washington, D.C., 1938.

Forshaw, J. H., and Patrick Abercrombie; *County of London Plan,* Macmillan & Co., Ltd., London, 1943.

Fowlkes, John Guy; *Planning Schools for Tomorrow,* Committee on Planning for Education, U.S. Office of Education, Washington, D.C., 1942.

Hjelte, George; *The Administration of Public Recreation,* The Macmillan Co., New York, 1939.

Hubbard, H. V.; *Parks and Playgrounds,* Proceedings, 14th National Conference on City Planning, 1922.

Isaacs, Reginald R.; *Are Neighborhoods Possible?* The Journal of Housing, July 1948.

——; *The "Neighborhood Unit" Is an Instrument for Segregation,* The Journal of Housing, August 1948.

Mayer, Albert; *Technique for Planning Complete Communities,* Architectural Forum, January, February 1937.

McKenzie, R. D.; *The Metropolitan Community,* McGraw-Hill Book Co., New York, 1933.

Meredith, L. Douglas; *Planning for Private Investment,* Architectural Forum, April, 1944.

National Housing Agency; *Public Housing Design,* Federal Public Housing Authority, Washington, D.C., June 1946.

National Park Service; *A Study of the Park and Recreation Problem of the U.S.,* U.S. Department of the Interior, Washington, D.C., 1941.

National Recreation Association; *Play Space in New Neighborhoods,* A Committee Report on Standards of Outdoor Recreation Areas in Housing Developments, New York, 1939.

National Resources Board; *Recreation Use of Land in the United States,* Vol. IX, Report of Land Planning Committee, Washington, 1938.

Neighborhoods, Schools, Recreation and Parks, The Metropolitan Planning Committee and the Winnipeg Town Planning Commission, Manitoba, Canada, 1947.

Nichols, J. C.; *Mistakes We Have Made in Community Development*, Technical Bulletin No. 1, Urban Land Institute, Washington, D.C., 1945.

Park Recreational Areas in U.S., Government Printing Office, Washington, D.C., 1928.

Perry, Clarence; *The Neighborhood Unit*, Vol. 7, Neighborhood and Community Planning, Regional Survey of New York and Its Environs, New York, 1929.

——; *Housing for the Machine Age*, Russell Sage Foundation, New York, 1939.

——; *Wider Use of the School Plant*, Russell Sage Foundation, New York, 1910.

Sert, José; *The Human Scale in City Planning*, The New Architecture and City Planning, Paul Zucker, Philosophical Library, New York, 1944.

Stonorov, Oscar, and Louis I. Kahn; *You and Your Neighborhood*, Revere Copper and Brass, Inc., New York, 1944.

Strayer, George D.; *The School Building Program an Important Part of the City Plan*, Proceedings, National Conference on City Planning, June 1922.

Sutherland, Robert L., and Julian L. Woodward; *Introductory Sociology*, J. B. Lippincott Co., New York, 1937.

United States Housing Authority; *Planning the Site*, Department of the Interior, Washington, D.C., 1939.

Waverly, A Study in Neighborhood Conservation, Federal Home Loan Bank Board, Washington, D.C., 1940.

Weir, L. H.; *Parks: A Manual of Municipal and County Parks*, A. S. Barnes & Co., New York, 1928.

Westchester County Parks; Annual Reports, Westchester County Park Commission, Bronxville, N.Y.

Whitten, Robert, and Thomas Adams; *Neighborhoods of Small Homes: Economic Density of Low-Cost Housing in America and England*, Harvard University Press, Cambridge, 1931.

Wirth, Louis; *Urbanism as a Way of Life*, American Journal of Sociology, Vol. XLIV, No. 1, July 1938.

Zucker, Paul; *The New Architecture and City Planning*, Philosophical Library, Inc., New York, 1944.

Commercial Centers

Bartholomew, Harland; *Urban Land Uses*, Harvard University Press, Cambridge, 1932.

Community Builders Council; *Shopping Centers—A Community Necessity*, Urban Land Institute, September, October and November 1944.

——; *Community Builders Handbook*, Urban Land Institute, 1947.

DeBoer, S. R.; *Shopping Districts*, American Planning and Civic Association, Washington, D.C., 1937.

Dowling, Robert; *Neighborhood Shopping Centers*, Architectural Forum, October 1943.

Ford, George B.; *Building Height, Bulk, and Form*, Harvard University Press, Cambridge, 1931.

Green, Howard Whipple; *Shopping Centers*, Cleveland Real Property Inventory, Cleveland, 1945.

Kingery, R.; *Determining the Size of Retail Districts in Zoning Cities and Villages*, American City, February 1927.

Mott, Seward, and Max S. Wehrly, *Shopping Centers: An Analysis*, Technical Bulletin No. 11, Urban Land Institute, Washington, D.C., 1949.

Morrow, C. Earl; *Community Shopping Centers*, Architectural Record, June 1940.

——; *Traffic Design*, Pencil Points, April 1944.

National Resources Committee; *Consumer Expenditures in the United States*, Washington, D.C., 1939.

——; *Consumer Incomes in the United States*, Washington, D.C., 1938.

Pepler, G. L.; *Proportion of Area Required for Industry*, Town Planning Review, Vol. 12, 1926.

Stein, Clarence, and Catherine Bauer; *Store Buildings and Neighborhood Shopping Centers*, Architectural Record, February 1934.

Villanueva, Marcel; *Planning Neighborhood Shopping Centers*, National Committee on Housing, Inc., New York, 1945.

Welch, Kenneth C.; *Regional Shopping Centers*, City Planning Commission, Grand Rapids, Michigan, 1948.

The Circulation System

American Automobile Association; *Parking and Terminal Facilities*, Washington, D.C., 1940.

——; *Parking Manual—How to Solve Community Parking Problems*, Washington, D.C., 1946.

American Public Works Association; *Airports: Location, Design, Financing, Zoning, and Control*, Chicago, 1945.

American Transit Association; *Moving People in Modern Cities*, New York, 1944.

Barnett, Joseph; *Express Highway Planning in Metropolitan Areas*, Transactions of the American Society of Civil Engineers, Vol. 112, 1947.

Bartholomew, Harland; *The Place of the Railroad in the City Plan*, Proceedings, National Conference on City Planning, 1926.

Bibbin, J. R.; *Planning for City Traffic*, American Academy of Political and Social Sciences, 1927.

Buckley, James C.; *Comprehensive Transportation and Terminal Planning for Large Urban Centers*, Journal of the American Institute of Planners, Winter, 1947.

Bureau of Public Roads; *Toll Roads and Free Roads*, Department of Agriculture, Washington, D.C., 1939.

Chamber of Commerce of the U.S.; *Urban Transportation*, Washington, D.C., May 1945.

——; *Making Better Use of Today's Streets*, Washington, D.C., 1947.

Civil Aeronautics Administration; *Small Airports*, Washington, D.C., September 1945.

——; *Airport Planning for Urban Areas*, Washington, D.C., 1945.

Electric Railway Journal.

Eno Foundation for Highway Control, *Traffic Quarterly*, Saugatuck, Conn.

Federal Highway Acts, U.S. Department of Agriculture, Washington, D.C., 1922.

Federal Works Agency, *State Laws Related to "Freeways*," Public Roads Administration, Washington, D.C., 1940.

Ford, George B.; *Building Height, Bulk, and Form*, Harvard University Press, Cambridge, 1931.

Freeways for the Region, County of Los Angeles, Regional Planning Commission, Los Angeles, 1943.

Geddes, Norman Bel; *Magic Motorways*, Random House, N.Y., 1940.

Giedion, Sigfried; *Space, Time and Architecture*, Harvard University Press, Cambridge, 1943.

Gubbels, J. L.; *American Highways and Roadsides*, 1938.

Halsey, Maxwell; *Traffic Accidents and Congestion*, John Wiley and Sons, New York, 1941.

Hammond, Harold J., and Leslie J. Sorenson; *Traffic Engineering Handbook*, Institute of Traffic Engineers and National Conservation Bureau, New York, 1941.

Herrey, Hermann; *Comprehensive Planning for the City: Market and Dwelling Place, Part I, Traffic Design*, Pencil Points, April 1944.

Hubbard, Henry V., Miller McClintock, Frank B. Williams; *Airports*, Harvard University Press, Cambridge, 1930.

Justement, Louis; *New Cities for Old*, McGraw-Hill Book Co., New York, 1946.

Kennedy, G. Donald; *Modern Highways*, Conference Committee on Urban Problems, U.S. Chamber of Commerce, Washington, D.C., 1944.

MacElwee, Roy S.; *Ports and Terminal Facilities*, McGraw-Hill Book Co., New York, 1926.

Master Plan of Airports; County of Los Angeles, Regional Planning Commission, Los Angeles, 1940.

Master Plan of Highways; County of Los Angeles, Regional Planning Commission, Los Angeles, 1941.

McClintock, Miller; *Short Count Traffic Surveys and Their Application to Highway Design*, Portland Cement Association, Chicago, 1935.

McKaye, Benton, and Lewis Mumford; *Townless Highways for the Motorist*, Harper's Magazine, August 1931.

Moulton, Harold G.; *The American Transportation Problem*, The Brookings Institution, Washington, D.C., 1933.

National Conservation Bureau; *Manual of Traffic Engineering Studies*, The Bureau, New York, 1945.

National Resources Planning Board; *Transportation and National Policy*, Washington, D.C., 1943.

Nolting, Orin F., and Paul Opperman; *The Parking Problem in Central Business Districts*, Public Administration Service, Chicago, 1938.

Parking Garages for San Francisco; Planning Commission, City and County of San Francisco, 1947.

Paver and McClintock; *Traffic and Trade.*

Recommended Practice for Street Lighting, Illuminating Engineering Society, New York, 1946.

Simonson, Wilbur H.; *The Mount Vernon Memorial Highway*, American City, October 1930.

Smith, Wilbur S., and Charles S. LeCraw; *Parking*, Eno Foundation for Highway Traffic Control, December 1946.

Spengler, Edwin H.; *Land Values in New York in Relation to Transit Facilities*, Columbia University Press, 1930.

Tratman, E. E. R.; *Unification of Railway Passenger Terminals*, Engineering News-Record, February 24, 1927.

Turner, D. L.; *The Fundamentals of Transit Planning for Cities*, Proceedings, 14th National Conference on City Planning, 1922.

Urban Land Institute; *Automobile Parking in Central Business Districts*, Technical Bulletin No. 6, Washington, D.C., 1946.

PART VI

Chapters 24, 25, 26

Abercrombie, Patrick; *Greater London Plan 1944*, His Majesty's Stationery Office, London, 1945.

Abrams, Charles; *Revolution in Land*, Harper & Brothers, New York, 1939.

Academy of Political and Social Sciences; *Building the Future City*, The Annals, Philadelphia, November 1945.

Ackerman, Frederick; *Controlling Factors in Slum Clearance and Housing*, Architectural Forum, February 1934.

——; *Debt As the Foundation for Houses*, Architectural Forum, April 1934.

Adams, Frederick J.; *Density Standards for Multi-Family Residential Areas*, American Institute of Planners, Cambridge, 1943.

American Institute of Planners; *Program for the Use of Tax Abandoned Land*, Chicago, 1942.

——; *Report of Committee on Urban Land Policies*, Journal of American Institute of Planners, Vol. XII, No. 2, 1946.

Armstrong, R. H., and Homer Hoyt; *Decentralization in New York City*, Urban Land Institute, Washington, D.C., 1941.

Barlow Report; Report of Royal Commission on Distribution of Industrial Population, H. M. Stationery Office, London, 1940.

Bartholomew, Harland; *The Present and Ultimate Effects of Decentralization Upon American Cities*, Urban Land Institute, Washington, D.C., 1940.

Boyd, John Taylor, Jr.; *Toward the Reconstruction of New York's Lower East Side*, Architectural Forum, January and August 1932.

Chamber of Commerce of the U.S.; *Balanced Rebuilding of Cities*, A Statement Issued by the Construction and Civic Development Department Committee, Washington, D.C., 1937.

Churchill, Henry; *Densities in New York City*, Citizens Housing Council of New York, New York, 1944.

Colean, Miles, and Arthur P. Davies; *Cost Measurement in Urban Redevelopment*, National Committee on Housing, New York, 1943.

Ford, G. B.; *Building Height, Bulk, and Form,* Harvard University Press, Cambridge, 1931.

Ford, Henry; *Ford Ideals,* being a Selection from "Mr. Ford's Page" in the *Dearborn Independent,* The Dearborn Publishing Company, Dearborn, Michigan, 1922.

Forshaw, J. H., and Patrick Abercrombie; *County of London Plan,* London County Council, Macmillan & Co., Ltd., London, 1943.

Fulmer, O. Kline; *Greenbelt,* American Council on Public Affairs, Washington, D.C.

Fortune Magazine; Articles on City Planning, 1943–44.

George, Henry; *Progress and Poverty,* New York, 1879.

Greer, Guy; *The Problems of the Cities and Towns,* Conference on Urbanism, Harvard University, March 5, 6, 1942.

——; *Your City Tomorrow,* The Macmillan Co., New York, 1947.

Gropius, Walter; *Rebuilding Our Communities,* Paul Theobald, Chicago, 1945.

Hansen, Alvin; *Financing Urban Redevelopment,* Architectural Forum, April 1944.

—— and Guy Greer; *Urban Redevelopment for Cities in the U.S.,* Federal Housing Administration, Washington, D.C., November 1941.

——; *Urban Redevelopment and Housing,* National Planning Association, Washington, D.C., 1941.

Harrison, Bernard J., Jr., Henry Whitney and Chloethiel Woodard; *From Rent to Space,* Architectural Forum, June 1936.

Holden, Arthur C.; *Gabriel Over Block 326–A,* Architectural Forum, January 1935.

——; *A Basis for Procedure in Slum Clearance,* Architectural Record, March 1933.

Holden, Thomas; *Practical Urban Redevelopment,* Architectural Record, November 1943.

Housing and Home Finance Agency; *Comparative Digest of the Principal Provisions of State Urban Redevelopment Legislation,* Washington, D.C., April 1947.

——; *Comparative Digest of State Statutes Authorizing Insurance Companies, Building and Loan Associations, and Savings Banks to Invest Funds Directly in Ownership and Operation, or Construction and Sale of Housing Accommodations,* Washington, D.C., January 1, 1948.

——; *Land Assembly for Urban Redevelopment,* Washington, D.C., 1945.

Journal of Land and Public Utility Economics, Quarterly, University of Wisconsin, Madison.

Justement, Louis; *New Cities for Old,* McGraw-Hill Book Co., New York, 1946.

Mayer, Albert; *Techniques for Planning Complete Communities,* Architectural Forum, January, February 1937.

National Resources Committee; *Urban Planning and Land Policies,* Vol. 2, Supplementary Report of the Urbanism Committee, Washington, D.C., 1939.

——; *Better Cities,* by Charles Ascher, Washington, D.C., 1942.

Reconstruction and Planning in Europe; Task, July–August 1948, Cambridge.

School of Architecture; *Discussions on Urbanism,* Columbia University, January 8 to April 23, 1943.

Simon, Sir E. D., and J. Inman; *Rebuilding of Manchester,* Longmans, Green and Co., New York, 1935.

Stein, Clarence; *The Price of Slum Clearance,* Architectural Forum, February 1934.

Stephenson, Gordon; *New Town Policies in Great Britain,* A brief description, Department of Civic Planning, Liverpool University, Liverpool, 1948.

Straus, Michael, and Talbot Wegg; *Housing Comes of Age,* Oxford University Press, New York, 1938.

Uthwatt Report; Report of the Expert Committee on Compensation and Betterment, Minister of Works and Planning, London, September 1942.

Walker, Mabel; *Urban Blight and Slums,* Economic and Legal Factors in Their Origin, Reclamation and Prevention, Harvard University Press, Cambridge, 1938.

Western Addition District Redevelopment Study, San Francisco City and County Planning Commission, San Francisco, 1947.

Woodbury, Coleman, and Frederick A. Gutheim, *Rethinking Urban Redevelopment,* Public Administration Service, Chicago, 1949.

Wright, Henry; *Rehousing Urban America,* Columbia University Press, New York, 1935.

Augur, Tracy; *Citizen Participation in City Planning*, The Annals, American Academy of Political and Social Sciences, November 1945.

Bauer, Catherine; *Cities in Flux*, The American Scholar, New York, Winter, 1943–44.

Bottoni, Piero; *Urbanistica*, Ulrico Hoepli Editore, Milano, 1938.

Burnham, Daniel H., and Edward H. Bennett; *Plan of Chicago*, edited by Charles Moore, Commercial Club, Chicago, 1909.

Chambless, Edgar; *Roadtown*, New York, 1910.

Chase, Stuart; *The Road We Are Travelling*, The Twentieth Century Fund, New York, 1942.

——; *For This we Fought*, The Twentieth Century Fund, New York, 1946.

Collection ASCORAL; *Les Trois Établissements Humains*, Denoël, 19 Rue Amelie, Paris, 1945.

Davidge, W. R., and Herbert Warren; *Decentralization of Population and Industry*, London, 1930.

Directive Committee on Regional Planning; *The Case for Regional Planning with Special Reference to New England*, Yale University, Yale University Press, New Haven, 1947.

Ferris, Hugh; *The Metropolis of Tomorrow*, New York, 1929.

Fitch, James Marston; *American Building*, Houghton Mifflin Co., Boston, 1948.

Geddes, Norman Bel; *Magic Motorways*, Random House, New York, 1940.

Giedion, Sigfried; *Space, Time and Architecture*, Harvard University Press, Cambridge, 1943.

Goodman, Percival and Paul; *Communitas*, University of Chicago Press, Chicago, 1947.

Goodrich, Carter; *Migration and Economic Opportunity*, Report on a study of Population and Distribution, Philadelphia, 1936.

Hegemann, Werner; *City Planning: Housing*, Vol. I, Historical and Sociological, Architectural Book Publishing Co., New York, 1936.

——; *City Planning: Housing*, Vol. II, Political Economy and Civic Art, Architectural Book Publishing Co., New York, 1938.

——; *City Planning: Housing*, Vol. III, A Graphic Review of Civic Art, Architectural Book Publishing Co., New York, 1938.

—— and Elbert Peets; *Civic Art: The American Vitruvius*, Architectural Book Publishing Co., New York, 1922.

Herrey, Hermann and Erna, and Constantine Pertzoff; *An Organic Theory of City Planning*, Architectural Forum, April 1944.

Hilberseimer, Ludwig; *The New City*, Paul Theobald, Chicago, 1944.

Huxley, Aldous; *On Living in a Revolution*, Harper & Brothers, New York, 1944.

Le Corbusier; *The City of Tomorrow*, The Architectural Press, London, 1929.

——; *La Ville Radieuse*, Boulogne, 1934.

——; *When the Cathedrals Were White*, Reynal & Hitchcock, New York, 1947.

——; *Concerning Town Planning*, Translated by Clive Entwistle from *Propos D'Urbanisme*, Yale University Press, New Haven, 1948.

——; *New World of Space*, Reynal & Hitchcock, New York, 1948.

—— and Pierre Jeanneret; *Oeuvre Complet, 1910–29*, Verlag Dr. H. Girsberger & Cie., Zurich, 1930. *1929–34*, Willy Boesiger, Zurich, Les Editions d'Architecture, Erlenbach, Zurich. *1934–38*, Max Bill, Editions Dr. H. Girsberger, Zurich, 1945. *1938–46*, Willy Boesiger, Les Editions d'Architecture, Zurich.

Lilienthal, David; *Democracy on the March*, Harper & Brothers, 1944.

Lorwin, Lewis L.; *Time for Planning*, Harper & Brothers, 1945.

MacKenzie, Findlay; *Planned Society, Yesterday, Today and Tomorrow*, New York, 1937.

McKaye, Benton; *The New Exploration: A Philosophy of Regional Planning*, Harcourt, Brace & Co., New York, 1928.

Mumford, Lewis; *Technics and Civilization*, Harcourt, Brace & Co., New York, 1934.

——; *The Culture of Cities*, Harcourt, Brace & Co., New York, 1938.

——; *The Condition of Man*, Harcourt, Brace & Co., New York, 1944.

——; *City Development*, Harcourt, Brace & Co., New York, 1945.

National Resources Planning Board; *Progressive Planning Studies*, Tacoma, Washington; Salt Lake City, Utah; Corpus Christi, Texas; published in New Pencil Points, August 1943.

Osborn, Frederick; *The Human Wealth of the United States*, New Horizons in Planning: Proceedings of the National Planning Conference, American Society of Planning Officials, Chicago, 1937.

Packard, Walter E.; *The Economic Implications of the Central Valley Project*, Adcraft, Los Angeles, 1942.

Planned Neighborhoods for 194X; Architectural Forum, October 1943.

Rodgers, Cleveland, and Rebecca B. Rankin; *New York: The World's Capital*, Harper & Brothers, New York, 1948.

Saarinen, Eliel; *The City: Its Growth, Its Decay, Its Future*, Reinhold Publishing Corp., New York, 1943.

Sanders, S. E., and A. J. Rabuck, *New City Patterns*, Reinhold Publishing Corp., New York, 1946.

Scott, Mel; *Cities Are for People*, Pacific Southwest Academy, Los Angeles, 1942.

Sert, José; *Can Our Cities Survive?* Harvard University Press, Cambridge, 1942.

Sharp, Thomas; *Town and Countryside*, New York, 1933.

——; *Town Planning*, Penguin Books, New York, Revised Edition, 1945.

Sitte, Camillo; *The Art of Building Cities*, translated by Charles Stewart, Reinhold Publishing Corp., New York, 1945.

Sullivan, Louis; *Kindergarten Chats*, Washington, D.C., 1934.

Survey Graphic; *Regional Planning Number*, May 1925.

Tennessee Valley Authority: 1933–37, Washington, D.C., 1937.

United Nations Bulletin 2, Department of Social Affairs, *Housing and Town and Country Planning*, Columbia University Press, New York, 1949.

United Nations Publication Sales No. 1948–IV–7, *Housing and Town and Country Planning*, Columbia University Press, New York, 1949.

Violich, Francis; *Cities of Latin America*, Reinhold Publishing Corp., New York, 1944.

Wagner, Otto; *Die Grosstadt: Eine Studie*, Vienna, 1911.

Whitaker, Charles Harris; *Ramses to Rockefeller*, Random House, New York, 1934.

Wright, Frank Lloyd; *When Democracy Builds*, University of Chicago Press, Chicago, 1945.

——; *The Disappearing City*, William Farquhar Payson, New York, 1932.

435

U. S. Housing Authority, 148, 152, 153, 154, 155, 156, 159, 207, 208
Unwin, Raymond, 72, 126, 197, 204, 352, 373
Urban Land Institute, 283, 296
Urban Redevelopment. *See* Redevelopment
Uthwatt, Hon. Augustus Andrewe, 351, 353
Utilities, in ancient cities, 6, 7, 10, 11, 13, 16, 19; Roman engineering for, 26; Roman domestic, 30, 31; in the medieval dwelling, 38, 39; in the middle ages, 41; nineteenth century development, 65, 69, 74; crowding of, 203, 204; extension of, 189, 190, 344; court decision, 88, 89; for domestic use, 214, 218; in subdivision, 257–260. *See* Water Supply, Sanitation
Utopians, 70, 72, 92

Valadier, 48
Valenciennes, France, 72
Vancouver, Wash., 161, 162
Vanport, Oregon, 162
Vatican, 43
Vauban, 45
Vaux, Calvert, 117
Venice, 40, 43, 44, 45, 403, 404
Verne, Jules, 415
Versailles, 45, 46, 48, 403
Vienna, 42, 45, 68, 192
Villanueva, Marcel, 296, 300, 301
Ville Contemporaine, 376
Ville Radieuse, 376, 378
Viollet-le-duc, 34
Virgin Islands, 152
Vitruvius, 27
Voisin Plan, 378
Voiture-omnibus, 64

Wagner-Ellender-Taft Housing Bill, 341
Wagner, Otto, 409
Waite, Justice, 89
Wall Street, 52, 54, 175, 291
War housing, World War I, 121, 122, 123; World War II, 159–162
Ware, James E., 67
Washington, D. C., 85, 399, 400; L'Enfant's plan, 55, 56; development of, 73, 81, 84; housing, 75, 136, 144, 147, 169, 214; transportation, 193, 404
Washington, George, 55, 56
Washington Sanitary Improvement Company, 75, 136
Washington Sanitary Housing Company, 75, 136

Water Supply, 10, 13, 16, 19, 26, 39, 41, 49, 396, 397; extension of, 88, 89, 257–260, 344
Watt, 63
Welwyn, 92, 95, 96, 353
Westchester County Parkways, 404
Westfield Acres, Camden, N. J., 150
Westwood Village, Los Angeles, 119, 184
Wickens, David L., 180
Wilhelm, Prince, 71
William and Mary, College of, 53, 54
Williamsburg, 53, 54
Williamsburg Houses, New York City, 148, 149
Willow Run, Michigan, 162, 299
Wilmington, Del., 123
Wilshire, Los Angeles, 184
Wisconsin, 55, 88
Wood, John, 48
World's Fairs, 81, 119
Works Progress Administration, 243
Wren, Christopher, 43, 46
Wright, Frank Lloyd, 392, 394
Wright, Henry, 123–129, 132, 135, 204
Wythenshawe, England, 95, 96, 97
Wyvernwood, Los Angeles, 142

Xenophon, 22

Yonkers, N. Y., 169
York, England, 72
Yorkship Village, N. J., 121

Zoning, 9, 168, 241, 265–276, 357, 358, 363, 380; origin of, 87, 88, 225, 226, 227; early laws, 87, 228, 229; work of Edward M. Bassett, 87, 88; court decisions on, 88, 229–233; Euclid case, 88, 234; population density in, 169, 170, 171, 174, 175, 176, 177, 351; mixed land uses in, 170, 172–175, 272, 273, 391, 394; retroactive, 170, 242; "strip," 170, 175, 271, 273, 276, 393; "spot," 174, 234; police power for, 227, 228, 229, 231, 232, 233, 234; fourteenth amendment and, 230, 233; comprehensive plan for, 229; interim ordinances in, 234; enabling acts for, 235, 236; for conservation, 236, 237, 271; administration of, 238, 239; districts, 265–268; parking requirements in, 268–270; transition, 271; non-conforming uses, 242; open space in, 271; quantity of land in, 272–276; for parking, 269–270
Zurich, 115, 187